REFUGEE LAW

SECOND EDITION

Other Books in the *Essentials of Canadian Law* Series

International Trade Law
Family Law
Copyright Law
The Law of Sentencing
Administrative Law
Securities Law
Computer Law 2/e
International Human Rights Law
Franchise Law
Legal Ethics and Professional Responsibility 2/e
National Security Law: Canadian Practice in International Perspective
Public International Law 2/e
Individual Employment Law 2/e
The Law of Partnerships and Corporations 3/e
Civil Litigation
Religious Institutions and the Law in Canada 3/e
Canadian Telecommunications Law
Intellectual Property Law 2/e
Animals and the Law
Income Tax Law 2/e
Fundamental Justice
Mergers, Acquisitions, and Other Changes of Corporate Control 2/e
Personal Property Security Law 2/e
The Law of Contracts 2/e
Youth Criminal Justice Law 3/e
Bank and Customer Law in Canada 2/e
The Law of Equitable Remedies 2/e
Environmental Law 4/e
Pension Law 2/e
International and Transnational Criminal Law 2/e
Remedies: The Law of Damages 3/e
Freedom of Conscience and Religion
The Law of Trusts 3/e
The Law of Evidence 7/e
Ethics and Criminal Law 2/e
Insurance Law 2/e
Immigration Law 2/e
Criminal Law 6/e
The Law of Torts 5/e
Bankruptcy and Insolvency Law 2/e
Legal Research and Writing 4/e
Criminal Procedure 3/e
Canadian Maritime Law 2/e
Public Lands and Resources in Canada
Conflict of Laws 2/e
Statutory Interpretation 3/e
Land-Use Planning
Constitutional Law 5/e
The Charter of Rights and Freedoms 6/e
Detention and Arrest 2/e

ESSENTIALS OF CANADIAN LAW

REFUGEE LAW

SECOND EDITION

SASHA BAGLAY
University of Ontario
Institute of Technology

MARTIN JONES
University of York (UK)

Refugee Law, second edition

Published in 2017 by

Irwin Law Inc.
14 Duncan Street
Suite 206
Toronto, ON
M5H 3G8

www.irwinlaw.com

ISBN: 978-1-55221-450-3
e-book ISBN: 978-1-55221-451-0

Library and Archives Canada Cataloguing in Publication

Jones, Martin (Martin David), author
Refugee law / Sasha Baglay (University of Ontario, Institute of Technology), Martin Jones (University of York (UK)). — Second edition.

(Essentials of Canadian law)
Revision of: Refugee law / Martin Jones, Sasha Baglay. — Toronto : Irwin Law, ©2007.
Includes bibliographical references and index.
Issued in print and electronic formats.

ISBN 978-1-55221-450-3 (softcover).—ISBN 978-1-55221-451-0 (PDF)

1. Refugees—Legal status, laws, etc.—Canada. 2. Emigration and immigration law—Canada. I. Baglay, Sasha, 1978–, author II. Title. III. Series: Essentials of Canadian law

KE4472.J65 2017 342.7108'3 C2017-901649-0
KF4483.I5J65 2017 C2017-901650-4

Printed and bound in Canada.

1 2 3 4 5 21 20 19 18 17

SUMMARY TABLE OF CONTENTS

DETAILED TABLE OF CONTENTS

CHAPTER 2:
LEGAL FRAMEWORK OF REFUGEE LAW IN CANADA *41*

CHAPTER 3:
CATEGORIES OF STATUS IN CANADIAN REFUGEE LAW 87

CHAPTER 4:
THE DEFINITION OF CONVENTION REFUGEE 139

CHAPTER 12:
REMOVAL FROM CANADA 408

CHAPTER 13:
CONCLUSIONS 443

PREFACE

A. INTRODUCTION

This book is intended as an introductory guide to Canadian refugee law and procedure for law students, legal practitioners, paralegals, and NGO staff. While it is at times technical in its language and procedural descriptions, it can also be used by those interested in refugee issues more generally.

The book defines "Canadian refugee law" fairly broadly to include not only the formal statutory and regulatory basis of the law but also the various policies, processes, and practices that are used to determine refugee law issues. Furthermore, the term is seen to include not only protection of individuals who are Convention refugees but also other categories of individuals who are in need of protection due to a potential violation of their human rights abroad.

While Canadian refugee law has emerged over the past several decades as an independent branch of law and discrete area of practice, inevitably it remains closely tied to immigration law and often requires cross-referencing to immigration law. Therefore, this book presents refugee law as a system subject to that discipline's internal logic and integrity, not a system of law that operates in isolation.

The principal objective of the book is to provide an accurate account of the basic features of Canadian refugee law, policy, and procedure. It is by no means exhaustive. No single book can describe, discuss, and resolve all of the details and nuances of the Canadian refugee system.

However, it is our hope that this account will provide a solid foundation from which the reader can begin to judge the merits and weaknesses of the existing system and will allow him or her to engage with the ongoing debate, both academic and popular, about the Canadian refugee system.

Much has been written about the explicit and implicit premises of refugee law. For the purposes of this book, Canadian refugee law is assumed to be based upon two premises: first, that states, including Canada, owe obligations to certain individuals who are at risk of persecution or serious human rights violations in their countries of origin and, second, that these obligations are governed, at a certain level, by the operation of international law and policy.

Both of these premises are embodied in the international treaty that continues to play a central role in refugee law, the *Convention Relating to the Status of Refugees* of 1951 (the *Refugee Convention*). The *Refugee Convention* defines a refugee as a person who:

> Owing to well-founded fear of being persecuted for reasons of race, religion, nationality, membership of a particular social group or political opinion, is outside the country of his nationality and is unable or, owing to such fear, is unwilling to avail himself of the protection of that country; or who, not having a nationality and being outside the country of his former habitual residence as a result of such events, is unable or, owing to such fear, is unwilling to return to it.[1]

The definition of a refugee set out in the *Refugee Convention* has been incorporated into Canadian law by section 96 of the *Immigration and Refugee Protection Act* (*IRPA*). It delineates those to whom Canada is required to offer protection and clearly excludes vast numbers of individuals who might appear to the lay person to be refugees. Individuals displaced by civil war, natural disaster, and famine are amongst those who are commonly excluded from the legal definition of refugee but who might otherwise be commonly perceived as refugees. Thus the converse to the first premise of refugee law is that, equally, states, including Canada, do *not* owe obligations to certain individuals. This will be seen explicitly in the discussion of exclusion, vacation, and cessation later in this book. An underlying discussion concerning the propriety of such a disavowal can also be seen in the ongoing debates of Canadian refugee law.

Thus, the availability of refugee protection is subject to certain definitional confines. In addition to these general principles, each national system devises special procedures for refugee determination and prin-

1 *Convention Relating to the Status of Refugees*, 28 July 1951, 189 UNTS 150, art 1A(2).

ciples of treatment of refugees. In this respect, Canadian refugee law and procedure can be viewed as a reflection of Canada's understanding of its humanitarian obligations.

B. OUTLINE

The book is divided into thirteen chapters, each focusing on a distinct aspect of Canadian refugee law. The chapters can be generally grouped into four topical clusters: the basics of Canadian refugee and immigration systems (Chapters 1 to 3); the criteria for refugee and other protection in Canada (Chapters 4 to 6); the procedures by which inland and overseas claims for refuge or protection are made and challenged (Chapters 7 to 10); and detention and removal (Chapters 11 to 12). Chapter 13 will address some contemporary debates in Canadian refugee law and provide some concluding remarks. In some ways, the organization of the book represents the arc of a refugee claim in Canada or abroad: the application, the assessment against definitional criteria, the determination of status, and the consequences of a grant or refusal of refugee protection.

The book begins, in Chapter 1, with an overview of the history of Canadian immigration and refugee policy. This provides a useful context for the analysis of Canada's current and future policies. Chapter 2 explores the legal structure of Canadian refugee law, including the constitutional, statutory, regulatory, and policy framework that governs refugee decision making. The chapter also examines the core international treaties, including the aforementioned *Refugee Convention*, that influence Canadian law and policy.

Chapter 3 examines the categories established in and relevant to the operation of Canadian refugee (and, more broadly, immigration) law. The legislation distinguishes three broad categories of persons — foreign nationals, permanent residents, and citizens — each of which enjoys different rights in Canada. The chapter primarily focuses on the subcategories of foreign national and how these subcategories affect the rights of those seeking protection in the most essential spheres of their lives such as procedural rights, right to work and study, social assistance, legal aid, and medical coverage.

Chapters 4 and 6 deal with the definitions of "refugee" and "persons in need of protection" which lie at the heart of Canadian refugee law. The constituent elements of the definition of a Convention refugee and a "person in need of protection" are examined. Chapter 5 focuses on the grounds of exclusion from refugee protection.

Chapters 7 and 8 deal with overseas refugee processing and inland refugee determination respectively. Both chapters provide a detailed description of the procedure to be followed and of the principles governing refugee protection decision making. Chapter 7 presents refugee resettlement from abroad as a unity of two processes: the approval of sponsoring organizations and groups in Canada and the selection of individuals abroad for resettlement in Canada. Chapter 8 follows the progress of a refugee claim through the inland refugee determination process: from making of the claim to the first instance decision at the Refugee Protection Division (RPD) of the Immigration and Refugee Board. It also discusses interdiction measures that seek to prevent asylum-seekers' entry to Canada, the *Safe Third Country Agreement* between Canada and the United States, and cessation and vacation of refugee protection by the RPD. Chapter 9, closely interconnected with Chapter 8, discusses some of the intricacies of legal representation of asylum-seekers. It specifically focuses on the role of counsel during the application process and at refugee hearings as well as issues of professional responsibility related to that role.

The remaining chapters describe the steps that usually follow a negative refugee determination, either before the Immigration and Refugee Board or by an immigration officer in Canada or abroad. Chapter 10 focuses on the procedures by which the Federal Court (and, less commonly, other courts) can review refugee-related decisions, including the power of the court to grant a stay of removal. Chapters 11 and 12 deal with the detention of refugee claimants and the removal of unsuccessful refugee claimants respectively. Chapter 11 offers an analysis of the grounds on which asylum seekers may be detained under the *IRPA* and the procedure and timing governing detention reviews. Chapter 12 is dedicated to the examination of pre-removal risk assessment and removal arrangements.

In Chapter 13, we attempt to outline some of the ongoing debates in Canadian (and international) refugee law and to draw some conclusions about Canadian refugee law and its relation to refugee law elsewhere in the world.

C. CURRENCY

This book reflects the state of legislation and caselaw as of 1 March 2017. While refugee law is constantly developing, the principles and frames of reference described in this text remain at the core of it.

ACKNOWLEDGEMENTS

While having our names on the cover indicates our willingness to accept full responsibility for any errors, a large number of individuals have assisted, supported, and inspired our writing of this book. The following is a necessarily incomplete list of these individuals.

Our first acknowledgement must go to our publisher. In particular, we are indebted to Jeffrey Miller who ever so patiently and with good humour dealt with our queries and requests for deadline extensions. Without his wholehearted commitment to this book, it would neither have been written nor published. We would also like to thank our editors Jo Roberts (the first edition of the book) and Kate Revington and Alisa Posesorski (the second edition) for managing to wrestle the stylistic peccadillos of two authors into the single unified text that is before you.

We would also like to thank our families, friends, and colleagues for all their support, love, and inspiration in our lives.

Beyond those whom we are able to thank explicitly are the countless individuals who have made it possible to write about the field of refugee law in Canada at all. The contributions of these advocates, jurists, and claimants are acknowledged too incompletely in the footnotes of this book. Ultimately, it is to these individuals who have come before us — and who will come after us — that this book is dedicated.

March 2017

Sasha Baglay
Toronto, Canada

Martin Jones
York, UK

LIST OF ABBREVIATIONS

CAT	*Convention Against Torture*
CBSA	Canada Border Services Agency
CIC	Citizenship and Immigration Canada
CSIS	Canadian Security Intelligence Service
H&C	humanitarian and compassionate consideration
IAD	Immigration Appeal Division (of the Immigration and Refugee Board)
ICCPR	*International Covenant on Civil and Political Rights*
IFA	internal flight alternative
IRB, or the Board	Immigration and Refugee Board (of Canada)
IRCC	Immigration, Refugees and Citizenship Canada (formerly Citizenship and Immigration Canada)
IRPA	*Immigration and Refugee Protection Act*
JAS	joint assistance sponsorship
PRRA	pre-removal risk assessment
PSEP	Public Safety and Emergency Preparedness (Department of)
RAD	Refugee Appeal Division (of the Immigration and Refugee Board)

RAP	Resettlement Assistance Program
RPD	Refugee Protection Division (of the Immigration and Refugee Board)
SAH	sponsorship agreement holder
SIN	social insurance number
UNHCR	United Nations High Commissioner for Refugees

CHAPTER 1

CANADIAN REFUGEE POLICY

A. INTRODUCTION

This chapter provides a concise account of the development of Canada's migration policies since Confederation. Although Canada gave refuge to dissidents and the persecuted since its early settlement, the history of its formal refugee determination system is rather young. Before the 1970s, refugees were admitted on an ad hoc basis in response to refugee crises and were often treated similarly to other migrants.

This chapter is divided into time periods defined in relation to the main mileposts of immigration and refugee regulation: 1969, when Canada became a party to the *Convention Relating to the Status of Refugees (Refugee Convention)*; 1978, when the *Immigration Act* came into force; 1985, the year of the seminal *Singh v Canada (Minister of Employment and Immigration)* decision, which established the right of refugee claimants to an oral hearing and consequently led to an overhaul of the refugee determination system; 1992, when further changes to inland refugee determination were made; 2002, when the new *Immigration and Refugee Protection Act* came into force; and 2012, when a series of changes to the refugee system were implemented. In addition to describing the evolution of the Canadian refugee protection regime, the chapter situates Canada's policies in a larger context of international migration trends and discourses on immigration and refugee law.

B. HISTORICAL OVERVIEW

1) Pre-1969

a) Until 1945

Since its early settlement, Canada has served as a place of refuge for various dissident and persecuted groups. Among the first political refugees were British Loyalists who moved to Canada between 1775 and 1784 in response to the American Revolution.[1] In the centuries that followed, forced migrants included Mennonites fleeing the Russification of Ukraine and universal military conscription;[2] Jews escaping the pogroms in Ukraine;[3] Doukhobors persecuted in Russia;[4] and Hutterites driven from the United States by xenophobic sentiments. However, in contrast to present-day refugees, these groups were, for the most part, treated like other immigrants, often having to satisfy the same requirements and undergo the same procedures.

The pre-Confederation period was characterized by relatively uncontrolled immigration,[5] although Nova Scotia, New Brunswick, and Lower Canada (now Quebec) exercised limited forms of immigration control such as collection of a head tax and health and quarantine screening.[6] At Confederation, the *Constitution Act, 1867* created concurrent federal–provincial jurisdiction over immigration. The Act thereby preserved the power of the provinces to regulate immigration matters within their territories, while also giving the federal government a new power to regulate immigration "into all or any of the Provinces."[7] The latter created preconditions for a more centralized approach to immigration regulation in Canada.

During the first decades after Confederation, immigration was viewed as key to industrial growth and nation-building. Therefore, it

---

1 Valerie Knowles, *Strangers at Our Gates: Canadian Immigration and Immigration Policy, 1540–1997* (Toronto: Dundurn Press, 1997) at 20.

2 *Ibid* at 53.

3 *Ibid* at 55.

4 *Ibid* at 70.

5 Norman Macdonald, *Canada: Immigration and Colonization, 1841–1903* (Toronto: MacMillan, 1966) at 90.

6 RA Vineberg, "Federal–Provincial Relations in Canadian Immigration" (1987) 30:2 *Canadian Public Administration* 299 at 300; Ninette Kelley & Michael Trebilcock, *The Making of the Mosaic* (Toronto: University of Toronto Press, 1998) at 40–50; Warren E Kalbach, *The Impact of Immigration on Canada's Population* (Ottawa: Dominion Bureau of Statistics, 1970) at 11.

7 *Constitution Act, 1867* (UK), 30 & 31 Vict, c 3, s 95, reprinted in RSC 1985, App II, No 5.

was actively promoted, and there were relatively few restrictions on admission.[8] The first Canadian *Immigration Act*, passed in 1869, primarily focused on ensuring the safety of passengers en route to and upon arrival in Canada by prescribing quarantine checks, limits on the number of passengers allowed aboard, and protection from extortion or fraud by captains, merchants, and innkeepers.[9] The few restrictions in place were dictated by the economic priorities of the time, namely, agricultural development and the settlement of the Prairies. Viewed as a means to land development, immigration was even included in the same chapter of the *Constitution Act* as agriculture.[10] Canada promoted immigration of farmers and agricultural workers, artisans and tradesmen, simultaneously discouraging the immigration of administrative occupations such as clerks and house servants.[11] Both federal and provincial authorities were engaged in immigrant recruitment: they advertised immigration opportunities in the same newspapers, canvassed the same groups of prospective immigrants, and employed overseas immigration agents, which led to waste of resources and unnecessary competition.[12] As a result, the 1874 federal–provincial immigration conference concluded that independent action by provinces was inefficient and decided to vest the federal minister of agriculture with the sole responsibility for immigrant recruitment overseas.[13]

By the early twentieth century, the arrival of a relatively high number of immigrants with different cultures, traditions, and religions began to raise concerns about demographic composition of the country and stimulated introduction of restrictions aimed at preserving Canada

---

8 The notable exception from this trend constituted the treatment of Japanese and Chinese who faced numerous restrictions of their rights, including employment and franchise. Many of these restrictions were introduced by provinces, particularly British Columbia. This provincial legislation produced a string of litigation with respect to constitutional division of powers over immigration, naturalization, and aliens. See, for example, *Union Colliery Co of British Columbia v Bryden*, [1899] AC 580 (JCPC); *Reference re: British Columbia Provincial Elections Act, 1897*, [1903] AC 151 (JCPC); *Reference re: Act to validate and confirm orders in council and provisions relating to the employment of persons on Crown property (British Columbia)* (1922), 63 SCR 293; *Brooks-Bidlake and Whittall v British Columbia (Attorney General)*, [1923] AC 450 (JCPC); and *R v Quong-Wing* (1914), 49 SCR 440.

9 Kelley & Trebilcock, above note 6 at 84.

10 Jamie Chai Yun Liew & Donald Galloway, *Immigration Law*, 2e (Toronto: Irwin Law, 2015) at 13.

11 Knowles, above note 1 at 45.

12 Macdonald, above note 5 at 90; Kelley & Trebilcock, above note 6 at 77.

13 Valerie Knowles, *Strangers at Our Gates: Canadian Immigration and Immigration Policy, 1540–1990* (Toronto: Dundurn Press, 1992) at 49.

as a white, predominantly British society. Chinese immigrants, many of whom were brought in for the construction of the Canadian Pacific Railway in the 1880s, were one of the targeted groups. British Columbia was particularly vigorous, passing more than 100 acts imposing various restrictions on Chinese immigrants.[14] Soon, a similar approach started gaining ground at the federal level. In 1885, the government passed the *Electoral Franchise Act* which excluded all Chinese persons, naturalized and non-naturalized alike, from participation in federal elections.[15] The same year, as the Canadian Pacific Railway was approaching completion, the federal *Chinese Immigration Act* was adopted. It imposed a $50 head tax on all Chinese immigrants and restricted the number of Chinese migrants that a ship could carry per every fifty tons of cargo.[16] Over the next eighteen years the head tax continued to rise, reaching $500 in 1903.[17] Nor was the anti-Asian immigrant sentiment purely legislative; in 1907, Vancouver was wracked by a large race riot that caused extensive damage to property occupied by Asian migrants.

The 1906 *Immigration Act* continued the trend of more restrictive immigration policies. It consolidated and revised all immigration legislation by providing a definition of an immigrant and establishing inadmissible and deportable classes of immigrants. For example, persons with mental or physical disabilities, individuals with contagious diseases, and those who were likely to become a public charge were barred from entry.[18] Canada was not alone in adopting restrictive immigration legislation at the time; in 1905, the United Kingdom adopted similar measures.[19]

---

14 Kelley & Trebilcock, above note 6 at 98.

15 *Ibid* at 97.

16 *Ibid*.

17 In 1999, a group of payers of Chinese head tax and/or their surviving spouses and descendants filed a class action lawsuit arguing that the head tax and exclusions of Chinese migrants were contrary to the *Canadian Charter of Rights and Freedoms*, Part 1 of the *Constitution Act, 1982*, being Schedule B to the *Canada Act 1982* (UK), 1982, c 11 [*Charter*]. The Ontario Superior Court dismissed the case, finding that the *Charter* could not be applied retroactively or retrospectively: *Mack v Canada (Attorney General)* (2001), 55 OR (3d) 113 (SCJ), aff'd [2002] OJ No 3488 (CA), leave to appeal to SCC refused, [2002] SCCA No 476. In 2006, Prime Minister Stephen Harper issued an apology for the implementation of the Chinese head tax and offered symbolic payments of $20,000 to the survivors or spouses of deceased payers of the tax. Prime Minister of Canada, News Release, "Prime Minister Harper Offers Full Apology for the Chinese Head Tax" (22 June 2006).

18 Knowles, above note 1 at 82–83.

19 *Aliens Act 1905* (in full "An act to amend the law with respect to aliens"), 5 Edw VII c 13.

In 1908, the "continuous journey" requirement was introduced. To be admitted, immigrants had to arrive in Canada directly from their countries of origin. Given the then-existing travel routes, the legislation effectively barred Indian and Japanese immigration.[20] In 1914, almost 400 migrants were deported from Vancouver after a lengthy and hostile standoff and much litigation. The reason for the refusal of entry was that they had arrived on the *Komagata Maru* after a "non-continuous journey" to Canada — a journey from India which, at the time, was physically impossible to undertake without a stopover.

In 1910, the list of excludable classes was expanded to "charity cases" (unless allowed by a special authorization)[21] and persons of "race deemed unsuitable to the climate and requirements of Canada."[22] In addition, new grounds of deportation — political and moral instability — were introduced.[23]

The start of the First World War fuelled hostility to the foreign born — potential immigrants and long-term residents of Canada alike. Entry was barred to immigrants from enemy countries such as Germany and the Austro-Hungarian empire; those already in Canada faced internment and disenfranchisement, and could be deported on suspicion of conspiring against the government of the United Kingdom or Canada. Following the end of the First World War, Canada's declining economy, rising unemployment, and labour unrest prompted by layoffs and wage cuts created further incentives to tighten up immigration controls. In 1919, to the list of inadmissible persons were added alcoholics, illiterate persons, anarchists, those who believed in the overthrow by force of the government of Canada, and people with peculiar customs, habits, and modes of living.[24] The latter restriction effectively barred from immigration to Canada such groups as the Doukhobors.[25] Increased attention was also paid to surveillance of ethnic and left-wing organizations as well as removal of political radicals, anarchists, and persons suspected of conspiring to overthrow the government.[26]

As the economy began to recover around 1921, some restrictions on immigration were gradually lifted. For example, Americans and

---

20 Knowles, above note 1 at 93.

21 *Ibid* at 85.

22 *Ibid* at 137.

23 Valerie Knowles, *Strangers at Our Gates: Canadian Immigration and Immigration Policy, 1540–2006* (Toronto: Dundurn Press, 2007) at 111 [Knowles, 2007].

24 Kelley & Trebilcock, above note 6 at 183–84.

25 Knowles, above note 1 at 106.

26 Reg Whitaker, *Canadian Immigration Policy since Confederation* (Ottawa: Canadian Historical Association, 1991) at 11.

northern Europeans could be admitted relatively freely if they had an occupation in demand; even "non-preferred" migrants from eastern and southern Europe were allowed to come on special permits; and "persons with peculiar customs, habits and modes of living" such as Hutterites, Mennonites, and Doukhobors were again permitted to immigrate to Canada.[27] Admissions, however, were strongly polarized along racial lines. This approach was epitomized by the 1923 *Chinese Immigration Act* which barred entry of Chinese persons so effectively that only about twenty-five Chinese migrants entered Canada between 1923 and the repeal of the Act in 1946.[28]

The Great Depression of the 1930s prompted another cycle of restrictions on admissions. In 1931, the classes of admissible immigrants were limited to British and Americans with sufficient capital; family members of Canadian residents; agriculturalists; and labourers with arranged employment in farming, mining, lumbering, or logging.[29] Admissions fell, but deportations increased: some 25,000 were deported between 1930 and 1937 — more than in the preceding seven-year period.[30] Such deportations were utilized as one means to decrease the pressure from growing unemployment and reliance on public welfare during the Depression.[31]

Canada's response to flows of refugees produced by the start of the Second World War was mixed at best. In 1939–40, it admitted several hundred highly skilled Czech and Polish refugees as well as about 1,500 Jewish children evacuated from Britain.[32] However, it remained unsympathetic to the plight of 930 German Jews aboard the ocean liner *St Louis* seeking refuge from the Nazi regime. *St Louis*'s passengers, originally destined for Cuba, were refused entry there. Having unsuccessfully attempted to gain admission to the United States and Canada, the ship had to sail back to Europe, where many of its passengers faced the horrors of the Nazi regime and perished.[33] The government attitude towards Jews fleeing Nazi Germany is summed up in the title of the landmark book on this phase of Canadian migration policy: *None Is*

27 Ninette Kelley & Michael Trebilcock, *The Making of the Mosaic*, 2d ed (Toronto: University of Toronto Press, 2010) at 191–92 [Kelley & Trebilcock, 2010].

28 Knowles, above note 1 at 107.

29 *Ibid* at 115.

30 Kelley & Trebilcock, 2010, above note 27 at 221.

31 Whitaker, above note 26 at 13; Knowles, 2007, above note 23 at 143.

32 Knowles, above note 1 at 120–21.

33 *Ibid* at 117.

Too Many.[34] During this major refugee event, which was formative for the post-war drafters of the *Refugee Convention*, Canada's record was among the poorest of any country.

Canada's involvement in the Second World War prompted increased attention to enemies from within. Under the *Defence of Canada Regulations*, persons suspected of subversive activities could be arrested and interned, certain organizations could be declared illegal, and press could be censored. Two major waves of internment took place.[35] First, following Canada's declaration of war, persons deemed to have pro-Nazi and pro-Italian sympathies were interned. Second, after the bombing of Pearl Harbor by the Japanese in December 1941, Japanese Canadians faced relocation to detention camps across Canada.[36]

As seen from the above, since the First World War, the policy focus began to shift from attracting immigrants to selecting only those that were viewed as the most desirable,[37] and in the 1930s, the policy transformed into a policy of exclusion.[38] These changes came about due to multiple pressures: racial and xenophobic sentiment, economic downturns and the need to reduce pressure on public funds, and concerns over political stability during the times of war and economic crisis. The restrictive admission policies accompanied by increased deportations were largely maintained until the mid-1940s.[39]

b) 1945 to 1969

The end of the Second World War marked a gradual liberalization of immigration policies and more favourable attitudes towards refugees. Canada's economy was rapidly growing, creating demand for skilled labour that the government sought to satisfy through the increased admission of immigrants and displaced persons from Europe. The general objectives of Canadian post-war immigration rested on the principles of population growth, "absorptive capacity" of the Canadian economy, and national prerogative for selection of potential immigrants.[40]

---

34 Irving M Abella & Harold M Troper, *None Is Too Many: Canada and the Jews of Europe, 1933–1948* (Toronto: Lester & Orpen Dennys, 1983).

35 See Kelley & Trebilcock, 2010, above note 27 at 279–92.

36 Knowles, 2007, above note 23 at 153. In 1988, a settlement was achieved where the federal government paid financial compensation for each Japanese Canadian who was mistreated between 1942 and 1949.

37 Kelley & Trebilcock, above note 6 at 248.

38 Kelley & Trebilcock, 2010, above note 27 at 252.

39 *Ibid* at 165, 217, 229, and 251.

40 Mackenzie King, "Statement before the House of Commons, 1 May 1947" in Citizenship and Immigration Canada, *Forging Our Legacy: Canadian Citizenship*

Between 1946 and 1962, refugees came to Canada either through contract-labour schemes or through sponsorship by relatives, the government, or religious groups.[41] Most refugee admissions took place under arranged labour schemes in response to labour shortages in particular industries (primarily logging, mining, and lumber) and agriculture.[42] The government dispatched five mobile teams of immigration officials to Germany and Austria to select persons in refugee camps on the basis of their economic potential, ethnic origin, and ideological views (for example, communists were routinely rejected). All in all, some 100,000 displaced persons were admitted due to these efforts.[43]

The bulk labour scheme started to lose momentum in the summer of 1948 when, due to its amended immigration legislation, the United States became a preferred immigration destination.[44] In 1950, an order in council expanded admissible classes to include all healthy skilled individuals who could be integrated into Canadian society. The notion of who could be integrated was strongly reflective of racial bias, however. White Americans, British, Australians, New Zealanders, and South Africans were among the most preferred classes, followed by northern, central, southern, and eastern Europeans; Jews, blacks, and Asians were among the least desired immigrants.[45] Small quotas for non-white populations from India, Pakistan, and Ceylon were introduced in response to bilateral agreements with the respective governments.[46]

In 1952, the government passed the *Immigration Act* which set out admission requirements and codified most of the existing executive practices. It gave significant discretionary powers to the Minister and placed a strong emphasis on the powers of exclusion, deportation, and removal. The Cold War also brought to the fore increased attention to the "red menace," prompting screening of immigrants for potential association with communists (at the same time, screening of Nazi war criminals was much less rigorous).[47]

Although various ad hoc initiatives had been launched to regularize and liberalize admission, immigration policies did not take a defined

---

and Immigration, 1900–1977, online: www.cic.gc.ca/english/department/legacy/index.html.

41 Kelley & Trebilcock, above note 6 at 337.

42 Knowles, above note 1 at 127.

43 Whitaker, above note 26 at 14.

44 Knowles, above note 1 at 136.

45 Kelley & Trebilcock, above note 6 at 442.

46 Freda Hawkins, *Canada and Immigration: Public Policy and Public Concern*, 2d ed (Kingston, ON: McGill-Queen's University Press, 1988) at 117.

47 Whitaker, above note 26 at 17.

and consistent direction until the 1960s. The haphazard state of immigration policy and the shifting priorities were reflected in the changing institutional structure of immigration management. Immediately after the Second World War, immigration was under the jurisdiction of the Department of Mines and Resources, highlighting its instrumental role in economic growth. In 1950, responsibility for immigration was transferred to the newly created Department of Citizenship and Immigration, which, in 1966, was transformed into the Department of Manpower and Immigration. These changes exemplified the tension between the long-term benefits of steady high immigrant intake advocated by the immigration department and the "tap on and off" admission lobbied for by the labour department.[48]

In the 1960s, ideological and economic factors led to the re-evaluation of the selection criteria for immigrants. The general promotion of liberal values in Canadian society motivated the eradication of various discriminatory admission policies. Economic considerations reinforced this motivation as the traditional sources of labour from Europe were no longer producing enough immigrants.[49] The needs of industrialization put an increased emphasis on the skills of would-be immigrants and resulted in the development of corresponding selection criteria. In 1962, Canada became the first major immigrant-receiving country to abolish (most of) its discriminatory admission policies. In 1967, the government introduced a skills-based points system for the selection of immigrants and established an Immigration Appeal Board to hear appeals on deportation and sponsorship cases.

Canada's refugee policy during the 1950s and 1960s showed few signs of a comprehensive, long-term approach. Although Canada admitted groups of refugees from various countries, all arrangements were made on an ad hoc basis and were often motivated by economic considerations. For example, among the most numerous admissions of the 1950s and 1960s were Hungarians fleeing the Soviet invasion (1956–57) and Czech refugees (1968–69). The government's willingness to resettle them in rather high numbers can be partially explained by the fact that most of the Hungarians and Czechs were young and highly skilled.[50]

The 1960s also saw the rise of Quebec as a more active player in immigration policy and decision making. Quebec's Quiet Revolution

48 *Ibid* at 112.

49 Jock Collins & Francis Henry, "Racism, Ethnicity and Immigration" in Howard Adelman et al, eds, *Immigration and Refugee Policy: Australia and Canada Compared* (Toronto: University of Toronto Press, 1994) 515 at 530.

50 Kelley & Trebilcock, above note 6 at 341.

supported the development of discourse on Quebec identity, drawing attention to the need to preserve the province's distinctiveness. Provincial say in immigration and settlement was, thus, seen as instrumental to maintaining French language and culture through attracting persons who speak French and encouraging learning of French by newcomers. In 1968, Quebec created its own department of immigration and sent representatives overseas to promote emigration of French-speaking individuals to Quebec. During the 1970s to 1990s, Quebec acquired powers over immigrant selection, reception, and integration services through a series of accords with the federal government. As a result, Quebec has its own selection and integration system, but the federal immigration department remains responsible for inadmissibility screening of prospective immigrants to Quebec (see more on this in Chapter 2, Section B(1)(a)).

2) 1969 to 1978

The 1960s brought about a change in immigration and refugee law that was rooted in the transformed post-Second World War self-understanding of Canada as a nation and its role in the global community.[51] The post-war period of economic growth and prosperity, which lasted until the early 1970s,[52] facilitated a more liberal stance on immigration and refugee admissions. Canada's part in the Second World War and the affirmation of its self-reliance boosted more vigorous nationalism and the desire to be recognized as a nation with a distinct identity. In this process, the adoption of the *Citizenship Act* in 1947 and the establishment of the Supreme Court of Canada as the court of the highest instance in 1949 were important symbolic landmarks. Subsequently, humanitarianism and internationalism emerged as distinct features of Canadian foreign policy.[53] In 1969, Canada acceded to the 1951 UN *Refugee Convention*[54] and the 1967 *Protocol Relating to the Status of Refugees*.[55] The nearly two-decade delay in acceding to the *Refugee Convention* was caused by Canada's position that the open-ended refugee definition and the non-*refoulement* principle ran contrary to its

51 Donald Galloway, *Immigration Law* (Toronto: Irwin Law, 1997) at 18.

52 Citizenship and Immigration Canada, *Forging Our Legacy*, above note 40.

53 Internationalism embraces a variety of activities, but can be generally characterized as active involvement in international affairs and constant co-operation with other states and international entities in enhancing universal values. See, generally, Don Munton & Tom Keating, "Internationalism and the Canadian Public" (2001) 34 *Canadian Journal of Political Science* 517.

54 28 July 1951, 189 UNTS 150 [*Refugee Convention*].

55 31 January 1967, 606 UNTS 267 [*Refugee Protocol*].

interests of immigration control and the ability to turn away undesirable migrants.[56] This concern continues to influence Canadian refugee policy to the present day.

In the years immediately following Canada's accession to the *Refugee Convention*, the country admitted several large groups of forced migrants, including Tibetans fleeing the occupation by China; Asians expelled from Uganda by Idi Amin's regime;[57] Chileans escaping after the violent overthrow of Salvador Allende's government;[58] and American draft dodgers and deserters refusing to participate in the Vietnam War. It should be noted, however, that the latter migrants were not treated as refugees, despite a public discourse that often portrayed them as such. The American military service evaders were simply allowed to apply for residency from within Canada on grounds having nothing to do with the reasons for their flight to Canada. In contrast, the current system requires American deserters (and others) who oppose war to go through a full refugee determination process.

The introduction of the policy of multiculturalism in 1971 prompted a review of immigration legislation and policies. The 1975 Green Paper and subsequent wide public consultations formed the basis for the 1976 *Immigration Act*, which came into force in 1978.

3) 1978 to 1985

The 1976 *Immigration Act* established many of the principles and procedures of contemporary Canadian immigration law, including classes of immigrants, refugee protection mechanisms, family reunification, and federal–provincial consultations. Of note was the federal minister's new power to enter into immigration agreements with the provinces. In 1978, this power was used to negotiate an agreement with Quebec (where immigration became a particularly hot issue under the separatist government of René Levesque). The agreement enabled the province to take a leading role in selection of immigrants destined

---

56 James C Hathaway, "The Conundrum of Refugee Protection in Canada: From Control to Compliance to Collective Deterrence" in Gil Loescher, ed, *Refugees and the Asylum Dilemma in the West* (University Park, PA: Pennsylvania State University Press, 1992) 71 at 73.

57 Knowles, above note 1 at 172.

58 However, compared to other groups of refugees, Chileans were accepted grudgingly and slowly. This was due to political and ideological reasons. Many refugees from the Pinochet regime supported left-wing or communist ideology and thus were viewed as undesirable for admission to Canada. Reg Whitaker, *Double Standard: The Secret History of Canadian Immigration* (Toronto: Lester & Orpen Dennys, 1987) at 257–61.

for Quebec, subject only to federal medical, criminality, and security checks. Over the years, immigration agreements were also signed with other provinces, but they were not as extensive as Quebec's.[59]

The *Immigration Act* provided for three avenues of refugee admission: (1) inland determination; (2) resettlement through private and government sponsorship; and (3) special programs for persons from specified countries.[60] Three special programs — for the Indochinese, Latin American political prisoners, and Eastern European self-exiles — allowed for admission of asylum seekers even if they did not fully satisfy the requirements of the *Refugee Convention*.[61] Significant numbers of Poles, Salvadorans, Chileans, Vietnamese, Laotians, and Kampucheans were able to benefit from these programs.[62]

The inland refugee determination process under the *Immigration Act* was complex and multi-stage.[63] If a person was out of status at the time of lodging a claim, she was subject to an immigration inquiry that was adjourned to allow for the refugee claim to be decided. The first stage of the determination process involved an examination of the claim by an immigration officer. Claimant's counsel could be present and could pose questions, but witnesses were not allowed. A transcript of the examination was sent to the claimant and her counsel as well as to the Refugee Status Advisory Committee (RSAC) in Ottawa. The committee was responsible for reviewing asylum claims and making recommendations to the Minister as to whether the claims should be accepted. These reviews and recommendations were based, in large part, upon transcripts of the claimants' interviews. Persons recognized as refugees were given Minister's permits and processed for landing as permanent residents. Rejected claimants could apply to the Immigration Appeal Board (IAB) for a re-determination of their claim, a process which involved an oral hearing. An IAB decision could be further challenged in the Federal Court of Appeal. If a person's claim was rejected by both the Minister and the Immigration Appeal Board and no court appeal was filed or it was unsuccessful, an immigration inquiry was reconvened and the person was ordered removed from Canada.[64]

---

59 Kelley & Trebilcock, 2010, above note 27 at 388.

60 Knowles, above note 1 at 405.

61 *Ibid* at 406.

62 Gerald E Dirks, *Controversy and Complexity: Canadian Immigration Policy during the 1980s* (Montreal & Kingston: McGill-Queen's University Press, 1995) at 70–71; Knowles, above note 1 at 174.

63 David Matas with Ilana Simon, *Closing the Doors* (Toronto: Summerhill Press, 1989) at 87.

64 *Ibid* at 87–103.

This determination and appeal system was designed to handle only a small number of refugee claims; it could not cope with the changing refugee realities of the 1980s. As a growing number of individuals sought protection through the inland determination,[65] pressure mounted, vividly exposing the system's inadequacies. A serious backlog of inland applications started accumulating when the annual number of asylum arrivals climbed from 200–400 people in the 1970s to 3,400–5,200 claimants in the 1980s.

In 1980, a Task Force on Immigration Practices and Procedures recommended some changes to the refugee determination process. In particular, the Task Force recommended conducting oral hearings and establishing an independent tribunal for refugee determination. The ministry accepted the recommendations and a year later announced a pilot project in Montreal and Toronto, where claims were heard before an RSAC member.[66] In 1984, a member of the Task Force, Ed Ratushny, produced another report that again recommended the implementation of oral hearings. A year later, yet another report commissioned by the federal government outlined various models for refugee determination, all of them having such common features as an oral hearing, an independent decision-making body, and an appeal process. Ultimately, the Supreme Court's 1985 landmark decision in *Singh v Canada (Minister of Employment and Immigration)*[67] became a major factor in the introduction of universal oral hearings for inland claimants.

4) 1985 to 1992

The period of 1985–92 was marked by two key developments that had serious implications for refugee policy: (1) the Supreme Court decision in *Singh* and (2) the arrivals of two boats with asylum seekers, one in 1986 and the other in 1987. Both developments sparked major debates on immigration and refugee matters and the consequent overhaul of certain policies and procedures.

---

65 Compare with past years: in 1980–98, 99 percent of all landed refugees came through resettlement; in 1991, 74 percent; in 1992, 42 percent; in 1993, 48 percent; in 1994, 60 percent; in 1995, 54 percent; and in 2002, 42 percent. See Citizenship and Immigration Canada, "Inland Determination Refugees before and after Landing" (2001) at 3; Citizenship and Immigration Canada, *The Changing Labour Market Prospects of Refugees in Canada* (2000) at 10, online: http://open.canada.ca/vl/en/doc/publications-263772.

66 Matas, above note 63 at 113–18.

67 [1985] 1 SCR 177 [*Singh*].

Singh dealt with the issue of procedural fairness in the inland refugee determination and the absence of a universal right to an oral hearing. As noted earlier, decisions on refugee claims were made on the basis of transcripts of claimants' interviews with immigration officers. This procedure did not allow claimants an opportunity to be heard before the Refugee Status Advisory Committee or to know and effectively challenge the information on which an RSAC decision was made. Given the seriousness of the consequences of a negative decision, the Supreme Court recognized that refugee claimants are entitled to fundamental justice under section 7 of the *Charter*, which, at a minimum, requires that a claimant has an adequate opportunity to state his or her case and to know the case to meet. The Court held that the absence of an oral hearing violated principles of procedural fairness and that it could not be saved under section 1 of the *Charter*.

The *Singh* decision required a complete restructuring of the system. To this effect, Bill C-55, which was passed in 1988, mandated the establishment of a new independent administrative tribunal — the Immigration and Refugee Board (IRB) — responsible for hearing refugee claims as well as appeals on sponsorship and removal cases.[68] The bill also proposed that immigration officers could turn away claimants who came from a safe third country and could have filed their claim there. This aspect of the bill, however, was never implemented. (See subsequent sections on the *Safe Third Country Agreement* between Canada and the United States as well as Chapter 8 for more details.)

The debate regarding the Canadian refugee system was further impassioned by the highly publicized arrivals of two boats with asylum seekers: 155 Sri Lankan Tamils in August 1986 and 174 Sikhs in July 1987. The Tamils claimed that they were abandoned in the North Atlantic and spent five days in lifeboats until rescued by Canadians. They received a warm welcome: the asylum seekers were issued one-year Minister's permits and were flown to Toronto and Montreal, where the Tamil community could provide the needed support. A subsequent investigation revealed that the Tamils came from West Germany where they enjoyed asylum and allegedly paid \$3,000 to \$5,000 US each to be brought to Canada.[69] This discovery contributed to the negative perception about refugees that had already been circulating in the media.[70]

---

68 Kelley & Trebilcock, above note 6 at 415–16.

69 Robert Martin & Graham Fraser, "152 Can Stay If Nationality Is Confirmed" *The Globe and Mail* (13 August 1986) A1.

70 In 1986, *The Globe and Mail* published ninety-two articles on refugees, twice as many as the year before. In 1987, many refugee stories — one out of five — made front-page news. Some 88 percent of these articles contributed to the negative

Less than a year after the Tamil arrival, 174 Sikhs landed in Nova Scotia. Unlike other arrivals, this group was first detained for over a week and then released under unprecedented conditions requiring that they reside with a sponsor, post a $5,000 bond, and report regularly to the authorities.[71] Furthermore, the arrival prompted an emergency session of Parliament in August 1987, which resulted in the introduction and eventual passage of Bill C-84. The bill sought greater powers of border control, detention of undocumented arrivals, deportation of security threats, and search and seizure to fight people-smuggling.[72] Bill C-84 originally included a provision that allowed authorities to turn away boats suspected of carrying bogus refugees, but this provision was dropped from the final version of the bill. The bill produced a heated debate both in Parliament and in the community at large. Many non-governmental organizations, including the Canadian Jewish Council, the Coalition for a Just Refugee and Immigration Policy, and the Canadian Civil Liberties Association, argued against provisions. However, the bill was passed, albeit with several amendments, by the conservative majority. Ironically, this took place only a year after Canada's efforts in refugee protection were recognized with the Nansen Medal.[73]

5) 1992 to 2002

The end of the 1990s and the start of the new millennium were marked by an increase in asylum arrivals in Canada. On the one hand, the expansion of international transportation facilitated the mobility of people, including asylum seekers, worldwide. The end of the Cold War furthered this trend, both by removing many exit restrictions and by allowing certain conflicts to intensify, which, in turn, started to generate greater refugee flows. On the other hand, the adoption of more restrictive immigration policies in Europe and the United States forced more asylum seekers to opt for other destinations, including Canada. Yet, the post-*Singh* refugee determination system was as multi-stage and cumbersome

---

portrayal of refugees. The coverage focused only on selected groups of asylum seekers: for example, the arrival of thousands of claimants from Portugal and Turkey in 1986–87 attracted little media attention, while at least forty-six stories were reported about a group of 155 Tamils. Gillian Creese, "The Politics of Refugees in Canada" in Vic Satzewich, ed, *Deconstructing a Nation: Immigration, Multiculturalism and Racism in '90s Canada* (Halifax: Fernwood, 1992) 123 at 131 and 135.

71 Creese, *ibid* at 137.

72 *Ibid* at 417.

73 Knowles, above note 1 at 181.

as the previous one and, hence, had limited ability to process a growing number of claimants effectively.

First, a claimant had to go through an immigration inquiry. After that, a credible basis hearing was held. If a credible basis was established, the case went to a full hearing before a two-member panel of the Convention Refugee Determination Division (CRDD) of the Immigration and Refugee Board. Rejected claimants could appeal to the Federal Court of Appeal (with leave) and further to the Supreme Court.

In 1992, the Law Reform Commission of Canada made seventy-two recommendations to improve the refugee determination system, including a suggestion to abolish credible basis hearings.[74] The latter recommendation, along with some others, was incorporated in Bill C-86, which came into force in February 1993. The credible basis hearings were eliminated, and refugee determination was transformed into a one-stage hearing process. Other changes included provision precluding claims by persons who arrived from a safe third country (not implemented[75]); the transfer of the responsibilities for judicial review from the Federal Court of Appeal to the Trial Division of the Federal Court;[76] and stricter inadmissibility and enforcement criteria, which reflected a growing preoccupation with health risks, criminality, and security.

The increasing concern over the risk dimensions of migration was also evident in the Conservative government's decision to shift immigration functions to the Public Security Ministry in 1993. The move provoked an explosion of criticism as it strengthened the association of immigration with threats to security, thereby reinforcing a backlash against immigrants. However, the reorganization did not last long: after the 1993 election the winning Liberals created the Department of Citizenship and Immigration, which became responsible for most immigration processing and policy making.[77]

A notable development in the 1993 election was the popularity of the Reform Party, which called for abandoning multiculturalism and reducing immigration by at least 50 percent. Although it maintained that Canada should continue accepting refugees, it also suggested giving more power to border officers to turn back refugee claimants.[78] Drawing on concern about the rising national debt and the high cost of the social safety net as well as appealing to the "good old days" of

74 Kelley & Trebilcock, above note 6 at 423.

75 Knowles, 2007, above note 23 at 239-241.

76 Kelley & Trebilcock, above note 6 at 424–25.

77 Knowles, above note 1 at 199.

78 Neil Bissoondath, *Selling Illusions: The Cult of Multiculturalism in Canada* (Toronto: Penguin, 1994) at 59.

budget surplus and cultural homogeneity, the Reform Party prospered. It gave voice to a sense of "drift and powerlessness" which some of the public attributed to multicultural policies.[79] It won fifty-two seats in Parliament, becoming the Official Opposition.[80]

In 1994–95, two publicized Toronto shootings committed by immigrants whose deportation orders had not been enforced created further pressure to tighten up enforcement measures.[81] Bill C-44, enacted in 1995, made it easier to remove permanent residents, including Convention refugees, with serious criminal records, and precluded persons with serious criminal records from claiming asylum in Canada.[82] In addition, the government undertook to conduct an independent review of the immigration legislation[83] (which ultimately led to the adoption of the *Immigration and Refugee Protection Act*[84] in 2001).

The Legislative Review Advisory Group formed in 1996 conducted wide consultations with provinces, territories, and major stakeholders, resulting in a report, *Not Just Numbers*. The report proposed introducing two separate pieces of legislation — one dealing with immigration and citizenship, and the other with refugee protection — to reflect the different goals of the two programs. With respect to refugee protection, some of the report's recommendations reflected a more sensitive approach to the needs of refugees, while others were likely to create additional barriers to claimants. For example, the report recommended assigning priority to the most vulnerable; abolishing the permanent residence processing fee for refugees; and introducing an avenue of appeal on protection decisions. At the same time, it recommended giving the Minister the authority to identify safe third countries, introducing time limits for filing a refugee claim inland, and reducing panels on refugee hearings from two members to one.[85]

---

79 *Ibid* at 57.

80 The Reform Party was briefly transformed into the Canadian Reform Alliance Party (before someone realized the implications of the acronym — see Bissoondath, *ibid* at 60) and became the Canadian Alliance in March 2000. In October 2003, the latter merged with the Progressive Conservative Party, forming the Conservative Party of Canada.

81 See, for detailed discussion, Solange Davis-Ramlochan, *The Intersection of Racialized Crime and the Forced Removal of "Foreign Criminals" from Canada: A Critical Analysis* (MA Thesis, Ryerson University, 2013), online: http://digital.library.ryerson.ca/islandora/object/RULA:2190.

82 Kelley & Trebilcock, above note 6 at 434.

83 Galloway, above note 51 at 315.

84 SC 2001, c 27 [*IRPA*].

85 Robert Trempe et al, *Not Just Numbers: A Canadian Framework for Future Immigration* (Ottawa: Minister of Public Works and Government Services Canada,

Following the release of *Not Just Numbers*, a further series of consultations was held, resulting in *Building on a Strong Foundation for the 21st Century: New Directions for Immigration and Refugee Policy and Legislation*.[86] With respect to refugee protection, this White Paper recommended consolidation of Convention and non-Convention grounds for protection decisions; introduction of a limitation period for making inland refugee claims; faster processing of claims from countries considered normally not refugee producing; more active application of cessation and vacation of refugee protection clauses; and a more transparent process for selection of IRB members.[87]

In addition to the above research and consultations, the content of the *IRPA* was influenced by the 2000 report of the Standing Committee on Citizenship and Immigration titled *Refugee Protection and Border Security: Striking a Balance*.[88] The report was prompted by the arrival of four boats with Chinese asylum seekers (599 persons, including 131 unaccompanied minors) in Canada between July and September 1999, which, once again, put into question the effectiveness of Canada's immigration controls. The reaction to the arrivals was mostly negative, painting them as security and health risks.[89] The Standing Committee report made several recommendations, including the detention of trafficked migrants and refugee claimants who refuse to co-operate with authorities in establishing their identities; front-end criminality and security checks, as well as fingerprinting and photographing of refugee claimants; hearing of refugee cases by one-member panels; creation of an appeal structure for rejected claimants; and introduction of a merit-based appointment system for the Immigration and Refugee Board. The

---

1998) at 77–100.

86 Citizenship and Immigration Canada, *Building on a Strong Foundation for the 21st Century: New Directions for Immigration and Refugee Policy and Legislation* (Ottawa: Citizenship and Immigration Canada, 1999).

87 *Ibid* at 43–44.

88 Standing Committee on Citizenship and Immigration, *Refugee Protection and Border Security: Striking a Balance* (March 2000), online: www.parl.gc.ca/InfoComDoc/36/2/CIMM/Studies/Reports/cimm02-e.htm.

89 Joshua Greenberg, "Opinion Discourse and Canadian Newspapers: The Case of the Chinese 'Boat People'" (2000) 25 *Canadian Journal of Communications* 517; Alison Mountz, "Embodying the Nation-State: Canada's Response to Human Smuggling" (2004) 23 *Political Geography* 323; Minelle Mahtani & Alison Mountz, *Immigration to British Columbia: Media Representation and Public Opinion* (Research on Immigration and Integration in the Metropolis, Working Paper No 02-15) (August 2002), online: mbc.metropolis.net/assets/uploads/files/wp/2002/WP02-15.pdf.

government accepted most of the committee's recommendations, many of which were reflected in the new legislation.

The *IRPA* (Bill C-31) was tabled in April 2000, but its adoption was interrupted by the election called in October 2000. It was reintroduced as Bill C-11 in February 2001 and received royal assent in December 2001. It came into force on 28 June 2002.

The harrowing events of September 11 occurred between the introduction of the *IRPA* and its coming into force. Although most of the *IRPA*'s provisions were drafted before 9/11, this event prompted even greater attention to security aspects of immigration. After the terrorist attacks in the United States, Canada implemented several new measures to enhance border control, monitor human movement across the border, and facilitate identification of individuals crossing the border. These measures included the development of the National Security Policy, biometric technology for border control, and the negotiation of Canada–US agreements on immigration, asylum, and security measures. In December 2001, the United States and Canada signed a *Smart Border Declaration* and a thirty-point Action Plan to increase public and economic security between the two countries. The Action Plan presupposed, *inter alia*, joint development of biometric identifiers; review of asylum practices to allow thorough screening for security risks; negotiation of a safe third country agreement; visa policy coordination; exchange of immigration and intelligence information; and joint enforcement activities.[90]

In December 2002, Canada and the United States signed a *Safe Third Country Agreement*, which came into force in December 2004. (The content and impact of the agreement on access to asylum in Canada is discussed in Chapter 8.) It should be noted, however, that an earlier attempt to negotiate such an agreement was made in the 1990s but was abandoned by the United States. The official justification was that the United States had to streamline all its resources into implementing changes brought by the 1996 amendments to the *Immigration and Naturalization Act*.[91] However, some argue that the United States was merely not interested as such an agreement was likely to be more beneficial for Canada than for it (more claimants travel via the United States to Canada than the other way around).[92] The events of 9/11 motivated the

---

90 US Department of State, *U.S. - Canada Smart Border/30 Point Action Plan Update*, online: http://2001-2009.state.gov/p/wha/rls/fs/18128.htm.

91 Judith Kumin, "Proposed US–Canada Accord Sparks Debate" (3 September 2002), online: www.unhcr.org/news/latest/2002/9/3d74ec864/feature-proposed-us-canada-accord-sparks-debate.html.

92 The number of claimants transiting from the United States to Canada far exceeds the number of claimants moving in the opposite direction. See Audrey

United States to change its position largely as a concession in order to gain Canada's greater co-operation in security matters.

6) 2002 to 2008

The *IRPA* and the *Immigration and Refugee Protection Regulations*[93] amended both procedural and substantive aspects of the Canadian refugee system. On a positive side, the *IRPA* broadened the grounds on which protection can be conferred, provided for a new Refugee Appeal Division of the Board, and placed more emphasis on protection needs in selection of refugees for resettlement. The Act, however, also introduced certain restrictions in relation to other aspects of refugee determination. For example, panels hearing refugee claims were reduced from two members to one; the requirement for leave for judicial review was extended with respect to decisions on resettlement; and referral from the UN High Commissioner for Refugees (UNHCR) or a sponsorship undertaking were made mandatory preconditions for resettlement from overseas. In respect to border control and security, the *IRPA* expanded powers of immigration arrest and detention, codified categories of inadmissibility, limited the right to appeal inadmissibility decisions, streamlined the security certificate process, and introduced tougher penalties for immigration offences. The peculiarities of these procedures and their impact on asylum seekers will be discussed in subsequent chapters of this book.

Among other notable developments at this time are the creation of the Canada Border Services Agency (CBSA) in 2003 and changes to the IRB appointment process in 2004 and 2007. The CBSA took over from Citizenship and Immigration Canada (CIC) the functions of intelligence, interdiction, and enforcement. It is currently the agency primarily responsible for traveller screening at the border, immigration detention, and removal. (The details of its work will be discussed in Chapters 11 and 12.)

As to the Immigration and Refugee Board, the changes were motivated by the long-standing criticism of political favoritism in the appointment process as well as increased public scrutiny of the issue due to highly publicized allegations of bribery and other misconduct by

---

Macklin, "Disappearing Refugees: Reflections on the Canada–US *Safe Third Country Agreement*" (2005) 36 *Columbia Human Rights Law Review* 365.

93 SOR/2002-227 [*Regulations*].

several IRB members.[94] In 2004[95] and 2007, changes were made to the selection of the members of the Refugee Protection and Immigration Appeal divisions of the Board. The new procedure seeks to ensure that appointment is merit based and includes the following steps:

1) preliminary screening for basic requirements such as education and experience;
2) review by the Selection Advisory Board (SAB);[96]
3) taking of a written test, which evaluates conceptual thinking, judgment/analytical thinking, decision making, and written communication;

---

94 For example, in June 2003, two IRB members in Montreal were alleged to have received bribes in return for favourable decisions. "Immigration Judges Took Bribes, Affidavit Alleges" *CBC News* (6 June 2003), online: www.cbc.ca/1.393283; "Minister Defends Immigration Board after Scandal" *CBC News* (7 June 2003), online: www.cbc.ca/1.379313. One of the Board members was convicted and sentenced to six years in prison. "A Good Start, but How Far Has the Rot Spread?" Editorial, *The Gazette* (3 July 2006) A14.

In the spring of 2004, one of the IRB staff alleged that Board members delegated writing of decisions to refugee protection officers in violation of Refugee Protection Division (RPD) rules. "Refugee Judges Delegate Decision, Complaint Says" *CBC News* (17 March 2004), online: www.cbc.ca/1.473965; Colin Freeze, "Wrote Rulings for Judges, Refugee Officer Declares" *The Globe and Mail* (18 March 2004) A7. In June 2004, four members of the IRB were reprimanded for "improper conduct," and Ed Ratushny was commissioned to investigate the situation. Michael Friscolati, "Four Refugee Board Judges Reprimanded" *National Post* (19 June 2004) A4.

In the fall of 2006, two IRB members were accused of sexual misconduct; one of them was facing criminal charges. Marina Jimenez, "Refugee Board to Reopen Cases after Complaints" *The Globe and Mail* (11 November 2006), online: www.theglobeandmail.com/news/national/refugee-board-to-reopen-cases-after-complaints/article4315792/.

95 Citizenship and Immigration Canada, News Release, "Minister Sgro Announces Reform of the Appointment Process for Immigration and Refugee Board Members" (16 March 2004).

96 As of 2017, there was no publicly available information on the composition of the SAB. However, in his testimony before the House of Commons Standing Committee on Citizenship and Immigration in 2009, Simon Coakeley, executive director of the IRB, indicated that the SAB consists of nine members: the chairperson of the IRB; four persons — jointly appointed by the Minister of Citizenship, Immigration and Multiculturalism and the IRB chairperson — from outside the IRB; and four persons appointed by the IRB chairperson from within IRB personnel. Testimony of Simon Coakeley, executive director of the IRB, before the House of Commons Standing Committee on Citizenship and Immigration (28 April 2009), online: www.parl.gc.ca/HousePublications/Publication.aspx?Language=e&Mode=1&Parl=40&Ses=2&DocId=3838654.

4) behaviour event interview by the SAB, which evaluates oral communication, information seeking, self-control, organizational skills, results orientation, and cultural competence;
5) reference checks.[97]

After completion of the above steps, the IRB Chairperson communicates names of successful candidates to the immigration minister, who, in turn, makes recommendations to the Governor in Council (federal Cabinet).[98]

In the realm of overall immigration policy, the period from about 2008 onwards was characterized by increased emphasis on promoting efficiency of immigrant selection and management as well as prevention of fraud and abuse in the immigration and refugee system. A notable development of 2008, which sought to advance this agenda, was the grant of a new power to the immigration minister to issue instructions to immigration officers with respect to processing of various applications. For example, such instructions can establish conditions that must be met before or during the processing of an application or request; prescribe an order for the processing of applications or requests; and set the number of applications or requests to be processed in a given year.[99] This power has been utilized on a number of occasions, with significant implications for applicants, primarily with respect to the economic class. For instance, Ministerial Instructions established (and revised several times) eligibility criteria for applications under the federal skilled worker class, revised existing immigration streams (e.g., the caregiver program), or introduced new application streams (e.g., start-up visa), and imposed suspensions on certain applications (e.g., in business class and in relation to sponsorship of parents and grandparents).[100] Although this power does not apply to the refugee determination process, it signified a move towards greater executive discretion and less transparent and publicly debated process for making changes to the immigration system.

7) 2008 to the Present

Since 2008, few areas of immigration, refugee, or citizenship laws have remained untouched by the flurry of changes introduced by the Conservative government (which was in power as a minority government

97 *Ibid.*
98 *Ibid.*
99 *IRPA*, above note 84, s 87.3(3).
100 See full list, online: www.cic.gc.ca/english/department/mi/.

from 2006 to 2011 and subsequently as a majority until October 2015).[101] The Conservative government's rhetoric prominently featured moral panic about external and internal threats and promoted responses to them through enhanced screening for dangerous and risky individuals, increased punishments and interventions by the police, border security, and intelligence services.[102] As some note, "[t]he Harper Conservatives see a social world of law-abiding Canadians, yet a world beset with problems of border security, child pornography, citizen's arrest, elder abuse, foreign criminals living in Canada, illicit drugs, gangs and youth-at-risk, human trafficking, money-laundering, prisons with drug problems, sex offenders, smuggling of tobacco, terrorism, and white collar crime."[103] This rhetoric has been vivid and influential in government's stance on immigration and refugee issues: immigration and citizenship fraud,[104] threats from criminals,[105] and "bogus" refugees[106] who violate of the integrity of this system. For example, in 2010, the government introduced "Cracking Down on Crooked Consultants Bill" to combat "fraud [which] remains a widespread threat to the integrity of our citizenship and immigration programs and costs us all."[107] In

---

101 For a useful review, see Naomi Alboim & Karen Cohl for Maytree, *Shaping the Future: Canada's Rapidly Changing Immigration Policies* (October 2012), online: maytree.com/wp-content/uploads/2012/10/shaping-the-future.pdf.

102 Michael J Prince, "Prime Minister as Moral Crusader: Stephen Harper's Punitive Turn in Social Policy-Making" (2015) 71 *Canadian Review of Social Policy/Revue canadienne de politique sociale* 53.

103 *Ibid* at 63.

104 Speaking notes for the Honourable Jason Kenney, Minister of Citizenship, Immigration and Multiculturalism, at a news conference to announce changes to spousal sponsorship (2 March 2012), online: www.cic.gc.ca/english/department/media/speeches/2012/2012-03-02.asp [Kenney, spousal sponsorship]; Speaking notes for the Honourable Jason Kenney, Minister of Citizenship, Immigration and Multiculturalism, at a news conference regarding Citizenship and Immigration fraud investigations (10 September 2012), online: www.cic.gc.ca/english/department/media/speeches/2012/2012-09-10.asp.

105 Speaking notes for the Honourable Jason Kenney, Minister of Citizenship, Immigration and Multiculturalism, at a news conference to announce the tabling of Bill C-43: *Faster Removal of Foreign Criminals Act* (20 June 2012), www.cic.gc.ca/english/department/media/speeches/2012/2012-06-20.asp [Kenney, Bill C-43].

106 Speaking notes for the Honourable Jason Kenney, Minister of Citizenship, Immigration and Multiculturalism, at a news conference following the tabling of Bill C-31, *Protecting Canada's Immigration System Act* (16 February 2012), online: www.cic.gc.ca/english/department/media/speeches/2012/2012-02-16.asp [Kenney, Bill C-31].

107 Speaking notes for the Honourable Jason Kenney, Minister of Citizenship, Immigration and Multiculturalism, on *Cracking Down on Crooked Consultants*

2012, changes to sponsorship of foreign spouses (including introducing a two-year conditional permanent residence) were implemented as a "part of the government's overarching strategy to tackle the growing problem of immigration fraud."[108] Also in 2012, Bill C-43, "Faster Removal of Foreign Criminals Bill," sought to streamline removal of inadmissible persons in order to help increase "[government's] ability to protect Canadians from criminal and security threats."[109] As explained by the then immigration minister, "[w]e have introduced a law that will stop foreign criminals relying on endless appeals in order to delay their removal from Canada during which time they continue to terrorize innocent Canadians . . . Canadians are generous and welcoming people, but they have no tolerance for criminals and fraudsters abusing our generosity."[110] Finally, in 2014, the *Strengthening Canadian Citizenship Act* (Bill C-24) was passed to "protect and strengthen the great value of [Canadian] citizenship" (*inter alia*, by increasing the residency requirement) and provide authorities with "stronger tools to counter citizenship fraud and, more generally, bolster the integrity of the system"[111] (through, for example, streamlining revocation of citizenship and introducing new grounds for revocation). Given the highly restrictive nature of the above-mentioned measures and their potentially negative impact on immigrant and refugee populations, numerous concerns have been highlighted by various advocacy groups.[112] However, the voices of advocacy groups not only had little impact on government policy response, but were, at times, criticized by the government as doing a disservice to Canada.[113]

Some groups, notably Roma claimants (from Hungary and the Czech Republic), were singled out in government rhetoric as "bogus"

(8 June 2010), online: www.cic.gc.ca/english/department/media/speeches/2010/2010-06-08.asp.

108 Kenney, spousal sponsorship, above note 104.

109 Kenney, Bill C-43, above note 105.

110 Immigration, Refugees and Citizenship Canada, "Minister Kenney Supports the *Faster Removal of Foreign Criminals Act*" (2012), online: IRCC http://news.gc.ca/web/article-en.do?nid=696319.

111 Speaking notes for Chris Alexander, Canada's Citizenship and Immigration Minister, for a keynote address entitled "Strengthening the Value of Canadian Citizenship" to the Canadian Club of Vancouver (18 February 2014), online: http://news.gc.ca/web/article-en.do?nid=831819.

112 For example, see Canadian Council for Refugees papers on refugee protection in Canada at http://ccrweb.ca/en/library.

113 Jason Kenney, Opinion Letters, *Welland Tribune* (23 May 2012), online: www.wellandtribune.ca/2012/05/23/immigration-minister-jason-kenny-responds.

refugees.[114] For example, Minister Kenney said that "refugee claims from Czechs make no sense because they could easily move to 26 other Western democracies in the European Union."[115] In 2009, the Immigration and Refugee Board issued the paper on state protection, "Czech Republic: Fact-finding Mission for Internal Relocation," which was subsequently relied upon to refuse claims by the Czech Roma.[116] In addition, visa restrictions and other measures have been used from time to time to deter "bogus" Roma arrivals. A visa requirement was imposed on Czech citizens in 1998 and lifted in 2007 to be reimposed again in 2009 and lifted in 2013. Similarly, a visa requirement was imposed on Hungarian citizens in 2001 (lifted in 2008). In 2013, Canadian authorities bought billboard space in Hungary to place warnings that those who make unfounded claims will be processed and removed from Canada faster.[117]

Two boat arrivals — the *Ocean Lady*, with seventy-six Tamils aboard in October 2009, and MV *Sun Sea*, with 492 Tamil passengers in August 2010 — further impassioned the debate about asylum, human smuggling, and security. Both arrivals received extensive and largely negative coverage in the media highlighting issues of criminality and terrorism.[118] The response from the government was also harsh. Although the 2009 arrivals were allowed to remain in the community on bail-like conditions, everyone from the *Sun Sea* was detained, including sixty-three women and forty-nine children, for at least several

---

114 For detailed discussion, see Petra Molnar Diop, "The 'Bogus' Refugee: Roma Asylum Claimants and Discourses of Fraud in Canada's Bill C-31" (2014) 30 *Refuge* 67.

115 "Kenney Defends Visa Rules for Czech Nationals" *CTV News* (15 July 2009), online: www.ctvnews.ca/kenney-defends-visa-rules-for-czech-nationals-1.416560.

116 A class action has been launched in relation to this report: see *Sivak v Canada (Minister of Citizenship and Immigration)*, 2011 FC 402, and related proceedings. See also Julianna Beaudoin, Jennifer Danch, & Sean Rehaag, *No Refuge: Hungarian Romani Refugee Claimants in Canada* (Osgoode Legal Studies Research Paper Series, Paper 94) (2015), online: http://digitalcommons.osgoode.yorku.ca/olsrps/94, which documents concerns about the IRB's institutional bias against Roma claimants.

117 Nicholas Keung, "Roma Refugees: Canadian Billboards in Hungary Warn of Deportation" *Toronto Star* (25 February 2013), online: www.thestar.com/news/canada/2013/01/25/roma_refugees_canadian_billboards_in_hungary_warn_of_deportation.html.

118 Ashley Bradimore & Harald Bauder, "Mystery Ships and Risky Boat People: Tamil Refugee Migration in the Newsprint Media" (Vancouver, BC: Metropolis British Columbia, Centre of Excellence for Research on Immigration and Diversity, 2011), online: http://mbc.metropolis.net/assets/uploads/files/wp/2011/WP11-02.pdf.

months.[119] A memo obtained by the Canadian Council for Refugees through an access-to-information request revealed that the CBSA was directing officers to use all legal means to detain the passengers as long as possible, despite also recognizing that many were likely to be refugees. This was said to be necessary in the interests of deterring future arrivals.[120] Eventually, some passengers were found to be refugees, others were rejected, and a number were determined inadmissible and issued removal orders.[121] Although in Canadian history boat arrivals were few (for example, since 1986, only eight boats reached Canada carrying a total of about 1,500 people, or 0.2 percent of all refugee arrivals[122]), they tended to create public hysteria about security and border control, frequently leading to harsh executive and legislative response. The arrivals of the *Ocean Lady* and the *Sun Sea* prompted some of the recent changes to the immigration detention regime.

In the fall of 2010, the Conservative government introduced Bill C-49, *Preventing Human Smugglers from Abusing Canada's Immigration System Act*.[123] While the title of the bill suggested that it targeted human smugglers, it also proposed measures that would have a negative impact on some refugee claimants. For example, it provided that refugee claimants who arrive without proper authorization would be subject to a mandatory twelve-month detention; face a five-year bar on application for permanent residence following a successful refugee claim; and have no right to appeal to the Refugee Appeal Division. These measures were such a dramatic departure from Canada's humanitarian tradition that it was unclear how the government intended to garner sufficient support for them to pass. Several advocacy groups voiced major concerns about the bill and mounted campaigns, including lobbying mem-

---

119 Amnesty International, Canadian Council for Refugees, Canadian Tamil Congress, International Civil Liberties Monitoring Group, Media Release, "Rights Advocates Decry Detention of Refugee Claimants from MV Sun Sea" (20 February 2011).

120 Canadian Council for Refugees, "Submission to the Senate Standing Committee on National Security and Defence for Its Study on the Policies, Practices, and Collaborative Efforts of Canada Border Services Agency in Determining Admissibility to Canada and Removal of Inadmissible Individuals" (April 2014) at 8, online: CCR http://ccrweb.ca/files/senate-inadmissibility-study-april-2014.pdf; memo obtained through access-to-information request is available, online: http://ccrweb.ca/files/atip-cbsa-sun-sea-strategy-next-arrival.pdf.

121 Keith Fraser, "Refugee Claimants Underwent 'Survival of the Fittest,' Prosecutor Tells Hearing" *The* [Vancouver] *Province* (6 February 2013).

122 Stephanie Silverman, "In the Wake of Irregular Arrivals: Changes to the Canadian Immigration Detention System" (2014) 30 *Refuge* 27 at 28.

123 The boat arrivals on the *Ocean Lady* and the *Sun Sea* were specifically referred to in the Sponsor's speech. See note 124, below.

bers of Parliament not to support the bill. Eventually, all opposition parties publicly stated that they would not support the bill. Given that the Conservative government had a minority at the time, the bill could not have been passed without some support from the opposition and, thus, was abandoned (it died on the order paper when Parliament was dissolved and an election called).

Interestingly, however, the failure of Bill C-49 surfaced (as least implicitly) as a useful tool in electoral rhetoric. For example, a 2011 Conservative Party's ad contained an image of a ship (presumably with "illegal arrivals") accompanied by the following accusation against rival parties: "Ignatieff [leader of the Liberal Party] and his reckless coalition — weak on border security . . . ." The Conservatives won a majority in May 2011.

It is in the above context that most of the recent changes to the refugee determination system were developed and implemented. The first step was taken in March 2010 when the government introduced Bill C-11, *Balanced Refugee Reform Act* (which received royal assent in June 2010). It contemplated the following key changes:

- an information-gathering interview no earlier than fifteen days after a claimant's arrival (in contrast to the past whereby claimants were provided with a personal information form to complete on their own (or with assistance of a counsel or a support person) within twenty-eight days);
- an initial hearing by public servant members of the IRB (in contrast to the past whereby claims were heard by the Governor in Council appointees);
- ministerial authority to designate countries of origin that are considered normally not refugee producing and fast tracking of claims from those countries;
- timelines for refugee hearings: within sixty days for claimants from designated countries of origin and within ninety days for others;
- implementation of the Refugee Appeal Division;
- new authority of the Refugee Protection Division to identify "manifestly unfounded claims," that is, claims considered to be clearly fraudulent (these claims were to be fast-tracked on appeal);
- a one-year bar on access to pre-removal risk assessment (PRRA) for rejected claimants (in contrast to the past system, which did not impose any temporal limitation on PRRA applications).

Bill C-11 provided for differentiation between groups of refugee claimants: those from designated countries of origin, those whose claims were found to be manifestly unfounded, and all other claimants.

The first two groups would be fast-tracked. As outlined by the then immigration minister Jason Kenney, the changes were necessary for the following reasons:

> Our refugee system is amongst the most generous in the world. It is internationally recognized for its fairness . . . .
>
> But for too many years, our generous asylum system has been abused by too many people making bogus refugee claims. Canadians take great pride in the generosity and compassion of our immigration and refugee programs. But they have no tolerance for those who abuse our generosity or take advantage of our country . . . .
>
> For too long, we have spent precious time and taxpayers' money on people who are not in need of our protection, at the expense of legitimate asylum seekers who have been forced to wait at the back of an unacceptably long queue . . . .
>
> To be blunt: Canada's asylum system is broken. That's why Parliament passed the *Balanced Refugee Reform Act* in 2010.[124]

Concerns over the slow and backlogged refugee determination system were long-standing. On average, it could take between one and two years to have a claim heard. By 2010, the backlog of claims before the Immigration and Refugee Board had reached some 63,000.[125] Further, rejected claimants could remain in Canada for prolonged periods (from four to six years[126]) if they pursued judicial review or pre-removal risk assessment or applied for humanitarian and compassionate consideration. Long delays had negative impact on claimants, leaving them in uncertainty about their future and prolonging separation from loved ones. The delays were also considered (by some) to create incentives for frivolous claims whereby individuals could benefit from social assistance, healthcare, and a work permit, while their cases were awaiting determination. Thus, changes to the system were necessary in order to make it faster, fairer, and more efficient.[127] The tools chosen by the

---

124 Kenney, Bill C-31, above note 106; see also the Sponsor's speech at second reading (23 April 2012), online: www.parl.gc.ca/HousePublications/Publication.aspx?Pub=Hansard&Doc=108&Parl=41&Ses=1&Language=E&Mode=1.

125 Legislative Summary of Bill C-11: *An Act to amend the Immigration and Refugee Protection Act and the Federal Courts Act (Balanced Refugee Reform Act)*, online: www.lop.parl.gc.ca/About/Parliament/LegislativeSummaries/bills_ls.asp?Language=E&ls=C11&Mode=1&Parl=40&Ses=3&source=library_prb.

126 For one such proposal, see Peter Showler, *Fast, Fair and Final: Reforming Canada's Refugee System* (Toronto: Maytree Foundation, 2009) at 8, online: www.maytree.com/wp-content/uploads/2009/07/FastFairAndFinal.pdf.

127 *Ibid.*

Conservative government to effectuate the change, however, were highly problematic.

It was expected that Bill C-11 would be implemented by 29 June 2012, but while it was being prepared for implementation, it became apparent that some changes would not work. For example, information-gathering interviews would be extremely time consuming and also raise a variety of due process concerns. Consequently, Bill C-31, *Protecting Canada's Immigration System Act*, introduced in February 2012, sought to amend Bill C-11 as well as incorporate certain provisions similar to those contained in Bill C-49.

Among the major changes resulting from Bill C-31 were these:

- differentiation between three groups of claimants: (1) claimants from designated countries of origin (DCOs); (2) designated foreign nationals; and (3) all other claimants (the first two groups would face serious restrictions in the refugee determination process) (for details on the definitions and differences among these groups, see Chapter 3);
- implementation of designated countries of origin list (that is, a list of countries that do not normally produce refugees);
- limitations on access to appeal to the Refugee Appeal Division for designated foreign nationals and claimants from DCOs;
- a new detention regime for designated foreign nationals (see Chapters 3, 8, and 11 for further details).

The bill was strongly criticized by advocacy groups,[128] but was passed with relatively few amendments. The changes took effect on 15 December 2012. In addition, cuts to the Interim Federal Health Program had been announced in June 2012, resulting in some claimants having virtually no access even to life-saving treatment (for more detailed discussion, see Chapter 3).

For a detailed comparison of pre-2012 and new refugee determination systems, see Chapter 8, Table 8.1.

128 Canadian Council for Refugees, "Protect Refugees from Bill C-31: Joint Statement" (March 2012), online: CCR http://ccrweb.ca/en/protect-refugees-c31-statement; Ontario Council of Agencies Serving Immigrants, "Bill C-31 Must Be Withdrawn," online: OCASI www.ocasi.org/bill-c-31-must-be-withdrawn; UNICEF, Brief to the House of Commons Standing Committee on Citizenship and Immigration, "Bill C-31: The *Protecting Canada's Immigration System Act*" (18 April 2012), online: www.unicef.ca/sites/default/files/imce_uploads/DISCOVER/OUR%20WORK/ADVOCACY/DOMESTIC/unicef_canada_bill_c-31_submission final.pdf.

In October 2015, the nearly ten-year rule of the Conservative Party ended. With the Liberal Party in the majority, it is unlikely that the past increasingly restrictive trends will continue. In fact, the Liberal Party promised to reverse a number of measures introduced by the Conservative government.[129] For example, it already has introduced Bill C-6, which proposes to remove some of the more burdensome requirements for citizenship that took effect in 2014 (such as lengthier residency requirement, declaration of intention to reside in Canada, and a citizenship and language test for individuals aged fourteen to sixty-four) as well as to abolish new grounds for citizenship revocation based on national security concerns.[130] It also announced an intention to remove a two-year conditional permanent residence for sponsored spouses, introduced in 2012.[131] Finally, between November 2015 and June 2016, the Liberal government resettled more than 28,000 Syrian refugees — a move that sharply contrasts with the Conservative government's commitment to resettle only 1,300 Syrian refugees in 2014.[132]

In terms of immigration plans and priorities for 2016–17, the Liberal government established a higher overall target for admissions: 280,000 to 305,000 new permanent residents in 2016[133] (compared to an average annual total of about 257,000 between 2008 and 2014[134]). Compared to past years, it has allocated more spaces to family and refugee streams and reduced targets for the economic class. In 2016, family stream accounted for 27 percent of all admissions (compared to, on average, 25 percent during 2008–14); refugee stream, 18 percent (compared to about 9 percent during 2008–14); and economic class, 54 per-

---

129 Liberal Party, Brochure, "A New Plan for Canadian Immigration and Economic Opportunity," online: www.liberal.ca/realchange/a-new-plan-for-canadian-immigration-and-economic-opportunity/?shownew=1.

130 For more on citizenship requirements and prohibitions, see Chapter 3, Section C(5).

131 Nicholas Keung, "Activists Hail Proposed Changes to Spousal Sponsorship Rules" *Toronto Star* (1 March 2016), online: http://on.thestar.com/1oWom/1oWKRkgKRk.

132 For more discussion of this, see Liew & Galloway, above note 10 at 240–42. See also Immigration, Refugees and Citizenship Canada, "#WelcomeRefugees: Milestones and Key Figures," online: IRCC www.cic.gc.ca/english/refugees/welcome/milestones.asp.

133 "Liberals Shift Immigration Focus to Family Reunification, Refugee Resettlement" *CBC News* (8 March 2016), online: www.cbc.ca/news/politics/liberals-immigration-levels-plan-2016-1.3479764.

134 For statistics on 2008–14 admissions, see Immigration, Refugees and Citizenship Canada, "Facts and Figures 2014 — Immigration Overview: Permanent Residents," online: IRCC www.cic.gc.ca/english/resources/statistics/facts2014/permanent/01.asp.

cent (compared to 60 to 63 percent during 2008–14).[135] For breakdown of annual admissions by immigration stream between 1996 and 2015, see Appendix C.

The department of Citizenship and Immigration Canada was re-branded as Immigration, Refugees and Citizenship Canada (IRCC): the latter name will be used throughout this book even when it describes activities of the immigration department before the name change.

C. ANALYTICAL OVERVIEW

Since the Second World War, Canada has admitted close to one million refugees and other humanitarian cases.[136] Its refugee protection system has evolved from ad hoc arrangements to orderly and extensive mechanisms of inland and overseas determination. However, the history of Canadian immigration policies attests not only to the evolution of humanitarianism, but also to the contradictions within the objective of population movement control inherent in migration law. While exemplifying the liberalization of certain aspects of migration control, it also demonstrates how surprisingly little has changed. The law no longer explicitly excludes "mentally retarded," "deaf and dumb," "blind," or "charity cases," but it makes inadmissible potential immigrants on the basis of lack of financial resources or likelihood of causing "excessive demand on health or social services."[137] The terminology has undoubtedly changed, but in real terms, the current system may still indirectly discriminate against certain groups (e.g., persons from poorer countries are likely to face greater difficulty satisfying financial requirements and paying processing and landing fees). Visa restrictions are frequently described as the new face of the various racial exclusion acts of an earlier time;[138] and the right of landing fee payable upon receipt of permanent residence can be analogized to the head tax. New racism disguises itself into more acceptable forms, without explicit invocation of race.[139]

135 *Ibid.*

136 Immigration, Refugees and Citizenship Canada, *Facts and Figures 2005 — Immigration Overview: Permanent and Temporary Residents*, online: IRCC http://publications.gc.ca/collections/Collection/Ci1-8-2005E.pdf.

137 *IRPA*, above note 84, s 38(1)(c).

138 See, for example, Cynthia Levine-Rasky et al, "The Exclusion of Roma Claimants in Canadian Refugee Policy" (2014) 48 *Patterns of Prejudice* 67.

139 See, generally, David Theo Goldberg, *Racist Culture: Philosophy and the Politics of Meaning* (Oxford and Cambridge, MA: Blackwell, 1993).

Although these practices do not deny the important extension of the *Charter* protection to non-citizens, they highlight the inherently discriminatory nature of migration law. The tension can be vividly traced in the overall framework of the *IRPA*, which ambivalently combines greater sensitivity to the circumstances of migrants in some aspects of the system (e.g., expanded grounds of refugee protection) with greater restrictions in others (e.g., a new detention regime for designated foreign nationals, fast-tracking of claims from designated countries of origin). The changes brought about by the Conservative government during the past decade exemplified a new era of restrictions and a shift in its approach to refugee protection. However, the election of the Liberal Party to power in October 2015 created a possibility of change in course. As seen throughout the discussion in this chapter, Canada's history of immigration and refugee regulation is one of fluctuations between more restrictive and more liberal policies, under the influence of a variety of domestic and international factors. While such factors are multiple, the following three sets create a useful context for understanding past and present immigration and refugee policies:

1) patterns and nature of international migration;
2) models of community membership; and
3) states' international human rights obligations.

1) Patterns and Nature of International Migration

Migration does not occur randomly; it is a social process patterned by a wide range of factors.[140] For example, Stephen Castles, speaking of migration generally, succinctly grouped factors into three categories:

- factors endemic to the migration process itself (such as the migration industry, network migration, and states' structural dependence on emigration or immigrant labour);
- factors linked to globalization, transnationalism, and the North–South divide;
- factors rooted in national political systems (such as interest groups, clientelist politics, civil society, and the welfare state).[141]

The above factors not only shape migration patterns, but also influence the effectiveness of state migration policies and their ability to achieve stated objectives.

140 Stephen Castles, "The Factors That Make and Unmake Migration Policies" (2004) 38 *International Migration Review* 852 at 870.

141 *Ibid* at 857.

The first group of factors encompasses structures that attract and sustain migration. For example, network migration, family, and community linkages provide social capital that enables migration. The migration industry, which includes travel agents, immigration lawyers and consultants, labour recruiters, and others, not only facilitates migration but also creates actors that have a strong interest in the continuation of migration.[142] In addition to official channels of movement, smuggling and trafficking networks constitute an important part of the migration industry. Given that asylum seekers frequently do not have a choice of a destination or do not even know where they are being taken, smugglers may help shape refugee flows. Further, migration flows are sustained by states' dependence on immigration or emigration. Many countries become dependent on migrant labour (e.g., Canada, with its greenhouse industry, is heavily dependent on Mexican seasonal agricultural workers[143]) and consequently are likely to maintain certain migration programs long term. In turn, for some developing countries, emigration becomes a way to reduce unemployment, stimulate development, and ensure flow of remittances (e.g., Mexico and the Philippines). A government's encouragement of emigration may lead to the development of a culture of emigration, thereby sustaining the outflow of persons to other countries.[144]

The second group of factors often determines the direction of migration flows. Countries of the global North are often considered to be a strong magnet for migrants from developing countries, forming corresponding migration patterns. Further, globalization creates incentives for people to move farther and migrate back and forth, not necessarily permanently.[145] By establishing ethnic communities in their countries of new residence and maintaining links with home countries, migrants facilitate the development of transnational communities that help facilitate migration.[146] Despite these developments, most global North states continue being only selectively open to migration. They compete for "the best and the brightest," consequently resulting in greater freedom of movement for highly skilled workers.[147] At the same time, they are less willing to admit lower-skilled workers, sponsored relatives, and

---

142 *Ibid* at 859–60.

143 Tanya Basok, "Post-national Citizenship, Social Exclusion and Migrants Rights: Mexican Seasonal Workers in Canada" (2004) 8 *Citizenship Studies* 47.

144 Castles, above note 140 at 860–61.

145 *Ibid* at 862.

146 *Ibid* at 863.

147 For a detailed account, see Ayelet Shachar, "The Race for Talent: Highly Skilled Migrants and Competitive Immigration Regimes" (2006) 81 *New York University*

refugees as those are often considered to have lower human capital and higher likelihood of becoming burdens on social and healthcare systems. Unauthorized migrants are perceived as not only undesirable, but also threatening to the sovereignty and good order of receiving states. They are "greeted" with new barriers on entry and other disincentives.[148] Refugees, who are often equated in the public imagination with illegal migrants and "queue jumpers" seeking to gain entry through the "back door," also often face barriers on entry. Further, some governments view the arrival of asylum seekers as a factor that frustrates their orderly humanitarian programs.[149]

The third group of factors considers the role of various stakeholders in shaping state migration policies and highlights frequent contradictions arising in the policy-formation process. For example, some interest groups (e.g., representing businesses) are often seen lobbying governments for extension of foreign worker programs, while others may lobby for the opposite. Further, the reasons for groups and individuals favouring or opposing immigration are numerous: economic, political, ideological, national identity, and others. A state needs to balance these various competing interests, often creating hidden agendas (e.g., professing strict border control policies, while tacitly accepting significant undocumented labour migration).[150]

Migration flows need to be understood in the complex context of the above-discussed factors, interconnected with issues of economic development, global inequality, and changing policies of major receiving states. Such interconnectedness can be vividly traced during the past century. For example, before the First World War, numerous refugees and immigrants were transiting through Europe on their way to America. Notwithstanding the constant and heavy influx of "outsiders,"

Law Review 148. See also, generally, Catherine Dauvergne, "Sovereignty, Migration and the Rule of Law in Global Times" (2004) 67 *Modern Law Review* 588.

148 It should be noted that much of the discussion on border control and migration management is presented from the perspective of developed states that feel the need and have the capacity to maintain such control. Some developing countries also implement visa requirements with respect to citizens of many countries, including developed countries. However, such controls can be more properly characterized as not purely defensive, but rather ideological (e.g., as a guard against Western expansion or as a way of retaliation against similar requirements implemented by developed states).

149 Such a position has been clearly articulated and maintained by the Australian government. See, for example, Honourable Philip Ruddock, "Refugee Claims and Australian Migration Law: A Ministerial Perspective" (2000) 23 *University of New South Wales Law Journal* 1 at 3.

150 Castles, above note 140 at 867.

European countries never closed their borders, knowing that these people had little intention of staying in their territory permanently.[151] The refugee crises first arose when the obsession with state sovereignty and border control stopped the free movement of people.[152] Once the United States and Canada closed their doors to transatlantic migration in the 1920s, European states not wanting to permanently host people who were no longer free to immigrate to the New World were compelled to act similarly. In the 1990s, Europe's shift to refugee deterrence and similar measures in the United States made Canada an increasingly attractive refugee destination.[153] In 2015–16, certain European Union countries (e.g., Hungary, Slovenia) started closing their borders with neighbouring states in an effort to divert major flows of refugees from Syria and other countries of the Middle East.

Stricter border control, interdiction, and deterrence may divert flows of asylum seekers from one country to the other or force more people to resort to illegal entry. However, they will not stop those flows, unless their underlying causes are addressed.

2) Notions of Community Membership

Immigration law is said to have a strong connection to national identity. It reflects the guiding values of a society expressly through the objectives of immigration legislation and judicial decisions[154] as well as implicitly through the design of immigration procedures and policy decisions. By prescribing the criteria for membership, immigration law creates an image of those who are desirable and those who are not. By regulating access to territory and access to membership, it constitutes the boundary of a community and shapes its identity. For example, the desire to preserve Canada as a white, British society was one of the determinative factors in imposition of racial restrictions during the late nineteenth to early twentieth century. Post Second World War, the ideas of humanitarianism and multiculturalism inspired the

151 Saskia Sassen, *Guests and Aliens* (New York: New Press, 1999).

152 *Ibid* at 78.

153 Raphael Girard, "Speaking Notes for an Address" (Paper delivered at the Conference on Refuge or Asylum: A Choice of Canada, York University, 1986) at 4 [unpublished], cited in James C Hathaway, "The Conundrum of Refugee Protection in Canada: From Control to Compliance to Collective Deterrence" in Gil Loescher, ed, *Refugees and the Asylum Dilemma in the West*, above note 56, 71 at 80.

154 In judicial decisions, national identity may be discussed directly (e.g., what it means to be Canadian) as well as indirectly through indicating which conduct will "shock national conscience" or "outrage standards of decency."

transformation of Canada's admission policies into some of the more inclusive and welcoming among developed countries. The idea of community membership is, thus, an underlying consideration in migration law: How do we determine who would make a good member of a host society? Whose interests are to be prioritized in admission decisions: those of the host community or of the migrant?

There are various theories of community membership. By way of example, we will note (in a rather cursory manner) key features of only three: (1) liberal, (2) communitarian, and (3) neo-liberal. Communitarian approach assigns special importance to the shared understanding, interests, values, history, culture, and memories of a community.[155] Immigration is tailored with the preservation of these peculiar characteristics in mind and consequently requires both relative closure of a community[156] and high selectivity towards potential members. Preference is often given to persons with perceived similar cultural heritage or family connection to the current members.[157] New members are expected to learn local language and culture as a precondition for their ability to maintain society's political practices and democratic traditions.[158] However, according to prominent communitarian theorist Michael Walzer, a community does have an obligation to open its borders for refugees. As long as the numbers of refugees are small, the principle of mutual aid will warrant similar treatment of all refugees. Nevertheless, once the numbers of refugees go up, states will be forced to choose among them, likely selecting those with closer connection to the host community's way of life.

The liberal approach is based upon the principles of liberty and equality of persons. The emphasis is placed not on the preservation of a particular "community of character," but on a more general goal of maintaining democratic discourse in a community. Therefore, immigration requirements are focused on evaluating "civic" characteristics of potential members and their ability to maintain the discourse. Theorists such as Joseph Carens have made a compelling case for open membership based on a liberal social contract.[159] Carens challenged the

155 Bhikhu Parekh, "Three Theories of Immigration" in Sarah Spence, ed, *Strangers and Citizens: A Positive Approach to Migrants and Refugees* (London: Rivers Oram Press, 1994) 91 at 94.

156 Michael Walzer, *Spheres of Justice: A Defence of Pluralism and Equality* (Oxford: Basil Blackwell, 1989) at 39.

157 *Ibid* at 41.

158 Parekh, above note 155 at 102.

159 Joseph Carens, "Aliens and Citizens: The Case for Open Borders" (1987) 49 *Review of Politics* 251 at 270.

moral right of states to restrict or deny entry to migrants and argued for generally open admissions, subject only to limitations necessary for maintaining public order and security. He noted that the culture or history of a given community should not be a relevant moral consideration for limiting migration. Open migration would change a community, but this should not be seen as a threat.

More recently, migration scholars started focusing on the impact of neo-liberalism on migration policies. Neo-liberalism is less concerned with the "civic" or "ethnic" values of prospective members, but more so with their ability to become efficient and self-sufficient workers. From this perspective, the national community is fostered not by cultural homogeneity but by promoting an entrepreneurial culture of autonomy and competitiveness.[160] As some suggest, the neo-liberal approach to immigration results in two major developments: (1) the use of "risk management" tools (such as points-based selection systems) which weed out those who lack market-based traits; and (2) the promotion of "responsabilization," whereby selected individuals are self-reliant and do not require state support and expenditures.[161] "Those admitted are constructed as the 'neoliberal citizen' who is disciplined, productive, industrious and acts as an 'entrepreneur of him or herself' by continuously investing in and enhancing their 'human capital.'"[162] In the Canadian context, this is evident, for example, in the 2008–15 changes to the selection of economic immigrants and overall strong priority given to the economic rather than family or humanitarian admissions.

In most states, migration regulation is not based purely on either of the above models; rather, features of all three exhibit themselves with different prominence, depending on the migration stream. For example, refugee protection can be considered to have a link to a liberal approach as membership is often granted on the basis of ideological similarity (e.g., support for human rights, freedom of speech, political opinion) between a host society and an asylum seeker. At the same time, requirements for permanent residence under the family class or for citizenship often reflect a more communitarian approach (e.g., knowledge of Canada test for future citizens). The neo-liberal approach is becoming particularly prominent in revision of criteria for selection of economic

160 James Walsh, "Quantifying Citizens: Neoliberal Restructuring and Immigrant Selection in Canada and Australia" (2011) 15 *Citizenship Studies* 861.

161 *Ibid.*

162 Colin Gordon, "Governmental Rationality" in Michel Foucault et al, eds, *The Foucault Effect* (Chicago: University of Chicago Press, 1991) 1 at 44.

immigrants as well as reduced funding for settlement supports.[163] The interaction between different models of membership is mediated by various government and non-government actors participating in policy debates as well as consideration of other economic, social, and demographic factors. For example, interests of employers and labour unions have long been among factors influencing Canada's selection criteria.[164] Further, federal and provincial interests as well as other institutional factors also play a role in shaping immigration law and policy.

3) International Law

The primary international treaties dealing specifically with refugees are the 1951 *UN Convention Relating to the Status of Refugees*[165] and the 1967 *Protocol Relating to the Status of Refugees*[166] to which the overwhelming majority of states are parties.[167] Refugee protection touches upon a wide spectrum of fundamental values, from the right to life and personal security to prohibition of torture, freedom of expression, freedom from arbitrary detention, and many other basic human rights. By virtue of this eclectic collection of interests and values that intersect in the context of refugee law, many other international instruments and corresponding state obligations are of relevance. For example, the *International Covenant on Civil and Political Rights*[168] and the *Convention Against Torture and Other Cruel, Inhuman or Degrading Treatment or Punishment*[169] form the basis for subsidiary grounds of protection (in addition the *Refugee Convention*). These instruments will be discussed in more detail in Chapter 2.

---

163 For example, since 2010, settlement funding allocation for Ontario has been decreasing. According to the existing formula, funding is allocated based on permanent resident arrival numbers. Although Ontario continues receiving some of the highest numbers of newcomers, its proportion has been declining over the recent years, resulting in cuts to settlement funding. Immigration, Refugees and Citizenship Canada, "Backgrounder—Government of Canada 2012–13 Settlement Funding Allocations," online: IRCC www.cic.gc.ca/english/department/media/backgrounders/2011/2011-11-25.asp.

164 Kelley & Trebilcock, 2010, above note 27 at 463–64.

165 Above note 54.

166 Above note 55.

167 As of 3 July 2016, 145 states were parties to both the 1951 *Refugee Convention* and the 1967 *Protocol*. It is interesting to note that the United States is a party to the 1967 *Protocol* only. Online: https://treaties.un.org/Pages/ViewDetailsII.aspx?src=TREATY&mtdsg_no=V-2&chapter=5&Temp=mtdsg2&clang=_en.

168 19 December 1966, 999 UNTS 171 [*ICCPR*].

169 December 1984, Can TS 1987 No 36, 23 ILM 1027.

International treaties signed and ratified by states create binding obligations on them; however, there is much debate about the impact of these obligations on state practices.[170] Some suggest that ratification of human rights treaties does little to improve human rights,[171] while others find some positive correlation between the two.[172] The extent of a given state's compliance depends on a range of factors such as its interests, resources, and foreign policy orientation. Some argue that states abide by their international obligations only when it is beneficial for them to do so.[173] Hence, considerations such as national security and the state's economic or other interests may trump human rights concerns. For instance, Canada's position that removal to torture may be justified in extraordinary circumstances can be seen as an example of such prioritizing of state interests.

In the realm of refugee law, the *Refugee Convention* and major human rights treaties have undoubtedly had an impact on state refugee determination procedures and assessment of individuals' protection needs. For example, the refugee definition has been nearly universally adopted by states as the criterion for determining one's need for protection. However, it is also not uncommon to see practices that openly contradict the spirit of the *Refugee Convention*. For instance, all developed countries practise at least some form of interdiction measures against asylum seekers and other "undesirable" migrants.

In some cases, the lack of implementation of international obligations may be due to the state's lack of resources, limited capacity of state institutions, civil wars, and other widespread violence.[174] Although all state parties have equal obligations of refugee protection under the *Refugee Convention* (unless they made reservations to certain

---

170 For detailed discussion of the impact of human rights treaties, see Oona Hathaway, "Do Human Rights Treaties Make a Difference?" in Beth Simmons, ed, *International Law* (London: Sage, 2008), vol 6 at 123.

171 Linda Keith, "The United Nations *International Covenant on Civil and Political Rights*: Does It Make a Difference in Human Rights Behaviour?" (1999) 36 *Journal of Peace Research* 95; Hathaway, above note 170.

172 Todd Landman, "The Politic Science of Human Rights" (2005) 35 *British Journal of Political Science* 549.

173 See, generally, David P Forsythe, *Human Rights in International Relations* (New York: Cambridge University Press, 2000); Jack Donnelly, *Realism and International Relations* (New York: Cambridge University Press, 2000); Jack L Goldsmith & Eric A Posner, *The Limits of International Law* (Oxford: Oxford University Press, 2005).

174 Emilie M Hafner-Burton, "A Social Science of Human Rights" (2014) 51 *Journal of Peace Research* 273 at 276; Emilie Hafner-Burton, *Making Human Rights a Reality* (Princeton, NJ: Princeton University Press, 2013) ch 6.

provisions), the burden of refugee assistance is distributed unequally. Most refugee-producing situations are found in Africa, Asia, and the Middle East, and most displaced persons do not move outside their region in search for safety. For example, in 2015, there were 65.3 million forced migrants worldwide, including 21.3 million refugees and 3.2 million asylum seekers.[175] Out of these, developing regions hosted some 86 percent of refugees[176] (and a similar trend has been observed over the past years).[177] The continuing pressure on developing countries to host large numbers of refugee populations makes it increasingly difficult for them to provide adequate supports for refugee populations in their territories.

D. CONCLUSION

This chapter provided an overview of the historical events and analytical issues that influence Canadian refugee law. As noted, many of these events are unhappy; Canada's history towards individuals seeking protection is not spotless. This chapter has also sketched out some of the factors that play a role in the formation of migration flows and state response to migration. The broader global phenomenon of migration is the context within which refugee law and policy must operate. The following chapters will elaborate on various aspects of the Canadian refugee protection system and its accessibility for refugee claimants.

175 UNHCR, "Global Trends 2015," online: www.unhcr.org/global-trends-2015.html.
176 *Ibid.*
177 See UNHCR annual "Global Trends" reports for the past five years.

CHAPTER 2

LEGAL FRAMEWORK OF REFUGEE LAW IN CANADA

A. INTRODUCTION

This book largely treats refugee law as a discrete field of law. While, as discussed in Chapter 1, this is increasingly true on a day-to-day basis, refugee law, like any legal field, is influenced by other branches of law. Domestic constitutional and administrative law, as well as international law, play a significant part in directing the development of refugee law.

Constitutional law provides the framework in which institutional roles are determined and decision making occurs. Although under the *Constitution Act, 1867*,[1] immigration is an area of shared federal–provincial jurisdiction, for most of the twentieth century, it has been de facto exercised by the federal government. While the past twenty years have seen an increased role for provinces and territories in selection of economic immigrants through provincial/territorial nominee programs, refugee processing and decision making remain strongly federal. At a deeper level, constitutional law provides various procedural and substantive protections to the subjects of refugee-related decisions. Of particular importance are the rights to life, liberty, security of person, and equality, as asserted in the *Canadian Charter of Rights and Freedoms*:[2] these are engaged in many aspects of refugee law. Administrative law

---

1 (UK), 30 & 31 Vict, c 3, reprinted in RSC 1985, App 11, No 5.

2 Part 1 of the *Constitution Act, 1982*, being Schedule B to the *Canada Act 1982* (UK), 1982, c 11 [*Charter*].

provides additional guidance on the procedure to be followed by decision makers and allows affected individuals a range of means to challenge those decisions. Finally, Canadian refugee law is informed by developments at the international level and in foreign jurisdictions. Refugee law in Canada is the product of the country's international commitments, notably under the *Convention Relating to the Status of Refugees*, the *International Covenant on Civil and Political Rights*, and the *Convention Against Torture and Other Cruel, Inhuman or Degrading Treatment or Punishment*. Increasingly, Canadian decision makers are seeking guidance from international treaties and jurisprudence, guidelines issued by international bodies such as the UN High Commissioner for Refugees (UNHCR), and comparative refugee determination practices and decisions in other jurisdictions.

This chapter will review the core constitutional, statutory, and other sources that provide the framework for Canadian refugee law. It will also provide an overview of the *Refugee Convention* as well as of two major human rights treaties — the *International Covenant on Civil and Political Rights* and the *Convention Against Torture* — that have proved to be of fundamental importance in the area of refugee protection.

B. CONSTITUTIONAL PROVISIONS

The Canadian Constitution contains three types of provisions of key relevance to immigration and refugee law:

1) federal–provincial division of powers with respect to immigration, aliens, and naturalization;
2) federal and provincial powers to establish judicial bodies (something that has implications for the system of judicial review of immigration and refugee decisions); and
3) individual rights and freedoms guaranteed in the *Charter*.

1) Federal–Provincial Division of Powers

a) Division of Powers over Immigration, Aliens, and Naturalization

The *Constitution Act, 1867* does not speak specifically of refugee issues, but does address two related subject matters: "immigration" and "naturalization and aliens." The latter falls within exclusive federal jurisdiction under section 91(25), while the former falls under section 95 concurrent federal/provincial jurisdiction. In addition, regulation of issues such as employment standards, education, social assistance, pension and other benefits, and legal aid have important implications for immigrants and refugee claimants. Therefore, the allocation of legislative powers between the two levels of government in relation to these subject matters also plays a role in shaping the overall regime of treatment of non-citizens in Canada and will be discussed where relevant in subsequent chapters (particularly, Chapter 3).

As for regulation of "immigration" proper, section 95 provides that provincial legislatures may regulate "immigration into the province," and the federal Parliament may enact legislation in relation to immigration into "all or any of the provinces." Where a federal and a provincial law conflict, the former prevails — or in the words of section 95, a provincial law governing immigration into a province is valid only so "long and as far as it is not repugnant to any Act of the Parliament of Canada."

Although conflicts between immigration-related federal and provincial legislation are not common now,[3] it is important to specify the threshold required to establish that a provincial statute is invalid. A high standard would allow both laws to coexist if their provisions can be applied without conflict.[4] This may be the case, for example, when provincial legislation contains more stringent immigration requirements than federal legislation. Since the enforcement of more stringent

---

3 However, this has not always been in case. For example, in the late nineteenth to early twentieth century, some provinces (particularly British Columbia) enacted various (mainly racially based) restrictions on non-citizens. Notable cases included provincial legislation barring the employment of Japanese citizens in government works, the employment of Chinese labourers in mines, the employment of Japanese and Chinese labourers in the timber industry, the employment of white women and girls by Chinese men, and the barring of Asian naturalized British subjects from voting. Some of these acts were challenged, albeit often unsuccessfully, on jurisdictional grounds (plaintiffs argued that the subject matter of legislation fell outside powers allocated to provinces by the Constitution). For example, in *R v Quong-Wing* (1914), 49 SCR 440 [*Quong-Wing*], the applicant made such an argument with respect to a Saskatchewan statute that prohibited Chinese men from employing white women and girls (this prohibition was said to protect the morals of white women and girls). The central question for the court was whether the statute dealt with the issue related to "aliens and naturalization" (federal jurisdiction) or constituted an issue of "property and civil rights" (provincial jurisdiction). The Supreme Court upheld the legislation. See also *Union Colliery Co of British Columbia v Bryden*, [1899] AC 580 (JCPC); *Reference re: British Columbia Provincial Elections Act, 1897*, [1903] AC 151 (JCPC); *Reference re: Act to validate and confirm orders in council and provisions relating to the employment of persons on Crown property (British Columbia)* (1922), 63 SCR 293; and *Brooks-Bidlake and Whittall v British Columbia (Attorney General)*, [1923] AC 450 (JCPC).

4 *Quong-Wing*, above note 3. See also Donald Galloway, *Immigration Law* (Toronto: Irwin Law, 1997) at 26.

provincial standards entails simultaneous enforcement of less restrictive federal rules, there will be no express contradiction between the two laws. In contrast, a low standard would invalidate provincial laws where they conflict with the federal legislative purpose. Even when the provisions of both acts could coexist, if their purposes conflict, the provincial statute will be declared repugnant.

At present, the precise threshold for repugnancy is subject to some debate. The high standard test has been suggested by Hogg and applied by the courts. However, the Supreme Court has also adopted the low standard test.[5] In *Law Society of British Columbia v Mangat*,[6] the Supreme Court wrote on a conflict between federal and provincial immigration-related legislation:

> In this case, there is an operational conflict as the provincial legislation prohibits non-lawyers to appear for a fee before a tribunal but the federal legislation authorizes non-lawyers to appear as counsel for a fee. At a superficial level, a person who seeks to comply with both enactments can succeed either by becoming a member in good standing of the Law Society of British Columbia or by not charging a fee. Complying with the stricter statute necessarily involves complying with the other statute. However, following the expanded interpretation given in cases like M & D Farm and Bank of Montreal, *supra*, dual compliance is impossible . . . . Where there is an enabling federal law, the provincial law cannot be contrary to Parliament's purpose. Finally, it would be impossible for a judge or an official of the IRB to comply with both acts.[7]

From the cited passage it is clear that while the Supreme Court is applying the low standard ("the provincial law cannot be contrary to Parliament's purpose"), it does not completely rule out the relevance of the high standard ("it would be impossible for a judge or an official of the IRB to comply with both acts").

Mangat involved a conflict between provincial legislation regulating the legal profession and federal legislation governing representation before the Immigration and Refugee Board (IRB). At the time, the federal *Immigration Act*[8] allowed individuals appearing before the IRB to be

5 *Bank of Montreal v Hall*, [1990] 1 SCR 121. See also Galloway, above note 4 at 27.

6 2001 SCC 67 [*Mangat*].

7 *Ibid* at para 72 (Gonthier J *per curiam*).

8 RSC 1985, c I-2. Various provisions of the *Immigration Act*, including ss 30 and 69(1), allow "other counsel" to represent individuals subject to immigration proceedings. Other provisions allowing "other counsel" can be found in the rules of the IRB's various divisions.

represented by immigration consultants (non-lawyers who were paid a fee). In contrast, the provincial *Legal Profession Act*[9] restricted the provision of "legal advice" (the broad definition of which would include representation of an individual before the Board) to barristers and solicitors. The substance of the matter simultaneously engaged federal jurisdiction over naturalization and aliens and provincial jurisdiction over civil rights and regulation of the practice of law. The Supreme Court acknowledged that it would be possible to comply with both requirements by complying with more restrictive provincial legislation. This, however, would defeat the federal objective of establishing an "informal, accessible (in financial, cultural, and linguistic terms), and expeditious process" before the IRB.[10] The Court pointed out that it may often be difficult to find lawyers who are fluent in foreign languages and familiar with different cultures. In this respect, paralegals who are often able to converse in client's native languages and understand their culture play an important role before the Board. Therefore, provincial law was contrary to the purpose of the federal law and was inoperative under the doctrine of paramountcy. Interestingly, several years after the *Mangat* decision, the federal government introduced a regulatory scheme for non-lawyers representing clients for a fee in immigration and refugee matters.[11]

i) Federal and Provincial/Territorial Agreements on Immigration

The *Immigration and Refugee Protection Act*, or *IRPA*, provides for the authority of the Minister of Immigration, Refugees and Citizenship to enter into agreements with provinces and to consult with them in regard to immigration and refugee policies.[12] Under this authority, the federal government has signed comprehensive agreements on immigration with eight provinces and one territory: British Columbia, Alberta, Saskatchewan, Manitoba, Ontario, Quebec, Nova Scotia, Prince Edward Island, and Yukon. In addition, agreements on specific immigration issues (such as provincial nominees) were signed with British Columbia, Alberta, Saskatchewan, Manitoba, Ontario, New Brunswick, Prince Edward Island, Newfoundland and Labrador, Northwest Territories,

9 SBC 1987, c 25 (now SBC 1998, c 9, ss 1, 15, and 85(5)–(8)).

10 *Mangat*, above note 6 at para 72.

11 For further information on this issue, see Chapter 9. The Law Society of Upper Canada unsuccessfully sought to declare such regulation *ultra vires*. *Law Society of Upper Canada v Canada (Minister of Citizenship & Immigration)*, 2006 FC 1489.

12 SC 2001, c 27, ss 8 and 10 [*IRPA*].

and Yukon.[13] The agreements on provincial/territorial nominee programs (PTNPs) allow provinces/territories to participate in selection of economic immigrants: they can prescribe selection criteria reflective of local needs and nominate the most suitable candidates for immigration into their territories. Although PTNPs focus on economic immigrants only and have no direct connection to refugee protection, it is important to be aware of the increasing role of provinces in immigration — a development that constitutes a significant departure from the pattern of federal exclusivity over immigration regulation during most of the twentieth century.

Quebec occupies a unique position in immigrant selection and settlement compared to other provinces. Not only did its involvement in immigrant selection start much earlier (in the 1960s compared to the late 1990s to early 2000s for other provinces), but its authority in relation to immigration issues is more extensive. The very objective of the *Canada–Quebec Accord on Immigration* reflects the particular significance of provincial control over immigrant selection: "to provide Québec with new means to preserve its demographic importance in Canada, and to ensure the integration of immigrants in Québec in a manner that respects the distinct identity of Québec." In addition to economic immigrants, Quebec can select refugees from overseas (subject to the federal inadmissibility requirements). The selection criteria for immigrants and refugees destined for Quebec are outlined in provincial immigration legislation.[14]

b) Powers to Establish Judicial Bodies

Under the *Constitution Act, 1867*, both federal and provincial governments have the power to set up courts, prescribe procedure before them, and appoint judges. Section 92(14) gives provinces exclusive jurisdiction over the administration of justice in each province, including creation of their own systems of provincial courts. Under section 101, the federal government also has power to create certain types of courts, namely, a "General Court of Appeal for Canada, and . . . any additional Courts for the better Administration of the Laws of Canada."

---

13 For their texts, see the website of Immigration, Refugees and Citizenship Canada: www.cic.gc.ca/English/department/laws-policy/agreements/index.asp.

14 *Loi sur l'immigration au Québec*, LRQ c I-0.2; *Règlement sur la sélection des ressortissants étrangers*, CQLR c I-0.2, r 4; *Règlement sur la pondération applicable à la sélection des ressortissants étrangers*, CQLR c I-0.2, r 2. Some other provinces also recently adopted immigration-related legislation (e.g., *Ontario Immigration Act, 2015*, SO 2015, c 8).

This power has been used to create, *inter alia*, the Supreme Court of Canada, the Federal Court, and the Federal Court of Appeal.

Decisions under the *IRPA* are subject to a statutory judicial review by the Federal Court. The jurisdiction of the Federal Court to hear such matters is provided in the *Federal Courts Act*:

> . . . the Federal Court has exclusive original jurisdiction
>
> (*a*) to issue an injunction, writ of *certiorari*, writ of prohibition, writ of *mandamus* or writ of *quo warranto*, or grant declaratory relief, against any federal board, commission or other tribunal; and
>
> (*b*) to hear and determine any application or other proceeding for relief in the nature of relief contemplated by paragraph (*a*), including any proceeding brought against the Attorney General of Canada, to obtain relief against a federal board, commission or other tribunal.[15]

Both decisions of the Immigration and Refugee Board and of other government officials, such as Immigration, Refugees and Citizenship Canada, fall within the definition of "federal board, commission or tribunal."[16] The right of judicial review of refugee-related decisions before the Federal Court is further defined in the *IRPA*, sections 72 to 75. In immigration and refugee cases, an applicant must first seek a leave to appeal (a permission from the court to have the case heard). If leave is granted, the case proceeds to judicial hearing. The Federal Court can either uphold the decision by the original decision maker or, where an error is found, send it back for re-determination. The decisions of the Federal Court can be appealed, upon certification of a question of general importance, to the Federal Court of Appeal[17] and then with leave to the Supreme Court.[18] Given that the Federal Court plays a central role in the resolution of refugee matters, the legislation and rules governing

---

15 RSC 1985, c F-7, s 18.1.

16 *Ibid*, s 2(1):

> federal board, commission or other tribunal means any body, person or persons having, exercising or purporting to exercise jurisdiction or powers conferred by or under an Act of Parliament or by or under an order made pursuant to a prerogative of the Crown, other than the Tax Court of Canada or any of its judges, any such body constituted or established by or under a law of a province or any such person or persons appointed under or in accordance with a law of a province or under section 96 of the *Constitution Act, 1867*.

17 The leave must be granted by the Federal Court per the *IRPA*, above note 12, s 74(d).

18 The leave may be granted by either the Federal Court of Appeal or the Supreme Court per the *Supreme Court Act*, RSC 1985, c S-26, ss 37.1 and 40.

the court will be discussed further in this chapter, and Chapter 10 will be devoted to a more detailed examination of the process of judicial review of refugee decisions.

Notwithstanding the language of section 18(1) of the *Federal Courts Act*,[19] superior provincial courts have concurrent jurisdiction in immigration and refugee-related matters due to their inherent jurisdiction. In addition, section 18(1) fails to grant jurisdiction to the Federal Court over the writ of *habeas corpus*. Thus, the provincial superior court continues to have exclusive jurisdiction to return a writ of *habeas corpus*. For more discussion on the overlapping jurisdictions of federal and provincial courts, see Chapter 10.

C. *CHARTER OF RIGHTS AND FREEDOMS*

The *Charter of Rights and Freedoms*, which constitutes an integral part of the *Constitution Act, 1982*, enshrines the most fundamental rights and freedoms of individuals in Canada. These rights and freedoms are divided into the following categories:

- fundamental freedoms (freedom of association, assembly, expression, religion);
- democratic rights (right to vote and to seek candidacy in elections);
- mobility rights (right to enter, remain in, and leave Canada as well as the right to interprovincial mobility);
- legal rights (fair hearing, protection from arbitrary arrest and detention, right to counsel, right of *habeas corpus*, presumption of innocence, and others); and
- equality rights.

Charter rights may be subject to limitations under section 1: "The guaranteed rights and freedoms are subject only to such reasonable limits prescribed by law as can be demonstrably justified in a free and democratic society."

Most *Charter* rights do not distinguish between citizens and non-citizens — referring to "everyone," "every individual," or "any person" — and thus can be invoked by refugee claimants and other migrants. Only two *Charter* rights are reserved exclusively for citizens: (1) democratic rights and (2) the right to enter, remain in, and leave Canada.

---

19 The *Federal Courts Act*, above note 15, s 18(1), refers to "exclusive" original jurisdiction.

The *Charter* protections are, however, limited in terms of their territorial application. As held in *Kindler v Canada (Minister of Justice)*,[20] the *Charter* generally does not have extraterritorial application.[21] Although the *Charter* does not expressly impose any territorial limits, the respect for state sovereignty dictates that it (as well as any other Canadian law) cannot be enforced in a foreign territory without the consent of the foreign state.[22] Thus, with respect to immigration and refugee matters, only non-citizens within Canada can benefit from *Charter* protections.

For non-citizens within Canada, the most frequently invoked *Charter* rights are section 7 (right to life, liberty, and security of person), section 10(b) (right to counsel), section 12 (prohibition of cruel and unusual treatment or punishment), and section 15 (equality). Below is a brief overview of the content of each of the four provisions. The discussion

---

20 [1991] 2 SCR 779 [*Kindler*].

21 However, as the Supreme Court held in *R v Cook*, [1998] 2 SCR 597 [*Cook*], the *Charter* can, in certain "limited and rare" circumstances, apply beyond Canada's territory. In this case, the accused was detained in the United States, but questioned by Canadian officers; the Court held that the *Charter* applied. Under *Cook*, the *Charter* may apply where the act falls within s 32(1) of the *Charter* and the application of the *Charter* does not interfere with the sovereign authority of the foreign state, thereby not generating any "objectionable extraterritorial effect." The Court, however, warned that the decision in *Cook* did not mean that *Charter* rights will be conferred on every person who in some respect implicated the exercise of Canada's authority abroad. It has generally been established that the *Charter* applies where there is a sufficient causal connection between the Canadian government's participation in a foreign investigation and the potential deprivation of *Charter* rights which a person in question faces as a result: *United States of America v Kwok*, 2001 SCC 18. In *R v Hape*, 2007 SCC 26, however, the majority of the Supreme Court revised its approach, formulating it in more nuanced and restrictive terms, noting that the *Charter* will apply only if there is an exception to state sovereignty. Finally, in *Canada (Justice) v Khadr*, 2008 SCC 28, the Supreme Court relied on an exception to find that the *Charter* applied to the actions of Canadian officials at the US military base in Guantánamo Bay, Cuba. The Court noted that the US military commission regime in place at the time constituted a clear violation of fundamental human rights and, hence, comity did not justify deference to the foreign state. In *Canada (Prime Minister) v Khadr*, 2010 SCC 3, the Supreme Court found that Canadian officials acting in Guantánamo Bay violated Khadr's section 7 rights. At the time of the interrogation, Khadr was a minor, and Canadian officials elicited statements from him about the most serious criminal charges while he was detained and without access to counsel, and while knowing that the results of the interrogations would be shared with the US prosecutors. The Court found that Canada's participation in what was at the time an illegal regime has contributed and continued to contribute to Khadr's detention; hence, the connection between Canada's actions and deprivation of rights under section 7 was established.

22 *Hape*, above note 21.

in this section is not intended as a comprehensive overview of relevant caselaw. Rather, it seeks only to outline the main parameters of the above-mentioned *Charter* sections and provide examples on how they have been utilized in the immigration and refugee context.

1) Section 7

Section 7 provides that "everyone has the right to life, liberty, and security of the person and the right not to be deprived thereof except in accordance with the principles of fundamental justice." It has been invoked in a variety of contexts ranging from the design of refugee procedures to conditions of immigration detention and issues of deportation. In general, section 7 would be engaged when immigration proceedings could have sufficiently severe impact on the applicant.[23] Section 7 limits state action, but it does not create a positive obligation on the government to act. For instance, it does not provide a positive right to refugee protection[24] or to healthcare.[25]

To establish a violation of section 7, an applicant must demonstrate that (1) there has been or could be a deprivation of the right to life, liberty, or security of person; and (2) the deprivation was not or would not be in accordance with the principles of fundamental justice.[26] If the two branches of the test are met, the onus shifts to the government to justify the deprivation under section 1 of the *Charter*.[27]

Madame Justice Wilson pointed out in *Singh v Canada (Minister of Employment and Immigration)* that "life, liberty and security of person" are three distinct interests.[28] Subsequent jurisprudence further elucidated the meaning of each interest. The "liberty" interest includes not only freedom from physical restraint, but also freedom to make fundamental life choices.[29] The "security of person" extends to both bodily and

---

23 *Charkaoui v Canada (Citizenship and Immigration)*, 2007 SCC 9 at paras 12–18 [*Charkaoui*].

24 *Febles v Canada (Citizenship and Immigration)*, 2014 SCC 68 at para 68.

25 For example, jurisprudence holds that the *Charter* does not confer a freestanding right to healthcare: *Chaoulli v Quebec (Attorney General)*, 2005 SCC 35 at para 105; *Auton (Guardian ad litem of) v British Columbia (Attorney General)*, 2004 SCC 78; *Toussaint v Canada (Attorney General)*, 2011 FCA 213; *Wynberg v Ontario* (2006), 82 OR (3d) 561 (CA); *Flora v Ontario (Health Insurance Plan, General Manager)*, 2008 ONCA 538.

26 Test originally set out in *R v Beare; R v Higgins*, [1988] 2 SCR 387 at 401.

27 *Charkaoui*, above note 23 at para 12.

28 [1985] 1 SCR 177 at 204–5 [*Singh*]; *Reference re: Motor Vehicle Act (British Columbia)*, [1985] 2 SCR 486 at 500 [*Re BC Motor Vehicle Act*].

29 *Blencoe v British Columbia (Human Rights Commission)*, 200 SCC 44 at para 49.

psychological integrity.[30] Establishing a deprivation of a right under section 7 does not require that all three interests be unduly restricted;[31] establishing deprivation of one of them will be sufficient.

The second element of section 7 analysis — the concept of "fundamental justice" — is rooted in "the basic tenets of [the Canadian] legal system."[32] In order to be considered a principle of fundamental justice, the following conditions must be met: (1) the principle must be a legal principle; (2) there must be sufficient consensus that this principle is fundamental to the society's notion of justice; and (3) the principle must be capable of being clearly formulated and applied to cases at hand.[33]

There is no one single list of principles of fundamental justice, and they cannot be defined in the abstract; rather, they are determined contextually, depending on the process in question and interests at stake.[34] In immigration context, relevant considerations may include the principles of immigration law (namely, that non-citizens do not have an unqualified right to enter and remain in Canada[35]); the fact that the distinction between citizens and non-citizens is authorized by the *Charter*, section 6;[36] societal interests;[37] and Canada's international obligations and values expressed in various international documents and customary norms.[38]

As the Supreme Court observed in *Charkaoui v Canada (Citizenship and Immigration)*,[39] "[s]ection 7 of the *Charter* requires not a particular type of process, but a fair process having regard to the nature of

30 *Ibid* at para 55. For example, serious state-imposed psychological stress can constitute a breach of the security of person. This may occur where a state interferes in the person's ability to control his physical or psychological integrity by prohibiting or limiting access to certain procedures such as abortion or assisted suicide. For example, *Rodriguez v British Columbia (Attorney General)*, [1993] 3 SCR 519 at 587.

31 *Singh*, above note 28 at para 42.

32 *Re BC Motor Vehicle Act*, above note 28 at 503.

33 *R v Malmo-Levine*, 2003 SCC 74 at para 113 [*Malmo-Levine*].

34 *R v Lyons*, [1987] 2 SCR 309 at 361; *Canada (Minister of Employment and Immigration) v Chiarelli*, [1992] 1 SCR 711 at paras 23–24 [*Chiarelli*]; *Charkaoui*, above note 23 at para 20; *Kindler*, above note 20 at 848; *R v Wholesale Travel Group Inc*, [1991] 3 SCR 154 at 226.

35 *Charkaoui*, above note 23 at para 24.

36 *Ibid*.

37 *Ibid* at para 20, citing to *Malmo-Levine*, above note 33 at para 98.

38 *Suresh v Canada (Minister of Citizenship and Immigration)*, [2002] 1 SCR 3 at para 46 [*Suresh*], citing to *United States of America v Burns*, [2001] 1 SCR 283 at paras 79–81 [*Burns*].

39 *Charkaoui*, above note 23 at para 20.

the proceedings and the interests at stake." Thus, contextual factors will play an important role in elucidating what would be fair in given circumstances. For example, in the case of deportation to the risk of torture, consideration should be given to such factors as the danger that a person presents to Canada, the personal circumstances of the potential deportee, and the threat of terrorism to Canada.[40] National security concerns may also inform the analysis of what is fundamentally unfair.[41]

For section 7 to be engaged, the person must be exposed to the imminent risk of deprivation of right to life, liberty, or security of person. Thus, for example, decisions that can be followed by further procedural stages prior to deportation are normally not considered to engage section 7. For instance, in *Poshteh v Canada (Minister of Citizenship and Immigration)*,[42] the Federal Court of Appeal found that a determination of inadmissibility did not engage section 7 because there were several more procedural stages prior to any deportation. Similarly, in *Nguyen v Canada (Minister of Employment and Immigration)*, the court held that declaration of ineligibility to have a hearing before the Refugee Protection Division (in the case at hand, it was due to serious criminality) did not in itself lead to any act that may affect a claimant's life, liberty, or security.[43]

As a general rule, there is no breach of section 7 in deporting a permanent resident who has committed serious crimes[44] or in surrendering a person for trial in a foreign country.[45] However, even though deportation of a non-citizen may not in itself engage section 7, some features associated with deportation, such as the possibility of torture in the destination country, may trigger its engagement.[46] As noted in *Canada v Schmidt*, the manner in which a foreign state would deal with a deported or surrendered person may be such that the surrender or deportation would be contrary to the principles of fundamental justice.[47] For example, extradition to the death penalty would violate section 7.[48]

For section 7 to apply to extradition or deportation, there must be a sufficient causal connection between the actions of the Canadian

---

40 *Suresh*, above note 38 at para 45.
41 *Charkaoui*, above note 23 at para 23.
42 2005 FCA 85 [*Poshteh*].
43 [1993] 1 FC 696 (CA) [*Nguyen*].
44 *Chiarelli*, above note 34.
45 *Canada v Schmidt*, [1987] 1 SCR 500 at 522 [*Schmidt*].
46 *Charkaoui*, above note 23 at para 17.
47 *Schmidt*, above note 45 at 522.
48 *Burns*, above note 38.

government and the resulting deprivation.[49] For example, in *Suresh v Canada (Minister of Citizenship and Immigration)*, the applicant was recognized as a Convention refugee but subsequently was determined to be a security risk due to his affiliation with the LTTE (an organization considered terrorist by Canada). Canadian authorities sought to remove Suresh back to Sri Lanka where he alleged he would be tortured. In commenting on the link between the actions of Canadian authorities and exposure to torture, the Supreme Court noted:

> At least where Canada's participation is a necessary precondition for the deprivation and where the deprivation is an entirely foreseeable consequence of Canada's participation, the government does not avoid the guarantee of fundamental justice merely because the deprivation in question would be effected by someone else's hand.[50]

2) Section 10(b)

The wording of the right to counsel in section 10 of the *Charter* is quite expansive and applies to all individuals facing any form of arrest or detention:

> Everyone has the right on arrest or detention
> (a) to be informed promptly of the reasons therefor;
> (b) to retain and instruct counsel without delay and to be informed of that right; and
> (c) to have the validity of the detention determined by way of *habeas corpus* and to be released if the detention is not lawful.

Since the guarantee under section 10 is restricted to individuals under arrest or in detention, much jurisprudence dealt with issues of what constitutes arrest and detention and the timing of their occurrence. Of course, when an order for detention is made, the situation is clear and the right to counsel arises. However, in other contexts, such as, for example, examination of a migrant at a port of entry, it may not be readily apparent if arrest or detention has taken place. In the leading case of *Dehghani v Canada (Minister of Employment and Immigration)*,[51] the Supreme Court held that the examination upon entry, including secondary examination,[52] was part of the general screening process for

---

49 *Ibid*, affirmed in *Suresh*, above note 38 at para 54.

50 *Suresh*, *ibid*.

51 [1993] 1 SCR 1053 [*Dehghani*].

52 "Secondary examination" is a term used to describe the questioning of an individual that occurs away from the primary examination kiosk at which the

persons entering Canada and did not amount to a detention. As a result, Dehghani's right to counsel under section 10(b) of the *Charter* was not engaged.[53] This decision was based, in part, on the Court's observation that "there is no right for non-citizens to enter or remain in Canada"[54] — an observation that was made despite the fact that Dehghani had sought refugee protection upon arrival. Later decisions of the Federal Court have tempered the decision in *Dehghani* by indicating that when the secondary examination becomes formal detention, the person must be advised of and provided with access to counsel. For example, in *Huang v Canada (Minister of Citizenship and Immigration)*,[55] the court found that a refugee claimant had been detained when she had been kept in custody under close supervision for three days and interviewed four times. In *Chen v Canada (Minister of Citizenship and Immigration)*,[56] the refugee claimant was considered to have been detained when he was kept in custody for two days and interviewed twice during that period. Similarly, in *Dragosin v Canada (Minister of Citizenship and Immigration)*,[57] a person who had spent two days in a correctional centre was considered detained for purposes of section 10(b).

Where a right to counsel does arise, jurisprudence established that it entails two components:

1) informational: This component requires that a person is not only advised of the right to counsel, but is also informed of the existence of legal aid and duty counsel.[58]
2) implementational: This component requires that the detainee be given an opportunity to exercise the right to counsel.

While the above components have been outlined in the criminal law context, they are equally applicable to immigration arrest and detention.[59] However, in practice, refugee claimants subject to detention may face obstacles to acting upon their section 10(b) rights. Despite

---

individual initially reports.

53 The Court also held that there was no right to counsel under s 7 of the *Charter* on the facts of the case: *Dehghani*, above note 51 at para 50.

54 *Ibid* at para 33.

55 2002 FCT 149 [*Huang*].

56 2006 FC 910 [*Chen*].

57 2003 FCT 81 [*Dragosin*].

58 *R v Brydges*, [1990] 1 SCR 190.

59 *Dragosin*, above note 57; *Chevez v Canada (Minister of Citizenship and Immigration)*, 2007 FC 709 [*Chevez*]. In *Chevez*, the applicant was informed of the right to counsel, but at the exclusion hearing the duty counsel was unavailable and the delegate proceeded without informing the applicant of the possibility of waiting or of other alternatives.

being advised of their rights, they may not fully appreciate the significance of access to counsel or of the proceedings to which they are being subjected. Furthermore, their frequent lack of a familial or social network within Canada will make it much more difficult for them to contact and retain counsel.

Where a violation of section 10(b) is established, a court may order remedies, most typically — in both immigration and criminal contexts — the exclusion of evidence obtained in violation of that right.[60] Thus, for example, inconsistent statements by a detained refugee claimant made in the absence of access to counsel can be excluded from evidence before the Immigration and Refugee Board, which can, in turn, lead to setting aside of the decision in question.[61]

The right to counsel under section 10(b) of the *Charter* should be distinguished from the right to counsel in other contexts where a person was not arrested or detained. For example, a right to be represented by counsel in Refugee Protection Division (RPD) proceedings does not have origin in section 10(b).

3) Section 12

Section 12 prohibits everyone from being "subjected to any cruel and unusual treatment or punishment." Most of the jurisprudence on section 12 originates in the criminal law context and deals primarily with issues of "punishment" rather than "treatment." In order to determine whether section 12 is violated, courts consider whether a particular act would "shock Canadian conscience"[62] or "outrage standards of decency," or whether punishment would be "grossly disproportionate" to the act committed.[63] In *Canadian Doctors for Refugee Care v Canada (Attorney General)*, the Federal Court summarized the approach to determining cruel and unusual treatment in the following way:

> In determining whether treatment or punishment is "cruel and unusual," Canadian courts have looked at a number of factors as part of a kind of "cost/benefit" analysis. These factors include whether the treatment goes beyond what is necessary to achieve a legitimate

---

60 *Charter*, above note 2, s 24(2).

61 *Huang*, above note 55; *Chen*, above note 56; *Dragosin*, above note 57. For example, in *Chen*, the IRB made a negative credibility finding based on inconsistencies between the narrative contained in the Personal Information Form (PIF) and Port of Entry (POE) Notes that were taken while Chen was in detention, in the absence of the counsel.

62 *Kindler*, above note 20; *Burns*, above note 38.

63 *R v Smith*, [1987] 1 SCR 1045 [*Smith*]; *R v Swain*, [1991] 1 SCR 933.

> aim, whether there are adequate alternatives, whether the treatment is arbitrary and whether it has a value or social purpose. Other considerations include whether the treatment in question is unacceptable to a large segment of the population, whether it accords with public standards of decency or propriety, whether it shocks the general conscience, and whether it is unusually severe and hence degrading to human dignity and worth.[64]

In the immigration and refugee context, section 12 has been most frequently invoked to challenge detention and deportation[65] provisions. Generally, caselaw holds that deportation of long-term residents on grounds of criminality does not violate section 12.[66] It does not constitute punishment and does not outrage standards of decency.[67] In fact, as noted by the Supreme Court in *Chiarelli v Canada (Minister of Employment and Immigration)*: ". . . it would tend to outrage such standards if individuals granted conditional entry into Canada were permitted, without consequence, to violate those conditions deliberately."[68]

However, where a protected person is facing removal due to having committed serious offences, consideration of additional factors is required. For example, one needs to consider the treatment that would await the applicant upon removal, the country conditions, and whether the change of regime in that country might affect the person's reasonable fear of persecution — "all measured against the . . . crimes he committed in this country [Canada]."[69] The deportation of an unsuccessful refugee claimant to a country engaged in an ongoing civil war does not constitute a violation of section 12 as long as a proper risk assessment is conducted and no potential risk is found.[70]

Immigration detention is not cruel and unusual treatment unless it violates accepted norms.[71] For example, denial of opportunity to challenge detention and the ensuing possibility of it becoming indefinite may contribute to detention being cruel and unusual. However, ex-

64 2014 FC 651 at para 614 [*Canadian Doctors for Refugee Care*].

65 In *Chiarelli*, above note 34, the Supreme Court observed that the *Concise Oxford Dictionary* (1990) defined "treatment" as "a process or manner of behaving towards or dealing with a person or thing." According to the Court, deportation may "come within the scope of a 'treatment' in s. 12" (at para 29).

66 *Chiarelli*, *ibid* at paras 28–31.

67 *Ibid* at para 29.

68 *Ibid* at para 31.

69 *Barrera v Canada (Minister of Employment and Immigration)*, [1993] 2 FC 3 at para 25 (CA).

70 *Sinnappu v Canada (Minister of Citizenship and Immigration)*, [1997] FCJ No 173 (TD).

71 *Charkaoui*, above note 23.

tended periods of immigration detention would not violate section 12 of the *Charter* if detainees are provided with regular detention reviews.[72]

Most recently, the Federal Court considered whether reduction of healthcare coverage for refugee claimants in Canada was a violation of section 12 (see Chapter 3 for more details). The summary of reasons provides useful insight into the application of section 12:

> . . . I have concluded that while it is open to government to assign priorities and set limits on social benefit plans such as the IFHP [Interim Federal Health Program], the intentional targeting of an admittedly poor, vulnerable and disadvantaged group takes this situation outside the realm of ordinary *Charter* challenges to social benefit programs.
>
> With the 2012 changes to the IFHP, the executive branch of the Canadian government has set out to make the lives of disadvantaged individuals even more difficult than they already are in an effort to force those who have sought the protection of this country to leave Canada more quickly, and to deter others from coming here. In light of the unusual circumstances of this case, I am satisfied that the affected individuals are being subjected to "treatment" as contemplated by section 12 of the *Charter.*
>
> I am also satisfied that this treatment is "cruel and unusual," particularly, but not exclusively, as it affects children who have been brought to this country by their parents. The cuts to health insurance coverage effected through the 2012 modifications to the IFHP potentially jeopardize the health, and indeed the very lives, of these innocent and vulnerable children in a manner that shocks the conscience and outrages our standards of decency. They violate section 12 of the *Charter.*[73]

4) Section 15

Section 15 provides that "every individual is equal before and under the law and has the right to the equal protection and equal benefit of the law without discrimination . . . based on race, national or ethnic origin, colour, religion, sex, age or mental or physical disability." As clarified by the Supreme Court in *R v Kapp*, the focus of section 15(1) of the *Charter* is on "preventing governments from making distinctions based on the enumerated or analogous grounds that: have the effect of perpetuating group disadvantage and prejudice; or impose disadvantage on the basis

---

72 *Ibid* at para 110.

73 *Canadian Doctors for Refugee Care*, above note 64 at paras 689–91.

of stereotyping."[74] Thus, the test for determining a section 15 violation involves two questions: (1) does the law create a distinction based on an enumerated or analogous ground? (2) does the distinction create a disadvantage by perpetuating prejudice or stereotyping?[75]

The concept of human dignity and focus on substantive equality are underlying considerations of section 15.[76] However, acknowledging the difficulty of applying human dignity as a legal test, the Supreme Court suggested that the analysis may more usefully focus on the indicators of discrimination and the impact on the person or group concerned.[77] For example, in *Canadian Doctors for Refugee Care*, the Federal Court concluded that the distinction between refugee claimants from designated countries of origin (DCO) (considered normally not refugee producing)[78] and those from non-DCO countries, providing a lesser level of health insurance coverage to the former, "puts their lives at risk and perpetuates the stereotypical view that they are cheats, that their refugee claims are 'bogus,' and that they have come to Canada to abuse the generosity of Canadians."[79] The court found violation of section 15.

In contrast, in other cases, section 15 claims were rejected because courts did not find that distinctions drawn by immigration law reflected stereotyping or prejudice. For example, in *Guzman v Canada (Minister of Citizenship and Immigration)*,[80] the applicant was barred from sponsoring a family member due to her reliance on social assistance and challenged it as violation of section 15. The court found that receipt of social assistance was not a personal characteristic and that the provision in question did not discriminate in a substantive sense as its effect was not demeaning to the applicant or others in receipt of social assistance. The court noted that the provision was based on legislators' assumption that persons on social assistance would not be able to provide for their sponsored relatives without further reliance on state assistance, and wrote: "Such an assumption does not reflect . . . the stereotypical view that people who receive social assistance are less worthy individuals . . . but instead is based on an informed general assumption that an individual on social assistance cannot provide the necessary financial support to aid a new immigrant to estab-

---

74 2008 SCC 41 at para 25.
75 *Ibid* at para 17.
76 *Ibid* at paras 20–21.
77 *Ibid* at para 23.
78 For more on the treatment of claimants from DCOs, see Chapter 3.
79 *Canadian Doctors for Refugee Care*, above note 64 at para 851.
80 2006 FC 1134.

lish himself in Canada."[81] In *Chesters v Canada (Minister of Citizenship and Immigration)*,[82] the plaintiff, who was denied permanent residence in Canada due to having multiple sclerosis, challenged provisions on medical inadmissibility as discriminating on the basis of disability. The Federal Court rejected the argument, reasoning that medical inadmissibility provisions focused on excessive demand on health services (due to applicants' medical conditions), not on disease or disability. It also noted that admission to Canada is a privilege and "its grant lies within the purview of the Canadian government which is entitled to establish entry standards, including an assessment of potential excessive demands on health services."[83]

At a more general level, caselaw holds that the fact that some procedures apply to non-citizens only (for example, deportation) does not, for that reason alone, violate section 15.[84] In *Chiarelli*, for example, the Supreme Court found it was not discriminatory that the deportation scheme applied to non-citizens but not to citizens.[85] A similar approach was taken in *Al Yamani v Canada (Minister of Citizenship and Immigration)* which dealt with inadmissibility of a person on security grounds[86] and *Catenacci v Canada (Attorney General)*, where a Canadian permanent resident was denied transfer from the US prison to Canada on the grounds that the *International Transfer of Offender Act* applied only to Canadian citizens.[87] The underlying rationale behind such conclusions is that section 6 of the *Charter* specifically allows for differential treatment of citizens and non-citizens in such matters as entry and stay in Canada.[88]

Although the above cases provided only very selective, patchwork illustrations to the invocation of *Charter* provisions in the immigration and refugee context, they do demonstrate the inalienable link that exists between constitutional law and immigration and refugee law. The *Charter* has been and remains an important tool for immigration/refugee advocates, but *Charter* arguments have had mixed success before courts. While several landmark cases significantly strengthened

81 *Ibid* at para 38.

82 2002 FCT 727.

83 *Ibid* at para 120.

84 *Charkaoui*, above note 23 at para 129.

85 *Chiarelli*, above note 34 at para 32.

86 2006 FC 1457.

87 2006 FC 539. The court determined that the pith and substance of the benefit that the applicant sought was about entry to Canada and as a result necessarily engaged s 6 of the *Charter*.

88 Only citizens have an unconditional right to enter and remain in Canada: *Charter*, above note 2, s 6(1).

non-citizens' rights, courts have generally been cautious to rigorously scrutinize immigration and refugee laws and policies.[89] September 11, in particular, motivated a more restrictive approach and provided strong justification to governments for giving priority to the interests of the host nation.[90]

D. LEGISLATIVE AND REGULATORY PROVISIONS

1) *Immigration and Refugee Protection Act*[91]

The *Immigration and Refugee Protection Act* came into force on 28 June 2002. It was the first complete revision of Canadian immigration and refugee legislation in almost a quarter century. As the primary source of Canadian immigration and refugee law, it establishes the objectives of immigration and refugee policy, classes of immigrants and refugees, criteria of inadmissibility, powers of immigration and refugee decision makers, and other essential elements of migration regulation.

Given that the *IRPA* is framework legislation, it stipulates only the general principles, criteria, and powers of immigration/refugee decision making. Further details of applicable definitions, procedures, and criteria are elaborated in the *Immigration and Refugee Protection Regulations*. In addition to the *Regulations*, bodies established under the *IRPA*, notably the Immigration and Refugee Board, have the power to develop rules and guidelines. Furthermore, each government body involved in immigration and refugee management adopts sets of manuals, guidelines, and policies that help to further promote the efficiency and consistency of their decision making.

a) Structure of the *IRPA*

The *IRPA* is divided into five parts:

Part 1, "Immigration to Canada," establishes the main principles of admission of persons to Canada and conditions of their stay in the

89 Francois Crépeau, "When Recourses Fail to Protect: Canadian Human Rights Obligations and the Remedies Offered to Foreigners against Immigration Decisions" (2005) 7 *European Journal of Migration and Law* 275 at 285.

90 See, for example, Francois Crépeau, "The Foreigner and the Right to Justice in the Aftermath of September 11th" (Paper delivered at the Breakfast on the Hill Lecture Series, Canadian Federation for the Humanities and Social Sciences, Ottawa, 19 May 2005), online: https://papers.ssrn.com/sol3/papers.cfm?abstract_id=2782144.

91 *IRPA*, above note 12.

country. In particular, it outlines the classes of immigrants and basic criteria for their selection, grounds of inadmissibility, rights and obligations of permanent and temporary residents, and grounds for loss of immigration status, detention, and removal of foreign nationals and permanent residents, as well as the process for appealing and judicially reviewing immigration decisions.

Part 2, "Refugee Protection," defines the terms "Convention refugee" and "person in need of protection," sets out eligibility criteria for accessing protection — both before the Board and through pre-removal risk assessment — and outlines grounds for vacation and cessation of refugee protection.

Part 3, "Enforcement," sets out penalties for human smuggling and trafficking, the use of false documents, misrepresentation, and other immigration-related offences.

Part 4, "Immigration and Refugee Board," outlines the IRB's powers, composition, and main principles of operation.

Part 5, "Transitional Provisions," resolves issues of application of the *IRPA* and the transition from the old *Immigration Act* to the *IRPA*.

b) Objectives of the *IRPA*

Section 3 of the *IRPA* stipulates the objectives — separately — for immigration and for refugee protection.

The immigration objectives are as follows:

(*a*) to permit Canada to pursue the maximum social, cultural and economic benefits of immigration;

(*b*) to enrich and strengthen the social and cultural fabric of Canadian society, while respecting the federal, bilingual and multicultural character of Canada;

(*b.1*) to support and assist the development of minority official languages communities in Canada;

(*c*) to support the development of a strong and prosperous Canadian economy, in which the benefits of immigration are shared across all regions of Canada;

(*d*) to see that families are reunited in Canada;

(*e*) to promote the successful integration of permanent residents into Canada, while recognizing that integration involves mutual obligations for new immigrants and Canadian society;

(*f*) to support, by means of consistent standards and prompt processing, the attainment of immigration goals established by the Government of Canada in consultation with the provinces;

(*g*) to facilitate the entry of visitors, students and temporary workers for purposes such as trade, commerce, tourism, international understanding and cultural, educational and scientific activities;

(*h*) to protect public health and safety and to maintain the security of Canadian society;

(*i*) to promote international justice and security by fostering respect for human rights and by denying access to Canadian territory to persons who are criminals or security risks; and

(*j*) to work in cooperation with the provinces to secure better recognition of the foreign credentials of permanent residents and their more rapid integration into society.[92]

With respect to refugee protection, the *IRPA* stipulates the following objectives:

(*a*) to recognize that the refugee program is in the first instance about saving lives and offering protection to the displaced and persecuted;

(*b*) to fulfil Canada's international legal obligations with respect to refugees and affirm Canada's commitment to international efforts to provide assistance to those in need of resettlement;

(*c*) to grant, as a fundamental expression of Canada's humanitarian ideals, fair consideration to those who come to Canada claiming persecution;

(*d*) to offer safe haven to persons with a well-founded fear of persecution based on race, religion, nationality, political opinion or membership in a particular social group, as well as those at risk of torture or cruel and unusual treatment or punishment;

(*e*) to establish fair and efficient procedures that will maintain the integrity of the Canadian refugee protection system, while upholding Canada's respect for the human rights and fundamental freedoms of all human beings;

(*f*) to support the self-sufficiency and the social and economic well-being of refugees by facilitating reunification with their family members in Canada;

(*g*) to protect the health and safety of Canadians and to maintain the security of Canadian society; and

(*h*) to promote international justice and security by denying access to Canadian territory to persons, including refugee claimants, who are security risks or serious criminals.[93]

92 *IRPA*, above note 12, s 3(1).

93 *Ibid*, s 3(2).

There is no official hierarchy among the above objectives. However, court jurisprudence suggests that security has acquired particular importance.[94] Chief Justice McLachlin summarized the spirit of the *IRPA* provisions in *Medovarski v Canada (Minister of Citizenship and Immigration); Esteban v Canada (Minister of Citizenship and Immigration)* in the following way:

> The objectives as expressed in the *IRPA* indicate an intent to prioritize security. This objective is given effect by preventing the entry of applicants with criminal records, by removing applicants with such records from Canada, and by emphasizing the obligation of permanent residents to behave lawfully while in Canada. This marks a change from the focus in the predecessor statute, which emphasized the successful integration of applicants more than security: e.g. see s. 3(1)(*i*) of the *IRPA* versus s. 3(*j*) of the former Act; s. 3(1)(*e*) of the *IRPA* versus s. 3(*d*) of the former Act; s. 3(1)(*h*) of the *IRPA* versus s. 3(*i*) of the former Act. Viewed collectively, the objectives of the *IRPA* and its provisions concerning permanent residents, communicate a strong desire to treat criminals and security threats less leniently than under the former Act.[95]

The statement of the objectives and interpretive provisions can provide important guidelines for the judicial analysis of *IRPA* provisions. The *IRPA*'s embodied distinction between immigration and refugee objectives attests to greater sensitivity towards the specific interests of refugee protection and needs of refugees. At the same time, it is important to note that both immigration and refugee objectives include the protection of the "health and safety and . . . the security of Canadian society" and the promotion of international justice and security "by denying access to Canadian territory to persons who are criminals or security risks." In addition, the *IRPA*'s general interpretive provision — section 3(3)(f) — sets out that the statute be construed so as to "comply with international human rights instruments to which Canada is signatory."[96]

The range of instruments covered by section 3(3)(f) may be gleaned from the website of the Office of the United Nations High Commissioner for Human Rights (UNHCHR) which lists both core international human rights instruments and other human rights instruments.[97] In

94 [2005] 2 SCR 539 [*Medovarski*].

95 *Ibid* at para 10. See also para 46.

96 *IRPA*, above note 12, s 3(3).

97 *De Guzman v Canada (Minister of Citizenship and Immigration)*, 2005 FCA 436 [*De Guzman*].

addition, regional multilateral human rights instruments, such as the *American Convention on Human Rights*, may fall within section 3(3)(f).

The Federal Court of Appeal decision in *De Guzman v Canada (Minister of Citizenship and Immigration)* provided important guidance on the application of section 3(3)(f). First, this section is an interpretive aid. It does not incorporate international human rights instruments signed by Canada into domestic law, but "merely directs that [the Act] must be construed and applied in a manner that complies with them."[98] This helps ensure that all new international conventions signed by Canada are included in the progressive interpretation of the *IRPA*.[99] Second, the weight given to various international human rights instruments in the interpretation of the *IRPA* depends on whether those instruments are binding. The instruments to which Canada is a signatory and which are binding[100] are determinative of the meaning of the *IRPA*, in the absence of a "clearly expressed legislative intention to the contrary."[101] Therefore, they have more than "mere ambiguity-resolving, contextual significance."[102] In contrast, non-binding instruments, while they may also be used in the interpretation of the *IRPA*, constitute only persuasive and contextual factors.[103]

2) *Immigration and Refugee Protection Regulations*[104]

Section 5 of the *IRPA* allows the Governor in Council (that is, the federal Cabinet) to make regulations. The *Immigration and Refugee Protection Regulations* are divided into twenty-one parts detailing the criteria, procedures, and requirements for each class of immigrants and temporary residents; inland and overseas refugee determination procedures; pre-removal risk assessment; detention; removal; the obligations of carriers; and the fees payable for various types of visas and permits. The *Regulations* are accompanied by regulatory impact analysis statements (RIAS) that outline the anticipated impact on persons concerned and anticipated benefits from the new regulations.[105] Although it is beyond

---

98 *Ibid* at para 73.

99 *Ibid*. See also *Charkaoui (Re)*, [2005] FCJ No 2038 at para 42 (FC).

100 The mere factor of signing does not make the instrument binding on Canada. As a rule, ratification is required. An international instrument will be binding if it has been ratified or if it does not require ratification.

101 *De Guzman*, above note 97 at paras 75, 87, and 108.

102 *Ibid* at para 82.

103 *Ibid* at para 89.

104 SOR/2002-227 [*Regulations*].

105 A regulatory impact analysis statement (RIAS) is a public document published along with the text of the regulation; it is required as a matter of government

the scope of this discussion to review the RIAS, they are beginning to be cited in the jurisprudence as a factor to consider in the interpretation of the *Regulations*.[106]

3) *Federal Courts Act*[107]

The Federal Court and the Federal Court of Appeal are creations of statute.[108] In keeping with section 101 of the *Constitution Act, 1867*, neither court is a court of general jurisdiction. Rather, the jurisdiction of the Federal Court system is confined to the subject matters stipulated in the *Federal Courts Act*.[109]

The Federal Court (or the Trial Division, as it was known before 2002) was originally given exclusive jurisdiction over a wide range of disputes involving the Crown. Since 1993, the Trial Division has also assumed responsibility for immigration and refugee matters.[110] Thus, the Federal Court now has concurrent original jurisdiction in all cases in which relief is claimed against the Crown[111] as well as cases involving Canadian maritime law, navigation and shipping,[112] aeronautics, bills of exchange and promissory notes, and interprovincial works and undertakings.[113]

The Federal Court also has "exclusive" jurisdiction[114] in a number of areas, including judicial review and provision of relief against decisions of federal boards, tribunals, and commissions[115] as well as

---

policy for all proposals to amend regulations or introduce new ones.

106 *Popal v Canada (Minister of Citizenship and Immigration)*, [2000] FCJ No 352 (TD); *Collier v Canada (Minister of Citizenship and Immigration)*, 2004 FC 1209; *Canada (Minister of Citizenship and Immigration) v Vong*, 2005 FC 855. See also France Houle, "Regulatory History Material as an Extrinsic Aid to Interpretation: An Empirical Study on the Use of RIAS by the Federal Court of Canada" (2006) 19 *Canadian Journal of Administrative Law & Practice* 151.

107 *Federal Courts Act*, above note 15, s 14.

108 Before the amendments of 2002, the federal courts were called the Federal Court—Trial Division and the Federal Court—Appeal Division.

109 Peter W Hogg, *Constitutional Law of Canada* (Scarborough: Carswell, 2005) at 198.

110 Michael S Whittington & Richard J Van Loon, *Canadian Government and Politics: Institutions and Processes* (Toronto: McGraw-Hill Ryerson, 1996) at 698.

111 *Federal Courts Act*, above note 15, s 17(1).

112 *Ibid*, s 22.

113 *Ibid*, s 23.

114 As noted previously, the "exclusive" jurisdiction of the Federal Court over relief against tribunals set out in the *Federal Courts Act* must be read in light of the broad inherent jurisdiction of provincial superior courts.

115 *Federal Courts Act*, above note 15, s 18.

issues of copyright, trademark, and patents.[116] In the opinion of some authors, the area of general administrative law where remedies are provided against federal agencies and tribunals constitutes likely the most important aspect of the Federal Court's work.[117] In fact, immigration matters constitute between 50 and 60 percent of the court's annual workload.[118]

The Federal Court of Appeal has the power to review decisions of the Federal Court and decisions of specified federal boards and tribunals such as the Pension Appeals Board and the National Energy Board.[119] Until 1993, the Federal Court of Appeal was the court of review for refugee decisions.[120] At present, the Federal Court of Appeal may review the decisions of the Federal Court in refugee and immigration matters only when the latter certifies that the case raises "a serious question of general importance."[121]

The procedure and filing deadlines before the Federal Court are generally governed by the *Federal Courts Rules, 1998*.[122] Cases involving immigration and refugee matters are subject to additional *Federal Courts Citizenship, Immigration and Refugee Protection Rules*.[123] The *IRPA* also contains provisions on judicial review of the decisions made under the Act. These provisions outline requirements for leave for judicial review and leave for appeal as well as for certification of "a serious question of general importance" for appeal. (For more on leave and certification requirements, see Chapter 10.)

4) *Citizenship Act*

The *Citizenship Act*[124] sets out the conditions of acquisition and loss of full membership in Canadian society. Citizenship status can play a

---

116 *Ibid*, s 20.

117 Whittington & Van Loon, above note 110 at 698.

118 Courts Administration Service, *Annual Report 2010–11*, online: http://cas-ncr-nter03.cas-satj.gc.ca/portal/page/portal/CAS/AR-RA_eng/AR-RA10-11_eng#link36; *Annual Report 2012–13*, online: http://cas-cdc-www02.cas-satj.gc.ca/portal/page/portal/CAS/AR-RA_eng/AR-RA12-13_eng#RA_02.2.

119 *Federal Courts Act*, above note 15, s 28.

120 For a review of the complicated and convoluted history of judicial review of refugee matters, see Mary C Hurley, "Principles, Practices, Fragile Promises: Judicial Review of Refugee Determination Decisions before the Federal Court of Canada" (1996) 41 *McGill Law Journal* 317.

121 *IRPA*, above note 12, s 74(d).

122 SOR/98-106.

123 SOR/93-22.

124 RSC 1985, c C-29.

crucial role in the fate of an immigrant or a refugee not only in terms of broader political and socio-economic rights that it provides, but, most crucially, for the individual's ability to remain in Canada. Generally speaking, only citizenship status guarantees that a person cannot be deported from Canada.[125] War crimes, criminality, and national security issues often trigger removal proceedings against non-citizens and may result in even refugees being removed from Canada.[126] The peculiarities of each membership status (permanent resident, citizen, refugee claimant, etc.), including the rules of their acquisition and loss, will be discussed in more detail in Chapter 3.

E. ADMINISTRATIVE GUIDELINES

1) Institutional Framework for Immigration and Refugee Protection Administration

The three government agencies central to the administration of immigration and refugee matters are (1) the Immigration and Refugee Board (IRB); (2) Immigration, Refugees and Citizenship Canada (IRCC) (formerly Citizenship and Immigration Canada (CIC)); and (3) the Canada Border Services Agency (CBSA). The *IRPA* outlines the authorities given to the IRCC[127] and the IRB; the CBSA is governed by the *Canada Border Services Agency Act*,[128] although a part of its authorities is also prescribed in the *IRPA*. Each agency has specific functions related to the refugee process. The IRB is an independent administrative tribunal

125 The qualification to this statement is that "every person registered as an Indian under the *Indian Act*" has a right to enter and remain in Canada.

126 The contrast between the difficulty of revoking citizenship and the relative ease of cancelling permanent residence or refusing status in Canada can be illustrated by the statistics under the Crimes Against Humanity and War Crimes Program. The authorities were successful in revoking citizenship on grounds of commission of war crimes only in six out of fifteen cases during 1995–2002. In contrast, they issued fifty-nine removal orders against permanent residents on the same grounds in 2001–02 alone. However, the 2014 amendments to the *Citizenship Act* streamlined the citizenship revocation process. In the past, citizenship could be revoked only by the Governor in Council, but currently this can be done by the minister (although a Federal Court declaration may be required in some cases). *Citizenship Act*, RSC 1985, c C-29, ss 10–10.1.

127 In addition, IRCC's mandate is governed by the *Department of Citizenship and Immigration Act*, SC 1994, c 31. As of 2008, IRCC is also responsible for administering the *Canadian Multiculturalism Act*, RSC 1985, c 24 (4th Supp).

128 SC 2005, c 38 [*CBSA Act*].

which is responsible for such matters as first-instance refugee determination, inadmissibility hearings, detention reviews, and appeals on immigration and refugee decisions. IRCC is a government department responsible for immigration and refugee policy-making as well as processing and decision making on all types of permanent and temporary resident applications (for example, economic immigration, family sponsorship, work and study permits, and humanitarian and compassionate applications). In relation to inland claimants, IRCC has a role at the initial and concluding stages of the claim process: for claims made inland, it determines if they are eligible for referral to the hearing at the IRB and decides on permanent resident applications of persons granted protection. IRCC also decides on applications for refugee resettlement from overseas. The CBSA is an enforcement agency in charge of border control, risk assessment, immigration detention, and removal. In addition, it determines eligibility of refugee claims made at the border.

These government agencies issue and use various administrative guidelines. These take the form of procedural manuals, policies, instructions, and other similar instruments. This "soft law" reflects the given agency's approach to a certain issue and allows flexible and timely adjustment in response to day-to-day experience.[129] For example, IRCC has created operational manuals concerning each aspect of refugee and immigration processing. The IRB has also developed a number of administrative guides, ranging from the Chairperson's Guidelines, to instructions and policies that seek to promote consistency and efficiency of decision making. Although the administrative guidelines of other departments and agencies are occasionally relevant to refugee matters, the focus of the present discussion will be on those developed by IRCC and the IRB.

2) Responsibility for the Administration of the *IRPA*

The *IRPA* prescribes that the Minister of Immigration, Refugees and Citizenship is primarily responsible for the administration of the Act.[130] In addition, the Minister of Public Safety and Emergency Preparedness (PSEP)[131] has a responsibility for the administration of provisions of the *IRPA* that relate to examinations at ports of entry; enforcement of the *IRPA*, including arrest, detention, and removal; development of policies with respect to enforcement and inadmissibility on grounds of security,

129 *Thamotharem v Canada (Minister of Citizenship and Immigration)*, 2007 FCA 198 at para 56 (CA) [*Thamotharem*].

130 *IRPA*, above note 12, s 4(1).

131 *CBSA Act*, above note 128, s 2.

organized criminality, or violation of human or international rights; and ministerial exemptions to inadmissibility.[132] Further, the Minister of Employment and Social Development may also be given some powers under the Act by the *Regulations*.[133]

Of course, ministers do not administer all *IRPA* matters personally. They delegate most of the tasks to officers of various levels (referred to as "minister's delegates").[134] Most of the responsibilities under the *IRPA* are given to IRCC officers, but some functions are also exercised by the CBSA. There are, however, powers that must be exercised by ministers personally and cannot be delegated. For example, they include signing of a security certificate under section 77(1) of the *IRPA*; designating irregular arrivals as designated foreign nationals; declaring that a foreign national cannot be admitted for temporary residence for public policy reasons; and granting exemptions to inadmissibility.[135]

3) Ministerial Instructions

In 2008, the IRCC minister was granted a new power to issue instructions to immigration officers with respect to processing of various applications. This power is formulated in the following way in section 87.3(3) of the *IRPA*:

> . . . the Minister may give instructions with respect to the processing of applications and requests, including instructions
>
> (a) establishing categories of applications or requests to which the instructions apply;
> (a.1) establishing conditions, by category or otherwise, that must be met before or during the processing of an application or request;
> (b) establishing an order, by category or otherwise, for the processing of applications or requests;
> (c) setting the number of applications or requests, by category or otherwise, to be processed in any year; and

132 *IRPA*, above note 12, s 4(2).

133 *Ibid*, s 4(2.1).

134 *Ibid*, ss 6(1) & (2); *CBSA Act*, above note 128, s 6(2).

135 *IRPA*, above note 12, s 6(3). See also Immigration, Refugees and Citizenship Canada, "Operation Manuals—Legislation," online: IRCC www.cic.gc.ca/english/resources/manuals/il/il03-menu.asp; Canada Border Services Agency, "Designation and Delegation by the Minister of Public Safety and Emergency Preparedness under the *Immigration and Refugee Protection Act* and *Immigration and Refugee Protection Regulations*—Amendment," online: CBSA www.cbsa-asfc.gc.ca/agency-agence/actreg-loireg/delegation/irpa-lipr-2016-07-eng.html.

(d) providing for the disposition of applications and requests, including those made subsequent to the first application or request.

Although not applicable to refugee context,[136] this power has very important implications for the immigration system. Under the Conservative government, it was used on multiple occasions not only to direct application processing, but also to alter substantive selection requirements under immigration subclasses. Among the most notable uses of the Instructions are these:

- establishment of a Start-up Visa Program;
- establishment of the Immigrant Investor Venture Capital Class;
- changes to the criteria for admission under the Caregiver Class;
- introduction of the Parent and Grandparent Super Visa;
- introduction of a two-year moratorium on applications to sponsor parents and grandparents.[137]

4) Immigration, Refugees and Citizenship Canada Operational Manuals

Immigration, Refugees and Citizenship Canada developed a series of operational manuals on all key aspects of immigration processing, including inland and overseas processing of immigration applications, temporary foreign workers, protected persons, citizenship, information sharing, and enforcement. Each departmental manual describes the minutiae of processing, refers to some common practices, and clarifies the specific application of the *IRPA* and the *Regulations* in various scenarios. Given that the manuals outline procedures in great detail, it is important to construe them in a way that does not fetter officers' discretion. As indicated in *Yhap v Canada (Minister of Employment and Immigration)*, guidelines are appropriate as long as they express "general policy" or "rough rules of thumb" and do not impose limitations on officers' discretion.[138]

In addition to offering detailed guidance to decision makers, the manuals and guidelines can play an important role in other aspects of the process. Although non-binding, they can provide some assistance in the interpretation of legislation.[139] They can also give rise to legitim-

136 *IRPA*, above note 12, s 87.3(1).

137 For the list of past and current instructions, see www.cic.gc.ca/english/department/mi/.

138 [1990] 1 FC 722 (TD).

139 *Hernandez v Canada (Minister of Citizenship and Immigration)*, 2005 FC 429; *Baker v Canada (Minister of Citizenship and Immigration)*, [1999] 2 SCR 817 at

ate expectations that an officer would consider certain factors or take an action outlined in a manual.[140]

5) Immigration and Refugee Board Division Rules

The IRB is comprised of four divisions:[141]

1) the Refugee Protection Division (RPD), which conducts refugee hearings and makes first-instance decisions on claims for protection;
2) the Immigration Division (ID), which holds inadmissibility hearings and detention reviews;
3) the Immigration Appeal Division (IAD), which hears appeals on family sponsorship cases and removal orders; and
4) the Refugee Appeal Division (RAD), which hears appeals on RPD decisions.

Each division has sole and exclusive jurisdiction to hear and determine all questions of law and fact, including questions of jurisdiction, in matters brought before it.[142] Each division is expected to deal with cases informally and quickly, but still observe the principles of fairness and natural justice.[143] None of the divisions is bound by legal or technical rules of evidence.[144]

Matters are usually decided by one-member panels, although a panel of three members may be constituted in any division, except the Immigration Division.[145] Each division will usually hold a hearing into the matter, although the statutory obligation to hold a hearing is not framed in the same way with respect to each division. The Refugee Protection Division must hold a hearing in all cases.[146] The Immigration Appeal Division is not obligated to hold a hearing in all cases, except where there is an appeal under section 63(4) of the *IRPA* (appeals regarding residency obligation).[147] The Immigration Division must, "where practicable," hold a hearing.[148] The Refugee Appeal Division "may" hold a hearing,[149] but most cases are decided on the basis

para 67 [*Baker*].

140 *Varela v Canada (Minister of Citizenship and Immigration)*, [2001] 4 FC 42 (TD).

141 *IRPA*, above note 12, s 151.

142 *Ibid*, s 162(1).

143 *Ibid*, s 162(2).

144 *Ibid*, ss 170(g), 171(a.2), 173(c), and 175(1)(b).

145 *Ibid*, s 163.

146 *Ibid*, s 170(b).

147 *Ibid*, s 175(1)(a).

148 *Ibid*, s 173(a).

149 *Ibid*, s 171.

of a written record. Parties may participate in a hearing in person or by video conference[150] and may be represented by a counsel.[151] Proceedings are usually conducted in public, except in cases of refugee claimants and refugees or where confidentiality may be required for other reasons.[152]

Each division has its own rules of procedure that outline applicable deadlines, disclosure requirements, procedure for making applications, and other issues.[153] In addition, the IRB has developed "soft law" instruments that provide guidance on substantive and procedural issues. These instruments include the following: (1) Chairperson's Guidelines; (2) jurisprudential guides; (3) persuasive decisions; (4) policies; and (5) Chairperson's Instructions. All of the above instruments may be addressed to all IRB divisions or may be individually tailored for one division. For example, as will be shown below, most of the current Chairperson's Guidelines are addressed to the Refugee Protection Division, while many of the policies apply to all divisions.

6) Immigration and Refugee Board Guidelines

Administrative agencies such as the IRB "are often required to be procedurally innovative in order to handle a heavy case load effectively and to make the most efficient use of scarce resources."[154] As acknowledged by the Federal Court, the Board has a "uniquely difficult mandate of administrative adjudication":[155] it has a heavy case load, has to keep up-to-date with rapidly changing conditions in many countries of origin, and operates under the scrutiny of political and public attention. Guidelines and other "soft law" techniques are particularly useful for achieving consistency within tribunals that enjoy discretion in performing their adjudicative functions.[156] Furthermore, even though manuals and guidelines are not binding, they can offer an opinion on the purpose or meaning of the legislation.[157]

---

150 *Ibid*, s 164.

151 *Ibid*, s 167.

152 *Ibid*, s 166.

153 The rules are issued by the IRB Chairperson. *IRPA*, above note 12, s 161.

154 *Geza v Canada (Minister of Citizenship and Immigration)*, [2006] FCJ No 477 at para 1 (CA) [*Geza*].

155 *Ibid* at para 55.

156 *Thamotharem*, above note 129 at para 60.

157 *Canada (Information Commissioner) v Canada (Minister of Citizenship and Immigration)*, 2002 FCA 270 at para 37; *Baker*, above note 139 at para 67.

In addition to procedural rules, the IRB Chairperson may issue "guidelines" pursuant to section 159(1)(h) of the *IRPA*. These guidelines establish a recommended approach to dealing with various subject matters or issues.

Although the Chairperson's Guidelines have no binding force and represent a recommended approach, it is expected that the members will consider them in appropriate cases. As in the case of the IRCC manuals, the content and language of the guidelines is subordinated to the following important principle: the guidelines must observe the duty of fairness and must not interfere with the Board's independence and impartiality.

Each guideline must also be understood in its historical context. The guidelines were issued at different stages of the development of the Board and related jurisprudence. While some may seem to deal with now well-settled law (such as Guideline 1 and, to a lesser extent, Guideline 4), when they were adopted, they represented an effort to direct the development of the law. To the extent that a guideline now appears uncontentious, it has succeeded.

At present, there exist seven guidelines:

Guideline 1: "*Civilian Non-combatants Fearing Persecution in Civil War Situations*" (1996)
This guideline addresses issues arising in cases involving civilian non-combatants fearing return to situations of civil war. In particular, it provides guidance to the RPD on assessing whether harm feared by claimants falls under the definition of the *Convention Relating to the Status of Refugees*,[158] what principles are to be considered, and what evidentiary elements to look for. The guideline advocates a non-comparative approach; that is, the assessment is not based on a comparison between the claimant's risk and the risk faced by other individuals or groups at risk for a *Convention* reason. Instead, the Board examines whether the claimant faces a risk of sufficiently serious harm linked to a *Refugee Convention* reason as opposed to the general, indiscriminate consequences of civil war.

Guideline 2: "*Detention*" (latest revision: 2013)
This guideline deals with several issues, including grounds for detention, long-term detention, alternatives to detention, and relevant evidence and procedure. It is intended primarily for use by the Immigration Division which is charged with detention reviews.

---

158 28 July 1951, 189 UNTS 150, art 1 [*Refugee Convention*].

Guideline 3: *"Child Refugee Claimants: Procedural and Evidentiary Issues"* (1996)
This guideline reflects the Board's recognition that the procedures followed for adult claimants are not always suitable for child claimants. It prescribes the procedure for designation of a representative for a child claimant, steps to be followed in processing claims made by unaccompanied minors, and the gathering and assessment of evidence in a child's claim.

Guideline 4: *"Women Refugee Claimants Fearing Gender-Related Persecution"* (1996)
Given that gender is not included in the *Refugee Convention* as an enumerated ground, the guideline assists the Board in determining the link between gender, feared persecution, and grounds of the *Refugee Convention*. (Currently, there is no Guideline 5.)

Guideline 6: *"Scheduling and Changing the Date or Time of a Proceeding"* (latest revision: 2012)
This guideline stipulates the criteria to be considered in decisions related to the change of date or time of hearings for all four divisions. While allowing for consideration of special circumstances, it emphasizes that the changes of date or time would be allowed only in exceptional circumstances.

Guideline 7: *"Concerning Preparation and Conduct of a Hearing in the Refugee Protection Division"* (2003; latest revision: 2012)
This guideline deals with case preparation, hearing preliminaries (oath, exhibits, pre-conference hearings), interpreters, and the order of questioning at an RPD hearing. It provides that, as a matter of standard practice (where a Minister is not a party to the hearing), the Board member begins questioning followed by a counsel for the claimant.[159] In exceptional circumstances (e.g., a child claimant, a survivor of torture), the Board may vary the order of questioning.[160]

Before the guideline was introduced, Board members exercised individual discretion in deciding how to proceed and often allowed counsel to question the claimant first. Being questioned by their counsel first could help put claimants at ease and tell their story, but, from

159 Immigration and Refugee Board, "Chairperson's Guideline 7: Concerning Preparation and Conduct of a Hearing in the Refugee Protection Division," s 5.3, online: www.irb-cisr.gc.ca/Eng/BoaCom/references/pol/guidir/Pages/GuideDir07.aspx [IRB, Guideline 7]. As of 2012, this order of questioning is also prescribed by the *Refugee Protection Division Rules*, SOR/2012-256, s 10. For more on the order of questioning, see Chapter 8.

160 IRB, Guideline 7, above note 159, s 5.6.

an administration perspective, it was considered inefficient and more time-consuming. Hence, Guideline 7 was put in place. The new order of questioning was challenged before courts.[161] The applicants argued that the guideline denied them the right to be heard, fettered the discretion of the Board members, and unlawfully distorted their adjudicative role. The applicants' argument succeeded before the Federal Court, but the decision was overturned on appeal. Thus, the guideline remains in effect.

Guideline 8: *"Concerning Procedures with Respect to Vulnerable Persons Appearing before the Immigration and Refugee Board of Canada"* (2006; latest revision: 2012)

Guideline 8 consolidates the Board's policies for dealing with vulnerable individuals and applies to all four divisions. "Vulnerable persons" are defined as "individuals whose ability to present their cases before the IRB is severely impaired."[162] They may include, but are not limited to, minors, the elderly, victims of torture, persons with mental disabilities, and victims of gender-related persecution or persecution based on sexual orientation and gender identity. The guideline sets out various procedural accommodations for vulnerable persons, including scheduling, order of questioning, and the use of expert evidence.[163]

7) Immigration and Refugee Board Jurisprudential Guides, Policies, and Instructions

Jurisprudential guides are issued by the IRB Chairperson under the same statutory provision as the guidelines. Jurisprudential guides are decisions of the Board which, in the Chairperson's view, "contain persuasive reasoning that should be followed."[164] Since decisions of any IRB division are not binding on the subsequent panels of that division, jurisprudential guides are used to suggest preferred means of analysis. Once a decision has been identified as a jurisprudential guide, members are expected to follow the reasoning of that decision when they deal with

161 *Thamotharem*, above note 129.

162 Immigration and Refugee Board, "Chairperson's Guideline 8: Procedures with Respect to Vulnerable Persons Appearing before the IRB," s 2.1, online: www.irb-cisr.gc.ca/Eng/BoaCom/references/pol/guidir/Pages/GuideDir08.aspx.

163 For discussion of the guideline, see Janet Cleveland, "The Guideline on Procedures with Respect to Vulnerable Persons Appearing before the Immigration and Refugee Board of Canada: A Critical Overview" (2008) 25 *Refuge* 119.

164 Immigration and Refugee Board, "Policy on the Use of Jurisprudential Guides" at para 4, online: IRB www.irb-cisr.gc.ca/Eng/BoaCom/references/pol/pol/Pages/PolJurisGuide.aspx.

similar cases. If a member does not adopt the reasoning of the jurisprudential guide, she must give reasons for not doing so.[165] The jurisprudential guides remain in effect until revoked by a Chairperson or overturned by a court. As of March 2017, one decision (TB4-05778) was designated as a jurisprudential guide (it discusses whether citizens of North Korea are deemed to be citizens of South Korea).

In addition to jurisprudential guides, the Board, under its statutory mandate, occasionally designates persuasive decisions. Decision makers are encouraged to rely upon these decisions in order to maintain consistency. However, unlike the expectation for jurisprudential guides, they are not required to provide reasons if they decide against following a persuasive decision.[166] As of March 2017, no decisions were designated as persuasive.

In addition to the guidelines, jurisprudential guides, and persuasive decisions, the IRB can adopt policies and instructions. These policies and instructions explain the purpose and mechanics of the Board's initiatives and set out specific responsibilities for decision makers and administrative personnel. The following policies apply to all IRB divisions:

- Policy on the Use of Social Media by Authorized Individuals at the IRB;
- Policy on Disclosing Information Regarding the Conduct of Authorized Representatives to Regulatory Bodies;
- Reasons Review Policy;
- Policy for Handling IRB Complaints Regarding Unauthorized, Paid Representatives;
- Policy on the Use of Chairperson's Guidelines;
- Policy on Court-Ordered Redeterminations;
- Policy on Higher Court Interventions;
- Policy on the Use of Jurisprudential Guides;
- Security Screening Measures Policy at IRB Controlled Premises.

A further number of policies specifically concern the Refugee Protection Division (RPD):

- Policy on Redeterminations Ordered by the RAD;
- Policy on the Expedited Processing of Refugee Claims by the RPD;
- Designation of Three-Member Panels — RPD Approach;
- Policy on the Transfer of Files for Hearings by Videoconference;
- Policy on Country-of-Origin Information Packages in Refugee Protection Claims;

165 *Ibid* at para 7.

166 Immigration and Refugee Board, "Persuasive Decisions," online: IRB www.irb-cisr.gc.ca/Eng/BoaCom/references/pol/persuas/Pages/index.aspx.

- Policy on the Treatment of Unsolicited Information in the RPD;
- Policy on Document Harmonization in Support of Jurisprudential Guides.

The following policy exists with respect to the RAD:

- Designation of Three-Member Panels — Refugee Appeal Division.

Chairperson's Instructions represent formal directions to IRB personnel to take or to avoid certain actions.[167] In contrast to policies, instructions are more limited in scope and usually concern a specific and narrow practice area. The instructions specific to the RPD include these:

- Instructions for Gathering and Disclosing Information for RPD Proceedings;
- Instructions Governing the Management of Refugee Protection Claims Awaiting Front End Security Screening;
- Instructions Governing Communication in the Absence of Parties between Members of the Refugee Protection Division and Refugee Protection Officers and between Members of the Refugee Protection Division and Other Employees of the Board.

The following document is specific to the RAD:

- Instructions for Gathering and Disclosing Information for Refugee Appeal Division Proceedings.

These policies and instructions complete the complex web of guidance given to IRB staff and decision makers.

F. INTERNATIONAL LAW

Several international instruments have particular significance for immigration and refugee law. They include the *Refugee Convention*,[168] the *International Covenant on Civil and Political Rights* (*ICCPR*),[169] the *Convention Against Torture and Other Cruel, Inhuman or Degrading Treatment or Punishment* (*CAT*)[170] and the *Convention on the Rights of the Child*.[171]

167 Immigration and Refugee Board, "Chairperson's Instructions," online: IRB www.irb-cisr.gc.ca/Eng/BoaCom/references/pol/instructions/Pages/index.aspx.

168 Above note 158 and surrounding text.

169 GA Res 2200A (XXI), 21 UN GAOR Supp (No 16) at 52, UN Doc A/6316 (1966), 999 UNTS 171 [*ICCPR*].

170 10 December 1984, [1987] Can TS No 36 [*CAT*].

171 GA Res 44/25, 1577 UNTS 3.

Canada has signed and ratified all four.[172] It should be noted that international treaties relevant to refugee law are by no means limited to those mentioned. Rather, these treaties establish the core framework and values that are most frequently invoked in refugee law. These conventions are significant not only by virtue of the rights enshrined in them, but also due to the international remedies that some of them afford. The *CAT*, the *ICCPR*, and the *Convention on the Rights of the Child* provide for the establishment of special committees that monitor states parties' compliance with their obligations, can issue interpretations of respective treaty provisions, and can hear and decide upon individual complaints alleging violation of the convention obligations by states parties.[173] Although non-binding, the decisions on individual complaints play an important role in interpreting international law and drawing attention to questionable actions of the states parties. (For more on complaints procedures, see Chapter 10.)

As a general rule, in dualist systems of law (such as Canada), international law is not a part of domestic law unless it has been incorporated by an act of legislature. This, however, does not prevent the use of international instruments (both binding and non-binding) as important tools for the interpretation of domestic law. Parliament is generally presumed to act in accordance with the customary and conventional international law: "These constitute a part of the legal context in which legislation is enacted and read. In so far as possible, therefore, interpretations that reflect these values and principles are preferred."[174] Canadian courts have, on a number of occasions, recognized the important role of international law in statutory interpretation[175] as well as in establishing internationally prevailing approaches on certain issues (e.g., voting rights of inmates;[176] death penalty[177]). As noted by the Supreme Court in *R v Keegstra*, Canada's international human rights

---

172 For ratification status, see online: Office of High Commissioner for Human Rights http://indicators.ohchr.org/.

173 In December 2011, the UN General Assembly approved a third Optional Protocol to the *Convention on the Rights of the Child*, which allows the Committee on the Rights of the Child to examine individual complaints. The Protocol opened for signature in February 2012 and entered into force in April 2014.

174 Ruth Sullivan, *Driedger on the Construction of Statutes*, 3d ed (Toronto: Butterworths, 1994) at 330, quoted with approval in *Baker*, above note 139 at para 70.

175 *Baker*, *ibid* at paras 69–71; *114957 Canada Ltée (Spraytech, Société d'arrosage) v Hudson (Town)*, 2001 SCC 40.

176 *Sauvé v Canada (Chief Electoral Officer)*, 2002 SCC 68.

177 *Kindler*, above note 20.

obligations reflect values and principles that underlie the *Charter*.[178] It further quoted to the pronouncement made in *Slaight Communications Inc v Davidson*:

> . . . Canada's international human rights obligations should inform not only the interpretation of the content of the rights guaranteed by the *Charter* but also the interpretation of what can constitute pressing and substantial s. 1 objectives which may justify restrictions upon those rights.[179]

In the following sections, we briefly review the *Refugee Convention*, the *ICCPR*, and the *CAT*.

1) *Refugee Convention*

The *Refugee Convention* that was negotiated after the Second World War initially sought to address the situation of refugees in Europe. In fact, it was limited in territorial and temporal scope — at its narrowest, to refugees produced by the "events occurring in Europe before 1 January 1951."[180] In 1967, the additional *Protocol* to the *Refugee Convention*[181] largely removed both these arbitrary limits on qualification as a refugee. The *Refugee Protocol* exists as an independent international legal instrument, but it is largely ignored when reference is made to the international legal basis of refugee law due to its perceived limited role in merely expanding the scope of refugee protection offered under the *Refugee Convention*.[182] There remain a small number of state parties to either or both the *Refugee Convention* and the *Refugee Protocol* who continue to restrict their interpretation of "refugee" either temporally (to those individuals whose fear arises out of pre-1951 events) or geographically (to those individuals whose fear arises out of events in Europe).[183]

---

178 *Slaight Communications Inc v Davidson*, [1989] 1 SCR 1038 at 1056–57, quoted in *R v Keegstra*, [1990] 3 SCR 697 at para 66 [*Keegstra*].

179 *Keegstra*, *ibid*.

180 State parties to the *Refugee Convention* had the option (under art 1B) of declaring that a refugee was an individual whose risk arose out of "events occurring in Europe before I January 1951" or "events occurring in Europe or elsewhere before 1 January 1951."

181 606 UNTS 267 (entered into force 4 October 1967) [*Refugee Protocol*].

182 This view has been criticized as legally inadequate. See James Hathaway, *The Rights of Refugees under International Law* (London: Cambridge University Press, 2005) at 111.

183 States with a temporal restriction: Madagascar and St Kitts and Nevis have adopted only the *Refugee Convention*. Thus, these states are required to accept only refugees arising out of events before 1 January 1951.

The *Refugee Convention* constitutes the core of international refugee law and has had a defining impact on domestic refugee decision making across the globe. First, it provides the definition of a refugee that for over sixty years has served the international community. It forms the basis for determining whether an asylum seeker should be granted protection (discussed in detail in Chapter 4). Second, it establishes the principle of non-*refoulement* (prohibition of expulsion or return). Article 33 prohibits expulsion of a refugee to a country where she may face persecution, unless there are "reasonable grounds" to consider her a danger to security or to the community of a host state. As a result of this principle, states' ability to remove refugees is more constrained than their ability to remove migrants of other categories. Third, the *Refugee Convention* imposes an obligation on states parties to ensure certain standards of treatment to refugees, namely, these:

- treatment equal to the treatment of nationals of a host state: This standard applies to access to the courts,[184] freedom of religion;[185] elementary education;[186] artistic and industrial rights;[187] rationing;[188] public relief and assistance;[189] labour legislation and social security.[190]
- the most favourable treatment accorded to non-nationals in the same circumstances: This standard applies to the rights of association[191] and employment.[192]
- treatment as favourable as possible and, in any event, not less favourable than that accorded to aliens generally in the same circumstances: This standard applies to acquisition and rights to movable and immovable property;[193] self-employment;[194] practice of liberal professions;[195] housing;[196] and education (other than elementary).[197]
- treatment accorded to non-nationals generally in the same circumstances: This standard applies to freedom of movement.[198]

---

184 *Refugee Convention*, above note 158, art 16.
185 *Ibid*, art 4.
186 *Ibid*, art 22.
187 *Ibid*, art 14.
188 *Ibid*, art 20.
189 *Ibid*, art 23.
190 *Ibid*, art 24.
191 *Ibid*, art 15.
192 *Ibid*, art 17.
193 *Ibid*, art 13.
194 *Ibid*, art 18.
195 *Ibid*, art 19.
196 *Ibid*, art 21.
197 *Ibid*, art 22.
198 *Ibid*, art 26.

However, the *Refugee Convention* does not establish a specific procedure for refugee determination that must be followed by a state party in deciding whether an individual is a refugee. It also does not impose on the parties an obligation to admit refugees or compel any particular long-term consequence of refugee status (e.g., for asylum to be permanent or to entail citizenship).[199] Moreover, unlike other major human rights treaties, the *Refugee Convention* provides no international authority to monitor states parties' compliance with the obligations under the *Refugee Convention*.

The Office of the UN High Commissioner for Refugees (UNHCR)[200] is a central non-political organ that promotes interstate co-operation in the field of refugee protection, but it has no power, either actual or formal, to enforce states' compliance with their obligations under the *Refugee Convention*. UNHCR is mandated to safeguard the well-being of refugees and to ensure that everyone can exercise the right to seek asylum or repatriate voluntarily. In its efforts to protect refugees and to promote solutions to their problems, UNHCR works in partnership with governments and regional, international, and non-governmental organizations. As a result of various UN General Assembly resolutions, UNHCR is now mandated to assist with the protection not only of "refugees" under the *Refugee Convention* but also other forced migrants of concern.

UNHCR has developed several handbooks (e.g., *Handbook on Voluntary Repatriation* and *Handbook on Procedures and Criteria for Determining Refugee Status*) to provide non-binding guidelines on its own procedures. UNHCR's *Handbook on Procedures and Criteria for Determining Refugee Status*,[201] which provides an interpretation of the terms used in defining a refugee and an outline of preferred practices in determining refugee status, is one of the most frequently referred to in the jurisprudence. The Canadian courts (and courts of other countries) have given much weight to the UNHCR Handbook:

> . . . while not formally binding upon signatory states such as Canada, the UNHCR Handbook has been formed from the cumulative knowledge available concerning the refugee admission procedures

199 The *Refugee Convention*, however, does prevail upon states to "as far as possible facilitate the assimilation and naturalization of refugees" (art 34).

200 UNHCR was established by resolution of the General Assembly in 1950. *Statute of the Office of the United Nations High Commissioner for Refugees*, GA Res 428 (V), annex, 5 UN GAOR Supp (No 20) at 46, UN Doc A/1775 (1950).

201 *Handbook on Procedures and Criteria for Determining Refugee Status under the 1951 Convention and the 1967 Protocol* HCR/IP/4/Eng/rev.1 (UNHCR, Geneva, 1979, re-edited January 1992).

> and criteria of signatory states. This much-cited guide has been endorsed by the Executive Committee of the UNHCR, including Canada, and has been relied upon for guidance by the courts of signatory nations. Accordingly, the UNHCR Handbook must be treated as a highly relevant authority in considering refugee admission practices. This, of course, applies not only to the Board but also to a reviewing court.[202]

However, notwithstanding the acknowledgement of the UNHCR Handbook's authority, the deference to it and other UNHCR positions regarding the *Refugee Convention* is not complete by either administrative decision makers or the courts. The disagreements between Canadian refugee law and refugee law as understood by UNHCR will be highlighted in the subsequent discussion of the interpretation of the meaning of "refugee" (see Chapter 4).

2) *International Covenant on Civil and Political Rights*

The *ICCPR* enshrines fundamental rights of individuals, regardless of their immigration or citizenship status: equality, liberty, and security of person, freedom of expression, freedom of association, freedom of religion, and many others.[203] The following *ICCPR* provisions are also of particular importance to the refugee context:

- article 2: the right to an effective remedy where *ICCPR* rights have been violated;
- article 6: the right to life and prohibition of arbitrary deprivation of life;
- article 7: the prohibition of cruel, inhuman, or degrading treatment or punishment;
- article 9: the right to liberty and security of person, freedom from arbitrary arrest and detention, and the right of every arrested or detained person to take proceedings before a court;
- article 12: the right of everyone staying lawfully in a territory of a state to move within that territory; freedom to leave a country, including one's own; prohibition of arbitrary deprivation of right to enter one's own country;
- article 13: the right of an alien lawfully in the territory of a state party to be expelled based only on a decision made according to the law, except where reasons of national security require otherwise —

---

202 *Chan v Canada (Minister of Employment and Immigration)*, [1995] 3 SCR 593 at para 46 (LaForest J, in dissent).

203 Only art 25 refers to "every citizen" in the context of right to unimpeded participation in the conduct of public affairs, elections, and access to public service.

an alien should be given an opportunity to present reasons against expulsion and to have his case reviewed before a competent authority;

- article 14: the equality of all individuals before any court or tribunal;
- article 18: the freedom of conscience and freedom to manifest religious beliefs;
- article 19: the right to hold and express opinions without interference.

Canada became a party to the *ICCPR* and its *First Optional Protocol*[204] in 1976. The *ICCPR* has multiple direct and indirect impacts on domestic law. The text of the Canadian *Charter* in many respects follows the tradition of the *ICCPR*, reflecting "a fusion of classic liberties and human rights."[205] In the area of refugee protection specifically, the *ICCPR* provisions both influence the interpretation of the term "refugee" and provide substantive rights to refugees in Canada. With respect to the former, a key element of the term "refugee" is the concept of "persecution": a refugee must be at risk of persecution in her country of nationality. Persecution is increasingly interpreted in light of the provisions of international human rights law, including the *ICCPR*: where an important international human right is at risk of serious violation, the case of persecution will likely be made out. With respect to the individual rights, the *ICCPR* not only describes rights refugees should have been granted in their country of nationality, but also directs what rights refugees (and refugee claimants) should be granted in Canada. Finally, the *ICCPR* guarantees of life and freedom from torture provide the basis for the *IRPA*'s definition of the "person in need of protection."[206]

Unlike the *Refugee Convention*, which does not provide for mechanisms to monitor and facilitate state compliance with their obligations, the *ICCPR* establishes a treaty body — the Human Rights Committee — to monitor and facilitate states parties' compliance. The powers of the committee include receiving periodic reports from states parties on compliance with the *ICCPR*, issuing interpretations of the *ICCPR* provisions, and considering interstate and individual complaints on alleged violations of the *ICCPR*. Over the years, the committee has adjudicated a number of complaints related to the treatment of refugees and refugee claimants.

---

204 *Optional Protocol to the International Covenant on Civil and Political Rights*, GA Res 2200A (XXI), 21 UN GAOR Supp (No 16) at 59, U Doc A/6316 (1966), 999 UNTS 302.

205 Hugh M Kindred, ed, *International Law Chiefly as Interpreted and Applied in Canada*, 6th ed (Toronto: Emond Montgomery, 2000) at 230.

206 *IRPA*, above note 12, s 97(1).

3) *Convention Against Torture*

The *CAT*, which came into force in 1987, provided an international definition of torture and prescribed a range of important obligations with respect to prevention of torture by states parties. Canada is a party to the Convention.[207] In combination with the noted provisions of the *ICCPR*, article 3 of the *CAT* provides the basis for the definition of the "person in need of protection" in the *IRPA*.[208]

The *CAT* defines torture in the following way:

> any act by which severe pain or suffering, whether physical or mental, is intentionally inflicted on a person for such purposes as obtaining from him or a third person information or a confession, punishing him for an act he or a third person has committed or is suspected of having committed, or intimidating or coercing him or a third person, or for any reason based on discrimination of any kind, when such pain or suffering is inflicted by or at the instigation of or with the consent or acquiescence of a public official or other person acting in an official capacity.[209]

The Convention contains an absolute prohibition of torture. Article 2(2) reads: "No exceptional circumstances whatsoever, whether a state of war or a threat of war, internal political instability or any other public emergency, may be invoked as a justification of torture." States parties are obliged not only to prevent and criminalize acts of torture within their jurisdictions, but also to abstain from expelling individuals to other states where there are substantial grounds to believe that they would be subject to torture.[210] The *CAT* prescribes the establishment of the Committee against Torture which has powers much like those of the *ICCPR*'s Human Rights Committee.

It is important to note that both the *CAT* and the *ICCPR* contain stronger obligations with regard to non-*refoulement* of refugees than the *Refugee Convention*. The *Refugee Convention* allows for expulsion for reasons of national security or public safety.[211] In contrast, the *CAT* prohibits all *refoulement* (albeit of the narrower class of individuals at risk of torture). Any enthusiasm for the protections provided to potential refugees by the *CAT* and the *ICCPR* must, however, be tempered by

---

207 Can TS 1987 No 36.

208 *IRPA*, above note 12, s 97(1).

209 *CAT*, above note 170, art 1.

210 *Ibid*, art 3.

211 *Refugee Convention*, above note 158, art 33.

the much quoted *obiter dicta* of *Suresh* in which the Supreme Court suggested a willingness to overrule Canada's international commitments:

> We do not exclude the possibility that in exceptional circumstances, deportation to face torture might be justified, either as a consequence of the balancing process mandated by section 7 of the *Charter* or under section 1. (A violation of section 7 will be saved by section 1 "only in cases arising out of exceptional conditions, such as natural disasters, the outbreak of war, epidemics and the like": see *Re B.C. Motor Vehicle Act*, *supra*, at p. 518; and *New Brunswick (Minister of Health and Community Services)* v. *G.(J.)*, [1999] 3 S.C.R. 46, at para. 99.) Insofar as Canada is unable to deport a person where there are substantial grounds to believe he or she would be tortured on return, this is not because article 3 of the *CAT* directly constrains the actions of the Canadian government, but because the fundamental justice balance under section 7 of the *Charter* generally precludes deportation to torture when applied on a case-by-case basis. We may predict that it will rarely be struck in favour of expulsion where there is a serious risk of torture. However, as the matter is one of balance, precise prediction is elusive. The ambit of an exceptional discretion to deport to torture, if any, must await future cases.[212]

While this passage has been the subject of much judicial and scholarly commentary,[213] at the very least it reminds us that both the *ICCPR* and the *CAT* exist in the Canadian jurisprudence at the behest of Canadian law. (For more discussion, see Chapter 3, Section C(1).)

G. CONCLUSION

Canadian refugee law consists of both national and international law. At a basic level, the provisions of the *Constitution Act, 1867* provide the authority for Parliament to enact immigration legislation such as the *IRPA*. The *IRPA*, in combination with its delegated legislation (most notably, the *Regulations*), provide a comprehensive scheme for the regulation of refugee matters. The IRB Chairperson further completes the regulatory scheme by setting out the procedures, principles, and cases that should guide refugee determination before the Board. In addition

212 *Suresh*, above note 38 at para 78.

213 Obiora Chinedu Okafor & Pius Lekwuwa Okoronkwo, "Re-configuring Non-*Refoulement*? The *Suresh* Decision, 'Security Relativism,' and the International Human Rights Imperative" (2003) 15 *International Journal of Refugee Law* 30.

to this statutory and regulatory scheme, government agencies such as the IRCC have developed policy manuals to assist them in execution of their statutory and regulatory mandate. The variety of statutory, regulatory, and administrative provisions governing refugee law demonstrates its high complexity. Such complexity and variety of regulation is particularly startling given that it was largely developed over the past sixty years. Both legislative and executive authority, including in immigration and refugee matters, must be exercised within the limits of the *Charter*.

At the international level, the *Refugee Convention* (along with the *Protocol*), the *ICCPR*, and the *CAT* all are immediately connected to refugee law. Further, the jurisprudence developed by the UN Human Rights Committee and the Committee against Torture provides important guidelines on the content of state obligations under the *ICCPR* and the *CAT* and, *inter alia*, the treatment of refugee claimants and refugees.

Currently, one of the most contentious aspects of refugee law appears at the junction of international and domestic norms. Although national refugee determination systems are based upon the *Refugee Convention*, their practices have not always been in full compliance with the spirit and letter of the Convention. Similarly, the *CAT* and the *ICCPR* have not always been regarded as binding upon domestic courts. As demonstrated in *Suresh*, the Supreme Court supported the prohibition on deportation to torture based on the domestic principles of fundamental justice rather than the *CAT*. The ambiguous role of international law in Canadian refugee law continues as the jurisprudence develops.

Refugee law represents a complex web of law. It has numerous sources, both within and outside of Canada, which can be organized in various ways into hierarchies. The hierarchical nature of immigration and refugee law can also be traced in the differentiation of citizenship/immigration statuses of individuals and the corresponding scopes of their rights: from most extensive for citizens to limited for foreign nationals. The next chapter, Chapter 3, discusses these different statuses.

CHAPTER 3

CATEGORIES OF STATUS IN CANADIAN REFUGEE LAW

A. INTRODUCTION

Canadian immigration law distinguishes three main categories of individuals: foreign nationals, permanent residents, and Canadian citizens.[1] These categories represent a hierarchy as each status denotes a different scope of rights — from the narrowest for foreign nationals to the fullest for citizens.

Citizenship represents full-fledged membership in the community, with unconditional rights of entry and residence as well as the widest scope of political, social, and economic entitlements in Canada.

Permanent residents, while usually retaining foreign citizenship, are also understood to be members of the Canadian community, albeit whose membership is contingent upon various factors, including their continued residence in the country and good behaviour. They have a qualified right to enter[2] and remain in Canada and possess most of the social and economic entitlements of citizens. They do not, however, have a constitutionally protected right to vote and to stand in elections.

---

1 Aboriginal persons can be seen as a special instance of Canadian citizen. *Immigration and Refugee Protection Act*, SC 2001, c 27, s 19(1) [*IRPA*]. The connection of Aboriginal identity and Canadian citizenship has been the subject of some critique (see, for example, Glen St Louis, "The Tangled Web of Sovereignty and Self-Governance: Canada's Obligation to the Cree Nation in Consideration of Quebec's Threats to Secede" (1996) 14 *Berkeley Journal of International Law* 380).

2 *IRPA*, above note 1, s 27(1).

Foreign nationals are individuals who are neither Canadian citizens nor permanent residents. They include visitors, foreign workers and students, refugee claimants, protected persons (who have not obtained permanent resident status), holders of temporary resident permits, and individuals under unenforceable removal orders. Unlike permanent residents and citizens, foreign nationals have no entitlement to be in Canada: they require special authorization for entry, study, or employment[3] and must depart Canada upon expiry of such an authorization. The scope of their entitlements is not only much narrower than for permanent residents, but is also specifically linked to the purpose of their admission to Canada: for instance, visitors are usually not allowed to either work or study in Canada; international students have limitations on the types and hours of employment (e.g., only part-time during the academic year); and foreign workers cannot engage in post-secondary studies unless they obtain a study permit.

This chapter will focus primarily on the category of foreign nationals and specifically on the treatment of refugee claimants and protected persons in Canada.

B. CATEGORIES OF STATUS IN CANADIAN REFUGEE LAW

By definition, the subjects of Canadian refugee law are either foreign nationals or permanent residents. Citizens of Canada are excluded from seeking refugee protection in Canada as a matter of policy.[4] International law also does not recognize an ability to seek refugee protection while within one's own country of nationality.[5] As to permanent residents, they theoretically may seek protection in Canada, but it is a rare occurrence.[6]

---

3 *Ibid*, ss 29(1), 30(1).

4 Immigration, Refugees and Citizenship Canada, "In-Canada Claims for Refugee Protection: Intake," online: IRCC www.cic.gc.ca/english/resources/tools/refugees/canada/intake/claims.asp. Notwithstanding the policy to this effect, the statutory scheme that deems an individual eligible unless determined ineligible would likely require an immigration officer to refer the claim to the Immigration and Refugee Board (IRB).

5 The definition of a "refugee" set out in the *Refugee Convention* requires an individual to be outside his or her country of nationality (or, in the case of a stateless person, his or her country of former habitual residence). See *Convention Relating to the Status of Refugees*, 28 July 1951, 189 UNTS 150, art 1A(2) [*Refugee Convention*].

6 For example, individuals who were formerly permanent residents (perhaps having lost their permanent residence status due to failure to maintain residence

For the purposes of refugee law, the category of foreign nationals can be subdivided into the following groups: refugee claimants, protected persons, rejected claimants, and foreign nationals under unenforceable removal orders. These subgroups are granted more extended rights and entitlements than foreign nationals generally. Some of these entitlements flow from Canada's international commitments; others from policy reasons related to the humanitarian purpose of the categories. Each of these statuses and related entitlements is discussed in turn, following a trajectory of refugee determination process: from making a claim to its resolution and in the case of a positive decision, further application for permanent residence and citizenship.

Please note that rights and entitlements of refugees resettled from abroad are not discussed in detail. As a rule, the processing of applications of resettled refugees is completed abroad and they become permanent residents upon arrival in Canada. Therefore, they immediately enjoy rather extensive rights given to permanent residents. In certain urgent cases, processing of applications cannot be completed before arrival in Canada (e.g., when a person's life is at risk and the individual must be resettled as soon as possible). In such a case, a resettled refugee is admitted to Canada on a temporary resident permit (TRP)[7] and can apply for permanent residence from within Canada.[8] As is the case for refugee claimants and protected persons, individuals on TRPs would have limited rights until they receive permanent residence.

The table below provides a brief overview of the main categories discussed in this chapter.

---

in Canada or misconduct) not infrequently seek protection during subsequent removal proceedings.

7 *Immigration and Refugee Protection Regulations*, SOR 2002/227, s 151.1 [*Regulations*].

8 Immigration, Refugees and Citizenship Canada, "Procedures for Processing Urgent Protection Cases: Temporary Resident Permits and Permanent Resident Status," online: IRCC www.cic.gc.ca/english/resources/tools/refugees/resettlement/processing/urgent/permit.asp.

Table 3.1: Categories of Status in Canadian Refugee Law

Category	Definition (as Used in This Book)	Access to Rights and Benefits
Refugee claimants: 1) Claimants from designated countries of origin (DCOs) 2) Designated foreign nationals (DFNs) 3) All other claimants	Persons who made a claim from within Canada and are awaiting a decision on it	• Can work in Canada with a work permit • Can study at a post-secondary institution with a study permit; have access to primary and secondary schooling (study permit not required) • Are protected from removal to countries of alleged persecution, torture, or risk to life until their claim is decided • Have access to healthcare through the Interim Federal Health Program (IFHP)
Protected persons: 1) Convention refugees 2) Persons in need of protection	Individuals whose claims have been accepted through the inland refugee determination process	• Can work in Canada with a work permit • Can study at a post-secondary institution with a study permit; have access to primary and secondary schooling (study permit not required) • Are protected from removal to countries of persecution, torture, or risk to life • Have access to healthcare through the IFHP • Are entitled to apply for permanent residence
Resettled refugees: 1) Convention refugees abroad 2) Country of asylum	Persons who have made an application overseas and have been approved for resettlement	• Become permanent residents on arrival • Enjoy the same rights as permanent residents • Have access to healthcare through the IFHP until they become eligible for provincial healthcare

Category	Definition (as Used in This Book)	Access to Rights and Benefits
Rejected claimants	Persons whose claims were rejected by the Refugee Protection Division (RPD)	• Can work in Canada with a work permit • Can study at a post-secondary institution with a study permit; have access to primary and secondary schooling (study permit not required) • Have access to healthcare through the IFHP • Are subject to removal (unless a stay of removal obtained)
Persons under unenforceable removal orders	Persons whose claims have been rejected but who cannot be removed from Canada (e.g., due to a temporary moratorium on removals to their country of origin)	• Can work in Canada with a work permit • Can study at a post-secondary institution with a study permit; have access to primary and secondary schooling (study permit not required) • Have access to healthcare through the IFHP
Permanent residents	Persons who have immigrated to Canada under family, economic, or refugee stream	• Have most economic and social rights of citizens • Have conditional right of entry and stay in Canada • Have full access to provincial healthcare
Canadian citizens	Persons who obtained Canadian citizenship by descent, birth, or naturalization	• Have full political rights (to vote, to run for office) • Have full economic and social rights • Have unconditional right of entry and stay in Canada • Have full access to provincial healthcare

1) Refugee Claimants

Refugee claimants (often referred to as "asylum seekers") are persons who have made a claim for refugee protection in Canada and whose claim has not yet been decided. The notion of refugee claimants refers only to individuals seeking refugee protection from within Canada; individuals who apply for Canada's protection outside Canada are not members of this category.[9] The basis for this distinction is both legal and practical. Most international conventions, including the *Refugee Convention*, require a state to offer protection only to individuals within their jurisdiction. An individual abroad is generally not within a state's jurisdiction.[10] For example, many of the protections for refugee claimants in Canadian law relate to the prohibition on removing a refugee claimant — a power that the government of Canada does not hold over individuals who are abroad. Other entitlements (such as, for example, access to elementary schooling and right to counsel) would also be difficult to provide to individuals abroad.

In the past, the refugee determination process was essentially the same for all refugee claimants. However, due to the changes that came into effect in December 2012, refugee claimants have been divided into three groups — each with different implications for the refugee determination process and individual entitlements. These groups are as follows:

1) claimants from designated countries of origin (DCOs);
2) designated foreign nationals;
3) all other claimants.

This section will provide an overview of each category, but procedural issues related to the refugee hearings, appeals, and judicial review will be discussed in Chapters 8 and 10.

a) Claimants from Designated Countries of Origin

The *Immigration and Refugee Protection Act* gives the Minister of Immigration, Refugees and Citizenship (IRCC) the power to identify desig-

---

9 The category of "refugee claimants" is not explicitly defined in either the *IRPA* or the *Regulations*. However, various sections refer to the more cumbersome phrase "individuals making a claim to refugee protection."

10 There has been much jurisprudential and scholarly debate over the extent of a state's "jurisdiction" and its consequent obligations under the *Refugee Convention*. Both the United Kingdom and Australia have seen litigation on this issue: *R v Immigration Officer at Prague Airport and another (Respondents) ex parte European Roma Rights Centre and others*, [2004] UKHL 55; and *Ruddock v Vadarlis*, 2001 FCA 1865 (Austl).

nated countries of origin (DCOs).[11] Such countries are considered to normally not produce refugees. There are two criteria for designation:[12]

1) *Quantitative*: This criterion is used where there are at least thirty finalized refugee claims from a given country in any consecutive twelve-month period in the three years preceding the designation. The designation will be triggered if
   - the Immigration and Refugee Board's (IRB) combined rejection, withdrawal, and abandonment rate of asylum claims from that country is 75 percent or higher; or
   - the IRB's combined withdrawal and abandonment rate of asylum claims from that country is 60 percent or higher.

2) *Qualitative*: If the number of finalized refugee claims from a given country is less than thirty in any consecutive twelve-month period during the three years prior to designation, then a qualitative criterion is used. A country may be designated if the Minister believes that in that country
   - there is an independent judicial system;
   - basic democratic rights and freedoms are recognized, and redress mechanisms are available if those rights or freedoms are infringed; and
   - civil society organizations exist.

Even if the above criteria are triggered, designation is not automatic. The final decision rests with the Minister.

Refugee claimants who are citizens of DCOs face some limitations in the refugee determination process.

- They have shorter hearing timelines than other claimants: their refugee hearing takes place thirty or forty-five days after the claim was referred to the IRB compared to sixty days for other claimants.[13]
- They may not apply for a work permit until their refugee claim is approved by the Refugee Protection Division (RPD) or until 180 days have passed since the referral of the claim to the RPD and the claim has not been decided.[14]

11 *IRPA*, above note 1, s 109.1(1).

12 *Ibid*, s 109.1(2); Minister of Citizenship and Immigration, *Order Establishing Quantitative Thresholds for the Designation of Countries of Origin* (2012), online: www.gazette.gc.ca/rp-pr/p1/2012/2012-12-15/html/notice-avis-eng.html. Please note that s 109.1 provides only general criteria, but the actual percentages are prescribed by the Ministerial Order.

13 *Regulations*, above note 7, s 159.9(1).

14 *Ibid*, s 206(2).

- They may not apply for a pre-removal risk assessment (PRRA) until thirty-six months have passed since the final decision on their case (compared to twelve-months for non-DCO claimants).[15]
- They are not granted an automatic stay (halt) of removal upon application for judicial review of a negative RPD decision.[16]

The DCO designation creates several challenges for an already vulnerable population of refugee claimants. Shorter timelines can be detrimental to their ability to retain counsel, properly prepare for a hearing, and obtain supporting documents, especially if those documents must be mailed from abroad. Further, designating a country as safe for all individuals does not take into consideration the peculiar circumstances of certain populations. For example, Hungary can be generally considered a safe and democratic country, but it is not a safe place for Roma. Although the DCO provisions convey an idea that claims from some countries are not well-founded, recent statistics show an encouraging trend that decisions makers do not summarily dismiss claims from designated countries of origin. In fact, the acceptance rate for claimants from some DCOs (notably, Hungary) went up since 2012 (see Appendix D, Table 3).

In addition to the above-mentioned restrictions, the 2012 amendments provided that claimants from DCOs would not have the right to file an appeal with the Refugee Appeal Division (RAD).[17] However, in July 2015, the Federal Court found that section 110(2)(d.1), which removed appeal rights from DCO claimants, was a violation of the *Charter*, section 15(1).[18] The court determined that the provision drew a clear and discriminatory distinction between refugee claimants from DCOs and others based upon national origin and perpetrated "the historical disadvantage of undesirable refugee claimants and the stereotype that their fears of persecution or discrimination are less worthy of attention."[19] Consequently, rejected refugee claimants from DCOs, whose RPD decisions were issued on and after 23 July 2015 (date of the Federal Court decision) may now file an appeal to the Refugee Appeal Division.[20]

---

15 *IRPA*, above note 1, ss 112(2)(b.1) & (c).

16 *Regulations*, above note 7, ss 231(1) & (2).

17 *IRPA*, above note 1, s 110(2)(d.1). They could apply for judicial review in the Federal Court, but there was no automatic stay of removal until the case is decided by the court, and an individual could be removed well before the case was heard.

18 *YZ v Canada (Minister of Citizenship and Immigration)*, 2015 FC 892 [*YZ*].

19 *Ibid* at para 128.

20 Immigration and Refugee Board, News Release, "Federal Court Decision Impacting the Right to Appeal to the Refugee Appeal Division" (20 August 2015),

b) Designated Foreign Nationals

The Minister of Public Safety and Emergency Preparedness is responsible for the administration of the *IRPA* in relation to several selected areas, including examination at ports of entry, arrest, detention, and removal.[21] In particular, the Minister may designate groups of irregular migrants as "designated foreign nationals" in any of the following circumstances:

- The examinations of the persons in the group (e.g., for establishing identity or determining inadmissibility) cannot be conducted in a timely manner.
- There are reasonable grounds to suspect that the group was smuggled to Canada for profit, or "for the benefit of, at the direction of or in association with a criminal organization or terrorist group."[22]

The implications of the designation are severe:

- All designated individuals who are sixteen years of age or older face mandatory detention.[23]
- Even in the case of a successful claim for protection, a designated individual is precluded from making an application for permanent or temporary resident status or for humanitarian and compassionate consideration for five years after the final determination on their refugee claim.[24]
- There is no right to appeal a negative RPD decision to the RAD.[25]
- There is no automatic stay of removal upon application for judicial review of a negative RPD decision.[26]
- Designated individuals who receive protected status cannot be issued a travel document as provided by the *Refugee Convention*, article 28, unless they become permanent residents or hold temporary resident permits.[27]
- If a designated individual comes from a designated country of origin, he also faces additional restrictions, such as a shorter hearing timeline and ineligibility for a PRRA for thirty-six months.

---

online: IRB www.irb-cisr.gc.ca/Eng/NewsNouv/NewNou/2015/Pages/craupd.aspx.

21 *IRPA*, above note 1, s 4(2).

22 *Ibid*, s 20.1(1).

23 *Ibid*, s 55(3.1).

24 *Ibid*, ss 11(1.1), 24(5), and 25(1.01).

25 *Ibid*, s 110(2)(a).

26 *Regulations*, above note 7, s 231(1) & (2).

27 *IRPA*, above note 1, s 31.1.

In 2012, fifteen people, including three minors, were detained under the above provisions; in 2013, ten were detained; in 2014, none.[28]

The rules on designated foreign nationals are notable as the first instance in recent Canadian history when mandatory and automatic detention of potential refugee claimants was introduced. Although periodic detention reviews are provided for, their timelines are longer than for other types of immigration detention. The first detention review for designated foreign nationals takes place fourteen days after initial detention and subsequently six months after each preceding review.[29] In contrast, for other types of immigration detention, the first review is within forty-eight hours, the second one during the seven days following the first review, and subsequently, at least once during each thirty-day period.[30] Even if a designated foreign national is released from detention, he is to be subject to conditions such as regular reporting to an immigration officer.[31] Failure, without a reasonable excuse, to comply with those conditions can lead to a further one-year delay (in addition to the five-year bar) on application for a permanent or a temporary resident status or for humanitarian and compassionate (H&C) consideration.[32] The issues of detention are discussed in detail in Chapter 11.

As with DCO claimants, the main objective is to deter refugee claimants from coming to Canada. While the changes are said to be motivated by the fight against human smugglers, in effect, they punish those who have been smuggled. The negative impact of detention on refugee claimants and refugees is well documented.[33] Other restrictions on designated foreign nationals are also likely to exacerbate their

---

28 This data comes from the authors' access-to-information request to the Canada Border Services Agency [on file with authors].

29 *IRPA*, above note 1, s 57.1.

30 *Ibid*, s 57.

31 *Ibid*, ss 58(4) and 98.1; *Regulations*, above note 7, s 174.1.

32 *IRPA*, above note 1, ss 11(1.3)(a), 24(7), and 25(1.03).

33 Derrick Silove et al, "No Refuge from Terror: The Impact of Detention on the Mental Health of Trauma-Affected Refugees Seeking Asylum in Australia" (2007) 44 *Transcultural Psychiatry* 359; Australian Human Rights Commission, "A Last Resort? National Inquiry into Children in Immigration Detention" (2014), online: www.humanrights.gov.au/publications/last-resort-national-inquiry-children-immigration-detention; Delphine Nakache, *The Human and Financial Cost of Detention of Asylum-Seekers in Canada* (2011), online: UNHCR www.unhcr.ca/wp-content/uploads/2014/10/RPT-2011-12-detention_assylum_seekers-e.pdf#_ga=1.268142733.2087847137.1484749201; Janet Cleveland & Cecile Rousseau, "Psychiatric Symptoms Associated with Brief Detention of Adult Asylum Seekers in Canada" (2013) 58 *Canadian Journal of Psychiatry* 409. See also more, online: www.fmreview.org/detention/cleveland%20#_edn2.

trauma due to uncertainty in their future, being watched by immigration authorities (due to conditions imposed upon release), and limitations on rights stemming from the lack of permanent resident status. The impact of the lack of status is discussed in more detail in Section C(4)(c), below in this chapter.

c) Other Claimants

Compared to the two above-discussed groups, this group of claimants faces fewer limitations in the refugee determination process. Nevertheless, the 2012 changes created new restrictions even for them. These claimants

- have a refugee hearing sixty days after referral of the claim to the IRB;[34]
- can, if granted protected status, apply for permanent residence without any waiting period (unlike designated foreign nationals);
- have access to the RAD;
- enjoy a stay of removal upon application for judicial review;
- are precluded from applying for a temporary resident permit or humanitarian and compassionate consideration for twelve months if their claim was rejected or determined withdrawn or abandoned (period beginning at the moment of decision);[35]
- are barred from applying for a PRRA (pre-removal risk assessment) for twelve months since the claim was rejected, withdrawn, or abandoned.[36]

Table 3.2: Comparison of Three Groups of Claimants

	Claimants from DCOs	**Designated Foreign Nationals**	**Other Claimants**
Timeline for a refugee hearing	Thirty days for claims made at inland IRCC office; forty-five days for claims made at a port of entry	Depends on whether they are from a DCO or not	Sixty days
Access to RAD	Yes	No	Yes
Access to judicial review	Yes	Yes	Yes

34 *Regulations*, above note 7, s 159.9(1)(b).

35 *IRPA*, above note 1, ss 24(4) and 25(1.2)(c).

36 *Ibid*, ss 112(2)(b.1) & (c).

	Claimants from DCOs	Designated Foreign Nationals	Other Claimants
Automatic stay of removal upon application for judicial review	No	No	Yes
Application for permanent residence	No waiting period	Five-year bar	No waiting period
Application for H&C or TRP	Three-year bar	Wait time depends on whether they are from a DCO or not	One-year bar
Access to PRRA	Three-year bar	Wait time depends on whether they are from a DCO or not	One-year bar
Detention	Possible, but not automatic (on grounds such as lack of identity, flight risk, danger to the public); detention review within forty-eight hours, then seven days and once every thirty days	Automatic detention review within fourteen days and then six months after each preceding review	Possible, but not automatic (on grounds such as lack of identity, flight risk, danger to the public); detention review within forty-eight hours, then seven days and once every thirty days
Application for a work permit	Ineligible to apply until the claim is granted or until 180 days have passed since the claim was referred to the IRB and it was not heard by the Board	Wait time depends on whether they are from a DCO or not	No waiting period

In addition to the above, persons whose claims were determined by the RPD to be manifestly unfounded or to have no credible basis as well as persons falling within the exceptions from the *Safe Third Country Agreement* do not have access to the RAD and have no automatic stay of removal upon application for judicial review.[37]

37 *IRPA*, above note 1, ss 110(2)(c) & (d); *Regulations*, above note 7, s 231.

As discussed in Chapter 1, the Conservative government claimed that the above changes to the refugee system were necessary in order to deter "bogus" claimants and prevent abuse of Canada's generosity.[38] The changes sought to deter claimants from DCOs from coming to Canada. In fact, IRCC boasted that since the introduction of the DCO list, the claims from those countries went down by 87 percent. In particular, claims from Hungary (a number-one source country for refugee claims in Canada in 2012) dropped from an average of 3,000 a year to under 100 in 2013.[39]

The system accelerated refugee proceedings (especially for DCOs), limited recourse on negative decisions, and aimed to remove rejected claimants quickly. As claimed by the immigration department, in 2014, rejected claimants were removed approximately within twenty-three days of their referral for removal and, overall, it took roughly four months from the moment a claim was made until a rejected claimant was removed.[40] In January 2014 the IRCC Minister reported that "more than $600,000 in welfare, education and health-care costs have been saved to date because of these reforms."[41] Such savings, however, come at the expense of refugee rights and safety. The implication of the changes will be discussed in greater detail in Chapter 8, in reference to each stage of the refugee determination process.

2) Protected Persons

The category of protected person can be subdivided into three groups based upon the grounds for protection:

---

38 Speaking notes for the Honourable Jason Kenney, Minister of Citizenship, Immigration and Multiculturalism, at a news conference to announce Senate passage for Bill C-11, the *Balanced Refugee Reform Act*, and launch a summer tour to promote refugee resettlement (29 June 2010), online: www.cic.gc.ca/english/department/media/speeches/2010/2010-06-29.asp; speaking notes for the Honourable Jason Kenney, Minister of Citizenship, Immigration and Multiculturalism, at a news conference following the tabling of Bill C-31, *Protecting Canada's Immigration System Act* (16 February 2012), online: www.cic.gc.ca/english/department/media/speeches/2012/2012-02-16.asp; see also Sponsor's speech at the second reading (23 April 2010), online: www.parl.gc.ca/HousePublications/Publication.aspx?Pub=Hansard&Doc=33&Parl=40&Ses=3&Language=E&Mode=1#int-3117372.

39 Speaking notes for Chris Alexander, Canada's Citizenship and Immigration Minister, at the news conference regarding Canada's asylum system (22 January 2014), online: http://news.gc.ca/web/article-en.do?nid=831769.

40 *Ibid.*

41 *Ibid.*

1) Convention refugees;
2) persons in need of protection; and
3) persons resettled through an overseas application.

The protected person status is conferred either by the Immigration and Refugee Board or the Minister of Immigration, Refugees and Citizenship.[42] If a person's application for refugee protection is successful, she will become a "protected person."

Protected persons include both permanent residents and non-permanent residents. The protected persons selected through the resettlement process will be permanent residents as they gain that status upon arrival in Canada.[43] In contrast, successful inland claimants will not necessarily have permanent resident status. As discussed in Chapter 8, a successful refugee claim does not automatically confer permanent residence on a protected person, but merely entitles the individual to apply for permanent residence. Thus, such protected persons remain foreign nationals, albeit with more extended rights than is normally accorded to foreign nationals in Canada, until their application for permanent residence is approved.

a) Convention Refugees

Convention refugees are individuals who fall within the definition set out in the *IRPA*, section 96. This section incorporates the definition of a refugee contained in the *Refugee Convention.*

In cases where an individual has been determined to be a refugee by the Board or the Minister, the principle of comity generally requires other states parties to the *Refugee Convention* to recognize the determination of Convention refugee status made by the Canadian government.[44] Thus, a person determined to be a Convention refugee possesses not only rights in Canada, but, in theory at least, rights elsewhere.

In the words of the Federal Court in *Buon-Leua v Canada (Minister of Employment and Immigration)*, however, membership in the category of Convention refugee depends upon an individual continuing to be a refugee.[45] Thus, an individual must not only fulfill the criteria set out in the definition of Convention refugee at the time of application

---

42 *IRPA*, above note 1, ss 95(1)(b) & (c).

43 *Ibid*, s 95(1)(a).

44 Article 28 of the *Refugee Convention*, above note 5, encourages states to issue travel documents to Convention refugees. Paragraph 7 of the *Schedule to the Refugee Convention* (detailing obligations concerning travel documents) requires states to "recognize the validity" of such refugee travel documents.

45 [1981] 1 FC 259 at 263–64 (CA) [*Buon-Leua*]. The decision in *Buon-Leua* was later critiqued by Wilson J in *Singh v Canada*, [1985] 1 SCR 177 at 190ff.

for protection but also must do so on a continuing basis. The *Refugee Convention* requires this: article 1C sets out a list of conditions which, if fulfilled, cause refugee status to cease. Canadian law has adopted this list of cessation conditions.[46]

b) Persons in Need of Protection

A person "in need of protection" is "a person in Canada" whose removal to the country of her nationality or former habitual residence would subject her to a risk of torture,[47] risk to life, or risk of cruel and unusual treatment or punishment.[48] Thus, unlike the category of Convention refugees, the "persons in need of protection" category is applicable explicitly to people who are inside Canada.[49] As with the category of Convention refugee, an individual must fulfill the criteria for membership in the category on an ongoing basis.

3) Foreign Nationals Subject to Unenforceable Removal Orders

In addition to refugee claimants and protected persons, foreign nationals in another category enjoy extended rights in Canada: persons subject to unenforceable removal orders. Most commonly, these are persons who are either excluded from refugee protection or whose claims have been rejected, but who, nevertheless, cannot be removed from Canada. The inability to remove them can be due to various circumstances such

---

46 *IRPA*, above note 1, s 108. Cessation may occur either before refugee protection is conferred by the Board or the Minister (in which case a negative decision is issued) or may be used to vacate refugee status (in which case a prior positive decision will be overturned).

47 Article 1(1) of the *Convention Against Torture and Other Cruel, Inhuman or Degrading Treatment or Punishment*, 10 December 1984, Can TS 1987 No 36, 23 ILM 1027 [*CAT*], defines torture as follows:

> For the purposes of this Convention, torture means any act by which severe pain or suffering, whether physical or mental, is intentionally inflicted on a person for such purposes as obtaining from him or a third person information or a confession, punishing him for an act he or a third person has committed or is suspected of having committed, or intimidating or coercing him or a third person, or for any reason based on discrimination of any kind, when such pain or suffering is inflicted by or at the instigation of or with the consent or acquiescence of a public official or other person acting in an official capacity. It does not include pain or suffering arising only from, inherent in or incidental to lawful sanctions.

48 *IRPA*, above note 1, s 97.

49 *Ibid*, s 97(1).

as the conditions in their countries of origin, impossibility of obtaining necessary travel or identity documents, or the fact that an individual is stateless. The legislation prescribes several scenarios that render a removal order unenforceable, ranging from statutory or regulatory stay of removal to moratoria on removal to certain countries and other circumstances. (For more detailed discussion of the removal process and stays of removal, please see Chapter 12.)

Figure 3.1: Categories of Status in Canadian Immigration and Refugee Law

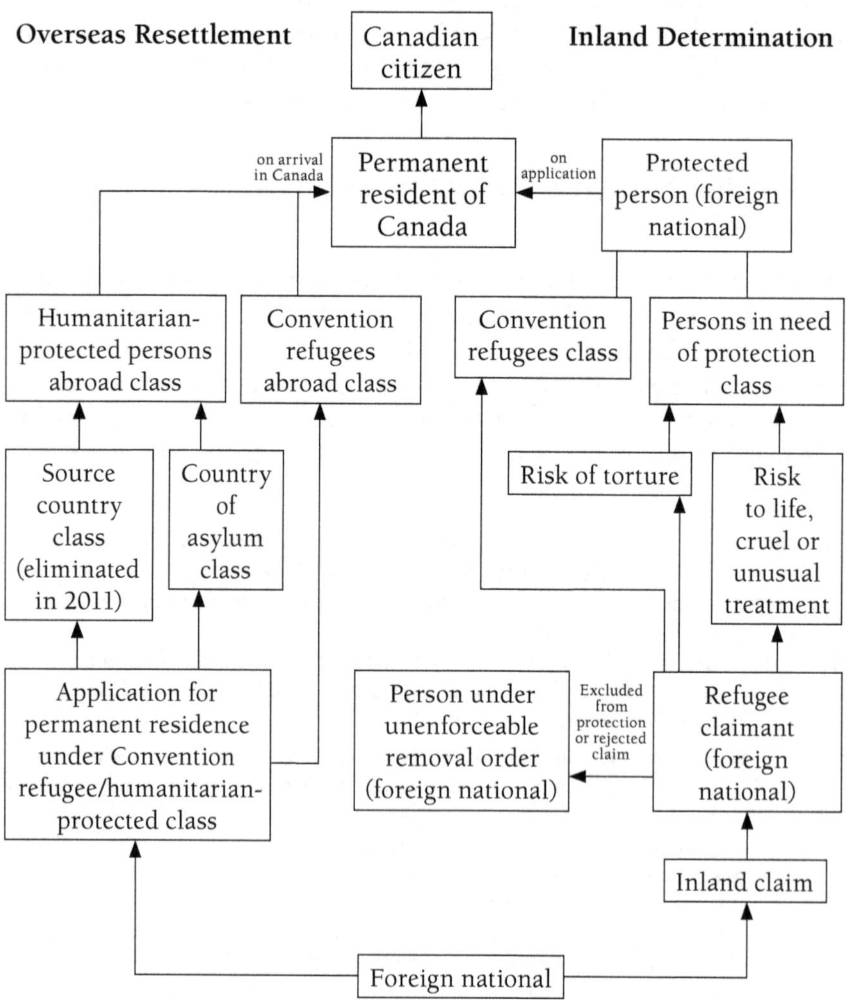

C. RIGHTS OF INDIVIDUALS IN CANADIAN LAW

Each of the above-discussed categories of foreign nationals provides for a different scope of rights and entitlements in Canada. Some of these categories bring with them fairly long-term and substantive rights and entitlements. Others simply provide temporary and procedural protections.

In this section, we will discuss and compare the rights of refugee claimants, protected persons, and persons under unenforceable removal orders as relates to the following key areas: non-*refoulement*, right to work, right to study, legal assistance, financial assistance, and access to permanent residence and citizenship. This section is not intended as a detailed examination of all rights of refugees and refugee claimants, but rather represents a broad overview of selected areas. The issues of non-*refoulement* and issuance of work and study permits, as well as applications for permanent residence and citizenship, are regulated and administered federally. Legal aid is within the jurisdiction of the provinces, and financial assistance is administered at federal and provincial levels: the federal government regulates pensions and child tax benefits, while provinces deal with welfare payments. Where a matter falls within provincial jurisdiction, eligibility criteria, practices, and procedures may vary across Canada. Given the uneven distribution of claimants across Canada, some provinces feel greater pressure to provide services and supports to claimants and protected persons.

1) Right to Non-*refoulement*

Of fundamental importance to all individuals seeking (or who have sought) protection in Canada is the right not to be *refouled* (expelled) from Canada. This right is protected by the *Refugee Convention* and the *Convention Against Torture and Other Cruel, Inhuman or Degrading Treatment or Punishment*, or *CAT*. Article 33 of the *Refugee Convention* prohibits expulsion of a refugee and, by extension, a refugee claimant, to a country where he may face persecution. This principle, thus, restrains state action and implicitly requires states to "tolerate" in their territory those who cannot be removed. However, the prohibition of *refoulement* under the *Refugee Convention* is not absolute: where "there are reasonable grounds to believe" that a refugee constitutes a danger to security or a danger to the community of a host state, that refugee can be expelled.[50] In contrast, the *CAT* provides absolute protection against *refoulement* to torture: *no* circumstances may justify removal to torture.[51]

Canadian legislation implemented the above provisions of international law, although with certain limitations. Both refugee claimants and protected persons enjoy protection against *refoulement* by statute. For refugee claimants, the *IRPA* provides an automatic stay of removal in the following circumstances:

- pending the determination of their refugee claim by the IRB;[52]
- pending the outcome of a pre-removal risk assessment;[53]
- during the judicial review of any negative decision on protection (this applies only to claimants who are not from DCOs and who are not designated foreign nationals).[54]

For protected persons, removal to any country in which they would be at risk of persecution, torture, or cruel and unusual treatment or punishment is prohibited.[55] However, the *IRPA* provides for two exceptions. The removal may be possible when

1) a protected person is inadmissible on grounds of serious criminality and constitutes, in the opinion of the Minister, a danger to the public in Canada; or
2) a protected person is inadmissible on grounds of security, violating human or international rights, or organized criminality and, in the opinion of the Minister, should not be allowed to remain in Canada due to the nature and severity of acts committed or of danger to the security of Canada.[56]

The application of the above exceptions will be discussed in Chapter 12.

As to the non-*refoulement* under the *CAT*, unfortunately, Canadian legislation does not contain an absolute prohibition on deportation to torture. The constitutionality of removing a protected person to torture was examined by the Supreme Court in *Suresh v Canada (Minister of Citizenship and Immigration)*.[57] The Court concluded that, as a rule, deportation to torture would violate section 7 of the *Charter*, but also

50 *Refugee Convention*, above note 5, art 33.
51 *CAT*, above note 47, art 3.
52 *IRPA*, above note 1, s 49(2).
53 *Ibid*, s 232.
54 *Regulations*, above note 7, s 231.
55 *IRPA*, above note 1, s 115(1).
56 *Ibid*, s 115(2).
57 [2002] 1 SCR 3 [*Suresh*].

found that such removal may still be possible in exceptional circumstances. The Court wrote:

> We do not exclude the possibility that in exceptional circumstances, deportation to face torture might be justified, either as a consequence of the balancing process mandated by s. 7 of the *Charter* or under s. 1 . . . . Insofar as Canada is unable to deport a person where there are substantial grounds to believe he or she would be tortured on return, this is not because Article 3 of the *CAT* directly constrains the actions of the Canadian government, but because the fundamental justice balance under s. 7 of the *Charter* generally precludes deportation to torture when applied on a case-by-case basis. We may predict that it will rarely be struck in favour of expulsion where there is a serious risk of torture. However, as the matter is one of balance, precise prediction is elusive. The ambit of an exceptional discretion to deport to torture, if any, must await future cases.[58]

The Court made it clear that only a few cases would be exceptional and that there must be evidence of a serious threat to national security. Nevertheless, the possibility of deporting Convention refugees and other protected persons to torture demonstrates the malleability of Canada's refugee protection and the competing interests permeating refugee law. For example, in 2006, Canada deported a refugee — Mostafa Dadar — to Iran notwithstanding the conclusion of the UN Committee against Torture that he may be subject to torture there and that deporting him to Iran would violate the *CAT*, article 3.[59] This case did not even involve a threat to national security. Dadar was convicted of several offences, including theft, assault, and aggravated assault. Correctional Services of Canada concluded that he represented low risk to the public, but immigration authorities nevertheless sought to remove him. They concluded that given the passage of time, he likely would not be of interest to the Egyptian authorities or, in the event they were in error regarding the risk of torture, Dadar's case fell within the *Suresh* exception.

The Committee against Torture has repeatedly highlighted its concern regarding the failure of Canada's domestic law to recognize the absolute nature of non-*refoulement* under article 3 of the *CAT*.[60] Canada's responses to the committee maintain that the possibility of removal to

---

58 *Ibid* at para 78.

59 *Mostafa Dadar v Canada*, Communication No 258/2004, UN Doc CAT/C/35/D/258/2004 (2005).

60 Committee against Torture, "Concluding Observations on Canada's Fifth Periodic Report" (2005), CAT/C/CR/34/CAN at para 4(a); Committee against

torture is largely theoretical, yet affirm that the government continues to reserve such a power.[61]

2) Access to Legal Assistance

The ability of refugee claimants to effectively exercise their rights to refugee determination, non-*refoulement*, and appeal often depends on the availability of qualified legal assistance. Consequently, the right to counsel and legal aid acquires utmost importance for refugee claimants and rejected claimants.

a) Right to Counsel

The right to counsel as provided for by the *Charter* is discussed in Chapter 2, Section C(2). The specific aspects of legal representation, as well as types of legal representatives, will be discussed in Chapter 9.

b) Access to Legal Aid

All provinces have established legal aid systems to allow low-income individuals to obtain legal advice free of charge and thereby promote access to justice. The provision of free legal assistance is usually done through the following channels: (1) private lawyers who are paid set fees by a legal aid agency for providing services to eligible individuals; and (2) legal aid clinics with full-time salaried lawyers that provide legal services on matters of primary concern for people of low income.[62] While specific requirements vary across provinces, as a rule, in order to be eligible for legal aid, an individual's income must be below a certain threshold, and his case must have merit. For example, a two-person household is eligible for legal aid in Ontario if gross annual income is under $30,337;[63] in British Columbia, if their monthly income is under

---

Torture, "Concluding Observations on Canada's Sixth Periodic Report" (2012), CAT/C/CAN/CO/6 at para 9.

61 For example, see Canada's responses to the list of issues adopted by the Committee against Torture in advance of the examination of Canada's Sixth Periodic Report on the *Convention against Torture and Other Cruel, Inhuman or Degrading Treatment or Punishment*, CAT/C/CAN/6 (2012) at paras 125–31, online: www.pch.gc.ca/DAMAssetPub/DAM-drtPrs-humRts/STAGING/texte-text/written-ResponseToCATLOI-Final-ForSubmission-May2012_1363340887503_eng.PDF?WT.contentAuthority=3.1.

62 RJ Gathercole, "Legal Services and the Poor" in Robert G Evans & Michael J Trebilcock, eds, *Lawyers and the Consumer Interest: Regulating the Market for Legal Services* (Toronto: Butterworths, 1982) at 417.

63 Legal Aid Ontario, "Am I Eligible for a Legal Aid Certificate?," online: www.legalaid.on.ca/en/getting/eligibility.asp.

$2,100;[64] in Alberta, if their monthly income is under $2,027 or yearly income is under 24,333;[65] in Saskatchewan, if their monthly income is under $1,150 or yearly income is under $13,800;[66] in Manitoba, if their annual income is under $27,000.[67] In Newfoundland and Labrador, there is no set income threshold and eligibility is determined on a case-by-case basis by intake workers.[68]

Immigration and refugee matters may be covered by legal aid, but its availability and scope depend on the refugee claimant's province of residence. For example, Saskatchewan, Nova Scotia, Prince Edward Island, New Brunswick, Northwest Territories, Yukon, and Nunavut provide no free legal support to refugee claimants.[69] In British Columbia, legal aid can cover filing of the forms, preparation for a hearing, and representation at a hearing.[70] In Alberta, legal aid may be available for refugee claims, judicial reviews of rejected refugee claims, and danger opinions for protected persons.[71] In Ontario, legal aid may cover completion of the Basis of Claim Form; representation at a refugee hearing; preparation for an appeal to the RAD; preparation of judicial review in the Federal Court; preparation of a motion for stay of removal in the Federal Court; and preparation of a danger opinion.[72]

3) Social and Economic Rights

For refugees, protection can be considered meaningful and effective only if it entails a degree of inclusion in a host society and access to certain key entitlements. As discussed in Chapter 2, the *Refugee Convention*

---

64 British Columbia Legal Services Society, "Do I Qualify for Legal Representation?," online: www.lss.bc.ca/legal_aid/doIQualifyRepresentation.php.

65 Legal Aid Alberta, "Eligibility," online: www.legalaid.ab.ca/help/eligibility/Pages/default.aspx.

66 Legal Aid Saskatchewan, "Am I Financially Eligible for Legal Aid?," online: www.legalaid.sk.ca/legal_help/eligible.php.

67 Legal Aid Manitoba, "Who Qualifies Financially," online: www.legalaid.mb.ca/getting-legal-aid/who-qualifies-financially.

68 Newfoundland & Labrador Legal Aid Commission, "Eligibility," online: www.legalaid.nl.ca/eligible.html.

69 Refugee Forum, "Legal Aid for Refugee Claimants in Canada," online: http://oppenheimer.mcgill.ca/IMG/pdf/University_of_Ottawa_Refugee_Forum_-_Legal_Aid_for_Refugee_Claimants_in_Canada_-_September_2012.pdf.

70 British Columbia Legal Services Society, "Immigration Problems," online: www.lss.bc.ca/legal_aid/immigrationProblems.php.

71 Legal Aid Alberta, "Immigration & Refugee Law," online: www.legalaid.ab.ca/help/Pages/Immigration-and-Refugee-Law.aspx.

72 Legal Aid Ontario, "Services for Refugee Claimants," online: www.legalaid.on.ca/en/getting/type_immigration_supportref.asp.

provides for four major standards of treatment of refugees (and by extension, refugee claimants) in relation to a range of areas such as the right to work and education, housing, public relief, freedom of religion, and freedom of association. This section provides a brief overview of the ways Canada has implemented these obligations in relation to work, education, financial assistance, and medical services.

a) Work in Canada

The *Refugee Convention* contains several provisions relating to the right to work. Article 17 requires that in regard to wage-earning employment, refugees lawfully staying[73] in a host state be accorded the most favourable treatment accorded to foreign nationals in the same circumstances. With respect to self-employment and the practice of liberal professions, states are to accord refugees treatment as favourable as possible and at the very least, no less favourable than that accorded to foreign nationals generally in the same circumstances.[74] With respect to the right to association, including trade unions, states are to provide refugees the most favourable treatment accorded to foreign nationals in the same circumstances.[75] Finally, they are to receive the same treatment as nationals with respect to labour legislation related to remuneration, hours of work, holiday pay, minimum wage, and related issues.[76] Canada, however, made a reservation to the latter provision of the *Refugee Convention*, stating that it interprets the phrase "lawfully staying'" as referring only to refugees admitted for permanent residence; claimants and protected persons who are not permanent residents will be accorded the same treatment as visitors generally.[77]

Refugee claimants, protected persons, and persons subject to unenforceable removal orders do not have an automatic right to engage in employment in Canada, but they are eligible to apply for and obtain a work permit.[78] Like other applicants for work permits, they must submit standard documents such as a completed application form, proof of immigration status in Canada, and a copy of identity documents.

---

73 Access to various types of gainful employment under the *Refugee Convention*, above note 5, is restricted to those Convention refugees who are "lawfully present" — hence, in the Canadian context, either refugee claimants or protected persons.

74 *Ibid*, arts 18–19.

75 *Ibid*, art 15.

76 *Ibid*, art 24.

77 United Nations Treaty Collection, *Convention relating to the Status of Refugees: Declarations and Reservations*, online: https://treaties.un.org/pages/ViewDetailsII.aspx?src=TREATY&mtdsg_no=V-2&chapter=5&Temp=mtdsg2&clang=_en [UNTC, *Reservations*].

78 *Regulations*, above note 7, ss 199, 206(1), 207(c), 209, and 215.

In addition, each refugee claimant must provide proof of submitting a Basis of Claim Form to the IRB and of being unable to support themselves without recourse to social assistance.[79]

Unlike other applicants for work permits, refugee claimants, protected persons, and persons subject to unenforceable removal orders enjoy a somewhat simpler procedure for issuance of work permits.[80] As a rule, when a foreign national applies for a work permit in Canada, an immigration officer must determine on the basis of an opinion provided by Employment and Social Development Canada (ESDC) if the job offer is genuine and if the employment of the foreign national is likely to have a neutral or positive effect on the labour market in Canada.[81] No opinion from ESDC is required for refugee claimants, persons subject to unenforceable removal orders, and protected persons.[82]

There is one important limitation on access to a work permit: claimants from DCOs are not eligible to apply until their refugee claim is approved by the RPD or until 180 days have passed since the claim was referred to the division.[83]

There is a $155 processing fee for work permits, but refugee claimants, protected persons, and their family members are exempt from payment.[84] The exemption does not, however, apply to rejected claimants and persons under unenforceable removal orders.

Notwithstanding the ability to obtain a work permit, refugee claimants and protected persons may face numerous barriers in entering the workforce.[85] Language, culture, lack of permanent resident status, and ongoing legal commitments (requiring attendance at the office of counsel, at the offices of the Minister of Immigration, Refugees and Citizenship or before the Board) make securing gainful employment very difficult.

b) Study in Canada

The *Refugee Convention* prescribes that refugees be given full access to primary education and "as favorable as possible and, in any event, not less favorable than that accorded to aliens generally" access to all

---

79 *Ibid*, s 206(1).

80 *Ibid*, s 200(2).

81 *Ibid*, s 203(1).

82 *Ibid*.

83 *Ibid*, s 206(2).

84 *Ibid*, ss 299(2)(a)&(b).

85 For example, a survey of refugees' experiences in Alberta between 1992 and 1997 found that those without permanent resident status faced major employment barriers, including discrimination on the part of employers. Harvey Krahn et al, "Educated and Underemployed: Refugee Integration into the Canadian Labour Force" (2000) 1 *Journal of International Migration and Integration* 59.

other levels and types of education.[86] Furthermore, the *Convention on the Rights of the Child* recognizes the right of all children to at least primary education.[87]

Depending on the level of study, foreign nationals may need to obtain a study permit. No permit is required for preschool, primary, and secondary schooling. Under the *IRPA*, all minor children of refugee claimants and protected persons, other than children of temporary residents not authorized to work or study in Canada, may study at the preschool, primary, or secondary level.[88] Further, provincial legislation frequently requires attendance at school by all children resident in the province.[89]

In order to engage in post-secondary studies in Canada, refugee claimants, protected persons, and persons subject to unenforceable removal orders must obtain a study permit.[90] An application for a study permit must include usual documents such as proof of status in Canada and identity documents as well as proof of the applicant's acceptance to a higher education institution[91] and proof of sufficient funds to pay tuition.[92] The latter requirement is likely to be a significant obstacle to refugee claimants, refugees, and persons under unenforceable removal orders because as foreign nationals, they usually have to pay high international student fees. In Ontario, Alberta, and Quebec, tuition fees are governed by provincial government policy, and those governments have recognized that protected persons should be given an exemption from international student fees. In contrast, in other provinces, each institution sets its own tuition fees, so practices vary.

The eligibility for federal and provincial student loans and financial assistance usually extends only to protected persons, but not to refugee claimants. Since August 2003, protected persons are eligible to apply for student financial assistance through the Canada Student Loans Program.[93] In addition, protected persons are now eligible for provincial student loans in the province of their residence.[94]

---

86 *Refugee Convention*, above note 5, art 22.

87 GA Res 44/25, annex, 44 UN GAOR Supp (No 49) at 167, UN Doc A/44/49 (1989), art 28.

88 *IRPA*, above note 1, s 30(2).

89 See, for example, Ontario *Education Act*, RSO 1990, c E.2, s 21.

90 *Regulations*, above note 7, s 215.

91 *Ibid*, s 219.

92 *Ibid*, s 220.

93 *Canada Student Financial Assistance Act, 1994*, SC 1994, c 28, s 2.

94 Government of Newfoundland and Labrador, StudentAid, online: www.aesl.gov.nl.ca/studentaid/; Government of Nova Scotia, Student Assistance, online: http://novascotia.ca/studentassistance/apply/New/EligibilityRequirements.asp;

The processing fee for a study permit is $150, but refugee claimants, protected persons, and their family members are exempt from payment.[95] However, rejected claimants and persons under unenforceable removal orders are not included in this exemption.

c) Financial Assistance: Federal and Provincial Programs

Canada provides a range of income-security measures for various people who need them. The assistance is delivered through federal programs such as the Canada Child Benefit, Employment Insurance (EI), Old Age Security pension, and Canada Pension Plan, as well as provincial social assistance programs. While most of these programs are intended for Canadian citizens and permanent residents, refugee claimants and protected persons can benefit from some of them. Many of such benefits are in keeping with Canada's commitments under the *Refugee Convention*.[96]

The *Refugee Convention* stipulates that refugees lawfully staying in a host state are to be provided the same treatment as nationals with respect to public relief and assistance,[97] labour legislation, and social security.[98] However, Canada has filed the following reservation with respect to the provisions on public relief: "Canada interprets the phrase 'lawfully staying' as referring only to refugees admitted for permanent residence: refugees admitted for temporary residence will be accorded the same treatment with respect to the matters dealt with in articles 23 [public relief] and 24 [labour legislation and social security] as is accorded visitors generally."[99] As visitors generally are accorded little or

---

Government of Alberta, Student Aid Alberta, online: http://studentaid.alberta.ca/before-you-apply/eligibility/; Government of Saskatchewan, Student Loans, online: www.saskatchewan.ca/residents/education-and-learning/student-loans; Government of British Columbia, StudentAidBC, online: https://studentaidbc.ca/apply/eligibility#basic-eligibility; Government of Manitoba, Manitoba Student Aid, online: www.edu.gov.mb.ca/msa/program/eligibility.html; Government of Ontario, Ontario Student Assistance Program, online: www.ontario.ca/page/how-get-osap#section-1; Government of Quebec, Student Financial Aid, online: www.mesrs.gouv.qc.ca/en/aide-financiere-aux-etudes/before-your-studies/assessment-parameters/; Government of New Brunswick, Student Financial Services, online: www2.gnb.ca/content/gnb/en/departments/post-secondary_education_training_and_labour/Skills/content/FinancialSupport/StudentFinancialServices.html; Government of Prince Edward Island, Student Financial Services, online: www.studentloan.pe.ca/.

95 *Regulations*, above note 7, s 300(2)(a) & (b).

96 The *Refugee Convention*, above note 5, requires the provision of social assistance to refugees under arts 20, 21, 23, & 24.

97 *Ibid*, art 23.

98 *Ibid*, art 24.

99 UNTC, *Reservations*, above note 77.

no access to public relief or social security, this reservation effectively removes Canada's obligation towards refugee claimants and protected persons. Notwithstanding the absence of an international legal commitment, as will be discussed, refugee claimants and protected persons in Canada can access various forms of government financial assistance.

Eligibility requirements vary depending on the program, but the basic and universal preconditions are legal immigration status in Canada, residence in Canada or in a particular province, and possession of a social insurance number (SIN).[100] A SIN is linked to a person's participation in work relations, and in the case of foreign nationals usually requires proof of permission to work in Canada by means of either a work permit, a study permit indicating authorization to work in Canada, or a visitor record indicating authorization for work in Canada. While applying for a SIN may seem mundane for a citizen of Canada, the documentary stipulations (particularly in relation to an individual's identity) and other requirements can be burdensome for a refugee claimant or even a protected person.

Some programs, such as pension plans and Employment Insurance, depend on a person's contributions, but do not necessarily require permanent residence in Canada as a precondition for eligibility; others, such as Old Age Security and social assistance, depend on residence. As the following descriptions of the programs will make clear, the ability of refugee claimants and protected persons to benefit from them is substantially limited by the residence and contribution requirements. For these reasons, provincial income assistance programs are likely to be the main source of subsistence for refugee claimants and protected persons. Further, immigrants and refugees may face indirect exclusion from social programs due to cultural or linguistic barriers as well as due to the emphasis on the length of Canadian residence and employment, which some non-citizens would not meet.[101]

i) *Canada Child Benefit*

The Canada Child Benefit (CCB) is a tax-free monthly payment to low- and middle-income families to assist with the costs of child rearing. The basic conditions of eligibility are residence of parents or guardians in Canada and their immigration status. A parent/guardian or her spouse or common law partner must be a Canadian citizen, permanent

100 A SIN is a nine-digit number necessary to work in Canada or to access government programs and benefits.

101 For detailed discussion, see Edward A Koning & Keith G Banting, "Inequality below the Surface: Reviewing Immigrants' Access to and Utilization of Five Canadian Welfare Programs" (2013) 39 *Canadian Public Policy* 581.

resident, protected person, or a temporary resident who has lived in Canada throughout the previous eighteen months, and who has a valid permit in the nineteenth month.[102] Refugee claimants are ineligible for CCB. The amount of the benefit depends on family income, number of children, their ages, and province or territory of residence. The CCB is administered automatically through the tax system, so, to receive benefits, a parent and any partner or spouse must file tax returns every year.

ii) Pension Support

There are two main government pension programs: the Old Age Security (OAS) program and the Canada Pension Plan. The OAS program provides a monthly payment to individuals who are sixty-five years of age or older. This program does not require individuals to directly contribute to it in order to subsequently receive benefits. To be eligible to apply for an OAS pension, a person must (1) be a Canadian citizen, permanent resident, or holder of a temporary resident permit (TRP); and (2) have lived in Canada for at least ten years after reaching the age of eighteen (or twenty years if the applicant is currently living abroad). The amount of pension depends on the length of residency in Canada. To receive full pension, the applicant must have resided in Canada for forty years. Persons who receive an OAS pension and have little or no other income are also eligible for a Guaranteed Income Supplement. Due to immigration status restrictions on eligibility, refugee claimants and protected persons without permanent resident status would not have access to this program. Even those who obtain permanent residence would not have immediate access to the OAS program, and many are unlikely to receive a full pension in their lifetime.

In contrast to the OAS program, the Canada Pension Plan (CPP) is a contributory social insurance program that assists in case of loss of income due to retirement, disability, or death. The contributions are made by both employee and employer: half and half. As a rule, everyone over eighteen who works in Canada outside Quebec (including foreign nationals) and earns more than $3,500 per year must contribute to the Plan.

Commonly, individuals start receiving CPP pension at the age of sixty-five, although it is also possible to take a permanently reduced pension as early as age sixty or a permanently increased pension after the age of sixty-five. The amount of retirement pension depends on the amount and length of one's CPP contributions. In 2015, the average

---

102 Canada Revenue Agency, "Canada Child Benefit," online: www.cra-arc.gc.ca/E/pub/tg/t4114/t4114-e.html.

monthly amount for new pension recipients (taken at age sixty-five) was $640.23.[103] Thus, although foreign nationals may be able to claim benefits under the CPP, their amount is likely to be relatively small, depending on earnings and length of contributory period.

iii) Employment Insurance

Employment Insurance[104] is available to persons who have lost their jobs through no fault of their own. It also provides additional benefits such as maternity, parental, and sickness benefits, and compassionate care benefits. Like the CPP, it is contributory. Applicants must meet several eligibility requirements, including having worked for a set number of insurable hours during the last fifty-two weeks before making a claim; being ready, willing, and capable of working; and actively looking for work. The number of required hours is based on a person's place of residence and the unemployment rate in the economic region at the time of filing the claim for benefits. Most people need between 420 and 700 hours of work to qualify for EI benefits.[105] Regular benefits can be paid from fourteen to a maximum of forty-five weeks depending on the unemployment rate in the person's region and the amount of insurable hours accumulated. The amount of a person's weekly benefit payment depends on total earnings before deductions.[106]

Refugee claimants, protected persons, and persons under unenforceable removal orders may have access to EI if they have accumulated the required number of insurable hours and can demonstrate their readiness and availability to work.[107]

---

103 Government of Canada, "Canada Pension Plan — Eligibility," online: www.canada.ca/en/services/benefits/publicpensions/cpp/cpp-benefit/eligibility.html.

104 *Employment Insurance Act*, SC 1996, c 23; *Employment Insurance Regulations*, SOR/96-332.

105 Service Canada, "Employment Insurance Regular Benefits," online: www.servicecanada.gc.ca/eng/ei/types/regular.shtml#eligible.

106 *Ibid*.

107 Some scholars documented that temporary foreign workers with job-specific work permits (not the case for refugee claimants, protected persons, or persons under unenforceable removal orders) had trouble accessing EI as some jurisprudence considered them not being available to work due to the restricted nature of their work permit. Delphine Nakache & Paula Kinoshita, "The Canadian Temporary Foreign Worker Program: Do Short-Term Economic Needs Prevail over Human Rights Concerns?" (2010) 5 *IRPP Study* 1 at 18–21.

iv) Provincial Social and Income Assistance

Each province has legislation on income assistance.[108] Applicants usually need to provide proof of identity, proof of status in Canada, a SIN, and information about their assets or earnings. As a rule, refugee claimants and protected persons may access provincial social assistance, although those who have arrived recently may have difficulty due to lack of a SIN or acceptable proof of identity.[109] Some provinces expressly addressed the latter situation. For example, British Columbia distinguishes two types of assistance: persons who satisfy citizenship, SIN, and proof of identity requirements receive income assistance, while those who are not eligible for income assistance for a variety of reasons (e.g., those who do not have a SIN or proper identification) can apply for hardship assistance.[110]

In addition to the above, applicants usually have to provide information on the status of their refugee claim. For example, under the *Ontario Works Act* and *Regulations*, refugee claimants, protected persons, and persons under unenforceable removal orders resident in Ontario are eligible to receive income assistance.[111] Claimants must provide proof that they have made a claim and are eligible for an RPD hearing. Rejected claimants may be eligible for Ontario Works assistance in the following circumstances: their PRRA is pending; their removal order has been stayed; they have been granted permission to stay under a humanitarian and compassionate consideration; or they are

---

108 For example, *Income and Employment Supports Act*, SA 2003, c I-0.5 and *Regulations* (Alberta); *Employment and Assistance Regulation*, BC Reg 263/2002 (British Columbia); *Family Income Security Act*, RSNB 2011, c 154 (New Brunswick); *Income and Employment Support Act*, SNL 2002, c I-0.1 (Newfoundland and Labrador); and *Ontario Works Act, 1997*, SO 1997, c 25, Sch A and *Regulations*.

109 In October 2014, the Conservative government introduced Bill C-43, which, among other things, allowed provinces to prescribe minimum residency requirements that refugee claimants must meet if they are to be eligible for social assistance. The bill came into force in December 2014 (*Act to implement certain provisions of the budget tabled in Parliament on February 11, 2014 and other measures*, SC 2014, c 39, s 173), amending s 25.1 of the *Federal–Provincial Fiscal Arrangements Act*, RSC 1985, c F-8, which sets out criteria for provinces' eligibility for Canada Social Transfer. As amended, s 25.1(2) of the Act stipulates that provinces cannot prescribe the minimum residency period only for the following groups of individuals: Canadian citizens, permanent residents, victims of human trafficking, and protected persons. However, to the authors' knowledge, provinces have not yet acted upon these provisions.

110 British Columbia, *Employment and Assistance Regulation*, above note 108, ss 39 and 41–42.

111 *Ontario Works Act, 1997*, above note 108; *General*, O Reg 134/98, s 6 [*Ontario Works Regulations*].

under an unenforceable removal order.[112] Persons ineligible to make a refugee claim or those whose claims were determined abandoned or withdrawn are ineligible for assistance.[113] Eligibility for assistance also ceases when a removal order against a person comes into force.[114]

The amount of assistance differs by province and depends on the number of persons in a household, their ability to work, and any other income a household receives. For example, in British Columbia, income support allowance for a single person varies from $235 to $531 a month depending on the age and employability of the recipient.[115] In Alberta, the income assistance for a single person is set at $304 for core essentials and at $323 for shelter.[116] In Nova Scotia, respective amounts are $255 and $300;[117] in Newfoundland and Labrador, $323 (for core essentials for a single adult living with relatives) and up to $372 for shelter.[118]

v) *Medical Coverage*

As a rule, most foreign nationals do not have access to provincial healthcare.[119] This can create difficulties for claimants and refugees who usually need medical and other related services due to physical and/or psychological trauma of the past, but have no financial resources to pay for them. Recognizing this gap, the Interim Federal Health Program (IFHP) was set up to provide temporary medical coverage for refugees, refugee claimants, rejected refugee claimants, and individuals under unenforceable removal orders.[120] These persons are eligible for the IFHP if not covered by any other public or private plan and un-

---

112 Ontario Works Policy Directives, "Section 3.1 — Residency Requirement" at 3–4 (January 2013), online: www.mcss.gov.on.ca/en/mcss/programs/social/directives/index.aspx#ow.

113 *Ontario Works Regulations*, above note 111, ss 6(1) & (2).

114 *Ibid*, s 6(1)(ii).

115 British Columbia, "BC Employment and Assistance Rate Table," *BCEA Policy & Procedure Manual*, online: www.eia.gov.bc.ca/mhr/ia.htm.

116 Alberta, "Schedule 5 Core Income Support Tables" (23 March 2012), online: http://humanservices.alberta.ca/AWonline/IESA/6435.html.

117 Nova Scotia, "Basic Income Assistance Rates," online: http://novascotia.ca/coms/employment/income_assistance/BasicAssistance.html.

118 Newfoundland and Labrador, "Program Overview," online: www.aesl.gov.nl.ca/income-support/overview.html.

119 Some provinces extend provincial healthcare coverage to foreign workers and international students (e.g., Ontario provides coverage to foreign workers if they are employed in the province full-time for at least six months: see www.health.gov.on.ca/en/public/publications/ohip/temp_foreign.aspx). For an overview and barriers to access, see Koning & Banting, above note 101 at 588.

120 Some other groups, such as persons only entitled to a PRRA, victims of human trafficking, and immigration detainees, were also covered.

able to pay for health services.[121] Coverage lasts until the person leaves the country or becomes eligible for provincial healthcare coverage (e.g., upon obtaining permanent residence and satisfying any applicable provincial residence period).

The IFHP covers essential health services for the prevention and treatment of serious medical and dental conditions; emergency dental and vision care; essential prescription medications; and contraceptive, prenatal, and obstetrical care.[122] All eligible individuals receive the same level of benefits.

In the past several years, the IFHP has been subject to some changes and controversies. In 2012, the Conservative government determined that the program had become too expensive and decided to reduce the coverage, creating three tiers of benefits of varying scope.[123] Under that system, government-assisted refugees and joint assistance sponsorship refugees (for definitions, see Chapter 7) enjoyed the most extensive coverage, which was similar to the previous IFHP. For others, however, only services of urgent or essential nature continued to be covered; medications and vaccines were covered only when needed to prevent or treat a disease posing a risk to public health or to treat a condition presenting a public safety concern. Refugee claimants whose claim was withdrawn or abandoned and persons who were eligible only for a PRRA received no coverage. However, the Minister of Citizenship and Immigration had the discretion to pay a person's medical expenses in "exceptional and compelling circumstances."[124]

The changes have been widely criticized.[125] The effects of reduced coverage were dramatic. If a refugee claimant had a certain condition that did not constitute a health or safety risk, even life-saving medication would not be provided. This could be the case, for example, if a

---

121 Immigration, Refugees and Citizenship Canada, "Interim Federal Health Program: Summary of Coverage," online: www.cic.gc.ca/english/refugees/outside/summary-ifhp.asp.

122 *Ibid.*

123 *Order Respecting the Interim Federal Health Program, 2012*, SI/2012-26 (30 June 2012); SI/2012-49 (18 July 2012).

124 *Ibid*, s 8.

125 Steve Barnes, "The Real Cost of Cutting the Interim Federal Health Program" (October 2013), online: www.wellesleyinstitute.com/wp-content/uploads/2013/10/Actual-Health-Impacts-of-IFHP.pdf; Canadian Doctors for Refugee Care, online: www.doctorsforrefugeecare.ca/the-issue.html; Canadian Council for Refugees, "Refugee Healthcare," online: http://ccrweb.ca/en/ifh; Andrea Evans et al, "The Cost and Impact of the Interim Federal Health Program Cuts on Child Refugees in Canada" (2014) 9 *PLOS ONE*, online: www.plosone.org/article/info%3Adoi%2F10.1371%2Fjournal.pone.0096902.

person required insulin or suffered a heart attack. Pregnancy was also not a condition that posed a risk to public health or public safety, and, thus, claimants from DCOs would have no coverage for prenatal or obstetrical care. Further, the scope of coverage would change over time, depending on the progression of a claim. For instance, once a woman's claim was rejected by the RPD, her coverage was reduced. Further, the 2012 changes created much confusion among healthcare providers; in some cases, care was denied despite patients' actual eligibility for IFHP coverage.[126] Some providers found the system too confusing and started to refuse seeing any IFHP patients.[127] In addition, reduced IFHP coverage for privately sponsored refugees affected the ability and willingness of private organizations to sponsor refugees for resettlement to Canada. According to the 2014 survey by Citizens for Public Justice, about a third of church-connected sponsorship agreement holders (for definition, see Chapter 7) decreased or ended their involvement in the sponsorship program as a result of the added liability for health costs.[128]

Some provinces (Ontario, Quebec, Alberta, Manitoba, Nova Scotia, and Saskatchewan) reinstated access to essential and urgent care for refugees and refugee claimants in order to address the gap created by the IFHP. The federal government, however, criticized such a move. For example, Minister Chris Alexander expressed regret with Ontario's

---

126 *Canadian Doctors for Refugee Care v Canada (Attorney General)*, 2014 FC 651 at paras 134–35 [*Canadian Doctors for Refugee Care*].

127 *Ibid* at para 136.

128 Citizens for Public Justice, "Private Sponsorship and Public Policy" (2014) at 6, online: CPJ www.cpj.ca/sites/default/files/docs/files/PrivateSponsorshipand-PublicPolicyReport.pdf. Some sponsoring organizations attempted a challenge to the order in council that brought about the change to the IFHP, but were unsuccessful. *Hospitality House Refugee Ministry Inc v Canada (Attorney General)*, 2013 FC 543. In 2011, the Hospitality House and the Synod of the Diocese of Rupert's Land undertook to sponsor 1,940 refugees through the private sponsorship program. At the time, the health services for privately sponsored refugees were covered by the IFHP. However, in 2012, the changes to the IFHP came into effect, reducing the coverage for privately sponsored refugees. The sponsoring organizations were concerned that they would need to find additional financial resources to cover the difference between the previous and the currently more limited coverage. They challenged the order in council, which brought about the change, arguing that it breached the sponsorship contract between them and the minister as well as the duty of fairness owed to them. The Federal Court concluded that the order did not breach any agreement between the applicants and the minister as the agreement did not specify any particular level of healthcare services. Further, given that the order was a legislative act, there was no legal duty on the Governor in Council to consult with the applicants prior to policy changes.

decision to reinstate healthcare to refugee claimants. He called this decision "irresponsible, as it makes Canada — and Ontario in particular — a magnet for bogus asylum seekers. It's also unfair to taxpayers, who have to foot the bill, while their own access to health care suffers."[129] Interestingly, when a similar argument was made before the Federal Court, the court did not find it convincing. Justice Mactavish wrote: ". . . it is hard to reconcile the respondents' argument that the availability of health care in Canada operates as a 'pull factor' for refugee claimants from DCO countries with their claim that refugee claimants from DCO countries do not need health insurance coverage while they are in Canada because they can get comparable health care back home."[130]

In 2013, a group of non-governmental organizations (Canadian Doctors for Refugee Care, the Canadian Association of Refugee Lawyers, and Justice for Children and Youth) along with two claimants challenged the government's decision to reduce IFHP coverage.[131] In July 2014, Mactavish J of the Federal Court determined that the cuts to refugee healthcare were "cruel and unusual treatment" and thus a violation of section 12 of the *Charter*. She wrote:

> With the 2012 changes to the IFHP, the executive branch of the Canadian government has set out to make the lives of disadvantaged individuals even more difficult than they already are in an effort to force those who have sought the protection of this country to leave Canada more quickly, and to deter others from coming here. In light of the unusual circumstances of this case, I am satisfied that the affected individuals are being subjected to "treatment" as contemplated by section 12 of the *Charter*.
>
> I am also satisfied that this treatment is "cruel and unusual," particularly, but not exclusively, as it affects children who have been brought to this country by their parents. The cuts to health insurance coverage effected through the 2012 modifications to the IFHP potentially jeopardize the health, and indeed the very lives, of these innocent and vulnerable children in a manner that shocks the conscience and outrages our standards of decency. They violate section 12 of the *Charter*.[132]

---

129 Speaking notes for Chris Alexander, Canada's Citizenship and Immigration Minister, at the news conference regarding Canada's asylum system (22 January 2014), online: http://news.gc.ca/web/article-en.do?nid=831769.

130 *Canadian Doctors for Refugee Care*, above note 126 at para 826.

131 *Ibid*.

132 *Ibid* at paras 690–91.

Justice Mactavish also found that the cuts violated section 15 of the *Charter* as they provided for different levels of coverage for DCO and non-DCO claimants. This distinction was based upon the national origin of the refugee claimants and perpetuated stereotypes that claimants from DCOs are "bogus" and that they have come to Canada to abuse Canada's generosity.

The Conservative government filed an appeal, but when the Liberal Party came to power in the fall of 2015, the new government announced it would not pursue the appeal.[133] The IFHP coverage has been restored, and the tier system has been eliminated.

4) Access to Permanent Residence

The goal of refugee protection may be considered achieved only if a recognized refugee is granted formal membership in a host community (in a form of secure immigration status) and certainty about the future in the country where protection has been granted. The *Refugee Convention* stipulates that states parties are to "as far as possible" facilitate the assimilation and naturalization of refugees, including by making every effort to expedite naturalization proceedings and to reduce as far as possible the charges and costs of such proceedings.[134] However, it does not establish an obligation to grant permanent residence to refugees. Taking advantage of this lacuna in the international refugee regime, some states (e.g., members of the European Union and Australia) have moved towards provision of temporary protection; others (e.g., Canada) separated the process of refugee determination from approval for permanent residence. Both temporary protection and the lag between refugee determination and conferral of permanent residence result in uncertainty about the long-term future of refugees and limitations on full enjoyment of rights to work, study, family reunification, and more.

In Canada, resettled refugees obtain permanent resident status at the time of their entry in Canada.[135] In contrast, persons who made a

---

133 Statement from the Minister of Immigration, Refugees and Citizenship and the Minister of Justice and Attorney General of Canada (16 December 2015), online: http://news.gc.ca/web/article-en.do?nid=1025029.

134 Article 34 of the *Refugee Convention*, above note 5, provides: "The Contracting States shall as far as possible facilitate the assimilation and naturalization of refugees. They shall in particular make every effort to expedite naturalization proceedings and to reduce as far as possible the charges and costs of such proceedings." However, this formulation does not presuppose that host states are under obligation to allow refugees to naturalize.

135 *IRPA*, above note 1, ss 95(1) & (2). For a detailed discussion of this class and relevant definitions, see Part 4.

successful inland claim receive protected status, but do not automatically gain permanent residence. To gain such status, they must file a separate application. They must

- make an application within 180 days of the decision about the conferral of the protected person's status;[136]
- provide proof of identity;[137]
- not be inadmissible on grounds of security, violation of human or international rights, serious criminality, organized criminality, or as a danger to public health or safety.[138]

However, as mentioned earlier, a designated foreign national is not eligible to apply for permanent residence for five years after the final determination on his refugee claim.[139]

An application for permanent residence is made to Immigration, Refugees and Citizenship Canada. The applicant may include a spouse or a common law partner and dependent children in the application for permanent residence in order to allow them to become permanent residents as well.[140] Applicants are exempt from some fees normally payable by other immigrants. For example, protected persons and resettled refugees do not pay the $490 right of landing fee.[141] Resettled refugees are also exempt from paying a processing fee for their permanent resident applications.[142] However, protected persons who apply for permanent residence after making a successful inland claim do have to pay a $550 processing fee.[143]

Some protected persons may not become permanent residents even if they meet the above requirements. These classes, prescribed in the *Regulations*, section 177, include persons

- whose refugee protection ceased or was vacated;
- who are already permanent residents of Canada;
- who have been recognized by any country, other than Canada, as Convention refugees and who would be allowed to return to that country;

---

136 *Regulations*, above note 7, s 175(1).
137 *IRPA*, above note 1, s 20(1); *Regulations*, above note 7, ss 50 and 178.
138 *IRPA*, above note 1, s 21(2).
139 *Ibid*, ss 11(1.1), 24(5), and 25(1.01)
140 *Regulations*, above note 7, s 176(1).
141 *Ibid*, ss 303(2)(c), (d), & (e).
142 *Ibid*, ss 295(2) and 301(1.1). The total fee payable by a family depends on the number and ages of the individuals included in the application.
143 *Ibid*, s 301. The total fee payable by a family depends on the number and ages of the individuals included in the application.

- who have citizenship of another country, other than the one they left due to fear of persecution; and
- who have permanently resided in a country, other than the country where they fear persecution, and who would be allowed to return to that country.

a) Proof of Identity

According to section 50(1) of the *Regulations*, a person seeking to become a permanent resident must hold one of the following identity documents: a passport or a travel or identity document issued by his country of citizenship or a specified international organization or entity. The IRCC Minister also has the power to designate, individually or by class, passports or travel/identity documents that are considered unreliable.[144] Such documents cannot be used as acceptable proof of identity. As of 2016, the following have been designated as unreliable: any passport purporting to have been issued by Somalia; non-machine readable passports issued by the Czech Republic; temporary passports issued by the Republic of South Africa; and provisional passports issued by Venezuela.[145]

Due either to the situation in many countries of origin or to the method of exit and travel to Canada, many protected persons do not possess an identity document within the meaning of section 50(1). Section 50(2) allows protected persons an exemption from the above requirement if they cannot obtain a passport or an identity or travel document referred to in section 50(1). In such a case, a protected person may establish her identity by any of the following means:

> (*a*) any identity document issued outside Canada before the person's entry into Canada; or
>
> (*b*) if there is a reasonable and objectively verifiable explanation related to circumstances in the applicant's country of nationality or former habitual residence for the applicant's inability to obtain any identity documents, a statutory declaration made by the applicant attesting to their identity, accompanied by
>
> (i) a statutory declaration attesting to the applicant's identity made by a person who, before the applicant's entry into Can-

---

144 *Ibid*, s 50.1.

145 Immigration, Refugees and Citizenship Canada, "Operational Bulletin 190 — March 12, 2010," online: IRCC www.cic.gc.ca/english/resources/manuals/bulletins/2010/ob190.asp; Immigration, Refugees and Citizenship Canada, "Determine Your Eligibility," online: IRCC www.cic.gc.ca/english/visit/apply-who.asp.

ada, knew the applicant, a family member of the applicant or the applicant's father, mother, brother, sister, grandfather or grandmother, or

(ii) a statutory declaration attesting to the applicant's identity made by an official of an organization representing nationals of the applicant's country of nationality or former habitual residence.[146]

The above documents must satisfy certain conditions to be accepted in lieu of normally required identity documents. Identity documents must be genuine, identify the applicant, and constitute credible evidence of the applicant's identity.[147] Statutory declarations must be consistent with any information previously provided to IRCC or the IRB and must constitute credible evidence of the applicant's identity.[148]

While the *IRPA* has attempted to increase flexibility in the means of establishing identity, some individuals may still face challenges meeting the proof of identity requirement.

b) Inadmissibility

In order to be granted permanent resident status, a person must not be inadmissible. Broadly speaking, inadmissibility refers to circumstances or conditions that make a person undesirable for temporary or permanent admission to Canada. It reflects concerns associated with potential danger that a person may represent to Canada or Canadians, their "bad" character, or the financial or other burden that they may impose on the host community. The *IRPA* outlines eleven grounds of inadmissibility:

- security;
- violation of human or international rights;
- criminality;
- serious criminality;
- organized criminality;
- health;
- financial reasons;
- misrepresentation;
- cessation of refugee protection;
- non-compliance with the *IRPA*;
- inadmissible family member.[149]

---

146 *Regulations*, above note 7, s 178(1).

147 *Ibid*, s 178(2)(a).

148 *Ibid*, s 178(2)(b).

149 *IRPA*, above note 1, ss 34–42.

Like other applicants, protected persons have to satisfy IRCC that they are not inadmissible. However, due to the humanitarian nature of their admission, they are exempt from two inadmissibility bars: (1) excessive demand on health or social services[150] and (2) inadmissible family member.[151]

The consequences of inadmissibility for refugee claimants and protected persons can be as follows: (1) if inadmissibility on grounds of security, violating human/international rights, serious criminality, or organized criminality is detected at the initial stages of the claim process, a person would be ineligible for a hearing before the RPD and would have access only to a PRRA (for more on eligibility and pre-removal risk assessments, please see Chapters 8 and 11, respectively); (2) some circumstances captured under inadmissibility grounds may also trigger issues of exclusion from refugee protection (for the discussion of the latter, please see Chapter 5); (3) if inadmissibility is detected or arises after a claimant has received protected person status, he may be precluded from obtaining permanent residence. Due to the current practice of front-end security and criminality checks for refugee claimants, the majority are likely to face consequence (1) or (2).

Due to constraints of space, not all of the above-mentioned grounds of inadmissibility will be discussed. Instead, we will briefly review only those that are likely to be most relevant to cases of protected persons.

i) *Security (Section 34(1) of the* IRPA*)*

According to section 34(1) of the *IRPA*, a person can be inadmissible on security grounds for

> (a) engaging in an act of espionage that is against Canada or that is contrary to Canada's interests;
> (b) engaging in or instigating the subversion by force of any government;
> (b.1) engaging in an act of subversion against a democratic government, institution or process as they are understood in Canada;
> (c) engaging in terrorism;
> (d) being a danger to the security of Canada;
> (e) engaging in acts of violence that would or might endanger the lives or safety of persons in Canada; or
> (f) being a member of an organization that there are reasonable grounds to believe engages, has engaged or will engage in acts referred to in paragraph (a), (b), (b.1) or (c).

---

150 *Ibid*, s 38(1)(c).
151 *Ibid*, s 42.

Section 34(1)(f) has been one of the most frequently encountered barriers in permanent residence applications by protected persons. It has been framed and interpreted rather broadly and hence can capture a range of activities, including those by national liberation movements. For example, members of the following groups have been routinely found inadmissible under section 34(1)(f): the Eritrean Liberation Movement, which fought a brutal Ethiopian dictatorship following the illegal annexation of Eritrea by Ethiopia in 1962; the Palestine Liberation Organization (PLO), which embodied the struggle of Palestinian people for self-determination and has been formally recognized as representative of the Palestinian people by several countries; the Frente Farabundo Marti para la Liberación Nacional (FMLN) in El Salvador, which is currently a political party leading the present government recognized by other countries, including Canada. This situation not only creates challenges for protected persons, but also highlights the tensions inherent in immigration and refugee law. Paradoxically, persons who have embodied the fight for recognized human rights may be denied permanent residence in Canada for that very reason.

Courts held that the term "member" is to be interpreted broadly.[152] In order to determine if a person is a member of an organization, it is necessary to examine the extent of the person's involvement in the organization, the length of their association with it, and the degree of commitment to its objectives.[153] In addition, decision makers need to consider whether a person has joined an organization under coercion, duress, or any other form of compulsion.[154] A person's status as a minor is also a relevant consideration as it relates to their requisite knowledge and capacity to understand the nature and acts of the organization.[155] The decision in *Ezokola v Canada (Citizenship and Immigration)* (see Chapter 5, Section F(1)) did not modify the test for membership under section 34(1)(f) to require complicity through contribution.[156]

---

152 *Poshteh v Canada*, 2005 FCA 85 at para 27 [*Poshteh*].

153 *TK v Canada (Minister of Public Safety and Emergency Preparedness)*, 2013 FC 327 at para 105 [*TK*]; *Krishnamoorthy v Canada (Minister of Citizenship and Immigration)*, 2011 FC 1342 at para 23; *Villegas v Canada (Minister of Citizenship and Immigration)*, 2011 FC 105 at para 44.

154 *TK*, above note 153 at para 114.

155 *Poshteh*, above note 152 at para 48. Although "minor" usually refers to a person under eighteen, in *Poshteh*, the Federal Court of Appeal noted, at para 48, that a finding of membership may be possible with respect to a minor of any age, although it would be highly unusual for a child under twelve.

156 *Kanagendren v Canada (Minister of Citizenship and Immigration)*, 2015 FCA 86, leave to appeal to SCC refused, [2015] SCCA No 264. In *Ezokola v Canada (Citizenship and Immigration)*, 2013 SCC 40, the Supreme Court examined exclusion

The breadth of the provision stems from two aspects of its interpretation. First, to be inadmissible under section 34(1)(f), it is sufficient that a person was merely a member of an organization. The person need not have actively participated in terrorist or subversive activities or had knowledge of those activities.[157] Thus, a person who was unaware of the organization's terrorist or subversive activities or who was engaged in serving purely humanitarian aims may still be rendered inadmissible.[158] Further, the issue of legitimacy or lawfulness of the use of force (e.g., in case of organizations fighting for self-determination or against oppressive regimes) is not a relevant consideration, and section 34 cannot be construed as excluding from its application organizations seeking to subvert a certain type of government in furtherance of an oppressed people's claimed right to self-determination.[159]

In determining whether an organization has engaged in terrorism, decision makers must first examine whether there are reasonable grounds to believe that an organization has committed the acts attributed to it and, second, determine whether those acts constitute terrorism.[160] It is not necessary that the organization officially sanctioned acts of terrorism in order to find that it has engaged in terrorism.[161] Further, the standard of "reasonable grounds to believe" is low: it is more than a mere suspicion, but less than the balance of probabilities.[162]

---

under art 1F(a) of the *Refugee Convention*, above note 5, where there are "serious reasons for considering that [an applicant has] committed a crime against peace, a war crime, or a crime against humanity." The Court distinguished between mere association and culpable complicity, finding that complicity arises by contribution; art 1F(a) requires serious reasons for considering that an individual has voluntarily made a significant and knowing contribution to a group's crime or criminal purpose.

157 *Tjiueza v Canada (Minister of Citizenship and Immigration)*, 2009 FC 1260.

158 *Kozonguizi v Canada (Minister of Citizenship and Immigration)*, 2010 FC 308. For example, for detailed discussion of the Eritrean Liberation Movement, see Catherine Bruce et al, "Out of the Fire and into the Pot: The Eritrean Liberation Movement, the Right to Self-Determination and the Over-Breadth of North American Immigration Security Provisions" (2011) 25 *Georgetown Immigration Law Journal* 859; Canadian Council for Refugees, "From Liberation to Limbo" (April 2010), online: ccrweb.ca/files/from_liberation_to_limbo.pdf. For some cases of FMLN members, see, for example, Oscar Vigil Campaign, online: http://vigilcampaign.ca/.

159 *Najafi v Canada (Public Safety and Emergency Preparedness)*, 2014 FCA 262, leave to appeal to SCC refused, [2015] SCCA No 2.

160 *Jalil v Canada (Minister of Citizenship and Immigration)*, 2007 FC 568 at para 18.

161 *Rizwan v Canada (Minister of Citizenship and Immigration)*, 2010 FC 781.

162 *Mugesera v Canada (Minister of Citizenship and Immigration)*, 2005 SCC 40 at para 114.

Second, there is no temporal limitation on the membership provision: one's period of membership need not overlap with the time when an organization engaged in terrorism or subversion.[163] A person would be inadmissible even if she joined an organization after it denounced violence as a means to advance its cause.[164]

However, a recent decision in *Figueroa v Canada (Minister of Citizenship and Immigration)*[165] (involving a former member of the FMLN in El Salvador), although made in the context of an H&C application, suggests that decision makers should take a more nuanced approach that considers the history of a given country, the nature of the organization in question, and the applicant's exclusively non-combatant role. The court wrote:

> The Delegate unreasonably referred to the FMLN as a "terrorist organization". That term is not used in s 34 and is not a term of art employed by the statute. The *IRPA* refers to membership in an organization that has, is or will engage in acts of terrorism. The FMLN was never a group for which political terror was a primary tactic. It had broad popular support and has now formed the government elected through democratic means. The organization attracted 80–100,000 members in a country of 5 million population. It was a broad based legitimate resistance group. The armed elements of the FMLN were primarily military forces engaged in a civil war against an oppressive regime much like the African National Congress in South Africa's struggle against apartheid. The FMLN has not been proscribed as a "terrorist entity" on the list maintained by the Government of Canada. The Government of Canada carries on normal relations with the Government of El Salvador, now led by the FMLN. Some consideration should have been given to all of this before the Delegate concluded that the applicant's membership in the FMLN was of such a serious nature that it outweighed the positive humanitarian and

---

163 *Gebreab v Canada (Minister of Public Safety and Emergency Preparedness)*, 2010 FCA 274.

164 For example, in *Haqi v Canada (Minister of Citizenship and Immigration)*, 2014 FC 1167, the Federal Court upheld an inadmissibility finding against an applicant who joined the Kurdish Democratic Party of Iran (KDPI) in 2006 — ten years after it made a public announcement to pursue autonomy by peaceful means. The KDPI was established in the 1940s to fight the repression of the Kurdish people, including by military means.

165 2014 FC 673 [*Figueroa*]. Note that his refugee claim was rejected and the inadmissibility arose in the context of application for permanent residence on H&C grounds.

compassionate factors in favour of granting the applicant an exemption.[166]

ii) Human or International Rights Violations (Section 35 of the IRPA*)*

Under section 35, a person can be inadmissible for having committed genocide, a war crime, or a crime against humanity, or for "being a prescribed senior official in the service of a government that, in the opinion of the Minister, engages or has engaged in terrorism, systematic or gross human rights violations, or genocide, a war crime or a crime against humanity."[167] "Prescribed senior officials" include heads of state or government and their senior advisors; members of the Cabinet or governing council and their senior advisors; senior members of the public service; senior members of the military and of the intelligence and internal security services; ambassadors and senior diplomatic officials; and members of the judiciary.[168]

In addition, a person may be inadmissible under section 35 where Canada has imposed travel or economic sanctions on certain individuals (e.g., with respect to senior officials of the Yanukovych government in Ukraine[169]).

The definitions of genocide, war crimes, and crimes against humanity can be found in international documents such as the *Statute of the International Criminal Court* as well as reflected in domestic legislation such as the *Crimes against Humanity and War Crimes Act*.[170]

iii) Criminality (Sections 35–37 of the IRPA*)*

The *IRPA* distinguishes three types of criminality: criminality, serious criminality, and organized criminality. Broadly speaking, a person can be inadmissible for criminality or serious criminality if he has been convicted of certain offences[171] in or outside Canada or has committed an act outside Canada that is an offence in the place where it was com-

166 *Ibid* at para 38.

167 *IRPA*, above note 1, s 35(1)(b).

168 *Regulations*, above note 7, s 16.

169 *Special Economic Measures (Ukraine) Regulations*, SOR/2014-60.

170 SC 2000, c 24.

171 The following fall under "serious criminality": conviction in Canada of an offence punishable by a maximum term of imprisonment of at least ten years, or of an offence for which a term of imprisonment of more than six months has been imposed; conviction outside Canada of an offence that, if committed in Canada, would be punishable by a maximum term of imprisonment of at least ten years; commission of an act outside Canada that amounts to an offence and, if committed in Canada, would be punishable by a maximum term of imprisonment of at least ten years.

mitted and, if committed in Canada, would constitute an offence of a certain type. If an offence was committed abroad, decision makers need to determine if a foreign offence is "equivalent" to an offence in Canadian law. Persons who have been granted an absolute or conditional discharge or a record of suspension (previously known as a "pardon") would not be inadmissible. Further, persons who have been convicted of an offence or have committed an offence outside Canada may overcome inadmissibility by demonstrating that they have rehabilitated.[172]

A person may be inadmissible on the grounds of organized criminality if she (1) is a member of an organization that "is believed on reasonable grounds to be or have been engaged" in planned and organized criminal activity; or (2) engaged, in the context of transnational crime, in activities such as people smuggling or trafficking or money laundering.[173] In *B010 v Canada (Citizenship and Immigration)*,[174] the Supreme Court examined whether persons who aided in their own illegal entry to Canada would be inadmissible for human smuggling under section 37(1). The case involved several Tamil claimants whose ship MV *Sun Sea* was abandoned by the smugglers, leaving the passengers to fend for themselves during a three-month long trip from Thailand to Canada. One of the applicants volunteered to work in the engine room, the other assisted navigation, and the third one was a cook and a lookout. The IRB found applicants inadmissible, but the Supreme Court disagreed with such broad interpretation of section 37(1):

> [Section] 37(1)(*b*) of the *IRPA* applies only to people who act to further illegal entry of asylum-seekers in order to obtain, directly or

---

The following fall under "criminality": conviction in Canada of an offence punishable by way of indictment, or of two offences under not arising out of a single occurrence; conviction outside Canada of an offence that, if committed in Canada, would constitute an indictable offence, or of two offences not arising out of a single occurrence; commission outside Canada of an act that constitutes an offence in the place where it was committed and that, if committed in Canada, would constitute an indictable offence; commission, on entering Canada, an offence under the *Criminal Code*, the *IRPA*, the *Firearms Act*, the *Customs Act*, or the *Controlled Drugs and Substances Act*.

The ground of serious criminality applies to permanent residents and foreign nationals; criminality, only to the latter group.

172 Depending on the type of an offence, a person may be deemed rehabilitated if five or ten years have elapsed since the completion of their sentence. Decision makers may also engage an individualized inquiry to determine if the person has been rehabilitated. *IRPA*, above note 1, s 36(3); *Regulations*, above note 7, ss 17–18.

173 *IRPA*, above note 1, s 37(1).

174 2015 SCC 58.

> indirectly, a financial or other material benefit in the context of transnational organized crime . . . . [A]cts of humanitarian and mutual aid (including aid between family members) do not constitute people smuggling under the *IRPA* . . . . The appellants can escape inadmissibility under s. 37(1)(*b*) if they merely aided in the illegal entry of other refugees or asylum-seekers in the course of their collective flight to safety.[175]

In a related case, *R v Appulonappa*,[176] which also involved arrivals on MV *Sun Sea*, the Supreme Court reiterated that human smuggling is to be understood to capture organized crime rather than humanitarian, mutual, or family assistance. Section 117 of the *IRPA*[177] was found unconstitutional insofar as it permitted prosecution for humanitarian aid to undocumented entrants, mutual assistance among asylum seekers, or assistance to family members.

iv) *Ministerial Exemption*

Persons who are found inadmissible under sections 34 (security), 35 (violating human or international rights), or 37(1) (being a member of an organized crime group) may nevertheless be able to obtain permanent resident status if they are granted a Ministerial exemption. On application or on his own initiative, the Minister of Public Safety and Emergency Preparedness may declare that the applicant's circumstances do not constitute inadmissibility, given that this is not contrary

---

175 *Ibid* at paras 5 and 72.

176 2015 SCC 59.

177 The section reads as follows:

> (1) No person shall knowingly organize, induce, aid or abet the coming into Canada of one or more persons who are not in possession of a visa, passport or other document required by this Act.
>
> (2) A person who contravenes subsection (1) with respect to fewer than 10 persons is guilty of an offence and liable
>
> (*a*) on conviction on indictment
>
> (i) for a first offence, to a fine of not more than $500,000 or to a term of imprisonment of not more than 10 years, or to both, or
>
> (ii) for a subsequent offence, to a fine of not more than $1,000,000 or to a term of imprisonment of not more than 14 years, or to both; and
>
> (*b*) on summary conviction, to a fine of not more than $100,000 or to a term of imprisonment of not more than two years, or to both.
>
> (3) A person who contravenes subsection (1) with respect to a group of 10 persons or more is guilty of an offence and liable on conviction by way of indictment to a fine of not more than $1,000,000 or to life imprisonment, or to both.

to the national interest.[178] In determining whether to make a declaration, "the Minister may only take into account national security and public safety considerations, but, in his or her analysis, is not limited to considering the danger that the foreign national presents to the public or the security of Canada."[179]

c) "Refugees in Limbo"

Some persons may be unable to satisfy one of the requirements for a permanent resident application or face long delays due to governmental concerns over, most commonly, inadmissibility. They are usually referred to as "refugees in limbo" due to the uncertainty about their future and the hardship caused by lack of permanent resident status.[180] They face numerous limitations: they are precluded from family reunification as only Canadian citizens and permanent residents can sponsor family members for immigration to Canada;[181] they are restricted in their ability to travel outside Canada and ability to return to Canada; and they cannot work or study without a permit. The lack of permanent resident status creates multiple barriers to protected persons' integration in Canada, from labour market access to mental health problems caused by uncertainty about the future and separation from loved ones.[182] In 2005, it was estimated that there were more than 20,000 protected persons in limbo in Canada.[183] Preliminary research suggested that the cost to the government of Canada of maintaining refugees in limbo exceeds $100 million per year and that the cost to refugees caught in limbo exceeds $300 million per year in foregone earned income.[184]

---

178 *IRPA*, above note 1, ss 42.1(1) & (2).

179 *Ibid*, s 42.1(3).

180 A fuller discussion of the topic of refugees in limbo can be found in Harry J Kits, "Betwixt and Between: Refugees in Limbo" (2005) 22 *Refuge* 3. The issue of limbo due to the lack of permanent resident status has received considerable attention from both academics and advocates in Canada. See, for example, Canadian Council for Refugees, "Refugees in Limbo: A Human Rights Issue" (1999), online: http://ccrweb.ca/en/refugees-limbo-human-rights-issue; Andrew Brouwer, "Permanent Protection: Why Canada Should Grant Permanent Residence Automatically to Recognized Refugees" (2005) 22 *Refuge* 88; Harvey Krahn et al, "Educated and Underemployed: Refugee Integration into the Canadian Labour Force" (2000) 1 *Journal of International Migration and Integration* 59.

181 *Regulations*, above note 7, s 130(1).

182 See, generally, Tim Coates & Caitlin Hayward, "The Costs of Legal Limbo for Refugees in Canada: A Preliminary Study" (2005) 22 *Refuge* 77.

183 *Ibid* at 77 (quoting data received from the Ministry of Citizenship and Immigration in 2004).

184 *Ibid*.

An illustrative example of limbo can be found in the case of Nawal Haj Khalil. She was recognized as a Convention refugee in Canada in 1994. In 1995, she applied for permanent residence, yet over a decade later, was still awaiting a decision. Haj Khalil was a member of Fatah and a journalist for a Fatah-controlled Palestine Liberation Organization (PLO) publication. Canadian immigration authorities concluded that she was inadmissible on security grounds, namely, membership in an organization that there are reasonable grounds to believe engages, has engaged, or will engage in terrorism (section 34(1)(f) of the *IRPA*). In the officers' opinion, Fatah had engaged in terrorism during Haj Khalil's employment and Haj Khalil would have been aware of the organization's ideology and terrorist actions.[185] After successful judicial review of the initial negative decision, Haj Khalil's case was sent for reconsideration (including for ministerial relief against inadmissibility). However, given the backlog that existed at the time, what is now Immigration, Refugees and Citizenship Canada decided to prioritize inadmissibility files and "park" ministerial relief cases. In 2007, the decision on Haj Khalil's case remained outstanding. She eventually sued IRCC for negligence in immigration processing, seeking damages for the harm suffered due to delays with the decision on her application (psychological distress (depression); economic loss; loss of guidance, care, and companionship of her husband). However, courts found that IRCC owed no duty of care[186] to Haj Khalil and that the causal link between the alleged harm and IRCC's negligence was not established.[187]

Following the conclusion of tort litigation, IRCC made a decision on Haj Khalil's application: she was found inadmissible and ministerial

---

185 Note that there have been several determinations on Haj Khalil's inadmissibility. During the first consideration of her file, an officer determined her inadmissible on the basis of membership in the Palestine Liberation Organization (PLO), but that conclusion was overturned on judicial review. A second officer also found Haj Khalil inadmissible on the basis of membership in and employment by the PLO. That decision was overturned on judicial review on consent of the minister. A third officer found Haj Khalil inadmissible due to her membership in Fatah. That conclusion was also overturned on judicial review on consent of the minister. Finally, a fourth officer found Haj Khalil to be inadmissible on the basis of her membership in Fatah. This decision was upheld as reasonable by the Federal Court. See *Khalil v Canada (Minister of Public Safety and Emergency Preparedness)*, 2011 FC 1332.

186 In tort law, the notion of the duty of care means that a person or an entity has a responsibility to avoid actions that can be reasonably foreseen to cause harm to others. This implies that a human being or private/government entity has to keep in mind others that may be affected by his/her actions.

187 *Haj Khalil v Canada*, 2007 FC 923, aff'd 2009 FCA 66.

relief was denied. Another judicial review[188] resulted in the case being sent for another re-determination only to be, once again, denied ministerial relief. Following one more round of judicial review, the last decision to deny Ministerial exemption was upheld by the Federal Court of Appeal.[189] Apart from symbolic stance on organizations that engage in terrorism, the denial of permanent residence to Haj Khalil seems to serve little purpose: if considered a danger, she has already been in Canada for more than twenty years and, as a stateless Palestinian and a Convention refugee, cannot be removed from the country.

It should be noted that there is no statutory duty to render a decision within a specific time or to meet a specific deadline in processing permanent resident applications. Although applicants are owed a duty of natural justice and procedural fairness, it is possible for the government to delay decision making, claiming that this is necessary for thorough investigation and related activities. There is currently little recourse for applicants like Haj Khalil, except for seeking an order of *mandamus* to compel a government authority to make a decision (for more on *mandamus*, see Chapter 10). However, an order of *mandamus* cannot address other needs of applicants such as promoting government accountability and obtaining damages for loss suffered. Had the duty of care been recognized, this would have created a more effective mechanism to compel immigration authorities to make decisions in a timely manner. The exact numbers of refugees in Haj Khalil's situation are unknown, but at least several similar cases have been reported.[190]

---

188 *Haj Khalil v Canada (Minister of Public Safety and Emergency Preparedness)*, 2011 FC 1332.

189 *Khalil v Canada (Minister of Public Safety and Emergency Preparedness)*, 2014 FCA 213.

190 For example, Suleyman Goven, a Kurdish refugee, has been in limbo over permanent residence for thirteen years due to allegations of terrorist activity in his country of origin. He was cleared of these allegations in 2000 by the Security Intelligence Review Committee, but his status was eventually granted only in 2006. In 2005, he filed a lawsuit against the Canadian government for damages. See, online: www.cpj.ca/en/exonerated-suspicion-still-limbo; Nicholas Keung, "Refugee Files Lawsuit over Status: Canada Gave Him Asylum 12 Years Ago but Landed Immigrant Status Refused" *Toronto Star* (9 November 2005) B01. See also *Goven v Canada (Attorney General)*, IMM-6730-05 (FC) (originated 8 November 2005). Some twenty more Kurdish refugees are said to be in a similar situation. Statement of Suleyman Goven (11 May 2000), online: www.cpj.ca/files/docs/statemnt.pdf. In *John Doe v Canada (Minister of Public Safety and Emergency Preparedness)*, 2006 FC 535, the Federal Court dealt with another case of delay in processing a permanent resident application by a refugee. John Doe was granted refugee status in 1986, but in 2006, there was still no decision on

5) Access to Naturalization

Access to citizenship is governed by the *Citizenship Act*. Canadian citizenship can be acquired in one of the following three ways: (1) by birth in Canada, (2) by descent (being born abroad to a Canadian citizen[191]), or (3) by naturalization. The latter is the mode of citizenship acquisition for immigrants and refugees.

The *Citizenship Act* was subject to significant amendments in 2014, which expanded some of the existing requirements for naturalization, introduced new ones (such as the requirement to file tax returns and to make a declaration of intention to reside in Canada), and prescribed new grounds for revocation of citizenship.

As a result of the above amendments, applicants must satisfy the following in order to obtain citizenship by naturalization:

- be at least eighteen years of age;
- reside in Canada as a permanent resident for a specified time (see below);
- demonstrate adequate knowledge of an official language;
- demonstrate adequate knowledge of Canada and of responsibilities and privileges of citizenship;
- file tax returns;
- make a declaration of an intention to reside in Canada; and
- not be under a removal order; subject to a declaration that a person constitutes a threat to the security of Canada or that a person has engaged, is engaging, or may engage in a pattern of criminal activity; or subject to any of the prescribed prohibitions.[192]

---

his permanent residence due to security concerns. The court ordered IRCC to make a decision within ninety days.

191 Since 2009, citizenship by descent is limited to first-generation children born abroad. Thus, a child born abroad will be a Canadian citizen only if her parent was either born in Canada or acquired citizenship by naturalization.

192 The following individuals shall not be granted citizenship: persons who are on probation, parole, or serving a sentence in a penitentiary, jail, prison, or reformatory; individuals serving a sentence outside Canada for an offence that, if committed in Canada, would constitute an offence; persons charged with or on trial for listed offences; persons under investigation for or charged with or on trial for an offence under the *Crimes Against Humanity and War Crimes Act*; persons convicted of an offence under the *Crimes Against Humanity and War Crimes Act*; persons who directly or indirectly misrepresent or withhold material circumstances, which induces or could induce an error in the administration of the *Citizenship Act*; persons whose citizenship was revoked due to convictions related to national security or due to participating in an armed conflict with Canada. *Citizenship Act*, RSC 1985, c C-29, s 20.

An applicant must have been physically present in Canada as a permanent resident for at least four years (1,460 days) out of the six years preceding the application and 183 days per year for four years out of six.[193] Prior to the amendments, the residency requirement was three out of four years preceding the application. In addition, the applicant must have filed tax returns with respect to four years within six years preceding the application.[194] Prior to the 2014 amendments, filing of tax returns was not a precondition for citizenship.

Applicants aged fourteen to sixty-four must demonstrate adequate knowledge of Canada and of one of the official languages. In the past, such a requirement applied only to persons eighteen to fifty-four. The following can be used as a proof of language competency: (1) results of an accepted third-party test (e.g., International English Language Testing System or Test d'Évaluation de Français); (2) proof of completion of a secondary or post-secondary program conducted in French or English, either in Canada or abroad; or (3) proof of achieving Canadian Language Benchmark/Niveaux de compétence linguistique canadiens (CLB/NCLC) level 4 or higher in speaking and listening skills through certain government-funded language training programs (e.g., Language Instruction for Newcomers to Canada or Cours de Langue pour Immigrants au Canada). The knowledge of Canada test is based largely on the content of a study guide titled *Discover Canada*[195] which contains information on Canada's history, geography, system of government, and other issues.

Applicants fourteen years or older must take a citizenship oath, which reads: "I swear (or affirm) that I will be faithful and bear true allegiance to Her Majesty Queen Elizabeth the Second, Queen of Canada, Her Heirs and Successors, and that I will faithfully observe the laws of Canada and fulfil my duties as a Canadian citizen."[196] The requirement to swear allegiance to the Queen was challenged as violating the freedom of conscience, religion, and expression as well as equality under the *Charter*.[197] However, courts did not find a violation. In the most recent decision, the Ontario Court of Appeal concluded that swearing allegiance to the Queen symbolizes commitment to Canada's

---

193 *Ibid*, s 5(1)(c).

194 *Ibid*, s 5(1)(c)(iii).

195 For the text of the guide, see online: www.cic.gc.ca/english/resources/publications/discover/index.asp.

196 *Citizenship Act*, above note 192, s 24.

197 *Roach v Canada (Minister of State for Multiculturalism and Culture)*, [1992] 2 FC 173 (TD) aff'd [1994] 2 FC 406 (CA); *McAteer v Canada (Attorney General)*, 2014 ONCA 578 [*McAteer*].

form of government and its democratic principles (the reference to the Queen in the oath is a reference to Canada's form of government).[198] The purpose of the oath is to inquire into an individual's commitment to Canada's form of government, not to compel expression. Further, it is possible for an individual to subsequently recant the objectionable elements of the oath without there being any effect on the applicant's citizenship status.[199] Similar reasoning was applied to dismiss the rest of the claim in relation to violation of freedom of conscience and religion as well as equality.

Some persons cannot be granted citizenship or be allowed to take a citizenship oath even if they meet the above requirements. These include persons who are in prison, on parole, or on probation in Canada; persons serving a sentence outside Canada; persons charged with or on trial for an indictable offence in Canada or an offence outside Canada; persons who have been convicted of an indictable offence in Canada or an offence outside Canada in the four years preceding application for citizenship; persons convicted of specified offences (war crimes, crime against humanity, genocide, treason, terrorism, certain offences under the *National Defence Act* and *Security of Information Act*); and persons who served as members of an armed force or of an organized armed group that was engaged in an armed conflict with Canada.[200]

The 2014 changes to the *Citizenship Act* introduced new grounds for revocation of citizenship. In the past, it could be revoked only from naturalized citizens and only on the basis of fraud, false representations, or knowingly concealing material circumstances. Currently, additional grounds include conviction of specified offences[201] (treason, terrorism, certain offences under the *National Defence Act* and *Security of Information Act*) and where the Minister has reasonable grounds to believe

198 *Ibid.*

199 For example, one of the applicants in *McAteer* held strong republican views and argued that the oath compelled him to convey a message with which he disagrees as well as constrains his future expression by precluding him from working towards the abolition of the monarchy. In fact, a plaintiff in previous citizenship oath litigation — Charles Roach — and one of the litigants in the *McAteer* challenge have disavowed their citizenship oaths. See Colin Perkel, "Man Set to Recant Oath to the Queen Right after Citizenship Ceremony" *The Globe and Mail* (29 November 2015), online: www.theglobeandmail.com/news/national/man-set-to-recant-oath-to-the-queen-right-after-citizenship-ceremony/article27521591/.

200 *Citizenship Act*, above note 192, s 22.

201 *Ibid*, s 10(2). The provision requires that, in addition to having been convicted of these offences, the person has been sentenced to imprisonment of specified length (at least five years or life, depending on the offence).

that a person served as a member of an armed force or of an organized armed group that was engaged in an armed conflict with Canada.[202] The Conservative government was quick to start using these provisions in relation to several persons convicted of terrorism.[203]

In has been noted that increased language and other requirements created new barriers to citizenship.[204] In February 2016, the new Liberal government introduced Bill C-6 that aims to reduce barriers to citizenship, in part, by rolling back some of the 2014 amendments.[205] As of March 2017, the Bill was still before Parliament and it is unknown when it will reach the final stage.

D. CONCLUSION

This chapter provided an overview of the main categories of status under Canadian immigration and refugee law. As a result of the changes to refugee and citizenship laws over the past several years, these categories have become more complex and less secure. Individuals may simultaneously be members of more than one category and will, over time, move between categories. The category an individual is in at any given moment largely defines the scope of his entitlements. These entitlements are both individually and cumulatively significant: for example, while the right to receive financial support from the government is inherently beneficial, it also assists an individual in pursuing her refugee claim and the related exercise of her right to non-*refoulement*. Without funds, a refugee claimant may not be able to retain counsel in situations where legal aid is not forthcoming and/or may not be able to devote time and energy to the pursuit of the claim. Thus, while these entitlements are described individually, they should be understood as providing a web of protection for individuals in Canada. Deficiencies

202 *Ibid*, s 10.1(2).

203 The Canadian Press, "Toronto 18's Zakaria Amara among 1st to Lose Citizenship under Bill C-24" *CBC News* (26 September 2015), online: www.cbc.ca/1.3245319.

204 Canadian Council for Refugees, "Barriers to Citizenship for Newcomers to Canada" (2014), online: CCR http://ccrweb.ca/en/barriers-citizenship; Anna Korteweg, "Citizenship Research Synthesis 2009–2013," online: http://ceris.ca/wp-content/uploads/2015/01/CERIS-Research-Synthesis-on-Citizenship.pdf.

205 Katharine Starr, "Changes Coming Soon to Citizenship Act, John McCallum Says," *CBC News* (18 February 2016), online: www.cbc.ca/1.3453658. This bill received second reading in the Senate 15 December 2016.

in any part of the web lead to weakening of the overall effectiveness of the system.

This chapter has also highlighted some of the enduring themes of refugee law which will be reiterated and examined in the subsequent parts of this book: the existence of hierarchies of membership; the different scopes of rights accorded to individuals depending on the type of their formal membership in a Canadian society; and the existence of varying provincial, national, and international approaches to the rights and entitlements of non-citizens.

CHAPTER 4

THE DEFINITION OF CONVENTION REFUGEE

A. INTRODUCTION

This chapter seeks to outline the definition of "Convention refugee" that lies at the heart of Canadian refugee law. As will be seen, the definition has been influenced by its origin in the *Convention Relating to the Status of Refugees*[1] and by subsequent developments in international law. In addition, the Canadian interpretation of the definition is informed by the jurisprudence applying identical or similar definitions of other countries that also offer protection to refugees.

But ultimately, the Canadian definition of refugee is just that: Canadian. It is most significantly informed, and ultimately governed, by a mass of domestic jurisprudence, ranging from the thousands of reported decisions by the first-instance decision makers of the Immigration and Refugee Board (IRB) to the countless decisions by the Federal Court and the Federal Court of Appeal and more than two dozen decisions of the Supreme Court on matters related to refugees. It is impossible to comprehensively summarize this mass of jurisprudence here. Instead, this chapter seeks simply to provide an outline of the elements of the definition and an overview of the debates that continue in the jurisprudence concerning their interpretation.

1 28 July 1951, 189 UNTS 150 [*Refugee Convention*].

B. TREATY AND STATUTORY DEFINITION

The definition of "refugee" in Canadian law is based on the definition adopted by the international community in the *Refugee Convention* which defines a refugee as a person who

> [a]s a result of events occurring before 1 January 1951 and owing to well-founded fear of being persecuted for reasons of race, religion, nationality, membership of a particular social group or political opinion, is outside the country of his nationality and is unable or, owing to such fear, is unwilling to avail himself of the protection of that country; or who, not having a nationality and being outside the country of his former habitual residence as a result of such events, is unable or, owing to such fear, is unwilling to return to it.[2]

Canada has adopted the essential elements of this definition into domestic law through the *Immigration and Refugee Protection Act*, section 96. Although worded slightly differently, the Canadian definition of "Convention refugee"[3] is equivalent to that set out in article 1A(2) of the *Refugee Convention* without its temporal limitation.[4] As noted previously, the temporal limitation was largely removed from international law by the *Refugee Protocol* of 1967[5] and does not exist in Canadian law.

---

2 *Ibid*, art 1A(2).

3 SC 2001, c 27, s 96 [*IRPA*].

> A Convention refugee is a person who, by reason of a well-founded fear of persecution for reasons of race, religion, nationality, membership in a particular social group or political opinion,
>
> (a) is outside each of their countries of nationality and is unable or, by reason of that fear, unwilling to avail themself of the protection of each of those countries; or
>
> (b) not having a country of nationality, is outside the country of their former habitual residence and is unable or, by reason of that fear, unwilling to return to that country.

4 The most obvious difference in wording between the two definitions relates to the mention in s 96 of "each of their countries of nationality" (as opposed to "the country of nationality" in art 1A(2)). However, this apparent difference is resolved in a later paragraph of art 1A(2), which states "the term 'the country of his nationality' shall mean each of the countries of which he is a national." Perhaps the most notable difference between the Canadian and *Refugee Convention* definitions of refugee has to do with the omission of exclusion from the Canadian definition on the basis of art 1D. For a fuller discussion of this issue and exclusion more generally, see Chapter 5.

5 31 January 1967, 606 UNTS 267 [*Refugee Protocol*].

The definition of Convention refugee is derived from an international treaty to which Canada has committed itself. As such, general principles of interpretation of international law provide the starting point of any interpretation of what the definition means.[6] Although it is beyond the scope of this book to provide a full explanation of these principles, the negotiating history of the *Refugee Convention*, the behaviour of other parties to the *Refugee Convention*, and the position of the United Nations High Commissioner for Refugees (UNHCR) serve as important considerations in interpreting the definition.

Judicial pronouncements on the meaning of "Convention refugee" made in other jurisdictions that are parties to the *Refugee Convention* can also be used to inform the interpretation of the term in Canada. It is this aspect of the interpretation of the definition which is particularly remarkable and is arguably peculiar to the field of refugee law.[7] Due to the increased volume and availability of decisions concerning what the definition means, especially over the last decade, a genuinely transnational jurisprudence on the meaning of "Convention refugee" has emerged. The decision makers in Canada have played an active role in the development of this jurisprudence. Canadian decisions, from those of the Refugee Protection Division (RPD) to those of the Supreme Court of Canada, are widely cited by decision makers in other jurisdictions. Equally, Canadian decision makers frequently refer to decisions elsewhere, particularly in other common law jurisdictions.[8]

The coincidental, if not deliberate, goal of this process is the increasingly uniform interpretation of the meaning of "Convention refugee." As stated most clearly by the Federal Court of Australia in the matter of *Rocklea Spinning Mills Pty Ltd v Anti-dumping Authority*,[9] the common interpretation of a treaty is inherent in its function as a treaty:

> [I]t is obviously desirable that expressions used in international agreements should be construed so far as possible in a uniform and

6 These principles are set out in the *Vienna Convention on the Law of Treaties*.

7 For a fuller discussion of the development (and limitations) of transnational refugee law in the European context, see Guy Goodwin-Gill & Hélène Lambert, eds, *The Limits of Transnational Law Refugee Law, Policy Harmonization and Judicial Dialogue in the European Union* (Cambridge: Cambridge University Press, 2013).

8 For example, the recent decision by the Supreme Court in *Febles v Canada (Citizenship and Immigration)*, 2014 SCC 68 (concerning exclusion from protection as a refugee), made reference to judgments by the national courts of Australia, Belgium, Canada, France, Germany, and New Zealand and the regional court of the European Union.

9 (1995), 56 FCR 406 (Austl).

> consistent manner . . . to avoid a multitude of divergent approaches in the territories of the contracting parties on the same subject matter.

Although commenting on a different treaty, this approach has increasingly been adopted by courts, including Canadian courts, in interpreting the meaning of "Convention refugee."[10] Jurisprudence from other jurisdictions is invariably a central consideration in the Canadian interpretation of the definition. However, the consideration of foreign jurisprudence comes with an obvious caveat: while the jurisprudence of other countries is regularly used to fill in the lacunae of Canadian refugee law, it will never outweigh binding domestic precedent.

C. LIMITATIONS OF THE DEFINITION AND ALTERNATIVE DEFINITIONS

When originally negotiated, the *Refugee Convention* was limited in application to refugees who were displaced due to "events occurring in Europe before I January 1951."[11] This distinction has largely disappeared since the negotiation of the *Refugee Protocol* in 1967 which extended protection to refugees displaced without temporal or geographic limitation. However, even without these limitations, the definition of "refugee" can be quite restrictive and is certainly much narrower than the colloquial usage of the term.

In response to the restrictions of the definition, various countries and regions have tried to reformulate the definition. One of the earliest such attempts was by the Organization of African Unity (OAU). In 1969, the OAU *Convention Governing the Specific Aspects of Refugee Problems in Africa* defined refugees as also including

> every person who, owing to external aggression, occupation, foreign domination or events seriously disturbing public order in either part or the whole of his country of origin or nationality, is compelled to leave his place of habitual residence in order to seek refuge in another place outside his country of origin or nationality.[12]

---

10 *R v Secretary of State for the Home Department ex parte Adan*, [2001] 2 AC 477 (HL); and *Sepet and Another v Secretary of State for the Home Department (Respondent)*, [2003] UKHL 15 [*Sepet*].

11 *Refugee Convention*, above note 1, art 1(B)(1).

12 Article 1(2) of the *Convention Governing the Specific Aspects of Refugee Problems in Africa*, 20 June 1974, 1001 UNTS 45.

More recently, the Organization of American States (OAS) issued the *Cartagena Declaration* which contained a similar expanded definition of "refugee."[13] While Canada is an OAS member, it has not explicitly endorsed the provisions of the *Cartagena Declaration*.[14]

UNHCR has not been unaffected by this trend towards a broader interpretation of the term "refugee." Its own mandate has gradually expanded to include not only refugees within the meaning of the *Refugee Convention* but also refugees within the meaning of the OAU Convention and the OAS *Cartagena Declaration*. In addition, it has a mandate to offer protection to a plethora of other "individuals of concern." These "individuals of concern" now include the stateless, the internally displaced, and other groups in need of humanitarian assistance. At present, there are more "persons of concern" receiving protection from UNHCR who fall outside the definition of refugee in the *Refugee Convention* than those who fall within the definition.[15]

While Canada continues to apply the definition set out in the *Refugee Convention*, it has also been offering protection to broader categories of individuals who do not fall strictly within the definition of "Convention refugee." Canada's overseas refugee resettlement program already offers protection to individuals who are not formally Convention refugees. In the inland process, the *IRPA* has expanded the RPD's jurisdiction to include the ability to offer protection to individuals fearing various serious human rights violations upon return to their country of

13 *Cartagena Declaration on Refugees*, 22 November 1984, Annual Report of the Inter-American Commission on Human Rights, OAS Doc OEA/Ser.L/V/II.66/doc.10, rev. 1 at 190–93 (1984–85) [*Cartagena Declaration*].

14 The *Cartagena Declaration* has been praised by UNHCR and in December 2014, twenty-eight countries and three territories of Latin America and the Caribbean met in Brasilia on the thirtieth anniversary of the 1984 *Cartagena Declaration* to reaffirm their commitment to it and its full implementation into domestic law. A majority of Latin American states have either incorporated the *Cartagena Declaration* into domestic law or apply it on a de facto basis. For more information on the current discussions concerning the *Cartagena Declaration*, see "A Framework for Cooperation and Regional Solidarity to Strengthen the International Protection of Refugees, Displaced and Stateless Persons in Latin America and the Caribbean" (Brasilia, 3 December 2014), online: www.acnur.org/cartagena30/en.

15 Statistics from UNHCR for 2014 indicate that Convention refugees represent 14.4 million (25 percent) of the 59.5 million forcibly displaced persons in the world. UNHCR anticipates that, in 2016 and 2017, 16.5 million (30 percent) out of 54.9 million persons of concern to UNHCR will be refugees, asylum seekers, or recently repatriated refugees: UNHCR, *Statistical Yearbook 2014*, 14th ed (2015), online: www.unhcr.org/statistics/country/566584fc9/unhcr-statistical-yearbook-2014-14th-edition.html; and UNHCR, *Global Appeal 2016–2017*, online: www.unhcr.org/ga16/index.xml.

reference ("persons in need of protection" under section 97 of the *IRPA*). These aspects of the expanded scope of protection will be discussed in detail in Chapters 6 (Persons in Need of Protection) and 7 (Overseas Protection).

D. BURDEN OF PROOF

The legal burden of proof is on a refugee claimant to establish that she falls within the definition of Convention refugee.[16] The satisfaction of the legal burden of proof is affected by various evidentiary presumptions at play. These two issues will be discussed in more detail below.

1) Legal Burden of Proof

This burden flows from the general proposition in international law that an individual seeking admission to a state must justify his admission.[17] Satisfaction of each component of the definition must be proven on a balance of probabilities. The discharge of the burden of proof can be assisted or hampered by the operation of various evidentiary presumptions, such as the presumption of state protection.

However, that each element must be proven on a balance of probabilities does not entail that each element requires proof of every fact on a balance of probabilities. The discharge of the burden of proof and the requirements of each component of the definition are analytically discrete; the Federal Court of Appeal has cautioned that the "standard of proof" must be differentiated from the "legal test to be met."[18] For example, the requirement of an objectively well-founded fear of persecution is that there be more than "a serious possibility" of persecution.[19] Discharge of the burden of proof of this element does not require proof that persecution will occur on a balance of probabilities; rather, it requires proof on a balance of probabilities that there is more likely than not a serious possibility of persecution.

---

16 Conversely, the burden of proof on exclusion rests with the government. For further discussion, please see Chapter 5.

17 Lassa Oppenheim, *Oppenheim's International Law*, 7th ed by Hersch Lauterpacht (London: Longmans Green, 1952) at 616. In the context of refugees, see Paul Weis, "Legal Aspects of the *Convention Relating to the Status of Refugees*" (1953) 30 *British Yearbook of International Law* 478 at 481.

18 *Li v Canada (Minister of Citizenship and Immigration)*, 2005 FCA 1 at para 10.

19 *Adjei v Canada (Minister of Employment and Immigration)*, [1989] 2 FC 680 (CA).

2) Evidentiary Presumptions

The legal burden of proof must be distinguished from the evidentiary presumptions that exist in refugee law. Various pieces of evidence may create or rebut presumptions of proof with respect to a particular fact. For example, the production of a passport may lead to the evidentiary presumption of citizenship.[20] A subsequent declaration from a consular official may rebut this evidentiary presumption. While the evidentiary burden with respect to proof of a particular fact may shift, the overall legal burden remains with the refugee claimant. At the end of the hearing, a refugee claimant must have established all required elements of her claim on a balance of probabilities.

A refugee claimant will typically seek to discharge the evidentiary burden of proof through his testimony about particular facts. Refugee proceedings are characterized by their reliance on the testimony of refugee claimants. While other types of proceedings rely heavily upon witnesses, it is rare for legal proceedings to rely so heavily on the testimony of a single witness. However, even accepting such testimony, it is often difficult for a refugee to establish all facts material to her claim — particularly those facts that relate to the general conditions in the country of reference to individuals such as the claimant. In recognition of the difficulty that refugee claimants face, the Canadian courts have adopted the "flexible" approach of the UNHCR *Handbook on Procedures and Criteria for Determining Refugee Status under the 1951 Convention and the 1967 Protocol*:

> Often, however, an applicant may not be able to support his statements by documentary or other proof, and cases in which an applicant can provide evidence of all his statements will be the exception rather than the rule. In most cases a person fleeing from persecution will have arrived with the barest necessities and very frequently even without personal documents. Thus, while the burden of proof in principle rests on the applicant, the duty to ascertain and evaluate all the relevant facts is shared between the applicant and the examiner. Indeed, in some cases, it may be for the examiner to use all the means at his disposal to produce the necessary evidence in support of the application.[21]

In practice, this flexible approach means that decision makers typically gather documentary evidence about the general conditions in

20 *Rodrik v Canada (Minister of Citizenship and Immigration)*, 2015 FC 654.

21 HCR/IP/4/Eng/rev.1 (1979; re-edited January 1992) at para 195 [UNHCR *Handbook*].

a refugee claimant's country of reference. It also means that decision makers may seek confirmation of specific facts or may conduct research about the general risk to refugee claimants in particular categories; the Research Directorate of the Immigration and Refugee Board, which responds to "information requests," is an example of this practice.[22]

3) Statutory Provisions Concerning the Burden of Proof

The burden of proof is influenced by statute. The *IRPA* reinforces the burden of proof upon refugee claimants, particularly concerning their identity. The *IRPA* reiterates that a refugee claimant must "produce all documents and information as required by the rules of the Board."[23] The failure to produce such documents as required may affect aspects of the claim beyond those with which the documents are concerned.[24]

With respect to identity, the *IRPA* requires the Board to take into account with respect to the credibility of a claimant

> whether the claimant possesses acceptable documentation establishing identity, and if not, whether they have provided a reasonable explanation for the lack of documentation or have taken reasonable steps to obtain the documentation.[25]

Notwithstanding this statutory requirement of evidence of identity, this provision is rarely used in isolation to deny a refugee claimant's claim.[26] Furthermore, it is to be read very narrowly as applying only to a claimant's own identity documents and only insofar as the claimant's own identity is in dispute.[27]

The issue of the identity of a refugee claimant is intertwined with most other aspects of her claim: the country of reference, her past persecution, and her well-founded fear. It is also intertwined with pub-

---

22 For more information, please see IRB's Research Program, online: IRB www.irb-cisr.gc.ca/Eng/ResRec/Pages/index.aspx.

23 *IRPA*, above note 3, s 106.

24 The most obvious way in which the failure to produce documents can affect unrelated aspects of a claim is through an adverse finding of credibility based on the (disbelieved) explanation for the failure to produce documents.

25 *IRPA*, above note 3, s 106. See also s 100(4) which imposes a general duty on a refugee claimant, upon referral to the Board, to "produce all documents and information as required by the rules of the Board."

26 A typical analysis wherein s 106 is used to support specific and general findings of non-credibility can be found in *RHQ (Re)*, [2003] RPDD No 99 (IRB). A critique of the at-times overzealous use of s 106 can be found in *PK v Canada (Minister of Citizenship and Immigration)*, 2005 FC 103.

27 *Kosta v Canada (Minister of Citizenship and Immigration)*, 2005 FC 994.

lic anxiety about refugees. A refugee claimant without an established identity is increasingly likely to be presumed to be a threat and subject to detention.[28] As indicated earlier in this chapter, the issue of identity has received particular attention when it comes to the burden of proof. In many ways, the establishment of a claimant's identity is a threshold issue — it is a necessary condition for a successful refugee claim.

A claimant may obviously testify to his identity. Documentary evidence, including not only identity documents but photographs and other ephemera of life, may also be tendered. In addition, friends, family, and acquaintances may testify as to his identity. Linguists, community members, and religious leaders may also provide evidence of aspects of the claimant's identity, including religious beliefs and ethnic or linguistic community. The Board may also seek to "test" the claimant's knowledge of facts that should be known to an individual of his putative identity.

Where the claimant presents identity documents issued by a government (typically that of the country of reference), the documents provide *prima facie* proof of her identity.[29] However, the presumed validity and accuracy of the documents may be rebutted by other evidence impeaching the validity of the documents and by serious inconsistencies, omissions, and contradictions on the face of the documents.[30] Although expert evidence may be used to impeach the validity of an identity document, it is not required.[31] The mere presence or absence of photographs on the identity document does not determine a document's validity; documents without pictures still have residual probative value.[32]

E. COUNTRY OF REFERENCE

The risk alleged by a refugee claimant must be judged against his "country of nationality." Where an individual is stateless, the country of his

28 An inability to establish identity is grounds for arrest and detention under both *IRPA*, above note 3, ss 55(2)(b) and 58(1)(d). For further discussion of the detention of refugee claimants, see Chapter 11.

29 *Ramalingam v Canada (Minister of Citizenship and Immigration)*, [1998] FCJ No 10 at para 5 (TD); *Kathirkamu v Canada (Minister of Citizenship and Immigration)*, 2003 FCT 409 [*Kathirkamu*].

30 *RKL v Canada (Minister of Citizenship and Immigration)*, 2003 FCT 116 at para 11.

31 *Allouche v Canada (Minister of Citizenship and Immigration)*, [2000] FCJ No 339 at para 5 (TD).

32 *Kathirkamu*, above note 29 at para 34.

"former habitual residence" will be the focus of analysis of risk. The interpretation of these terms has been the subject of much jurisprudence. The terms will be collectively described as the "country of reference."[33]

The country of reference must be distinguished from the country to which the claimant may be returned. The *Regulations* set out broad criteria for identifying countries to which a claimant may be removed, including various countries through which she transited before arriving in Canada.[34] Thus, although a refugee claimant may have his fear of persecution assessed by the Refugee Protection Division against the country of his nationality, he may be removed to a completely different country. This discrepancy is mitigated somewhat by the existence of a pre-removal risk assessment (PRRA) once the country of removal has been determined. However, the consequences of the discrepancy between country of reference and country of removal have yet to be fully explored in the jurisprudence.

1) Country of Nationality

The country of reference is usually the country of nationality of a refugee claimant. "Nationality" has been interpreted quite narrowly as "citizenship."[35] In most cases, the country of reference will be uncontroversial. Most refugees possess only one country of nationality and have resided in that country for most or all of their lives.

The peculiar characteristics of the law of nationality make the task of formally establishing the country of nationality quite formidable. The definition of "nationality" is solely a matter of domestic law. It is frequently regulated by both constitutional and statutory means and, like any type of law, changes over time. To obtain a completely accurate determination of an individual's nationality, her status must be at the very least "traced" from the time of birth to the present day. In states where nationality is determined by descent, the tracing may need to predate the birth of the individual (that is, be conducted upon the in-

---

33 The singular usage of this term has been chosen for convenience. As will be seen, there are many situations where there are "countries" of reference.

34 Unsuccessful refugee claimants may be removed, according to *Immigration and Refugee Protection Regulations*, SOR/2002-227, s 241 [*Regulations*], to any of the following countries: the country from which they came to Canada; the country in which they last permanently resided before coming to Canada; a country of which they are a national or citizen; the country of their birth; or, in the absence of any of the foregoing countries being willing to accept the individual, "any country that will authorize entry within a reasonable time."

35 *Hanukashvili v Canada*, [1997] FCJ No 356 (TD) [*Hanukashvili*].

dividual's parents).[36] At every change in the law of nationality of the prospective country of nationality, the status of the individual must be re-evaluated. This may also require examining the nationality laws of successor states.

Such a process is time consuming and requires grounding in the interpretive peculiarities of the law of the country of prospective nationality. As a result, decision makers and claimants more often seek to rely upon documentary proof of nationality. An original passport will generally provide *prima facie* proof of nationality.[37] More generally, the caselaw asserts that "birth in a country can create a rebuttable presumption that the claimant is a national of that country."[38] This general presumption is rooted in a parochial importance of the place of birth in Canadian citizenship law[39] and ignores divergent practice in other countries. In countries that follow the principle of *jus solis*, proof of birth in the country will provide evidence of nationality. However, in countries that follow the principle of *jus sanguinis*, proof of the nationality of the claimant's parents is required to provide evidence of nationality.

While in most refugee claims, proof of identity is dealt with in a rather perfunctory manner, in a small number it can become very problematic.[40] Incomplete documents and the absence of original documents may lead to adverse inferences by the Board.[41] In some cases, the evidence of consular officials regarding the nationality of the claimant may be required.[42]

---

36 See *Lobaina v Canada (Minister of Citizenship and Immigration)*, 2006 FC 369 [*Lobaina*], for a case where the failure to adequately trace the nationality of a parent led to the court overturning the Board's decision.

37 *Adar v Canada (Minister of Citizenship and Immigration)*, [1997] FCJ No 695 at para 14 (TD); *Mathews v Canada (Minister of Citizenship and Immigration)*, 2003 FC 1387 at para 11; for a situation where the possession of a passport was not found to indicate nationality, see *Karsoua v Canada (Minister of Citizenship and Immigration)*, 2007 FC 58.

38 *Sviridov v Canada (Minister of Citizenship and Immigration)*, [1995] FCJ No 159 (TD); *QTT (Re)*, [2010] RPDD No 5 (IRB).

39 In Canadian citizenship law, persons born in Canada are generally entitled to citizenship. Children born abroad may obtain Canadian citizenship through their parents, but it is limited to the first generation born abroad: *Citizenship Act*, RSC 1985, c C-29, ss 3(1)(a) & (b), and 3(3).

40 The perfunctory manner with which the country of reference is dealt is typified by the following boilerplate and solitary reference to identity in many RPD decisions: "The claimant presented a [passport, birth certificate] as proof of identity."

41 Although photocopies and incomplete documents may not be rejected capriciously: *Rasheed v Canada (Minister of Citizenship and Immigration)*, 2004 FC 587.

42 See, for example, *T(VF) (Re)*, [1993] CRDD No 197 (IRB), and *JZQ (Re)*, [2003] RPDD No 184 (IRB), on general information provided by consular officials; and

a) Multiple Nationalities

An individual may have more than one country of nationality. In such a case, there may be more than one country of reference. Where an individual has several countries of nationality, his risk must be judged against each country separately.[43] It is in the interests of a claimant to limit her countries of reference. Thus, the jurisprudence often sees cases where the RPD (and, at times, the Minister's representative) alleges, and the claimant denies, a second or third nationality.[44]

The analysis is made more complicated by the factors noted above in relation to the determination of nationality. A further difficulty is posed by the interpretation and application of the still frequent prohibitions on multiple nationalities in the nationality laws of various states. The analysis of multiple nationalities (like the analysis of "single" nationality) is almost always concerned with "formal" nationality. Once the nationalities are established, the analysis proceeds to determine whether the requirements of the definition of "refugee" are satisfied with respect to each country of reference. The caveat to this statement can be found in a small number of cases where it was alleged that the "formal" nationality of at least one of the countries of nationality was illusory and did not constitute "effective" nationality.[45] However, in order to be successful, such an argument must be founded upon a risk in the country of nationality of being returned to another country of nationality in which the claimant would be in danger.[46] At first sight, such a factual situation seems to go against the very idea of nationality.[47]

L(DC) (Re), [1993] CRDD No 29 (IRB), and *RHQ (Re)*, [2003] RPDD No 99 (IRB), on claimant-specific or claimant-initiated enquiries to consular officials.

43 This is inherent in the wording of the definition of "Convention refugee" found in the *IRPA*, above note 3, s 96(a). See also the *Refugee Convention*, above note 1, art 1(A)(2); and *Canada (Minister of Employment and Immigration) v Akl*, [1990] FCJ No 254 (CA).

44 At its extreme, a claimant may deny any country of nationality (alleging statelessness).

45 *OM (Designated Representative) v Canada (Minister of Citizenship and Immigration)*, [1996] FCJ No 790 (TD) [*OM*]; for the analysis concerning countries of reference for stateless claimants, see *Thabet v Canada (Minister of Citizenship and Immigration)*, [1998] FCJ No 629 (CA) [*Thabet*].

46 *OM*, above note 45 at para 12 *et seq* (quoting with approval James C Hathaway, *The Law of Refugee Status* (Toronto: Butterworths, 1991) at 59).

47 Such a situation is perhaps possible where there is close political connection between the two countries at issue, which may result in extradition or some other type of expulsion. The jurisprudence has yet to provide a clear example of formal, but ineffective nationality. Although not argued explicitly on this basis, see perhaps *Drozdov v Canada (Minister of Citizenship and Immigration)*, [1995]

b) Country of Prospective Nationality

In the context of the determination of the country of reference, a refugee claimant's nationality (or nationalities) will also include any prospective nationality which the claimant could nearly automatically acquire. Thus, where the acquisition of nationality is "within the control of the applicant," it will be considered as a country of reference.

Previous cases have used various terms to describe the ease with which a claimant may be able to acquire nationality in a country of prospective nationality: acquisition of citizenship in a "non-discretionary manner"[48] or acquisition by "mere formalities."[49] In *Williams v Canada (Minister of Citizenship and Immigration)*, the Federal Court of Appeal outlined the new "control" test for prospective nationality:

> The true test, in my view, is the following: if it is within the control of the applicant to acquire the citizenship of a country with respect to which he has no well-founded fear of persecution, the claim for refugee status will be denied. While words such as "acquisition of citizenship in a non-discretionary manner" or "by mere formalities" have been used, the test is better phrased in terms of "power within the control of the applicant" for it encompasses all sorts of situations, it prevents the introduction of a practice of "country shopping" which is incompatible with the "surrogate" dimension of international refugee protection recognized in *Ward* and it is not restricted, contrary to what counsel for the respondent has suggested, to mere technicalities such as filing appropriate documents.[50]

The control test does not represent a complete departure from previous conceptions of prospective nationality. Rather, it is simply a reformulation that centres on the personal ability of the claimant to acquire another nationality. Subsequent caselaw has found this test to be satisfied in situations where a refugee claimant has an "inherent right" to acquire citizenship[51] and where only a simple consular procedure is required.[52] However, the actual practice of a state, not simply

---

FCJ No 20 (TD), where the claimants feared loss of citizenship due to misrepresentation.

48 *Grygorian v Canada (Minister of Citizenship and Immigration)*, [1995] FCJ No 1608 at para 7 (TD).

49 *Bouianova v Canada (Minister of Employment and Immigration)*, [1993] FCJ No 576 at para 8 (TD).

50 [2005] FCJ No 603 at para 22 [*Williams*].

51 *MRA v Canada (Minister of Citizenship and Immigration)*, [2006] FCJ No 252 at para 9 (FC).

52 *Lobaina*, above note 36.

the wording of its laws, must be taken into consideration.[53] A past but now lapsed ability to acquire another nationality is not relevant for the determination of country of reference.[54] While a previously refused application for citizenship provides good evidence against a country of nationality, there is no requirement that a claimant make or have made an application for citizenship.[55]

Although the ability to acquire a prospective nationality will sometimes be the result of a conscious action of a refugee claimant (such as marriage), it will most likely be brought about due to the unconscious actions of his forebears. In some cases, the acquisition of prospective nationality can be brought about through the passage of legislation in a country with which the claimant and even her forebears have only a tenuous connection. In this last category of cases is the "Law of Return" of Israel which was for a while interpreted as conferring prospective nationality upon all Jews, whether or not they wished to immigrate to Israel.[56] Thus, Ukrainian Jews fleeing persecution in Ukraine were required to establish a well-founded fear of persecution in Israel as well as in Ukraine. In recent years, a more extensive analysis by the RPD of the application of Law of Return by Israel has convinced the RPD to more narrowly construe the law.[57] However, the cases on the Law of Return indicate both the difficulty and the importance of fully evaluating both the text of foreign nationality laws and their practical application.

More recently, a similar question arose in relation to North Koreans' access to South Korean citizenship. In *Kim v Canada (Minister of Citizenship and Immigration)*,[58] the Federal Court noted that while the claimant may have control over whether to apply for citizenship, it remains within the control of the state whether to grant citizenship. The

53 *Dolma v Canada (Minister of Citizenship and Immigration)*, 2015 FC 703 [*Dolma*].

54 Implied by the court in *Mijatovic v Canada (Minister of Citizenship and Immigration)*, [2006] FCJ No 860 at para 32 (FC). However, the past failure to apply for or acquire citizenship may possibly lead to questions regarding an individual's past subjective fear (and consequently her credibility); such an approach was rejected in *Basmenji v Canada (Minister of Citizenship and Immigration)*, [1998] FCJ No 39 (TD); and *Pavlov v Canada (Minister of Citizenship and Immigration)*, [2001] FCJ No 923 (TD).

55 *Dolma*, above note 53.

56 See *DAP (Re)*, [1997] CRDD No 58 (IRB), for an example of the analysis. This approach was particularly problematic as the Law of Return states that "the desire to settle in Israel is a requirement for immigration": *Katkova v Canada (Minister of Citizenship and Immigration)*, [1997] FCJ No 549 at para 5 (FC) [*Katkova*], a requirement that was glossed over in most of the CRDD jurisprudence at the time.

57 *Katkova*, *ibid*.

58 2010 FC 720 [*Kim*].

court concluded that it was not "automatic" or "within the control" of the applicants that they would receive South Korean citizenship; it was for state officials to determine, for example, if the applicants met the condition that they "will and desire" to live in South Korea.[59]

The assessment of countries of prospective nationality includes countries in which the acquisition of nationality may lead to the loss of another nationality. Thus, the mere fact that the acquisition of a prospective nationality will lead to the loss of another nationality does not prevent the Board from using it as a country of reference.[60] This recent development in the jurisprudence seems to conflict with the well-established proposition that the arbitrary loss of nationality is a violation of an individual's human rights.[61] On the facts of the cases thus far, however, the loss of nationality was not legally "arbitrary."[62] It remains to be seen whether the arbitrary loss of nationality as a result of an individual availing himself of a prospective nationality will prevent the country of prospective nationality from becoming a country of reference.[63]

2) Country of Former Habitual Residence

The country of reference of a stateless refugee claimant will be her "country of former habitual residence." This will also be the country

59 However, in 2016, the RAD departed from the conclusions in *Kim*, *ibid*. It noted that the Kim decision relied heavily on the 2008 IRB document on access to South Korean citizenship, the accuracy of which has been subsequently questioned. In light of new information, which confirmed that North Koreans are deemed to be citizens of South Korea, the RAD reached a different conclusion. *RAD File No TB4-05778*, [2014] RADD No 1335 (IRB). In December 2016, this decision was designated as a jurisprudential guide.

60 *Williams*, above note 50.

61 *Universal Declaration of Human Rights*, GA Res 217(III), UNGAOR, 3d Sess, Supp No 13, UN Doc A/810, (1948), art 15; *International Covenant on Civil and Political Rights*, 19 December 1966, 999 UNTS 171, art 5(d)(iii) [*ICCPR*]; and *Human Rights and Arbitrary Deprivation of Nationality*, 11 April 1997, CHR Res 1997/36, Supp No 3 UN Doc E/CN.4/1997/36, at 122.

62 In *Williams*, above note 50, the renunciation of already vested (Rwandan) nationality was required in order to acquire prospective (Ugandan) nationality. There was no evidence that this requirement was applied in an arbitrary or discriminatory manner. The case may also be distinguished based upon the possibility of the individual automatically reacquiring Rwandan citizenship in the future, should he so desire.

63 In the context of already acquired nationalities, this issue was argued (but not addressed) by the Federal Court in its decision in *De Sousa v Canada (Minister of Citizenship and Immigration)*, 2004 FC 267.

of reference for an individual whose nationality cannot be "clearly established."[64]

A country of habitual residence has been interpreted, as much as possible, along the same lines as a country of nationality:

> [T]he concept of "former habitual residence" seeks to establish a relationship to a state which is broadly comparable to that between a citizen and his or her country of nationality. Thus the term implies a situation where a stateless person was admitted to a given country with a view to continuing residence of some duration, without necessitating a minimum period of residence.[65]

Habitual residence has been understood as establishing a home or, more technically, making a place "his abode or the centre of his interests."[66] At the very least, it requires a physical presence in the country.[67] Hathaway has suggested that this entails a period of residence of at least one year (although the jurisprudence has been hesitant to accept such a formulistic approach). While the jurisprudence has not yet outlined the precise requirements of habitual residence, in *Maarouf v Canada (Minister of Employment and Immigration)*, the court also considered whether the person was admitted into the country for the purpose of continuing residence of some duration. In *Marchoud v Canada (Minister of Citizenship and Immigration)*, the court held that living in a country during one's childhood without any significant subsequent legal connection or physical visits does not constitute habitual residence.[68]

The *IRPA* refers to the country of habitual residence in the singular; there are no provisions dealing with multiple countries of former habitual residence (unlike multiple nationalities). Notwithstanding this statutory language, the jurisprudence has placed the stateless in a situation analogous to that of nationality: all countries of former habitual residence will be countries of reference. As the Federal Court of Appeal stated in *Thabet v Canada (Minister of Citizenship and Immigration)*:

> Where a claimant has two nationalities he or she does not have to show two separate instances of persecution. It will suffice to show

---

64 *Kochergo v Canada (Minister of Employment and Immigration)*, [1994] FCJ No 368 (TD). See also UNHCR *Handbook*, above note 21 at para 89.

65 *Maarouf v Canada (Minister of Employment and Immigration)*, [1993] FCJ No 1329 at para 38 (TD) [*Maarouf*].

66 Atle Grahl-Madsen, *The Status of Refugees in International Law* (Leyden: AW Sijthoff, 1966) vol 1 at 160 (quoted with approval in *Maarouf*, *ibid* at para 18).

67 *Kadoura v Canada (Minister of Citizenship and Immigration)*, 2003 FC 1057.

68 [2004] FCJ No 1786 (FC).

> that one state is guilty of persecution, but that both states are unable to protect the claimant. Likewise, where a claimant has been resident in more than one country it is not necessary to prove that there was persecution at the hands of all those countries. But it is necessary to demonstrate that one country was guilty of persecution, and that the claimant is unable or unwilling to return to any of the states where he or she formerly habitually resided . . . . Stateless people should be treated as analogously as possible with those who have more than one nationality.[69]

The somewhat convoluted result of this approach is that a stateless individual must (1) establish that she would suffer persecution in at least one country of former habitual residence, and (2) establish that she cannot return to any of her other countries of former habitual residence.[70]

Yet, unlike the case of a country of citizenship, a refugee claimant need not be able to be deported to his country of habitual residence: the ability (or lack thereof) to be admitted to a country does not determine whether the country qualifies as a country of habitual residence.[71] This somewhat absurd situation underscores the occasional detachment of Canadian refugee determination from reality. This approach entails that even if a persecuting state prevents a refugee from re-entering, it will remain a country of reference. Thus, a persecuting state may not frustrate a refugee claim by removing the right of re-entry. By disconnecting the real possibility of return from the analysis of country of reference, however, the analysis risks becoming overly abstract. As pointed out at the outset of this section, the country of reference and the country of removal are two different concepts in Canadian refugee law. However, the fact that the refugee claimant cannot be deported to his country of habitual residence may later assist him in establishing a well-founded fear of persecution insofar as the denial of admission to his country of habitual residence may be inherently persecutory.[72]

---

69 Above note 45 at paras 28 & 29.

70 *Ibid*. Applied in *Elbarbari v Canada (Minister of Citizenship and Immigration)*, [1998] FCJ No 1286 (TD), and in *Popov v Canada (Minister of Citizenship and Immigration)*, 2009 FC 898.

71 *Maarouf*, above note 65; *Shaat v Canada (Minister of Employment and Immigration)*, [1994] FCJ No 1149 (TD). The rationale behind this approach is that it allows an individual who is stateless to benefit from refugee protection and to cite the refusal to allow him to return to the country as an act of persecution; without this approach, a stateless individual may have no country of reference.

72 *Maarouf*, above note 65.

It should be noted that the determination of the country of reference for a stateless individual is quite different from that of an individual with one or more nationalities. In addition to this difference, there are several other significant differences between the treatment of the stateless and other refugee claimants in the application of the definition of Convention refugee.

F. WELL-FOUNDED FEAR

Embodied in the colloquial meaning of the term "refugee" is the concept of someone fleeing danger. The equivalent of this concept in the definition of Convention refugee is the requirement that a refugee claimant have a "well-founded fear." In the context of the definition, this fear of danger has been understood in two ways: (1) that there is an objective danger, and (2) that the refugee claimant possesses a personal fear. These elements of "well-founded fear" have been described as, respectively, the "objective" basis and the "subjective" basis of the claim. While this bifurcation of the analysis has been criticized by jurists,[73] it remains an accepted feature of qualification as a refugee under Canadian law.

1) Objective Basis

The phrase "well-founded fear" has been interpreted as containing an objective component. This objective component requires that a claimant establish a "serious possibility" of persecution in the country of reference. The nature of refugee protection is forward looking: it is designed to prevent a claimant from being returned to a country where she would suffer a risk of persecution in the future.[74] The objective component must be established as of the date of the hearing. As the objective component requires only the establishment of a risk of persecution (a "serious possibility"), all that must be established as of the date of the hearing is that the claimant might suffer persecution.

The objective basis of a claim cannot be determined in isolation from the other elements of the definition. In particular, the state's ability to

73 See Hilary Evans Cameron, "Risk Theory and 'Subjective Fear': The Role of Risk Perception, Assessment, and Management in Refugee Status Determinations" (2008) 20 *International Journal of Refugee Law* 567.

74 *Longia v Canada (Minister of Employment and Immigration)*, [1990] FCJ No 425 (CA).

protect the claimant should also be considered in assessing whether there is a serious possibility of the claimant suffering persecution. The Supreme Court has stated that "if a state is able to protect the claimant, then his or her fear is not, objectively speaking, well-founded."[75]

While the objective basis of the claim will generally be supported by "objective" sources (e.g., government reports, newspaper articles, NGO reports), there is no requirement that it be established only by such sources. For example, the testimony of the claimant may be used to establish the objective basis of the claim. Similarly, objective evidence may be used to establish the subjective basis of the claim.[76]

a) Level of Risk

A refugee claimant need not establish that there is a certainty of persecution. Conversely, a refugee claimant must provide evidence that his risk of persecution is real and not merely speculative. Between these two points is a "serious possibility of persecution." In short, the level of risk required is somewhat less than a civil standard of proof:

> "Good grounds" or "reasonable chance" is defined in *Adjei* as occupying the field between upper and lower limits; it is less than a 50 per cent chance (i.e., a probability), but more than a minimal or mere possibility. There is no intermediate ground: what falls between the two limits is "good grounds."[77]

The articulation of a precise level of risk has been hampered by use of various terms to describe the level of required risk: "a reasonable chance," "good grounds," "more than a minimal possibility," and "reasonable possibility." In addition, the precise calculation of risk is impossible. While the level of risk of persecution will never have a precise mathematical expression, both American and British jurisprudence have described it as falling somewhere between the "less than 10 percent" chance of occurring represented by pure speculation and the "51 percent" chance represented by a likelihood.[78]

---

75 *Canada (Attorney General) v Ward*, [1993] 2 SCR 689 at 712 [*Ward*].

76 *Lai v Canada (Minister of Employment and Immigration)* (1989), 8 Imm LR (2d) 245 at 246 (CA).

77 *Ponniah v Canada (Minister of Citizenship and Immigration)*, [1991] FCJ No 359 (CA).

78 *INS v Cardozo Fonseca*, 480 US 421 (1987). Quoted with approval by Lord Keith in *R v Secretary of State for the Home Department, ex parte Sivakumaran*, [1988] AC 958 (HL).

b) Past and Future Risk

The definition of "Convention refugee" has been described as "forward looking." A Convention refugee is someone who has a well-founded fear of persecution in the future. Past persecution need not have occurred; the absence of past persecution is not a bar to recognition as a Convention refugee.[79]

Past persecution is only important insofar as it may assist in establishing whether future persecution will occur. However, contrary to what has been said in some of the jurisprudence, there is no "rule" that past persecution will result in an automatic presumption of future persecution.

> [T]his claim is an example of a situation where one can accept that past persecution occurred without accepting that it will continue in the future. Consequently, the presumption of well foundedness of persecution depends upon more than proof of past persecution and lack of state protection. It requires one to assume that there is no valid reason why past conduct will not be repeated in the future.[80]

The Federal Court of Appeal has explicitly rejected the notion of a "rebuttable presumption" that a person has well-founded fear of being persecuted if she has already been the victim of persecution.[81] Absent evidence that the situation in the past continues to be the case, there can be no logical inference of future persecution. However, even with this caveat, past persecution can still be "a most effective means" of establishing future risk.[82]

Conversely, in some cases, the absence of past persecution may strongly suggest that no persecution is likely in the future inasmuch as common sense allows us to infer that the future will be similar to the past. Once again, however, this is the case only where both the claimant's actions and the country's conditions will be equivalent to the past in the future. Where a claimant was in hiding in the past, and as a result did not suffer persecution, but will not be in hiding in perpetuity,

---

79 *Salibian v Canada (Minister of Employment and Immigration)*, [1990] 3 FC 250 at 258 (CA).

80 *Sman v Canada (Minister of Citizenship and Immigration)*, 2002 FCT 891 at para 20 (quoted with approval in *Fernandopulle v Canada (Minister of Citizenship and Immigration)*, [2004] FCJ No 491 at para 9 (FC)).

81 *Fernandopulle v Canada (Minister of Citizenship and Immigration)*, 2005 FCA 91.

82 *Marchant v Canada (Minister of Employment and Immigration)*, [1982] 2 FC 779 (CA); *Saka v Canada (Minister of Citizenship and Immigration)*, [1996] FCJ No 1005 (TD); *Thevasagayam v Canada (Minister of Citizenship and Immigration)*, [1997] FCJ No 1406 (TD).

such an inference is inappropriate. Similarly, where a claimant's future activities will be materially different (either more public or less so), such an inference is also inappropriate.

c) Location of Risk

The required location of the risk to the refugee claimant in her country of reference has resulted in a plethora of caselaw. In short, the jurisprudence asks this question: "How widespread must be the risk in the claimant's country of reference in order for her to be allowed to gain protection in Canada?" The question can also be phrased in this way: "How small must the claimant's internal flight alternative, or IFA,[83] be before Canada can be required to offer protection?" The notion of IFA has been widely, but often quite differently, adopted in the practice of other states, though often using different terms: "internal relocation alternative," "relocation principle," and "internal protection alternative."[84]

Applying the idea that refugee protection is subsidiary to national protection, it would seem that wherever a claimant can find safety within his own country he will not qualify as a refugee. Until relatively recently, however, the caselaw suggested that such an individual could nonetheless qualify as a refugee if the IFA was unreasonable in the circumstances of the claimant.[85] The reasonableness of an IFA depended on the claimant's background, the ability of the claimant to settle in the new location, the presence of family in the putative IFA location, and many other considerations.

---

83 Hathaway has argued that the term "internal flight alternative" should be replaced with the term "internal protection alternative" in order to ensure that the enquiry focus on the issue of protection of the claimant; however, this book deliberately adopts the term "IFA" in recognition of its use in the Canadian jurisprudence (but without comment on the validity of Hathaway's argument about either nomenclature or analysis, neither of which has yet been embraced by the Canadian caselaw). See James C Hathaway "The Michigan Guidelines on the Internal Protection Alternative" (1999) 21 *Michigan Journal of International Law* 131.

84 See James C Hathaway & Michelle Foster, "Internal Protection/Relocation/Flight Alternative as an Aspect of Refugee Status Determination" in Erika Feller et al, eds, *Refugee Protection in International Law: UNHCR's Global Consultations on International Protection* (Cambridge: Cambridge University Press, 2003); and UNHCR, *Guidelines on International Protection: "Internal Flight or Relocation Alternative" within the Context of Article 1A(2) of the 1951 Convention and/or 1967 Protocol relating to the Status of Refugees*, HCR/GIP/03/04 (23 July 2003).

85 *Rasaratnam v Canada (Minister of Employment and Immigration)*, [1992] 1 FC 706 (CA).

In recent years, the reasonableness approach towards an IFA has been largely abandoned as the analysis of the IFA is integrated into the analysis of risk:

> First, the Board must be satisfied that there is no serious possibility of the claimant being persecuted in the IFA found to exist. Second, it must be objectively reasonable to expect a claimant to seek safety in the part of the country considered to be an IFA.[86]

While this approach makes reference to being "reasonable" in its second branch, the core issue is the safety of the claimant.

The first issue for any IFA is whether it would truly provide safety for the claimant. In relation to safety, the new location must not only remove the claimant's objective basis but must also not create a new objective basis; further, it must be realistically accessible to the claimant.[87] If the new location is accessible and safe, it will be presumed to be "reasonable" for the claimant to relocate to the IFA instead of seeking international protection.[88] A claimant may rebut this presumption and show that it would be unreasonable to expect her to seek safety in the IFA. However, the jurisprudence has found an IFA to be reasonable in the absence of "conditions which would jeopardize the life and safety of a claimant."[89] Despite the less generous approach to IFAs, the jurisprudence continues to require that any finding of an IFA be founded in a specified geographic location where prevailing conditions are clearly and precisely assessed in the context of the claimant's identity, including gender.[90] As with establishing the claim more generally, the burden in establishing a lack of an IFA lies with the claimant.[91]

2) Subjective Basis

The requirement of a subjective basis of the claim can be traced to the interpretation of the word "fear" in the definition of Convention refu-

---

86 *Zablon v Canada (Minister of Citizenship and Immigration)*, 2013 FC 58 at para 20 [*Zablon*].

87 *Thirunavukkarasu v Canada (Minister of Employment and Immigration)*, [1993] FCJ No 1172 (CA).

88 *Ibid.*

89 *Ranganathan v Canada (Minister of Citizenship and Immigration)*, [2001] 2 FC 164 at para 15 (CA).

90 *Rabbani v Canada (Minister of Citizenship and Immigration)* (1997), 125 FTR 141 at para 16 (TD); on the importance of considering gender, see *Syvyryn v Canada (Minister of Citizenship and Immigration)*, 2009 FC 1027.

91 *Zablon*, above note 86 at para 20; *Odurukwe v Canada (Minister of Citizenship and Immigration)*, 2015 FC 613 at para 44.

gee.[92] The doctrinal requirement of subjective fear has been questioned in the academic literature by leading jurists;[93] the empirical basis for many of the views expressed in the jurisprudence about the expected behaviour of those in fear has been similarly critiqued.[94] The act of making a refugee claim is an expression of subjective fear; similarly, the direct testimony of a claimant that she fears returning to the country of reference is *prima facie* proof of subjective fear.[95]

Claims are frequently refused by the RPD based on a lack of subjective fear by the claimant when what is missing is credibility rather than subjective fear. In some of these cases, subjective fear is used to dismiss the claims in order to avoid a longer analysis of the credibility of the claimant or his risk of persecution. In a particularly problematic subset of these cases, the lack of subjective fear, based upon unarticulated credibility concerns, is later tautologically used to support a finding of non-credibility. Overall, the concern over this fixation on subjective fear as a ground for denying refugee protection has been best expressed by Hugessen J:

> I find it hard to see in what circumstances it could be said that a person who, we must not forget, is by definition claiming refugee status could be right in fearing persecution and still be rejected because it is said that fear does not actually exist in his conscience. The definition of a refugee is certainly not designed to exclude brave or simply stupid persons in favour of those who are more timid or more intelligent.[96]

---

92 The element of subjective fear is absent from the definition of person in need of protection under the *IRPA*, s 97. *Ghasemian v Canada (Minister of Citizenship and Immigration)*, 2003 FC 1266.

93 For a critique of the requirement of subjective fear, see James C Hathaway & William S Hicks, "Is There a Subjective Element in the *Refugee Convention*'s Requirement of 'Well-Founded Fear'?" (2005) 26 *Michigan Journal of International Law* 505; and more recently, James Hathaway & Michelle Foster, *The Law of Refugee Status*, 2d ed (Cambridge: Cambridge University Press, 2014) at 92 *et seq*. For the jurisprudential requirement of subjective fear, see *Ward*, above note 75 at 723.

94 Cameron, above note 73.

95 *Parada v Canada (Minister of Citizenship and Immigration)*, [1995] FCJ No 353 (TD); *Hatami v Canada (Minister of Citizenship and Immigration)*, [2000] FCJ No 402 at para 25 (TD).

96 *Yusuf v Canada (Minister of Employment and Immigration)*, [1992] 1 FC 629 (CA); subsequently distinguished in *Tabet-Zatla v Canada (Minister of Citizenship and Immigration)*, [1999] FCJ No 1778 at para 6 (TD), and *Maqdassy v Canada (Minister of Citizenship and Immigration)*, 2002 FCT 182 at para 8; followed in *Balendra v Canada (Minister of Citizenship and Immigration)*, 2003 FC 1078.

The requirement of subjective fear, like all other requirements of the definition, must be satisfied at the time of the hearing.[97] Thus, even refugee claimants who have, in the past, failed to have a subjective fear may nonetheless have a subjective fear. Decision makers need to be alert to the fact that an otherwise unfearful or opportunistic claimant may develop a fear of persecution during her refugee status determination.

a) Timing of Claim

The timing of the making of a claim to refugee protection is often seen as an indicator of the presence, or absence, of subjective fear. The earlier the claim, the greater the fear; conversely, the later the claim, the lesser the fear. However, as most refugee claimants do not travel to Canada directly and most refugee claimants do not seek protection immediately upon their arrival in Canada, delay of some amount is present in almost all refugee claims in Canada.[98]

Although any delay must be understood in its own factual context, it can in the end contribute to a negative determination:

> The importance that one gives to this "relevant" element of delay depends on the circumstances of the case. The more inexplicable the delay, the greater the probability that subjective fear is absent. Sometimes the circumstances are such that the element not only is relevant but assumes a decisive role. In these circumstances, delay in making a refugee claim can be a decisive factor in turning down a claim . . . .[99]

Whether delay in and of itself can result in a negative decision is open to some debate. In its decision in *Huerta v Canada (Minister of Employment and Immigration)*, the Federal Court of Appeal suggested that delay "is not a decisive factor in itself" but is nonetheless "a relevant element which the tribunal may take into account in assessing

---

97 Technically, the requirements of the definition must be fulfilled at the time of the decision (declaration) that a refugee claimant is a Convention refugee. However, as the hearing effectively represents the last moment at which evidence is collected, the decision reflects the fulfillment (or lack thereof) of all elements of the definition at that time.

98 Historically, over the past decade, about half of all refugee claims have been made inland, which, by definition, signifies a period of time after the refugee claimants' arrival in Canada. Canadian Council for Refugees, "Closing the Front Door on Refugees: Report on the First Year of the *Safe Third Country Agreement*" (Montreal: CCR, 2005) at 3 (Table 1).

99 *VPV (Re)*, [2002] RPDD No 480 at para 13 (IRB).

both the statements and the actions and deeds of a claimant."[100] Subsequent caselaw seems to suggest that, in some cases, delay can in and of itself result in a finding of no subjective fear and hence a negative determination.[101] The more accurate formulation is that delay cannot be determinative, but a lack of subjective fear that is established (if only by delay) can in and of itself found a negative determination.[102] In simpler language, a lengthy delay can be determinative of the fact that the claimant has no subjective fear.[103] Nevertheless, while being a relevant factor to consider, the delay does not automatically mean the absence of subjective fear.[104] The circumstances and explanations for the delay must be considered.[105] For example, in *Gurung v Canada (Minister of Citizenship and Immigration)*, a Nepalese citizen fearing persecution by the Maoists came to Canada as a live-in caregiver and expected to eventually obtain permanent residence on that basis. Through no fault of her own, that option did not work out and she subsequently made a refugee claim. The Federal Court concluded that under these circumstances, her behaviour and delay in making a refugee claim could not be interpreted as showing lack of subjective fear.

In some cases, a refugee claimant will not have the capacity to have a subjective fear. Legally incapable adults can have their subjective fear expressed by their designated representative.[106] Although the Board and the courts have never explicitly discussed the subjective fear of children, it is presumably also derived from their designated representative (usually their parents).

With respect to the delay in making a claim, there are two scenarios that arise in refugee claims: (1) individuals who arrive in Canada after having passed through various countries en route to Canada

100 [1993] FCJ No 271 (CA); *Aragon v Canada (Minister of Citizenship and Immigration)*, 2008 FC 144.

101 *Duarte v Canada (Minister of Citizenship and Immigration)*, [2003] FCJ No 1259 at para 15 (FC); *Espinosa v Canada (Minister of Citizenship and Immigration)*, [2003] FCJ No 1680 at para 17 (FC).

102 The consequence of this formulation is that the Board cannot base a finding of no subjective fear upon delay *simpliciter*, but rather must cite evidence concerning the unreasonable delay. In the absence of such evidence (including an absence caused by a lack of enquiry by the Board), a finding of no subjective fear will be set aside: *Singh v Canada (Minister of Citizenship and Immigration)*, [2001] FCJ No 426 at para 8 (TD).

103 *DHW (Re)*, [2004] RPDD No 27 at para 21 (IRB).

104 *Gurung v Canada (Minister of Citizenship and Immigration)*, 2010 FC 1097.

105 *Ibid* at paras 21–23.

106 *Rosales v Canada (Minister of Employment and Immigration)*, [1993] FCJ No 1454 at para 14 (TD).

without seeking protection, and (2) individuals who, after arriving in Canada, allowed time to pass before seeking protection.[107] The nuances of each situation will be discussed in further detail below.

i) Failure to Claim Elsewhere

As noted at the outset of this section, most refugee claimants who arrive in Canada have passed through other countries before arriving in Canada. In some sense, the failure to claim elsewhere is an issue in all inland refugee claims. Generally, the failure to claim elsewhere is but a factor to be considered in determining a refugee claim, and, in particular, the presence or absence of subjective fear. It is not a bar to refugee protection:

> The fact that a person does not seize the first opportunity of claiming refugee status in a signatory country may be a relevant factor in assessing his or her credibility, but it does not thereby constitute a waiver of his or her right to claim that status in another country.[108]

The one exception to this proposition are refugee claimants who seek protection in Canada at a land border with the United States. Such claimants are covered by the *Safe Third Country Agreement* and their passage through the United States to Canada bars them from seeking protection in Canada. The *Safe Third Country Agreement* will be discussed in more detail in Chapter 8.

Although technically an issue in almost all refugee claims, failure to claim elsewhere will usually be dealt with in a fairly perfunctory manner as it can be easily explained. The inability to seek protection in a country is a complete answer to the charge of failing to claim elsewhere; such a failure is relevant only where there is evidence that protection would have been offered, such as by proof that the country is a signatory to the *Refugee Convention*.[109] Where a claimant honestly (and perhaps mistakenly) believes that he would not be able to seek protection in a country, the charge of failing to claim elsewhere is answered.[110] The time

---

107 Although the following discussion is phrased in terms of inland claims, the same analysis can technically be applied to individuals seeking refugee protection from Canada through the overseas process who have delayed in seeking protection. However, there has yet to be any jurisprudence indicating that this is frequently invoked as a basis for refusal in the overseas process.

108 *Gavryushenko v Canada (Minister of Citizenship and Immigration)*, [2000] FCJ No 1209 at para 11 (TD) [*Gavryushenko*].

109 *Tung v Canada (Minister of Employment and Immigration)*, [1991] FCJ No 292 (CA).

110 *Raveendran v Canada (Minister of Citizenship and Immigration)*, [2003] FCJ No 116 at para 29 (TD).

an individual spends in a country of transit and his risk of apprehension by authorities in that country (and consequently of being *refouled* to the country of reference) are also relevant considerations.

Similarly, the personal circumstances of the claimant in another country, including relative youth, inexperience, and absence of family, can provide a full explanation. Refugee claimants can receive advice from other individuals against claiming asylum in certain countries. Many refugee claimants have never travelled abroad and can hardly be expected to know how or where to claim protection; such claimants frequently have little personal autonomy while en route to Canada, having surrendered decision making to community leaders, family members, or smuggling agents. In all these cases, the delay caused by failure to claim elsewhere has been disregarded. In other cases, however, where relatively worldly refugee claimants spend periods of time in countries that are well known to be signatories to the *Refugee Convention*, the RPD and the Federal Court are much less forgiving.[111]

ii) Delay in Claiming upon Arrival

As with failure to claim elsewhere, delay in claiming is technically an issue in most refugee claims. A significant and unexplained delay upon arrival in Canada can in and of itself result in a lack of subjective basis:

> The delay in claiming refugee status, which is not explained, as in this case, is an important factor in determining the lack of a subjective fear of persecution. In my opinion, this factor alone was, in the circumstances, sufficient to allow the Refugee Division to reasonably infer that the applicant did not have a subjective fear of persecution in Algeria, and sufficient to result in the dismissal of his claim.[112]

Although, on the facts, the delay in this case was lengthy (thirty months after arrival in Canada), less lengthy delays have resulted in similar consequences for claimants.[113] It must be emphasized that even lengthy delays may be adequately explained, however; the Federal Court has quashed findings by the Board of a lack of subjective fear in cases where the delay has been up to fourteen years.[114] The personal

111 *Saleem v Canada (Minister of Citizenship and Immigration)*, 2005 FC 1412 (one month in the United States and the United Kingdom).

112 *Gamassi v Canada (Minister of Citizenship and Immigration)*, [2000] FCJ No 1841 at para 6 (TD) [references omitted].

113 *Bhandal v Canada (Minister of Citizenship and Immigration)*, 2006 FC 426 (twenty-one months).

114 *Robinson v Canada (Minister of Citizenship and Immigration)*, [2006] FCJ No 588 (FC).

circumstances of the refugee claimant must be assessed to determine whether she presents a credible account of the delay.[115] As with other factors considered in the analysis of subjective fear in the jurisprudence, delay in claiming has also been found to undermine a claimant's credibility.[116]

In *sur place* cases, where the fear of persecution arises after arrival in Canada, the relevant point for counting the period of delay is the inception of the fear rather than arrival in the country of asylum.[117]

b) Delay in Departure

A variation on the issue of delay in claiming upon arrival in Canada (or failure to seek protection elsewhere) is a delay in flight from the country of reference, in which the risk of persecution has emerged. In many ways, the basis of the analysis remains the same: the inconsistency between a subjective fear of persecution and a failure to flee the persecution. This common foundation is reflected in the fact that the jurisprudence on delay in departure often cross-references the caselaw on delay in claiming.[118] As with other aspects of delay, the Board need not explicitly flag the issue of delay in claiming as long as it brings its concerns to the attention of the claimant and provides him with an opportunity to respond to them.[119]

Unlike a delay in claiming, which is measured from a relatively precise moment (day of arrival), a delay in departure may be linked to a much more indeterminate event: the decision to flee one's country. This decision may not be linked to the first act of mistreatment, particularly where the mistreatment escalates over time and only in cumulative effect becomes persecutory. In such a case, delay in departure (or at least

---

115 The RPD must be "particularly alert and alive to the cultural context and to the need to properly and genuinely apply the *Chairperson's Guideline 4*, Women Refugee Claimants Fearing Gender-Related Persecution . . . .": *Charles v Canada (Minister of Citizenship and Immigration)*, 2007 FC 103 at para 14.

116 It is often left unclear whether the delay affects general credibility or simply credibility concerning subjective fear: *Ilie v Canada (Minister of Citizenship and Immigration)* (1994), 88 FTR 220 (TD); *Gavryushenko*, above note 108. More recent caselaw suggests that delay cannot be the sole basis for determining a claimant not to be generally credible: *Islam v Canada (Minister of Citizenship and Immigration)*, 2015 FC 1246.

117 *Gabeyehu v Canada (Minister of Citizenship and Immigration)*, [1995] FCJ No 1493 at para 7 (TD).

118 In some cases, the issues of delay in fleeing and delay in claiming are both raised on the facts. *Karakaya v Canada (Minister of Citizenship and Immigration)*, 2014 FC 777.

119 *Rios v Canada (Minister of Citizenship and Immigration)*, 2012 FC 276 at para 77ff.

delay when measured from the first incident) cannot be a "significant factor" in doubting a claimant's subjective fear:

> Cumulative acts which may amount to persecution will take time to occur. If a person's claim is actually based on several incidents which occur over time, the cumulative effects of which may amount to persecution, then looking to the beginning of such discriminatory or harassing treatment and comparing that to the date on which a person leaves the country to justify rejection of the claim on the basis of delay, undermines the very idea of cumulative persecution.[120]

G. PERSECUTION

The term "persecution" is left undefined in both the *Refugee Convention* and the *IRPA*. Nonetheless, a risk of persecution must be established by all successful refugee claimants. It has seldom been defined in a comprehensive manner in the jurisprudence; the Board and the courts prefer to adjudicate on whether persecution has been made out on the facts of a particular case. As a result, the jurisprudence seldom goes beyond the ordinary meaning of the term as set out in the dictionary — a habit dating back to the case of *Rajudeen v Canada (Minister of Employment and Immigration)*. The dictionary definition used in that case defined "persecution" as follows:

> To harass or afflict with repeated acts of cruelty or annoyance; to afflict persistently, to afflict or punish because of particular opinions or adherence to a particular creed or mode of worship.

and,

> A particular course or period of systematic infliction of punishment directed against those holding a particular (religious belief); persistent injury or annoyance from any source.[121]

From these definitions, the jurisprudence has established the outlines of persecution. Persecution must be harm that is both serious and systematic; it must be a fundamental violation of human dignity. Persecution must also not be harm that is within the legitimate purview

---

120 *Ibrahimov v Canada (Minister of Citizenship and Immigration)*, 2003 FC 1185 at para 19, applied in *Soto v Canada (Minister of Citizenship and Immigration)*, 2008 FC 354; and *Rojas v Canada (Minister of Citizenship and Immigration)*, 2015 FC 250.

121 [1984] FCJ No 601 (CA) [*Rajudeen*] (quoting the *Living Webster Encyclopedic Dictionary* and the *Shorter Oxford English Dictionary*).

of the state to inflict, such as prosecution and punishment for criminal activity. Each of these aspects of persecution will be discussed below.

1) Violation of a Human Right

Although in some cases the persecution feared (or suffered in the past) will be horrendous and appalling, there is no requirement that mistreatment rise to such a level to constitute persecution (although such extreme mistreatment may give rise to special relief).[122] The seriousness of the harm must be judged based upon the interest that is being violated and the extent to which it is being violated. A minor violation of a minor interest is not equivalent to a major violation of a major interest. The interests that are subject to violation amounting to persecution are generally defined in terms of human rights: refugee law requires "the general notion [of persecution] to be related to developments within the broad field of human rights."[123] Human rights set the minimum level of treatment required for an individual to maintain her human dignity.

However, as there is a plethora of human rights this notion does not in and of itself allow the significance of an interest to be assessed. In order to organize the interests that are potentially subject to violation and to distinguish between those whose violation may amount to persecution and those whose violation will not, a more comprehensive analytical framework is required. James Hathaway, in his seminal book on refugee law, suggested that persecution can be understood as a "serious" violation of a claimant's human rights.[124] It can be quite difficult, however, to determine how to delineate a serious violation. Several different approaches have been adopted, legislatively and in the jurisprudence. One approach is to construct a hierarchy linked to the normative strength of the human rights obligation: strong rights (unqualified and non-derogable) are placed at the top while weaker rights (qualified and derogable) are placed in the lower levels.[125] At the bottom

---

122 *El Khatib v Canada (Minister of Citizenship and Immigration)*, [1994] FCJ No 1415 (TD), aff'd [1996] FCJ No 968) (CA) [*El Khatib*]. Individuals who have suffered particularly appalling past persecution may gain additional relief under the *IRPA*, s 108(4). Please see the discussion of this relief under Section K(3), below in this chapter.

123 Guy S Goodwin-Gill, *The Refugee in International Law*, 2d ed (Oxford: Clarendon Press, 1996) vol 1 at 38 (quoted with approval in *Ward*, above note 75 at 734).

124 Hathaway, *The Law of Refugee Status*, above note 46.

125 Article 9 of the European Union's Qualification Directive: *Directive 2011/95/EU of the European Parliament and of the Council of 13 December 2011 on standards for the qualification of third-country nationals or stateless persons as beneficiaries of interna-*

of the hierarchy are putative rights which have never been formally recognized in treaties. Using this hierarchy of rights as a predictive tool, the closer a violation of human rights is to the top of the hierarchy, the more likely that an act of persecution will be found.[126]

This hierarchy is more useful than simply being an objective guide for determining whether a particular mistreatment qualifies as persecution. It serves to keep the analysis of persecution grounded in international human rights law; any argument about mistreatment must be articulated in terms of international human rights. Doing this helps to avoid relativistic debates over whether particular cultural practices are persecutory or not — though there may be substantive debates over the extent to which human rights law recognizes a particular "emerging right."[127] Of course, on this latter point of relativism, in applying the hierarchy, care must be taken in ensuring that the enumerated right is at risk of violation. Many of the noted human rights are much more qualified than their colloquial meanings may lead us to believe. For example, the freedom of expression may be limited by "respect of the rights or reputations of others"[128] and freedom of association may be restricted for reasons of "public safety."[129] However, while a hierarchical view of rights is useful, the jurisprudence in recent years does not formally link its analysis to it.[130]

---

tional protection, for a uniform status for refugees or for persons eligible for subsidiary protection, and for the content of the protection granted, [2011] OJ, L 337/9.

126 While this hierarchy is attributed to Hathaway (he sets it out in *The Law of Refugee Status*, above note 46 at 105ff), his most recent review of the topic rejects a "mechanistic" exercise and a "rigid classification of relevant harms": Hathaway & Foster, above note 93 at 207.

127 See, for example, the discussion within the compulsory military service caselaw on the "emerging right to conscientious objection"; a similar issue is raised with respect to the various rights associated with non-binary gender identities. *Hinzman v Canada (Minister of Citizenship and Immigration)*, 2007 FCA 171 [*Hinzman*]; *Sepet*, above note 10.

128 *ICCPR*, above note 61, art 19(3).

129 *Ibid*, art 22(2).

130 The last decision explicitly referencing Hathaway's articulation of a "hierarchy of rights" was *AWC (Re)*, [2003] RPDD No 71 (IRB).

Figure 4.1: Hierarchy of Human Rights

Category of Rights	Particular Rights
First Order: Absolute and non-derogable	• Freedom from arbitrary deprivation of life • Protection against torture or cruel, inhuman, or degrading punishment or treatment • Freedom from slavery • Freedom of thought, conscience, and religion
Second Order: Absolute and derogable	• Freedom from arbitrary arrest or detention • Equal protection of the law • Fair criminal proceedings • Family privacy • Freedom of internal movement • Freedom of opinion, expression, assembly, and association • Right to vote • Access to public employment
Third Order: Qualified and derogable	• Right to work • Right to essential food, clothing, and housing • Right to healthcare • Right to basic education • Right to cultural expression
Fourth Order: Rights not formally recognized in treaty	• Right to private property • Protection from unemployment

2) Repetition, Combination, and Impact

The requirement that persecution be not only serious but also systematic has led to the general proposition that it cannot constitute an isolated incident. This proposition can be traced back to *Rajudeen* and has support in various later Federal Court of Appeal decisions.[131] It suggests that "[an] element of repetition and relentlessness [is] found at the heart of persecution."[132] However, while this proposition serves as a good guide to what constitutes persecution, there is no formal requirement that an act of mistreatment be repeated to constitute persecution. Indeed, particularly serious acts of mistreatment may, by definition, be able to occur only once — freedom from the arbitrary deprivation of life being the obvious example. Rather, the requirement of repetition

131 *Valentin v Canada (Minister of Employment and Immigration)*, [1991] 3 FC 390 (CA) [*Valentin*].

132 *Sedigheh v Canada (Minister of Citizenship and Immigration)*, [2003] FCJ No 239 (FC), quoting *Valentin*, *ibid*.

should be understood as simply underscoring the necessity that persecution be a *serious* interference with an individual's human dignity.

It is rare that a refugee claimant fears a single discrete act upon return to the country of reference. Rather, she usually fears a series of mistreatments. The basis of most refugee claims is that a series of mistreatments has already begun and would continue upon return to the country of reference. Frequently, the acts of mistreatment trace an escalating pattern, often triggering the flight of the claimant. At times, however, no such escalation occurs: the mistreatment remains at a constant level. In such a situation, none of the past or feared mistreatments may rank particularly high on the rights hierarchy discussed above. Each individual mistreatment may be a relatively minor breach of a low-level human right. The jurisprudence has adopted a holistic approach to the evaluation of such mistreatments; even if individual acts of mistreatment do not qualify as persecution, a series of such acts may together constitute persecution.[133] The "seriousness" of the mistreatment is derived from the totality of the acts. The jurisprudence acknowledges, without providing much principled guidance, that "the dividing line between persecution and discrimination or harassment is difficult to establish."[134]

While so far the analysis of persecution has focused on the alleged right being violated by the act of mistreatment, the alternative approach is to focus instead on the effect of the act of mistreatment and of the violation of right on the individual. This approach finds persecution in an act's impact upon an individual:

> Where measures of discrimination are, in themselves, not of a serious character, they may nevertheless give rise to a reasonable fear of persecution if they produce, in the mind of the person concerned, a feeling of apprehension and insecurity as regards his future existence.[135]

While such an approach values the idea of "human dignity" that lies at the core of the international human rights regime, it disregards the limits set on such a concept by the various accepted human rights. Human rights violations are generally defined by a concrete act rather than a subjective consequence. Thus, freedom of expression is violated when there is an unpermitted interference with expression rather than

133 *Madelat v Canada (Minister of Employment and Immigration)*, [1991] FCJ No 49 (CA).

134 *Sagharichi v Canada (Minister of Employment and Immigration)*, [1993] FCJ No 796 (CA); *Warner v Canada (Minister of Citizenship and Immigration)*, 2011 FC 363.

135 UNHCR *Handbook*, above note 21 at para 54.

when there is merely a perception that an expression is not valued or encouraged. In most cases, a preferable approach would be to expand the scope of the human rights considered to be violated. Such was the situation in *He v Canada (Minister of Employment and Immigration)*, where the Board rejected the claim based up an alleged violation of the right to employment as not amounting to persecution. In overturning the decision, the Federal Court cited a much wider range of rights subject to violation:

> To permanently deprive a teacher of her profession and to forever convert an educated young woman into a farm hand and garment worker, constituted persecution. In addition, to permanently deprive the Applicant of her mobility and her freedom to choose where she would live also amounted to persecution. I have concluded that the Board committed a fundamental error of law in its application of the accepted definitions of persecution to the facts of this case.[136]

A broader range of rights reduces the reliance upon the subjective suffering of an individual, although, in some cases, the impact of the act upon the individual may be inherent in the definition of the human right in question.[137]

3) Prosecution of a Law of General Application

As noted previously, attention must be paid to the formal limits of the human rights upon the violation of which the claim of persecution is based. For example, freedom of expression may be restricted by law as necessary to ensure "respect of the rights or reputations of others" and to protect the "national security," "public order," "public health," or "morals" of society.[138] An interference with the freedom of expression that legitimately falls within this limitation will not constitute persecution.

From this rather simple observation that human rights can be legitimately limited, a large body of jurisprudence has developed, assessing under what circumstances the limitations will be considered "legitimate." A key desire of the drafters of the *Refugee Convention* was to prevent "ordinary criminals" from using it to avoid proper punishment. To paraphrase the language of the UNHCR *Handbook*, such individuals are fugitives from justice rather than actual or potential

136 [1994] FCJ No 1243 at para 14 (TD).

137 For example, the prohibition on torture and other cruel, inhuman, and degrading treatment defines all terms fundamentally in relation to their impact on the individual.

138 *ICCPR*, above note 61, art 19(3).

victims of injustice which the *Refugee Convention* seeks to protect.[139] Conversely, however, such laws cannot be allowed to "[cloak] persecution with a veneer of legality" and thereby prevent an individual from gaining international protection.[140] This is particularly important given the contemporary trend towards the use of legislation, including criminal law, to illegitimately restrict the activities of civil society, including political dissidents.[141]

Colloquially, in refugee law this issue is referred to as the issue of a "law of general application." A law of general application — and hence, a legitimate restriction on a human right — can be imposed only by a government. In almost all cases, these limitations will need to be applied by formal law.[142] Prosecution under a law of general application does not remove the possibility that a refugee claimant may also be subject to related but extra-judicial mistreatment and an unfair process. Such acts of mistreatment must be considered outside the law of general application analysis (and may found a successful refugee claim). The law of general application analysis also applies only to state agents of persecution. By definition, a law of general application must apply to the entire population.[143]

The analysis of a law of general application is derived from an early case concerning forced military service. On the facts, an Iranian soldier fled his conscripted service into military action against dissident Iranian Kurds.[144] The analysis of whether he was a refugee hinged on whether he could be legitimately compelled to perform his military service and as a consequence, whether he could be legitimately punished for his desertion from that service. In determining that he was

---

139 UNHCR *Handbook*, above note 21 at para 54; *Patabanthi v Canada (Minister of Citizenship and Immigration)*, [2002] FCJ No 1772 at para 34.

140 *Cheung v Canada (Minister of Employment and Immigration)*, [1993] 2 FC 314 at 322 (CA).

141 UN Special Rapporteur on the Situation of Human Rights Defenders, *Use of Legislation to Regulate Activities of Human Rights Defenders*, UNGAOR, 67th Sess, UN Doc A/67/292 (2012).

142 The definition of "arbitrary" (and hence, unacceptable) in relation to most human rights is that, *inter alia*, it is not properly authorized by law (e.g., arbitrary arrest and detention). The possible exception to the requirement that a law of general application be a "formal" law is the use of the residual powers of the executive or Crown in times of national emergency.

143 While this will not be an issue for most quasi-criminal laws prohibiting certain acts, the jurisprudence is split over how to understand "general" in the context of laws imposing obligations.

144 *Zolfagharkhani v Canada (Minister of Employment and Immigration)*, [1993] FCJ No 584 (CA) [*Zolfagharkhani*].

a refugee, the Federal Court of Appeal set forth four principles against which laws of general application should be assessed:

> (1) The statutory definition of Convention refugee makes the intent (or any principal effect) of an ordinary law of general application, rather than the motivation of the claimant, relevant to the existence of persecution.
> (2) But the neutrality of an ordinary law of general application, *vis-à-vis* the five grounds for refugee status, must be judged objectively by Canadian tribunals and courts when required.
> (3) In such consideration, an ordinary law of general application, even in non-democratic societies, should, I believe, be given a presumption of validity and neutrality, and the onus should be on a claimant, as is generally the case in refugee cases, to show that the laws are either inherently or for some other reason persecutory.
> (4) It will not be enough for the claimant to show that a particular regime is generally oppressive but rather that the law in question is persecutory in relation to a Convention ground.[145]

Although the analysis of the Federal Court of Appeal in *Zolfagharkhani v Canada (Minister of Employment and Immigration)* can be criticized for taking some liberties with the facts of the claim, the legal principles it cites have been followed in more than five dozen reported decisions.[146]

At the core of the *Zolfagharkhani* analysis are two issues: (1) the intent or primary effect of the law, and (2) the consequences of the law for the claimant. A link between the former and one of the five enumerated grounds[147] must be established; the latter must be shown to be serious enough as to constitute persecution. Proof of the intent or effect of the law is often difficult. Disproportionate punishment may itself provide implicit proof of both the discriminatory intent of the law and its persecutory consequences. In addition, a claimant who fears being subject to a law of general application must avail himself of opportunities within the law that might grant an exemption from or mitigate the effects of any prosecution.[148]

---

145 *Ibid* at paras 20–23.

146 For a critique of *Zolfagharkhani*, see Martin Jones, "The Refusal to Bear Arms as Grounds for Refugee Protection in the Canadian Jurisprudence" (2008) 20 *International Journal of Refugee Law* 123.

147 See Section H, below in this chapter.

148 *Hinzman*, above note 127 at para 50; *Goltsberg v Canada (Minister of Citizenship and Immigration)*, 2010 FC 886.

H. REQUIREMENT OF NEXUS

To qualify as a Convention refugee, a refugee claimant must establish that her well-founded fear of persecution occurs "for reasons of" one of five enumerated grounds: (1) race, (2) religion, (3) nationality, (4) political opinion, or (5) membership in a particular social group. This requirement is commonly referred to as the requirement of "nexus."

In order to establish a nexus, there must be evidence that the enumerated ground has caused the well-founded fear. Causation may take several forms. It may occur directly, such as where the actions of the agent of persecution are directly motivated by the enumerated ground. Such is the case when an individual assaults a refugee claimant because he has expressed political opinions. Causation, however, may also occur indirectly. Such is the case when a refugee claimant suffers an assault and the police then subsequently refuse to offer any assistance because of her expressed political opinions. Nexus can be found either directly in the perceptions of the agent of persecution or indirectly in the perceptions of the state agents who are responsible for offering protection.[149]

Key in the analysis is the perception of the agent of persecution or agent of the state responsible for protection. As the nexus is understood as the cause of the danger of persecution, the perceptions of the persecutor and the protector are paramount. In relation to the former (although equally true of the latter), the following has been said:

> the persecutor may perceive that the claimant is a member of a certain race, nationality, religion, or particular social group or holds a certain political opinion and the claimant may face a reasonable chance of persecution because of that perception. This perception may not conform with the real situation.[150]

The requirement of nexus prevents many individuals who have a well-founded fear of persecution from receiving protection. Victims of natural disasters, famine, and generalized violence will normally not satisfy the nexus requirement. In order to address this problem, as discussed earlier in this chapter, several regional international legal instruments have been negotiated since the *Refugee Convention*. Canada

---

149 For a more detailed discussion of the duty of the state to offer protection, see Section I, below in this chapter.

150 Immigration and Refugee Board, "Interpretation of the Convention Refugee Definition in the Case Law" (31 December 2010) at para 4.1, online: www.irb-cisr.gc.ca/Eng/BoaCom/references/LegJur/Pages/RefDef04.aspx (citing *Ward*, above note 75 at 747 in support).

is not a party to any of these instruments, however. Nonetheless, some of these individuals may be eligible for protection as "persons in need of protection" or in some categories of individuals eligible for protection overseas.

The meanings of most of the enumerated grounds are quite straightforward. While each has been interpreted fairly broadly, the list of five grounds is not seen as encompassing all possible grounds of persecution. The last two enumerated grounds — "political opinion" and "membership in a particular social group" — have attracted the most controversy.

1) "For Reasons Of"

Before discussing the enumerated grounds, the often overlooked core of the requirement of nexus — the phrase "for reasons of" — should be discussed more fully. Clearly, this phrase requires a linkage between the well-founded fear of persecution and one of the five enumerated grounds. The full nature of this linkage is rarely directly discussed in the jurisprudence. It must certainly be causal. However, whether it must also be intentional is a matter of some dispute:

> [T]here is frequent confusion or conflation of the elements of causation and intent as elements of the nexus analysis, which can make it difficult and somewhat artificial in many cases to isolate the causation standard as an issue of discussion. As mentioned above, it is well recognized that the nexus clause denotes a causal link. Curiously however, while it is recognized that causation does not necessarily involve any element of intent in other areas of the law, in the refugee context courts frequently introduce it unselfconsciously into the equation as though it were an inevitable aspect of a causal determination. That is, the causal link is often held not to be established unless the applicant is able to establish that the (past or future) persecutor intends to inflict serious harm because of the applicant's race, political opinion, or other protected status. This leap from causation to intention is seldom identified or justified.[151]

In discussing intention, the jurisprudence frequently seeks a nexus in the intentions of both the refugee claimant and the agents of per-

151 Michelle Foster, "Causation in Context: Interpreting the Nexus Clause in the *Refugee Convention*" (2002) 23 *Michigan Journal of International Law* 265 at 268 and 269 [footnotes omitted].

secution.[152] While such an approach is generous, it is not analytically consistent. From the structure of the definition, the focus must be on the refugee claimant's predicament and the feared prospective persecution. Such a focus requires an exclusive focus on the motivation of the agents of persecution and/or the agents of state protection.[153] This principle is underscored in the first principle enunciated in *Zolfagharkhani*, discussed earlier. In extreme cases, this may entail that an individual who is motivated by profound political beliefs to assist a political cause at great risk may be denied protection as a refugee. An extreme example of this was a supporter of the Angolan guerilla movement who provided sensitive military intelligence to the movement and was later charged with treason.[154] He was clearly motivated by his support of the guerillas (and an equivalent dislike of the government); however, as his agents of persecution were found to be uninterested in his motives, his persecution was found to have no nexus.

The "for reasons of" clause has been interpreted as simply requiring some linkage between the risk and an enumerated ground. In Canadian law, there is no requirement that a single enumerated ground provide the "nexus." Rather, there may be multiple links between the risk of persecution and the enumerated grounds. There may also be links between the risk of persecution and non-enumerated grounds:

> "People frequently act out of mixed motives, and it is enough for the existence of political motivation that one of the motives was political." Similarly, the fact that the acts of persecution of which the applicant says he was the target may have been engaged in for personal or pecuniary reasons does not exempt the Board from its duty as a decision-maker, to examine whether in fact, according to the evidence in the record, some political opinions had or might have been imputed to the applicant by the governmental authority.[155]

The jurisprudence has yet to establish the minimum level of connection required in a case of "mixed motives." Indeed, some of the

---

152 *Shahiraj v Canada (Minister of Citizenship and Immigration)*, [2001] FCJ No 734 (FC); *Zhu v Canada (Minister of Employment and Immigration)*, [1994] FCJ No 80 (CA) [*Zhu*].

153 James C Hathaway, "International Refugee Law; The Michigan Guidelines on Nexus to a Convention Ground" (2002) 23 *Michigan Journal of International Law* 210 at 215.

154 *Antonio v Canada (Minister of Employment and Immigration)*, [1994] FCJ No 1414 (TD).

155 *Sopiqoti v Canada (Minister of Citizenship and Immigration)*, [2003] FCJ No 136 at para 14 (TD) (quoting *Zhu*, above note 152 at para 2).

jurisprudence suggests that any mixed motivation is sufficient if the motivation is merely in part linked to a *Convention* ground.[156] Based on the more general interpretation of the definition, the issue should remain whether there is a "serious possibility of persecution on one or more Convention ground."[157] While the mixed motive approach is often used to fulfill a nexus where at least one motive of persecution is not linked to a Convention ground, the opposite can also occur: "[the claimant's race, membership in a particular social group, and perceived political opinion] were not sufficient to establish a nexus to the Convention ground of race on their own, however, when taken together they cumulatively established a serious possibility of risk of persecution upon return."[158] Other signatories to the *Refugee Convention* have taken a less generous approach to this issue. Both the United States and Australia have statutorily required that the risk of persecution be nearly exclusively for reasons of one of the enumerated grounds.[159]

2) Proof of Nexus

Many refugee claimants are unaware of the quite legalistic requirement of nexus. The Basis of Claim, or BOC, Form requires the claimant to indicate the enumerated ground(s) which he believes to provide a nexus.[160] Although this is a required element of the refugee definition, a claimant need not be able to articulate his precise nexus. Instead, the

---

156 *Cabarcas v Canada (Minister of Citizenship and Immigration)*, [2002] FCJ No 396 at para 6 (TD); *Katwaru v Canada (Minister of Citizenship and Immigration)*, 2007 FC 612.

157 This approach was adopted by the RAD in *RAD File No TB4-02212*, [2014] RADD No 1134 (IRB), though on the facts the test was not satisfied.

158 *Canada (Minister of Citizenship and Immigration) v B344*, 2013 FC 447 at para 45 [*B344*].

159 Australia's *Migration Act 1958*, s 91R(a), requires that one or more of the enumerated grounds provide "the essential and significant reason(s)" for the risk of persecution. For the United States, s 101(a)(3) of *An Act Making Emergency Supplemental Appropriations for Defense, the Global War on Terror, and Tsunami Relief, for the fiscal year ending September 30, 2005, and for other purposes*, Pub L No 109-13 (US) (Division B of which, including s 101, is also known as the *Real ID Act* 2005), amended s 208(b)(1) of the *Immigration and Nationality Act*, 8 USC § 1158(b)(1), to require that "race, religion, nationality, membership in a particular social group, or political opinion was or will be a central reason for persecuting the applicant."

160 In question 2(a), the BOC Form asks: "What do you think was the reason for the harm or mistreatment or threats that occurred?" Previously, the personal information form (PIF) specifically required the claimant to identify the nexus of their claim.

decision maker has a duty to consider each possible nexus based upon the facts of the claim.[161]

Although the courts frequently denounce the speculations of claimants regarding nexus, it is inherently difficult to determine the perceptions and motivations of another individual or institution. In the jurisprudence there is given an allowance that actions may be the result of mixed motives.

3) Enumerated Grounds

The definition enumerates five grounds to which a claimant's fear of persecution must be linked: nationality, race, religion, political opinion, and membership in a particular social group. The meaning of each of the enumerated grounds will be discussed in turn.

a) Nationality

Nationality as an enumerated ground is not restricted to legal status. In this way, its usage as a ground of nexus must be distinguished from its usage in determining the country of reference.[162] While the ground of nationality can include its narrower meaning of citizenship, its broader meaning of "ethnic group" is more frequently invoked regarding nexus.[163] Like any other ground, nationality can also include the mistaken perception that an individual has a particular nationality.[164] Decisions of the Board have considered, *inter alia*, the following groups as based upon nationality: Azeri-Russians (in Azerbaijan),[165] Armenians (in Russia),[166] the Romani,[167] and members of the Brava clan (in Somalia).[168]

---

161 *Ward*, above note 75 at 745.

162 *Hanukashvili*, above note 35 at para 8.

163 Where the narrow ground of "nationality" is invoked, the refugee claimant is typically in a situation where he is residing in a country other than his country of nationality. As such, the country of nationality is a country of reference and it is impossible to establish that the mistreatment in the country of residence will continue in the country of nationality. Absent another basis for the claim, such a claim will fail.

164 VA2-00238 (unreported).

165 MA1-01064 (unreported).

166 TA5-03359 (unreported).

167 MA1-05556 (unreported).

168 MA3-08450 et al (unreported).

b) Race

Race has been understood very broadly by international law. The international *Convention on the Elimination of All Forms of Racial Discrimination*[169] defines race as including "race, colour, descent, or national or ethnic origin."[170] The approach to race in refugee law adopts a similarly broad construction of the idea of race.

There is scant Canadian jurisprudence concerning race as a ground of nexus. Decisions of the Board have considered, *inter alia*, the following groups as potentially "racial": Jews,[171] Tutsis,[172] Chinese (in Peru),[173] Tamils (from Sri Lanka),[174] and blacks (in Colombia).[175] The Romani have been found to be both a racial group as well a national group, as noted above — a not infrequent occurrence in the jurisprudence on race and nationality.[176] Presumably, Indigenous peoples would also be included under race. In the sole Federal Court decision on the subject, the court upheld a finding of refugee status for a young Tamil citizen of Sri Lanka based upon a nexus of race.[177] There is frequent overlap between the nexus of race and that of nationality in the caselaw. Not infrequently the (non-enumerated) ground of "ethnicity" is pleaded.

c) Religion

Freedom of religion is understood very broadly by international human rights law. The *International Covenant on Civil and Political Rights*, article 18, protects "freedom of conscience" and protects both religious belief and behaviour that arises from that belief. The Human Rights Committee has commented that religious belief should be understood to include "theistic, non-theistic and atheistic beliefs," "the right not to profess any religion or belief," "traditional religions or to religions and beliefs with institutional characteristics," and non-traditional and non-institutionally defined religions and beliefs.[178]

---

169 660 UNTS 195.

170 Article 1 (defining "racial discrimination").

171 *IRX (Re)*, [2002] RPDD No 423 (IRB) (Jews in Ukraine); and *AXJ (Re)*, [2003] RPDD No 228 (IRB) (Jews in Israel).

172 *GVT (Re)*, [2003] RPDD No 31 (IRB).

173 *SBO (Re)*, [2003] RPDD No 17 (IRB).

174 *B344*, above note 158.

175 *VYI (Re)*, [1996] CRDD No 250 (IRB).

176 *ZFP (Re)*, [2002] CRDD No 330 (IRB).

177 *Canada (Minister of Citizenship and Immigration) v Manoharan*, 2005 FC 1122 at para 29, aff'g [2004] RPDD No 629 (IRB) (the Board's decision also found a nexus to nationality).

178 UN Human Rights Committee, "General Comment No 22: The Right to Freedom of Thought, Conscience and Religion (art 18)" CCPR/C/21/Rev.1/Add.4 (1993).

The Canadian jurisprudence has equivocated about whether "devil worship" can constitute a religion. The cases in question concern the Ogboni "cult" from Nigeria which has variously been described as a "secret society,"[179] "pagan religion," and a "criminal cabal." In *Nosakhare v Canada (Minister of Citizenship and Immigration)*, the Federal Court accepted that feared mistreatment for refusing to join the Ogboni could constitute persecution due to religious belief.[180] However, in other decisions the court has refused to overturn decisions of the Board arriving at a contrary conclusion.[181] Other jurisdictions have also grappled with the issue of claims related to Ogboni persecution. Most famously, the Court of Appeal in the United Kingdom denied such a basis of claim (although based as much on its interpretation of "for reasons of" as on its finding that the Ogboni were not a religious group).[182]

d) Political Opinion

Political opinion provides the nexus for the archetypal refugee: the political dissident. The ambit of political opinion as a nexus certainly includes such individuals. The Supreme Court of Canada has famously construed political opinion as "any opinion on any matter in which the machinery of state, government, and policy may be engaged."[183] At a basic level, this has been found to include political dissidents,[184] government employees fearing persecution from guerillas,[185] community activists,[186] and individuals supporting the prosecution of perpetrators of genocide.[187] More than any other ground of nexus, political opinion is frequently based on the (often untrue) perceptions of the refugee claimant by the agent of persecution. Religious beliefs, ethnic membership, familial affiliation, and occupation have all been found to plausibly ground inferences about a refugee claimant's political opinion. More concretely, agents of persecution frequently impute political opinions to sons based on the conduct of fathers and to individuals based upon the general beliefs of the community in which they live.

---

179 *Efese v Canada (Minister of Citizenship and Immigration)*, [2002] FCJ No 639 (TD) [*Efese*].

180 [2001] FCJ No 1120 (TD).

181 *Efese*, above note 179; *Oloyede v Canada (Minister of Citizenship and Immigration)*, [2001] FCJ No 453 (TD).

182 *Omoruyi v Secretary of State for the Home Department*, [2001] Imm AR 175 (CA).

183 *Ward*, above note 75 at 693.

184 T98-01067 (unreported).

185 TA1-20210 et al (unreported).

186 TA1-12841 (unreported).

187 AA1-00250 et al (unreported).

Unfortunately, it is rare for agents of persecution to double-check their prejudices, assumptions, and inferences about a claimant's belief.

In recent years, however, the jurisprudence has expanded political opinion beyond the archetypal political dissident. In *Klinko v Canada (Minister of Citizenship and Immigration)*, the Federal Court of Appeal was asked to answer the following question:

> Does the making of a public complaint about widespread corrupt conduct by customs and police officials to a regional governing authority, and thereafter, the complainant suffering persecution on this account, when the corrupt conduct is not officially sanctioned, condoned or supported by the state, constitute an expression of political opinion as that term is understood in the definition of Convention refugee in subsection 2(1) of the *Immigration Act*?[188]

The court responded in the affirmative. On the facts, the refugee claimant had suffered retaliation (and a risk of further future retaliation) as a result of formally complaining about corrupt practices in the Ukrainian government. Applying the logic of *Klinko*, individuals who suffer mistreatment because of expressed opinions about a wide variety of matters on which the government has taken a position will fall within the nexus of political opinion. While in *Klinko* the expression was in the form of a formal complaint, even an informal expression can bring a claimant within the ambit of political opinion.[189]

Notwithstanding the potential breadth of political opinion, it is still limited by the need for the mistreatment to be linked to an expression.[190] Furthermore, the expression in question must be perceived as political; where an expression is perceived as purely personal, it will not fall within the ambit of *Klinko*.[191]

e) Membership in a Particular Social Group

Membership in a particular social group was the last enumerated ground added in the drafting of the *Refugee Convention*. It was added without much explanation or debate. The silence of the drafters on its meaning led to almost a half-century of divergent jurisprudence.

---

188 [2000] FCJ No 228 at para 1 (CA) [*Klinko*].

189 *Stefanov v Canada (Minister of Citizenship and Immigration)*, [2002] FCJ No 954 (TD).

190 *Bencic v Canada (Minister of Citizenship and Immigration)*, [2002] FCJ No 623 at para 16 (TD).

191 *Gonzales v Canada (Minister of Citizenship and Immigration)*, [2002] FCJ No 1683 (TD); *Rivera v Canada (Minister of Citizenship and Immigration)*, [2003] FCJ No 1634 (FC).

Finally, in Canada and elsewhere, in the 1990s a consensus emerged concerning its meaning. The leading case on the meaning of membership in a particular social group, both in Canada and the rest of the world, is *Canada (AG) v Ward*.[192]

In *Ward*, the Supreme Court of Canada concluded that the term must be both limited in scope and analogous — but not identical — to the other four enumerated grounds. Proceeding upon this basis, the Court identified three types of "particular social groups":

1) groups defined by an innate or unchangeable characteristic;
2) groups whose members voluntarily associate for reasons so fundamental to their human dignity that they should not be forced to forsake the association;
3) groups associated by a former voluntary status, unalterable due to its historical permanence.

The Court went on to elaborate upon these three types of particular social groups as follows:

> The first category would embrace individuals fearing persecution on such bases as gender, linguistic background and sexual orientation, while the second would encompass, for example, human rights activists. The third branch is included more because of historical intentions, although it is also relevant to the anti-discrimination influences, in that one's past is an immutable part of the person.[193]

The approach taken in *Ward* has been described as the "protected characteristics approach." Each of the three categories of groups outlined is defined by either an immutable characteristic or one that an individual should not be required to change. This combination of immutable characteristics and changeable but protected characteristics in the *Ward* groups has been criticized as analytically inconsistent insofar as it conflates two categories of groups that should be protected for quite different reasons.[194] Furthermore, the "association" that is required of the second and third categories of groups has not always been required in the jurisprudence; notably in La Forest J's decision in *Chan v Canada (Minister of Employment and Immigration)* allowing prospective parents opposed to forced sterilization as a social group.[195] At the very least, all of the groups are defined in relation to "internal"

192 Above note 75.

193 *Ibid* at 739.

194 See Nicole Laviolette, "The Immutable Refugee: Sexual Orientation in *Canada (A.G.) v. Ward*" (1997) *University of Toronto Faculty of Law Review* 1.

195 [1995] 3 SCR 593 (the majority decision did not address this aspect of the claim).

characteristics — features shared by members of the group — as opposed to the "external" perception of the group.[196]

Since the decision in *Ward*, numerous particular social groups have been recognized in the Canadian jurisprudence, most notably the particular social group of "women." In addition, the following social groups have been found to exist: homosexuals,[197] trade unionists,[198] children (and various subgroups),[199] the poor,[200] and various other finely described groups. Yet, as the Board put it shortly after the *Ward* decision, a social group cannot be "some vague, amorphous, mass of humanity . . . [such as] all the bald-headed bespectacled heterosexual men in Turkey, all the homosexuals in Argentina or all the tea-drinkers in China, for that matter!"[201] Although the reference to homosexuals in Argentina has been reversed by the caselaw, the exasperated warning about defining arbitrary social groups remains apt. Since the date of the warning, the courts have gone further and have prohibited even non-arbitrary social groups defined only by the persecution that they suffer.[202] The rationale behind this prohibition is that to allow such groups would be to allow the definition of refugee to be turned into a tautology: a refugee is a person who has a well-founded fear of persecution by reason of her membership in particular social group X which has a well-founded fear of persecution by agent Y. Notwithstanding the preclusion of such tautologies, the courts have struggled with whether

---

196 T Alexander Aleinikoff, "'Membership in a Particular Social Group': Analysis and Proposed Conclusions" (Background Paper for "Track Two" of the Global Consultations) (Geneva: UNHCR, nd) at 10.

197 *Tchernilevski v Canada (Minister of Citizenship and Immigration)*, [1995] FCJ No 894 (TD).

198 *Zubita v Canada (Minister of Employment and Immigration)* (31 October 1979) Action No 79-1034 (Immigration Appeal Board); *Barraza v Canada (Minister of Employment and Immigration)* (23 March 1979) Action No 77-9449 (Immigration Appeal Board); *Hartley v Canada (Minister of Citizenship and Immigration)*, [2000] FCJ No 631 (TD) (in *obiter*).

199 *Canada (Minister of Citizenship and Immigration) v Li*, [2001] FCJ No 620 (TD) (in *obiter* as the issue concerned whether the named subset of children was a valid social group). Recognized subgroups of children include impoverished children (*JDJ (Re)*, [1998] CRDD No 12 (IRB)); second children in violation of family planning law (*Cheung v Canada (Minister of Employment and Immigration)*, [1993] 2 FC 314 (CA)); and orphans (*WBT (Re)*, [1999] CRDD No 119 (IRB)).

200 *Sinora v Minister of Employment and Immigration*, [1993] FCJ No 725 (CA) (arguably based upon a misreading of *Orelien v Canada (Minister of Employment and Immigration)*, [1992] 1 FC 592 (CA)).

201 *U(BT) (Re)*, [1992] CRDD No 286 (IRB).

202 *Mason v Canada (Secretary of State)*, [1995] FCJ No 815 (TD).

a group may be only partially defined by the persecution that members jointly fear.[203]

The most controversial social group in recent years is that of family. Applying *Ward*, a family group would seem to qualify under any of the three categories. "[O]ne cannot imagine a closer-knit or easier to confirm unit than the family,"[204] the Federal Court has stated. Indeed, family members of individuals who are at risk because of another enumerated ground regularly gain protection on the basis of their "familial association."[205] The controversy arises when a refugee claimant seeks protection as a result of familial association *simpliciter* — or more specifically when she seeks protection as a result of her familial association with someone who is at risk because of no enumerated ground.

In general, the caselaw rules against such a refugee claimant.[206] The Federal Court Trial Division in *Klinko* expressed it this way: "[W]hen the primary victim of persecution does not come within the Convention refugee definition, any derivative Convention refugee claim based on family group cannot be sustained."[207] No other enumerated ground has had such a qualification read into it. Despite what is stated in the jurisprudence, the requirement that the familial association be underpinned by a nexus to another enumerated ground suggests that familial association does not per se provide a nexus but rather provides a quasi-evidentiary presumption that the agent of persecution will "perceive"

---

203 The best recent example of such a struggle is expressed in the line of cases concerning Tamil refugee claimants aboard the MV *Ocean Lady* and MV *Sun Sea*. These cases struggle with whether passengers on the vessels can constitute a "particular social group," the possibility of a nexus of perceived political opinion, and the impact of the mixed motive doctrine. The struggle of the Federal Court resulted in several (unpursued) certified questions and substantially diverging outcomes and reasonings. See *Canada (Minister of Citizenship and Immigration) v A011*, 2013 FC 580 at para 11, where Harrington J pronounced: "[I]t is a great injustice that passengers on these two ships should be treated so differently. There is no sound basis for predicting who will be welcomed here as a refugee and who will be thrown out."

204 *Casetellanos v Canada (Solicitor General)*, [1994] FCJ No 1926 at para 24 (TD).

205 *Macias v Canada (Minister of Citizenship and Immigration)*, [2004] FCJ No 2132 (FC).

206 *Al-Busaidy v Canada (Minister of Employment and Immigration)*, [1992] FCJ No 26 (CA).

207 *Klinko v Canada (Minister of Citizenship and Immigration)*, [1998] FCJ No 561 (TD) (the Federal Court of Appeal did not address this issue in its decision). Quoted with approval in *Gonzalez v Canada (Minister of Citizenship and Immigration)*, [2002] FCJ No 456 (CA). *Granada v Canada (Minister of Citizenship and Immigration)*, [2004] FCJ No 2164 at para 16 (FC); SM v *Canada (Minister of Citizenship and Immigration)*, 2011 FC 949 at para 11.

the refugee claimant in the same light as the familial member who faces a risk due to an enumerated ground. In addition, as a matter of proof of nexus, the absence of persecution taken against some family members often results in an inference that family is not the reason for the persecution in question.[208]

Other jurisdictions have taken a less restrictive approach. Australia, which has adopted statutory measures to restrict other liberal interpretations of "membership in a particular social group,"[209] recognizes family as a particular social group in all situations.[210]

The decision in *Ward* has been quoted in the jurisprudence in countless other countries; together with the cases in which it was cited, it is probably the pre-eminent example of the development of a transnational refugee law jurisprudence. It remains to be seen whether in coming years the flow of jurisprudential influence will reverse and whether, particularly in relation to family as a social group, the Canadian jurisprudence will draw upon more liberal approaches elsewhere.

I. AVAILABILITY OF STATE PROTECTION

It is the duty of all states to offer protection to their nationals. Refugee protection becomes available only when a state fails in the performance of its duty, including at the extreme participating in the persecution of its own nationals. The refugee definition requires each refugee to establish that he "is unable, or owing to [his well-founded] fear, is unwilling to avail himself of the protection of that country."[211] Thus, as

---

208 *El Achkar v Canada (Minister of Citizenship and Immigration)*, 2013 FC 472.

209 *Migration Act 1958*, above note 159, s 93S, limits the inferences that can be made concerning claims based upon familial association. The *Migration Legislation Amendment Bill* (No 3) 1995, s 2(3), stated: "The fertility control policies of the government of a foreign country are to be disregarded in determining if a non-citizen is a member of a particular social group (within the meaning of the *Refugee Convention* as amended by the *Refugee Protocol*) for the purpose of considering an application for a protection visa." The bill was never passed into law.

210 The leading case was re-litigated on multiple occasions. Four slightly different iterations of the High Court's judgment concerning family and social group can be found in *Sarrazola v Minister for Immigration & Multicultural Affairs (No 1)*, 1999 FCA 101 (Hely J); *Minister for Immigration & Multicultural Affairs v Sarrazola* (1999), 95 FCR 517 (Einfeld, Moore, & Branson JJ); *Sarrazola v Minister for Immigration & Multicultural Affairs*, 2000 FCA 919 (Madgwick J); *Sarrazola v Minister for Immigration & Multicultural Affairs (No 4)* (2001), 107 FCR 184 (Heerey, Sundberg, & Merkel JJ).

211 *Refugee Convention*, above note 1, art 1A(2); and *IRPA*, above note 3, s 96(a).

noted previously, one of the guiding principles of international refugee protection is the concept of subsidiarity. The protection of an individual becomes the obligation of the international community, *qua* Convention refugee, only if his state of nationality is unable to offer protection or the refugee claimant is unwilling to avail himself of the state's protection.[212]

1) Scope of State Protection

State protection is just that: protection by agents of the state. The jurisprudence is somewhat ambivalent as to whether "agents of the state" will include the individuals and institutions of civil society within the state. *Thakur v Canada (Minister of Employment and Immigration)* suggests that assistance by "civil rights groups" is irrelevant in the determination of state protection.[213] Subsequent cases have reached a similar conclusion with respect to both domestic[214] and international[215] "human rights organizations." Oddly, the caselaw has suggested that despite the irrelevancy of civil society to the state protection analysis, state protection may be provided by foreign armed forces in alliance with the government of the state.[216] All of this does not suggest that the presence of other avenues of protection in the country of reference is completely irrelevant. Their presence (and the refugee claimant's interaction with them) may be used in the assessment of the subjective and objective fear of the claimant — along with his credibility. The efforts of a non-state or international actor to develop a state's ability to offer protection may also improve a state's operational ability to offer protection.[217]

It must be noted that at international law a duty of protection is owed by the state to its own nationals. The stateless who are habitually resident in a state are not owed the same duty. Thus, the requirement of state protection for the stateless is formulated quite differently than that for persons possessing a nationality. State protection per se does

212 *Ward*, above note 75 at 709.

213 [1993] FCJ No 600 (TD).

214 *Mendoza v Canada (Minister of Citizenship and Immigration)*, [1996] FCJ No 90 (TD).

215 *Mohacsi v Canada (Minister of Citizenship and Immigration)*, [2003] FCJ No 586 (TD).

216 *Chebli-Haj-Hassam v Canada (Minister of Employment and Immigration)* (1996), 203 NR 222 (CA); *Isufi v Canada (Minister of Citizenship and Immigration)*, 2003 FC 880.

217 The important consideration is less the "effort" of such actors and more its outcome: *EYMV v Canada (Minister of Citizenship and Immigration)*, 2011 FC 1364 at paras 14–16.

not exist for the stateless individual. Instead, she must simply establish that she is "unable or, by reason of that fear, unwilling to return to [the country of reference]."[218] The peculiarities of this requirement will be discussed further below.

2) Inability and Unwillingness

The "inability to offer protection" is distinguished in the definition from the "unwillingness [of a claimant] to seek protection." The UNHCR *Handbook* describes the distinction in the following terms:

> 98. Being *unable* to avail himself of such protection implies circumstances that are beyond the will of the person concerned. There may, for example be a state of war, civil war or other grave disturbance, which prevents the country of nationality from extending protection or makes such protection ineffective. Protection by the country of nationality may also have been denied to the applicant. Such denial of protection may confirm or strengthen the applicant's fear of persecution, and may indeed be an element of persecution.
>
> . . .
>
> 100. The term *unwilling* refers to refugees who refuse to accept the protection of the Government of the country of their nationality. It is qualified by the phrase "owing to such fear." Where a person is willing to avail himself of the protection of his home country, such willingness would normally be incompatible with a claim that he is outside that country "owing to well-founded fear of persecution." Whenever the protection of the country of nationality is available, and there is no ground based on well-founded fear for refusing it, the person concerned is not in need of international protection and is not a refugee.[219]

Although a useful distinction, in practice, both "unable" and "unwilling" get conflated into a single question: can the actions of the state mitigate the risk to the claimant enough so as to remove her well-founded fear? The utility of the distinction is that it highlights the type of evidence that a claimant may be able to produce to indicate the absence of state protection. "Inability" cases are characterized by evidence of the state's failure to provide adequate resources to the executive agen-

218 *Refugee Convention*, above note 1, art 1A(2); and *IRPA*, above note 3, s 96(b).
219 Quoted with approval in *Ward*, above note 75 at 718.

cies that might protect an individual. In contrast, the "unwilling" cases largely rely upon the proximity of the state to the agents of persecution.

3) Proof of Inadequacy of State Protection

A claimant must present "clear and convincing proof" of the country of reference's inability to protect.[220] Clear and convincing proof can be based on the personal experiences of the refugee claimant or the experiences of other "similarly situated individuals." Just as inferences about future persecution can be drawn from past persecution, so, too, can inferences about future lapses in state protection be drawn from past lapses. Similarly situated individuals can include not only individuals known to the claimant but also individuals reported in the documentary material. Clear and convincing proof must generally include a request to the state for protection — unless such an approach would be objectively unreasonable.[221] While there is no absolute requirement that the applicant approach the state for protection, it will be difficult for a claimant to discharge the burden of presenting clear and convincing proof of an inability to protect without such an approach (where such an approach would be reasonable).[222]

It has also been suggested that "the more democratic" a country of reference, the stronger the presumption that it will offer adequate state protection — although the factual linkage between the means of selecting a government and the control of actions within the state by that government seems factually questionable.[223]

Absent a complete breakdown of the machinery of state, a state is presumed to be capable of providing protection to its nationals. The jurisprudence provides few examples of a "complete breakdown": Lebanon during its civil war in the 1980s[224] and parts of Somalia[225] are the most cited examples. The Board and the courts are, as a general

220 *Ibid* at 726.

221 *Ibid* at 724.

222 *Doka v Canada (Minister of Citizenship and Immigration)*, 2004 FC 449; *Espinoza v Canada (Minister of Citizenship and Immigration)*, 2005 FC 343.

223 *NK v Canada (Minister of Citizenship and Immigration)*, [1996] FCJ No 1376 at para 5 (TD); *Minister of Employment and Immigration v Satiacum* (1989), 99 NR 171 at 176 (CA); *Ward*, above note 75 at 725.

224 *Zalzali v Canada (Minister of Employment and Immigration)*, [1991] FCJ No 341 (CA) [*Zalzali*].

225 *P(MP) (Re)*, [1993] CRDD No 187 (IRB); *AMH (Re)*, [1998] CRDD No 46 (IRB) (although numerous decisions arrived at the opposite conclusion; see, for example, *Roble v Canada (Minister of Employment and Immigration)*, [1994] FCJ No 587 (CA)).

rule, reluctant to make a finding of a breakdown of the machinery, even during the devastating (and ongoing) civil wars of Colombia, Ethiopia, and Afghanistan.

Nor is a government required to provide perfect protection.[226] As the courts repeatedly indicate, such protection does not even exist in Canada, let alone in any country of reference. The jurisprudence provides the following not so helpful guide: "State protection cannot be held to a standard of perfection but it must be adequate."[227] At the very least, an "adequate" response will require action, investigation (where factually possible), and not simply assistance in fleeing the country. Even inadequate protection by a particular institution or group of employees of the state will not rebut the presumption of state protection where there were other institutions or employees from which the claimant could have sought protection.[228]

The question of appropriate test for assessing availability of state protection has been subject to much judicial and academic debate. The perspectives on the test range from a more liberal approach that asks whether the applicant's well-founded fear is eliminated as a result of the state's efforts to a more restrictive "due diligence" approach, which focuses on whether the state has done everything that can be reasonably expected of it.[229] The former requires an inquiry into the effectiveness of protection measures, while the latter can be satisfied by establishing that the state has a system of protection and is able or ready to operate it.[230] Over the past several years, the jurisprudence of the Federal Court has become less homogeneous in its approach to the test for state protection. A series of cases suggested that the analysis needs to examine the extent to which state efforts are successful and translate into actual adequate protection.[231] In contrast, others on the

---

226 *Canada (Minister of Citizenship and Immigration) v Villafranca*, [1992] FCJ No 1189 (CA); *Zalzali*, above note 224.

227 *BR v Canada (Minister of Citizenship and Immigration)*, [2006] FCJ No 337 (FC).

228 *Kadenko v Canada (Solicitor General)* (1996), 143 DLR (4th) 532 (FCA).

229 Penelope Mathew et al, "The Role of State Protection in Refugee Analysis" (2003) 15 *International Journal of Refugee Law* 444.

230 *Ibid* at 449–50.

231 Such language is found, for example, in *EB v Canada (Minister of Citizenship and Immigration)*, 2011 FC 111 at para 9; *Beri v Canada (Minister of Citizenship and Immigration)*, 2013 FC 854 at paras 36–37; *Orgona v Canada (Minister of Citizenship and Immigration)*, 2012 FC 1438; *Buri v Canada (Minister of Citizenship and Immigration)*, 2014 FC 45 at para 62; *Hercegi v Canada (Minister of Citizenship and Immigration)*, 2012 FC 250 at para 5; *Stark v Canada (Minister of Citizenship and Immigration)*, 2013 FC 829 at paras 10–11; *EYMV v Canada (Minister of Citizenship and Immigration)*, 2011 FC 1364.

court profess restraint, emphasizing deference to the special expertise of the Immigration and Refugee Board in assessing country of origin information and cautioning against expanding state protection analysis beyond "due diligence" issues.[232] Despite these emerging divisions within the Federal Court, Canada's current approach to the evaluation of state protection continues to gravitate closer to the "due diligence" approach.

4) Interaction with Other Elements of the Definition

As noted previously, the determination of objective basis is closely tied to the issue of state protection. Two "presumptions" are often cited in describing the symbiotic relationship between objective basis and state protection:

- First Presumption: If a refugee claimant's fear of persecution is credible AND if there is an absence of state protection, then there is a presumption that there is a well-founded fear of persecution.
- Second Presumption: If a state is not in a situation of complete breakdown, there is a presumption of adequate protection that can only be rebutted through the presentation of "clear and convincing" evidence of the state's inability to protect.[233]

These two presumptions were first enumerated in *Ward*. The first presumption indicates that the absence of state protection is a sufficient condition for a well-founded fear. The second presumption indicates that the absence of "clear and convincing evidence" of a failure of state protection is enough to show that the fear is not well-founded.

As mentioned in Section H, above in this chapter, the absence of state protection can be brought into the analysis of nexus. Insofar as the absence of state protection creates a well-founded fear, where the absence is caused "for reasons of" one of the five enumerated grounds, it can provide a nexus.

---

232 *Mudrak v Canada (Minister of Citizenship and Immigration)*, 2015 FC 188.

233 *Ward*, above note 75 at 722 and 726; see also Immigration and Refugee Board, "Interpretation of the Covention Refugee Definition in the Case Law" (31 December 2010) at para 6.1.5, online: www.irb-cisr.gc.ca/Eng/BoaCom/references/LegJur/Pages/RefDef.aspx.

J. STATELESS PERSONS

As noted previously, the *Refugee Convention* constructs the duty of a state to offer protection around the concept of nationality. Individuals who are merely in a state as habitual residents fall outside the duty of protection.

In *El Khatib v Canada (Minister of Citizenship and Immigration)*, the Federal Court wrote: "In my view the distinction . . . is that the stateless person is not expected to avail himself of state protection when there is no duty on the state to provide such protection."[234] While this statement is consistent with the structure of the *Refugee Convention*, the "duty" of a state to offer protection arises independently of the *Refugee Convention*. More recent jurisprudence has begun to require that the absence of state protection be proven by stateless persons, albeit often couched as part of the "objective basis of the claim."[235]

Even if there was a differential duty of protection between nationals and aliens at the time of the drafting of the *Refugee Convention*, the duty of protection that exists now relates to the shared humanity of the prospective victims of persecution.

The ability of the country of reference of a stateless person to offer protection will affect his risk of persecution even if it is not considered in a manner identical to that for a claimant with nationality.

K. CESSATION

The *Refugee Convention* contains five provisions that act to end an individual's qualification for Convention refugee status. These provisions have been incorporated into Canadian law as part of the *IRPA*:

> A claim for refugee protection shall be rejected, and a person is not a Convention refugee or a person in need of protection, in any of the following circumstances:
>
> (a) the person has voluntarily reavailed themself of the protection of their country of nationality;
> (b) the person has voluntarily reacquired their nationality;
> (c) the person has acquired a new nationality and enjoys the protection of the country of that new nationality;

---

234 *El Khatib*, above note 122; *Thabet*, above note 45.

235 *Popov v Canada (Minister of Citizenship and Immigration)*, 2009 FC 898.

(d) the person has voluntarily become re-established in the country that the person left or remained outside of and in respect of which the person claimed refugee protection in Canada; or
(e) the reasons for which the person sought refugee protection have ceased to exist.[236]

These five grounds are grounds upon which both protection as a Convention refugee may be refused and the RPD may vacate any past finding of refugee status.[237] While being grounds of refusal in and of themselves, the circumstances that each of the clauses describes may also lead to adverse inferences about other aspects of the refugee definition. For example, re-availment may also lead to doubts about subjective fear.[238]

1) Re-availment and Re-establishment

Re-availment of the protection of a refugee claimant's country of nationality may take several forms. At its most obvious level, re-availment can occur when a claimant approaches her country of nationality for protection from persecution. This may be accomplished directly by a refugee claimant, at a diplomatic mission of her country of nationality, or indirectly in her country of origin by an agent, such as a family member. Re-availment may be inferred where a claimant has returned to his country after the basis of his claim arose.[239] At a much less obvious level, re-availment can occur with the issuance of a passport or other document relating to personal status.[240] However, where such documents were requested for use in refugee proceedings or otherwise due to necessity, re-availment would not have occurred. At its core, any re-availment must be voluntary and must result in protection;[241] it must also not be merely "occasional or incidental."[242]

Re-establishment occurs when an individual returns to her country of reference. Re-establishment, unlike re-availment, requires a physical

---

236 Above note 3, s 108(1).

237 *Ibid*, s 108(2).

238 *WBS (Re)*, [2000] CRDD No 503 at para 15 (IRB); CA4-00158 et al, [2004] RPDD No 741 at para 15 (IRB).

239 *Caballero v Canada (Minister of Employment and Immigration)*, [1993] FCJ No 483 (CA).

240 *QCW (Re)*, [2001] CRDD No 453 at para 18 (IRB), rev'd on other grounds (*sub nom El Kasim v Canada (Minister of Citizenship and Immigration)*), 2002 FCT 1087.

241 *Nsende v Canada (Minister of Citizenship and Immigration)*, 2008 FC 531.

242 *Romero v Canada (Minister of Citizenship and Immigration)*, 2014 FC 671 at para 41.

presence in the country of reference. Re-establishment also requires an intention to remain for a protracted time in the country; a brief presence in the country will not qualify as re-establishment. There has yet to be significant jurisprudence on re-establishment in Canada.[243]

In the past, the issues of re-availment and re-establishment became somewhat moot after a refugee claimant received a positive decision since most such protected persons went on to receive permanent residence in Canada. In such a case, vacation proceedings would not affect the permanent residence status of the protected person. However, as a result of the 2012 changes to the *IRPA*, cessation due to circumstances outlined in sections 108(1)(a) to (d) or vacation of refugee status now automatically results in loss of permanent resident status.[244] Thus, if a claimant's protection ceases due to any listed circumstances, except change in country conditions, the claimant would be under risk of removal from Canada. According to the Canadian Council for Refugees, after 2012, the CBSA's applications for cessation of refugee status became more frequent.[245] Currently, only acquisition of Canadian citizenship constitutes a protection against the risk of removal stemming from cessation of refugee status.

2) Reacquisition of Nationality and Acquisition of New Nationality

As the analysis of a refugee claim revolves around the conditions for the refugee claimant in the country of reference, it is not surprising that a change in the country of reference will affect the Convention refugee status either in the process of being determined or already acquired. Where, after gaining refugee protection, an individual reacquires a formerly held nationality, the mere act of reacquisition can lead to the commencement of vacation proceedings and ultimately the loss of refugee status. Where an individual acquires a *new* nationality, the act of acquisition will affect refugee status only where the new country of nationality can offer protection. The discrepancy between these two provisions (former versus new nationality) has never been adequately explored in the jurisprudence. In both cases, the reacquisition or acquisition of new nationality must be conscious. For the reasons noted

243 *RPD File No TB0-15804*, [2011] RPDD No 765 (IRB); *RPD File No VB3-00408*, [2014] RPDD No 70 (IRB).

244 *IRPA*, above note 3, ss 46(1)(c.1) and (d).

245 Canadian Council for Refugees, "Cessation: Stripping Refugees of Their Status in Canada" (May 2014), online: CCR ccrweb.ca/sites/ccrweb.ca/files/cessation-report-2014.pdf.

above in relation to re-establishment and re-availment, reacquisition and acquisition of nationality have not been frequently used to vacate refugee status, but this may be changing.

3) Change in Circumstances and Compelling Reasons

The situation in any country is subject to change. As a refugee claimant's risk is tied to this fluctuating situation, it is possible for an individual who once had a very high level of risk in the country of reference to later have a much lower level of risk. A "change in circumstances" is both a reason for a claimant to be found not to be a refugee under section 108(1) as well as a basis for the vacation of previously conferred refugee status under section 108(2). Only the former will be discussed in this section.

While relevant changes in circumstances are listed in the *IRPA*, it is basically a reiteration of the central question of fact that lies at the heart of all refugee determination:

> We would add that the issue of so-called "changed circumstances" seems to be in danger of being elevated, wrongly in our view, into a question of law when it is, at bottom, simply one of fact. A change in the political situation in a claimant's country of origin is only relevant if it may help in determining whether or not there is, at the date of the hearing, a reasonable and objectively foreseeable possibility that the claimant will be persecuted in the event of return there. That is an issue for factual determination and there is no separate legal "test" by which any alleged change in circumstances must be measured. The use of words such as "meaningful," "effective," or "durable" is only helpful if one keeps clearly in mind that the only question, and therefore the only test, is that derived from the definition of Convention Refugee in s. 2 of the Act: does the claimant now have a well founded fear of persecution?[246]

As noted by the Federal Court of Appeal, the jurisprudence has applied the ideas of durability and significance to assess the changes. Durability can be assessed, in part, through the passage of time, with more recent changes being the most suspect. Significance must be assessed against the particular situation of the claimant; for example, a change in the leadership of the government may not remove a claimant's fear of persecution at the hands of the police.

---

246 *Yusuf v Canada (Minister of Employment and Immigration)*, [1995] FCJ No 35 at para 2 (TD).

The effect of the change in circumstances and cessation provisions can be quite severe. An individual genuinely fearing persecution may flee long distances and suffer great hardship only to be required to return to her country of reference due to changed circumstances. In order to temper this severity, the Board may, in a limited number of cases, grant refugee protection to an individual who has ceased to be a refugee. Despite the fact that reasons for which the refugee claimant sought protection have ceased to exist, the *IRPA*, section 108(4), requires the Board to offer protection to

> a person who establishes that there are compelling reasons arising out of previous persecution, torture, treatment or punishment for refusing to avail themselves of the protection of the country which they left, or outside of which they remained, due to such previous persecution, torture, treatment or punishment.

This provision is modelled on the *Refugee Convention*, article 1(C)(5).[247] In all cases where the Board finds the claimant to have suffered past persecution and there to have been a change in circumstances, the Board must consider whether the claimant falls within section 108(4) due to compelling reasons.[248]

The preconditions of this exemption from the cessation provisions are that an individual must have suffered past persecution and have qualified at some point as a refugee.[249] Traditionally, only atrocious past persecution such as sexual assault and torture was considered sufficient to create compelling reasons.[250] However, in the 2005 decision in *Suleiman v Canada (Minister of Citizenship and Immigration)*, the court reversed its approach:

> The formulative question to ask in regard to "compelling reasons" is, should the claimant be made to face the background set of life

247 Interestingly, the "compelling reasons" exception of art 1(C)(5) applied only to refugees who, under art A(1) of the *Refugee Convention*, had been "grandfathered" into the protection of the *Refugee Convention*: the largely Jewish, Armenian, and Russian and wartime refugees protected by the International Refugee Organization.

248 *Yamba v Canada (Minister of Citizenship and Immigration)* (2000), 254 NR 388 at para 6 (CA).

249 This latter precondition will not be met, for example, where an individual who suffered past persecution never fled her country of nationality or former habitual residence until *after* the change in circumstances: *Nadjat v Canada (Minister of Citizenship and Immigration)*, 2006 FC 302.

250 *Arguello-Garcia v Canada (Minister of Employment and Immigration)* (1993), 70 FTR 1 (TD); *Velasquez v Canada (Minister of Employment and Immigration)* (1994), 76 FTR 210 (TD).

> which he or she left, even if the principal characters may no longer be present or no longer be playing the same roles? The answer lies not so much in established determinative conclusive fact but rather more to the extent of travail of the inner self or soul to which the claimant would be subjugated. The decision, as all decisions of a compelling nature, necessitates the view that it is the state of mind of the refugee claimant that creates the precedent — not necessarily the country, the conditions, nor the attitude of the population, even though those factors may come into the balance.[251]

Although atrocious and appalling persecution may still cause compelling reasons, it is an error of law to limit compelling reasons to such a subset of persecution.[252]

L. FAMILY UNITY

Frequently, entire families seek protection as refugees; however, the risk of persecution is often unevenly distributed among the family members. Sometimes, only one or two family members may be genuinely at risk. However, the refusal to grant protection to family members of refugees can seem unduly harsh. The final act of the conference of plenipotentiaries who drafted and signed the *Refugee Convention* recommended that states extend protection to close family members:

> THE CONFERENCE, CONSIDERING that the unity of the family, the natural and fundamental group unit of society, is an essential right of the refugee, and that such unity is constantly threatened
>
> . . .
>
> RECOMMENDS Governments to take the necessary measures for the protection of the refugee's family, especially with a view to:
>
> (1) Ensuring that the unity of the refugee's family is maintained particularly in cases where the head of the family has fulfilled the necessary conditions for admission to a particular country:
> (2) The protection of refugees who are minors, in particular unaccompanied children and girls, with special reference to guardianship and adoption.[253]

---

251 [2005] 2 FCR 26 at para 19 (FC).

252 *Ibid* at para 21.

253 Final Act of the United Nations Conference of Plenipotentiaries on the Status of Refugees and Stateless Persons, Part B.

The "principle of family unity," as it has subsequently become known, is not recognized in Canadian law.[254] Family members of refugees are not automatically recognized as such. However, where one member of a close family is at risk, it is generally plausible that other members will also be at risk. In addition, the family members of successful refugee claimants within Canada and resettled refugees from abroad may be granted permanent residence based upon their familial relations.[255]

M. *SUR PLACE* CLAIMS

The preceding discussion of the requirements of the definition of "refugee" is largely premised upon a situation where a claimant faces an increasing level of risk in the country of reference, flees to Canada, and then seeks protection as a refugee. This sequence of events, however, is not required by the definition. In some cases, the refugee claimant's departure may precede any risk. "A person becomes a refugee '*sur place*' due to the circumstances arising in his country of origin during his absence."[256] The archetype of such a "*sur place*" claim is the pro-government political activist who is outside his country of reference when a revolution occurs.

The sequence of flight and risk is irrelevant as far as satisfying the legal requirements of the definition of "refugee." However, the sequence can reveal important aspects of the underlying facts upon which the claim is based. In situations where the flight precedes the risk, the facts will likely need to establish that there has been a significant change in circumstances since the claimant's departure from the country of reference. Such a change can relate to either the situation in the country — as is the case with revolution — or the claimant. With respect to the former, the post-departure discovery of the claimant's activities, the further activities of associates of the claimant, and a change in policy by the government may all cause a risk to arise after a claimant

---

254 While the *IRPA*, s 3(1)(d) (and previous provisions in the *Immigration Act*) recognizes the principle of family unity in Canadian immigration law more generally, this has been found not to affect the interpretation of the definition of "refugee." *Casetellanos v Canada (Solicitor General)*, [1994] FCJ No 1926 (TD); *Carrillo v Canada (Minister of Citizenship and Immigration)* 2012 FC 1228 at para 15.

255 A protected person may apply for permanent residence and include all immediate family members on his application. An individual applying for resettlement may include her immediate family members on her application.

256 UNHCR *Handbook*, above note 21 at para 95.

has departed the country of reference. With respect to the latter, the post-departure activities of the claimant are the most obvious way in which the claimant may alter how she is perceived and, hence, increase her risk. There are limits to how much a claimant may "change" subsequent to departure; a claimant may not manufacture risk by flagrantly bringing himself to the attention of potential agents of persecution after his departure from the country of reference. However, this "prohibition" is best understood as arising from the lack of subjective fear and credibility concerns that such behaviour raises than as arising from a prohibition on such a post-departure change of behaviour.[257]

N. CONCLUSION

As the foregoing discussion has illustrated, the definition's less than a hundred words have produced a much more wordy discourse about what types of circumstances fall within it. Almost every sentence in this chapter could be expanded and nuanced into a paragraph. However, while the explanation of the definition is not complete, it provides an outline of the essential elements of the definition.

To qualify as a refugee, an individual must establish a strong likelihood of persecution in his country (or countries) of reference. The persecution must be a serious interference with important human rights from which the government of the country of reference cannot offer him protection. Finally, either the persecution itself or the lack of protection must be linked to the individual's nationality, race, religion, political opinion, or membership in a particular social group — or the perception thereof by his persecutors. Unless all these conditions are fulfilled, an individual, no matter how much at risk or otherwise deserving, will not qualify as a refugee.

It was noted at the outset of this conclusion that the explanation of the definition provided is incomplete. On a practical level, the current volume of jurisprudence and pace of developments would make completion difficult. However, on a more abstract level, there is an underlying, deliberate dynamism in the definition of "refugee" that prevents it from becoming fixed. The definition is constantly reinterpreted in light of the evolving meaning and scope of its terms and of other areas of international law, including, in particular, emerging concepts in

---

257 *Zewedu v Canada (Minister of Citizenship and Immigration)*, [2000] FCJ No 1369 (TD); *De Corcho Herrera v Canada (Minister of Employment and Immigration)*, [1993] FCJ No 1089 at para 10 (TD).

international human rights law. The definition of refugee is very much a *living* definition. For this reason, more than any practical obstacles, any effort to delimit the definition will ultimately be frustrated.

CHAPTER 5

EXCLUSION FROM REFUGEE PROTECTION

A. INTRODUCTION

Not everyone who satisfies the provisions of the definition of refugee will be considered a refugee. The *Convention Relating to the Status of Refugees*[1] and Canadian law set out various categories of individuals who are to be excluded from status as refugees. Exclusion is not discretionary; it is mandatory. For example, from 2008 to 2011, the federal government raised an issue of exclusion in, on average, ninety refugee cases before the Immigration and Refugee Board (IRB).[2] The Board considers exclusion on its own motion in an unknown, but likely larger, number of further cases. All individuals who fall within any of the "exclusion" provisions will be automatically deemed not to be refugees so will not benefit from any of the protections offered to refugees.

As discussed further below, refugee claimants may be excluded based on their lack of need of protection (article 1E) or their being undeserving of protection (article 1F).[3] The *Refugee Convention* also excludes a

1 28 July 1951, 189 UNTS 150 [*Refugee Convention*].

2 Canada Border Services Agency, *Canada's Program on Crimes against Humanity and War Crimes, 12th Report: 2008–2011*, online: CBSA www.cbsa-asfc.gc.ca/security-securite/wc-cg/wc-cg2011-eng.html#c5x1. For example, in 2011, the CBSA intervened in eighty-eight cases and investigated intervening in almost 600 other cases.

3 Sections 1E and 1F of the *Refugee Convention*, Schedule to the *Immigration and Refugee Protection* Act, SC 2001, c 27 [*IRPA*] (pursuant to s 2(1) *q.v.* "*Refugee Convention*").

subset of Palestinian refugees who are not seen to be in need of protection (article 1D), but Canada has not incorporated this exclusion into domestic law. The exclusion provisions express two key ideas found in the *Refugee Convention*: (1) that international protection is subsidiary to national protection, and (2) that international protection obligations do not trump national and international interests. These ideas will be discussed further in the analysis of articles 1E and 1F, below.

The consequences of exclusion are severe. As stated by the Supreme Court of Canada in the leading case of *Pushpanathan v Canada (Minister of Citizenship and Immigration)*,[4] the profound consequences of the exclusion provisions must inform their interpretation and application:

> By contrast, persons falling within article 1F of the Convention are automatically excluded from the protections of the Act. Not only may they be returned to the country from which they have sought refuge without any determination by the Minister that they pose a threat to public safety or national security, but their substantive claim to refugee status will not be considered. The practical implications of such an automatic exclusion . . . are profound . . . . It is against this background that the interpretation of the exclusion contained in article 1F(c) of the Convention must be considered.[5]

One immediate consequence of this approach is the narrow interpretation of the exclusion provisions that has been adopted in the jurisprudence. The exclusion provisions are exhaustive and must be interpreted strictly so as not to frustrate the intention of the *Refugee Convention* to provide protection. As stated in UNHCR's *Handbook on Procedures and Criteria for Determining Refugee Status under the 1951 Convention and the 1967 Protocol*: "Considering the serious consequences

---

E. This Convention shall not apply to a person who is recognized by the competent authorities of the country in which he has taken residence as having the rights and obligations which are attached to the possession of the nationality of that country.

F. The provisions of this Convention shall not apply to any person with respect to whom there are serious reasons for considering that:
   (a) he has committed a crime against peace, a war crime, or a crime against humanity, as defined in the international instruments drawn up to make provision in respect of such crimes;
   (b) he has committed a serious non-political crime outside the country of refuge prior to his admission to that country as a refugee;
   (c) he has been guilty of acts contrary to the purposes and principles of the United Nations.

4 [1998] SCJ No 46 at para 13 [*Pushpanathan*].

5 *Pushpanathan*, above note 4.

of exclusion for the person concerned, however, the interpretation of these exclusion clauses must be restrictive."[6] This statement is echoed in the Canadian jurisprudence.[7]

Nonetheless, the idea of certain individuals being undeserving of protection as refugees sits uneasily with conceptions of universality embodied in international human rights law. The core protections of most international human rights instruments are unqualified: they include, for example, the freedom from arbitrary deprivation of life[8] and the prohibition against torture.[9] This dissonance serves as a useful reminder that refugee law is often better understood as a subset of immigration law than as a subset of human rights law. It is arguably against the self-interest of a state and of the international community to grant protection to individuals viewed as undeserving.[10]

Although the grounds of exclusion are explicitly taken from the *Refugee Convention* and absent from subsequent international human rights treaties, the *Immigration and Refugee Protection Act* statutorily extends exclusion to refugee claimants seeking protection as persons in need of protection.[11] Thus, a refugee claimant fearing torture will be excluded from protection if she falls within the provisions of article 1E or 1F. Depending on the ground of exclusion, such individuals may, through a pre-removal risk assessment (PRRA), qualify either as a protected person (article 1E) or for a stay of removal (article 1F).[12] In either case, by virtue of the statutory extension, exclusion in Canada is not simply an issue for "Convention refugees."

---

6 HCR/IP/4/Eng/rev.1 (1979; re-edited January 1992) at para 149 [UNHCR *Handbook*].

7 *Ramirez v Canada (Minister of Employment and Immigration)*, [1992] 2 FC 306 (CA) [*Ramirez*]; *Zrig v Canada (Minister of Citizenship and Immigration)*, [2001] FCJ No 1433 at para 102 (TD) [*Zrig*] (in reference to art 1F, aff'd by the Federal Court of Appeal in *Zilenko v Canada (Minister of Citizenship and Immigration)*, 2003 FC 846).

8 *International Covenant on Civil and Political Rights*, 19 December 1966, 999 UNTS 171, art 6(1) [*ICCPR*].

9 *Convention Against Torture and Other Cruel, Inhuman or Degrading Treatment or Punishment*, 10 December 1984, Can TS 1987 No 36, 23 ILM 1027, art 2 [*CAT*].

10 Of course, the argument can be made that a longer-term or "higher self-interest" of both a particular state and the international community is served by the adoption of universal human rights, and the extension of protection on that basis.

11 Above note 3, s 98.

12 Under the *IRPA*, *ibid*, s 113(d)(ii), the analysis of who should be excluded under art 1F requires a balancing of a claim as a "person in need of protection" against "whether the application should be refused because of the nature and severity of acts committed by the applicant or because of the danger that the applicant constitutes to the security of Canada."

Although this chapter, like Chapter 4, will frequently refer to "refugee claimants," the exclusion provisions apply equally to overseas applicants. However, as indicated in the previous paragraph, the consequences of exclusion and the alternative avenues for protection to someone who has been excluded will be different for overseas applicants and inland refugee claimants.

B. RELATION TO INCLUSION

The example of an individual at risk of torture who is excluded from protection raises the question of whether the analysis of exclusion should include a consideration of the degree of mistreatment that an individual would face upon return to the country of reference.

Even though falling within an exclusion provision precludes a person from being granted protection as a refugee, the decision maker will, as a matter of practice, normally canvass and determine both exclusion and (in the alternative) inclusion. This has the practical effect of allowing any court sitting in review to overturn errors in the exclusion analysis without necessarily requiring a rehearing of the claim. Despite the fact that exclusion and inclusion will frequently be discussed in the same decision, the analyses of the two do not overlap. The degree of well-founded fear possessed by a claimant has no impact upon whether he will be excluded from protection. A refugee claimant will be excluded from protection if she falls within article 1E or 1F of the *Refugee Convention*, even if she is at certain risk of an extremely serious human rights violation under one of the enumerated grounds upon return to her country of nationality. UNHCR has campaigned, without much success, against this hard-hearted application of the exclusion provisions.[13] However, in *Gonzalez v Canada (Minister of Employment and Immigration)*,[14] the Federal Court of Appeal ruled that making a determination does not involve a balancing of the persecution that may be suffered by the refugee claimant against the consequences of his exclusion. As a consequence, an individual will be excluded even if he faces horrendous mistreatment in the country of reference.

---

13 Canada's approach is also followed in most common law countries. In the opinion of the authors, UNHCR's position largely ignores the clear debate contained in the *travaux préparatoires* about whether to make the exclusion provisions mandatory or discretionary. In short, the parties had a clear intention to make the provisions mandatory; UNHCR's suggested approach is more consistent with discretionary exclusion provisions.

14 (1994), 115 DLR (4th) 403 (FCA).

C. BURDEN OF PROOF

There is no onus on a refugee claimant to establish that she should not be excluded. Rather, any exclusion must be established on the evidence. In practice, this means that the burden of proof lies upon the government.[15] This burden is typically met by raising the issue through the Minister's participation in proceedings before the Board which may involve issues of exclusion.[16] In the overseas process, this burden can be met through the gathering of background information about the claimant through criminal and security checks. In the absence of an allegation, the Board may consider exclusion on its own motion.[17] In all cases, the evidence must establish that the requirements of exclusion are met.

The obvious corollary of the proposition that there is no requirement that a refugee claimant establish his non-exclusion is that a claimant must be advised if exclusion becomes an issue so that he may introduce evidence to address it. Failure to provide the claimant with a reasonable opportunity to present evidence concerning his exclusion will fatally flaw the decision.[18] The Board must generally notify the Minister if exclusion is an issue in a claim.[19]

The wordings of articles 1E and 1F of the *Refugee Convention* impose different standards of proof. Article 1E states that the protections of the *Refugee Convention* do not apply to a person if certain criteria are fulfilled. Article 1F, on the other hand, states that the protections of the *Refugee Convention* do not apply to a person if there are "serious reasons for considering" that various criteria are fulfilled. The difference between the wordings of the two articles has been interpreted as requiring a lower standard of proof for article 1F. The applicability of article 1E must be established on a balance of probabilities; concretely,

15 *Ezokola v Canada (Citizenship and Immigration)*, 2013 SCC 40 at para 29 [*Ezokola*]. Officers of the Canada Border Services Agency represent the government in exclusion matters before the Board as "Minister's representatives."

16 For more on the intervention of the minister, please see Chapter 8.

17 *Fletes v Canada (Secretary of State)* (1994), 83 FTR 49 (TD); *Gutierrez et al v Canada (Minister of Employment and Immigration)* (1994), 84 FTR 227 (TD); *Ashari v Canada (Minister of Citizenship and Immigration)*, [1999] FCJ No 1703 at para 7 (CA).

18 *Kone v Canada (Minister of Employment and Immigration)*, [1994] FCJ No 699 (TD); *Malouf v Canada (Minister of Citizenship and Immigration)*, [1994] FCJ No 1623 (TD), aff'd [1995] FCJ No 1506 (CA).

19 *Refugee Protection Division Rules*, SOR/2012-256, r 23. The notification is mandatory if the Board becomes aware that exclusion is an issue before the commencement of the hearing (r 23(1)); notification is discretionary after the commencement of the hearing (r 23(2)).

this requires "clear evidence" of the individual's status elsewhere.[20] Article 1F's applicability must be established at the lesser standard of "reasonable grounds to believe," which has been described as "a bona fide belief in a serious possibility based on credible evidence."[21] An arrest warrant or evidence of prosecution for an international crime may establish "serious reasons for considering." However, there must be some meaningful analysis of the underlying evidence or an analysis of indicia of reliability of the foreign body or process; a slavish adherence simply to the final judgment of a foreign court will ordinarily be insufficient.[22]

Exclusion must be established against each individual who is sought to be excluded. The exclusion of one refugee claimant does not automatically lead to the exclusion of that claimant's associates or family members. To paraphrase the Federal Court of Appeal in *Moreno v Canada (Minister of Employment and Immigration)*, exclusion clauses cannot serve as a means of effectively promoting retributive justice at the expense of the innocent.[23]

D. ARTICLE 1D

The *Refugee Convention* contains a controversial exclusion of Palestinian refugees. This exclusion is contained within article 1D:

> This Convention shall not apply to persons who are at present receiving from organs or agencies of the United Nations other than the United Nations High Commissioner for Refugees protection or assistance.
>
> When such protection or assistance has ceased for any reason, without the position of such persons being definitively settled in accordance with the relevant resolutions adopted by the General Assembly of the United Nations, these persons shall ipso facto be entitled to the benefits of this Convention.

The only category of individuals who were in receipt of assistance from other agencies of the United Nations were those people who had been displaced due to the Arab-Israeli War of 1948. In December 1949,

---

20 *Canada (Minister of Citizenship and Immigration) v Choovak*, [2002] FCJ No 767 (TD) [*Choovak*].

21 *Chiau v Canada (Minister of Citizenship and Immigration)*, [2001] 2 FC 297 (CA).

22 *Ching v Canada (Minister of Citizenship and Immigration)*, 2015 FC 860.

23 [1993] FCJ No 912 (CA) [*Moreno*].

the United Nations established the United Nations Relief and Works Agency (UNRWA) to deal with this population, now known as Palestinians. The UNRWA remains in existence today.

The most common explanation of this provision is that it was intended to allow the Arab-Israeli conflict to be resolved outside the framework of refugee protection.[24] Not surprisingly, like most other issues concerning Israel/Palestine, the exclusion of Palestinians from the protections of the *Refugee Convention* has occasioned much commentary and controversy. States have relied upon very restrictive interpretations of the terms of article 1D to deny many Palestinians protection within the terms of the *Refugee Convention*.[25]

Canada has not incorporated article 1D into domestic law. The protection of Palestinian refugees by UNRWA usually emerges as an evidentiary issue rather than one of exclusion: as evidence of identity and prior recognition elsewhere of status as a refugee.[26] The narrow debate over the meaning of article 1D terms is not relevant to Canadian law. The Canadian jurisprudence must deal with some of these issues elsewhere in its analysis of the definition: to what extent should states offer protection to those whose needs are already being met by the international community? More generally, article 1D raises the question, which states are just now beginning to deal with, of the interrelationship between the granting of refugee protection and the reconstruction of conflict-torn societies.

E. ARTICLE 1E

Article 1E of the *Refugee Convention* excludes a refugee claimant "who is recognized by the competent authorities of the country in which he has taken residence as having the rights and obligations which are attached to the possession of the nationality of that country." The exclusion is based upon the person's lack of need of international protection:

---

24 Whether this motivation should be framed benignly (as evidencing a desire not to confound the search for a solution) or malignantly (as evidencing a desire not to offer protection to the millions of displaced Arabs) is the subject of much debate.

25 BADIL Resource Center, "Closing Protection Gaps: A Handbook on Protection of Palestinian Refugees in States Signatories to the 1951 Refugee Convention," 2d ed (Bethlehem: BADIL Resource Center, 2011).

26 *El Bahisi v Canada (Minister of Employment and Immigration)* (1994), 72 FTR 117 (TD).

> If A faces such a threat in his own country, but is living in another country, with or without refugee status, and there faces no threat of persecution for Convention reasons, or put another way, A there enjoys the same basic rights of status as nationals of the second country, the function of Article 1E is to exclude that person as a potential refugee claimant in a third country.[27]

Following this example, exclusion under article 1E will not occur when A fears persecution in the second country. Rather, it is designed to prevent a person from "asylum shopping" while entitled to status in a "safe" country.[28]

Article 1E necessitates an analysis of the rights of the refugee claimant in her country of former residence. The "rights which are attached to the possession of the nationality of that country" have been interpreted as consisting of the core entitlements of citizenship:

1) the right to return to and reside for an unlimited time in the country of residence;
2) the right to study;
3) the right to work; and
4) the right to access basic social services in that country.[29]

At issue with respect to each of these core rights is the degree to which the refugee claimant's status has been "assimilated" to that of a national.[30] The precise list of rights that need to be considered will vary depending on the circumstances of the refugee claimant and the degree to which they can be limited under international law. The absence or limitation of one of these rights will not necessarily prevent a finding of exclusion under article 1E.

Of these four enumerated domains of rights, the jurisprudence is overwhelmingly concerned about the first right: the right to enter and reside. Unfortunately, it is difficult to generalize about the status required to fulfill the first core entitlement of entry and residency. Temporary discretionary renewable status will be insufficient;[31] permanent

---

27 *Kroon v Canada (Minister of Employment and Immigration)*, [1995] FCJ No 11 at para 10 (TD).

28 *Zeng v Canada (Minister of Citizenship and Immigration)*, 2010 FCA 118 [*Zeng*].

29 *Shamlou v Canada (Minister of Citizenship and Immigration)*, [1995] FCJ No 1537 (TD); *Kanesharan v Canada (Minister of Citizenship and Immigration)*, [1996] FCJ No 1278 (TD); *Choezom v Canada (Minister of Citizenship and Immigration)*, [2004] FCJ No 1608 (TD).

30 *CRD (Re)*, [2000] CRDD No 160 at para 11 (IRB).

31 *Canada (Minister of Citizenship and Immigration) v Alsha'bi*, 2015 FC 1381.

residence status will likely be sufficient.[32] There is clearly a continuum between these two positions: the intermediary points must be defined according to their own particular facts. As a general rule, however, the individual must be "fully protected against deportation or expulsion."[33]

Despite the general rule that the elements of the refugee definition must be fulfilled at the time of the hearing, a temporally "fluid" approach is adopted in the case of an assessment of rights under article 1D.[34] In particular, an assessment of the right to enter and reside must consider whether status was possessed previously, including at the time of the refugee claimant's request for refugee status.[35] The antedating of the assessment of this requirement is for policy reasons: to prevent a claimant from delaying his hearing in order to allow his status to expire in the country of former residence and to thereby prevent article 1E from being established.[36] The resulting sequential analysis was set out by the Federal Court of Appeal in *Zeng v Canada (Minister of Citizenship and Immigration)*:

> Does the claimant have status, substantially similar to that of its nationals, in the third country? If the answer is yes, the claimant is excluded. If the answer is no, the next question is whether the claimant previously had such status and lost it, or had access to such status and failed to acquire it. If the answer is no, the claimant is not excluded under Article 1E. If the answer is yes, the RPD must consider and balance various factors. These include, but are not limited to, the reason for the loss of status (voluntary or involuntary), whether the claimant could return to the third country, the risk the claimant would face in the home country, Canada's international obligations, and any other relevant facts.[37]

The jurisprudence is still somewhat confused about how the loss of status in the country of former residence after making a refugee claim is relevant. It has been suggested that if such a loss of status is established, the refugee claimant must explain why "having allowed the permanent residency to expire, [he or] she could not have re-applied

---

32 *Zeng*, above note 28.

33 CRD (Re), above note 30 at para 11 (quoting UNHCR *Handbook*, above note 6 at para 144ff).

34 *Zeng*, above note 28 at para 13ff.

35 *Mahdi v Canada (Minister of Citizenship and Immigration)*, [1995] FCJ No 1623 at para 12 (CA).

36 *Choovak*, above note 20 at para 37.

37 *Zeng*, above note 28 at para 28.

and obtained [a renewal or continuation of status]."[38] This proposition begs the question, which has not yet been clearly answered, of what would be a satisfactory explanation. The wording of the proposition suggests that any proof of an inability to regain status would be sufficient. Recent jurisprudence, however, has suggested that the inability to regain status is less important than evidence that the claimant is not "asylum shopping."[39] It can be suggested that the preferable approach would be to abandon the temporal fluidity of the consideration of status. In any case, in some situations antedating the assessment will assist in asylum shopping (as is the case where a refugee claimant abandons an application for status elsewhere that subsequently vests him with rights after his arrival in Canada).[40] Concerns about asylum shopping, which are likely overblown in any case, could then be dealt with through the tools of credibility and subjective fear.[41]

F. ARTICLE 1F

Article 1F excludes individuals who are "undeserving of protection" due to their past misconduct. The sub-clauses of article 1F provide an exhaustive list of past misconduct that is sufficiently deplorable as to warrant exclusion. The evidentiary threshold for establishing exclusion under any element of article 1F is proof of "serious reasons for believing." As noted earlier, this standard is lower than a balance of probabilities, but more than mere suspicion or conjecture.[42]

The three grounds for exclusion under article 1F are as follows: (1) commission of a crime against peace, a war crime, or a crime against humanity; (2) commission of a serious non-political crime outside the country of refuge; and (3) commission of an act contrary to the purposes and principles of the United Nations. Each of these grounds for exclusion will be discussed in detail below.

---

38 *Romero v Canada (Minister of Citizenship and Immigration)*, [2006] FCJ No 647 at para 8 (TD).

39 *Canada (Minister of Citizenship and Immigration) v Manoharan*, [2005] FCJ No 1398 (FC).

40 *Mohamed v Canada (Minister of Citizenship and Immigration)*, [1997] FCJ No 400 (TD).

41 *Shahpari v Canada (Minister of Citizenship and Immigration)*, [1998] FCJ No 429 (TD).

42 *Moreno*, above note 23.

1) Article 1F(a)

Article 1F(a) excludes individuals who have committed serious crimes against the international community:

> F. The provisions of this Convention shall not apply to any person with respect to whom there are serious reasons for considering that:
>
> (a) He has committed a crime against peace, a war crime, or a crime against humanity, as defined in the international instruments drawn up to make provision in respect of such crimes . . .

Each of three categories of crimes listed in article 1F(a) has a precise meaning in international law. Furthermore, article 1F(a) requires these crimes to be defined by reference to international instruments. The international instrument most frequently used to define these crimes is the *Charter of the International Military Tribunal*, which is also known as the *London Charter*;[43] the *Rome Statute of the International Criminal Court* is also increasingly being used to define crimes against humanity.[44] All terms must be interpreted in accordance with what was a crime at the date of alleged commission — not merely what was a crime when the *Refugee Convention* was drafted or what is a crime at the date of the hearing.[45] In addition to the elements of the crime being rooted in international law, the potential modes of commission (and defences) must also be grounded in the quickly developing field of international criminal law.[46]

a) Crimes against Peace

A crime against peace is defined by the *Charter of the International Military Tribunal*, article 6, as including the following acts:

> planning, preparation, initiation or waging of a war of aggression, or a war in violation of international treaties, agreements or assurances, or participation in a common plan or conspiracy for the accomplishment of any of the foregoing.

43 82 UNTS 279 (1945), also known as the *London Charter*.

44 2187 UNTS 90 (1998) [*Rome Statute*].

45 For example, the *Rome Statute*, *ibid*, entered into force on 1 July 2002. Its provisions therefore cannot be used in and of themselves to define a crime before that date.

46 *Ezokola*, above note 15 at para 43.

While the *Rome Statute* makes reference to "the crime of aggression," the Court has not yet taken jurisdiction over such a crime.[47] Based upon the historic and current agreed-on definitions, however, it is clear that only the instigation of an international conflict will come within the terms of crime against peace (or crime of aggression). So far, there have been no cases considering crimes against peace before the Board or the Federal Court.[48]

b) War Crimes

War crimes are also defined in the *Charter of the International Military Tribunal*, article 6, and include the following acts:

> violations of the laws or customs of war. Such violations shall include, but not be limited to, murder, ill-treatment or deportation to slave labor or for any other purpose of civilian population of or in occupied territory, murder or ill-treatment of prisoners of war or persons on the seas, killing of hostages, plunder of public or private property, wanton destruction of cities, towns or villages, or devastation not justified by military necessity.

More recently, the *Rome Statute* has refined the definition of war crimes. Article 8 defines war crimes as including "grave breaches" of the *Geneva Conventions* in international conflicts, "serious violations" of common article 3 of the *Geneva Conventions* in non-international conflicts, and other "serious violations" of the laws and customs applicable in either international or national armed conflict. The parties to the Statute have further elaborated upon the definition of war crimes in the International Criminal Court's "Elements of Crimes" document, negotiated pursuant to article 9 of the Statute.[49] In addition, there is a growing body of jurisprudence further elaborating upon the legal ele-

---

47 *Rome Statute*, above note 44, arts 5(1)(d) & (2). The definitions and the conditions for the exercise of jurisdiction over the crime of aggression were adopted by consensus at the 2010 Kampala Review Conference by the states parties to the International Criminal Court. However, this amendment to the *Rome Statute* can enter into force only once, (1) at least thirty state parties have ratified it and, (2) after 1 January 2017, the assembly of states parties makes a decision to activate the ICC's jurisdiction over the crime of aggression. As of February 2017, more than thirty states had ratified the amendment, but no decision on activation of jurisdiction had yet been made.

48 It is unlikely that an individual who potentially committed a crime against peace contrary to art 1F(a) would have a hearing before the Board as he would be very likely to be ineligible for referral to the Board due to inadmissibility on security grounds or due to human or international rights violations. *IRPA*, above note 13, ss 34, 35, and 101.

49 UN Doc PCNICC/2000/1/Add.2 (2000).

ments of war crimes from the ad hoc international criminal tribunals for the former Yugoslavia and Rwanda and, in the future, the International Criminal Court.[50]

Unlike crimes against peace, war crimes are not restricted to international conflicts. However, the definition of what constitutes a war crime varies between international and non-international conflicts.

c) Crimes against Humanity

Article 6 of the *Charter of the International Military Tribunal* defines crimes against humanity as including the following acts:

> namely, murder, extermination, enslavement, deportation, and other inhumane acts committed against any civilian population, before or during the war; or persecutions on political, racial or religious grounds in execution of or in connection with any crime within the jurisdiction of the Tribunal, whether or not in violation of the domestic law of the country where perpetrated.

As with war crimes, the *Rome Statute* specifies eleven acts that qualify as crimes against humanity.[51] A precondition of any such act is that it is committed as "part of a widespread or systematic attack directed against any civilian population, with knowledge of the attack."[52] Canadian law has also criminalized many of these acts.[53] Although both international and Canadian law distinguish between "crimes against humanity" and "genocide," the jurisprudence and UNHCR policy often merge the two together in their analysis.[54]

A distinction must be made between war crimes and crimes against humanity. While even an isolated act may qualify as the former, only an

---

50 On the importance of considering this international caselaw when assessing acts, see *Mugesera v Canada (Minister of Citizenship and Immigration)*, [2005] SCJ No 39 [*Mugesera*] (albeit, on the facts, in the context of inadmissibility). Of particular usefulness is the jurisprudence of the Appeals Chamber of the International Criminal Tribunal for the former Yugoslavia (which also hears appeals from the International Criminal Tribunal for Rwanda).

51 *Rome Statute*, above note 44, art 7.

52 *Ibid.*

53 *Crimes against Humanity and War Crimes Act*, SC 2000, c 24, ss 4 and 6 (formerly the *Criminal Code*, RSC 1985, c C-46, ss 7(3.76) & 7(3.77)).

54 The *Convention on the Prevention and Punishment of the Crime of Genocide* (General Assembly resolution 260 A (III) of 9 December 1948), entered into force in 1951 just as the *Refugee Convention* was being negotiated. On genocide qualifying as a crime against humanity, see "Guidelines on International Protection: Application of the Exclusion Clauses: Art 1F of the 1951 *Convention Relating to the Status of Refugees*," HCR/GIP/03/05 (2003) at para 13.

act that is part of a larger pattern of wrongful action will qualify as the latter. A crime against humanity must be a single prohibited act within a larger group of acts which are either a "widespread" or "systematic" attack against a civilian population. Both of these terms have been defined in the jurisprudence, most recently in the Supreme Court's decision in *Mugesera v Canada (Minister of Citizenship and Immigration)*.[55] In that case, the Court interpreted "widespread" as a "massive, frequent, large-scale action, carried out collectively with considerable seriousness and directed against a multiplicity of victims."[56] The key to an act being widespread is its consequence: both numerous less serious acts and a single very serious act would qualify as "widespread." Whereas a widespread attack need not be organized, a systematic attack is defined as being "thoroughly organised and follow[ing] a regular pattern on the basis of a common policy involving substantial public or private resources."[57]

d) Complicity and Intent

Complicity is the international legal equivalent of being a "party" to a crime under Canadian law. The Federal Court of Appeal has commented that in almost all cases involving exclusion under article 1F(a) "argument turned not on the existence of a crime but on the latter's nature or on the participation of the person concerned in its perpetration."[58]

The complicity of an individual who commits the act that constitutes the prohibited act under article 1F(a) is uncontested. In greater dispute is the complicity of those who assisted the individual in the commission of the act or who supported him through active participation in the organization of which they are both members. More concretely, the torturer is obviously excluded under article 1F(a), but what about the officer who guards the door of the room in which the torture occurs and the secretary who files the confessions produced by torture? The Supreme Court has held that while complicity can result in exclusion, mere association cannot: "[i]ndividuals may be excluded from refugee protection for international crimes through a variety of modes of commission. Guilt by association, however, is not one of them."[59]

For the most part, mere membership in an organization will not suffice to make a claimant complicit in an article 1F(a) act. The exception to this rule is a situation where the nature of the organization

55 *Mugesera*, above note 50 at paras 154 & 155.
56 *Ibid* at para 154.
57 *Ibid* at para 155.
58 *Ibid* at para 1.
59 *Ezokola*, above note 15 at paras 2 &3.

is such that its entire purpose is directed at acts of the type that fall within article 1F(a). In such a case, membership will "by necessity involve personal and knowing participation in persecutorial acts" and be sufficient to bring a claimant within the scope of article 1F(a).[60] Secret police organizations are often cited as the archetype of such an organization. However, this remains an evidentiary presumption and may still be rebutted by evidence to the contrary.[61]

The "personal and knowing participation" test developed in *Ramirez v Canada (Minister of Employment and Immigration)* has recently been narrowed and replaced by a "contribution-based approach": an individual may be excluded only where he has "voluntarily made a significant and knowing contribution to a group's crime or criminal purpose."[62] This approach is drawn from the provisions in the *Rome Statute* that define war crimes and crimes against humanity that create criminal liability where a person "[i]n any other way contributes to the commission or attempted commission of such a crime."[63]

The contribution must be voluntary and must be made knowingly; the Supreme Court (as well as some international jurisprudence) has suggested that mere recklessness will likely be insufficient.[64] A knowing contribution is made with the awareness that the "conduct will assist in the furtherance of the crime or criminal purpose."[65] A significant contribution is one that is either "directed to specific identifiable crimes" or "directed to wider concepts of common design."[66] While any analysis must take account of the particular circumstances of the case at hand (and focus on the role of the claimant), the following

---

60 *Ramirez*, above note 7.

61 *Moreno*, above note 23.

62 *Ezokola*, above note 15 at para 8. The courts have been uncertain whether this approach should be extended to the interpretation of other explicit or implicit references to international crimes in the *IRPA*, particularly concerning inadmissibility. *Canada (Minister of Citizenship and Immigration) v Halindintwali*, 2015 FC 390; *Haqi v Canada (Minister of Public Safety and Emergency Preparedness)*, 2015 FCA 256; *Joseph v Canada (Minister of Citizenship and Immigration)*, 2013 FC 1101; *Kanagendren v Canada (Minister of Citizenship and Immigration)*, 2015 FCA 86.

63 Article 25(3)(d) of the *Rome Statute*, above note 44. The other provisions of art 25(3) create criminal liability for other, more direct and conventional, forms of involvement in the commission of an international crime (e.g., direct commission; ordering; aiding and abetting; attempting; and, in the case of genocide, incitement).

64 *Ezokola*, above note 15 at para 60.

65 *Ibid* at para 89.

66 *Ibid* at para 87, quoting with approval *R (JS (Sri Lanka)) v Secretary of State for the Home Department*, [2010] UKSC 15.

are important considerations in determining whether there has been a voluntary, significant, and knowing contribution to an international crime:

(i) the size and nature of the organization;
(ii) the part of the organization with which the refugee claimant was most directly concerned;
(iii) the refugee claimant's duties and activities within the organization;
(iv) the refugee claimant's position or rank in the organization;
(v) the length of time the refugee claimant was in the organization, particularly after acquiring knowledge of the group's crime or criminal purpose; and
(vi) the method by which the refugee claimant was recruited and the refugee claimant's opportunity to leave the organization.[67]

Notwithstanding the adoption of the contribution-based approach, mere membership in an organization with a "limited brutal purpose" may still result in exclusion.[68] In order to make a determination of exclusion in such a case, the conduct of the claimant in committing, condoning, or encouraging acts prohibited by article 1F(a) must be assessed. A mere bystander will not be complicit in a crime, but "a person who aids in or encourages the commission of a crime may be responsible therefore."[69] Indicia of complicity can include remaining in a position within an organization after learning of prohibited acts, holding a senior position in the organization, being in close association with the perpetrators of the prohibited acts, and not making efforts to either prevent the prohibited acts or leave the organization after the commission of the prohibited acts.[70]

e) Defences

As with domestic criminal law, a refugee claimant accused of committing an excludable act may admit the commission of the act but proffer a defence that absolves her of criminal liability for the act. Such defences

---

67 *Ezokola*, above note 15 at para 91.

68 *Betoukoumesou v Canada (Minister of Citizenship and Immigration)*, 2014 FC 591 [*Betoukoumesou*].

69 *Mohammad v Canada (Minister of Citizenship and Immigration)* (1995), 115 FTR 161 at 178 (TD) [*Mohammad*].

70 *Sivakumar v Canada (Minister of Employment and Immigration)*, [1994] 1 FC 433 (CA); *Penate v Canada (Minister of Employment and Immigration)*, [1994] 2 FC 79 (CA); *Mohammad*, above note 69; *Shrestha v Canada (Minister of Citizenship and Immigration)*, [2002] FCJ No 1154 (TD).

typically attempt to remove the intentional component of the crime by pointing to some overriding circumstance that compelled the act. With respect to article 1F(a), the most commonly proffered defences are the defences of duress, military necessity, and superior orders.

Duress is the most frequently invoked defence. A variation of the general defence of necessity, the defence of duress attempts to vitiate the required voluntary intent by pointing to an imminent physical threat that compelled the claimant to commit the act in question. However, like the defence of necessity in domestic criminal law,[71] limits are placed upon the defence of duress:

> First, in order for the defense of duress to apply, the act which the applicant was compelled to take must be driven by a grave and imminent peril which is sought to be avoided . . . . The second necessary element to the application of the defense of duress incorporates the notion of proportionality, that is, the harm inflicted on the victim . . . must not be in excess of that which would otherwise have been directed at the applicant.[72]

The immediacy of duress will require clear risk of sanction. It will also likely be impossible to fulfill the proportionality requirement where the victims were tortured and/or killed.[73] While the Supreme Court reiterated the availability of the defence of duress in *Ezokola v Canada (Citizenship and Immigration)*, it remains unclear whether its requirement of voluntariness as part of the criminal complicity will allow a narrower form of duress to vitiate rather than excuse criminal liability.

The jurisprudence frequently discusses at great length whether the claimant fled the situation "at the first available opportunity." This requirement is often listed as a separate requirement. Analytically, it would seem to be better treated as an element of both immediacy (whether the claimant "sought to avoid" the situation) and the credibility of the claimant's testimony thereof. At times, the jurisprudence has also suggested that the situation cannot be brought about through the misdeeds of the claimant; whether the claimant volunteered for the position that he held is relevant in determining this aspect of duress.[74] This proposition is the analogue of the domestic criminal preclusion of

---

71 *Perka v The Queen*, [1984] 2 SCR 232.

72 *Kathiravel v Canada (Minister of Citizenship and Immigration)*, [2003] FCJ No 882 at paras 45–47 (TD) [*Kathiravel*].

73 *Arica v Canada (Solicitor General)*, [2005] FCJ No 1149 at para 25 (FC).

74 Compare *Kathiravel*, above note 72, to *Canada (Minister of Citizenship and Immigration) v Asghedom*, [2001] FCJ No 1350 at para 42 (TD) (conscripted).

the defence of necessity in cases where the accused was acting illegally. Again, this component of the analysis can be similarly incorporated into the analysis of immediacy.

The defence of necessity can overlap with the defence of duress; the lack of any other option at the core of necessity can be the result of duress. However, necessity can also take another form: the military necessity of committing a particular prohibited act. As most war crimes and crimes against humanity are defined by their lack of any direct link to military necessity — insofar as they involve, for example, targeting the civilian population — the defence of military necessity is unlikely to be established on the facts of most cases.[75] In short, the defence of military necessity will be available only where the crime itself provides for an exception in the case of military necessity.[76]

The defence of obedience to superior orders has been thoroughly excoriated in international criminal law over the past fifty years. It remains present in theory, although it is rarely successfully invoked. In order to bring himself within the defence, a claimant must establish that he was under an obligation to obey the order, that he did not know the order was illegal, and that the order was not "manifestly illegal."[77] The defence has been described as relying on a factual basis akin to duress: "there was such an air of compulsion and threat to the accused that the accused had no alternative but to obey the orders."[78] It will in practice be restricted to war crimes as all orders to commit crimes against humanity will be manifestly unlawful.[79] Orders to commit war crimes that "[offend] the conscience of every reasonable, right thinking person" will similarly be manifestly unlawful.[80]

2) Article 1F(b)

Article 1F(b) excludes ordinary criminals who seek refugee status to avoid prosecution:

---

75 The *Charter of the International Military Tribunal*, above note 43, defines war crimes as excluding acts justified by military necessity. While this exclusion has not been explicitly followed in the *Rome Statute*, above note 44,it remains implicit in the selection of acts that qualify as war crimes.

76 *P(IJ) (Re)*, [1990] CRDD No 731 (IRB).

77 *Crimes against Humanity and War Crimes Act*, above note 53, s 14(1). See also *R v Finta*, [1994] 1 SCR 701 [*Finta*].

78 *Betoukoumesou*, above note 68 at para 31, quoting with approval Cory J in *Finta*, above note 77.

79 *Crimes against Humanity and War Crimes Act*, above note 53, s 14(2).

80 *Finta*, above note 77.

> F. The provisions of this Convention shall not apply to any person with respect to whom there are serious reasons for considering that:
>
> (b) He has committed a serious non-political crime outside the country of refuge prior to his admission to that country as a refugee;

A "serious non-political crime" is a term used in extradition treaties. Despite its frequent use, there is no universal consensus on its meaning nor does the application of article 1F(b) depend on the existence of any extradition treaty. Article 1F(b) is statutorily deemed to be established in certain cases where the Minister of Justice has ordered the surrender of an individual following extradition proceedings.[81] In addition, some refugee claimants who fall within the provisions of article 1F(b) (who are also inadmissible due to serious criminality) will not have access to a refugee hearing before the Board.[82]

Article 1F(b) does not require that an individual be convicted of a crime. For an inland claimant, the crime must have occurred (1) outside Canada, and (2) before the refugee claimant sought protection in Canada. For an overseas applicant, article 1F(b) is more ambiguous. It is unclear how to apply article 1F(b) where an overseas applicant has not been formally "admitted" as a refugee to her country of residence; it is also unclear whether Canada or the country of residence should be taken as the "country of refuge."[83] That the refugee claimant is not wanted for the crime or has already served her sentence is not determinative of the article 1F(b) assessment.[84] Similarly, whether the individual poses a "present or future danger to the host society or post-crime rehabilitation or expiation" are factors that are extraneous to the analysis.[85] Arguably, even an individual acquitted of a crime could fall within article 1F(b).[86]

---

81 *IRPA*, above note 13, s 105(3).

82 *Ibid*, s 101(1)(f). In addition, some of these individuals will also be precluded from gaining refugee protection as a result of a pre-removal risk assessment (*ibid*, s 112(3)(b)).

83 Immigration, Refugees and Citizenship Canada's operational manual on overseas processing is silent on this issue. It is more likely that most such cases are dealt with by findings of inadmissibility due to criminality under the *IRPA*, *ibid*, s 36.

84 *Zrig*, above note 7 at paras 118–29, Nadon J; *Febles v Canada (Citizenship and Immigration)*, 2014 SCC 68 at para 60 [*Febles*].

85 *Febles*, *ibid* at para 60.

86 Acquittal requires only a "reasonable doubt" about the commission of the crime, which presumably in many cases leaves room for "serious reasons for considering" that the individual committed the crime.

The seriousness of the crime will be assessed in relation to the penalty imposed, the maximum penalty, and, where applicable, the Canadian equivalent.[87] It has been suggested that a crime with a maximum sentence of ten years or longer will result in a presumption that the crime was serious; conversely, a misdemeanour or summary conviction is unlikely to be serious enough to satisfy article 1F(b).[88] Such an approach has the advantage of being consistent with the statutory provisions defining "serious" criminality.[89] However, crimes where there is a high maximum but a wide range of sentencing can be particularly problematic.[90] Further, as the maximum penalty may vary over time, the relevant moment of assessment is the determination of status (not the commission of the crime).[91]

Whether the crime falls within the "political crime exception" requires a more detailed assessment, including both the motives of the claimant and the nature of the crime.[92] In certain cases, where there are no other avenues for political action, even violent actions may fall within the exception.[93] Ultimately, the issue is whether the "political element" of the act "outweigh[s] the common law character of the offence."[94]

There remain lacunae to be explored by the jurisprudence. Whether an international offence such as the importation of narcotics into Canada qualifies as an offence outside of Canada prior to admission as a refugee claimant remains to be resolved.[95] The Australian Federal Court has ruled that such an offence would result in exclusion.[96] With the expansion of extraterritorial criminal jurisdiction, this issue will likely only increase in importance.

---

87 *Xie v Canada (Minister of Citizenship and Immigration)*, 2003 FC 1023, aff'd [2005] 1 FCR 304 (CA).

88 *Febles*, above note 84 at para 62. For factors to consider when determining the seriousness of a crime, see *Jayasekara v Canada (Minister of Citizenship and Immigration)*, 2008 FCA 404 (confirmed as still generally applicable post-*Febles* in *Jung v Canada (Minister of Citizenship and Immigration)*, 2015 FC 464 [*Jung*]).

89 *IRPA*, above note 3, s 36(1).

90 See, for example, *Jung*, above note 88.

91 *Sanchez v Canada (Minister of Citizenship and Immigration)*, 2014 FCA 157 at para 6 (Austl).

92 *Gil v Canada (Minister of Employment and Immigration)*, [1995] 1 FC 508 (CA) [*Gil*].

93 *Ibid*.

94 *Ibid*.

95 This issue was discussed in *Zrig*, above note 7.

96 *Ovcharuk v Minister for Immigration and Multicultural Affairs* (1998), 158 ALR 289 (FCA).

3) Article 1F(c)

Article 1F(c) excludes individuals who in some other way have acted contrary to the principles of international comity that gave rise to the United Nations and the *Refugee Convention*. Article 1F(c) states as follows:

> F. The provisions of this Convention shall not apply to any person with respect to whom there are serious reasons for considering that:
>
> (c) He has been guilty of acts contrary to the purposes and principles of the United Nations.

Of all article 1F grounds of exclusion, article 1F(c) is the most unclear at first sight. The potential scope of the "purposes and principles of the United Nations" is quite broad. For several years in the mid-1990s, the Canadian jurisprudence adopted a fairly expansive approach to article 1F(c). Among those excluded during that period were persons convicted of drug trafficking while in Canada. The rationale at the time was that the United Nations, albeit under much pressure from the United States, had adopted a series of resolutions and treaties aimed at trade in illicit narcotics.

The Supreme Court of Canada had occasion to consider the interpretation of article 1F(c) in the matter of *Pushpanathan*.[97] In that case, a drug trafficker had been excluded on that basis. The Court overturned Pushpanathan's exclusion on the ground that article 1F(c) should be interpreted in light of the UN's fundamental devotion to the cause of human rights. If the "purposes and principles of the United Nations" are interpreted in keeping with its commitment to the protection of human rights, article 1F(c) will exclude only "those individuals responsible for serious, sustained or systemic violations of fundamental human rights which amount to persecution in a non-war setting."[98]

More precisely, the Court set out two categories of acts that fall within article 1F(c). The first category consists of acts that can be characterized as "serious, sustained and systemic violations of fundamental human rights constituting persecution."[99] The second category of acts contrary to the purposes and principles of the United Nations includes any act that violates a "widely accepted international agreement or [where a] United Nations resolution declares that the commission of [the act] is contrary to the purposes and principles of the United

97 *Pushpanathan*, above note 4.

98 *Ibid* at para 64, Bastarache J.

99 *Ibid* at para 70.

Nations."[100] Thus, absent explicit indication to the contrary through an international agreement or UN resolution, article 1F(c) will be limited to acts that are serious violations of international law, including international human rights law.

In its comments, the Supreme Court acknowledged that terrorist activities could fall within either category of excludable acts. However, some states have, for more certainty, statutorily deemed various types of international terrorists excludable under article 1F(c).[101] The jurisprudence has more recently applied the contribution-based approach outlined in *Ezokola* (see Section F(1)(d), above in this chapter) to complicity in acts contrary to the purposes and principles of the United Nations (article 1(F)(c)).[102]

G. CONCLUSION

The exclusion provisions in the *Refugee Convention* operate within the larger framework of immigration law. Many of the grounds of exclusion are also grounds of inadmissibility, which can prevent referral of a claim for determination of refugee status to the Immigration and Refugee Board and limit the protection available through other reviews of risk.

By definition, the exclusion provisions exclude individuals who would otherwise qualify for protection. While the act of exclusion has become an almost mundane aspect of refugee law, exclusion reveals underlying concepts within refugee law that may otherwise remain hidden behind its general focus on human rights. Thus, even though exclusion directly affects only a minority of refugee claimants, it is key to an understanding of refugee law.

Articles 1E and 1F set out the categories of individuals who are seen as either not in need of or undeserving of receiving Canada's protection. The list of individuals who are undeserving is not surprising: those with status elsewhere, those perceived as criminals, and those whose acts have created refugees. Concerning this last category of persons

---

100 *Ibid* at para 66.

101 The *USA Patriot Act*, Pub L No 107-56 (2001) contained provisions that excluded from protection, in effect under art 1F(c), various categories of individuals who "materially support" terrorist groups. These provisions have been used most controversially to exclude Colombian refugee claimants who have paid "taxes" to the rebel (putatively terrorist) FARC group in Colombia. The United Kingdom has adopted a similar approach with its *Immigration and Asylum Act 2006* (UK), c 13.

102 *Alam v Canada (Minister of Citizenship and Immigration)*, 2014 FC 556.

who are excluded, a further comment must be made. While this book is generally written from the point of view of the refugee claimant and her advocate, this does not necessarily mean that the advocate should confine himself to the point of view of the particular refugee claimant facing exclusion. Exclusion is also very much about protecting other refugees in Canada from running into their former persecutors here.

CHAPTER 6

PERSONS IN NEED OF PROTECTION

A. INTRODUCTION

As noted in Chapter 2, the *Immigration and Refugee Protection Act* created a new category of individual: "persons in need of protection."[1] These individuals are defined as persons who, if removed from Canada, would be at risk of torture, would have their life placed at risk, or would be at risk of cruel and unusual treatment or punishment. This chapter will

---

1 SC 2001, c 27, s 97(1) [*IRPA*].

97. (1) A person in need of protection is a person in Canada whose removal to their country or countries of nationality or, if they do not have a country of nationality, their country of former habitual residence, would subject them personally

(a) to a danger, believed on substantial grounds to exist, of torture within the meaning of Article 1 of the *Convention Against Torture*; or

(b) to a risk to their life or to a risk of cruel and unusual treatment or punishment if

(i) the person is unable or, because of that risk, unwilling to avail themself of the protection of that country,

(ii) the risk would be faced by the person in every part of that country and is not faced generally by other individuals in or from that country,

(iii) the risk is not inherent or incidental to lawful sanctions, unless imposed in disregard of accepted international standards, and

(iv) the risk is not caused by the inability of that country to provide adequate health or medical care.

explore the criteria that must be satisfied if a refugee claimant is to be recognized as a person in need of protection. In international law, this aspect of refugee status determination is known as "complementary" or "subsidiary" protection; in Canadian jurisprudential parlance, the criteria for being defined as a person in need of protection are known as the "consolidated grounds" for protection.[2]

Persons in need of protection may be granted protection by either the Immigration and Refugee Board (IRB) after a refugee hearing or by the Minister after a pre-removal risk assessment review. As a result of a determination by either the Board or the Minister, a person in need of protection becomes a protected person and benefits from the statutory prohibition on *refoulement*.[3]

Before the *IRPA*, the Board did not have jurisdiction to grant protection to the category of persons in need of protection. Rather, failed refugee claimants were considered for membership in a similarly defined category but only as a part of a post-determination process.[4] The post-determination process was plagued by strict deadlines and an extremely low acceptance rate.[5] At the very least, the relocation of the consideration of non-Convention refugee types of risk from a post-claim process to the actual determination of the claim improves the efficiency of the refugee determination process.[6] Given that the Board must already conduct a detailed analysis of the evidence underlying the claim, it would appear to be a good time to determine whether the claimant may face other types of risk upon return. It also (at least for claims determined by the Board) improves the quality of the decision making.[7] Those claimants not eligible for determination by the Board, and rejected claimants, will have their membership in the category of

---

2 The term "consolidated grounds" reflects the historical reality that these grounds were added ("consolidated" with the Convention refugee grounds) to the jurisdiction of the Board by the *IRPA*.

3 Interestingly, in relation to persons in need of protection, the statutory prohibition of s 115(1) prohibits only removal (1) to torture, and (2) to cruel and unusual treatment or punishment. Despite individuals who face a risk to life qualifying as persons in need of protection (and hence, after a determination, as protected persons), there is no statutory bar on removal of individuals to such a situation.

4 The Post-Determination Refugee Claimants in Canada (PDRCC) class.

5 In its early days, the PDRCC acceptance rate was as low as 0.5 percent (or conversely, the refusal rate was a staggering 99.5 percent): see *Sinnappu v Canada (Minister of Citizenship and Immigration)*, [1997] FCJ No 173 at para 34 (FC) [*Sinnappu*].

6 Catherine Dauvergne, "Evaluating Canada's New Immigration and Refugee Protection Act in Its Global Context" (2003) 41 *Alberta Law Review* 725 at 729.

7 Claims are determined by the Board after an oral hearing before what is a quasi-judicial and independent decision-making body. These characteristics of deter-

persons in need of protection determined as part of the pre-removal risk assessment process (discussed further in Chapter 12).

By definition, the category of persons in need of protection applies only to individuals "in Canada."[8] Unlike Chapter 5 (when, for convenience, the term "refugee claimant" was used to refer to both inland claimants and overseas applicants), the use of "refugee claimant" in this chapter should be understood to apply only to those within Canada.

Section 97(2) of the *IRPA* allows the category of persons in need of protection to be expanded by means of regulations, but again, any expanded definition would apply only to those in Canada. The purpose of this provision was apparently to allow the government to easily extend the category (without the need to amend the statute) to include protections offered by future human rights conventions.[9] The power to extend the category has not yet been used.

Like claims for Convention refugee status, claims in the category of "person in need of protection" may be based on circumstances that arose since a claimant's departure from the country of reference. In particular, a claim may be based on the very fact that the claimant has sought protection in Canada; the UN's Committee against Torture has recognized that some returnees may face a risk of torture as a result of seeking protection abroad.[10] The Board's equivalent in the United Kingdom has recognized that, in some cases, such a situation may result in a risk of torture or of cruel and unusual treatment.[11]

---

mination by the Board improve the quality of decision making (as compared with the PDRCC process).

8 *IRPA*, above note 1, s 97(1).

9 Appendix 2 (Excerpts from proceedings and evidence of the Standing Committee on Citizenship and Immigration) of *Charkaoui (Re)*, [2005] FCJ No 2038 (FC). Since the entry into force of the *IRPA*, three new human rights treaties have come into force: (1) the *International Convention on the Protection of the Rights of All Migrant Workers and Members of Their Families*; (2) the *International Convention for the Protection of All Persons from Enforced Disappearance*; and (3) the *Convention on the Rights of Persons with Disabilities*. Canada has become party to only the third listed treaty (as of 11 March 2010).

10 *Pauline Muzonzo Paku Kisoki v Sweden*, Communication No 41/1996, UN Doc CAT/C/16/D/41/1996 (1996).

11 *AA (Risk for Involuntary Returnees) Zimbabwe v Secretary of State for the Home Department*, CG [2006] UKAIT 00061.

B. INFLUENCE OF INTERNATIONAL LAW

As with the definition of Convention refugee found in the *IRPA*, the definition of persons in need of protection is based upon international treaties. The category of persons in need of protection attempts to give domestic force to Canada's treaty obligations under the *International Covenant on Civil and Political Rights* and the *Convention Against Torture and Other Cruel, Inhuman or Degrading Treatment or Punishment*.

Both of these UN Conventions, the *ICCPR* and the *CAT*, for short, establish supervisory committees (treaty bodies) consisting of recognized human rights experts.[12] These committees — the Human Rights Committee and the Committee against Torture, respectively — are charged with the consideration of the periodic reports of signatories, the receipt of complaints by states against other states parties, and the receipt of complaints by individuals against a state party or states parties.[13] These latter two functions may be performed only by the respective committee if a state has previously declared that it has accepted the jurisdiction of the committee over such complaints.[14] Canada has recognized the jurisdiction of both committees to receive such complaints.

Although the precise legal status of pronouncements by the committees — particularly in response to individual complaints — is the subject of much debate, they at the very least provide "persuasive authority."[15] Accession to the *ICCPR* and the *CAT* indicates an "acceptance of the supervisory mechanisms written into the treaty that monitor the treaty's implementation."[16] The result is that the reports, comments, and decisions of the committees form an important subsidiary body of law which can inform the interpretation of the criteria for "persons in need of protection."

---

12 *International Covenant on Civil and Political Rights*, 19 December 1966, 999 UNTS 171, art 27 [*ICCPR*]; *Convention Against Torture and Other Cruel, Inhuman or Degrading Treatment or Punishment*, 10 December 1984, Can TS 1987 No 36, 23 ILM 1027, art 17 [*CAT*].

13 *ICCPR*, above note 12, arts 40 & 41, and *Optional Protocol to the International Covenant on Civil and Political Rights*, GA Res 2200A (XXI), 21 UN GAOR Supp (No 16) at 59, UN Doc A/6316 (1966), 999 UNTS 302, art 1 [*ICCPR Optional Protocol*]; *CAT*, above note 12, arts 10–22.

14 *ICCPR*, above note 12, art 41, and *ICCPR Optional Protocol*, above note 13, art 1; *CAT*, above note 12, arts 21 & 22.

15 Joanna Harrington, "Punting Terrorists, Assassins and Other Undesirables: Canada, the Human Rights Committee and Requests for Interim Measures of Protection" (2003) 48 *McGill Law Journal* 55 at 65.

16 *Ibid* at 63.

The jurisprudence is divided on the issues of the authority that this subsidiary body of law has in the domestic context. Generally, in the jurisprudence concerning individuals seeking protection in Canada, the pronouncements of the committees have been influential (if not determinative).[17] However, where Canada itself is the subject of an international complaint, the courts (perhaps not surprisingly) have been much more sanguine about accepting the committees' pronouncements:

> In signing the Protocol, Canada did not agree to be bound by the final views of the Committee, nor did it even agree that it would stay its own domestic proceedings until the Committee gave its views . . . . The party states that ratified the Covenant and the Optional Protocol turned their minds to the question of whether they should agree to be bound by the Committee's views, or whether they should at least agree to refrain from taking any action against an individual who had sought the Committee's views until they were known. They decided as a matter of policy that they should not, leaving each party state, on a case-by-case basis, free to accept or reject the Committee's final views, and equally free to accede to or not accede to an interim measures request.[18]

The use of the committees as forums to hear complaints (particularly from rejected refugee claimants) will be discussed further in Chapter 10. However, there remains a dichotomy in the jurisprudence concerning its willingness to accept the committees' interpretive role and its unwillingness at times to accept their adjudicative role.[19]

In addition to the *ICCPR* and the *CAT*, almost identical provisions guaranteeing the rights noted in the definition of persons in need of protection can be found in numerous other international treaties, including the *European Convention on Human Rights*,[20] the *American Convention on Human Rights*,[21] the *African Charter on Human and Peoples' Rights*,[22]

---

17 *Suresh v Canada (Minister of Citizenship and Immigration)*, [2002] SCJ No 3 at para 73 [*Suresh*]; *Li v Canada (Minister of Citizenship and Immigration)*, [2003] FCJ No 1934 at paras 34–39 (FC), aff'd [2005] FCJ No 1 (CA): see paras 20 & 21 [*Li*].

18 *Ahani v Her Majesty the Queen, The Attorney General of Canada et al*, [2002] OJ No 431 at para 32 (CA).

19 See also *Dadar v Canada (Minister of Citizenship and Immigration)*, [2006] FCJ No 486 (FC); and *Sogi v Canada (Minister of Citizenship and Immigration)*, [2006] FCJ No 970 (FC).

20 ETS no 5, 213 UNTS 222.

21 OAS Treaty Series No 36, 1144 UNTS 123.

22 OAU Doc CAB/LEG/67/3 rev 5, 21 ILM 58 (1982).

and the *Convention on the Rights of the Child.*[23] All of these treaties have supervisory bodies that have the jurisdiction to issue reports, comments, and decisions in individual cases. The International Criminal Court also has jurisdiction over the prosecution of the crime of torture (insofar as it can constitute a crime against humanity).[24] All of these bodies are useful sources of interpretive guidance concerning the meaning of the criteria that must be fulfilled by persons in need of protection. Unfortunately, a review of the IRB's decisions of the first eight and a half years since the enactment of the *IRPA* revealed that international law, including the decisions and guidance of treaty bodies, is referenced in a small minority of decisions and relied upon "in an infinitesimal number of decisions."[25]

In a significant departure from the international human rights treaties upon which the categories for person in need of protection are based, the exclusion provisions of the *Refugee Convention*, discussed in Chapter 5, have been extended to the category of persons in need of protection.[26] Thus, for example, an individual facing a substantial risk of torture may be excluded from being a person in need of protection because of his terrorist activities. This approach, if it resulted in *refoulement*, would conflict with Canada's obligations under article 3 of the *CAT.*[27] The only protection for such an individual within the *IRPA* would be from the

---

23 GA Res 44/25, annex, 44 UN GAOR Supp No 49 at 167, UN Doc A/44/49 (1989).

24 *Statute of the International Criminal Court*, UN Doc A/CONF.183/9, arts 7(1)(f) and 7(2). For further discussion of "crimes against humanity," please see Chapter 5, Section F(1)(c).

25 Catherine Dauvergne, "International Human Rights in Canadian Immigration Law: The Case of the Immigration and Refugee Board of Canada" (2012) 19 *Indiana Journal of Global Legal Studies* 305 at 326.

26 *IRPA*, above note 1, s 98(1).

27 Whether Canada could ever deport an individual to face torture was much discussed in the aftermath of *obiter* comments by the Supreme Court in *Suresh*, above note 17 at para 45:

> Deportation to torture, for example, requires us to consider a variety of factors, including the circumstances or conditions of the potential deportee, the danger that the deportee presents to Canadians or the country's security, and the threat of terrorism to Canada. In contexts in which the most significant considerations are general ones, it is likely that the balance will be struck the same way in most cases. It would be impossible to say in advance, however, that the balance will necessarily be struck the same way in every case.

See also Audrey Macklin, "Mr. Suresh and the Evil Twin" (2002) 20 *Refuge* 15.

statutory principle of non-*refoulement* and the related pre-removal risk assessment process, both of which are limited.[28]

C. COUNTRY OF REFERENCE

As with the definition of Convention refugee, the determination of whether a refugee claimant falls within the category of protected person requires, as a condition precedent, a determination of the country (or countries) of reference. Section 97(1) specifies a list of countries that may qualify as countries of reference: (1) country or countries of nationality, and (2) the country of former habitual residence, if no country of nationality.

Given the similar wording of the definition of Convention refugee, the jurisprudence concerning country or countries of reference for Convention refugees is applicable to cases of persons in need of protection.

D. PERSONAL RISK

Removal of persons to their countries of reference must "subject them personally" to risk if they are to obtain protection as persons in need of protection. In some ways, this is an odd requirement as the risk of torture, risk of cruel and unusual punishment, and risk to life are inherently the most personal of risks. The phrase has been interpreted in the international jurisprudence as focusing the inquiry on the situation of the individual; proof of the presence (or absence) of patterns of torture in the country of reference is not determinative.[29] While this observation about the use of objective evidence is valid, the phrase is perhaps better understood as underscoring the burden of proof: "There are no substantial grounds for believing that someone is at risk of torture unless it is

---

28 *IRPA*, above note 1, s 115(1) and ss 112–14, respectively. See Chapter 12, Section D, below, for a discussion of the pre-removal risk assessment process. The appropriateness of this scheme was upheld by the Federal Court of Appeal in *Xie v Canada (Minister of Citizenship and Immigration)*, 2004 FCA 250.

29 Immigration and Refugee Board of Canada, Legal Services Department, "Consolidated Grounds in the *Immigration and Refugee Protection Act*: Persons in Need of Protection, Risk to Life or Risk of Cruel and Unusual Treatment or Punishment" (May 2002), online: IRB www.irb-cisr.gc.ca/Eng/BoaCom/references/LegJur/Pages/ProtectLifVie.aspx [IRB, "Consolidated Grounds in the *IRPA*"] (referring in support to *Kisoki v Sweden*, CAT Communication No 41/1996, and *KN v Switzerland*, CAT Communication No 94/1997).

established that he or she personally will run such a risk in the State to which he or she will be returned."[30]

The requirement of personal risk is re-emphasized for refugee claimants who fear a risk to their life, or cruel and unusual punishment or treatment.[31] These claimants are specifically precluded from being persons in need of protection if the risk is "faced generally by other individuals in or from that country."[32] The significance of this provision of the definition will be detailed below in the discussion of section 97(1)(b).

E. RISK OF TORTURE

Section 97(1)(a) defines a person in need of protection as including an individual who would be at risk of torture upon removal from Canada:

> A person in need of protection is a person in Canada whose removal to their country or countries of nationality or, if they do not have a country of nationality, their country of former habitual residence, would subject them personally
>
> (a) to a danger, believed on substantial grounds to exist, of torture within the meaning of Article 1 of the *Convention Against Torture*;

Stemming from this definition are two requirements. First, there must be a risk of torture to the individual upon return to the country of reference. Second, the risk must rise to the level of there being "serious reasons for believing" that torture will occur. Both requirements will be discussed in turn below.

1) Definition of Torture

Section 97(1)(a) of the *IRPA* explicitly defines torture as acts "within the meaning of article 1 of the *Convention Against Torture*." Article 1 of the *CAT*[33] defines torture:

> For the purposes of this Convention, the term "torture" means any act by which severe pain or suffering, whether physical or mental, is intentionally inflicted on a person for such purposes as obtaining

30 *Enrique Falcon Ríos v Canada*, Communication No 133/1999, UN Doc CAT/C/33/D/133/1999 (2004) at para 4.6 (referring to the State Party's Observations).

31 *IRPA*, above note 1, s 97(1)(b).

32 *Ibid*, s 97(1)(b)(ii).

33 *CAT*, above note 12.

> from him or a third person information or a confession, punishing him for an act he or a third person has committed or is suspected of having committed, or intimidating or coercing him or a third person, or for any reason based on discrimination of any kind, when such pain or suffering is inflicted by or at the instigation of or with the consent or acquiescence of a public official or other person acting in an official capacity. It does not include pain or suffering arising only from, inherent in or incidental to lawful sanctions.

The term "torture" is reserved for deliberate treatment causing particularly cruel suffering, mainly acts by which severe pain or suffering, either physical or mental, is intentionally inflicted.[34] Torture cannot be the result of accident or negligence.[35] Rather, torture must be the result of a deliberate act of will, although this act of will may be manifest by a deliberate omission (such as not providing food or medical care). The act of will must either intentionally seek to inflict suffering or at least be performed in the knowledge that suffering would be the likely consequence.[36]

It is a testament to both the success and failure of the *CAT* that most individuals can provide a fairly lengthy list of well-accepted examples of torture.[37] The following quotation provides some standard examples from the international jurisprudence:

> Severe beatings (often of the feet) with wooden or metal sticks or bars without breaking the bones or causing lesions, yet causing intense pain and swelling, are torture — indeed . . . "[t]o characterize such behaviour as torture is uncontroversial: it is classic, having been 'known for centuries.'" Torture also includes the combination of being made to stand all day for days at a time, beatings and withholding food; beatings and being buried alive; electric shocks, beatings, being hung with arms behind one's back, having one's head forced under water until nearly asphyxiated, and being made to stand for hours.[38]

34 *IOS (Re)*, [2003] RPDD No 108 at para 30 (IRB) (referring with approval to *Ireland v the UK*, Series A, Number 25, 18 January 1978, ECHR).

35 Anthony Cullen, "Defining Torture in International Law: A Critique of the Concept Employed by the European Court of Human Rights" (2003) 34 *California Western International Law Journal* 29 at 33.

36 IRB, "Consolidated Grounds in the *IRPA*," above note 29 at para 5.1.4.

37 The success of the *CAT* is that most individuals understand what torture is and that it is prohibited; its failure is that torture still occurs.

38 John T Parry, "What Is Torture, Are We Doing It, and What If We Are?" (2003) 64 *University of Pittsburgh Law Review* 237 at 240 [footnotes omitted].

To this list can be added rape.[39] There is no requirement that torture leave any "marks on the body." In fact, some techniques of torture deliberately seek to leave no marks.[40]

All of these acts share a "special stigma" of cruelty.[41] While torture is traditionally conceived of in physical terms, the infliction of mental suffering can also be torture. For example, intimidation and threats can be acts of torture, depending on their severity.[42] Acts that do not rise to the level of torture may nonetheless qualify as "cruel and unusual treatment or punishment" under section 97(1)(b).[43]

The definition of torture in reference to the subjective suffering of the victim distinguishes it from persecution. Whereas persecution is defined primarily by the breach of a quite objectively defined human right, torture is defined as a breach of a human right with an inherently subjective component. Thus, the experience of the victim must be a primary consideration; the list above provides a starting point but it is not complete without a consideration of "all the circumstances of the case."[44] The expression of such an experience in writing and at a hearing is fraught with personal and legal complexity.[45]

The definition of torture requires that the act be motivated by "such purposes as obtaining from him or a third person information or a confession, punishing him for an act he or a third person has committed or is suspected of having committed, or intimidating or coercing him or a third person, or for any reason based on discrimination of any kind."[46] The requirement that an act of torture have a purpose is consistent with it being an intentional act. As with the motives of agents of persecution in the definition of Convention refugee, the purpose pursued by the torturer need not be attainable, grounded in fact, or conscious. The list of purposes of torture enumerated in article 1 is not exhaustive;

---

39 United Nations Commission on Human Rights, Res 1998/38, UNESCOR, 1998, Supp No 3, UN Doc E/CN.4/1998/38 (1998) at para 22 [UNCHR, Res 1998/38]. The recognition of rape as torture is a recent phenomenon. For a fuller discussion of rape constituting torture, see Evelyn Mary Aswad, "Torture by Means of Rape" (1996) 84 *Georgetown Law Journal* 1913.

40 *Cetinkaya v Canada (Minister of Citizenship and Immigration)*, 2012 FC 8 (discussing *falaka*, or the beating of the soles of the feet).

41 *Ireland v United Kingdom*, App No 5310/71, 2 Eur HR Rep 25 at 174 (1980) (ECHR).

42 United Nations Commission on Human Rights, "Torture and Other Cruel, Inhuman or Degrading Treatment or Punishment," E/CN.4/RES/2001/62 at para 2.

43 *Ibid*.

44 *Cruz Varas v Sweden*, 201 Eur Ct HR (Ser A) at 31 (1991) (ECHR).

45 For more on this, see Chapter 8.

46 *CAT*, above note 12, art 1.

the opening clause ("such purposes as") indicates that the enumerated purposes are examples, but not a complete list, of the required purposes of torture. Although there is evidence that the drafters of the *CAT* intended any non-enumerated purposes to be similar to those listed,[47] the prevalent interpretation is now that the examples "should be regarded as merely representative."[48]

2) Level of Risk Required

Although article 1 of the *CAT* defines and prohibits torture, it is article 3 which prohibits *refoulement* to torture. The phrase "serious reasons for believing" is taken from article 3.

Protection from a risk of torture requires proof that there are "substantial grounds" for believing the risk to exist. The Board's initial interpretation of this standard was that it "requires the same standard of proof as in Convention refugee claims": a serious possibility.[49] However, the Federal Court and Federal Court of Appeal have reversed this interpretation and adopted a position more in keeping with the wording of article 1 of the *CAT*: "the danger or risk must be such that it is more likely than not that she would be tortured."[50] Interestingly, this finding was based in large part on an analysis of the use of the introductory wording of section 97(1) of the *IRPA*[51] rather than the phrase "substantial grounds" in section 97(1)(a).[52]

Unlike the *Refugee Convention*, which, through its "compelling reasons" clause, provides relief for former refugees who have suffered

---

47 Cullen, above note 35 at 34, stated: "According to Burgers and Danelius [two drafters of the *CAT*], for ill treatment to qualify as torture its purpose must have 'some — even remote — connection with the interests or policies of the State and its organs.' (Quoting J Hermann Burgers & Hans Danelius, *The United Nations Convention Against Torture: A Handbook on the Convention Against Torture and Other Cruel, Inhuman or Degrading Treatment or Punishment* (Norwell, MA: Kluwer Academic, 1988) at 119.)

48 *Prosecutor v Delalic et al*, ICTY Case No IT-96-21-T, Trial Chamber Judgment, P 470 (1998).

49 *ZJA (Re)*, [2002] RPDD No 175 (IRB). This decision was subsequently designated as a "persuasive decision" by the Chairperson of the Board.

50 *Li*, above note 17 at para 50 (FC), reaffirmed in *Selliah v Canada (Minister of Citizenship and Immigration)*, [2005] FCJ No 755 (CA), applied in *Rajaratnam v Canada (Minister of Citizenship and Immigration)*, 2014 FC 1071.

51 *IRPA*, above note 1, s 97(1), states that persons in need of protection are individuals whose removal to their country or countries of nationality or their country of former habitual residence (in the case of stateless persons) "would" subject them to a prohibited risk (e.g., under s 97(1)(a)) of torture.

52 *Li* (CA), above note 17 at para 22.

persecution but are no longer at risk, the *CAT* does not provide such a remedy. By statute, however, the *IRPA* extends the compelling reasons relief to past victims of torture.[53]

3) Agent of Torture

To qualify as torture, the suffering must be "inflicted by or at the instigation of or with the consent or acquiescence of a public official or other person acting in an official capacity."[54] Thus, all "torture" within the meaning of a person in need of protection must have a linkage to the state: "it is the official nature of the conduct which gives rise to torture."[55]

Such acts must be performed in or acquiesced to the person's official capacity.[56] The doctrine of imputability states that "the action or inaction of state officials is imputable to the state."[57] This is true even where an official acts in an official capacity against the "will" of the state, or contrary to its policies. Acquiescence to known torture will also result in the imputation of responsibility to the state.[58] By definition, the acts of guerilla, anti-government, and rebel forces cannot qualify as state actions.[59] Mere state indifference to the torture will not provide a sufficient level of involvement.[60] In requiring a state agent of

53 *IRPA*, above note 1, s 108(4).

54 *CAT*, above note 12, art 1.

55 *Kazemi Estate v Islamic Republic of Iran*, 2014 SCC 62 at para 96 (LeBel J for the majority; see the dissenting view of Abella J on this point at para 229).

56 *Ivaneishvili v Canada (Minister of Citizenship and Immigration)*, 2014 FC 1056.

57 Dawn J Miller, "Holding States to Their Convention Obligations: The United Nations *Convention Against Torture* and the Need for a Broad Interpretation of State Action" (2003) 17 *Georgetown Immigration Law Journal* 299 at 305 (referencing Ian Brownlie, *Principles of Public International Law*, 5th ed (Oxford, UK: Clarendon Press, 1998) at 449).

58 *Ibid.*

59 *WXY (Re)*, [2003] RPDD No 81 at para 13 (IRB).

60 *IHK (Re)*, [2002] RPDD No 196 (IRB) (although on the facts the indifference was isolated and the claimants were faulted for not pursuing redress through other avenues of state protection). Some authors urge for a broader interpretation of "acquiescence" to include situations where a state is unable or disinclined to protect the person. See Jane McAdam, *Complementary Protection in International Refugee Law* (New York: Oxford University Press, 2007) at 116. See also *Torture and Other Cruel, Inhuman or Degrading Treatment or Punishment: Report of the Special Rapporteur*, UN Doc E/CN.4/1986/15 (1986) at para 38 [*Report of the Special Rapporteur*]; *Dzemajl v Yugoslavia*, Communication No 161/2000, UN Doc CAT/C/29/D/161/2000 (11 November 1999) at para 9.2. It could be argued that the expelling states must examine foreseeable consequences of removal, which would include considering not only whether the risk emanates from the state,

persecution, the definition of torture contrasts sharply with the definition of Convention refugee. An individual may fall within the latter definition if he or she is at risk from either state or non-state agents of persecution.[61] The lack of concern in the refugee definition jurisprudence about whether an agent of persecution is linked to the state or is a non-state agent has resulted, until the *IRPA*, in a lack of domestic jurisprudence on this issue.

4) Lawful Sanction Exception

According to the definition of torture in the *CAT*, article 1, suffering that results from a lawful sanction does not qualify as torture. At a minimum, a lawful sanction must be legal in and imposed according to the procedures set out in the law of the country of reference. However, the "lawfulness" of a sanction in the country of reference is not sufficient. The lawfulness must also be assessed in relation to international law.[62] The following mistreatments that may result from otherwise lawful sanction have been suggested to constitute torture: punishment involving intentional withholding of medical treatment,[63] the infliction of corporal punishment,[64] the imposition of very severe prison conditions,[65] and prolonged incommunicado detention.[66] Whether a sanction is lawful can be determined by reference to the various international instruments governing the administration of justice and the detention of prisoners.[67] Simply establishing that the treatment to be received under a sanction will be worse than the treatment accorded in Canada is insufficient to constitute torture.[68]

---

but whether effective protection is available against the risk posed by non-state agents.

61 For a fuller discussion of this point, see Chapter 4.

62 IRB, "Consolidated Grounds in the *IRPA*," above note 29 at para 5.4.1.2.

63 Office of the High Commissioner for Human Rights, "Fact Sheet No. 4: Combating Torture" (Rev.1) [OHCHR, "Fact Sheet No. 4"] at 35.

64 UNCHR, Res 1998/38, above note 39.

65 OHCHR, "Fact Sheet No. 4," above note 63 at 36.

66 UNCHR, Res 1999/32 at para 5.

67 *Standard Minimum Rules for the Treatment of Prisoners* (adopted by the First United Nations Congress on the Prevention of Crime and the Treatment of Offenders, held at Geneva in 1955, and approved by the Economic and Social Council by its resolution 663 C (XXIV) of 31 July 1957 and 2076 (LXII) of 13 May 1977); *Basic Principles for the Treatment of Prisoners*, GA Res 45/111 of 14 December 1990; *Body of Principles for the Protection of All Persons under Any Form of Detention or Imprisonment*, GA Res 43/173 of 9 December 1988.

68 *PFQ (Re)*, [2003] RPDD No 5 (IRB).

In one of its first decisions dealing with the issue of "lawful sanction," the Board held that an Argentinian civil servant who faced charges of criminal libel would face particularly harsh treatment while in prison:

> Sentencing the claimant to imprisonment for the crime of libel would certainly be a lawful sanction in his country. But his exposure to cruel or unusual treatment or torture in prison could not be described as arising from, inherent in or incidental to that lawful sanction. That risk would rather arise from the dangerous prison system in his country and the systematic recourse by officers of the state to torture as a means of punishment within the prisons.[69]

The risk of torture in prisons is widespread in much of the world. While the documentary evidence was particularly strong in the case of Argentina, many "criminals" might qualify for protection on this basis. It is important to recall, however, that those claimants with respect to whom there are serious reasons for believing that they have committed a serious non-political crime will be excluded under article 1F(b).[70]

The Board has suggested that the onus of establishing that an act of torture does not fall within the lawful sanction provision is on the refugee claimant.[71] Albeit in an adversarial process, the international jurisprudence suggests that once a claimant has established that an act qualifies as torture, the burden shifts to the state party to establish that it was a lawful sanction.[72] While the analogy with non-adversarial proceedings is not perfect, this suggests that once a claimant has satisfied the other elements of the definition of torture the burden shifts to the Board or the Minister to establish that the act in question was a lawful sanction. Presumably the burden of proof, whoever bears it, is to be determined on a balance of probabilities.

F. RISK OF OTHER SERIOUS HUMAN RIGHTS VIOLATIONS

The category of protected persons extends to cover more than simply those at risk of torture. In section 97(1)(b), the *IRPA* also considers as a

---

69 *JXP (Re)*, [2002] RPDD No 182 (IRB).

70 For a full discussion of exclusion under art 1F(b), see Chapter 5.

71 IRB, "Consolidated Grounds in the *IRPA*," above note 29 at para 5.4.2.

72 *Womah Mukong v Cameroon*, Communication No 458/1991, UN Doc CCPR/C/51/D/458/1991 (1994) at para 9.2.

"person in need of protection" a refugee claimant whose life is at risk or who is at risk of cruel and unusual treatment:

> 97. (1) A person in need of protection is a person in Canada whose removal to their country or countries of nationality or, if they do not have a country of nationality, their country of former habitual residence, would subject them personally
>
> . . .
>
> (b) to a risk to their life or to a risk of cruel and unusual treatment or punishment . . .

There, the *IRPA* also imposes qualifying conditions on such risks:

> (i) the person is unable or, because of that risk, unwilling to avail himself of the protection of that country,
> (ii) the risk would be faced by the person in every part of that country and is not faced generally by other individuals in or from that country,
> (iii) the risk is not inherent or incidental to lawful sanctions, unless imposed in disregard of accepted international standards, and
> (iv) the risk is not caused by the inability of that country to provide adequate health or medical care.

Some of these conditions are embedded in the definition of torture and will be familiar from the discussion of section 97(1)(a); others are similar to limitations contained within the definition of Convention refugee. Only the limitation on risk arising from lack of adequate medical care is unique to section 97(1)(b), and even this condition has parallels in other aspects of refugee law. Both the categories of risk and the limitations will be discussed below.

1) Risk to Life

In international human rights law, every individual has the "inherent right to life."[73] This includes the right not to be "arbitrarily deprived of his [or her] life."[74] The clear Canadian analogue to this right is found in section 7 of the *Canadian Charter of Rights and Freedoms*;[75] for example, extradition to the death penalty has been found to be a violation of the

73 *ICCPR*, above note 12, art 6(1).

74 *Ibid.*

75 Part 1 of the *Constitution Act, 1982*, being Schedule B to the *Canada Act 1982* (UK), 1982, c 11 [*Charter*]

Charter.[76] In this context, it would be difficult to see how a risk to life created by capital punishment would be saved by the "lawful sanction" exception discussed below. In most cases other than those involving capital punishment, risk to life is pleaded along with varying "lesser" risks, such as torture and cruel and unusual treatment or punishment.

2) Risk of Cruel and Unusual Treatment or Punishment

A risk of "cruel and unusual treatment or punishment" may also qualify a refugee claimant as a person in need of protection. The phrase "cruel and unusual" is often associated with torture: the *CAT* also requires states to prevent cruel, inhuman, or degrading treatment or punishment,[77] and the *ICCPR* prohibits such treatment or punishment.[78]

Neither the *CAT* nor the *ICCPR* defines cruel, inhuman, or degrading treatment or punishment. The distinction between torture and cruel, inhuman, or degrading treatment or punishment lies in differences in the method, purpose, and severity of treatment.[79] Some acts, while extremely egregious, may fall outside the definition of torture either because they did not possess the degree of severity or did not meet the purposive element of the definition of torture.[80] For example, in assessing whether "torture" occurred in *Ireland v United Kingdom*, the European Court of Human Rights considered that the nature of the ill-treatment inflicted, the means and methods employed, the repetition and duration of such treatment, the sex and the condition of the person exposed to it, and the likelihood that such treatment might injure the physical, mental, and psychological condition of the person exposed to it are important factors.[81]

Domestically, section 12 of the *Charter* provides the right "not to be subjected to any cruel and unusual treatment or punishment," but the jurisprudence on the term "cruel and unusual treatment or punishment" can be described only as incomplete. As a result of the bulk

---

76 *United States v Burns*, [2001] 1 SCR 283 [*Burns*]. The applicability of *Burns* to pre-removal risk assessment was raised but not determined in *Liang v Canada (Minister of Citizenship and Immigration)*, 2003 FCT 751.

77 *CAT*, above note 12, art 16.

78 *ICCPR*, above note 12, art 7.

79 *Report of the Special Rapporteur*, above note 60 at paras 33–35.

80 Malcolm D Evans, "Getting to Grips with Torture" (2002) 51 *International and Comparative Law Quarterly* 365 at 375.

81 Above note 41 at para 162. It should be noted that the case was decided on the basis of the *European Convention on Human Rights*, which contains prohibition of torture in art 3: "No one shall be subjected to torture or to inhuman or degrading treatment or punishment."

of the caselaw to date concerning extradition, the overwhelming majority of cases have dealt with "punishment" rather than "treatment." Furthermore, that the two terms should be understood as different categories with different analyses is still open to debate. Nonetheless, the *Charter* jurisprudence does make this distinction, although the Board has not thus far clearly adopted such an analysis.

For punishment to be cruel and unusual, it must be disproportionate:

> The standard to be applied in determining whether punishment is cruel and unusual is whether the punishment is so excessive as to outrage standards of decency and surpass all rational bounds of punishment. The test seems to be one of proportionality: is the punishment disproportionate to the offence and the offender?[82]

Punishment is understood quite narrowly as a lawfully imposed penalty for an offence. Not all lawful governmental sanctions, such as deportation, for example, will constitute punishment.[83] The analysis of punishment will consider such factors as the imposition of mandatory minimum sentences, the use of indeterminate detention, confinement due to mental illness, pre-trial custody, prison conditions, parole and mandatory supervision, and the likelihood of repeated prosecutions.[84] The "standards of decency" referred to in the test are Canadian standards.[85]

In cases involving treatment, a different set of questions must be asked as there is no obvious penal objective that must be proportionate with the criminal or otherwise sanctioned act. Rather, the jurisprudence suggests that the following (not completely dissimilar questions) must be asked:

> 1. Is it not in accord with public standards of decency and propriety?
>
> . . .
>
> 2. Is it unnecessary because of the existence of adequate alternatives?
> 3. Can it not be applied upon a rational basis in accordance with ascertained or ascertainable standards?[86]

---

82 *R v Smith*, [1987] 1 SCR 1045 [*Smith*] (quoted with approval in *El Moussa v Canada (Minister of Citizenship and Immigration)*, [2003] RPDD No 633 at para 24 (IRB)).

83 *Canada (Minister of Employment and Immigration) v Chiarelli*, [1992] 1 SCR 711 at para 29.

84 IRB, "Consolidated Grounds in the *IRPA*," above note 29 at para 4.47.

85 *Smith*, above note 82; *Canada (Minister of Citizenship and Immigration) v Harvey*, 2013 FC 717 [*Harvey*].

86 *Soenen v Thomas* (1983), 8 CCC (3d) 224 at para 26 (Alta QB).

While the tests applied with respect to both punishment and treatment are different, they both apply the overlapping standard of "public decency and propriety."[87] In assessing decency and propriety, both analyses seek to preclude acts towards the claimant that will be "inhuman or degrading."[88] Looking more generally at the scope of inhuman and degrading acts the Board has stated as follows (borrowing from the Supreme Court jurisprudence on extradition):

> Treatment that is inhuman or degrading has been equated with cruel and unusual treatment. Inhuman treatment has been described as premeditated, applied for hours at a stretch and causing, if not bodily injury, intense physical and mental suffering. Degrading treatment has been described as arousing in its victims feelings of fear, anguish and inferiority capable of humiliating and debasing them and possibly breaking their physical and moral resistance.[89]

The Refugee Appeal Division has attempted to consolidate the comments of the Board in its decisions and the guidance derived from other areas of practice, such as extradition, as follows:

> The factors examined by Canadian courts to determine whether treatment or punishment is cruel and unusual include whether the treatment goes beyond what is necessary to achieve a legitimate aim, whether there are adequate alternatives, whether the treatment is arbitrary, and whether it has a value or social purpose. Other relevant considerations include whether the treatment in question is unacceptable to a large segment of the population, whether it accords with public standards of decency or propriety, whether it shocks the general conscience, and whether it is unusually severe and hence degrading to human dignity and worth.[90]

As with torture, this approach also defines "cruel and unusual" as involving an assessment of an act's impact upon a claimant. Cruel and unusual treatment has been found by the Board to include the following

---

87 Walter Tarnopolsky, "Just Deserts or Cruel and Unusual Treatment or Punishment? Where Do We Look for Guidance?" (1978) 10 *Ottawa Law Review* 1.

88 It is open to question whether the term "inhuman and degrading" is equivalent to "cruel and unusual." The texts of international treaties (including arguably the *European Convention on Human Rights*) suggest that "inhuman and degrading" is more akin to torture than to cruel and unusual punishment and treatment.

89 *IDQ (Re)*, [2002] RPDD No 189 at para 34 (IRB).

90 *RAD File No MB4-02156*, [2014] RADD No 488 at para 74 (IRB), referencing *Canadian Doctors for Refugee Care v Canada (Attorney General)*, 2014 FC 651, and *Smith*, above note 82.

acts: kidnapping,[91] the kidnapping of one's children,[92] and the receipt of "vindictive threats" which are likely to be consummated.[93] It has been suggested that the mere receipt of "threats and extortion" will not constitute cruel and unusual treatment.[94] The fact that a claimant faces merely ostracism amounting to "discrimination" (but not to persecution) does not qualify as cruel and unusual treatment.[95] Deportation to a country of reference in which an adult claimant has not lived since childhood and in which he suffered torture will not necessarily amount to cruel and unusual treatment.[96]

Some European jurisprudence has suggested that a complete lack of healthcare may constitute cruel and unusual punishment.[97] The Canadian jurisprudence, however, has been more skeptical, although perhaps because of less compelling facts.[98] The statutory bar on such a basis for claim in section 97(1)(b)(iv) of the *IRPA* would seem to render this issue moot, but these cases do suggest that even situations that may arise without any direct human agency (such as the consequences of illness) may bring about "cruel and unusual treatment."

The foregoing explanation of "cruel and unusual" is necessarily haphazard. The refugee law jurisprudence is only beginning to develop beyond the constraints of the extradition caselaw which has until now provided the bulk of analysis on this topic. Clearly many of the constraints imposed by an analysis centred around extradition are inapplicable in the context of refugee determination. Furthermore, the *Charter*, section 12, will likely continue to play an important role in the interpretation of "cruel and unusual treatment or punishment." International human rights precedents will probably figure more prominently in the future.

91 *IDQ (Re)*, above note 89; *VSI (Re)*, [2004] RPDD No 284 (IRB).

92 *Ibid.*

93 *USC (Re)*, [2002] RPDD No 190 (IRB).

94 This proposition is consistent with *Kanthasamy v Canada (Citizenship and Immigration)*, 2015 SCC 61, which held that it was appropriate for an officer deciding a humanitarian and compassionate application to consider threats insofar as they would not be excluded from consideration under s 25(1.3) of the *IRPA* (which precludes considering matters that could result in protection as a refugee or person in need of protection).

95 *Omoregbe v Canada (Minister of Citizenship and Immigration)*, [2003] RPDD No 487 (IRB) [*Omoregbe*].

96 *Kim v Canada (Minister of Citizenship and Immigration)*, [2005] FCJ No 540 (FC).

97 *D v United Kingdom* (1997), 24 EHRR 423 (ECHR). On the other side, see some of the subsequent jurisprudence of the European Court of Human Rights, such as *Bensaid v United Kingdom* (2001), 33 EHRR 205, and *N(FC) v Secretary of State for the Home Department*, [2005] UKHL 31.

98 See, for example, *Omoregbe*, above note 95 and *QZP (Re)*, [2004] RPDD No 281 (IRB).

It must also be noted that the jurisprudence is limited by the facts of the cases that are presented. Cases that might involve "cruel and unusual punishment" by the state are more frequently dealt with under the risk of torture. Cases involving non-state actors are more frequently determined on a concurrent risk to the life of the claimant.

3) Level of Risk Required

The standard of proof under section 97(1)(b) is the same as for the risk of torture.[99]

4) Fulfilling the Required Conditions

In order for a risk to life or a risk of cruel and unusual treatment or punishment to qualify an individual as a person in need of protection, the conditions listed in sections 97(1)(b)(i) to (iv) must be fulfilled. Each of these conditions is necessary for qualification as a person in need of protection under section 97(1)(b). The conditions are not unfamiliar; state protection, and risk in all parts of a country, are part of the Convention refugee and risk of torture analyses. Generalized risk and whether the risk arises from lawful sanction do not preclude protection under either the risk of torture analysis or the Convention refugee analysis, but have been the subject of much discussion, particularly in the Convention refugee caselaw. Only the last condition, that the risk not arise from the lack of medical and healthcare, is peculiar to persons in need of protection.

Each of the conditions of section 97(1)(b) will be discussed in further detail below. The conditions will be discussed in the order listed in the subsection.

a) Lack of State Protection

Section 97(1)(b)(i) requires that a risk to life or of cruel and unusual treatment or punishment may qualify an individual for protection only if "the person is unable or, because of that risk, unwilling to avail themself of the protection of that country." This requirement will be familiar from the discussion of the Convention refugee definition; it replicates almost verbatim the "state protection" requirement of that definition.[100]

---

99 The Board followed the same approach to the burden of proof in s 97(1)(b) as it did for s 97(1)(a). The case of *USC (Re)*, above note 93, was designated as "persuasive" and subsequently overruled by *Li* (CA), above note 17 at para 50.

100 For a full discussion of this issue, see Chapter 4.

b) Risk in Every Part of Country

Despite the suggestion from the statute, the concept of internal flight alternative (IFA) is not particular to the section 97(1)(b) grounds. An individual at risk of torture must similarly establish that she would be at risk throughout the country of reference. A Convention refugee must also show that he would be unable to pursue an IFA upon return to his country. Although Convention refugees may eliminate an IFA from consideration if it is "unreasonable," this term is now interpreted very narrowly, as the above discussion of recent cases in Chapter 4 indicated. As with the IFA analysis in the Convention refugee definition, care must be taken both that a putative IFA is real and that it does not create a new risk for the claimant.

c) Risk Not Faced Generally by Others

Unlike the definition of refugee in section 96, the protection of section 97 "is not predicated on the individual demonstrating that he or she is [at risk] . . . for any of the enumerated grounds of section 96."[101] Notwithstanding this general proposal, the risk to life or a risk of cruel and unusual punishment or treatment must not be a risk faced "generally by other individuals in or from that country."[102] Risks arising from natural disasters are the most frequently cited examples of general risks that fall within this prohibition.[103] A risk of random violence can also lead to a finding that it is faced generally by others. Similarly, the Board has found that the risk of general terrorist attack is "indiscriminate or random" and does not qualify an individual as a person in need of protection.[104] Where a civil war places all individuals in a country at risk, such a risk also will not qualify an individual for protection.[105]

The extent of individualization of the threat that is required is unclear. The Board has categorized as a general risk threats that apply to a minority that is nonetheless a numerically significant portion of the population.[106] However, where a generalized risk brings into existence a specific threat — such as where widespread criminality may

---

101 *Li*, above note 17 at para 33 (FCA).

102 *IRPA*, above note 1, s 97(1)(b)(ii).

103 IRB, "Consolidated Grounds in the *IRPA*," above note 29 at para 3.1.7 (referencing *Sinnappu*, above note 5).

104 *UFQ (Re)*, [2005] RPDD No 78 (IRB); *USE (Re)*, [2003] RPDD No 41 (IRB).

105 *WVZ (Re)*, [2003] RPDD No 106 (IRB).

106 See, for example, *Diaz v Canada (Minister of Citizenship and Immigration)*, [2004] RPDD No 309 (IRB), where the Board found that a risk applying to the group of "all able-bodied adult males in Colombia who have completed their mandatory military service" was nonetheless a general risk.

cause a particular criminal to threaten violence — the risk will no longer be "faced generally by others."[107] In addition, even where the risk arises generally, if the claimant remains at risk while the general population does not, this risk will meet the requirement of an individualized threat. Thus, where there is rampant crime and the police refuse to assist a particular segment of the population or an individual, the risk will no longer be "faced generally by others"[108] although simply being "targeted more frequently" will be insufficient.[109] A claimant at greater risk than the general population risk due to his particular characteristics will also be facing a risk not faced generally by others.[110] The mere fact that an individual is personally targeted is not determinative.[111] Although not setting out general principles, the caselaw appears to require a "personalized" or "individual" risk to be qualitatively (not quantitatively) different in "nature or degree"[112] from that faced by the general population (for example, a risk of gang violence rooted in a perception that a claimant is a police informant[113] or a risk to life rather than merely a risk of violence).[114] Such an analysis will necessarily require a particularized assessment of the source and level of risk faced by an individual, and its outcome may change over time.[115]

Notwithstanding the bar on qualification as a person in need of protection based upon a generalized risk, such a risk to a population in a country of reference may lead to the Minister imposing a stay of removals to the country.[116]

---

107 *UKR (Re)*, [2002] RPDD No 188 (IRB).

108 *SVK (Re)*, [2004] RPDD No 32 (IRB) (although on the facts of the case, such a risk was not established).

109 *Prophète v Canada (Minister of Citizenship and Immigration)*, 2008 FC 331, aff'd 2009 FCA 31 [*Prophète*]. For a slightly different view, see *Wankhede v Canada (Minister of Citizenship and Immigration)*, 2015 FC 265 at paras 33 & 34, which left open the possibility that the targeting of the wealthy might for some individuals in some countries not be generalized violence.

110 *Mijatovic v Canada (Minister of Citizenship and Immigration)*, [2006] FCJ No 860 at para 35ff (FC).

111 *Correa v Canada (Minister of Citizenship and Immigration)*, 2014 FC 252; *Flores v Canada (Minister of Citizenship and Immigration)*, 2015 FC 201 at para 21.

112 *Prophète*, above note 109 at paras 16–22.

113 *Ibid*; *Pineda v Canada (Minister of Citizenship and Immigration)*, 2011 FC 403 at paras 12–14.

114 *Portillo v Canada (Minister of Citizenship and Immigration)*, 2012 FC 678.

115 *Guerrero v Canada (Minister of Citizenship and Immigration)*, 2011 FC 1210 at para 28.

116 *Immigration and Refugee Protection Regulations*, SOR/2002-227, s 230(1).

d) Risk Not Inherent or Incidental to Lawful Sanctions

As with the risk of torture, any risk "inherent or incidental to lawful sanctions" will not qualify under section 97(1)(b). The statutory language of this criterion precludes the consideration of any sanction "imposed in disregard of accepted international standards." An otherwise lawful sanction, such as incarceration subsequent to criminal conviction, may run afoul of the latter requirement if the sentence imposed is internationally disproportionate or the conditions of detention are poor.[117] That a risk constitutes "cruel and unusual punishment" will not render this element redundant; an international analysis is key to this provision (unlike the analysis of cruel and unusual punishment).[118] The jurisprudence on the similar provision with respect to the risk of torture is applicable to the interpretation of section 97(1)(b)(iii).

e) Risk Not Due to Inadequate Healthcare

By the statutory terms of section 97(1)(b)(iv) of the *IRPA*, a risk to life or of cruel and unusual treatment that arises because of an inability to "provide adequate health or medical care" in the country of reference does not automatically qualify a claimant as a person in need of protection. While the stated policy grounds for this exclusion were that such considerations "can be more appropriately assessed through other means in the Act and are excluded from this definition," the clear policy motivation was to prevent a wave of claimants seeking to benefit from the Canadian healthcare system.[119] Based largely upon the clear meaning of the statutory language, the Federal Court of Appeal has held that the words "inability to provide adequate medical services" must include "situations where a foreign government decides to allocate its limited public funds in a way that obliges some of its less prosperous citizens to defray part or all of their medical expenses."[120]

Notwithstanding this intent, however, the jurisprudence does suggest that, as with generalized violence, where inadequate healthcare is exacerbated by a characteristic peculiar to the claimant (or a subset of the population), it may qualify under section 97(1)(b). Thus, in the case of a gay man fearing lack of medical care in Chile, the Board commented that

---

117 *Klochek v Canada (Minister of Citizenship and Immigration)*, 2010 FC 474.

118 *Harvey*, above note 85 at para 51.

119 *Singh v Canada (Minister of Citizenship and Immigration)*, [2004] FCJ No 346 at para 21 (FC) (quoting the clause-by-clause analysis of Bill C-11 tabled in Parliament). The linkage between the clause and preventing a flood of demands upon the Canadian healthcare system is noted in *Covarrubias v Canada (Minister of Citizenship and Immigration)*, [2005] FCJ No 1470 at para 58 (FC) [*Covarrubias*].

120 *Covarrubias*, *ibid* at para 38.

the claimant could qualify for protection if the evidence established that the "claimant's sexual orientation would result in discrimination in the provision of health care in Chile."[121]

In assessing the facts of a case, the jurisprudence distinguishes between an "inability" to provide medical and healthcare, and an "unwillingness"; only the former is precluded by the terms of the statute. A risk to life or of cruel and unusual treatment caused by unwillingness (e.g., due to prejudice against gay and lesbian people) will bring an individual within the scope of a person in need of protection:

> I am not satisfied that the section 97(1)(b)(iv) exclusion is so wide that it would preclude from consideration all situations involving a person's inability to access health care in his country of origin. Where access to life-saving treatment would be denied to a person for persecutorial reasons not otherwise caught by section 96 of the *IRPA*, a good case can be made out for section 97 protection.[122]

As with the other elements of a right to life claim, a claimant bears the onus of establishing denial for persecutorial reasons — and only in "rare cases would the onus on the applicant be met."[123] The analysis of the Federal Court of Appeal suggests that a *Charter* challenge to this restriction will be unsuccessful.[124]

G. CONCLUSION

This chapter has discussed the subsidiary forms of protection that the *IRPA* offers to refugee claimants who do not fall within the definition of Convention refugee. These protections are offered further to Canada's international human rights obligations. As discussed, these obligations have created a growing body of international law, including a form of international jurisprudence.

Individuals at risk of torture, at risk of loss of life, and at risk of cruel and unusual punishment may qualify for protection. As with the

---

121 *QZP (Re)*, above note 98 at para 20. Of course, the Board's suggested use of other sufferers of the same disease as a comparator is problematic insofar as it may obscure a larger bias in the provision of health services.

122 *AB v Canada (Minister of Citizenship and Immigration)*, [2006] FCJ No 667 at para 27 (FC); upheld in *Covarrubias*, above note 119 at para 39.

123 *Ibid* at paras 31 and 39.

124 The Federal Court of Appeal did not explicitly rule on this issue in *Covarrubias* as there was no factual foundation and the decision maker in question (a PRRA officer) did not have jurisdiction to consider *Charter* issues.

definition of Convention refugee, the category of those who may qualify for protection is limited by factors that emphasize that Canadian (or international) protection must come as a last resort and only if no possibility of safety within the country of reference exists. Unlike the Convention refugee definition, some of these factors are spelled out in the statute, although these are familiar from the analysis of Convention refugee.

In this chapter, the jurisprudence has been discussed only insofar as it can be used to inform the interpretation of "person in need of protection." However, the significance of this jurisprudence is not simply interpretive. A significant portion of it represents efforts by failed refugee claimants to seek a remedy from an international body after failing to receive protection in Canada. As of March 2016, the number of complaints filed against Canada with the Human Rights Committee was the highest among other states parties (218 out of 2,756 total complaints). As of August 2015, the number of complaints against Canada before the Committee against Torture was the third highest among states parties (124 out of 697 total complaints).[125] Most of these complaints were made by rejected refugee claimants seeking to prevent their removal. This topic will be discussed further in Chapter 10.

125 Statistical survey of individual complaints dealt with by the Human Rights Committee under the *ICCPR Optional Protocol*, above note 13 (March 2016); and statistical survey of individual complaints dealt with by the Committee against Torture under the procedure governed by art 22 of the *CAT* (August 2015). Both documents are available, online: www.ohchr.org/EN/HRBodies/CCPR/Pages/CCPRIndex.aspx and www.ohchr.org/en/hrbodies/cat/pages/catindex.aspx.

CHAPTER 7

OVERSEAS PROTECTION

A. INTRODUCTION

There are two main routes for obtaining refugee protection in Canada: (1) inland refugee determination (see Chapter 8) and (2) resettlement from overseas. Despite the current prevalence of inland asylum claims over applications for protection from overseas, Canada continues to play an important part in global resettlement, including through its participation in the resettlement program of the United Nations High Commissioner for Refugees (UNHCR). Between 1995 and 2005, Canada resettled, on average, ten thousand refugees annually.[1] Since 2005, the numbers have somewhat increased to between ten and twelve thousand annually.[2] As one of twenty-seven states participating in the UNHCR resettlement program,[3] Canada usually ranks among the top three

---

1 Immigration, Refugees and Citizenship Canada, "Facts & Figures: Immigration Overview 2003" at 2, and "Facts & Figures: Immigration Overview 2004" at 2; both online: IRCC www.cic.gc.ca.

2 Immigration, Refugees and Citizenship Canada, "Facts and Figures 2014 — Immigration Overview: Permanent Residents," online: IRCC www.cic.gc.ca/english/resources/statistics/facts2014/permanent/02.asp.

3 United Nations High Commissioner for Refugees, "Frequently Asked Questions about Resettlement," online: UNHCR www.unhcr.org/protection/resettlement/524c31666/frequently-asked-questions-resettlement.html. By 2013, the following countries had established or announced establishment of resettlement programs: Argentina, Australia, Austria, Belgium, Brazil, Bulgaria, Canada, Chile, the Czech Republic, Denmark, Finland, France, Germany, Hungary,

recipients of resettled refugees in any given year.[4] This high ranking is a testament both to the relatively large number of refugees resettled by Canada and to the very small number of refugees resettled by most other states. For example, in 2015, UNHCR estimated global resettlement needs at nearly one million,[5] but states participating in resettlement programs accepted only slightly more than 100,000 refugees.

Despite being driven by the same humanitarian ideals as inland determination, resettlement possesses several peculiar characteristics. Resettlement applies only to individuals outside of Canada. Applications are assessed by Immigration, Refugees and Citizenship Canada (IRCC) officers at Canadian missions abroad and applicants must secure referral from UNHCR or the support of a sponsor to assist in their settlement in Canada. In addition, applicants must pass mandatory medical, security, and criminality checks and generally demonstrate an ability to become successfully established in Canada. Individuals who are selected for resettlement are issued permanent resident visas and become permanent residents upon arrival in Canada. The resettlement program is coordinated by the federal government, except for Quebec which, under the *Canada–Quebec Accord*, is responsible for its own resettlement process and admission targets.

Due to its design, resettlement is much more amenable to planning and state control; it is often contrasted with the more "spontaneous" and "self-selected" nature of the inland claims. Unlike the numbers of inland refugee claims, which can fluctuate dramatically from year to year in response to a variety of factors in countries of origin and destination, the numbers of resettled refugees usually remain relatively constant over time. Every year, the Canadian government establishes annual targets for resettlement. For example, annual immigration plans for 1996–2013 set a target of admitting between 10,000 and 12,000 or 10,000 and 14,000 refugees (as a rule, approximately 7,000 to 7,500 gov-

---

Iceland, Ireland, Japan, Netherlands, New Zealand, Norway, Portugal, Romania, Spain, Sweden, Switzerland, United Kingdom, Uruguay, and the United States. Other countries also accept refugees for resettlement, but on an ad hoc basis.

4 United Nations High Commissioner for Refugees, *UNHCR Statistical Yearbook 2001*, *UNHCR Statistical Yearbook 2002*, *UNHCR Statistical Yearbook 2003*, and *UNHCR Statistical Yearbook 2004*, online: UNHCR www.unhcr.org. For example, Canada accepted 10 percent of refugees resettled by industrialized countries during the 1992–2001 period. United Nations High Commissioner for Refugees, *UNHCR Global Trends* 2010; 2011; 2012; 2013; 2014; online: UNHCR www.unhcr.org.

5 United Nations High Commissioner for Refugees, "Refugee Resettlement Trends 2015," online: UNHCR www.unhcr.org/protection/resettlement/559ce97f9/unhcr-refugee-resettlement-trends-2015.html.

ernment-assisted refugees and 3,000 to 5,000 privately sponsored).[6] In addition to annual targets, the Liberal government resettled 25,000 Syrian refugees between November 2015 and February 2016. It continued the resettlement efforts throughout 2016 and, as of 2 January 2017, a total of nearly 40,000 Syrian refugees had been resettled in Canada.[7]

Resettlement is comprised of two temporally and geographically distinct processes: (1) the in-Canada process, by which private sponsors are screened and approved to resettle refugees; and (2) the overseas process of screening and selecting the sponsored refugee(s). Only after both steps of the process are completed and the refugee and the sponsoring entity (private or government) are matched can a refugee be resettled to Canada.

Given the two-prong nature of resettlement, this chapter is divided into two corresponding parts: the first part describes the resettlement process from the perspective of a sponsor, focusing on requirements to sponsoring organizations/groups and the procedures to be followed; the second part describes the overseas processing of refugee applications. However, before the two aspects of the process of sponsorship are discussed, a few words need to be said about the various types of sponsorship.

B. TYPES OF REFUGEE SPONSORSHIP

As a rule, all resettled refugees must be sponsored either by a government or by private actors. However, refugees who possess sufficient financial resources of their own may also be resettled as self-supporting immigrants.

There are three types of refugee sponsorship arrangements: (1) government, (2) private, and (3) joint government and private. Government assistance and joint government and private sponsorship usually are used for the most vulnerable refugees; less demanding cases are typically covered by private sponsorships.

Under any of the sponsorship arrangements, the resettled refugees must be provided with comprehensive integration assistance ranging from financial support to orientation to life in Canada. Sponsoring groups are responsible, *inter alia*, for financing the food, rent, cloth-

---

6 Immigration, Refugees and Citizenship Canada, "Reports on Plans and Priorities," online: IRCC www.cic.gc.ca/english/resources/publications/rpp/.

7 Immigration, Refugees and Citizenship Canada, "#WelcomeRefugees: Canada Resettles Syrian Refugees," online: IRCC www.cic.gc.ca/english/refugees/welcome.

ing, and other household and day-to-day expenses of the sponsored refugees; selecting a family physician and dentist; enrolling children in school; linking refugees to people with similar interests; providing orientation on banking, transportation, and other peculiarities of life in Canada; and helping adult refugees look for work during the sponsorship period. In financial terms, sponsors are expected to provide a level of support equal or greater to that of social assistance in the community of settlement. The sponsorship period is limited to one year or until a refugee becomes self-sufficient, whichever comes first. In exceptional circumstances, an IRCC officer assessing a sponsorship application may require that the duration of this period be more than one year, but in no case can it be longer than three years.[8]

The nature of sponsor–refugee relations presupposes that during a sponsorship period a refugee will reside in the community where a sponsor is located. However, a refugee is not bound to live where he was originally resettled and can move elsewhere during the sponsorship period. Such relocation is called "secondary movement."[9] Given the importance of sponsorship support for refugees, secondary movement in cases of private sponsorship usually requires finding a new sponsor in the area of the refugee's relocation to take over the responsibility for support. The relationship with the original sponsor may be preserved, however, if the sponsor is willing to maintain sponsorship over distance. If a refugee becomes self-sufficient before the expiration of a sponsorship period and decides to move, the sponsor is discharged of its obligations.

1) Government Sponsorship

The resettlement of government-assisted refugees is fully funded by the government of Canada or the government of Quebec. Refugees falling under the Convention Refugee Abroad class (for definition, see discussion below) are usually designated as government-assisted refugees. The assistance provided to these refugees once they arrive in Canada is delivered through IRCC-supported non-governmental agencies, the

8 *Immigration and Refugee Protection Regulations*, SOR/2002-227, ss 154(2) & (3) [*Regulations*].

9 Ideally, refugees should be sent to places where they will enjoy the support of someone they know. The lack of consideration for refugees' preferred destinations has been found to be one of the reasons for the secondary migration of government-assisted refugees. Laura Simich, Martin Beiser, & Farah N Mawani, "Paved with Good Intentions: Paths of Secondary Migration of Government-Assisted Refugees in Ontario" (2002) 28 *Canadian Public Policy* 597 at 598.

service-provider organizations participating in the Resettlement Assistance Program (RAP).

The RAP includes financial assistance as well as support services. The income support component of the RAP is administered through regional and local IRCC offices. Government-assisted refugees are provided monthly financial assistance as well as special allowances for pregnant women, newborn, and school start-up. The amount of monthly income support varies slightly from province to province because it is based on provincial social assistance rates.

The RAP service providers are responsible for support services, which include meeting refugees at the airport, transporting them to the place of temporary accommodation, and ensuring that all their immediate needs are met. Several days after arrival, refugees are interviewed by IRCC staff, given a list of settlement agencies to contact if further help is needed, and issued income support cheques. Within the first four to six weeks after arrival in Canada, service-provider organizations provide an orientation to refugees, including information on everyday life in Canada; assistance with finding permanent accommodation; information on federal and provincial programs, such as the Canada Child Benefit, Interim Federal Health Program,[10] and provincial healthcare system, as well as referrals to other settlement programs.

2) Private Sponsorship

Private sponsorship can be undertaken by non-governmental organizations, community groups, and groups of individuals. There are three types of private sponsorship: (1) sponsorship by sponsorship agreement holders (SAHs) and their constituent groups, (2) community sponsorship, and (3) sponsorship by groups of five or more Canadian citizens or permanent residents (Groups of Five).

Groups or organizations that wish to participate in one of the three types of sponsorship must submit an application to IRCC. Once an application is approved, a group or an organization can proceed to make further arrangements for resettlement. All sponsors, except sponsorship agreement holders, must complete an application and obtain approval from IRCC every time they wish to resettle a refugee or a family of refugees. In the case of SAHs, the master "sponsorship agreement" between

10 The Interim Federal Health Program provides temporary medical coverage for Convention refugees and humanitarian-protected persons resettled from abroad who are in need of assistance before they become eligible for provincial healthcare coverage (which can be up to ninety days). See Chapter 3 for more details on the program.

the SAH and IRCC sets out the details and obligations of the anticipated sponsorships.

Three general requirements apply to all private sponsors:

1) The sponsoring entity must be located or have representatives in the community where resettled refugees are expected to reside.[11]
2) The sponsor must possess sufficient funds and human resources to meet the needs of the sponsored refugees and put in place adequate arrangements for settlement support.[12]
3) The sponsor must not be and must not include an individual or an organization that was a party to an undertaking on which they defaulted and remain in default.[13]

In addition to these basic requirements, each type of sponsorship entity — a SAH, a community sponsor, or a Group of Five — must satisfy other criteria, outlined in the sections below.

Each sponsorship application must include a set of documents that prove the sponsor's ability to satisfy the above-mentioned requirements; there is a slightly different procedure for SAHs and constituent groups. An application must include an undertaking, a settlement plan, a sponsor assessment, and proof of funds. A settlement plan outlines the logistics of settlement assistance delivery, including the nature of the accommodation provided; the anticipated monthly expenses of the refugees; and the anticipated involvement of the sponsoring group, settlement agencies, and community volunteers in the settlement of the refugees. An undertaking is a written commitment of an entity or a group to the Minister to provide settlement assistance, lodging, and other necessities to a refugee and her accompanying family members (as well as non-accompanying family members who may join the principal applicant later) for the duration of the sponsorship period.[14] An undertaking must be signed by each party to the sponsorship; it makes them both jointly and severally or solidary liable for the undertaking.[15]

Certain individuals cannot be parties to a sponsorship: persons detained in a penitentiary, jail, reformatory, or prison; persons convicted

---

11 *Regulations*, above note 8, s 153(1)(a).

12 *Ibid*, s 154(1).

13 *Ibid*, s 153(1)(c). Default can be ended in several ways: (1) default on a financial obligation: by reimbursing a party to the sponsorship or the government; (2) on a non-financial obligation: by satisfying an officer that the party is in compliance with the obligation; (3) for an organization: once five years have elapsed since the time of default. (*Regulations*, above note 8, s 153(4).)

14 *Ibid*, s 138.

15 *Ibid*, ss 153(2) & (3).

of murder or other serious offence[16] in or outside Canada if less than five years have elapsed since the completion of their sentence (unless acquitted or received a record of suspension); persons subject to a removal order; persons subject to a revocation of citizenship; and persons who are in default on any support payment obligations ordered by a court.[17]

a) Sponsorship Agreement Holders

To facilitate the sponsorship process, a number of religious, ethnic, community, and service organizations have signed sponsorship agreements with IRCC. These sponsorship agreement holders (SAHs) are pre-approved sponsors; that is, they do not have to undergo assessment and IRCC approval every time they wish to resettle a refugee. By signing an agreement, SAHs undertake overall responsibility for their sponsorships. A standard agreement includes provisions detailing settlement plans; financial requirements; the standard of conduct expected of the sponsor; reporting requirements; and the grounds for suspending or cancelling the agreement.[18] A SAH must complete a settlement plan for each refugee being sponsored but is not required to submit the plan for approval to the local IRCC office (unless it is a new SAH that signed its agreement less than two years previously). The majority of privately sponsored refugees come through assistance of SAHs and their constituent groups.

Organizations wishing to become SAHs must submit an application to IRCC. Sponsorship agreements with IRCC are usually signed by incorporated organizations with extensive expertise, resources, and personnel to sponsor refugees on a continuing basis. Most commonly, SAHs are religious or cultural organizations or other humanitarian agencies of local, regional, or national scale. There are more than 100 SAHs across Canada allowed to sponsor refugees destined to any province other than Quebec.[19] Many SAHs are churches or church-connected groups.[20] In 2011, a SAH association was formed with a view of representing the

---

16 The list of such offences is outlined in the *Corrections and Conditional Release Act*, SC 1992, c 20, Schedules I and II, and include, for example, hijacking, prison breach, sexual assault, and trafficking in controlled substances.

17 *Regulations*, above note 8, s 156.

18 *Ibid*, s 152(1).

19 Citizens for Public Justice, "Private Sponsorship and Public Policy" (2014) at 10, online: CPJ www.cpj.ca/sites/default/files/docs/files/PrivateSponsorshipand PublicPolicyReport.pdf [CPJ]. For a complete list of SAHs, refer to the IRCC website: www.cic.gc.ca/english/refugees/sponsor/list-sponsors.asp. Quebec has its own agreement holders' list and process.

20 CPJ, above note 19 at 3.

collective voice of SAHs when engaging with IRCC, UNHCR, and other agencies.[21]

In addition to sponsoring refugees themselves, SAHs may authorize constituent groups to do so under their agreements. Constituent groups are usually comprised of SAH members. Constituent groups wishing to resettle a refugee must submit a settlement plan and an undertaking to a SAH; the SAH then issues a letter of approval authorizing the group to sponsor a case under its agreement. Each SAH establishes its own rules for authorizing and overseeing undertakings by constituent groups.

b) Community Sponsorship

Other organizations that do not meet the criteria for SAHs can nevertheless participate in a sponsorship process under a different arrangement: community sponsorship. Community sponsorship is open to any organization, whether incorporated or non-incorporated, for-profit or not-for-profit. However, unlike SAHs and constituent groups, community sponsors are allowed to have only two sponsorship applications approved annually and must have their financial and settlement plans assessed by a local IRCC office each time they wish to bring refugees to Canada. As of October 2012, community sponsors may sponsor only applicants who are recognized as refugees by either UNHCR or a foreign state. In September 2015, the IRCC Minister established a temporary public policy exemption for Syrian and Iraqi refugees: they can be sponsored by Groups of Five and community sponsors even if they are not recognized as refugees by UNHCR or a foreign state.[22]

c) Co-sponsorship

SAHs, constituent groups, and community sponsors may set up formal partnerships with other organizations or individuals who will then "co-sponsor" a specific refugee or a group of refugees. These formal partnerships are made through signing an undertaking whereby co-sponsors share in the responsibility for sponsorship and become liable for the fulfillment of the undertaking.

---

21 For more on the Canadian Refugee Sponsorship Agreement Holders Association, see www.sahassociation.com/.

22 Immigration, Refugees and Citizenship Canada, "Temporary Public Policy to Facilitate the Sponsorship of Syrian and Iraqi Refugees by Groups of Five and Community Sponsors," online: IRCC www.cic.gc.ca/english/department/laws-policy/syria-iraq.asp [IRCC, "Temporary Public Policy"]

d) Groups of Five

Groups of five or more Canadian citizens or permanent residents can join together to sponsor refugees for resettlement to Canada.[23] To be eligible as sponsors, individuals must be at least eighteen years of age, live in the community where the sponsored refugee will reside, and personally provide settlement assistance and support.[24] Each member of the group must sign an undertaking, and becomes jointly and severally liable for its performance.[25] Not all members are obliged to contribute financially, but those who do so must complete a financial profile and provide proof of employment income or other sources of income that will be used to support the sponsored refugee. The group, as a whole, must submit a settlement plan and complete a financial assessment.[26] As of October 2012, Groups of Five may sponsor only applicants who are recognized as refugees by either UNHCR or a foreign state. In September 2015, the IRCC Minister established a temporary public policy exemption for Syrian and Iraqi refugees allowing sponsorship by Groups of Five even if they are not recognized as refugees by UNHCR or a foreign state.[27]

e) Joint Government–Private Sponsorships

Joint assistance sponsorships (JAS) provide an opportunity for the government and private sponsors (SAHs or constituent groups) to work together in the resettlement of refugees with special needs who require additional care and time to rebuild their lives in Canada.[28] The *Regulations* define an individual with "special needs" as "a person [who] has greater need of settlement assistance than other applicants for protection abroad owing to personal circumstances, including (a) a large number of family members; (b) trauma resulting from violence or torture; (c) medical disabilities; and (d) the effects of systemic discrimination."[29]

Due to the high vulnerability of the above-mentioned categories of individuals, the JAS period is usually up to two years and, in exceptional circumstances, up to three years.[30]

---

23 *Regulations*, above note 8, s 138.

24 *Ibid*.

25 *Ibid*, ss 153(2) & (3).

26 Immigration, Refugees and Citizenship Canada, "Guide to Private Sponsorship of Refugees Program," online: IRCC www.cic.gc.ca/english/resources/publications/ref-sponsor/section-2.asp#a2.1 [IRCC, "Guide to Private Sponsorship"].

27 IRCC, "Temporary Public Policy," above note 22.

28 Groups of Five and community sponsors are not eligible to participate in JAS.

29 *Regulations*, above note 8, s 157(2).

30 Immigration, Refugees and Citizenship Canada, "Joint Assistance Program — Sponsoring Refugees with Special Needs," online: IRCC www.cic.gc.ca/english/

Under a JAS, the responsibilities for sponsorship are divided between the government and private sponsors. Typically, the government delivers income support through the Resettlement Assistance Program, while the tasks of orientation, settlement, and emotional support are assigned to a private sponsor.

f) Blended Visa Office–Referred Program

In 2013, IRCC launched the Blended Visa Office–Referred (BVOR) Program, which matches refugees identified for resettlement by UNHCR with private sponsors in Canada.[31] These programs are referred to as "blended" because they involve cost sharing between the government and the private sector. The federal government provides up to six months of income support through the RAP, and private sponsors provide another six months of financial support and up to a year of social and emotional support.[32] Only SAHs and their constituent groups are eligible to participate in this program (except in relation to sponsorship of Syrian refugees where community groups and Groups of Five can also participate).

g) Self-Supporting Refugees

The resettlement of self-supporting refugees has many parallels with independent immigration and may be viewed as a hybrid between refugee protection and independent immigration. Like refugees applying for resettlement under government or private sponsorship, self-sponsored applicants must satisfy the requirements for refugee or humanitarian protection, demonstrate an ability to become successfully established in Canada, and pass medical, security, and criminality checks. Similar to independent immigrants, they also must provide proof of sufficient funds to cover, without outside financial support, the cost of transportation to Canada, lodging, and other start-up expenses until they become self-sufficient (that is, employed) in Canada. The precise amount of funds required is usually determined in reference to the prescribed start-up costs and income support that government-assisted refugees would receive through the RAP over the same period of time.[33]

---

refugees/sponsor/jas.asp.

31 Immigration, Refugees and Citizenship Canada, "Blended Visa Office–Referred Program — Sponsoring Refugees," online: IRCC www.cic.gc.ca/english/refugees/sponsor/vor.asp.

32 *Ibid.*

33 IRCC, Processing Manual, "Overseas Selection and Processing of Convention Refugees Abroad Class and Members of the Humanitarian-Protected Persons

The onus is on the applicant to demonstrate the possession of "sufficient financial resources." If a visa officer determines that the required proof of funding has not been provided, he is not obliged to assess the applicant's eligibility as a Convention refugee.[34] An officer is under no obligation to make further inquiries where an application is incomplete, including when proofs of funds are not satisfactory or are outstanding.[35]

Once in Canada, self-sponsored refugees are eligible to take part in government programs for newcomers such as language and orientation services but will not receive financial assistance.

C. THE SPONSOR–REFUGEE MATCHING PROCESS

A special procedure has been established to match overseas applicants and sponsoring entities. It serves a dual purpose: to find sponsors for already approved overseas applicants and to help organizations wishing to sponsor refugees find suitable cases. The matching usually occurs either through referral from a visa office (visa office–referred cases) or through referral from a sponsoring entity (sponsor-referred cases).

Under the sponsor-referred scheme, a sponsor obtains information about a potential refugee through its overseas or domestic contacts and puts forward a sponsorship application to bring the refugee and her family to Canada. Such an application must be submitted to an IRCC office in Canada which then decides on acceptance or refusal of an undertaking.[36] As a 2007 IRCC study showed, the refusal rate for private sponsorship is rather high: it has averaged 49 percent since 1998.[37]

As mentioned earlier, a sponsorship application in Canada is only one part of the resettlement process. A candidate for resettlement must also complete a permanent resident application, which will be assessed by a respective Canadian visa office abroad. If the candidate

---

Abroad Classes" at 67–68, online: IRCC www.cic.gc.ca/english/resources/manuals/op/op05-eng.pdf.

34 *Dardic v Canada (Minister of Citizenship and Immigration)*, [2001] FCJ No 326 (TD).

35 *Beganovic v Canada (Minister of Citizenship and Immigration)*, [2004] FCJ No 406 (FC); *Tahir v Canada (Minister of Citizenship and Immigration)* (1998), 159 FTR 109 (TD).

36 IRCC, "Guide to Private Sponsorship," above note 26.

37 Immigration, Refugees and Citizenship Canada, "Summative Evaluation of the Private Sponsorship of Refugees Program" (2007), online: IRCC www.cic.gc.ca/english/resources/evaluation/psrp/psrp-summary.asp#summary.

is determined to be in need of protection, and is not inadmissible, he and his family are resettled to Canada.

The processing time depends greatly on individual circumstances and an overseas visa office. For example, in 2016, for privately sponsored refugees, the processing time for applications made in Lebanon was eight months, while in Egypt, it was fifty-six months; in India, sixty-nine months; and in Pakistan, seventy-three months.[38] The processing delays have been a long-standing issue of concern.[39]

Visa office–referred cases include applicants who have been determined to be refugees or similarly situated persons by Canadian missions abroad and have met all statutory requirements, except for sponsorship support. Such refugees are matched with potential sponsors through the Matching Centre at IRCC headquarters in Ottawa, which maintains a database inventory of visa-referred cases. Sponsorship groups can either search the database through a secure website or request profiles from IRCC. Only one group may review a profile at a time; potential sponsors are encouraged to make decisions as soon as possible. Visa office–referred cases typically travel to Canada within one to four months from the sponsorship approval.[40]

D. QUALIFICATION FOR OVERSEAS PROTECTION

In order to qualify for resettlement, an applicant must satisfy the following requirements:

- be in need of protection;
- be outside Canada;[41]
- seek to establish permanent residence in Canada;[42]

---

38 Immigration, Refugees and Citizenship Canada, "Processing Times for Privately Sponsored Refugee Applications," online: IRCC IRCC www.cic.gc.ca/english/information/times/perm/ref-private.asp.

39 See, generally, Canadian Council for Refugees, "No Faster Way? Private Sponsorship of Refugees: Overseas Processing Delays" (October 2004), online: CCR http://ccrweb.ca/sites/ccrweb.ca/files/nofasterway.pdf; CPJ, above note 19 at 5.

40 IRCC, "Guide to Private Sponsorship," above note 26. Please note, however, that another IRCC page says that visa office–referred refugees are ready to travel to Canada within four to twelve months (see online: www.cic.gc.ca/english/refugees/sponsor/apply-after.asp).

41 *Regulations*, above note 8, s 139(1)(a).

42 *Ibid*, s 139 (1)(c).

- have no reasonable prospect, within a reasonable time, of a durable solution outside Canada;[43]
- be supported by a private or government entity or have own financial resources for resettlement to Canada;[44]
- be able to become successfully established in Canada (unless determined to be vulnerable or in urgent need of protection);[45]
- not be inadmissible.[46]

Given the assumption that refugees intend to settle in Canada permanently, they are designated as a special class of permanent resident visa applicants.[47] Applications for resettlement are assessed by visa officers in Canadian missions overseas. All the above requirements must be satisfied before applicants are issued immigration visas authorizing admission to Canada. Certain deviations from this procedure may be allowed in situations of urgent need of protection.

1) Persons Who Can Be Resettled

The immigration legislation distinguishes two classes of persons who can be granted protection through resettlement: (1) Convention Refugees Abroad and (2) Humanitarian-Protected Persons Abroad.[48] Similarly to

---

43 *Ibid*, s 139 (1)(d). For the purpose of this provision, the following are considered durable solutions: voluntary repatriation to the refugee's country of nationality or habitual residence, resettlement, or an offer of resettlement to a country other than Canada.

The non-signatories to the *Convention Relating to the Status of Refugees* and the *Protocol* are presumed to provide no durable solutions. It should be noted that even signatories to the *Refugee Convention* and *Protocol* do not always provide adequate protection for refugees. For example, Turkey, which is a signatory to both the *Refugee Convention* and the *Protocol*, has introduced a geographical limitation which denies protection to refugees fleeing from outside Europe: *Resettlement out of Signatory Countries: Policy Position* (October 2000), online: http://ccrweb.ca/sites/ccrweb.ca/files/static-files/signatory.htm.

44 *Regulations*, above note 8, s 139(1)(f).

45 *Ibid*, ss 139(1)(g) and 139(2).

46 *Ibid*, s 139(1)(i). According to the *Immigration and Refugee Protection Act*, SC 2001, c 27, s 38 [*IRPA*], a person may be found inadmissible to Canada if she is likely to be a danger to public health or to public safety or is likely to cause excessive demand on health or social services. Convention Refugees Abroad and Humanitarian-Protected Persons Abroad are exempt from the latter requirement: *IRPA*, s 38(2); *Regulations*, above note 8, s 139(4). They are also exempt from inadmissibility on the basis of misrepresentation: *Regulations*, *ibid*, s 22.

47 *Regulations*, *ibid*, s 70(2)(c).

48 *Ibid*, ss 144 and 146. It is interesting to note that the *Regulations* classify applicants from abroad as Convention Refugees Abroad or Humanitarian-Protected

the inland refugee determination process, this classification reflects the grounds on which protection is granted. The Convention Refugees Abroad class is constituted by persons who satisfy the *Refugee Convention* definition. The Humanitarian-Protected Persons Abroad class applies to persons in refugee-like situations who do not meet one of the *Refugee Convention* criteria, but are nevertheless in need of protection. Within both subclasses, the *Regulations* also take note of persons in particularly vulnerable circumstances or in urgent need of protection;[49] these individuals are subject to expedited processing and the waiver of such regulatory requirements as successful establishment in Canada.[50]

a) Convention Refugees Abroad

To be recognized as a member of a Convention Refugees Abroad class, a person must be outside Canada and must satisfy the *Refugee Convention* definition, as outlined in Chapter 4.[51]

b) Humanitarian-Protected Persons Abroad

Individuals who do not fall within the definition of Convention refugees may still qualify for resettlement under the Humanitarian-Protected Persons Abroad class. This class currently consists of "country of asylum" applicants, namely, people who are outside all countries of their nationality and/or habitual residence and who have been and continue to be "seriously and personally" affected by civil war, armed conflict, or massive human rights violations in those countries.[52] Thus, a member of the country of asylum class need not establish a nexus between risk of persecution and any of the five grounds enumerated in the definition of refugee as is required of those in the Convention Refugees Abroad class.[53]

Until 2011, the Humanitarian-Protected Persons Abroad class also included applicants from designated source countries, namely, persons at risk who were still in their country of nationality or habitual residence. The following countries were designated as source countries:

Persons Abroad, while the *IRPA* refers to the same categories as Convention refugees and persons in similar circumstances. For the purposes of s 12(3) of the *IRPA*, a person "in similar circumstances" is a member of the country of asylum class.

49 *Regulations*, above note 8, s 138.

50 *Ibid*, s 139(2).

51 *IRPA*, above note 46, s 96.

52 *Regulations*, above note 8, s 147.

53 *Ibid*, s 147; *Saifee v Canada (Minister of Citizenship and Immigration)*, 2010 FC 589 [*Saifee*].

Colombia, Democratic Republic of Congo, El Salvador, Guatemala, Sierra Leone, and Sudan. Applicants had to demonstrate that they were seriously and personally affected by civil war or armed conflict in the source country; or had been detained, imprisoned with or without charges, or subjected to some other form of penal control for an act that, in Canada, would be considered a legitimate exercise of freedom of expression or civil rights pertaining to dissent or trade union activity; or satisfied the Convention refugee definition (except for the condition of being outside their country of nationality or habitual residence).[54] However, the source country class was eliminated by the Conservative government in 2011.

c) Persons in "Urgent Need of Protection" and "Vulnerable" Persons

The immigration legislation recognizes that some persons may be in urgent need of protection or be particularly vulnerable. These groups enjoy expedited processing as well as flexibility in the application of some of the requirements for resettlement (notably, the waiver of the requirement for successful establishment).

A refugee in "urgent need of protection" is defined as one whose "life, liberty or physical safety is under immediate threat and, if not protected, the person is likely to be (a) killed; (b) subjected to violence, torture, sexual assault or arbitrary imprisonment; or (c) returned to their country of nationality or . . . former habitual residence."[55] "Vulnerable" persons are defined as persons who by virtue of their particular circumstances face a heightened risk to their physical safety and are in greater need of protection than other applicants for resettlement.[56]

The "urgent need of protection" cases are typically referred to Canadian offices by UNHCR. A decision on whether to accept the case for processing is usually taken within twenty-four to forty-eight hours, and approved applicants are usually en route to Canada within three to five days of referral.[57] Due to the nature of urgent processing, it is often impossible to complete inadmissibility checks (medical, security, and criminality) prior to the refugee's arrival in Canada. In most cases, such a refugee will be issued a permit under the Protected Temporary Resident class. Upon arrival, she will need to apply for permanent resident status from within Canada. Persons in urgent need of protection are usually designated as government-assisted refugees or JAS cases.[58]

---

54 *Regulations*, above note 8, s 148(1)(b).

55 *Ibid*, s 138.

56 *Ibid*.

57 IRCC, "Guide to Private Sponsorship," above note 26.

58 *Ibid*.

If a private sponsor is needed and one has not been found by the time of relocation, such refugees are sent to reception centres in Canada where they will wait for a match.[59]

Taking into consideration that women refugees often find themselves in particularly precarious or desperate circumstances, the government established a special program, Women at Risk. Since 1988, the Women at Risk program has addressed the needs of women and their children who have been left without support and protection of family, friends, or local authorities and are therefore exposed to a heightened risk of violence or harassment. Women at Risk cases pertain to persons deemed to be in "urgent need of protection" or "vulnerable"; they are often designated as JAS cases.[60]

E. APPLICATION FOR PROTECTION FROM OVERSEAS

The qualification for resettlement (as per criteria outlined in Section D, above in this chapter) is established on the basis of a submitted application, documentary evidence, and an interview. Only the principal applicant must establish his qualification for resettlement. Once he is determined to have qualified for protection, he and his family proceed to inadmissibility screening (medical, security, and criminality checks).

1) Application Procedure

An application for permanent residence as a Convention refugee or as a Humanitarian-Protected Person is assessed abroad by a Canadian visa office that services the applicant's place of residence. The application must be accompanied either by a referral from UNHCR[61] or by an undertaking of private sponsorship.[62] These access criteria correspond to the types of sponsorships described above whereby refugees referred by UNHCR often constitute more complicated cases in need of government assistance. It also generally prevents refugees from applying for

---

59 *Ibid.*

60 *Ibid.*

61 UNHCR is the referral organization, but the minister can enter into memoranda of understanding with other organizations for the purpose of locating and identifying refugees abroad: *Regulations*, above note 8, s 143.

62 *Ibid*, ss 140.2 & 140.3(1).

resettlement directly to the Canadian mission without having a prearranged sponsorship.

The inability to apply directly to the Canadian mission abroad unfairly prejudices refugees in areas where UNHCR and other organizations are unable to operate, and hence, unable to issue referrals. Consequently, in exceptional circumstances, the Minister may designate certain regions as areas of direct access where applicants are exempt from the requirement to submit a referral or an undertaking together with their applications.[63] As of 2017, no areas had been designated for direct access.

An application for resettlement asks candidates to provide detailed information about themselves, their family members, and de facto dependants, and describe instances of persecution, conditions in the country to which the applicants have fled (namely, whether the applicant is threatened there), and other circumstances relevant to determination of their protection needs. The application also asks candidates to list skills and personal qualities that would help them become successfully established in Canada.

For the purposes of refugee resettlement, the *Regulations* distinguish between family members, non-accompanying family members, and de facto dependants. A family member is an applicant's spouse or common law partner, and their dependent children.[64] De facto dependants are persons who are integral members of the applicant's family and depend on his support financially and/or emotionally, yet do not meet a prescribed definition of a family member. The category of de facto dependants is applicable exclusively to resettled refugees. De facto dependants may or may not be blood relatives of the principal applicant and her family. The definition of a de facto family member is culturally determined. It can include, for example, unmarried adult daughters where it is traditional for them to remain dependent on the family until marriage, widowed sisters, parents of any age if they have no other means of support, or elderly relatives. Although such members may be considered for resettlement as a part of the family of the principal applicant at the time of application for landing, they may not be sponsored or otherwise resettled based on their family relationship.

The legislation is sensitive to the fact that by virtue of the circumstances of forced migration, refugee families may get separated and that

---

63 *Ibid*, ss 140.3(2) & (3).

64 A "dependent child" is a biological or adopted child who is (1) single and under nineteen years of age; or (2) is nineteen or older and is dependent on a parent's financial support since before the age of nineteen and not self-supporting due to physical or mental disability: *ibid*, s 2.

not all family members can be resettled at the same time and from the same place. To facilitate family reunification, the legislation provides for a special category of non-accompanying family members and a one-year window for their resettlement. The one-year window opportunity waives the requirement for a referral or undertaking normally applied to applications for resettlement.[65] A non-accompanying family member can benefit from the one-year window opportunity if the following conditions are met:

- The non-accompanying family member was included in the principal applicant's original application for resettlement or was added to that application before the principal applicant's departure for Canada.
- The non-accompanying family member applied for resettlement within one year from the date when protection was conferred on the principal applicant.
- The non-accompanying member is not inadmissible.
- A visa officer is satisfied that the principal applicant's sponsor has been notified and that adequate financial resources are available for resettlement of the non-accompanying family member.[66]

Family members who wish to be resettled after one year has elapsed may apply as refugees in their own right or may be sponsored by relatives in Canada under the family class.

2) Interview

The assessment of resettlement applications is conducted on the basis of documentary evidence and an interview. Once a refugee's initial eligibility is established through a submitted application, a visa officer schedules an interview to determine an applicant's need for protection and potential for successful establishment in Canada.[67] In exceptional circumstances (such as urgent need of protection or very clear and credible cases of persecution), an officer can exercise his discretion to waive an interview.

An interview in many ways serves the same purpose as a refugee determination hearing before the Refugee Protection Division; the two procedures, however, are far from identical.

---

65 *Ibid*, s 141(2).

66 *Ibid*, s 141(1).

67 IRCC guidelines for interviewing applicants are outlined in "Resettlement from Overseas: Conducting Interviews" (25 February 2013), online: www.cic.gc.ca/english/resources/tools/refugees/resettlement/processing/interviews.asp.

First, there are fewer participants in an interview process: usually only the applicant, a visa officer, and an interpreter. In certain circumstances, a duty of fairness may require that the applicant's counsel be allowed to attend an interview as an observer and take notes (for example, when the applicant's ability to effectively participate in an interview would be inhibited without a counsel present).[68] This, however, does not mean that counsel are permitted to attend all interviews or that they are allowed to make oral submissions or intervene in the process, as legal representatives in refugee hearings can.

Second, in addition to protection needs, visa officers must evaluate an applicant's potential to become successfully established in Canada. The decision involves assessing the likelihood that a person "will be able to provide for themselves and their dependants, and does not have any impediments to joining the full-time labour force, even if it is at minimum wage."[69] In making this evaluation, officers consider the following factors prescribed in the *Regulations*:

- resourcefulness and other similar qualities that assist in the applicant's integration in a new society;
- presence of relatives or a sponsor in the expected community of resettlement;
- potential for employment in Canada, given the applicant's education, work experience, and skills;
- ability to learn to communicate in one of Canada's official languages.[70]

If an officer is not satisfied as to the applicant's ability to become successfully established in Canada within three to five years of arrival, the application may be refused. However, the IRCC Manual instructs officers to first consider whether an applicant may be able to become established if given extra support through JAS or extended sponsorship.[71]

While the adaptability of candidates for resettlement is an important consideration, the strict application of "ability to establish" creates inequality in treatment of resettled refugees and inland applicants. Inland refugee claimants need only to demonstrate the need for protection. This inequity

---

68 For example, when an officer puts forward questions of a legal nature that an applicant cannot be expected to understand or properly convey to his counsel for the purpose of being addressed in written submissions.

69 Immigration, Refugees and Citizenship Canada, "Determining Eligibility: Determining Whether the Applicant Has the Ability to Establish," online: IRCC www.cic.gc.ca/english/resources/tools/refugees/resettlement/eligibility/establish.asp [IRCC, "Determining Eligibility"].

70 *Regulations*, above note 8, s 139(1)(g).

71 IRCC, "Determining Eligibility," above note 69.

underscores the distinction made in much of international refugee law between refugees in general and refugees within a state's own jurisdiction.

The interview is crucial for an applicant's approval for resettlement. Despite some procedural differences from inland refugee hearings, Canadian courts tend to require of it many of the same characteristics of a full and fair hearing.[72] As in inland hearings, the applicant's ability to effectively participate in an interview is imperative for fair and open determination of a claim, particularly in respect to credibility assessment. Assessing credibility is within the expertise of the visa officer,[73] but her conclusions must be supported by the evidence.[74]

The central importance of the duty of fairness lies in the participatory rights of those affected by a decision to put forward their views and relevant evidence before a decision maker.[75] For example, an applicant must be provided with an opportunity to comment on the officer's findings about conditions in the country of the applicant's citizenship.[76] An officer must seek to clarify the applicant's answers and to record the interview fully and fairly.[77] An officer also must provide an environment conducive to an open and fair exchange during an interview.[78] However, the fact that an officer used a harsh tone and made a few intemperate remarks does not automatically indicate apprehension of bias.[79] If any extrinsic evidence is consulted, the applicant must be given an opportunity to comment on it; failing to do so constitutes violation of the duty

---

72 *Jallow v Canada*, [1996] FCJ No 1452 (TD) [*Jallow*]; *Smajic v Canada*, [1999] FCJ No 1904 (TD); *Oraha v Canada*, [1997] FCJ No 788 (TD) [*Oraha*].

73 *Aguebor v Canada (Minister of Employment and Immigration)*, (1993), 160 NR 315 (FCA).

74 *Mboudu v Canada (Minister of Citizenship and Immigration)*, 2012 FC 881.

75 *Baker v Canada (Minister of Citizenship and Immigration)*, [1999] SCJ No 39.

76 In *Phan v Canada (Minister of Citizenship and Immigration)*, [2000] FCJ No 728 (TD), the Federal Court held that the immigration officer's failure to provide the applicant with an opportunity to respond to "objective information" about the situation in his country of residence that contradicted applicant's testimony constituted a denial of natural justice. An officer must provide an applicant with an opportunity to be heard when possible and to provide material in support of his or her claim. See also *Jallow*, above note 72 at para 18.

77 *Muhazi v Canada (Minister of Citizenship and Immigration)*, 2004 FC 1392. For example, the Federal Court determined that an interview was not recorded fully and fairly where an officer made notes five days after the interview, did not reconstruct questions but provided only a summary (which contained inconsistencies), and issued a formal letter of refusal three and a half months after an actual decision was made.

78 *Mengesha v Canada (Minister of Citizenship and Immigration)*, [1999] FCJ No 1322 at para 48 (TD).

79 *Ibid*.

of fairness.[80] When assessing plausibility of applicants' stories, visa officers must be careful not to judge them by Canadian standards, but rather assess whether the stories are plausible when considered within the "claimant's milieu."[81]

A resettlement statutory scheme that provides no appeal on the merits and has great significance for applicants arguably requires a higher level of procedural fairness.[82] The factual reality for overseas claimants is that they are much more likely to suffer ill-treatment if the wrong decision is made. Furthermore, they have much less of an opportunity to challenge wrongful decisions than their inland equivalents — despite the fact that the *IRPA* does not formally discriminate between the two groups with respect to judicial review. Arguably, the duty of fairness to them should be higher because its violation may deprive a person of the sole opportunity to be relieved from danger.

In determining a person's eligibility for resettlement, a visa officer has a duty to consider all potential grounds of persecution raised by a claimant's application.[83] Officers are to consider both the Convention refugee abroad and the country of asylum definitions.[84] The assessment of a claim must be done with the knowledge and consideration of country conditions.[85]

In addition to considering the protection grounds, officers are to take into account whether an applicant has a prospect of a durable solution outside of Canada. The onus is on the applicant to establish that no such reasonable prospect exists.[86] The assessment of a reasonable prospect of a durable solution in another country needs to include the examination of the applicant's personal circumstances and the conditions in the applicant's country of residence.[87] For example, in *Al-Anbagi v*

---

80 *Mushimiyimana v Canada (Minister of Citizenship and Immigration)*, 2010 FC 1124 [*Mushimiyimana*]; *Toma v Canada (Minister of Citizenship and Immigration)*, 2006 FC 780.

81 *Ye v Canada (Minister of Employment and Immigration)*, [1992] FCJ No 584 (CA); *Ghirmatsion v Canada (Minister of Citizenship and Immigration)*, 2011 FC 519 at para 71.

82 *Ha v Canada (Minister of Citizenship and Immigration)*, [2004] 3 FCR 195 at paras 46–69 (CA) (analysis of the duty of fairness based on the *Baker* factors: see above note 75). See also *Krikor v Canada (Minister of Citizenship and Immigration)*, 2016 FC 458 at para 13.

83 *Adan v Canada (Minister of Citizenship and Immigration)*, 2011 FC 655 at para 30.

84 *Saifee*, above note 53.

85 *Ibid*.

86 *Barud v Canada (Minister of Citizenship and Immigration)*, 2013 FC 1152 at para 15 [*Barud*]; *Dusabimana v Canada (Minister of Citizenship and Immigration)*, 2011 FC 1238 at para 54.

87 *Mushimiyimana*, above note 80 at para 21.

Canada (Minister of Citizenship and Immigration),[88] the Federal Court found the officer's conclusion that applicants had a durable solution in Jordan unreasonable. Jordan is not a signatory to the *Refugee Convention* and, hence, is under no legal obligation to offer the applicants long-term residence. In fact, the applicant had only a temporary one-year permit, which did not protect him from *refoulement* to Iraq, especially in light of evidence that renewal procedures in Jordan are not fair and change constantly. Further, the applicant's status in Jordan was strongly contingent on his ability to run a successful business: if that business failed, his residency permit would likely not be renewed and he would face removal to Iraq. In contrast, in *Barud v Canada (Citizenship and Immigration)*,[89] the Federal Court upheld refusal of a resettlement application due to the existence of a durable solution in a third country. Barud fled from Somalia to South Africa where he acquired rights akin to citizenship. The applicant claimed that he was discriminated against and targeted by gangs and the police in South Africa, but the officer concluded that a durable solution was available as South Africa was making efforts at improving the treatment of foreigners. In upholding the officer's decision, the Federal Court noted that a durable solution differs from the test for state protection: "In the latter case, the question is whether the claimant will face a well-founded fear of persecution on return to his or her country of origin, given the state's resources and willingness to protect the person. In the case of a 'durable solution,' the state's plans and intentions, as compared to its existing capacity and desire, is far more relevant."[90]

3) Arrangements for Travel to Canada

If a person's application for resettlement is approved, he and his family are issued permanent resident visas to travel to Canada. Resettled refugees are supposed to pay for travel and other related expenses (e.g., medical examination, travel documents). However, if they do not have necessary funds, they may receive loans for transportation and inadmissibility checks from the Canadian government. Decisions on loans are made by visa officers abroad. While refugees are usually expected to repay the loan, sometimes a visa officer may ask a sponsoring group to pay some or all of the costs if she has concerns about the refugee's ability to repay.[91]

---

88 2016 FC 273.

89 *Barud*, above note 86.

90 *Ibid* at para 16.

91 IRCC, "Guide to Private Sponsorship," above note 26.

In addition to loan approval, visa offices abroad make other arrangements for refugee travel. For example, they can issue a temporary travel document to a refugee if he does not have one and would otherwise be unable to travel to Canada.[92]

F. CONCLUSION

Refugees can be resettled to Canada through government or private sponsorship. A range of possible sponsorship arrangements facilitate the involvement not only of government agencies, but also of various community organizations and private individuals in the resettlement process. A 2007 IRCC evaluation of private refugee sponsorship found that the program provided solid supports to facilitate refugee integration, and privately sponsored refugees were becoming self-supporting faster than government-assisted refugees.[93] Together with government sponsorship, the program assisted more than 10,000 refugees annually on an ongoing basis, and Canada has been one of the most active participants in resettlement in the world.

Applicants for resettlement, however, must meet a higher threshold than inland refugee claimants. This is most evident in the requirement to demonstrate the ability to become successfully established in Canada, a criterion for assessment which has no parallel in the inland process. In addition, applicants from overseas may be prejudiced in their access to the application process due to the requirement for a UNHCR referral or a sponsorship undertaking. Further, during the process, applicants from overseas have limited entitlement to the assistance of counsel (particularly during the interview) and are entitled to only a low level of procedural fairness. The existence of double standards for overseas and inland determination serves as yet another reminder of the state's desire to keep a tight grip on migration. As mentioned at the beginning of the chapter, resettlement is more amenable to state control than asylum arrivals, and the state takes full advantage of this feature of resettlement. The access to resettlement is likely to be even more restrictive due to recent changes, such as the elimination of the source country class and decision that Groups of Five and community sponsors are

---

92 *Regulations*, above note 8, s 151.

93 See also Jennifer Hyndman, "Research Summary on Resettled Refugee Integration in Canada" (2011), online: www.unhcr.org/4e4123d19.html; Jennifer Marchbank et al, *Karen Refugees after Five Years in Canada — Readying Communities for Refugee Resettlement* (2014), online: https://issbc.org/wp-content/uploads/2015/02/Karen_Refugees_After_Five_Years_in_Canada_CS.pdf.

limited to sponsoring only refugees recognized by UNHCR or other states.[94] However, the Liberal government elected into power in October 2015 has been strongly supportive of higher resettlement targets, particularly for Syrian refugees.[95] For example, the resettlement target for 2016 was increased to nearly 45,000 — in part, to allow completing Canada's earlier commitment to assist Syrian refugees.[96] For 2017, the target is lower — 25,000[97] — but it is still significantly higher than the 10,000 to 12,000 annual target maintained over the past decade.[98]

94 See, generally, the Canadian Council for Refugees on these concerns: CCR http://ccrweb.ca/en/changes-private-sponsorship-refugees.

95 See Global News, "Trudeau's Welcoming of Refugees Making International Headlines" (12 December 2015), online: http://globalnews.ca/news/2397754/trudeaus-welcoming-of-refugees-making-international-headlines/; Global News, "Governor General Welcomes Latest Batch of Syrian Refugees in Toronto" (18 December 2015), online: http://globalnews.ca/news/2410681/governor-general-welcomes-latest-batch-of-syrian-refugees-arriving/.

96 IRCC, "Key Highlights - 2016 Immigration Levels Plan," online: http://news.gc.ca/web/article-en.do?nid=1038709.

97 IRCC, "Key Highlights – 2017 Immigration Levels Plan," online: http://news.gc.ca/web/article-en.do?nid=1145319.

98 See above note 2.

CHAPTER 8

INLAND PROTECTION

A. INTRODUCTION

The overwhelming majority of refugees in the world are located outside of Canada. As we have seen in Chapter 7, some of those individuals can receive Canada's protection through resettlement. In addition to resettlement, the second avenue of gaining protection is through an inland refugee determination system designed for those who have made it to Canada and applied for protection from within the country. Such claimants are subject to a complicated process of examination, which consists of two main stages: (1) the determination of their eligibility for a hearing before the Refugee Protection Division (RPD) of the Immigration and Refugee Board (IRB), and (2) the determination of the substantive merit of their claims. This process is not designed to determine whether an individual is generally in need of protection; rather, it is designed to determine whether she falls within the limited grounds on which Canada promises to offer protection, namely, risk of persecution, risk to life, and risk of torture. Canada does not accept all individuals who claim to have fear on one of these grounds. Rather, after a process of examination and deliberation, Canadian authorities ultimately provide protection to less than half of individuals who seek protection in Canada.[1]

---

1 The calculation of the exact acceptance rate is quite complex, as it must combine the various acceptance rates at the various levels of decision making. During the

In the past decade, the Canadian government has adopted policies that make it more difficult for refugee claimants to successfully travel to Canada and has also introduced various measures that are expected to deter them from choosing Canada as a destination to claim asylum. The annual number of claims referred to the RPD has fluctuated, but since 2013, the number has been at its lowest in a decade: under 17,000 (for a detailed yearly breakdown, see Appendix D, Table 1).[2] In addition, the 2012 changes to the refugee determination system (particularly shorter hearing timelines) are likely to make it more difficult to succeed even for those who managed to overcome barriers to entry.

This chapter first examines the barriers and deterrents on access to refugee protection in Canada and then discusses the details of the refugee determination process for inland claimants.

B. ACCESS TO INLAND PROTECTION

The *Convention Relating to the Status of Refugees* imposes an explicit obligation on states parties not to expel a refugee to a country where he might be subject to persecution, and to guarantee certain rights to refugees in state party territory. However, there is no corresponding explicit obligation to admit potential refugee claimants who are outside a state party's territory. Due to this gap in the *Refugee Convention*, states have tried to limit their protection obligations by erecting barriers on refugee claimants' access to their territories.

1) Interdiction

The term "interdiction" refers to a variety of state measures designed to prevent non-citizens, including asylum seekers, from entering state territory. These measures encompass, but are not limited to, the use of carrier sanctions, the imposition of visa requirements, and the interception of incoming vessels. Canada is not alone in pursuing interdiction. Both the United States and Australia pioneered such practice in relation to refugee claimants in the 1980s and 1990s. Interdiction is now practised by the European Union and most developed nations.

---

past decade, on average, only slightly over 40 percent of refugee claims were accepted by the RPD [access-to-information request to the RPD, on file with authors]. The acceptance rates at other levels of decision making (including through the pre-removal risk assessment process) add much less than 10 percent to this total.

2 Access-to-information request to the IRB No A-2014-04527 [on file with authors].

Most of Canada's interdiction measures, except for visa requirements, are coordinated by the Canada Border Services Agency (CBSA) and are carried out at both Canadian ports of entry and overseas departure points. The CBSA employs the "multiple borders strategy," which "strives to 'push the border out' so that people posing a risk to Canada's security and prosperity are identified as far away from the actual border as possible, ideally before a person departs their country of origin."[3] As the image below shows, a border is viewed ". . . not as a geo-political line but rather a continuum of checkpoints along a route of travel from the country of origin to Canada . . . ."[4]

Figure 8.1: Multiple Borders Strategy

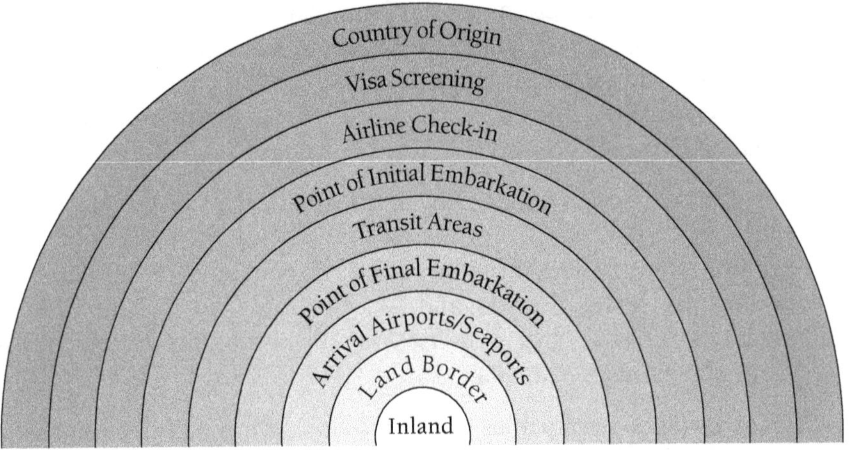

Source: Canada Border Services Agency, Admissibility Screening and Supporting Intelligence Activities — Evaluation Study (2009).

As part of this strategy, the CBSA's liaison officers abroad engage in risk assessment, interdiction, information collection, and training, working together with transportation carriers and foreign immigration and law enforcement authorities. In addition, special agreements on advance passenger information and other types of data sharing can assist CBSA officers in pre-departure screening. For example, in 2003, Canada and the United States signed a Statement of Mutual Understanding on Information Sharing,[5] which also includes an annex on

---

3 Canada Border Services Agency, "Admissibility Screening and Supporting Intelligence Activities — Evaluation Study" (2009).

4 Statement of Mutual Understanding on Information Sharing, online: www.cic.gc.ca/english/department/laws-policy/smu/smu-ins-dos.asp.

5 See text of SMU, online: www.cic.gc.ca/english/department/laws-policy/smu/smu-ins-dos.asp.

sharing information regarding asylum and refugee claims. In 2013, Canada and the European Union concluded an agreement on the transfer and processing of Passenger Name Record Data,[6] which allows the CBSA to receive advance passenger information, screen, and issue board/no-board messages for all travellers and crew members before flight departures for Canada.[7] Between 2001 and 2012, the CBSA Liaison Officer Program intercepted, on average, between six and seven thousand persons annually.[8]

In addition to relying upon its own personnel, the CBSA co-operates with transportation companies in screening and interdicting improperly documented passengers. This co-operation is ensured through two main mechanisms: (1) legislatively prescribed obligations of transportation companies and sanctions for non-compliance; and (2) memoranda of understanding (MOUs) between Canadian immigration authorities and carriers operating regular routes to Canada.

Under current law, the major obligations of transportation companies include the following:

1) provision of access to passenger information to immigration authorities;
2) prohibition on carrying improperly documented or other prescribed persons to Canada; and
3) payment of fines and expenses for bringing improperly documented persons to Canada.

Transportation companies must provide immigration authorities with advance passenger information and, on request, other personal information (e.g., a copy of a passenger's ticket, itinerary, and passport number) regarding anyone who is being carried to Canada.[9] Section 148(1)(a) of the *Immigration and Refugee Protection Act*, or *IRPA*, prescribes that transportation companies must not carry to Canada persons who do not possess proper documentation. Furthermore, if a transportation company has reasonable grounds to believe that a person might destroy documents before arrival in Canada, it must seize the person's

6 Online: www.treaty-accord.gc.ca/text-texte.aspx?id=105046.

7 Canada Border Services Agency, "Report on Plans and Priorities 2014–15," online: CBSA www.cbsa-asfc.gc.ca/agency-agence/reports-rapports/rpp/2014-2015/report-rapport-eng.html.

8 Harvard Immigration and Refugee Clinic, *Bordering on Failure: Canada–U.S. Border Policy and the Politics of Refugee Exclusion* (Cambridge, MA: Harvard Immigration and Refugee Law Clinical Program, 2013) at 34 [HIRC, *Bordering on Failure*].

9 *Immigration and Refugee Protection Regulations*, SOR/2002-227, ss 264 and 269 [*Regulations*].

documentation and present that person and documents for examination at the port of entry.[10] In addition, transporters must provide and maintain facilities at ports of entry for the holding and examination of persons carried to Canada.[11] Ultimately, a transportation company that has brought inadmissible or other prescribed persons to Canada[12] is responsible for their removal and the payment of any removal-related costs, including accommodation, meals, visa fees, and an escort if one is required.[13] In addition to these expenses, transportation companies are liable to pay an "administration fee" of $3,200 for each improperly documented person brought to Canada.[14]

Under memoranda of understanding, carriers undertake to co-operate closely with Canadian authorities in several areas, document screening, training of personnel in document screening, fraud prevention, gate checks, information exchange, and interdiction of inadmissible persons among them.[15] The *Immigration and Refugee Protection Regulations* provide an incentive for carrier co-operation by prescribing lower administration fees for signatories of MOUs. The fee is reduced proportionately to the degree of a carrier's compliance with an MOU and their success in interdiction of improperly documented or other prescribed persons.[16]

Another common means of interdiction is the imposition of visa requirements on refugee-producing countries. For example, high volumes of refugee claims from Mexico and the Czech Republic have been expressly cited as the reason for Canada's imposition of visas on citizens of those countries in 2009.[17] To obtain a visa, applicants usually

---

10 SC 2001, c 27, s 148 [*IRPA*]; *Regulations*, *ibid*, ss 260–61.

11 *IRPA*, above note 10, s 148(1)(e); *Regulations*, above note 9, s 271.

12 *Regulations*, *ibid*, s 273(1). According to this provision, transportation companies will be liable for those foreign nationals (or, in some cases, permanent residents) who are inadmissible by virtue of the *IRPA*, ss 40(1), 41, & 42, and will (depending on their removal destination) be required to effect their physical removal. The categories of individuals include those inadmissible due to misrepresentation or non-compliance with the provisions of the *IRPA* (or *Regulations*) and family members of the inadmissible (who are, on that basis, inadmissible). Obviously, those with inadequate documents will, *inter alia*, be inadmissible under the second ground (non-compliance through breach of the *IRPA*, s 20(1)(a), via s 259 of the *Regulations*).

13 *Regulations*, *ibid*, s 278.

14 *Ibid*, ss 279 & 280(1).

15 *Ibid*, s 280(3).

16 The fee can be reduced up to a zero. *Ibid*, s 280(2).

17 Immigration, Refugees and Citizenship Canada, News Release, "Canada Imposes a Visa on Mexico" (13 July 2009), online: IRCC http://news.gc.ca/web/article-en.do?nid=466839. During 2008–09, Mexico ranked as the top country of origin of refugee claimants in Canada; the Czech Republic was among the

must demonstrate a legitimate purpose for their trip, supported by a letter of invitation, and proof of availability of financial resources for the trip; they must also satisfy a visa officer that they will not remain in Canada past the authorized length of stay. An intention to claim asylum would not be considered a legitimate purpose for a trip, and other requirements are unlikely to be met as well, thus, effectively precluding potential claimants from such legal routes of entry to Canada. Data suggest that visa requirements indeed lead to a decrease in arrivals. For instance, a 2003 report by the IRB cited the imposition of visas on Hungary and Zimbabwe as one reason for a decline in the overall number of inland claims.[18] Similarly, the numbers of claimants from Mexico and the Czech Republic have dropped following introduction of visa requirements.[19]

2) *Safe Third Country Agreement*

The Canada–US *Safe Third Country Agreement* was signed on 5 December 2002 and entered into force on 29 December 2004.[20] It is said to pursue the objectives of promoting the sharing of responsibility for refugee protection between the United States and Canada, preventing "asylum shopping," and maintaining the integrity of the parties' refugee determination systems.[21] The *Safe Third Country Agreement* helps determine which state should adjudicate an individual's claim for protection: whether it should be the country in which the person first arrived (the arrival state) or the country in which the person seeks protection (the receiving state). In many cases, these two states will be the same: for instance, a person will arrive in Canada without passing through the United States and will seek protection in Canada shortly after her arrival. The Agreement governs situations where the arrival state and the receiving state

---

top ten countries of origin: United Nations High Commissioner for Refugees, *Asylum Levels in Industrialized Countries: 2009* (2010) at 33–34, online: www.unhcr.org/statistics/unhcrstats/4ba7341a9/asylum-levels-trends-industrialized-countries-2009-statistical-overview.html. For general discussion of visa requirements for Roma, see also Cynthia Levine-Ransky et al, "The Exclusion of Roma Claimants in Canadian Refugee Policy" (2014) 48:1 *Patterns of Prejudice* 67.

18 *Ibid.*

19 HIRC, *Bordering on Failure*, above note 8 at 42.

20 *Agreement between the Government of Canada and the Government of the United States of America for Co-operation in the Examination of Refugee Status Claims from Nationals of Third Countries*, 5 December 2002, art 4, online: www.cic.gc.ca/english/department/laws-policy/safe-third.asp [*Safe Third Country Agreement*].

21 Canada Border Services Agency, "Department Performance Report 2004–05," at 24, online: http://publications.gc.ca/collections/collection_2012/sct-tbs/BT31-4-91-2005-eng.pdf.

are different. It has been incorporated into Canadian law through an amendment to the *Immigration and Refugee Protection Regulations*.[22]

The Agreement applies only to claims made at the port of entry land border between Canada and the United States and sets out as a general principle that the state in which a refugee claimant first arrived should be responsible for determining the claim. Thus, a refugee claimant who arrives at a Canadian port of entry on the land border and makes a refugee claim will generally be sent back to the United States for the determination of his claim. The same rule applies to refugee claimants who transit through Canada before arriving at an American land-border post and seeking asylum.

The Agreement provides for a limited number of exceptions to the above rule. In regard to the following four categories of individuals, the responsibility of refugee determination rests with the receiving state, not the state of first arrival:

1) unaccompanied minors;
2) claimants who have a family member whose refugee claim was granted or who has lawful status (other than a visitor) in the receiving state;
3) claimants who have a family member who is at least eighteen years old and has a refugee claim pending in the receiving state;
4) claimants who arrived in the receiving state's territory on a valid visa or who do not require a visa.[23]

In addition to the four exceptions above, the parties may exempt other categories of claimants from the general rule on the basis of public interest.[24] For example, Canada decided not to apply the *Safe Third Country Agreement* in respect to claimants who have been charged with or convicted of an offence in another country, including the United States, which carries a death penalty.[25] The Agreement also does not apply to Canadian and US citizens as well as stateless persons habitually resident in one of the two countries.[26]

A claimant must satisfy an immigration officer on a balance of probabilities that he is subject to an exemption from the application of the Agreement.[27] If exemption on the basis of family member in the

22 *Regulations Amending the Immigration and Refugee Protection Regulations*, PC 2004-1157 (2004).

23 *Safe Third Country Agreement*, above note 20, art 4; and *Regulations*, above note 9, s 159.5.

24 *Safe Third Country Agreement*, above note 20, art 6.

25 *Regulations*, above note 9, s 159.6.

26 *Safe Third Country Agreement*, above note 20, art 2.

27 Immigration, Refugees and Citizenship Canada, "Processing in-Canada Claims for Protection: The *Safe Third Country Agreement*," online: IRCC www.cic.gc.ca/english/resources/tools/refugees/canada/processing/stca.asp.

receiving state is claimed, article 1 of the Agreement and section 159.1 of the *Regulations* define a "family member" to include a spouse, a common law partner, sons, daughters, parents, legal guardians, siblings, grandparents, grandchildren, aunts, uncles, nieces, and nephews.[28]

The Agreement provides that claimants refused access to protection should not be removed to any country other than the United States or Canada. Further, neither party shall remove a claimant until his claim is determined.[29] The presence of these two components in the *Safe Third Country Agreement* seeks to ensure claimants' access to refugee determination and to preclude the occurrence of "chain *refoulement*" and "refugees in orbit."[30] Due to the existence of these guarantees, Canada deems it unnecessary to allow claimants to apply for pre-removal risk assessment (see Chapter 12) before removing them to the United States.

In 2006, what was then Citizenship and Immigration Canada (CIC) released a report titled "A Partnership for Protection," which examined the first year of the Agreement's implementation.[31] It pronounced the Agreement a success and an effective tool for the sharing of responsibility. According to the CIC Minister Joe Volpe, cases were handled in a "generous and efficient manner . . . . Nor has there been any increase in inland claims or any indication that individuals are being denied protection as a result of the *Agreement*."[32] The critics, however, point to the numerous adverse effects of the Agreement on asylum seekers.[33] For example, instead of enhancing security and regularizing refugee flows, the *Safe Third Country Agreement* may force claimants to resort to illegal entry. Fewer claimants will be willing to present themselves at the border,[34]

28 *Safe Third Country Agreement*, above note 20, art 1; and *Regulations*, above note 9, s 159.1 *sub verbo* "family member."

29 *Safe Third Country Agreement*, above note 20, art 3.

30 Audrey Macklin, "Disappearing Refugees: Reflections on the Canada–US *Safe Third Country Agreement*" (2005) 36 *Columbia Human Rights Law Review* 365 at 373.

31 Immigration, Refugees and Citizenship Canada, "A Partnership for Protection: Year One Review" (2006) [IRCC, "A Partnership for Protection"].

32 Notes for an address by the Honourable Joe Volpe, Minister of Citizenship and Immigration, at a meeting with la Table de concertation au service des réfugiés et des immigrants (18 March 2005), online: www.cic.gc.ca/english/department/media/speeches/2005/tcri.asp.

33 See, for example, United Nations High Commissioner for Refugees, *Monitoring Report: Canada-United States "Safe Third Country" Agreement* (2005), online: UNHCR www.unhcr.org/455b2cca4.pdf; Canadian Council for Refugees, "Closing the Front Door on Refugees: Report on the First Year of the *Safe Third Country Agreement*" (2005), online: CCR http://ccrweb.ca/en/closing-front-door-refugees-report-first-year-safe-third-country-agreement [CCR, "Closing the Front Door on Refugees"].

34 CCR, "Closing the Front Door on Refugees," *ibid* at 12.

thus making the border less secure.[35] The concerns about security were considered by the Standing Committee on Citizenship and Immigration which recommended that the government should be ready to suspend or terminate the Agreement if it led to an increase in illegal entries.[36] In response, "A Partnership for Protection" indicated that Canadian and US enforcement agencies observed no appreciable shifts in irregular migration; the apprehensions of irregular migrants attempting to cross the border in both directions declined in 2005 compared to 2004.[37] However, a subsequent government report (which was not made public, but was obtained under the *Access to Information Act*) documented a rise in smuggling operations through the Canada–US border and a higher apprehension rate of smugglers in 2011 compared to 2010.[38]

Further, the *Safe Third Country Agreement* is likely to expose many claimants to less favourable treatment in the United States than that accorded to refugee claimants in Canada. For example, the United States is more likely to detain asylum seekers, including minors,[39] and to provide less sensitive (even if substantively similar) consideration to gender-based claims.[40] Moreover, the Agreement makes these problems invisible as claimants never reach Canadian territory and thus cannot attract media or judicial attention.[41] For example, the report "A Partnership for Protection" showed that the number of refugee claims made at the land border had decreased by about 55 percent — from 8,896 claims in 2004 to 4,033 in 2005 — which can be partially attributed to the Agreement.[42] Concerns were also raised about inconsistent and

---

35 Macklin, above note 30 at 423–24. United Nations High Commissioner for Refugees, *UNHCR Comments on the Draft Agreement between Canada and the United States of America "for Co-operation in the Examination of Refugee Status Claims from Nationals of Third Countries"* (2002), online: www.refworld.org/docid/3d4e69614.html.

36 House of Commons, Standing Committee on Citizenship and Immigration, *The Safe Third Country Regulations: Report of the Standing Committee on Citizenship and Immigration* (December 2002), online: www.parl.gc.ca/HousePublications/Publication.aspx?Language=e&Mode=1&Parl=37&Ses=2&DocId=1032292.

37 IRCC, "A Partnership for Protection," above note 31.

38 HIRC, *Bordering on Failure*, above note 8 at 100.

39 CCR, "Closing the Front Door on Refugees," above note 33 at 2–5; HIRC, *Bordering on Failure*, above note 8 at 68–78.

40 The research commissioned by the government in respect to concerns about gender-based claims found that the body of US caselaw was broadly supportive of gender-based claims: *Regulations Amending the Immigration and Refugee Protection Regulations*, PC 2004-1157 (29 May 2004), Regulatory Impact Analysis Statement, online: http://gazette.gc.ca/rp-pr/p2/2014/2014-06-18/html/sor-dors133-eng.php.

41 CCR, "Closing the Front Door on Refugees," above note 33 at ii; Macklin, above note 30.

42 See also HIRC, *Bordering on Failure*, above note 8 at 89–90, for more statistics on preceding and subsequent years.

rigid application of exceptions under the Agreement, which at times led to eligible claimants being turned away at the Canadian border.[43]

Not surprisingly, the *Safe Third Country Agreement* has not gone without a legal challenge. On the first anniversary of the Agreement coming into force, the Canadian Council for Refugees, Amnesty International, and the Canadian Council of Churches, along with a Colombian asylum seeker in the United States, launched a case seeking a declaration "that the designation of the United States of America as a 'Safe Third Country' for asylum seekers . . . was invalid and unlawful."[44] They argued that the United States is not safe because it does not respect its obligations under the *Convention Against Torture* and the *Refugee Convention* and that by returning refugee claimants to the United States, Canada is violating its international obligations and the claimants' rights to life, liberty and security, and to equality under the *Charter of Rights and Freedoms*.[45] The Federal Court found that the operation of the *Safe Third Country Agreement* indeed was contrary to the *Charter*.[46] It also concluded that the federal Cabinet acted unreasonably in concluding that the United States complied with non-*refoulement* obligations under the *Refugee Convention* and the *Convention Against Torture*. The decision was, however, overturned by the Federal Court of Appeal[47] (leave to appeal to the Supreme Court denied) and, consequently, the Agreement remains in force.

C. OVERVIEW OF REFUGEE DETERMINATION PROCESS

In December 2012, significant changes to the inland refugee determination system were implemented. They did not alter the substantive criteria such as eligibility for a hearing before the Refugee Protection Division (RPD) or the grounds on which protection can be conferred, but they changed many procedural aspects (such as hearing timelines, eligibility for appeal, and stays of removal) as well as the scope of entitlements for refugee claimants (see Chapter 3).

---

43 *Ibid* at 91–96.

44 *Canadian Council for Refugees v Canada*, 2007 FC 1262 (the quotation is from the application for leave and for judicial review).

45 Part I of the *Constitution Act, 1982*, being Schedule B to the *Canada Act 1982* (UK), 1982, c 11 [*Charter*].

46 *Canadian Council for Refugees v Canada*, above note 44.

47 *Canadian Council for Refugees v Canada*, 2008 FCA 229, leave to appeal to SCC refused, [2008] SCCA No 422.

Before December 2012, all claimants went through the same refugee determination process. If a person's claim was eligible for a hearing before the RPD, she was given a personal information form (PIF) to complete and submit to the IRB within twenty-eight days. The PIF asked claimants to provide detailed information about themselves, including education and employment history, travel route to Canada, and most important, their story and reasons for requesting protection. After receipt of the PIF, the Board scheduled a hearing, but there were no prescribed time limits within which a hearing had to take place. Given the backlog of claims in the system, a claimant could wait up to two years for his hearing.[48] If a claim was accepted, the person received protected person status and could apply for permanent residence. Rejected claimants could apply for judicial review (with leave) to the Federal Court. Although the *IRPA* provided for the establishment of the Refugee Appeal Division (RAD) within the IRB, the provision was not implemented until 2012. Hence, judicial review was the only avenue of recourse for rejected claimants. If judicial review application was granted, the case was sent back for re-determination to the RPD. A person's removal was stayed until judicial review was completed. If judicial review was unsuccessful or if a claimant did not pursue it, the claimant would become removal ready and would be provided with a pre-removal risk assessment (PRRA). A successful PRRA could lead to a protected person status and entitle the claimant to apply for permanent residence. In addition to PRRA, rejected claimants could apply for permanent residence on humanitarian and compassionate (H&C) grounds, arguing that return to their country of origin would subject them to undue, undeserved, or disproportionate hardship. Their removal could be stayed pending the outcome of an H&C application. As a result of these applications and stays, a rejected claimant could remain in Canada, on average, for four to six years from the date of making the refugee claim to removal.[49]

Since 15 December 2012, many aspects of the above-described process have changed. First, legislation started to differentiate between the following three groups: (1) claimants from designated countries of origin (DCOs); (2) claimants who are designated foreign nationals; and (3) all other claimants who do not fall within the first two categories (for details on the differences between the three groups, see Chapter 3). Second, somewhat different procedures were introduced for making an

---

48 Peter Showler, *Fast, Fair and Final: Reforming Canada's Refugee System* (Toronto: Maytree Foundation, 2009) at 4.

49 *Ibid.*

inland claim versus a claim at the border. Third, the PIF was replaced with a Basis of Claim (BOC) Form and the timeline for its submission was shortened. Fourth, timelines for refugee hearings have been legislatively prescribed and they vary, depending on whether the claimant comes from a DCO and whether the claim was made at the border or inland. Fifth, the Refugee Appeal Division (RAD) was established, but claimants from DCOs and designated foreign nationals do not have access to it. Sixth, designated foreign nationals and claimants from DCOs may apply for judicial review of a negative decision, but their removal is not stayed while the application is examined. Seventh, a provision was made specifically for designated foreign nationals precluding them from applying for permanent residence for five years after the date of a positive decision on their claim. Eighth, rejected claimants can no longer apply for a PRRA once they are removal ready: claimants from DCOs face a three-year bar and other claimants, a one-year bar.

Table 8.1: Comparison of Pre-2012 and Current Refugee Determination System

Pre-2012 System	Current System
1) Eligibility determination.	1) No change.
2) Completion of a personal information form (PIF) within twenty-eight days.	2) The PIF is replaced with the Basis of Claim (BOC) Form. Persons who make a claim inland must bring a completed BOC Form to the officer. Persons who make a claim at the border are given fifteen days to complete a BOC Form.
3) Hearing before an independent decision maker (an RPD member); no legislatively prescribed timelines for a hearing.	3) Hearing by a permanent public servant (RPD member) within a) thirty days for claimants from DCOs who made a claim inland; b) forty-five days for claimants from DCOs who made a claim at the border; c) sixty days for all other claimants.
4) No appeal to the Refugee Appeal Division (the division was not yet established).	4) Appeal to the RAD (except for designated foreign nationals and claimants from DCOs).

Pre-2012 System	Current System
5) Judicial review; stay of removal until the case is decided. Rejected claimants may also make a humanitarian and compassionate (H&C) application to remain in Canada.	5) Judicial review of RPD decision for claimants from DCOs and designated foreign nationals; no stay of removal. Judicial review of RAD decision for others; removal stayed until the case is decided. One-year bar on H&C applications, except in cases where removal poses a risk to person's life due to home country's inability to provide healthcare or where removal would have an adverse impact on the best interests of the child directly affected.
6) A pre-removal risk assessment (PRRA) application may be submitted once an individual is removal ready (regardless of when the decision on their refugee claim was made).	6) Three-year bar on PRRA applications (since the date of the last IRB decision on their case) for designated foreign nationals; one-year bar for others.

While the details of the refugee process and recourses available to rejected claimants are described in detail in subsequent sections as well as in Chapters 10 and 12, here is a brief overview of the life of a refugee claim:

1) **Making of a claim.** A refugee claim can be made at any time, at the border or from within Canada. The only persons who are not even entitled to make a claim are those who have already received a removal order and persons who have been ordered surrendered pursuant to extradition proceedings.[50]

---

50 *IRPA*, above note 10. Section 99(3) states that "a claim for refugee protection made by a person inside Canada . . . may not be made by a person who is subject to a removal order . . . ." Section 105(5) states a similar prohibition for those who are being surrendered as a result of extradition proceedings. Presumably, the reason that individuals with removal orders and individuals subject to extradition are excluded from even making a refugee claim (as opposed to simply being ineligible to make a refugee claim) is because generally even the issuance of an eligibility (or rather, in these cases, an ineligibility) decision gives rise to a stay on a person's removal. Despite these provisions, the preclusion of individuals from making a refugee claim has led to a large quantity of litigation, particularly those challenging removal orders. See notably *Raman v Canada (Minister of Citizenship and Immigration)*, [1999] 4 FC 140 (CA), and the more recent case, among many others, of *Dragosin v Canada (Minister of Citizenship and Immigration)*, 2003 FCT 81. As

A claim must be made to an officer.[51] If it is made at the border, it will be a CBSA officer; if inland, an Immigration, Refugees and Citizenship Canada (IRCC) officer. If a claim is made inland, a claimant must bring a completed BOC Form.[52] If a claim is made at the border and is found eligible for an RPD hearing, a claimant is given a BOC Form to complete within fifteen days and submit to the IRB.[53]

2) **Eligibility determination.** The first step after a refugee claim is made is to determine whether it should be referred to the RPD for a hearing. Eligibility of claims made at the Canadian border is determined by the CBSA; eligibility of claims made from within Canada's territory is determined by IRCC. For eligible claims, an officer will set a date for a refugee hearing as follows:
   - For claimants from DCOs: within forty-five days from the date of determination of eligibility for claims made at the border and within thirty days for claims made inland;
   - For other claimants: within sixty days from the date the claim was determined eligible.[54]
3) **Referral of the claim to the RPD.** Using the BOC, the RPD determines relevant issues to be considered at a hearing and collects information on the claimant's country of origin.
4) **Hearing before the Refugee Protection Division (RPD).** (See detailed description below.)
5) **Claim accepted.** If a claim is accepted, the claimant receives protected status and may apply for permanent residence. Designated foreign nationals can apply for permanent residence only five years after the protection is conferred.
6) **Claim rejected.** If a claim is rejected, the claimant may pursue one or both of the following options (depending on whether the claimant is a designated foreign national or from a DCO):
   - appeal to the RAD (not available to claimants from DCOs and to designated foreign nationals) (see Chapter 10);
   - judicial review before the Federal Court (see Chapter 10).
7) **Pre-removal Risk Assessment (PRRA).** Designated foreign nationals and non-DCO claimants who have not been removed within one year after the final rejection of their claim can make a PRRA application; in the case of claimants from DCOs, the bar is three years (see Chapter 12).

---

will be discussed below, more restrictive statutory provisions govern challenging surrender orders of those subject to extradition.

51 *IRPA*, above note 10, s 99(3).

52 *Ibid*, s 99(3.1).

53 *Regulations*, above note 9, s 159.8(2).

54 *Ibid*, s 159.9(1).

8) **Removal.** If a person's appeal and/or judicial review has been rejected and she is not eligible for a PRRA or if the PRRA is unsuccessful, arrangements are made by the CBSA to effectuate the person's removal.

Figure 8.2: Canada's Inland Refugee Determination System

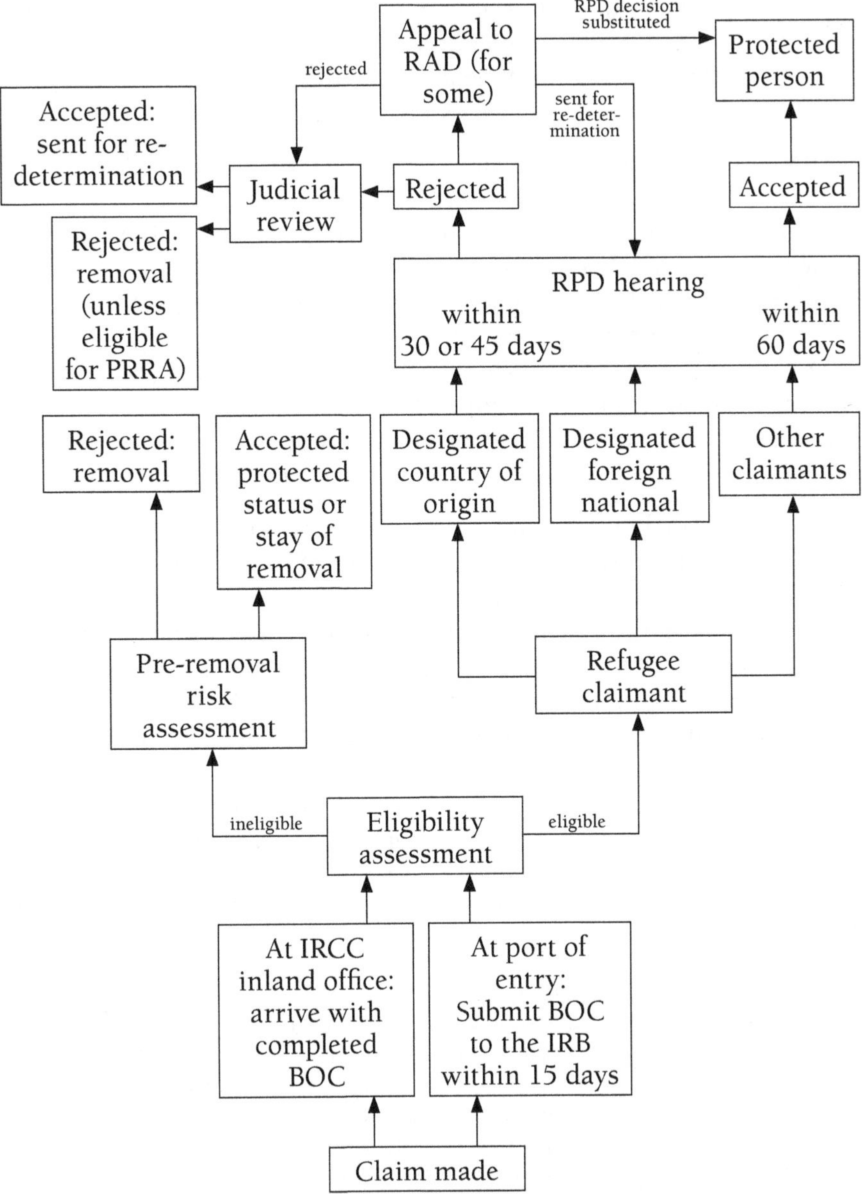

D. ELIGIBILITY FOR REFERRAL TO THE BOARD

After receiving a claim, an officer must perform an initial screening and determine whether the refugee claimant in question is eligible to have the claim heard by the RPD. The burden of proving eligibility rests upon a claimant who is obliged to answer all questions truthfully and provide the required documentation and information.[55]

Most individuals are eligible for a hearing; however, section 101 of the *IRPA* also prescribes several categories of ineligibility as follows:

- Refugee protection has already been conferred under the Act.
- A claim has been rejected by the IRB.
- A prior claim has been determined ineligible for referral to the RPD, withdrawn, or abandoned.
- A claimant has been recognized as a Convention refugee by another country and can be returned to that country.
- A claimant came from a safe third country (the United States is currently the only safe third country).
- A claimant is inadmissible on the grounds of security, violating human or international rights, serious criminality, or organized criminality.[56]

Although ineligible claimants do not get an RPD hearing, they do have some opportunity to present their case of risk and/or persecution. Most of them are entitled to a pre-removal risk assessment (see Chapter 12) which, in the case of a positive decision, protects a person from *refoulement* and may entitle her to apply for permanent residence.

Eligibility requirements have been unsuccessfully challenged in the courts. In *Berrahma v Canada (Minister of Employment and Immigration)*, the Federal Court said: "I do not see how it can be said that by limiting the right to claim refugee status in an objective and non-discriminatory manner — as it did, Parliament infringed the provisions of s. 7."[57] Subsequently, in *Nguyen v Canada (Minister of Employment and Immigration)*, the Federal Court held that a declaration of ineligibility per se did

---

55 *IRPA*, above note 10, s 100(1.1).

56 *Ibid*, s 101(1). Note that a person will be ineligible due to serious criminality only if she has been convicted of an offence in Canada punishable by a maximum term of imprisonment of at least ten years; or in case of a foreign conviction, of an offence that, if committed in Canada, would be punishable by a maximum term of imprisonment of at least ten years: *IRPA*, *ibid*, s 101(2). Further, if a person is found inadmissible for international or human rights violations on the basis of a decision or resolution of an international organization, he would not be eligible for an RPD hearing: *IRPA*, s 101(1)(f).

57 [1991] FCJ No 180 at para 13 (CA).

not lead to any act that might affect the claimant's life, liberty, or security.[58] In *Raza v Canada (Minister of Citizenshi and Immigration)*, drawing on *Nguyen*, the Federal Court concluded that the *Charter* argument did not need to be entertained further as eligibility screening did not engage section 7.[59]

1) Deemed Eligibility and Suspension of Consideration of Eligibility

As a rule, a decision on eligibility must be made within three working days from the day when the claim was made.[60] The decision must be made in writing and provided to the claimant. A copy of the decision will be necessary to ensure the claimant's access to health coverage, social assistance, and, where available, other social services. The referring officer will also set a date for the claimant's hearing before the RPD.[61]

If the three-day deadline lapses without a determination of eligibility, a claim is statutorily deemed to be eligible and is referred to the RPD.[62] A failure to refer a claim within the deadline may be caused by the complexity of issues involved in the determination, the volume of refugee claims during the three-day period, and simple administrative oversight. Although the *IRPA* does not provide for extension of the three-day deadline, it allows for the suspension of the consideration of eligibility in the following circumstances:

- a report has been referred for an admissibility hearing to determine if the claimant is inadmissible on grounds of security, violating human or international rights, serious criminality, or organized criminality; or
- the officer considers it necessary to wait for a court decision with respect to a claimant who is charged with an offence punishable by a maximum term of imprisonment of at least ten years.[63]

In both cases, the three-day time limit is suspended and resumes after the determination referred to above is made.

58 [1993] 1 FC 696 (CA) [*Nguyen*].
59 [1999] 2 FC 185 (TD).
60 *IRPA*, above note 10, s 100(1).
61 *Ibid*, s 100(4.1).
62 *Ibid*, s 100(3).
63 *Ibid*, s 100(2).

2) Re-determination of Eligibility

Re-determination takes place when an officer obtains information that changes an applicant's eligibility to have a claim referred to the RPD. Under the *IRPA*, section 104, an officer may notify the RPD that a claim is no longer eligible for consideration on one of the following grounds:

- the claim is ineligible under section 101(1) (see grounds of ineligibility discussed earlier in this section);
- the claim was referred as a result of directly or indirectly misrepresenting or withholding relevant material facts and that the claim was not otherwise eligible for referral to the RPD; or
- this refugee claim is not the first made by the claimant in question.[64]

Before making a re-determination, an officer needs to advise the claimant about her concerns and give an opportunity to respond to them.[65]

3) Extradition

Extradition involves surrender of a person by one state to another state or international tribunal (such as the International Criminal Court) for the purpose of prosecuting that person, imposing a sentence on that person, or enforcing a sentence imposed. Extraditions are governed by the *Extradition Act*[66] and extradition agreements that Canada has concluded with other states.[67]

Persons subject to extradition proceedings for serious offences (namely, those that carry a maximum sentence of at least ten years of imprisonment) will not be able to benefit from refugee protection in Canada. Rather, the RPD (or the RAD, if the claim is on appeal) will not commence or will suspend the consideration of their claim pending the outcome of the extradition proceedings.[68]

A decision to surrender a person in extradition proceedings is deemed to be a rejection of that person's refugee claim on the basis of the exclusion clause under article 1F(b) of the *Refugee Convention*.[69] In such a way, the person's *refoulement* to a location in which he might suffer persecution is not considered a violation of Canada's obligations under

---

64 *Ibid*, s 104(1).

65 *Cishahayo v Canada (Minister of Public Safety and Emergency Preparedness)*, 2012 FC 1237.

66 *Extradition Act*, SC 1999, c 18.

67 For a list of extradition partners, see Schedule to the *Extradition Act*.

68 *IRPA*, above note 10, s 105(1).

69 *Ibid*, s 105(3). The Schedule to the *IRPA* includes the relevant parts of art 1 of the *Convention Relating to the Status of Refugees*.

the *Refugee Convention*. However, before an individual is surrendered, the Minister of Justice may consider submissions relating to the individual's risk of mistreatment upon surrender. Furthermore, the Minister must refuse to surrender the individual where

> the request for extradition is made for the purpose of prosecuting or punishing the person by reason of their race, religion, nationality, ethnic origin, language, colour, political opinion, sex, sexual orientation, age, mental or physical disability or status or that the person's position may be prejudiced for any of those reasons.[70]

A deemed rejection of a refugee claim for reasons of exclusion cannot be appealed or subject to judicial review, except to the extent that a judicial review of the order of surrender is provided for under the *Extradition Act*.[71] As noted previously, if a person has not made a refugee claim before an order for surrender is issued, she is no longer entitled to do so.[72]

E. PROCEEDINGS BEFORE THE REFUGEE PROTECTION DIVISION OF THE BOARD

The consideration of the substantive merits of a claim begins upon referral to the RPD. While some information about the basis of claim is normally collected in advance, upon referral to the RPD the process accelerates and the consideration of the claim against the statutory criteria for protection begins.

1) Pre-hearing Process

Although the oral hearing is very much the centrepiece of the Canadian inland refugee determination process, several steps must be fulfilled before a claimant has his claim scheduled for a hearing; namely, the completion of a Basis of Claim (BOC) Form and the disclosure of all documentary evidence.

---

70 *Extradition Act*, above note 66, s 44(1)(b).

71 *IRPA*, above note 10, s 105(4).

72 *Ibid*, s 105(5). Article 1F(b) reads: "The provisions of this Convention shall not apply to any person with respect to whom there are serious reasons for considering that . . . he has committed a serious non-political crime outside the country of refuge prior to his admission to that country as a refugee."

a) Basis of Claim Form

The procedure for submission of a BOC Form varies, depending on whether the refugee claim is made at the border or inland. In case of the former, if the claim is eligible, a claimant is provided with a BOC Form, which she must complete within fifteen days and submit to the IRB.[73] In contrast, when a claim is made following admission to Canada, a claimant is expected to bring a completed BOC Form to the IRCC office, which will then determine the issue of eligibility.[74] Technically, the claimant who makes an inland application is not subject to a particular timeline for completion of the BOC. Given the short hearing timelines, it may be advantageous for claimants to enter Canada, prepare their BOC and all supporting documents, and only then file a claim officially. However, claimants have to be cautious not to significantly delay making of the claim as this may create questions about their well-founded fear at the refugee hearing (see Chapter 4, Section F(2)(a)(ii)).

A claimant may apply for an extension to complete the form but must show a valid reason to justify the extension; an extension must be requested at least three days before expiration of the deadline.[75] If a properly completed BOC Form is not received before the expiry of the fifteen-day (or any extended) deadline, the RPD may commence abandonment proceedings.[76]

The comparison of the contents of the BOC Form to the oral testimony of a claimant is one of the Board's "primary" methods of determining credibility.[77] The strong correlation of a complete and accurate BOC with a positive decision is abundantly obvious from the jurisprudence, as is the converse. The Board may consider omissions from the applicant's BOC Form and base adverse credibility findings upon those omissions.[78] Even omissions or inconsistencies seemingly collateral or not relevant to the basis of claim may support adverse credibility findings.[79] In addition, omissions or inconsistencies resulting from

---

73 *Regulations*, above note 9, s 159.8(2); *Refugee Protection Division Rules*, SOR/2012-256, r 7(2) [*RPD Rules*].

74 *RPD Rules*, *ibid*, r 7(1).

75 *Ibid*, r 8(2).

76 *Ibid*, r 65.

77 *Castroman v Canada (Secretary of State)*, [1994] FCJ No 962 (TD).

78 *Grinevich v Canada (Minister of Citizenship and Immigration)*, [1997] FCJ No 444 (TD); *Lobo v Canada (Minister of Citizenship and Immigration)*, [1995] FCJ No 597 (TD); *El Masalati v Canada (Minister of Citizenship and Immigration)*, [2005] FCJ No 1592 (FC); *Joseph v Canada (Minister of Citizenship and Immigration)*, [2000] FCJ No 49 (TD), aff'd [2001] FCJ No 1484 (CA).

79 *Basseghi v Canada (Minister of Citizenship and Immigration)*, [1994] FCJ No 1867 (TD). However, for example, in *Cao v Canada (Minister of Citizenship and Immigra-*

incompetent counsel will not necessarily prevent adverse inferences.[80] Furthermore, the duty to provide a complete and accurate BOC Form has been interpreted as an ongoing one. A claimant must amend and update his BOC if circumstances change or new information comes to light; in the absence of such amendments, adverse inferences can be drawn.[81]

However, that a claimant must provide an accurate and complete account does not entail that every possible detail of all events be listed in the BOC. Rather, the obligation in the BOC is to provide all "significant" details;[82] further "minor or elaborative" details may be provided in oral testimony.[83] Further, the Board must not engage in a microscopic analysis of the information in the BOC and use "technical" errors (such as mentioning living in city X in one part of the BOC but not in another part of the BOC) as the basis of an adverse credibility finding.[84]

b) Pre-hearing Disclosure of Documentary Evidence

Claimants are under a statutory duty to provide documents in support of their claim to the Board in accordance with its rules.[85] All claimant-specific and other documentary material must be disclosed well in advance of the hearing. Although this requirement is usually applied generically to all documents, the *Refugee Protection Division Rules* and the *IRPA* do distinguish between various types of documents.

Categories of documents set out in the *RPD Rules* and the *IRPA* include "acceptable documents establishing [claimant's] identity";[86] "acceptable documents establishing . . . other elements of the claim";[87] and any other document that a party "wants to use . . . in a hearing."[88] While these categories of documents clearly overlap, the obligation of

---

tion), 2012 FC 694, the Federal Court overturned the RPD's rejection of the claim, which was based on negative inference from BOC omissions that did not go to the heart of the claim.

80 *Robles v Canada (Minister of Citizenship and Immigration)*, [2003] FCJ No 520 (TD).

81 This obligation arises, in part, from the practice of a claimant adopting her BOC as "true and complete" at the start of the hearing. In the absence of amendments to include new evidence, such an adoption is inaccurate (at least if worded in the present tense).

82 *Ahangaran v Canada (Minister of Citizenship and Immigration)* (1999), 168 FTR 315 (TD).

83 *Akhigbe v Canada (Minister of Citizenship and Immigration)*, [2002] FCJ No 332 (TD).

84 *Li v Canada (Minister of Citizenship and Immigration)*, [2006] FCJ No 1104 (TD).

85 *IRPA*, above note 10, s 100(4).

86 *RPD Rules*, above note 73, r 11; *IRPA*, above note 10, s 106.

87 *RPD Rules*, above note 73, r 11.

88 *Ibid*, r 34(1).

disclosure technically arises at a distinct point for each category. Similarly, the consequences of non-disclosure may be different. Indeed, for certain categories of documents, the failure to disclose the document may result in an adverse inference being drawn about the claim.

Despite the reference in the *RPD Rules* and the *IRPA* to these overlapping categories, there are two larger types of documents presented to the RPD: (1) documents that are specific to the individual claimant and relate to the proof of his identity and/or past (mis)treatment, and (2) documents that relate more generally to the situation in the country of reference. Documents of the former type include birth certificates, passports, employment or school records, and medical reports. Documents of the latter type include reports by non-governmental organizations and other bodies on the situation in the country of reference.

Disclosure must occur in advance of the hearing. In almost all cases, disclosure must be accomplished no less than ten days before the hearing.[89] Disclosure that occurs after ten days, unless it is in response to another party's disclosure, may not be admitted into evidence by the Board. The Board has the discretion to waive the disclosure deadline and will consider the following factors in deciding whether to exercise this discretion:

(a) the document's relevance and probative value;
(b) any new evidence it brings to the hearing; and
(c) whether the party, with reasonable effort, could have provided the document as required by the Rules.[90]

Absent a specific duty to provide specific documentary evidence or a request from the Board, a claimant is not obliged to provide documentation to substantiate her claim; in the absence of contradictory evidence, the Board cannot link a failure to offer documentation to a lack of credibility.[91] Notwithstanding this general statement, the failure to provide an adequate explanation for why a document was not sought or disclosed can lead to a negative finding of credibility.

---

89 *Ibid*, r 34(3). The only automatic exception to this rule is for documents that are "provided to respond to another document provided by a party or the Division" under r 29(4)(b), which must be provided no less than five days before the hearing. As always, the Board has the discretion to waive the disclosure time limits under r 36.

90 *Ibid*, r 36.

91 *Ahortor v Canada (Minister of Employment and Immigration)*, [1993] FCJ No 705 (TD).

c) Designated Representative

Individuals without legal capacity require the appointment of a *guardian ad litem*. The *IRPA* requires that the Board appoint a "designated representative" in all claims involving a claimant "under 18 years of age or unable, in the opinion of the applicable Division, to appreciate the nature of the proceedings."[92] Under rule 20(1), an officer or a counsel for the claimant is under an obligation to notify the Board whenever he is of the belief that a designated representative is required.

In the case of children, a designated representative is usually the child's caregiver or a close relative of the child. Similarly, in the case of an adult unable to appreciate the nature of proceedings, a relative is the most common designated representative. An individual is not barred from acting as a designated representative simply because she is also a refugee claimant. Where no relative is available, a member of the community (typically one involved in activities with immigrants or refugees) is appointed as the designated representative.

> To be designated as a representative, a person must
> (a) be 18 years of age or older;
> (b) understand the nature of the proceedings;
> (c) be willing and able to act in the best interests of the claimant or protected person; and
> (d) not have interests that conflict with those of the represented person.[93]

A designated representative has the following duties:

> (a) deciding whether to retain counsel and then instructing counsel or assisting the represented person in instructing counsel;
> (b) making decisions regarding the claim or application or assisting the represented person in making those decisions;
> (c) informing the represented person about the various stages and procedures of the refugee determination process;
> (d) assisting in gathering evidence to support the represented person's case and in providing evidence and, if necessary, being a witness at the hearing;
> (e) protecting the interests of the represented person and putting forward the best possible case to the RPD;
> (f) informing and consulting the represented person to the extent possible when making decisions about the case; and
> (g) filing and perfecting an appeal to the RAD, if required.[94]

---

92 *IRPA*, above note 10, s 167(2).

93 *RPD Rules*, above note 73, r 20(4).

94 *Ibid*, r 20(10).

d) Joinder of Claims

The claims of close family members are automatically "joined" by the Board, "unless it is not practicable to do so."[95] Specifically, the claims of spouses, common law partners, children, parents, brothers, sisters, grandchildren, and grandparents are automatically joined.[96] Joinder entails that the claims are determined together based on a common pool of evidence.

The Board may also, upon request by a party, join or separate the claims of any two or more individuals after considering "any relevant factors, including whether

> (a) the claims or applications to vacate or to cease refugee protection involve similar questions of fact or law;
> (b) allowing the application to join or separate would promote the efficient administration of the Division's work; and
> (c) allowing the application to join or separate would likely cause an injustice."[97]

Notwithstanding the Board's power to join claims beyond those of family members, the exercise of such a power is rare and usually occurs only upon the request of counsel or the claimant.

2) Hearings before the Refugee Protection Division

The centrepiece of the Canadian refugee determination process is the oral hearing of the claim. Arising out of the landmark decision of the Supreme Court of Canada in *Singh v Canada (Minister of Employment and Immigration)*,[98] the hearing allows the achievement of two principal objectives: (1) it provides the claimant with an opportunity to state his case and know the case he has to meet, and (2) it allows the Board to assess the credibility of the claimant.[99] Refugee hearings are non-adversarial, except where issues of exclusion are raised.

The Board must hold a hearing in all refugee proceedings.[100] The date for the hearing is set by the IRCC or the CBSA officer at the time

---

95 *Ibid*, r 55(1).
96 *Ibid*, r 49(1).
97 *Ibid*, r 56(5).
98 [1985] 1 SCR 177 [*Singh*].
99 Both aspects of these features of oral hearings were emphasized as significant by Wilson J in *Singh*, *ibid* (see paras 57–64).
100 *IRPA*, above note 10, s 170(b). However, s 170(e) provides that a claim may be allowed without a hearing where "the Minister has not notified the Division,

when the claim is referred to the RPD.[101] The legislation prescribes specific timelines for hearings. For claimants from DCOs, a hearing must be set within forty-five days of eligibility determination if the claim was made at the border and thirty days if the claim was made inland.[102] For all other claimants, the hearing must be scheduled within sixty days of eligibility determination.[103]

All hearings before the RPD are conducted in camera.[104] The Board may open a refugee hearing to the public only in exceptional circumstances and almost always with the consent of the claimant.[105] In recent years, several high-profile refugee claims have been heard in public, including the claims of US military deserters Jeremy Hinzman and Brandon Hughey; US marijuana campaigner Steven Kubby and his family; and Chinese businessman Lai Cheong Sing and his family. These claims were heard in public with the consent of the claimants. Although most hearings are conducted in person, the Board also occasionally conducts hearings via video conference.

3) Procedure at the Hearing

A refugee hearing is not dissimilar to any other administrative hearing: the parties are present, witnesses are examined, and submissions are made. Despite the Board's own description of its hearing process as "informal," the reality for claimants is that it is decidedly formal.

a) Participants in the Hearing

Most refugee hearings are heard by one member of the RPD.[106] However, the Chairperson of the Board may designate claims to be heard by panels of three members.[107] Such designations are relatively rare and are made for training purposes only.[108]

---

within the period set out in the rules of the Board, of the Minister's intention to intervene."

101 *RPD Rules*, above note 73, r 3; *Regulations*, above note 9, s 159.9.

102 *Regulations*, *ibid*.

103 *Ibid*.

104 *Ibid*, s 166(c).

105 The factors the Board must consider in determining to open a refugee hearing to the public are set out in the *IRPA*, above note 10, s 166(b).

106 *Ibid*, s 163.

107 *Ibid*.

108 Immigration and Refugee Board, "Designation of Three-Member Panels — Refugee Protection Division Approach" (September 2015), online: IRB www.irb-cisr.gc.ca/Eng/BoaCom/references/pol/pol/Pages/PolRpdSpr3MemCom.aspx.

The claimant (or, in the case of joined claims, all claimants) must be physically present at a hearing unless excused from attendance by the Board. In addition, claimants have the right to be represented at the hearing by counsel.[109] An interpreter will be present at most hearings to interpret for the claimant (and possibly any other witnesses).

The Minister of Immigration, Refugees and Citizenship Canada (IRCC) and the Minister of Public Safety and Emergency Preparedness (PSEP) may intervene at any stage of refugee proceedings, including at a hearing. The RPD must provide "the Minister a reasonable opportunity to present evidence, question witnesses, and make representations."[110] In such a case, the Minister will be represented by counsel, either from IRCC or the CBSA, at the hearing. Generally speaking, the Minister intervenes in claims where exclusion grounds are raised or where, for various reasons, the Minister wishes to oppose the individual's request for protection.

In cases where the Minister is intervening, his representative must provide written notice to the RPD and the claimant.[111] The Minister usually intervenes either by filing written submissions, or by filing written submissions and attending at the hearing. The Minister's representative must make explicit reference to any grounds of exclusion that may be alleged.[112] As a party to the claim, the Minister must adhere to any disclosure requirements.[113]

b) Receipt of Evidence

The RPD is not bound by any strict rules of evidence.[114] Furthermore, the panel enjoys wide latitude in the conduct of a hearing. For example, if the *RPD Rules* do not regulate a particular issue that has arisen at the hearing, the panel "may do whatever is necessary to deal with the matter."[115] The panel may also waive requirements, change rules and deadlines, and otherwise act on its own initiative (however, only after giving parties notice and an opportunity to object).[116]

Overall, the burden rests on the claimant to prove that she falls within the definition of "Convention refugee" or "person in need of protection." Only if a person falls within either category can the RPD

109 *IRPA*, above note 10, s 167(1).
110 *Ibid*, s 170(e).
111 *RPD Rules*, above note 73, r 29(1).
112 *Ibid*, r 29(3).
113 *Ibid*, r 29(4).
114 *IRPA*, above note 10, s 170(g).
115 *RPD Rules*, above note 73, r 69.
116 *Ibid*, r 70.

grant protection. In the majority of cases, the turning point in determining whether to grant protection is the credibility of the claimant. As noted in Section E(1)(a), above in this chapter, credibility is often assessed by reviewing the consistency of the information provided in the BOC and oral testimony.[117]

The relaxed rules of evidence and procedure at refugee hearings have both advantages and disadvantages. On the one hand, they provide necessary flexibility for the panel and the claimant to explore the relevant aspects of the claim. They also allow the proceedings to be conducted in a relatively informal manner according to the needs of the particular claim and claimant.[118] On the other hand, a single-member panel with such broad latitude makes refugee proceedings relatively subjective and unpredictable. The informality of proceedings opens the door to quite subjective, if not capricious, decisions. This possibility is particularly worrisome in light of the documented inability of some Board members to understand cultural differences and insensitivity to avoidance reactions and other psychological consequences of trauma demonstrated by claimants during testimonies.[119] In fact, statistical analysis of RPD decisions by Professor Sean Rehaag showed disturbing disparities in grant rates: for example, in 2006, some members accepted only some 7 percent of heard claims, while for others, the acceptance rate was over 90 percent.[120] Similar disparities were observed by Rehaag after the 2012 changes to the refugee determination system. Unfortunately, for some

---

117 Cécile Rousseau et al, "The Complexity of Determining Refugeehood: A Multidisciplinary Analysis of the Decision-Making Process of the Canadian Immigration and Refugee Board" (2002) 15 *Journal of Refugee Studies* 43 at 53. It is very unfortunate that a refugee hearing often becomes simply a mechanical testing of the consistency of the BOC Form and oral testimony.

118 The characterization of proceedings before the RPD as "informal" is found in much of the jurisprudence. Despite this characterization — and its relative truth when RPD proceedings are compared to, for example, criminal proceedings — a hearing before the RPD remains, for a claimant, a formal affair.

119 Rousseau et al, above note 117.

120 Sean Rehaag, "Troubling Patterns in Canadian Refugee Adjudication" (2008) 39 *Ottawa Law Review* 335; see also his subsequent yearly analysis of RPD decisions at the Canadian Council for Refugees website: "2013 Refugee Claim Data and IRB Member Recognition Rates," online: http://ccrweb.ca/en/2013-refugee-claim-data; "2014 Refugee Claim Data and IRB Member Recognition Rates," online http://ccrweb.ca/en/2014-refugee-claim-data; "2015 Refugee Claim Data and IRB Member Recognition Rates," online: http://ccrweb.ca/en/2015-refugee-claim-data. Similar concerns have been found in the United States: see Jaya Ramji-Nogales, Andrew Schoenholtz, & Philip G Schrag, *Refugee Roulette: Disparities in Asylum Adjudication and Proposals for Reform* (New York: New York University Press, 2011).

claimants (namely, those from DCOs and designated foreign nationals) the only remedy to improper use of the broad discretion as to evidence and procedure of the RPD is judicial review — an option which, as will be discussed in greater detail in Chapter 10, is quite limited.

c) Evidence of the Claimant

The testimony of the claimant will generally constitute the bulk of the evidence presented at the hearing. It is common for the claimant to be the only witness at a refugee hearing. Furthermore, it is equally common for the allegations of the claimant to not be specifically corroborated by any other evidence, including documentary evidence. Thus, a determination of the credibility of a claimant is at the heart of almost all refugee hearings. The claimant's evidence, like any evidence given under oath, must be presumed to be credible unless there are good reasons to determine it otherwise. Even where a portion of the claimant's evidence is disregarded because of credibility concerns, the Board must still assess the remainder of her evidence to determine whether there remains a basis for the claim.[121]

There are many ways in which the credibility of the claimant is judged at a hearing. Obviously, the consistency of the claimant's oral testimony to his written testimony is an important consideration. However, additional indicia of credibility (or incredibility) are frequently invoked by the Board: candour, demeanour, and plausibility.[122] The difficulty of using such indicia to judge credibility in the context of interpreted proceedings that have as their subject matter events in a distant country has been the subject of much commentary in the jurisprudence:

> A tribunal must be careful when rendering a decision based on a lack of plausibility because refugee claimants come from diverse cultures, and actions which appear implausible when judged from Canadian standards might be plausible when considered from within the claimant's milieu.[123]

---

121 *Mahmud v Canada (Minister of Citizenship and Immigration)* (1999), 167 FTR 309 (TD).

122 For analysis of the complexities of interaction between claimants and decision makers and challenges to the reliability of these indicia of credibility, see, for example, Walter Kalin, "Troubled Communication: Cross-Cultural Misunderstandings in the Asylum-Hearing" (1986) 20 *International Migration Review* 230; Peter Showler, "Bridging the Grand Canyon: Deciding Refugee Claims" (2007) 114 *Queen's Quarterly* 29; and Hilary Evans Cameron, "Refugee Status Determinations and the Limits of Memory" (2010) 22 *International Journal of Refugee Law* 469.

123 *Valtchev v Canada (Minister of Citizenship and Immigration)*, [2001] FCJ No 1131 at para 7 (TD).

Just as the Board may not judge claimants by Canadian cultural standards, it may also not create "speculative" cultural standards for the country of reference and thereby judge the claimant. In *Ali v Canada (Minister of Citizenship and Immigration)*, the Federal Court overturned the Board's determination that the claimant's account was implausible because "[g]enerally culturally in Pakistan in a joint family, all the males would go together [to the site of vandalism]."[124] In addition, credibility findings based on the plausibility of a claimant's account may impose on the Board a duty to provide greater detail and explanation than may normally be required.[125]

d) Order of Questioning of Claimant

In the past, the questioning of the claimant often proceeded like that of any other witness: the claimant testified first and then was questioned by other participants in the hearing. However, in 2004, the IRB Chairperson's Guideline 7 substantially revised the order of questioning.[126] According to it, the "standard practice" is for the claimant to be first questioned by the RPD member and then by their counsel (also known as "reverse order questioning"). Where the Minister intervenes in a claim, the Minister's representative will either begin the questioning or question the claimant immediately before counsel depending on whether an issue of exclusion is raised.[127] In 2012, this order of questioning was also incorporated into the *RPD Rules*.[128]

Guideline 7 has been the subject of severe criticism by refugee advocates and even former members of the Board. It not only creates disadvantages for the claimant, but, also arguably, denies claimants their right to a fair hearing. The opening of the hearing with questions that are likely to focus on inconsistencies or gaps in the BOC allows the claim to become defined by allegations of non-qualification for protection. In addition, beyond mere disadvantage, medical evidence suggests that beginning the hearing with hostile questioning or, at the very least, questioning by strangers, may traumatize some claimants.[129]

---

124 [2003] FCJ No 1288 at para 24 (FC).

125 *Leung v Canada (Minister of Employment and Immigration)* (1994), 81 FTR 303 (TD).

126 Immigration and Refugee Board, "Chairperson's Guideline 7: Concerning the Preparation and Conduct of a Hearing in the Refugee Protection Division" (December 2003), online: IRB www.irb-cisr.gc.ca/Eng/BoaCom/references/pol/guidir/Pages/GuideDir07.aspx.

127 *RPD Rules*, above note 73, rr 10(2) and (3).

128 *Ibid*, r 10.

129 See the medical evidence presented in *Benitez v Canada (Minister of Citizenship and Immigration)*, 2006 FC 461 (appeal dismissed by the Federal Court of Appeal,

Unfortunately, efforts to challenge the reverse order questioning have largely failed.[130] However, while the Federal Court has refrained from requiring the RPD to follow a particular order of questioning, it has consistently ruled that individual members of the division must have the discretion to depart from the order of questioning set out in Guideline 7 where appropriate.[131] Furthermore, no matter when she asks her questions, the RPD member must be careful in asking questions not to lose her judicial distance and objectivity. The Board must not, through intrusive or aggressive questioning, descend into the battle of proving or disproving the basis of the claim.[132]

The order of questioning may be changed in "exceptional circumstances."[133] For example, IRB Chairperson's Guideline 8 provides for various procedural accommodations for vulnerable claimants, including varying of the order of questioning (for more on Guideline 8, see Chapter 2).

e) Presentation of Other Evidence

Evidence is typically presented in *viva voce* form at the hearing. Witnesses are sworn or affirmed and then questioned. In addition to the claimant, who almost without exception testifies at a hearing, the parties to a hearing may call other witnesses and may introduce documentary evidence. As with the disclosure issues related to the production of documentary evidence, a party wishing to call a witness must provide notice to the RPD.[134]

f) Interpretation of Testimony

Most claimants require the proceedings, including their own evidence, to be interpreted. Interpretation at an RPD hearing is arranged by the

---

2007 FCA 199) [*Benitez*] and *Thamotharem v Canada (Minister of Citizenship and Immigration)*, 2007 FCA 198 [*Thamotharem*].

130 *Thamotharem*, *ibid*; *Benitez*, above note 129.

131 Although the court's initial decision in *Thamotharem*, above note 129, found that the method by which Guideline 7 was implemented by the RPD had resulted in an improper fettering of the discretion of RPD members to control proceedings, the additional evidence about the RPD's practice provided to the court in *Benitez*, above note 129, resulted in the opposite conclusion.

132 *Osuji v Canada (Minister of Citizenship and Immigration)* (1999), 169 FTR 120 (TD). See also other cases where a decision was quashed due to interruptions or intrusive questioning by the Board member: *Reginald v Canada (Minister of Citizenship and Immigration)*, 2002 FCT 568; *Vlad v Canada (Minister of Citizenship and Immigration)*, 2004 FC 260.

133 *RPD Rules*, above note 73, r 10(5).

134 *Ibid*, r 44.

RPD and performed by accredited interpreters.[135] The immediate practical effect of interpretation is to elongate proceedings, effectively doubling the length of all questioning: the questions and answers must be consecutively interpreted from and into English or French. The use of interpretation also can create a psychological distance between the claimant and the other participants, as the RPD and other participants must react not to the words of the claimant as they are spoken but rather to their delayed interpretation. Perhaps the most legally significant consequence of the widespread use of interpretation is the confusion and misunderstanding that can be introduced into the proceedings due to the difficulty of accurately and consistently interpreting terms of art, idioms, and even dates.[136] This confusion, especially given the importance of credibility to the determination of a claim, directly affects the outcome of a claim.

Although there is a substantial jurisprudence establishing a *Charter* right to accurate interpretation in the context of criminal proceedings,[137] there has been a notable reluctance by the Federal Court to extend such a comprehensive protection to refugee claimants. Although the finding in *R v Tran* concerning the right to "continuous, precise, impartial, competent and contemporaneous" interpretation has been applied to refugee proceedings, the Federal Court has also frequently lowered the threshold for waiver of the right.[138] A claimant must complain at the earliest available opportunity — if the claimant is having difficulty understanding the interpreter, then during the hearing itself — about the quality of interpretation or risk losing his right to challenge any subsequent decision on that basis.[139]

The key principles governing issues of interpretation have been succinctly summarized in *Singh v Canada (Minister of Citizenship and Immigration*:[140]

---

135 The term "accredited" is somewhat misleading in this context as there is no national or provincial body with the authority to regulate interpreters. Consequently, the RPD administers its own interpretation proficiency test.

136 With respect to dates, many claimants, particularly those from Iran or other Middle Eastern countries, do not use the Gregorian calendar. Interpretation of dates is rendered quite complicated due to the shifting impact of leap-years in both calendar systems.

137 *R v Tran*, [1994] 2 SCR 951.

138 *Mohammadian v Canada (Minister of Citizenship and Immigration)*, 2001 FCA 191 [*Mohammadian*]. However, see *Thambiah v Canada (Minister of Citizenship and Immigration)*, [2004] FCJ No 14 (FC), for a more generous approach to waiver.

139 *Mohammadian*, above note 138.

140 2010 FC 1161 at para 3 (referring to *Mohammadian*, *ibid*).

a. The interpretation must be precise, continuous, competent, impartial and contemporaneous.
b. No proof of actual prejudice is required as a condition of obtaining relief.
c. The right is to adequate translation not perfect translation. The fundamental value is linguistic understanding.
d. Waiver of the right results if an objection to the quality of the translation is not raised by a claimant at the first opportunity in those cases where it is reasonable to expect that a complaint be made.
e. It is a question of fact in each case whether it is reasonable to expect that a complaint be made about the inadequacy of interpretation.
f. If the interpreter is having difficulty speaking an applicant's language and being understood by him is a matter which should be raised at the earliest opportunity.

g) Receipt of Post-hearing Evidence

Following the conclusion of the hearing, the RPD retains jurisdiction to receive evidence until it has rendered its decision. A claimant or other party to the hearing who wishes to present additional evidence after the hearing must seek the RPD's permission.[141] The criteria for the receipt of post-hearing evidence are similar to the long-established grounds at common law by which an individual may tender new evidence on appeal. Specifically, in determining whether to receive the evidence the RPD must consider

(a) the document's relevance and probative value;
(b) any new evidence the document brings to the proceedings; and
(c) whether the party, with reasonable effort, could have provided the document [as required by the *RPD Rules*].[142]

h) Judicial Notice and Specialized Knowledge

The Board may take notice of "any facts that may be judicially noticed, any other generally recognized facts and any information or opinion that is within its specialized knowledge."[143] Judicial notice concerns facts that are considered to be "common knowledge"[144] or are "generally known,

---

141 *RPD Rules*, above note 73, r 43.
142 *Ibid*, r 43(3).
143 *IRPA*, above note 10, s 170(i).
144 *El-Bahisi v Canada (Minister of Employment and Immigration)*, [1994] FCJ No 2 at para 6 (TD).

reasonably unquestionable or easily verifiable."[145] The fact that university education is conducted in the language of the country in which it is located has been cited as an appropriate matter for judicial notice.[146] No notice is required for facts of which judicial notice is taken. In contrast, when the Board applies its "specialized knowledge" it must provide the parties to the proceeding with an opportunity to make submissions and tender evidence concerning the reliability of and the propriety of using the specialized knowledge.[147]

4) Decision of the Refugee Protection Division

Ultimately, after hearing a claim, the RPD must issue a decision. A decision of the RPD may be issued either orally or in writing.[148] Decisions must be accompanied by reasons, either orally or in writing.[149] Where the decision is negative, any negative oral decision and reasons must be subsequently issued in writing.[150] Where the decision is positive, only the decision itself will be subsequently issued in writing.[151] Any subsequent written decision must be substantially the same as the oral decision.[152]

a) Positive or Negative Decision

The RPD must accept a claim where it "determines that the claimant is a Convention refugee or person in need of protection."[153] Conversely, where the RPD determines that the claimant is neither a Convention refugee nor a person in need of protection, it must issue a negative determination. In addition to determining a claim, the Board is under an obligation to provide the reasons for its determination. These reasons provide the basis for any challenge to the decision (through judicial

145 *Cheng v Canada (Minister of Employment and Immigration)*, [1993] FCJ No 1036 at para 6 (TD).

146 *Hassan v Canada (Minister of Citizenship and Immigration)*, [1996] FCJ No 250 at para 3 (TD) (although countless exceptions to this proposition can be cited).

147 *RPD Rules*, above note 73, r 22.

148 However, r 10(8) of the *RPD Rules*, *ibid*, seems to encourage oral decisions: "A Division member must render an oral decision and reasons for the decision at the hearing unless it is not practicable to do so."

149 *IRPA*, above note 10, s 169(b).

150 *Ibid*, s 169(d). In addition, a decision on vacation or cessation of refugee protection must also be in writing: *RPD Rules*, above note 73, r 67(2)(c).

151 Unless the claimant or the Minister requests the RPD to issue the reasons in writing within ten days of the oral decision: *RPD Rules*, *ibid*, s 169(e).

152 *Thanni v Canada (Minister of Citizenship and Immigration)*, [2001] FCJ No 582 (TD).

153 *IRPA*, above note 10, s 107(1).

review or appeal) and for subsequent applications (such as the pre-removal risk assessment). Combined, positive and negative decisions account for over 80 percent of decisions rendered by the Board (see Appendix D, Table 1). However, there are two additional methods by which the RPD may dispose of a claim: an allowance of withdrawal and a declaration of abandonment.

b) Withdrawal

In certain circumstances, claimants may wish to withdraw a claim. This may happen, for example, if they have otherwise acquired status in Canada or if they wish to leave Canada. A claim may be withdrawn either before or after referral to the RPD. While a withdrawal still prevents another future refugee claim[154] (as it is also a ground of ineligibility), it provides a residual opportunity to request a reinstatement of the claim at a future date.

To effectuate withdrawal, a claimant must either complete a declaration form (if withdrawing before a claim is referred to the RPD) or express his decision in writing or orally to the RPD.[155] If a claimant does not do this and merely departs Canada, a claim will be declared by the RPD as abandoned. The withdrawal or abandonment of a claim leads to the claimant's conditional departure order coming into force.

In some cases, particularly where a hearing into the claim has already commenced, the RPD may refuse an individual's request for withdrawal. The RPD must do so where withdrawal would constitute "an abuse of process" and would "likely have a negative effect on the Division's integrity."[156] In such cases, the RPD will continue with its consideration of the claim and ultimately render a decision.

c) Abandonment

The RPD may also declare a claim to be abandoned. A determination that a claim has been abandoned means that the claimant is "in default in the proceedings"[157] and has the effect that the refugee claim is re-

---

154 Please note that if the claim is withdrawn prior to referral to the RPD, this is not considered withdrawal under s 101 of the *IRPA*. If an individual decides to make a refugee claim in the future, that claim would not be considered ineligible for the purpose of s 101. Immigration, Refugees and Citizenship Canada, "Processing in-Canada Claims for Refugee Protection: Withdrawals and Suspensions," online: IRCC www.cic.gc.ca/english/resources/tools/refugees/canada/processing/withdrawal.asp.

155 *RPD Rules*, above note 73, r 59(2).

156 *Ibid*, r 59(1).

157 *IRPA*, above note 10, s 168(1).

jected.[158] In deciding whether a claim should be determined abandoned, the Board must consider "the explanation given by the claimant and any other relevant factors, including the fact that the claimant is ready to start or continue the proceedings."[159]

Unlike the withdrawal of a claim, the RPD's abandonment of a claim will generally occur only after a hearing.[160] Most declarations of abandonment occur because a claimant failed to complete and submit a BOC. However, a significant number of declarations of abandonment occur after a claimant fails to appear for a hearing. Although technically a claim may be declared abandoned for any default, including the failure to file documents, only the most serious defaults will generally lead to abandonment proceedings.

As abandonment decisions turn largely on the claimant's awareness of the requirements of having her claim heard by the Board, there are frequently factual disputes about notice and about instructions to and from counsel. Absent clear evidence to the contrary, the Board is entitled to draw inferences from the failure of the claimant to provide the BOC or to attend a hearing.[161] However, while it will be presumed that a notice of hearing mailed to the claimant (or counsel) provides adequate notice, where the evidence establishes that the notice was not in fact received, any abandonment determination will be set aside.[162] More than in any other area of refugee law, the Federal Court (if not the Board) has shown a willingness to overturn abandonment decisions where there is evidence of negligence on the part of counsel.[163]

d) No Credible Basis and Manifestly Unfounded Claims

Beyond simply determining that an individual does not qualify for protection, the RPD may make a determination of "no credible basis"[164] or "manifestly unfounded."[165] Both of these findings have severe consequences for a claimant; notably, they remove the right to appeal to the RAD and the automatic stay of removal pending judicial review.[166]

---

158 *Regulations*, above note 9, s 171.

159 *RPD Rules*, above note 73, r 65(4).

160 *Ibid*, r 65(1). A special hearing on abandonment must be held no later than five working days after the day on which the completed BOC Form was due (r 65(2)).

161 *Serrahina v Canada (Minister of Citizenship and Immigration)*, [2003] FCJ No 622 (FC).

162 *Anwar v Canada (Minister of Citizenship and Immigration)*, [2004] FCJ No 1441 (FC).

163 *Taher v Canada (Minister of Citizenship and Immigration)*, [2002] FCJ No 1327 (TD); *Masood v Canada (Minister of Citizenship and Immigration)*, [2004] FCJ No 1480 (FC).

164 *IRPA*, above note 10, s 107(2).

165 *Ibid*, s 107.1.

166 *Ibid*, s 110(1.1)(c); *Regulations*, above note 9, s 231.

In the case of *Rahaman v Canada (Minister of Citizenship and Immigration)*, the Federal Court of Appeal struggled with the meaning of "no credible basis," particularly in light of a lack of international consensus on the treatment of such claims.[167] It concluded that the Board "should not routinely state that a claim has 'no credible basis' whenever it concludes that the claimant is not a credible witness."[168] However, despite this statement, the Court of Appeal implicitly endorsed a fairly expansive interpretation of no credible basis:

> [W]hen the only evidence linking the applicant to the harm he or she alleges is found in the claimant's own testimony and the claimant is found to be not credible, the Refugee Division may, after examining the documentary evidence make a general finding that there is no credible basis for the claim. In cases where there is independent and credible documentary evidence, however, the panel may not make a no credible basis finding . . . [however] the "independent and credible documentary evidence" . . . must have been capable of supporting a positive determination of the refugee claim.[169]

Despite the potentially broad scope of the provision, the Board has generally adopted a "cautious" approach to the use of no credible basis.[170]

The RPD may determine a claim to be "manifestly unfounded" where "it is of the opinion that the claim is clearly fraudulent."[171] So far, jurisprudence has not developed detailed guidance on the interpretation of this concept. However, *Rahaman*[172] provided a useful overview of international and comparative approaches to its interpretation, noting the lack of consensus on the issue:

---

167 The relevant term in international refugee law is "manifestly unfounded."

168 [2002] 3 FC 537 (CA) [*Rahaman*].

169 *Ibid*, quoting *Foyet v Canada (Minister of Citizenship and Immigration)* (2000), 187 FTR 181 (TD).

170 Immigration and Refugee Board of Canada, Refugee Protection Division, "Assessment of Credibility in Claims for Refugee Protection" (31 January 2004), s 3.6, online: IRB www.irb-cisr.gc.ca/Eng/BoaCom/references/LegJur/Pages/Credib.aspx. The exception to this proposition was the targeted use of "no credible basis" findings by the Board (in combination with special expedited processing procedures) against claimants from various countries of origin, most notably Chile. See John Frecker, *Immigration and Refugee Legal Aid Cost Drivers*, Legal Aid Research Series (Ottawa: Department of Justice Canada, 2004), online: www.justice.gc.ca/eng/rp-pr/other-autre/ir/rr03_la17-rr03_aj17/index.html.

171 *IRPA*, above note 10, s 107.1.

172 *Rahaman*, above note 168 at paras 45–47.

There is no doubt that some international instruments appear to give a very restricted meaning to the term "manifestly unfounded." For example, paragraph (d) of Conclusion 30, *supra*, defines claims that are "manifestly unfounded" as "those which are clearly fraudulent or not related to the criteria for the granting of refugee status laid down in the 1951 . . . Convention . . . nor to any other criteria justifying the granting of asylum."

More recent pronouncements, however, are less categorical, no doubt in response to a growing number of genuine and bogus refugee claims. For example, Article 28 of the EU Council Resolution, *supra*, provides a longer list of the grounds on which a Member State may dismiss a refuge claim as manifestly unfounded, although the absence of credible evidence supporting the claim is not among them. However, the inclusion of two grounds on which a claim must not be considered as manifestly unfounded suggests that the longer list of what makes a claim manifestly unfounded is not intended to be exhaustive.

In addition, the recent report arising from the Global Consultations process of the United Nations canvasses the various approaches adopted by states to the definition of "manifestly unfounded": *supra*, at paragraphs 28-31. In particular, it says that some states have "factored credibility, or the absence thereof, into the original assessment of manifest unfoundedness," while others have taken the position that a claim may be manifestly unfounded if made with the intention of misleading the national authorities. Evidence that there is as yet no international consensus on the scope of the term, "manifestly unfounded" is provided by paragraph 26 of this document, which states:

> There is a need, in UNHCR's assessment, to promote a more common understanding of the types of claim which would merit the presumption that they are manifestly unfounded or clearly abusive, and which could be examined under the accelerated procedure.

5) Reopening Decisions of the Refugee Protection Division

Decisions of the RPD may be remedied through appeal or judicial review. Like other decision makers, the RPD is bound by the doctrine of *functus officio*. Furthermore, as a creature of statute it has no residual jurisdiction to offer relief. Nonetheless, despite these limitations, the RPD has reopened decisions where it has later learned that the decision was arrived at due to a breach in natural justice.[173] The jurisdiction of the RPD to reopen its own decisions will be discussed further in Chapter 10.

E. CESSATION AND VACATION OF REFUGEE STATUS

The Board also has jurisdiction to remove refugee status from an individual to whom refugee protection has already been granted. The removal of refugee protection is an extraordinary power of the Board and is relatively rarely invoked. There are two separate grounds that may result in the loss of refugee protection: (1) the "cessation" of the need for protection, and (2) the "vacation" of protection due to misrepresentation. Cessation and vacation proceedings before the Board are governed by special procedures and considerations.

As mentioned in Chapter 4, the consequences of vacation or cessation of protection are severe: not only is the person's protected status removed, but an individual's permanent resident status (if one was obtained) is also automatically removed.[174] This is particularly worrisome in light of the CBSA's announced commitment to "increase[e] the number of cessation or vacation cases referrals to the IRB, while ensuring that in successful cessation or vacation cases, the removal orders are enforced as soon as possible."[175]

1) Cessation of Refugee Protection

Cessation grounds may be invoked during refugee proceedings. In such a case, the Board may find that although an individual may have been a refugee in the past, he has ceased to be a refugee. The grounds of cessation, all of which relate to a material change in either the risk of persecution or the availability of state protection, are listed in the *IRPA*, section 108(1). (This aspect of the cessation provisions of the

---

173 *RPD Rules*, above note 73, ss 62(6) and 63(6).

174 *IRPA*, above note 10, ss 46(1)(c.1) and (d). The only exception in relation to a cessation decision is if cessation was due to the change in the circumstances in the protected person's country of origin.

175 Canada Border Services Agency, "Report on Plans and Priorities, 2014–15," above note 7. The CBSA's "2015–16 Report on Plans and Priorities" stated at 44: "In 2015–16, the Agency will continue investigating and referring cessation and vacation cases to the IRB, while enforcing removal orders for successful cessation or vacation applications." Online: CBSA www.cbsa-asfc.gc.ca/agency-agence/reports-rapports/rpp/2015-2016/rpp-2015-2016-eng.pdf.

IRPA is discussed in detail in Chapter 4.) Cessation grounds may also be invoked, however, after a claimant has received refugee protection and can then be used to remove protection from the individual.

2) Vacation of Refugee Protection

Whereas the ground of cessation does not imply any malfeasance on the part of the individual, the ground of vacation is based on the allegation that the individual provided incomplete or inaccurate information in order to obtain refugee protection. The act of misrepresentation or withholding of information does not need to be deliberate.[176] Although these acts need not be deliberate or done in bad faith, the record of vacation proceedings suggests that this is the characteristic that most often prompts the initiation of vacation proceedings.[177]

As stated in section 109(1) of the *IRPA*:

> The Refugee Protection Division may, on application by the Minister, vacate a decision to allow a claim for refugee protection, if it finds that the decision was obtained as a result of directly or indirectly misrepresenting or withholding material facts relating to a relevant matter.

Once any form of misrepresentation or withholding of a fact is established, the only other requirement for vacation is that the fact was material to the decision. At its most expansive this would include facts that, were they not misrepresented, would have led to different conclusions about the refugee claimant's credibility.[178] More commonly, and less controversially, it includes facts much closer to the determination of status, such as the claimant's identity, the claimant's status in various countries, and the timing and details of the alleged past persecution.

3) Procedure for Loss of Refugee Status before the Board

As noted at the outset of this section, the Board has jurisdiction to remove refugee protection. The Board may remove refugee protection that

---

176 *Zheng v Canada (Minister of Citizenship and Immigration)*, [2005] FCJ No 749 at para 27 (FC) [*Zheng*].

177 For an example of proceedings initiated in large part because of the perception that the refugee claimant conspired to deliberately manipulate the process of refugee determination, see *Naqvi v Canada (Minister of Citizenship and Immigration)*, [2004] FCJ No 1941 (FC).

178 *Canada (Minister of Citizenship and Immigration) v Rahman*, [2005] RPDD No 116 (IRB).

it has granted as well as protection that was granted through another inland process (such as the pre-removal risk assessment) or through an overseas application.[179]

The Minister must initiate loss of status proceedings by filing an application with the RPD.[180] The application triggers a hearing. Whereas under the *Immigration Act*, loss of status proceedings required a three-member panel, under the *IRPA* only a single member is required.[181] A hearing will be held, and evidence concerning the allegation of cessation or vacation will be received. Although the caselaw largely ignores the standard of proof, the allegations must presumably be established on a balance of probabilities. Ultimately, the Board will determine whether the application has succeeded. In the case of an application for vacation, the Board will then consider whether other evidence before the original panel may nonetheless have allowed for the individual to be granted refugee protection.[182]

A vacation or cessation proceeding examines a fairly narrow legal and factual issue. It does not amount to a "re-litigation" of the claim. Thus, where the grounds of cessation or vacation are established, the Board will not broadly re-determine whether there are grounds upon which protection might be granted. However, where an application to vacate is granted, the Board must consider whether "other sufficient evidence was considered at the time of the first determination to justify refugee protection."[183]

This consideration of "other evidence" is restricted to evidence that was previously before the decision maker at the time of the first decision: "In other words, even if there was a misrepresentation or a withholding of material facts on a relevant matter, was there other evidence available when the refugee decision was made to justify protection?"[184] As the focus of the enquiry is on the evidence before the original panel, any evidence before the new panel concerning the misrepresentation (and its reasons) will not be considered at this stage of the enquiry.[185] The reasons for the decision of the new panel need not conform to the analy-

179 For an example of the less common loss of status proceedings against an individual who received protection overseas, see *DRO (Re)*, [2005] RPDD No 52 (IRB).

180 *RPD Rules*, above note 73, r 64.

181 *IRPA*, above note 10, s 163.

182 *Ibid*, s 109(2). The same analysis is in a sense contained within each of the grounds of cessation.

183 *IRPA*, above note 10, s 109(2).

184 *Zheng*, above note 176 at para 26.

185 *Canada (Minister of Citizenship and Immigration) v Yaqoob*, [2005] FCJ No 1260 at para 19 (FC).

sis and assumptions of the original panel; the new panel may reassess evidence that was before the original panel, providing the reassessment is confined to that evidence.[186]

In cases of loss of status, beyond the provision for consideration of "other evidence" in cases of vacation, the Board does not retain any residual discretion over whether to remove refugee protection.[187] As with a refugee claim, an application to vacate or cease refugee status may be withdrawn. The same criteria that apply to the withdrawal (and reinstatement) of refugee claims apply to the withdrawal and reinstatement of applications for loss of refugee status.[188]

F. CONCLUSION

The inland refugee determination process is the centrepiece of Canadian refugee law. It provides the process through which membership in the categories of Convention refugee and persons in need of protection is determined. In a two-step process, a refugee claimant has her eligibility to make a claim determined and then has her claim referred to the Board (or, in some cases, a delegate of the Minister). After receiving a referral, the Board collects both information and documentation from the claimant. Ultimately, the inland refugee determination process culminates in an oral hearing before the Board.

However, while the process of inland determination remains important, an understanding of inland refugee determination is increasingly not just about how those who make claims in Canada are processed but also about how so many of those who try to travel to Canada to seek protection never make it to Canadian soil.

186 *Cooramaswamy v Canada (Minister of Citizenship and Immigration)*, [2002] 4 FC 501 (CA).

187 *Canada (Minister of Citizenship and Immigration) v Pearce*, [2006] FCJ No 646 (FC).

188 *RPD Rules*, above note 73, r 59.

CHAPTER 9

RIGHT TO AND ROLE OF COUNSEL

A. INTRODUCTION

The right to representation in refugee proceedings before the Immigration and Refugee Board (IRB) is established in the *Immigration and Refugee Protection Act*. The Act provides:

> Both a person who is the subject of Board proceedings and the Minister may, at their own expense, be represented by a barrister or solicitor or other counsel.[1]

A similar provision governs individuals pursuing pre-removal risk assessments.[2] The right to representation in other refugee matters, including overseas applications, flows from general principles of common law and constitutional law. With respect to the latter, Pinard J has found that the section 7 *Charter* rights involved in inland refugee proceedings include "the right to be represented by competent and careful counsel."[3] Note that this provision neither guarantees that a claimant

1 SC 2001, c 27, s 167(1) [*IRPA*].

2 *Immigration and Refugee Protection Regulations*, SOR/2002-227, s 161(1) [*Regulations*].

3 *Mathon v Canada (Minister of Employment and Immigration)* (1988), 38 Admin LR 193 at 208 (TD) [*Mathon*]. On the facts of the case, the emphasis was very much on the term "competent and careful."

will receive a publicly funded representative nor requires that a representative be a lawyer.[4]

There is no requirement for refugee claimants to have a representative; however, the use of a representative is usually desirable both personally and institutionally as it provides better protection of the rights of a claimant and enhances the efficiency of the determination process. The IRB practice shows that an absence of representation has caused delay and adjournment of Refugee Protection Division (RPD) hearings.[5] Some also point out that where legal aid is available at early stages of refugee determination, fewer cases must be litigated through judicial review, thus relieving the strain on the judicial system.[6]

A claimant must notify Immigration, Refugees and Citizenship Canada (IRCC) and the IRB about his representative or change of a representative by completing a special form. Although a claimant may use both legal and non-legal representatives in proceedings before the IRB, only legal professionals may represent claimants before the courts. Thus, if a claimant applies for judicial review of an RPD decision, he will need to retain a legal representative.[7]

This chapter will explore both the extent of the "right to counsel" in refugee proceedings and the meaning of the term "competent and careful." However, before dealing with these issues, it will discuss the methods by which counsel are regulated.

B. THE REGULATION OF COUNSEL

Before the introduction of regulations governing who may act as counsel pursuant to the *IRPA*,[8] there was some controversy over whether and how counsel should be regulated and who should regulate counsel. Many lawyers' associations and law societies complained that while

4 Sean Rehaag "The Role of Counsel in Canada's Refugee Determinations System: An Empirical Assessment" (2011) 49 *Osgoode Hall Law Journal* 71 at 79.

5 Sean Fine, "IRB Furor Reflects on Lawyers" *The Globe and Mail* (10 December 1994) A10.

6 Dagmar Soennecken, "Justice Served? Legal Aid and Access to the Courts for Refugees in a Comparative Context" (Paper delivered at the AGM of the Law and Society Association, Chicago, 27 May 2004) at 21, online: www.researchgate.net/publication/237532818_Justice_Served_Legal_Aid_and_Access_to_the_Courts_for_Refugees_in_a_Comparative_Context.

7 It is technically possible to pursue judicial review as a self-represented claimant, but few claimants proceed in such a manner and almost no such judicial reviews are successful.

8 *Regulations*, above note 2, s 2, *sub verbo* "authorized representative," and s 13.1.

lawyers were subject to regulation, the other "counsel" (e.g., immigration consultants) were wholly unregulated. In the case of *Law Society of British Columbia v Mangat*,[9] the Law Society of British Columbia challenged this state of affairs and argued that it violated the constitutional division of powers. Under the division of powers, a province is entitled to regulate professional activities. In British Columbia, the province had done so by granting a broad monopoly to the members of the Law Society on the provision of legal services. The Law Society argued that the allowance under the (then) *Immigration Act* of representation by "counsel" (that is, not only lawyers, but also other representatives) violated this constitutional division of powers.

Ultimately, the Supreme Court of Canada held that the participation of non-legal counsel in proceedings before the Board was a matter of federal jurisdiction which did not necessarily give rise to an obligation to regulate consultants.[10] Consequently, the allowance in the *Immigration Act*, and now the *IRPA*, of representation by non-lawyer counsel is constitutionally valid. Despite this ruling, the federal government chose to regulate non-legal counsel in April 2004 by adopting regulations specifying that "representation for a fee" is restricted to lawyers[11] and to members of the Canadian Society of Immigration Consultants. At the end of June 2011, provisions in Bill C-35 (*Act to Amend the Immigration and Refugee Protection Act*), which had previously formed part of the *Cracking Down on Crooked Consultants Act*, came into force. These provisions extended the scope of the regulation of immigration consultants, increased penalties, and gave the Minister more power to intervene in the regulation of immigration consultants.

The difficulty in allowing representation by non-lawyers has less to do with their possibly lower level of skill or knowledge and more to do with their, until recently, lack of regulation. Thus, while a lawyer is obliged to behave in a particular manner with respect to the collection of fees and the provision of services, a non-legal representative is largely free to behave in any manner.[12] The result of non-regulation can be particularly severe for persons seeking protection who are already in a very vulnerable position. Indeed, the jurisprudence and reports on this

---

9 [2001] 3 SCR 113 [*Mangat*].

10 *Ibid* and *Robles v Canada*, [2003] FCJ No 520 at para 27 (TD).

11 Members of a provincial bar or members of the Chambre des notaires du Quebec.

12 While any service provider is subject to provincial statutes and regulation governing the trade in services, these laws generally do not prevent non-legal counsel from continuing to provide services. Nor do these laws generally provide an avenue for a dissatisfied client to collect anything other than financial compensation.

topic are replete with instances where this vulnerability was exploited for flagrant pecuniary gain.[13]

Ironically, Mangat, the litigant who gave rise to the Supreme Court's decision and, in no small part, the subsequent regulation of non-legal counsel, subsequently became a lawyer.[14] His qualification as a lawyer underscores that there is not always a large difference between the skills and knowledge of lawyers and those of non-legal counsel. Many non-legal counsel have qualified as lawyers in other jurisdictions or have acted in senior positions in the Canadian immigration bureaucracy. The Supreme Court itself acknowledged the utility of non-legal representatives in immigration matters:

> Non-lawyers may provide a very useful service to people who are subject to IRB proceedings. It may be difficult to find lawyers who are fluent in other languages, as well as familiar with different cultures . . . . The possibility to choose to be represented by a non-lawyer may be conducive to informality and expeditiousness.[15]

While there may not be a gap between the skills of consultants and lawyers, the empirical evidence suggests that individuals represented by immigration consultants face a higher rate of withdrawal and abandonment and a lower rate of success than those represented by lawyers.[16]

C. NON-LEGAL REPRESENTATIVES

Since April 2004, non-legal representatives have been subject to a regulatory scheme. However, the regulatory scheme is not complete as it differentiates between unpaid and paid non-legal representatives; the latter are regulated, but the former are not.[17]

Unpaid non-legal representatives include members of non-governmental organizations, members of religious organizations, and friends and family of a claimant. The rationale behind not regulating such representatives is that they are, by definition, devoid of any financial motive. It also recognizes that, in some cases, where an individual is unable to afford paid representation, almost any unpaid representation

13 *NJU (Re)*, [1996] CRDD No 310 (IRB).

14 Mangat became a member of the Law Society of Alberta.

15 *Mangat*, above note 9 at para 60.

16 Rehaag, above note 4 at 86–87.

17 *IRPA*, above note 1, s 91(1).

may be better than no representation. The lack of regulation of unpaid non-legal representatives, however, does underscore that the regulation of immigration consultants is very much the regulation of commercial activity dealing with a vulnerable population, not the regulation of a professional activity per se. In any case, formal representation by unpaid representatives is quite rare in refugee proceedings.[18]

Paid non-legal representatives, or as they are commonly known "immigration consultants," are now regulated by the Immigration Consultants of Canada Regulatory Council (ICCRC).[19] Previously, immigration consultants were regulated by the Canadian Society of Immigration Consultants (CSIC). After the entry into force of Bill C-35, the Minister tabled regulations transferring regulatory authority from the CSIC to the ICCRC.[20] The ostensible rationale behind this transfer was the lack of public confidence in the CSIC and its disciplinary inactivity.[21]

The ICCRC is a federally incorporated society. As a society rather than a statutory body, the ICCRC has jurisdiction only over its membership. It has no ability to sanction or restrain individuals who are not ICCRC members, though the practice of such individuals before the IRB can be regulated by the Board.[22] In this respect, the ICCRC differs from almost all provincial law societies which have broad statutory power to regulate the provision of legal advice by any individual

---

18 The notable exception to this proposition is representation of inland refugee claimants in Halifax by the Halifax Refugee Clinic.

19 The ICCRC became the regulatory body for consultants providing immigration advice across the country on 30 June 2011. More recently, as of 30 June 2015, the regulatory scope of the ICCRC was extended to the provision of citizenship advice. In addition, the federal transfer of regulatory authority from the CSIC to the ICCRC was accompanied by similar provincial transfers, most notably in Quebec. See "Décret 190-2015 (18 mars 2015)" 147e année, no 13 (1 avril 2015) 707-10.

20 *Regulations Designating a Body for the Purposes of Paragraph 91(2)(c) of the Immigration and Refugee Protection Act*, SOR/2011-142. The CSIC unsuccessfully challenged these regulations in *Canadian Society of Immigration Consultants v Canada (Minister of Citizenship and Immigration)*, 2011 FC 1435, aff'd 2012 FCA 194.

21 Nicholas Keung, Surya Bhattacharya, & Jim Rankin, "How to Stay in Canada by Cooking Up a Story" *Toronto Star* (17 June 2007); House of Commons, Standing Committee on Citizenship and Immigration, *Regulating Immigration Consultants* (39th Parl, 2nd Sess, June 2008) (Chair: Norman Doyle).

22 The IRB has issued orders prohibiting the practice of various individuals before the Board even where no fee is charged: *Decision in the Matter of Ken Miller* (Lois D Figg, Toronto, 16 December 2011) and *Decision in the Matter of Charles Wallace* (Lois D Figg, Toronto, 11 October 2011).

within the province and to restrain the provision of legal advice by non-lawyers. The ICCRC has adopted a much more public disciplinary role, with twenty-five cases examined in 2016 alone.[23]

D. LEGAL REPRESENTATIVES

Barristers and solicitors of any province in Canada and notaries in the province of Quebec may represent refugee claimants. So, too, may refugee claimants be represented by students-at-law of any of the foregoing. Students-at-law who act under the supervision of a member in good standing of a provincial bar or Chambre des notaires du Quebec are deemed to be non-paid representatives.[24] Technically, any of the foregoing may represent a claimant anywhere in Canada or abroad. However, professional insurance and Law Society regulations may somewhat limit the geographic scope of practice.[25]

Studies show strong correlation between the presence of legal representation and refugee claim acceptance rates. For example, between July 2002 and March 2012, the overall acceptance rate before the IRB's Refugee Protection Division (RPD) was 53 percent, but it was significantly lower (only 16 percent) for unrepresented claimants.[26] The low acceptance rate is likely due to the claimants' inability to fully and effectively present their cases on their own, in the absence of proper advice from counsel.[27]

Luckily, in most cases, claimants do have legal representation. Between July 2002 and March 2012, only 6 percent were unrepresented in hearings before the RPD.[28] For those who find counsel, the next key question is about quality of representation.

---

23 See "Recent Decisions and Orders," online: http://iccrc-crcic.info/recent-decisions-and-orders/.

24 *Regulations*, above note 2, s 13.1(3).

25 The ability to represent individuals outside the province in which one is a qualified lawyer has expanded greatly over the past decade thanks to various bilateral and multilateral agreements between provincial law societies.

26 Michael Barutciski, *The Impact of the Lack of Legal Representation in the Canadian Asylum Process* (Ottawa: UNHCR, 2012) at 24, online: UNHCR www.unhcr.ca/wp-content/uploads/2014/10/RPT-2012-06-legal_representation-e.pdf. See also Rehaag, above note 4.

27 Barutciski, above note 26.

28 *Ibid*. Rehaag, above note 4 at 86, provides somewhat different statistics. According to him, between 2005 and 2009, only some 87 percent of refugee claimants in matters decided by the Refugee Protection Division were represented by either a lawyer or consultant.

E. THE RIGHT TO COUNSEL

Notwithstanding the invocation of significant constitutional and common law principles in some of the jurisprudence, the right to counsel is not without qualification. Many of these qualifications are concrete: most subjects of refugee law do not have the resources to retain counsel, and few counsel are available to represent them. Nor is the right to counsel supported by concomitant duties: there is no duty to advise an individual of his right to counsel and no duty to stay proceedings unless counsel is present.

First, the right to representation is qualified by the requirement that individuals hire a representative "at their own expense." The indigence of most refugee claimants prevents them from bearing such an expense. Provincial legal aid schemes assist some refugee claimants with the expense of counsel, but coverage can be quite limited in terms of the type of assistance and the type of claimant covered.

Eligibility for legal aid is determined on the basis of asset and income tests. All recipients of social assistance usually qualify without detailed testing.[29] However, refugee claims are not funded if a family member can be reasonably expected to pay for an applicant's legal fees. In many cases, eligibility for legal aid also involves an assessment of the merits of the claim; this is especially true for legal aid funding for judicial review and other post-hearing legal services. Furthermore, the availability of legal aid and the scope of covered services vary from province to province. Legal aid is available for claimants in six out of ten provinces; namely, Alberta, British Columbia, Manitoba, Newfoundland and Labrador, Ontario, and Quebec.[30] Some provinces, such as Nova Scotia, used to provide legal aid, but cancelled the programs in the late 1990s during budgetary cuts.

Services are usually provided in the following categories: general advice and assistance, legal advice, legal representation, duty counsel representation, public legal education, and translation and language

29 Social Planning and Research Council of British Columbia, *An Analysis of Immigration and Refugee Law Services in Canada* (Ottawa: Department of Justice Canada, 2005) at 22, online: www.justice.gc.ca/eng/rp-pr/other-autre/ir/rr03_la18-rr03_aj18/index.html.

30 University of Ottawa Refugee Forum, "Legal Aid for Refugee Claimants in Canada" (September 2012), online: http://oppenheimer.mcgill.ca/IMG/pdf/University_of_Ottawa_Refugee_Forum_-_Legal_Aid_for_Refugee_Claimants_in_Canada_-_September_2012.pdf. See also Immigration and Refugee Board, "List of Legal Aid Offices," online: www.irb-cisr.gc.ca/Eng/RefClaDem/Pages/ClaDemGuideLegAidJur.aspx.

assistance. British Columbia, Ontario, and Quebec have the widest coverage, delivering all above-mentioned services.[31] Most provinces usually provide coverage for the most essential issues of the refugee determination process: completion of a Basis of Claim Form, representation at a refugee determination hearing, appeal to the Refugee Appeal Division, judicial review of a negative IRB decision, and pre-removal risk assessment.[32] In provinces where legal aid is not available, volunteer legal aid clinics and non-governmental organizations provide assistance with legal referrals, general advice, and language services.[33] Legal aid schemes apply only to inland refugee claimants; refugees seeking resettlement will almost never have counsel.[34]

Second, the right to counsel is qualified by the competing statutory obligations of other actors in refugee determination. Practical and statutory considerations require both the immigration officer and the RPD to deal with claims in an expeditious manner. For example, the RPD is required to hear most claims within sixty days.[35] Consequently, hearings can be scheduled without consulting counsel and often on short notice.[36] In fact, IRB Chairperson's Guideline 6 reads:

> 3.3.4 The IRB attempts to accommodate counsel's calendar based on the dates provided; however, the IRB is not bound by counsel's availability, and these attempts cannot interfere with the IRB's ability to schedule its proceedings efficiently, fairly, and within legislated timeframes . . . .
>
> 3.3.6 If counsel is retained in so many proceedings before the IRB that the IRB cannot schedule cases efficiently or within the legislated timeframes taking counsel's availability into account, the IRB may schedule proceedings on dates when counsel is not available.[37]

---

31 University of Ottawa Refugee Forum, above note 30. In recent years, legal aid funding for representation in immigration matters has been the subject of intense federal–provincial bickering. The result has been the curtailment of funding for many refugee claimants, particularly those from countries of origin with low rates of acceptance by the Board.

32 *Ibid.*

33 *Ibid.*

34 Of course, the organization that is involved in sponsoring the refugee may have counsel.

35 *IRPA*, above note 1, s 100(4.1); *Regulations*, above note 2, s 159.9.

36 Most pre-removal risk assessment interviews will be scheduled without any consultation. Before the RPD, only abandonment hearings will be scheduled without any consultation.

37 Immigration and Refugee Board, Chairperson's Guidelines, "Guideline 6: Scheduling and Changing the Date or Time of a Proceeding" (2012), online: IRB www.irb-cisr.gc.ca/Eng/BoaCom/references/pol/GuiDir/Pages/GuideDir06.aspx.

Thus, a practical obstacle to representation may be created due to the unavailability of counsel on short notice.

The scheduling of matters without regard to the schedule of counsel, and the related problem of proceeding in the absence of unavailable counsel, has initiated much jurisprudence. While the Federal Court has recognized that the right to counsel is not absolute, the Board (and immigration officers) must be flexible in their approach. Ultimately, the determination of whether it is appropriate to proceed in the absence of counsel must be made based upon the specific circumstances of the case and the claimant:

> The following principles can therefore be drawn from the case law: although the right to counsel is not absolute in an administrative proceeding, refusing an individual the possibility to retain counsel by not allowing a postponement is reviewable if the following factors are in play: the case is complex, the consequences of the decision are serious, the individual does not have the resources — whether in terms of intellect or legal knowledge — to properly represent his interests.[38]

Third, the right to counsel is qualified by the practical availability of counsel. As a result, at least in part, of the deteriorating legal aid coverage provided for refugee claimants, many counsel are unwilling to take on such cases. In addition, claimants located outside major urban centres may find it difficult to locate counsel able or willing to represent them.

Overseas applicants face even more significant obstacles to representation. Where overseas claimants do find representation, however, there is an obligation on Immigration, Refugees and Citizenship Canada to consider, where appropriate, allowing counsel to attend the claimant's interview. Until recently, IRCC policy has been to explicitly limit the ability of counsel to attend the interview: "The general approach is to limit attendance at interviews to the individual applicants."[39] In the case of *Ha v Canada (Minister of Citizenship and Immigration)*, the Federal Court of Appeal struck down such an approach as an improper fetter on the discretion of an immigration officer.

Fourth, the right to counsel is qualified by the absence of any duty that an individual be informed of the right to counsel. In some circumstances, notably the arrest or detention of the claimant, such a duty is

38 *Mervilus v Canada (Minister of Citizenship and Immigration)*, [2004] FCJ No 1460 at para 25 (FC).

39 *Ha v Canada (Minister of Citizenship and Immigration)*, [2004] FCJ No 174 at para 74 (CA) (quoting policy of what was then Citizenship and Immigration Canada).

constitutionally required.[40] However, unlike predecessor statutes, the *IRPA* does not require that a claimant or overseas applicant be notified of her right to counsel.[41] Although advising an individual of the right to counsel is sound practice, absent a statutory duty, the failure to do so will not give rise to complaint; such a failure is problematic only insofar as it may be symptomatic of a larger failure to ensure that an individual is aware of the nature and consequences of proceedings.[42] As a matter of practice, the notices of hearing sent by the Board to claimants advise them of the right to counsel.

F. COMPETENT AND CAREFUL COUNSEL

As previously noted, refugee claimants are a particularly vulnerable group of individuals. They generally do not speak either English or French. They are typically without significant financial resources. They often know little about the mechanics of the Canadian refugee determination system, the role of legal counsel, or the Canadian legal system generally. The lack of familiarity with the proper role of counsel and even the lack of awareness of the difference between the words "counsel" and "lawyer" can make it difficult for claimants to even become aware of any problems with their representation.[43] And finally, they are anxious about gaining status in Canada. For all of these reasons, issues of professional responsibility are particularly important for anyone representing refugee claimants.

With the introduction of the regulation of immigration consultants, most individuals representing refugee claimants will have been required to undergo some training or pass an examination. However, given the gravity of the consequences of any mistakes made by counsel, the issue arises as to what remedies are available for a claimant if an error, either deliberate or inadvertent, is made by counsel. Unfortunately,

---

40 *Canadian Charter of Rights and Freedoms*, Part 1 of the *Constitution Act, 1982*, s 10(b), being Schedule B to the *Canada Act 1982* (UK), c 11.

41 *Immigration Act, 1976*, SC 1976-77, c 52, s 30, required that "[e]very person with respect to whom an inquiry is to be held shall be informed of the person's right to obtain the services of a barrister or solicitor or other counsel and to be represented by any such counsel at the inquiry and shall be given a reasonable opportunity, if the person so desires, to obtain such counsel at the person's own expense."

42 *Cha v Canada (Minister of Citizenship and Immigration)*, [2006] FCJ No 491 (CA).

43 *Shirwa v Canada (Minister of Employment and Immigration)*, [1994] 2 FC 51 (TD) [*Shirwa*].

the courts have largely set a very high threshold for individuals who challenge decisions because of the (mis)deeds of (in)competent and (un)careful counsel. Generally, the courts have held clients liable for the misconduct of counsel: "It is well recognized that a person has to accept the consequences of their choice of counsel."[44] Only when the incompetence of counsel rises to a very high level will a miscarriage of justice be found to have occurred.[45] Further, there must be clear and sufficiently specific evidence demonstrating the incompetence or negligence of counsel.[46]

The courts have distinguished between cases where the misconduct has denied an individual a hearing of his claim or application, and cases where the misconduct affected the quality of the presentation of the claim or application. In the former category are cases where counsel has failed to notify a client of a hearing.[47] In the latter category are cases where counsel has been poorly prepared for a client's hearing or has filed poorly prepared submissions.[48] While the distinction may be analytically coherent, in practice, it is often difficult to determine at what point counsel's incompetence or inattention rises to the level of denying a client the opportunity to be heard.

In most cases, a client is not completely denied a hearing by the misconduct of counsel. Rather, the quality of the hearing is diminished because of the misconduct. In such cases, the court has been reluctant to intervene:

> [W]here a hearing does occur, the decision can only be reviewed in "extraordinary circumstances," where there is sufficient evidence to establish the "exact dimensions of the problem" and where the review is based on a "precise factual foundation." These latter limitations are necessary, in my opinion, to heed the concerns expressed by

---

44 *Williams v Canada (Minister of Employment and Immigration)* (1994), 74 FTR 34 (TD).

45 Such a breach would usually occur only in "extraordinary circumstances." *Huynh v Canada (Minister of Employment and Immigration)* (1993), 65 FTR 11 (TD) [*Huynh*]. See also *Shirwa*, above note 43; *Sheikh v Canada (Minister of Citizenship and Immigration)*, [1990] 3 FC 238 (CA); *Fatima v Canada (Minister of Citizenship and Immigration)*, [2000] FCJ No 308 (TD).

46 For example, in *Memari v Canada (Minister of Citizenship and Immigration)*, [2010] FCJ No 1493 (TD), the Federal Court found a miscarriage of justice. It determined that the Board might have reached a different conclusion on the applicant's credibility had he not been prejudiced by counsel's inadequate representation.

47 *Mathon*, above note 3; *Shirwa*, above note 43; *Gulishvili v Canada (Minister of Citizenship and Immigration)*, 2002 FCT 1200.

48 *Huynh*, above note 45.

> Justices MacGuigan and Rothstein that general dissatisfaction with the quality of representation freely chosen by the applicant should not provide grounds for judicial review of a negative decision. However, where the incompetence or negligence of the applicant's representative is sufficiently specific and clearly supported by the evidence such negligence or incompetence is inherently prejudicial to the applicant and will warrant overturning the decision, notwithstanding the lack of bad faith or absence of a failure to do anything on the part of the tribunal.[49]

In the end, it must be shown that but for the incompetence of counsel, the result of the proceeding would have been different.[50]

Where a client is seen to have connived in or condoned the (mis)conduct of counsel, equitable principles will almost always result in a denial of relief. Furthermore, the past misconduct of the client — through the provision of false testimony or forged documents — can be used to disbelieve his allegations of misconduct by counsel.[51] As a matter of procedure, the Board and the Federal Court will entertain the issue of incompetence of counsel only if proof of notice of the complaint has been given to the counsel in question.[52]

G. COMPLAINTS ABOUT THE CONDUCT OF COUNSEL

Generally, complaints about the conduct of counsel must be directed to the appropriate regulatory body, either the provincial law society or the ICCRC. A complaint against an immigration consultant is investigated and then reviewed by the ICCRC's Complaints Review Committee, which decides whether to refer the case further to the Discipline

---

49 *Shirwa*, above note 43.

50 The exact standard of proof that must be met has been the subject of judicial debate. *Shirvan v Canada (Minister of Citizenship and Immigration)*, [2005] FCJ No 1864 (FC), established that the test was that there was a "reasonable probability" that the outcome would be different. More recently, *Srignanavel v Canada (Minister of Citizenship and Immigration)*, 2015 FC 584 (drawing support from *Thamotharampillai v Canada (Minister of Citizenship and Immigration)*, 2011 FC 438), has suggested that this test is too high and that a (lower) threshold of "fairly arguable case" is sufficient.

51 *ZGU (Re)*, [2005] RPDD No 50 (IRB).

52 *Nunez v Canada (Minister of Citizenship and Immigration)*, [2000] FCJ No 555 at para 19 (TD); *Yang v Canada (Minister of Citizenship and Immigration)*, 2015 FC 1189.

Committee. If no settlement is reached by the ICCRC and the member, the Discipline Committee conducts a hearing. Where a finding of misconduct is made, the committee may order a range of measures, including a reprimand, rehabilitative measures, suspension of membership, restrictions on the member's practice, or revocation of membership.[53]

A similar process is established by provincial law societies to investigate and address complaints against lawyers and paralegals. Where misconduct is found, the penalties may include a formal warning and a temporary suspension, a fine, or revocation of licence.[54] For example, such a finding was made in the much publicized 2015 case of Viktor Hohots. He was retained in the cases of some 900 Roma refugee claimants from Hungary (together with their families comprising between 4,000 and 5,000 individuals), but he did not meet many of his clients and left the interpreter to prepare claimants' personal information forms (predecessor to the Basis of Claim Form), resulting in numerous mistakes, omissions, and lack of detail in their narratives. Such inadequate preparation resulted in adverse credibility findings and rejection of several of his clients' cases before the IRB.[55] The Law Society Tribunal imposed a five-month suspension, a two-year restriction on practising refugee law, an order to participate in a practice review upon his return to practice, and $15,000 in costs.[56] This penalty was criticized as inadequate by some refugee advocates and by Hohots's former clients.[57]

The same year, the Law Society Tribunal found that another refugee lawyer — Erzsebet Jaszi — had committed serious misconduct. She "virtually ignored her obligations as a lawyer . . . to act competently in her clients' best interests" and was "dishonest with clients, the IRB and LAO [Legal Aid Ontario]."[58] At the disciplinary hearing, the lawyer did not show "remorse, acceptance of responsibility or an appreciation of the impact of her misconduct on others."[59] The Tribunal ordered

---

53 For more details on the complaints process, see the ICCRC website, online: http://iccrc-crcic.info/sample-page/.

54 See, for example, the Law Society of Upper Canada, online: www.lsuc.on.ca/subject-of-a-complaint/.

55 *Law Society of Upper Canada v Hohots*, 2015 ONLSTH 72.

56 *Law Society of Upper Canada v Hohots*, 2015 ONLSTH 205.

57 Maureen Brosnahan, "Toronto Lawyer Suspended for Five Months for Misconduct Involving Roma Refugees" *CBC News* (12 May 2015), online: www.cbc.ca/1.3071343; Neil Etienne, "Refugee Lawyers Disciplined for Failing to Serve Roma Clients" *Law Times* (21 December 2015), online: http://lawtimesnews.com/201512215135/headline-news/refugee-lawyers-disciplined-for-failing-to-serve-roma-clients.

58 *Law Society of Upper Canada v Jaszi*, 2015 ONLSTH 211 at para 36.

59 *Ibid* at para 31.

revocation of her licence to practise law, a payment of $50,000 in investigation costs to the Law Society, and a reimbursement to Legal Aid Ontario for overbilling services that she did not provide.

Obviously, in the case of unpaid non-legal representatives and in the case of immigration consultants who are not members of the ICCRC, there is no regulatory body to which to complain, though there is the possibility of criminal prosecution. As was seen previously, whether a formal complaint has been made to a regulatory body may be considered when the misconduct of counsel has been cited in proceedings challenging a decision.

In exceptional cases, the IRB or Immigration, Refugees and Citizenship Canada may act upon a complaint or its own initiative to prevent an individual from continuing to act as counsel. In the matter of *Rezaei v Canada (Minister of Citizenship and Immigration)*,[60] the Board learned of serious allegations of misconduct by an immigration consultant.[61] After an investigation into Rezaei's conduct, the Board banned him from representing individuals before it. In dismissing Rezaei's attempt to overturn this ban, the Federal Court stated:

> Given the procedural framework of the IRB, I accept its submission as intervener that it has the inherent jurisdiction to monitor its own procedures in order to ensure its integrity. Indeed, denial of the jurisdiction of the IRB to ensure the integrity of its processes would be a disservice to its stakeholders . . . .
>
> . . . it is not limited to banning the applicant from specific hearings on a case-by-case basis, contrary to what the applicant suggests in his submissions. If the IRB is of the view that a broader ban on the applicant is necessary to preserve the integrity of its process as a tribunal, such a remedy is open to it. It may impose a general ban provided that its conclusion that the sanction is necessary is based on consideration of all the evidence before it.[62]

Although the proceedings against Rezaei were conducted under the *Immigration Act*, the RPD continues to be able to bar counsel from representing individuals. The practical effect of the ICCRC, however, is that the RPD will no longer be required to perform such a regulatory task as complaint to and sanction by the ICCRC will usually achieve the same ends.

---

60 [2003] 3 FC 421 (TD) [*Rezaei*].

61 Rezaei had been charged with four counts of attempting to organize the coming into Canada of certain persons on false Canadian visas. He was later convicted but the convictions were overturned on appeal. He had "engaged in acts or omissions constituting misconduct" in a long list of matters before the Board.

62 *Rezaei*, above note 60 at paras 70 & 71.

H. CONCLUSION

The representation of refugee claimants by qualified counsel is an important part of the Canadian refugee determination process. The availability and expertise of counsel brings significant benefits to both the claimants and the overall efficiency and legitimacy of the process. The representation of refugee claimants is also an expression of a fundamental constitutional and common law value: that individuals facing complicated legal proceedings with serious consequences should be allowed to be represented so as to ensure that there is a full and fair hearing.

The exigencies of real life, however, serve to somewhat limit this laudable value. The affordability of, access to, and availability of counsel are all limited. Equally, a claimant may not be aware of his right to counsel — and may also not be able to judge whether his counsel is adequately ensuring that he receives a full and fair hearing. Unfortunately, largely in the interests of judicial finality, the courts have been reluctant to intervene where the determination of a claim or application is alleged to have been tainted by incompetent counsel.

It should be remembered that despite the foregoing statements about lapses in the quality and honesty of counsel, the overwhelming majority of claimants and applicants are represented (or otherwise assisted) by knowledgeable and dedicated counsel.[63] In fact, empirical analysis has confirmed that claimants with legal representation (particularly by lawyers) are significantly more likely to receive a positive determination than unrepresented claimants.[64] The presence of such a strong body of representatives has no doubt contributed to the advancement of Canadian refugee law and has resulted in a more complex and nuanced jurisprudence that could not have been developed without them. The overriding concern of this chapter that the right to counsel has received inadequate care and attention by the courts is not an indictment of refugee counsel in Canada, but rather, an argument in their support and defence.

---

63 Between 2005 and 2009, more than 87 percent of refugee claimants in matters decided by the Refugee Protection Division were represented by either a lawyer or a consultant: Rehaag, above note 4 at 86. See also Barutciski, above note 26 at 24.

64 See, generally, Rehaag, above note 4; and Barutciski, above note 26.

CHAPTER 10

APPEALS AND JUDICIAL REMEDIES

A. INTRODUCTION

The rendering of a negative decision in a refugee matter can have a profound impact on an individual. For those seeking protection in Canada, a negative decision can lead to the loss of status and, ultimately, removal from Canada. For those seeking protection from abroad, a negative decision not only bars them from resettlement in Canada, but also leaves them residing in potentially dangerous conditions. The ability to challenge negative decisions through appeals and other judicial remedies is important for those affected by the decisions as well as for the overall integrity of the refugee status determination process.

As discussed previously, the *Convention Relating to the Status of Refugees* is largely silent on matters of procedure.[1] That it fails to delineate the scope of a rejected refugee claimant's appeal rights is not surprising. However, the Executive Committee of the United Nations High Commissioner for Refugees (UNHCR) has adopted the following conclusion mandating that rejected refugee claimants be allowed to seek review of their refugee status determination:

> If the applicant is not recognized, he should be given a reasonable time to appeal for a formal reconsideration of the decision, either to

1 28 July 1951, 189 UNTS 150 [*Refugee Convention*]. The exception to this proposition is found in art 32 which requires, generally, that the expulsion of a recognized refugee occur only "in accordance with due process of law."

> the same or to a different authority, whether administrative or judicial, according to the prevailing system.[2]

Furthermore, access to such a right of review is not limited to a subset of rejected refugee claimants, but rather extends to even those refugee claimants whose claims have been determined to be "manifestly unfounded."[3]

Depending on the statistics used, about half of all refugee claimants have their claim denied by the Refugee Protection Division (RPD) of the Immigration and Refugee Board (IRB) (see Appendix D, Table 1). Some overseas refugee applicants are also refused, although for practical reasons these individuals are much less likely to challenge their negative decisions. The *Immigration and Refugee Protection Act* along with the *Refugee Protection Division Rules* and the *Refugee Appeal Division Rules* provides three major mechanisms by which a rejected claimant may challenge a negative decision: (1) a motion to reopen, (2) an appeal, and (3) a judicial review. In addition, rejected claimants who have exhausted all domestic remedies may seek redress through various international human rights mechanisms.

With the exception of the international mechanisms, each of these avenues of redress may also be invoked by the government of Canada to challenge a decision of the Board to grant protection. Not infrequently, decisions to grant refugee protection by the RPD are challenged by the Minister either through a motion to reopen or, more likely, through appeal or judicial review. For obvious reasons, the decisions of immigration officers concerning protection may not be similarly challenged.

In the remainder of this chapter, each of the various mechanisms through which a rejected refugee claimant and/or an overseas applicant may challenge a negative determination will be discussed.

B. MOTION OR REQUEST TO REOPEN

In general, the doctrine of *functus officio* prevents a decision maker from revisiting his decision. It applies primarily to judicial and quasi-judicial decision makers; hence, there is greater flexibility with respect of immigration officers' decisions. The doctrine was described in the

2 UNHCR Executive Committee, "Conclusion No 8 (XXVIII) Determination of Refugee Status (1977)," 8(e)(vi).

3 UNHCR Executive Committee, "Conclusion No 30 (XXXIV) The Problem of Manifestly Unfounded or Abusive Applications for Refugee Status or Asylum (1983)."

following terms by the Supreme Court in *Chandler v Alberta Association of Architects*:

> As a general rule, once such a tribunal has reached a final decision in respect to the matter that is before it in accordance with its enabling statute, that decision cannot be revisited because the tribunal has changed its mind, made an error within jurisdiction or because there has been a change of circumstances.[4]

Absent statutory authorization to the contrary, the only situations in which a decision can be revisited are (1) where there has been a "slip in drawing up the formal judgment," (2) "where there was an error in expressing the manifest intention of the Court," and (3) where there has been a breach of natural justice.[5] As the third situation is typically invoked in a request to reopen a decision, it bears greater elaboration. It has been described and justified in the following terms:

> If the error which renders the decision a nullity is one that taints the whole proceeding, then the tribunal must start afresh . . . . [if there was] a denial of natural justice which vitiated the whole proceeding. The tribunal was bound to start afresh in order to cure the defect.[6]

Based upon the foregoing, the doctrine of *functus officio* will not be circumvented by a simple allegation that new evidence has arisen or that not all possible evidence was before the decision maker.[7] Nor will *functus officio* be circumvented by proof of a substantive error in the decision. In such cases, a pre-removal risk assessment (PRRA) application and an application for judicial review are the appropriate remedies. The reopening of a case is seen as the means to uphold natural justice. This is made explicit in the *Refugee Protection Division Rules* and the *Refugee Appeal Division Rules*, which contain identical wording: "The Division must not allow the application unless it is established that there was a failure to observe a principle of natural justice."[8] Thus, the power to reopen a refugee claim is very limited:[9] if the division finds that an applicant has been afforded a fair hearing, there are no grounds

4 [1989] SCJ No 102 at para 20, Sopinka J [*Chandler*].

5 *Ibid*.

6 *Ibid*.

7 *Longia v Canada (Minister of Employment and Immigration)*, [1990] 3 FC 288 (CA); and, *inter alia*, *Iqbal v Canada (Minister of Citizenship and Immigration)* (1996), 33 Imm LR (2d) 179 (FCTD).

8 *Refugee Protection Division Rules*, SOR/2012-256, r 62(6) [*RPD Rules*]; *Refugee Appeal Division Rules*, SOR/2012-257, r 49(6) [*RAD Rules*].

9 *Huseen v Canada (Minister of Citizenship and Immigration)*, 2015 FC 845 [*Huseen*].

for reopening a claim.[10] However, where the "opportunity to be heard" was denied, a motion to reopen can be granted. The denial of an opportunity to be heard may be the result of errors by the RPD, including the failure to notify the claimant of a hearing. Such a denial may also occur due to clerical errors (e.g., notice of a hearing sent to a wrong address) or defects in the proceedings. For example, in *Kurija v Canada (Minister of Citizenship and Immigration)*,[11] the claimant, a minor, was not given the benefit of having a designated representative at the hearing, and his claim as well as a subsequent request to reopen were denied. The Federal Court concluded that the refusal to reopen the case was an error.[12] Further, even where an applicant misses a deadline or a hearing, all circumstances must be considered in order to decide whether reopening may nevertheless be warranted.[13] For example, in *Huseen v Canada (Minister of Citizenship and Immigration)*, the applicant missed the deadline for filing the Basis of Claim (BOC) Form and missed her abandonment hearing. The court concluded that the RPD's refusal to reopen the case was unreasonable as the division did not consider significant factors at play,[14] namely, that the applicant had no counsel during the period in question; attended the IRB office in Calgary to present the new address and change of venue request (she had made a claim at Pearson airport in Toronto, but then immediately moved to Calgary); mistakenly believed that proceedings were suspended until a decision on the change of venue request was made; had difficulty finding a lawyer between the move to Alberta on 18 December 2013 and the 7 January 2014 abandonment hearing due to the Christmas holiday season; and immediately addressed the missed BOC deadline after the

---

10 *Gurgus v Canada (Minister of Citizenship and Immigration)*, 2014 FC 9.

11 2013 FC 1158.

12 The claimant was fifteen, but claimed to be eighteen and that age appeared on his passport. At the hearing, counsel informed the Board that the claimant was under eighteen, but the Board proceeded to find that that applicant was eighteen and ordered a designated representative to leave the proceedings. Subsequently, the Board refused a request to reopen as it determined that there was no breach of natural justice.

13 *Andreoli v Canada (Minister of Citizenship and Immigration)*, 2004 FC 1111; *Matondo v Canada (Minister of Citizenship and Immigration)*, 2005 FC 416; *Albarracin v Canada (Minister of Citizenship and Immigration)*, 2008 FC 1143.

14 The *RPD Rules* and the *RAD Rules* also outline some of the factors that must be considered in decisions to reopen, namely, whether the application to reopen was made in a timely manner and the justification for any delay; and the reasons why the applicant did not make an appeal to the RAD (if he had such a right) or an application for judicial review. *RPD Rules*, above note 8, r 62(7); *RAD Rules*, above note 8, r 49(7).

first meeting with counsel and informed the IRB that she never had any intention to abandon the claim. As put by the Federal Court:

> . . . the door should not slam shut on all those who fail to meet ordinary procedural requirements. Such a restrictive reading would undermine Canada's commitment to its refugee system and underlying international obligations (section 3(2) of the Act) . . . . The opportunity to free a family from the scourge of persecution, the actors of which presumably caused the death of their husband and father, should not rest on an overly rigid application of procedural requirements.[15]

Finally, a denial of natural justice may also occur as a result of circumstances extrinsic to the proceedings that have as a consequence the silencing of the claimant, including most famously in the case of *Kaur v Canada (Minister of Employment and Immigration)* threats of violence against an individual.[16]

There is, however, a limitation on reopening of cases: the RPD cannot reopen on any ground — even a failure to observe a principle of natural justice — if the Refugee Appeal Division (RAD) or the Federal Court has made a final determination on the case.[17] Similarly, the RAD cannot reopen on any ground if the Federal Court has made a final determination on the case.[18] Thus, if a claimant became aware of a breach of natural justice after a RAD or a Federal Court decision was made, he would not be able to remedy that breach via reopening of the case.

Despite the possibility of bringing an application to reopen, relatively few such applications are made. The tight filing deadlines for appeal and judicial review make it impossible to first seek to reopen a decision and then to challenge the same decision through appeal or judicial review.

An application to reopen may be made to any decision maker with respect to any decision. The decisions of an immigration officer with respect to eligibility, the need for protection (under a PRRA), and qualification for overseas protection may all be challenged through a request to reopen the decision. Arguably, an immigration officer has a greater ability to reopen a decision given his status as a mere "administrative"

15 *Huseen*, above note 9 at paras 16–17.
16 [1990] 2 FC 209 (CA).
17 *Immigration and Refugee Protection Act*, SC 2001, c 27, s 170.2 [*IRPA*].
18 *Ibid*, s 171.1.

decision maker.[19] Iin practice, however, requests to reopen are made only to and usually granted only by the RPD or the RAD.

C. REFUGEE APPEAL DIVISION

The *IRPA* provides for a right of appeal by some refugee claimants to the Refugee Appeal Division (RAD) of the Immigration and Refugee Board (IRB).[20] RAD appeal is available to inland claimants only; applicants for resettlement from overseas do not have such a recourse and may seek only judicial review of an IRCC officer's decision (and/or may make an application to reopen).

Although the creation of the RAD was provided for in the 2002 *Immigration and Refugee Protection Act*, or *IRPA*, the respective provisions were not implemented until ten years later. Many refugee advocates were extremely frustrated by the failure to introduce the RAD.[21] The RAD was seen as the element of the *IRPA* regime which balances the switch from two-member panels used for first-instance refugee determination under the *Immigration Act* to one-member panels under the *IRPA*.[22] It has been argued that the support of refugee advocates (and, to a lesser extent, of UNHCR) for this latter change was contingent upon the introduction of the RAD. While, during the ten-year delay in RAD implementation, judicial review was available for rejected claimants, this option was quite limited in scope. A judge on judicial review has almost no capacity to receive new evidence and has only a limited capacity to substantively revisit factual determinations.[23] Furthermore, the relatively formal and legalistic nature of judicial review makes it relatively inaccessible to refugee claimants.

---

19 *Nouranidoust v Canada (Minister of Citizenship and Immigration)*, [2000] 1 FC 123 (TD).

20 *IRPA*, above note 17, ss 110–11 and 171.

21 Letter of 9 May 2002 from Judith Kumin (UNHCR Representative in Canada) to Minister Coderre, as quoted in Canadian Council for Refugees, "The Refugee Appeal: Is No One Listening?" (31 March 2005) at 4; UN Committee against Torture, "Conclusions and Recommendations of the Committee against Torture," CAT/C/CO/34/CAN at para 5(c); and Inter-American Commission on Human Rights, *Report on the Situation of Human Rights of Asylum Seekers within the Canadian Refugee Determination System*, OEA/Ser.L/V/II.106 (2000) (28 February 2000) at para 174ff, online: www.cidh.org/countryrep/Canada2000en/table-of-contents.htm.

22 The previous provisions of the *Immigration Act* required two-member panels unless a claimant consented to the hearing of his case by a single-member panel.

23 See below for further discussion of the limitations of judicial review.

1) The Nature of the Refugee Appeal Division

The RAD is intended to provide a full appeal on the merits, in relation to matters of fact, law, and of mixed law and fact,[24] and bring finality to the resolution of a case. As put by the Federal Court of Appeal in *Hugurlica v Canada (Minister of Citizenship and Immigration)*, "[t]he RAD was essentially viewed as the safety net that would catch all mistakes made by the RPD, be it on the law or the facts."[25] Claimants' removal is stayed while their appeal is being examined by the RAD.[26]

A number of important similarities and differences exist between the RPD and the RAD.[27] On the one hand, the RAD and the RPD have "essentially the same powers."[28] As a division of the IRB, the RAD is governed by the general jurisdictional provisions that apply to all divisions.[29] Both the RPD and the RAD can take judicial notice of any facts, of any other generally recognized facts, and of information or opinion that is within their specialized knowledge.[30] On the other hand, there are differences in the composition and procedure before the two divisions. Unlike members of the RPD, RAD members are Governor in Council appointees.[31] At least 10 percent of the members of the RAD must be lawyers or notaries.[32] (There is no similar requirement for members of the RPD.) While the RPD "must hold a hearing,"[33] oral hearings at the RAD are rare. Further, the RAD can consider only new evidence from the claimant, which has arisen after an RPD hearing or was not reasonably available for that hearing. Finally, when an appeal is heard by three members of the RAD, such a decision has precedential value binding all RPD members, as well as any one-member panel of the RAD.[34]

---

24 *IRPA*, above note 17, s 110(1).
25 2016 FCA 93 at para 98 [*Hugurlica*].
26 *IRPA*, above note 17, s 49(1)(c).
27 *Hugurlica*, above note 25 at para 56, usefully outlined some similarities and differences between the RPD and the RAD.
28 *Ibid*.
29 *IRPA*, above note 17, ss 162–69.
30 *Ibid*, ss 170(i) and 171(b).
31 *Ibid*, s 153(1)(a).
32 *Ibid*, s 153(4).
33 *Ibid*, s 170(b).
34 *Ibid*, s 171(c).

2) Right to Appeal

As a general rule, both a refugee claimant and the Minister can appeal an RPD determination to the RAD.[35] However, no appeal may be made with respect to the following:

- an RPD decision on a claim by a designated foreign national;[36]
- a refugee claim determined withdrawn or abandoned;[37]
- a refugee claim determined to have no credible basis or to be manifestly unfounded;[38]
- an RPD decision with respect to a claim that is subject to an exception to the *Safe Third Country Agreement*;[39]
- an RPD decision on a claim made by a national of a designated country of origin (DCO);[40]
- an RPD decision on cessation or vacation of refugee protection;[41]
- a refugee claim that was referred to the RPD prior to the relevant provisions of the new system coming into force in December 2012;
- a refugee claim deemed to be rejected because an order of surrender was issued under the *Extradition Act*.[42]

As research indicates, in 2013, the majority of claimants denied access to the RAD fell under the following categories: exception to the *Safe Third Country Agreement* (23.1 percent of claims referred to the RPD); claimants from designated countries of origin (DCOs) (8.6 percent of claims finalized by the RPD); and no credible basis or manifestly unfounded declarations (2.2 percent of claims finalized by the RPD).[43]

It is important to note that, in July 2015, the Federal Court determined that the limitation on the right to appeal for claimants from DCOs was unconstitutional. Hence, claimants whose RPD decisions were issued on and after 23 July 2015 (the date of the Federal Court

---

35 *Ibid*, s 110(1). The right of appeal includes refugee determination decisions as well as decisions concerning vacation and cessation. Decisions concerning withdrawal and abandonment may not be appealed to the RAD.

36 *Ibid*, s 110(2)(a).

37 *Ibid*, s 110(2)(b).

38 *Ibid*, s 110(2)(c).

39 *Ibid*, s 110(2)(d).

40 *Ibid*, s 110(2)(d.1).

41 *Ibid*, ss 110(2)(e)–(f).

42 *Ibid*, s 105(4).

43 Angus Grant & Sean Rehaag, "Unappealing: An Assessment of the Limits on Appeal Rights in Canada's New Refugee Determination System" (2015) 49 *UBC Law Review* 203 at 225.

decision) and who are not otherwise barred from appealing to the RAD may now file an appeal.[44]

In the past years, most RAD appeals (96.8 percent for 2013 and 2014) were made by refugee claimants on negative RPD decisions, and the remainder were Minister's appeals on positive decisions.[45] Appeals by the Minister had a 75.6 percent success rate and those by claimants, 26.4 percent.[46] For claimants who do not have a right to a RAD appeal, the main avenue to challenge an RPD decision is through judicial review in the Federal Court. By comparison, the success rate on judicial review of negative RPD decisions is much lower: only 7.8 percent.[47]

3) Timelines and Procedure

A notice of appeal must be filed within fifteen days from the day on which written reasons for the RPD decision have been received.[48] After that, an applicant has a further fifteen days to perfect the appeal.[49] The RAD has the power to grant an extension to the timeline "for reasons of fairness and natural justice."[50] In deciding on an extension, the RAD is to consider the following factors:

(a) whether the application was made in a timely manner and the justification for any delay;
(b) whether there is an arguable case;
(c) prejudice to the Minister, if the application was granted; and
(d) the nature and complexity of the appeal.[51]

The procedural rules are framed in an asymmetrical manner, prescribing fixed and restrictive timelines and requirements for claimants, while allowing significant flexibility to the Minister. For example, the Minister may intervene in an appeal at any time before the RAD makes its decision.[52] In contrast to the claimant who is limited to providing

---

44 Immigration and Refugee Board, "Federal Court Decision Impacting the Right to Appeal to the Refugee Appeal Division," online: IRB www.irb-cisr.gc.ca/Eng/NewsNouv/NewNou/2015/Pages/craupd.aspx.

45 Grant & Rehaag, above note 43 at 221–22.

46 *Ibid.*

47 *Ibid.*

48 *Immigration and Refugee Protection Regulations*, SOR/2002-227, s 159.91(1)(a) [*Regulations*].

49 *Ibid*, s 159.91(b).

50 *Ibid*, s 159.91(2).

51 *RAD Rules*, above note 8, r 12(6).

52 *IRPA*, above note 17, ss 110(1.1), 171(a.4); *RAD Rules*, above note 8, r 4(1).

new evidence only,[53] the Minister "may, at any time before the Division makes a decision, submit documentary evidence and make written submissions in support of the Minister's appeal or intervention in the appeal."[54]

4) RAD Hearing and Nature of RAD Review

The RAD review of an appeal usually occurs without a hearing and is based upon the written submissions of the parties and the record of the proceedings before the RPD.[55] A hearing may be held, however, where there is documentary evidence

(a) that raises a serious issue with respect to the credibility of the person who is the subject of the appeal;
(b) that is central to the decision with respect to the refugee protection claim; and
(c) that, if accepted, would justify allowing or rejecting the refugee protection claim.[56]

The RAD is not required to hold an oral hearing simply because it admits new evidence; the above three criteria must be met in order to warrant a hearing.[57]

Proceedings are generally conducted by a single-member panel.[58] However, the IRB Chairperson has the power to appoint three-member panels, in which case, the decision would have explicit precedential value.[59] As at the RPD, RAD proceedings are conducted in private.[60]

Like the RPD, the RAD is not bound by any legal or technical rules of evidence[61] and generally may base its decision on any evidence that "is adduced in the proceedings and considered credible or trustworthy in the circumstances."[62] However, the *IRPA*, section 110(4), limits the type of evidence that a claimant may present to the RAD. The limitation is similar to that applicable to pre-removal risk assessments (PRRAs) (see Chapter 12), namely, "only evidence that arose after the rejection

53 *IRPA*, above note 17, s 110(4).
54 *Ibid*, s 171(a.5).
55 *Ibid*, s 110(3).
56 *Ibid*, s 110(6).
57 *Singh v Canada (Minister of Citizenship and Immigration)*, 2016 FCA 96 at para 71 [*Singh*].
58 *IRPA*, above note 17, s 163.
59 *Ibid*, s 171(c).
60 *Ibid*, s 166(c).
61 *Ibid*, s 171(a.2).
62 *Ibid*, s 171(a.3).

of their claim or that was not reasonably available, or that the person could not reasonably have been expected in the circumstances to have presented, at the time of the rejection."[63]

Given the existence of a similar limitation with respect to evidence presented at a PRRA, the courts have drawn on PRRA jurisprudence to clarify what constitutes "new evidence" for the purpose of a RAD appeal. The leading case of *Raza v Canada (Minister of Citizenship and Immigration)* outlined the following criteria to be considered by decision makers (in PRRA context):

1. Credibility: Is the evidence credible, considering its source and the circumstances in which it came into existence? If not, the evidence need not be considered.
2. Relevance: Is the evidence relevant to the PRRA application, in the sense that it is capable of proving or disproving a fact that is relevant to the claim for protection? If not, the evidence need not be considered.
3. Newness: Is the evidence new in the sense that it is capable of:
   (a) proving the current state of affairs in the country of removal or an event that occurred or a circumstance that arose after the hearing in the RPD; or
   (b) proving a fact that was unknown to the refugee claimant at the time of the RPD hearing; or
   (c) contradicting a finding of fact made by the RPD (including a credibility finding)?

If not, the evidence need not be considered.

4. Materiality: If the evidence is material, in the sense that the refugee claim probably would have succeeded if the evidence had been made available to RPD? If not, the evidence need not be considered.
5. Express statutory conditions:
   (a) If the evidence is capable of proving only an event that occurred or circumstances that arose prior to the RPD hearing, then has the applicant established either that the evidence was not reasonably available to him or her for presentation at the RPD hearing, or that he or she could not reasonably have been expected in the circumstances to have presented the evidence at the RPD hearing? If not, the evidence need not be considered.

---

63 *Ibid*, s 110(4). The only exception to this rule is in relation to evidence that is presented in response to evidence presented by the Minister: *IRPA*, *ibid*, s 110(5).

(b) If the evidence is capable of proving an event that occurred or circumstances that arose after the RPD hearing, then the evidence must be considered (unless it is rejected because it is not credible, not relevant, not new or not material).[64]

In *Singh v Canada (Minister of Citizenship and Immigration)*, the Federal Court of Appeal concluded that "[s]ubject to . . . necessary adaptation, . . . the implicit criteria identified in *Raza* are also applicable in the context of subsection 110(4)."[65] Thus, in determining admissibility of new evidence, the RAD must comply with the explicit requirements of the *IRPA*, section 110(4), as well as consider the implicit factors of *Raza* such as credibility, relevance, newness, and materiality. The "adaptation" of *Raza* to the RAD context occurs primarily in relation to the materiality factor.[66] The Court of Appeal observed:

> As for the fourth implicit criterion identified by this Court in *Raza*, namely, the materiality of the evidence, there may be a need for some adaptations to be made. In the context of a PRRA, the requirement that new evidence be of such significance that it would have allowed the RPD to reach a different conclusion can be explained to the extent that the PRRA officer must show deference to a negative decision by the RPD and may only depart from that principle on the basis of different circumstances or a new risk. The RAD, on the other hand, has a much broader mandate and may intervene to correct any error of fact, of law, or of mixed fact and law. As a result, it may be that although the new evidence is not determinative in and of itself, it may have an impact on the RAD's overall assessment of the RPD's decision.
>
> Under subsection 110(6) of the *IRPA*, a RAD hearing may be held, subject to three conditions associated with the existence of new documentary evidence. The principle whereby the RAD proceeds without holding a hearing, as set out in subsection 110(3), is subject to an exception only where the documentary evidence "(a) [. . .] raises a serious issue with respect to the credibility of the person who is the subject of the appeal; (b) [. . .] is central to the decision with respect to the refugee protection claim; and (c) [. . .] if accepted, would justify allowing or rejecting the refugee protection claim." These three conditions are unquestionably related to the materiality of the new documentary evidence that the RAD could be required

64 2007 FCA 385 at para 13 [*Raza*].

65 *Singh*, above note 57 at para 49.

66 Except for the materiality of new evidence, "it is not necessary to interpret subsection 110(4) and paragraph 113(a) differently." *Singh*, *ibid* at para 64.

> to consider. If such is the case, as one would have reason to believe, it would be redundant to require materiality of evidence for it to be admissible as new evidence, to then subject the conduct of a hearing to the same criterion.[67]

Much discussion unfolded regarding the standard that the RAD is to use on review of RPD decisions. In 2016, this issue was finally clarified by the Federal Court of Appeal decision in *Hugurlica*.[68]

The Court of Appeal concluded that the RAD must apply the correctness standard of review with respect to the RPD's findings of law, fact, and mixed fact and law that raise no issues of credibility of oral evidence. In such cases, the RAD analyzes the RPD's record to determine if there was an error and either upholds or substitutes a decision of the RPD. In contrast, cases that raise issues of credibility and of weight to be given to testimony require a case-by-case approach to determine the level of deference to the RPD. In such cases, the RAD is to consider if "the RPD truly benefited from an advantageous position [of hearing testimony firsthand], and if so, whether the RAD can nevertheless make a final decision in respect of the refugee claim."[69]

5) RAD Decision

Unlike judicial review, an appeal to the RAD could, if successful, result in a final decision. The RAD is not required to remit the matter back to the RPD for re-determination, as is most often the case in the Federal Court. Upon review of a case, the RAD can confirm the decision of the RPD, set it aside and substitute the proper decision, or refer the matter back to the RPD with appropriate directions.[70] The *IRPA* suggests that the latter option should be used only in limited circumstances, namely, when the RPD's decision is wrong in law, in fact, or in mixed law and fact, and where the RAD cannot make a decision on appeal without hearing evidence that was presented to the RPD.[71] This provision acknowledges that "in some cases where oral testimony is critical or determinative in the opinion of the RAD, the RAD may not be in a position to confirm or substitute its own determination to that of the RPD."[72]

---

67 *Ibid* at paras 47–48.

68 Above note 25.

69 *Ibid* at para 70.

70 *IRPA*, above note 17, s 111(1).

71 *Ibid*, s 111(2).

72 *Hugurlica*, above note 25 at para 69.

The RAD must give a decision on an appeal, except in cases where an oral hearing is held, within ninety days after the appeal was perfected.[73] If it is not possible to reach a decision within the prescribed time limit, it must make a decision "as soon as feasible after that time limit."[74]

D. JUDICIAL REVIEW IN THE FEDERAL COURT OF CANADA

The *IRPA* provides for judicial review in the Federal Court of decisions of the RPD, the RAD, and all other decisions made under the *IRPA*[75] (e.g., a decision on a PRRA application, a decision on an application for resettlement from overseas, a decision on a permanent or temporary resident application). Judicial review of immigration decisions, including decisions relating to refugee claimants, constitutes a significant portion of the Federal Court's caseload.[76]

The current scheme, which requires leave before judicial review, is the most restrictive of a long line of statutory regimes which have progressively limited access to judicial review. In previous eras, individuals challenging protection decisions had a right of judicial review by the Supreme Court, the Federal Court of Appeal, and the Federal Court. As recently as 2002, decisions made with respect to protection overseas did not require leave.[77] Now review is by the Federal Court and only by leave of the court. Although the decisions of the Federal Court can still be appealed to higher courts, this is possible only upon certification of serious issues that need to be resolved by higher judicial instances. The increasing restrictions on access to judicial review have been mitigated

---

73 *Regulations*, above note 48, s 159.92(1).

74 *Ibid*, s 159.92(2).

75 Among the decisions most frequently judicially reviewed are pre-removal risk assessment decisions and eligibility decisions. Special procedures for judicial review apply to individuals against whom security certificates have been issued; for a discussion of these individuals and the procedures involved, see Chapter 11.

76 For example, in the past years, 50 to 60 percent of proceedings at the Federal Court related to immigration matters. Courts Administration Service, *Annual Report 2010–11*, online: http://cas-ncr-nter03.cas-satj.gc.ca/portal/page/portal/CAS/AR-RA_eng/AR-RA10-11_eng#link36; *Annual Report 2012–13*, online: http://cas-cdc-www02.cas-satj.gc.ca/portal/page/portal/CAS/AR-RA_eng/AR-RA12-13_eng#RA_02.2; *Annual Report 2014–15*, online: www.cas-satj.gc.ca/en/publications/ar/2014-15/courts-fc_en.html.

77 The *Immigration Act* did not require leave for the judicial review of decisions of visa officers.

slightly by the broader scope of judicial review now performed by the Federal Court.

There are several key differences between an appeal to the RAD and judicial review. First, no new evidence can be introduced on judicial review and it is usually confined to consideration of the evidence that was before the first-instance decision maker. Second, the remedies are different. The Federal Court can only send the matter back for reconsideration, while the RAD can also substitute an RPD decision. There is automatic stay of removal on a RAD appeal and judicial review of RAD decisions. Claimants who are not eligible for a RAD appeal, however, do not have automatic stay of removal upon application of judicial review of an RPD decision. Such applicants may apply for a court-ordered stay. If a stay is not granted, they may be removed prior to determination of their judicial review application, which may also moot the remedies ordered by the Federal Court.

1) Jurisdiction of the Federal Court of Canada

Section 101 of the *Constitution Act, 1867*[78] allows for the establishment of statutory courts.[79] The *Federal Courts Act* establishes the Federal Court and provides it with jurisdiction in all matters involving the *IRPA*.[80] In most cases where an individual seeks review of a negative determination by the RPD or the RAD, the Federal Court has exclusive original jurisdiction.[81]

---

78 Previously, the *British North America Act, 1867* (UK), 30 & 31 Vict c 3.

79 Section 101 of the *Constitution Act, 1867* states as follows: "The Parliament of Canada may, notwithstanding anything in this Act, from Time to Time provide for the Constitution, Maintenance, and Organization of a General Court of Appeal for Canada, and for the Establishment of any additional Courts for the better Administration of the Laws of Canada."

80 No explicit mention of the *IRPA* is found in the *Federal Courts Act*, RSC 1985, c F-7; ss 17 & 18 provide the court with jurisdiction over the types of claims raised by decisions and actions pursuant to the *IRPA*.

81 The Federal Court has exclusive original jurisdiction in all matters involving "any federal board, commission or other tribunal": *Federal Courts Act*, *ibid*, s 18(1)(a). Most applications for judicial review of final determinations of the RPD or the RAD will fall into this category. However, the Federal Court also has concurrent original jurisdiction in all matters against "any person for anything done or omitted to be done in the performance of the duties of that person as an officer, servant, or agent of the Crown" (*Federal Courts Act*, s 17(5)(b)). Any application for judicial review that did not fall within the exclusive original jurisdiction of the Federal Court would, at the very least, fall within its concurrent original jurisdiction.

The jurisdiction of the Federal Court is quite broad. Section 18.1(4) of the *Federal Courts Act* sets out the court's jurisdiction upon judicial review as follows:

> (4) The Federal Court may grant relief under subsection (3) if it is satisfied that the federal board, commission or other tribunal
> (a) acted without jurisdiction, acted beyond its jurisdiction or refused to exercise its jurisdiction;
> (b) failed to observe a principle of natural justice, procedural fairness or other procedure that it was required by law to observe;
> (c) erred in law in making a decision or an order, whether or not the error appears on the face of the record;
> (d) based its decision or order on an erroneous finding of fact that it made in a perverse or capricious manner or without regard for the material before it;
> (e) acted, or failed to act, by reason of fraud or perjured evidence; or
> (f) acted in any other way that was contrary to law.

More generally, the Federal Court has jurisdiction to determine the constitutionality of provisions of the *IRPA*. It also has jurisdiction to determine whether there has been a violation of an individual's rights under the *Canadian Charter of Rights and Freedoms.*[82]

Judicial review of matters under the *IRPA* can occur only with the leave of a judge of the Federal Court.[83] Consequently, an application for judicial review is in fact an application first, for leave for judicial review and, only after leave has been granted, for judicial review. In addition to the *IRPA*, the *Federal Courts Act*, the *Federal Court Rules*, and the *Federal Court Immigration and Refugee Protection Rules* all govern proceedings before the court. Any attempt to seek judicial review can occur only after all other appeals provided for in the *IRPA* have been exhausted.[84]

2) Application for Leave

The requirement that an individual apply for leave for judicial review is unusual. All other matters in the Federal Court occur without leave. The requirement is a relatively recent development dating back to 1993;

---

82 Part 1 of the *Constitution Act, 1982*, being Schedule B to the *Canada Act 1982* (UK), 1982, c 11 [*Charter*]. Under s 24(2), such a jurisdiction falls to "courts of competent jurisdiction."

83 *IRPA*, above note 17, s 72(1).

84 *Ibid*, s 72(2)(a).

it is clearly designed to decrease the volume of review applications dealt with by the court.[85] Historically, only about 10 percent of applications for leave were granted.[86] However, in the past several years, figures (specifically for immigration and refugee applications) tended to vary between 15 and 20 percent, with 2015 documenting the highest grant rate of 33 percent.[87] Unfortunately, as the leave process is entirely paper based, it can lead to applications being refused without an individual ever obtaining her "day in court." Despite scholarly commentary to the contrary, the requirement for leave has repeatedly been held to be constitutionally valid.[88]

For matters arising within Canada, an application for leave for judicial review must be filed within fifteen days of receipt of the decision

---

85 From 1970 to 1978, orders made against persons claiming refugee protection could be appealed with leave of the Federal Court of Appeal. From 1978 to 1989, determinations of refugee status could be judicially reviewed as of right by the Federal Court of Appeal. From 1989 to 1991, determination of refugee status could be judicially reviewed with leave by the Federal Court of Appeal. In 1992, jurisdiction over refugee matters was split, depending on the stage of the proceedings, between the Federal Court of Appeal as before and the Federal Court Trial Division concerning determinations of credible basis. Since 1993, all refugee matters could be judicially reviewed with leave by the Federal Court Trial Division or, as it is now known, the Federal Court. For a full history, see Mary C Hurley, "Principles, Practices, Fragile Promises: Judicial Review of Refugee Determination Decisions before the Federal Court of Canada" (1996) 41 *McGill Law Journal* 317.

86 Inter-American Commission on Human Rights, above note 21 at para 83 (quoting the submissions of the government of Canada). Even within the report there are cited various discordant figures (all obtained from the government) regarding the percentage of successful applications for leave. Historically, the figures have not varied much. Hurley, above note 85, cites figures between 10 and 20 percent in the period between 1989 and 1996.

87 The leave grant rate was approximately 33 percent in 2015 (Federal Court, "Activity Summary — January 1 to December 31, 2015"); 21 percent in 2014 (Federal Court, "Activity Summary — January 1 to December 31, 2014"); 16 percent in 2013 ("Activity Summary — January 1 to December 31, 2013"); 12 percent in 2012 ("Activity Summary — January 1 to December 31, 2012"); 16 percent in 2011 ("Activity Summary — January 1 to December 31, 2011"); and 16 percent in 2010 ("Activity Summary — January 1 to December 31, 2010"). All annual statistical reports are available, online: http://cas-cdc-www02.cas-satj.gc.ca/portal/page/portal/fc_cf_en/Statistics.

88 *Bains v Canada (Minister of Employment and Immigration)* (1989), 109 NR 239 (FCA) [*Bains*], and *Krishnapillai v Canada (Minister of Citizenship and Immigration)*, 2001 FCA 378 [*Krishnapillai*]. However, Heckman disputes the Court of Appeal's brief ruling in *Bains* and its longer ruling in *Krishnapillai* as contrary to international law and the *Charter*, above note 82, s 15. See Gerald P Heckman, "Unfinished Business: *Baker* and the Constitutionality of the Leave and Certification Requirements under the *Immigration Act*" (2002) 27 *Queen's Law Journal* 683.

which is the subject of the application; as for matters arising outside Canada, the application must be filed within sixty days of receipt of the decision.[89] The *IRPA* describes the receipt of the decision as "the day on which the applicant is notified of or otherwise becomes aware of the matter."[90] Not surprisingly, this phrase has been the subject of considerable jurisprudence.[91] However, the court may, upon request, extend the initial fifteen- or sixty-day filing deadline for "special reasons." Any request for an extension of the deadline must be pleaded in the initiating application.[92] The evidentiary and legal basis for such a request must then be set out in the materials filed in support of the application.[93] The court will determine the request at the same time as it determines the application for leave.[94]

Within thirty days of filing the application for leave for judicial review, the applicant must file a memorandum of fact and law containing various documents, supporting evidence, and legal arguments.[95] The respondent then has thirty days to respond to the applicant's memorandum.

The *IRPA* requires the court to "dispose of the application without delay and in a summary way."[96] Consequently, it is rare for the court to issue written reasons regarding its determination of leave; personal appearances are also rare. Although the *IRPA* does not prescribe a test for the determination of leave, the application for leave is judged by the following standard:

> On a leave to commence proceedings application the task is not to determine, as between the parties, which arguments will win on the merits after a hearing. The task is to determine whether the applicants have a fairly arguable case, a serious question to be determined.

---

89 *IRPA*, above note 17, s 72(2)(b).

90 *Ibid.*

91 Much of this jurisprudence arises out of motions for a stay of removal as a result of the individual in question falling within one of the automatic stay provisions (which require filing within the fifteen-day deadline of the *IRPA*, *ibid*, s 72(2)(b)).

92 *IRPA*, *ibid*, s 72(2)(c); *Federal Court Immigration and Refugee Protection Rules*, SOR/93-22 (25 January 1993), r 6(1) [*Federal Court IRPR*].

93 *Ibid*, r 6(2).

94 *Ibid.*

95 The thirty-day time limit may be extended where the applicant has not received a written copy of the decision being challenged; in this case, the thirty-day time limit begins when the applicant subsequently receives the written copy of the decision.

96 *IRPA*, above note 17, s 72(2)(d).

> If so then leave should be granted and the applicants allowed to have their argument heard.[97]

In other words, an application for leave should be granted "unless it is plain and obvious that the applicant would have no reasonable chance of succeeding."[98] While this standard may seem permissive, in practice, only a relatively small number of applications for leave for judicial review of decisions under the *IRPA* are granted. Research revealed significant disparities in the leave grant rates among Federal Court justices.[99] Further, most disturbingly, outcomes of leave applications seemed to depend largely on which judge was assigned to the case.[100] This arbitrary barrier on access to judicial review appears particularly problematic given that decisions on leave applications cannot be appealed.[101]

The leave and certification (for further appeal) procedures are screening mechanisms that allow courts to carry out their tasks with greater efficiency. The leave is supposed to prevent individuals from abusing the process, while the certification procedure is intended to help better allocate scarce resources by limiting the flow of appeals to serious questions only.[102] Some scholars argued that both requirements discriminate against non-citizens.[103] However, the courts disagreed. The Federal Court and the Federal Court of Appeal held that the requirement of leave did not deny refugee claimants access to the Federal Court and did not impair their rights under either section 7 or 15 of the *Charter*.[104] Similarly, the certification requirement was found to be consistent with section 15. The court noted that "[o]f necessity, the *Immigration Act* deals differently with citizens and non-citizens, including refugee claimants. Citizens have a constitutionally protected right to enter Canada, whereas the only right of non-citizens to do so flows from the *Immigration Act* itself. Accordingly, citizenship is not an irrelevant personal characteristic."[105]

---

97 *Wu v Canada (Minister of Employment and Immigration)*, [1989] FCJ No 29 at para 11 (TD).

98 *Saleh v Canada (Minister of Employment and Immigration)*, [1989] FCJ No 825 (TD).

99 Sean Rehaag, "Judicial Review of Refugee Determinations: The Luck of the Draw?" (2012) 38 *Queen's Law Journal* 1.

100 *Ibid.*

101 *IRPA*, above note 17, s 72(2)(e).

102 Heckman, above note 88 at 699.

103 *Ibid.*

104 *Bains*, above note 88; *Krishnapillai*, above note 88.

105 *Huynh v Canada (Minister of Citizenship and Immigration)*, [1996] 2 FC 976 at para 7 (CA).

3) Application for Judicial Review

While the application for leave is a paper process, once leave is granted an oral hearing on the underlying judicial review application is scheduled. According to the *IRPA*, a hearing must be scheduled between thirty and ninety days after the granting of leave.[106] In practice, this can lead to delays in the formal granting of leave as the court is unable to formally grant leave until it is able to physically accommodate the hearing of the application within this time frame. Upon granting leave, the court requests the "record of proceedings" from the decision maker in question.

Although judicial review is principally concerned with the evidence as it was at the date of the decision, it is possible to present new evidence. The most common form of "new" evidence is evidence of a defect in the proceedings that led to the decision being challenged. More specifically, most new evidence attempts to establish either deficient interpretation or prejudicial comments or occurrences that are not otherwise reflected in the record. In many respects, such evidence is not strictly "new" as it relates to matters that were before the decision maker at the time of the decision and events in which the decision maker participated. The court is much less favourably disposed to other types of new evidence, particularly documentary material that the applicant failed to present at an earlier occasion.

In any case, such evidence is presented in the form of sworn affidavits. Either party may challenge the new evidence presented by the opposing party either by motion, in argument at the hearing, or by cross-examination. In addition, in advance of the hearing of the judicial review, either party may provide additional submissions of legal argument.

Hearings of judicial review applications typically last no more than two hours. During this time counsel for the parties present legal arguments and respond to questions from the judge. Decisions are then made either orally from the bench or, more commonly, at a subsequent date in writing. Judicial review hearings are conducted in open court.

4) Standard of Review

Standard of review can be characterized as the "degree of rigour with which a court will scrutinize an agency's decision."[107] As set out in

---

106 *IRPA*, above note 17, s 74(b) (unless the parties agree to an earlier date).

107 John Swaigen, *Administrative Law: Principles and Advocacy*, 2d ed (Toronto: Emond Montgomery, 2010) at 358.

the Supreme Court decision in *Dunsmuir v New Brunswick*,[108] there are two standards of review: (1) reasonableness and (2) correctness. The reasonableness standard focuses on "the existence of justification, transparency and intelligibility within the decision-making process" and considers "whether the decision falls within a range of possible, acceptable outcomes which are defensible in respect of the facts and law."[109] This standard gives some deference to the original decision maker. While the reasonableness standard acknowledges that there may be more than one reasonable outcome,[110] the correctness standard connotes that there is only one correct answer to a given question and allows no deference to the original decision maker.

The standard of review will vary according to the nature of the alleged error and the specific topic of the question under review.[111] For example, decisions of the Immigration Division of the Board, which for refugee claimants largely concern issues of detention, will be held to a different standard of review than decisions of the RPD or RAD.[112] If a standard of review with respect to a particular type of question has not been specified in enabling legislation or has not been already settled by prior caselaw, the proper standard is determined based on the following factors:

- presence or absence of a privative clause;
- the purpose of the agency, as set out in the enabling legislation;
- the nature of the question at issue: law, fact, mixed law and fact;
- the expertise of the agency.[113]

The following factors usually point to the reasonableness standard: presence of a privative clause; special expertise of the original decision maker; and the review being in relation to questions of law that are within the specialized expertise of the original decision maker.[114] The standard of correctness would usually be employed in relation to constitutional issues; issues of law that fall outside the specialized expertise of the administrative decision maker; and questions of jurisdiction.

---

108 2008 SCC 9 [*Dunsmuir*].

109 *Ibid* at para 47; see also *Canada (Citizenship and Immigration) v Khosa*, 2009 SCC 12 at paras 59 and 62 [*Khosa*].

110 *Khosa*, *ibid* at para 88.

111 *Canada (Minister of Citizenship and Immigration) v Thanabal*, [2004] 3 FCR 523 (FC); *Khosa*, above note 109 at para 36.

112 For example, the members of the IRB's Immigration Division are employees of the Ministry and career civil servants, not Governor in Council temporally limited appointments as is the case with the RAD.

113 *Dunsmuir*, above note 108 at para 55.

114 *Ibid* at para 55.

Jurisprudence has already established the standards applicable to review of various types of issues arising in immigration and refugee context. For example, the following are reviewed on the standard of correctness: issues of procedural fairness;[115] findings of law by CBSA officers in relation to eligibility of refugee claims;[116] and fettering of discretion by the Board or immigration officers.[117] For the following, the standard of reasonableness has been used: RPD assessments of credibility and factual findings;[118] RPD decisions on applications to reopen;[119] RPD decisions regarding existence of an internal flight alternative;[120] RPD decisions regarding nexus to a Convention ground;[121] and decisions of officers pertaining to pre-removal risk assessments and humanitarian and compassionate (H&C) grounds.[122]

5) Relief upon Judicial Review

It is rare for the court to make an order determining an individual to be a Convention refugee or person in need of protection upon successful judicial review. Most decisions of the court simply quash the decision

---

115 *Mission Institution v Khela*, 2014 SCC 24 at para 79 [*Khela*]; *Khosa*, above note 109 at para 43; *Liu v Canada (Minister of Citizenship and Immigration)*, 2008 FC 836.

116 *Canada (Minister of Citizenship and Immigration) v Tobar Toledo*, 2013 FCA 226.

117 *Zaki v Canada (Minister of Citizenship and Immigration)*, 2005 FC 1066; *Benitez v Canada (Minister of Citizenship and Immigration)*, 2006 FC 461; *Thamotharem v Canada (Minister of Citizenship and Immigration)*, 2007 FCA 198.

118 *Qarizada v Canada (Minister of Citizenship and Immigration)*, 2008 FC 1310 at para 17; *Nassima v Canada (Minister of Citizenship and Immigration)*, 2008 FC 688 at paras 8–9; *Singh*, above note 57 at para 29; *Hugurlica*, above note 25 at para 35; *Gebremichael v Canada (Minister of Citizenship and Immigration)*, 2016 FC 646 at para 8; *Ghauri v Canada (Minister of Citizenship and Immigration)*, 2016 FC 548 at para 22; *Voloshyn v Canada (Minister of Citizenship and Immigration)*, 2016 FC 480 at para 15; *Sui v Canada (Minister of Citizenship and Immigration)*, 2016 FC 406 at para 14; *Ketchen v Canada (Minister of Citizenship and Immigration)*, 2016 FC 388 at para 20; *Zacarias v Canada (Minister of Citizenship and Immigration)*, 2012 FC 1155; *Lakatos v Canada (Minister of Citizenship and Immigration)*, 2014 FC 785 [*Lakatos*].

119 *Gurgus v Canada (Minister of Citizenship and Immigration)*, 2014 FC 9 at para 19; *Yan v Canada (Minister of Citizenship and Immigration)*, 2010 FC 1270.

120 *Jimenez v Canada (Minister of Citizenship and Immigration)*, 2014 FC 780; *Aramburo v Canada (Minister of Citizenship and Immigration)*, 2013 FC 984.

121 *Balachandran v Canada (Minister of Citizenship and Immigration)*, 2014 FC 800; *Melendez v Canada (Minister of Citizenship and Immigration)*, 2014 FC 700.

122 *Wang v Canada (Minister of Citizenship and Immigration)*, 2010 FC 799 at para 11; *Aleziri v Canada (Minister of Citizenship and Immigration)*, 2009 FC 38 at para 11; *Din v Canada (Minister of Citizenship and Immigration)*, 2013 FC 356 at para 5; *Kisana v Canada (Minister of Citizenship and Immigration)*, 2009 FCA 189 at para 18.

being challenged and refer the matter back to a new member of the RPD or the RAD, or a new immigration officer. Occasionally, the court will give directions to the new decision maker as to how to consider the matter in arriving at a new decision. With the exception of judicial reviews that succeed based upon a failure in natural justice, and absent any directions by the court to the contrary, a matter referred back to the RPD or the RAD will be determined by a new Board member.[123]

6) Doctrine of Mootness

As discussed further below in relation to interlocutory motions, mootness can be an issue where an applicant is challenging a decision that triggers his removal from Canada and, by the time of the determination of the application for judicial review, he has already been removed. This situation arises most frequently when the individual is not protected by an automatic statutory or regulatory stay of removal and fails to obtain a judicial stay of removal.

The general rules on mootness were formulated by the Supreme Court of Canada in *Borowski v Canada (Attorney General).*[124] A case is moot where it fails to meet a "live controversy" test. The doctrine of mootness prescribes that a court may decline to decide a case that raises merely a hypothetical or an abstract question. In other words, a court should not decide a case where a decision would not have any practical effect on the rights of the parties.[125]

To determine whether to proceed with a case, courts follow the two-step *Borowski* test. First, a court is to determine whether the tangible and concrete dispute has disappeared and the issues have become merely academic. Thus, the way a given controversy is characterized will be largely determinative of the issue of mootness.[126] If the answer to the first question is in the affirmative, the court proceeds to the second step and decides whether to nevertheless exercise its discretion to hear the case. A decision whether to exercise discretion hinges on the consideration of the reasons upon which the doctrine of mootness is based: the need for an adversarial context, the concern for judicial economy, and the need for the court to demonstrate a measure of

---

123 Immigration and Refugee Board, Policy on Court Ordered Redeterminations (2013), online: IRB www.irb-cisr.gc.ca/Eng/BoaCom/references/pol/pol/Pages/PolOrderOrdon.aspx.

124 [1989] 1 SCR 342 [*Borowski*].

125 *Ibid* at paras 15–16.

126 *Baron v Canada (Minister of Public Safety and Emergency Preparedness)*, 2009 FCA 81 at para 29.

awareness of its proper law-making function.[127] In light of these rationales, discretion may be justified where a decision would have collateral consequences for the parties, where a case involves issues of public importance, or where issues, although moot, are recurring.

In the immigration and refugee context, the most frequently arising question is: does an applicant's removal from Canada effectively render his pending application for judicial review moot? Recent jurisprudence provided some answers, highlighting that much depends on the nature of the underlying judicial review application. Where judicial review concerns a PRRA application, removal of the applicant makes the application moot.[128] This is so because

> [. . .] Parliament intended that the PRRA should be determined before the PRRA applicant is removed from Canada, to avoid putting her or him at risk in her or his country of origin. To this extent, if a PRRA applicant is removed from Canada before a determination is made on the risks to which that person would be subject to in her or his country of origin, the intended objective of the PRRA system can no longer be met. Indeed, this explains why section 112 of the Act specifies that a person applying for protection is a "person in Canada."
>
> By the same logic, a review of a negative decision of a PRRA officer after the subject person has been removed from Canada, is without object.[129]

Where judicial review concerns an RPD decision, the answer depends on whether the challenged determination involves section 96 or section 97 of the *IRPA*. By definition, section 97 (as well as section 112, which concerns PRRAs) deals with risks to a person "in Canada." Thus, like a judicial review of a negative determination under section 112, a review of a negative decision with respect to section 97 becomes moot once the applicant is removed from Canada.[130] The situation is different, however, when a claim is made under section 96, which requires

127 *Borowski*, above note 124 at paras 29–42.

128 *Perez v Canada (Minister of Citizenship and Immigration)*, 2009 FCA 171 [*Perez*]; *Lakatos*, above note 118; *Rosa v Canada (Minister of Citizenship and Immigration)*, 2014 FC 1234 at paras 34–35 [*Rosa*]. However, the court may nevertheless exercise its discretion to hear the matter. *Shpati v Canada (Minister of Public Safety and Emergency Preparedness)*, 2011 FCA 286 at para 30 [*Shpati*].

129 *Perez*, above note 128 at para 5, quoting the lower court's decision.

130 *Ibid*; *Shpati*, above note 128 at para 30.

only that the claimant be outside her country of nationality.[131] As the Federal Court stated in *Rosa v Canada (Citizenship and Immigration)*:

> In a judicial review of a negative PPRA [*sic*] decision, there would be little point in sending the matter back for redetermination by a different PRRA officer, because the applicant would no longer be "in Canada," as required by those provisions. In that context, it is readily apparent that the judicial review would be without object (*Solis Perez*, above).
>
> The same cannot be said with respect to a judicial review of a negative decision by the RPD under section 96. There is no specific requirement in section 96 that the refugee claimant still be in Canada at the time of the redetermination. In the absence of clear wording in the *IRPA* to the contrary, I reject the Respondent's position that the RPD does not have the jurisdiction to reconsider an application under section 96 once the applicant has properly been removed from Canada, even if this Court determines that the RPD committed a reviewable error in denying the application . . . .
>
> In my view, the RPD does have the jurisdiction to reconsider an application initially made pursuant to section 96 and in accordance with subsection 99(3) in such circumstances, provided that the applicant is outside each of his or her countries of nationality. Contrary to the respondent's position, there continues to be a "live controversy" in respect of the application in those circumstances, and therefore, an application for judicial review of the RPD's initial decision is not moot.[132]

It is important to note that in *Rosa*, the applicant was removed from Canada, but, at the time of examination of his judicial review application was outside his country of alleged persecution (and nationality). Would the same conclusion on mootness be reached where an applicant was removed to and remains in her country of nationality? In *Molnar v Canada (Citizenship and Immigration)*, the Federal Court determined that such application for judicial review was not moot. It wrote:

> . . . I am not prepared to find that the rights conferred on the Applicants by the *IRPA* are lost simply because the Applicants were involuntarily removed from Canada following a removal order executed by the Respondent, in accordance with its statutory obligations

131 *Rosa*, above note 128; *Molnar v Canada (Minister of Citizenship and Immigration)*, 2015 FC 345 at para 24 [*Molnar*]; *Magyar v Canada (Minister of Citizenship and Immigration)*, 2015 FC 750.

132 *Rosa*, above note 128 at paras 35–37.

> under the *IRPA*. It is important to note that the Applicants were successful in their application for leave to seek judicial review. The fact that their judicial review application could be defeated simply by reason of the enforcement of a removal order would render their rights illusory. It also opens the door to removal orders being enforced with the intent of depriving this Court of the opportunity to exercise its supervisory jurisdiction.[133]

The *Molnar* decision is currently on appeal with the following question certified: "Is an application for judicial review of a decision of the Refugee Protection Division moot where the individual who is the subject of the decision has involuntarily returned to his or her country of nationality, and, if yes, should the Court normally refuse to exercise its discretion to hear it?"

E. MOTIONS FOR INTERLOCUTORY RELIEF

The Federal Court also has jurisdiction to grant relief while a proceeding is in progress. This includes relief related to the proceeding itself, such as variation of deadlines and disclosure of evidence, as well as matters outside the proceeding. What is most important for those in the process of challenging a decision related to refugee protection is that the court has the jurisdiction to stay the effect of an immigration/refugee decision. In practical terms, this allows the court to prevent the removal of an individual from Canada until the outcome of his judicial review application is determined.

While in many instances the operation of a decision related to protection is stayed by statute or regulation until the resolution of judicial review (see Chapter 12), in some cases, an individual must seek an explicit injunction.[134] As a result of the 2012 legislative changes, higher numbers of rejected refugee claimants no longer enjoy automatic stay of removal. While in the past, all rejected claimants (except for those whose claims were determined to have no credible basis) received automatic stay upon application for judicial review, claimants from designated countries of origin[135] and designated foreign nationals[136] are currently excluded. In addition, the following groups also must seek

---

133 *Mrda v Canada (Minister of Citizenship and Immigration)*, 2016 FC 49.

134 For a more detailed discussion of statutory and regulatory stays of removal, see Chapter 12.

135 *Regulations*, above note 18, ss 231(1) & (2).

136 *Ibid*.

court-ordered stay: claimants whose claims were determined by the RPD as having "no credible basis" or being "manifestly unfounded," individuals inadmissible on grounds of serious criminality, or individuals resident in the United States or St Pierre and Miquelon.[137] Decisions on refugee claims' eligibility, PRRA decisions, and RPD decisions on abandonment and withdrawal of claims are also not included in automatic stay of removal.[138] Further, all applications for judicial review of RPD or RAD decisions which are filed after the limitation period do not benefit from an automatic stay.[139]

Injunctions (particularly on removal) benefit the individual challenging the decision insofar as they allow her to remain in Canada pending the outcome of her challenge. A court-ordered stay of removal may also be legally necessary for the success of the challenge: as discussed above, the removal of an individual from Canada has been repeatedly found by the Federal Court to render the challenge of certain protection-related decisions moot.[140] Unless there has been an error in the exercise of the court's jurisdiction, decisions upon interlocutory motions, including stays of removal, are final.[141]

In order to obtain an injunction, according to the criteria laid out in the much-cited case of *Toth v Canada (Minister of Employment and Immigration)*,[142] the moving party must establish three elements:

1) that there is a serious question to be tried;
2) that the moving party would suffer irreparable harm if the injunction were not granted; and
3) that the balance of convenience is in favour of the moving party.

The first component of the *Toth* test requires the applicants to establish that the underlying judicial review application raises a serious issue. The threshold for this issue is relatively low: the issue must not be frivolous and there must be at least some prospect of success.[143] At the very least, there must be a direct challenge to the removal or a decision concerning the individual's status in Canada.[144] The existence of

137 *Ibid*, s 232(3).

138 Abandonment and no credible basis decisions are, respectively, not covered by the regulatory stay of the *Regulations*, *ibid*, s 232(1).

139 *Ibid*, s 231(4).

140 As discussed above, this is so with respect to PRRA decisions or RPD decisions on protection under s 97 of the *IRPA*. *Perez*, above note 128 at para 5; *Shpati*, above note 128 at para 30.

141 *Razzaq v Canada (Solicitor General)*, 2006 FC 442.

142 (1988), 86 NR 302 (FCA) [*Toth*].

143 *Abazi v Canada (Minister of Citizenship and Immigration)*, [2000] FCJ No 429 (TD).

144 *Okolo v Canada (Minister of Citizenship and Immigration)*, [2001] FCJ No 23 (TD).

a court application by itself does not constitute a serious issue to be tried.[145]

With respect to the second branch of the *Toth* test, irreparable harm can refer either to (1) personal harm that will befall the claimant if the injunction is not granted, or (2) the legal consequences for the challenge if the injunction is not granted. The threshold for the first type of irreparable harm is relatively high: harm must be personal and must be proven on the balance of probabilities with clear and non-speculative evidence.[146] For example, where applicants are challenging the IRB's assessment of risk in their country of origin, they may also rely on the same risk to demonstrate irreparable harm.[147] However, normal consequences of deportation do not amount to irreparable harm.[148] As noted by the court in *Melo v Canada (Minister of Citizenship and Immigration)*:

> But if the phrase irreparable harm is to retain any meaning at all, it must refer to some prejudice beyond that which is inherent in the notion of deportation itself. To be deported is to lose your job, to be separated from familiar faces and places. It is accompanied by enforced separation and heartbreak. There is nothing in Mr. Melo's circumstances which takes it out of the usual consequences of deportation . . . . As unhappy as these circumstances are, they do not engage any interests beyond those which are inherent in the nature of a deportation.[149]

With respect to the second type of irreparable harm, some caselaw has recognized that sometimes the very refusal to grant a stay pending judicial review will constitute irreparable harm by effectively preventing the court from determining the underlying application.[150] Such an irreparable harm is of legal as opposed to physical nature: the harm will be caused by the application becoming legally moot and hence unable to be determined by the court. The evolution of this understanding of irreparable harm can be traced to the court's increasing use of the doctrine of mootness, as discussed earlier, to dismiss applications for judicial review. Courts, however, made sure to emphasize that the

---

145 *Akyol v Canada (Minister of Citizenship and Immigration)*, [2003] FCJ No 1182 (FC).

146 *Radji v Canada (Citizenship and Immigration)*, 2007 FC 100.

147 *Ahmed v Canada (Minister of Citizenship and Immigration)*, 2015 FC 936 at para 12.

148 *Ali v Canada (Minister of Citizenship and Immigration)*, 2007 FC 751; *Atwal v Canada (Minister of Citizenship and Immigration)*, 2004 FCA 427; *Thanabalasingham v Canada (Minister of Public Safety and Emergency Preparedness)*, 2006 FC 486.

149 [2000] FCJ No 403 at para 21 (TD).

150 *Suresh v Canada*, [1998] OJ No 296 (Gen Div).

potential mootness of the underlying judicial review application due to the applicant's removal does not always and automatically constitute irreparable harm.[151] Otherwise, it would apply in virtually all removal cases and "would essentially deprive the Court of the discretion to decide questions of irreparable harm on the facts of each case."[152] Whether removal would result in irreparable harm depends on the circumstances of the case and on how courts exercise their discretion. (As mentioned above, a court may decide to hear even a moot application if, for instance, it raises issues of a recurring nature.)

The balance of convenience branch of the *Toth* test is most commonly decided along the same lines as the determination of whether there will be irreparable harm. In cases where the failure to grant a stay will result in irreparable harm, the balance of convenience will usually favour the individual remaining in Canada. The exception to this proposition are individuals who pose a risk to the public[153] or have behaved deceitfully in the past. Where no irreparable harm has been established, the balance of convenience will never favour a stay of removal (although technically the consideration of the third branch of the *Toth* test in such a case is moot).[154]

F. FURTHER APPEAL OF FEDERAL COURT DECISIONS IN JUDICIAL REVIEW

An appeal to the Federal Court of Appeal may be made only if the matter in question has been judicially reviewed in the Federal Court. In such a case, an appeal to the Federal Court of Appeal can occur if the judge determining the matter certifies that a "serious question of general importance" is involved and states that question.[155] A certified question is both material to the outcome of the matter at hand and relevant beyond the immediate matter:

> In order to be certified pursuant to s. 83(1), a question must be one which, in the opinion of the motions judge, transcends the interests

---

151 *El Ouardi v Canada (Solicitor General)*, 2005 FCA 42 at para 8 [*El Ouardi*]; *Palka v Canada (Minister of Public Safety and Emergency Preparedness)*, 2008 FCA 165 at para 20.

152 *El Ouardi*, above note 151 at para 8.

153 *Sittampalam v Canada (Minister of Citizenship and Immigration)*, 2010 FC 562.

154 *Perry v Canada (Minister of Public Safety and Emergency Preparedness)*, [2006] FCJ No 473 (FC).

155 *IRPA*, above note 17, s 74(d).

of the immediate parties to the litigation and contemplates issues of broad significance or general application.[156]

Notwithstanding that the judge has certified a particular question, the Federal Court of Appeal is not restricted to the consideration of that question. As stated in *Pushpanathan v Canada (Minister of Citizenship and Immigration)*, the certification of a question of general importance is the "trigger" by which an appeal is justified: "The object of the appeal is still the judgment itself, not merely the certified question."[157] Further appeal lies to the Supreme Court of Canada by leave.[158]

G. ACCESS TO PROVINCIAL COURTS

Provincial superior courts and the Federal Court have concurrent jurisdiction to deal with constitutional or *Charter* issues arising in immigration matters.[159] Thus, in some cases, applicants have turned to provincial courts to seek relief in relation to immigration matters. However, the routine resort to provincial courts could raise concerns over forum-shopping, inconsistency, and multiplicity of proceedings.[160] Of particular concern to the courts has been the use of provincial superior courts as a forum for relief after the admittedly limited federal judicial remedies are exhausted. Thus, jurisprudence generally established that where primarily immigration matters are concerned, the Federal Court is the proper forum.[161] The deference of provincial superior courts to the Federal Court has been described as follows:

---

156 *Canada (Minister of Citizenship and Immigration) v Liyanagamage*, [1994] FCJ No 1637 at para 4 (CA).

157 [1998] 1 SCR 982 at para 25.

158 *Supreme Court Act*, RSC 1985, c S-26, ss 39.1 and 40.

159 *Reza v Canada*, [1994] 2 SCR 394 at para 21 [*Reza*]; *Francis (Litigation Guardian of) v Canada (Minister of Citizenship and Immigration)* (1999), 49 OR (3d) 136 (CA) [*Francis*]. The inherent jurisdiction of the provincial superior courts cannot be disturbed by federal legislation. *Canada (Attorney General) v Law Society of British Columbia*, [1982] 2 SCR 307.

160 Justice Abella's dissent in *Reza v Canada*, [1992] OJ No 2300 (CA). For example, in *Jaballah v Canada (Attorney General)*, [2005] OJ No 3681 at para 49 (SCJ) [*Jaballah*], an Ontario court echoed the same concern, stating that "[a]ny such inconsistency between this [provincial] Court and the Federal Court on such important legal issues for the implementation of *IRPA* is not in the public interest and may undermine the public confidence in the administration of justice."

161 Justice Abella's dissent in *Reza v Canada*, above note 160; *May v Ferndale Institution*, 2005 SCC 82; *Mohammad v Canada (Attorney General)*, 2013 ONSC 2936.

> This court has expressed the view that, generally, immigration matters are best dealt with under the comprehensive scheme established under that Act. Judicial review of decisions made under that Act are best left to the Federal Court. That is not to say that the provincial superior court should always yield to the jurisdiction of the Federal Court. There will be situations in which the Federal Court is not an effective or appropriate forum in which to seek the relief claimed. In those rare cases, the superior court can properly exercise its jurisdiction.[162]

It is also recognized that the Federal Court possesses extensive expertise in immigration and administrative law.[163] Thus, provincial superior courts will generally decline to grant relief, including under writs of *habeas corpus*, unless it can be shown that review in the Federal Court will be less advantageous. Although there is a requirement for leave to the Federal Court this does not automatically render it less advantageous.[164] An applicant cannot use a superior court to challenge an immigration matter simply because there is little hope for success in the Federal Court.[165] This is known as the *Peiroo* exception: "where a complete, comprehensive and expert statutory scheme provides for a review that is at least as broad as and no less advantageous than *habeas corpus*, *habeas corpus* is precluded."[166]

However, as recently decided in *Chaudhary v Canada (Minister of Public Safety and Emergency Preparedness)*,[167] the *Peiroo* exception is not a blanket exclusion of *habeas corpus* in all matters related to immigration law. In *Chaudhary*, the appellants challenged not a core immigration issue (as was the case in *Peiroo v Canada (Minister of Employment and Immigration)*), but sought the determination of the legality of their continued detention. They argued that the detention had become illegal because of its length (they were detained between two and eight years while awaiting deportation) and the uncertainty of its continued

162 *Francis*, above note 159 at para 12 (quoted with approval in *Wozniak v Brunton*, [2003] OJ No 1679 at para 41 (SCJ)). See also *Reza v Canada* (dissenting opinion of Abella J), above note 160, aff'd by the SCC, above note 159 at paras 10 and 18; *Sittampalam v Canada (Attorney General)*, 2010 ONSC 3205.

163 Justice Abella's dissent in *Reza v Canada*, above note 160, aff'd by the SCC, above note 159; *Jaballah*, above note 160 at para 45.

164 *Peiroo v Canada (Minister of Employment and Immigration)* (1989), 69 OR (2d) 253 at 259 (CA) [*Peiroo*].

165 *Francis (Litigation guardian of) v Canada (Attorney General)* (2003), 171 OAC 198 at para 5 (CA).

166 *Peiroo*, above note 164.

167 2015 ONCA 700 [*Chaudhary*].

duration and that, in this context, the *Peiroo* exception did not apply. The Ontario Court of Appeal agreed and concluded that the appellants had a right to choose whether to have their detention-related issues heard in the Federal Court through judicial review of the Immigration Division's decision, or in the Superior Court through a *habeas corpus* application.[168]

It is worth noting that issuing a writ of *habeas corpus* is not included in the list of remedies that can be provided by the Federal Court under the *Federal Courts Act*.[169] As concluded by the Supreme Court, "habeas corpus was 'deliberately omit[ted]' from the list of writs set out in s. 18 of the *FCA*. This means that although the Federal Court has a general review jurisdiction, it cannot issue the writ of habeas corpus . . . . Jurisdiction to grant *habeas corpus* with regard to inmates remains with the provincial superior courts."[170] In the recent case of *Warssama v Canada (Minister of Citizenship and Immigration)*,[171] the Federal Court engaged in detailed discussion, in *obiter*, on the issue of *habeas corpus*, noting that it seemed "somewhat peculiar" that the Federal Court cannot issue a writ of *habeas corpus*, despite dealing with detention in immigration and penitentiary matters "day in and day out." In the words of Harrington J: "Perhaps the last word [on Federal Court's jurisdiction over *habeas corpus*] has yet to be written, either by the courts or by Parliament."[172]

H. INTERNATIONAL REMEDIES

In addition to the various domestic mechanisms of recourse, there also exist international legal remedies since Canada is a party to numerous regional and international human rights treaties. While these remedies provide additional options for individuals refused protection, they also suffer from certain limitations (including, most notably, their ambiguous status in domestic law). These will be discussed below.

---

168 *Ibid* at para 113.

169 Section 18(1) of the *Federal Courts Act*, above note 80, reads: "Subject to section 28, the Federal Court has exclusive original jurisdiction . . . to issue an injunction, writ of certiorari, writ of prohibition, writ of *mandamus* or writ of *quo warranto*, or grant declaratory relief, against any federal board, commission or other tribunal." *Habeas corpus* is provided for as a remedy only "in relation to any member of the Canadian Forces serving outside Canada" under s 18(2).

170 *Khela*, above note 115 at para 32.

171 2015 FC 1311.

172 *Ibid* at para 56.

1) Available International Forums

The available international forums from which an individual may seek a remedy may be grouped into two categories: (1) forums related to Canada's membership in the United Nations, and (2) forums related to specific treaty obligations undertaken by Canada. The former group includes the UN Human Rights Council, which conducts Universal Periodic Review of UN member states' human rights records, and the various special procedures it has established. The latter group is comprised of both UN and regional treaty bodies which are empowered to monitor states parties' compliance with their obligations under the respective treaties and to receive complaints on non-compliance. Each of these forums will be discussed briefly below.

a) Universal Periodic Review

The Universal Periodic Review (UPR) is a state-driven process that involves periodic review of the human rights records of all UN member states. It was established in 2006 by a UN General Assembly resolution. Reviews are conducted on a cycle by the UPR Working Group, which consists of forty-seven members of the UN Human Rights Council. The review is based on information provided by the state under review; information contained in the reports of UN Special Procedures (see Section H(1)(b), below), human rights treaty bodies, and other UN entities; and information from other stakeholders, including non-governmental organizations. A state's human rights record is assessed on the standards set out in the *Charter of the United Nations*,[173] the UN *Universal Declaration of Human Rights*,[174] human rights instruments to which that state is party, voluntary pledges and commitments made by the state, and international humanitarian law.

The Working Group is assisted by "troikas" of states who serve as rapporteurs. A review session takes the form of an interactive dialogue where not only the Working Group, but also any UN member state can participate. During the discussion, states can pose questions, make comments, and provide recommendations to the state under review. Upon completion of the session, an outcome report containing a summary of the discussion, comments, and recommendations is produced. Although the UPR examines the whole human rights record of a given state and not just immigration or refugee-related issues, it can spotlight the latter matters and offer recommendations for improvement.

---

173 26 June 1945, Can TS 1945 No 7 [UN *Charter*].

174 GA Res 217(III), UNGAOR, 3d Sess, Supp No 13, UN Doc A/810, (1948).

b) UN Special Procedures

In addition to the Universal Periodic Review, the UN has established various other bodies, under the jurisdiction of its *Charter*, to monitor specific human rights issues.[175] The system of Special Procedures is one such mechanism. Under this system, independent human rights experts appointed by the UN (Special Rapporteurs, Independent Experts, and Working Groups) are mandated to report and advise on various human rights issues either thematically or by country. They can undertake country visits; act on individual cases and concerns of a structural nature; conduct thematic studies; convene expert consultations; engage in advocacy and public awareness campaigns; and provide advice and support for technical co-operation.

In 2015, there were forty-one thematic mandates and fourteen country mandates. The Special Procedures most relevant to individuals seeking refugee protection include the Working Group on Arbitrary Detention; the Working Group on Enforced or Involuntary Disappearances; the Special Rapporteur on extrajudicial, summary, or arbitrary executions; the Special Rapporteur on the situation of human rights defenders; the Special Rapporteur on the rights of internally displaced persons; the Special Rapporteur on the human rights of migrants; the Special Rapporteur on torture and other cruel, inhuman, or degrading treatment or punishment; and the Special Rapporteur on violence against women, its causes and consequences. Additional mechanisms defined by country mandates may also be appropriate for individuals facing return to those countries.

The Special Procedures bodies have the power to intervene on behalf of individuals by sending a communication to a given government in relation to an alleged violation. These communications can relate to a human rights violation that has already occurred, is ongoing, or which has a high risk of taking place. Any individual, group, or civil-society organization can submit information on alleged violations to the Special Procedure. However, intervention is discretionary and the criteria that must be fulfilled for intervention vary from one procedure to the other.

c) UN Treaty Monitoring Bodies

The most legally meaningful international forums in which to seek an individual remedy stem from Canada's international treaty obligations. The *Convention Against Torture and Other Cruel, Inhuman or Degrading*

175 For the list of Special Procedures, see www.ohchr.org/EN/HRBodies/SP/Pages/Welcomepage.aspx.

Treatment or Punishment[176] and the *International Covenant on Civil and Political Rights*[177] have been most frequently used to challenge various immigration and asylum measures (such as removal to alleged countries of persecution or torture, or the prolonged detention of asylum seekers). In addition to stipulating states parties' obligations, the *Convention Against Torture* and the *Optional Protocol to the ICCPR* establish committees entrusted with monitoring states parties' compliance with their obligations and receiving individual complaints of violations: the Committee against Torture deals with obligations under the *Convention Against Torture*, and the Human Rights Committee deals with obligations under the *ICCPR*. Canada has accepted the jurisdiction of the Committee against Torture and of the Human Rights Committee to adjudicate individual complaints. Consequently, individuals may petition a respective treaty body if they believe that Canada has failed to meet its obligations under the *Convention Against Torture* or the *ICCPR*. These two bodies have received many complaints concerning Canada.[178]

As the jurisdiction of treaty-monitoring bodies is circumscribed by the terms of the treaty, any complaint will go through a two-step process: (1) a determination of its admissibility; and (2) if it is admissible, a determination of its merits. Admissibility requirements vary by treaty but usually include the following: (1) the state in question recognizes the competence of the committee;[179] (2) all domestic remedies have been exhausted;[180] (3) a complaint is not anonymous;[181] (4) a complaint is not ill-founded or an abuse of process; and (5) the same matter

176 10 December 1984, [1987] Can TS No 36 [*Convention Against Torture*].

177 GA Res 2200A (XXI) 21 UN GAOR Supp (No 16) at 52, UN Doc A/6316 (1966), 999 UNTS 171 [*ICCPR*].

178 As of March 2016, the number of complaints filed against Canada with the Human Rights Committee was the highest among other states parties (218 out of 2,756 total complaints): Human Rights Committee, "Statistical Survey on Individual Complaints" (as of March 2016), online: www.ohchr.org/EN/HRBodies/CCPR/Pages/CCPRIntro.aspx. As of August 2015, the number of complaints against Canada was the third highest among complaints received by the Committee against Torture (124 out of 697 total complaints): Committee against Torture, "Statistical Survey on Individual Complaints" (as of 15 August 2015), online: OHCHR www.ohchr.org/EN/HRBodies/CAT/pages/catindex.aspx.

179 *Convention Against Torture*, above note 176, art 22(1); *Optional Protocol to the International Covenant on Civil and Political Rights*, GA Res 2200A (XXI), 21 UN GAOR Supp (No 16) at 59, UN Doc A/6316 (1966), 999 UNTS 302, art 1 [*ICCPR Optional Protocol*].

180 *Convention Against Torture*, above note 176, art 22(4)(b); *ICCPR Optional Protocol*, above note 179, art 2.

181 *Convention Against Torture*, above note 176, art 22; *ICCPR Optional Protocol*, above note 179, art 3.

has not been, and is not being, examined under another procedure of international investigation or settlement.[182]

For reasons of expediency, information concerning both the admissibility and merits of the complaint may be gathered at the same time. As in domestic legal procedures, the complainant will receive disclosure of the state's response to his complaint and will, through the filing of additional submissions and evidence, be a participant in the determination of the complaint. Unlike domestic remedies, international remedies do not generally preclude the receipt of new evidence. On the contrary, the absence of new evidence may result in a determination of inadmissibility based upon the complaint being "insufficiently substantiated."[183] However, unlike in domestic context, the claimant does not attend an oral hearing; the application is decided on the basis of written submissions.

Canada has not escaped criticism by the Human Rights Committee and the Committee against Torture. Their evolving jurisprudence not only highlights problematic aspects of domestic rules and procedures, but also helps develop a more nuanced approach to the interpretation and assessment of Canada's international obligations. For example, in *Roger Judge v Canada*,[184] Canada was found to be in violation of the right to life under article 6(1) of the *ICCPR* when it deported the applicant to the United States, where he was under sentence of death, without seeking assurances that the death penalty would not be carried out. Although Canada has not itself imposed the death penalty, its action to deport the person in question made possible his exposure to the death penalty risk. In *Boily v Canada*, the Committee against Torture found that the complainant's extradition to Mexico was in violation of the *Convention Against Torture*. Although Canada sought diplomatic assurances of proper treatment from Mexico, in the opinion of the committee, "the agreed system of diplomatic assurances was not carefully enough designed to effectively prevent torture."[185] In *Mansour Ahani v Canada*, the Human Rights Committee found several aspects of the certificate procedure and its application to the complainant to be inconsistent with the *ICCPR*.[186] In *Arthur Kalonzo v Canada*,[187] the Com-

182 *Convention Against Torture*, above note 176, art 22(4)(a). This is not a requirement under the *ICCPR Optional Protocol*.

183 *Singh v Canada*, Communication No 1315/2004, UN Doc CCPR/C/86/D/1315/2004 (2006).

184 Communication No 829/1998, UN Doc CCPR/S/78/D/829/1998 (2003).

185 Communication No 327/2007, UN Doc CAT/C/47/D/327/2007 (2011).

186 Communication No 1051/2002, UN Doc CCPR/C/80/D/1051/2002 (2004) [*Ahani*].

187 Communication No 343/2008, UN Doc CAT/C/48/D/343/2008 (2012).

mittee against Torture noted that the discretionary nature of moratoria on removals to countries marred by generalized violence was not consistent with the spirit of article 3 of the *Convention Against Torture* (for details on regulatory stays of removal, see Chapter 12). The committee noted that such a stay should apply to everyone without distinction and should not exclude people due to their criminal record. In *Singh v Canada*,[188] the Committee against Torture found, among other things, that the applicant's right to an effective remedy (article 22 of the Convention) was violated because Canada did not provide for judicial review of the merits (but only review of the reasonableness) of decisions to expel an individual to a risk of torture.[189] In *Jama Warsame v Canada*,[190] the Human Rights Committee offered useful interpretation of the concept of one's "own country" and commented on deportation of long-term permanent residents for reasons of criminality. Warsame had lived in Canada since the age of four, but never obtained citizenship. He was convicted of robbery and of possession of a controlled substance for the purpose of trafficking and, as a result, was determined inadmissible for serious criminality and ordered deported from Canada to Somalia. The committee found, among other things, violation of *ICCPR* article 12(4) (not to be arbitrarily deprived of the right to enter one's own country). It concluded that Canada was Warsame's "own country": he had lived in Canada for most of his life, received his entire education in Canada, his nuclear family lives in Canada, and he has no ties to Somalia (his country of citizenship). Further, the committee concluded that deportation to Somalia (which also effectively prevents him from subsequently returning to his "own country") was disproportionate to the aim of crime prevention and was arbitrary.

Most treaty bodies have mechanisms in place to either expedite the investigation of a complaint or to request interim measures such as a stay of removal from a state party. As evident from the discussion of the matter of Ahani in Section H(2), below in this chapter, a treaty body's ability to request interim measures does not entail that a state will comply with the request. Sometimes even the committee's conclusion that deportation would violate Canada's international obligations is insufficient to prevent removal.[191] For example, in 2006, Canada deported a recognized refugee, Mostafa Dadar, to Iran where he alleged

---

188 Communication No 319/2007, UN Doc CAT/C/46/D/319/2007 (2011).

189 Same point made in an earlier case: *TI v Canada*, Communication No 333/2004 (2010).

190 Communication No 1959/2010, UN Doc CCPR/C/102/D/1959/2010 (2011).

191 *Mostafa Dadar v Canada*, Communication No 258/2004, UN Doc CAT/C/35/D/258/2004 (2005).

risk of torture. The deportation order followed Dadar's conviction for aggravated assault and the consequent conclusion that he constituted a danger to the public. It was carried out notwithstanding the decision of the Committee against Torture that removal would violate article 3 of the *Convention Against Torture*.[192]

d) Regional Mechanisms

In addition to the bodies established under international conventions, there also exist similar treaty bodies under regional conventions (such as the Inter-American Commission on Human Rights under the *Charter of the Organization of American States*, the Inter-American Court of Human Rights under the *American Convention on Human Rights*, and the European Court of Human Rights under the *European Convention on Human Rights*). Canada is not a signatory to the *American Convention on Human Rights* and therefore is not subject to the court's jurisdiction. However, the Inter-American Commission on Human Rights can receive and investigate individual complaints on Canada's alleged violations of the *American Declaration of the Rights and Duties of Man*, perform site visits, and make recommendations for the improvement of human rights protections. For example, in 2000, the commission produced a special report on the rights of asylum seekers in Canada.[193] Over the years, it has also produced thematic reports, some of them specifically focusing on rights of migrants and refugees: these include *Refugees and Migrants in the United States: Families and Unaccompanied Children* (2015), *Human Rights of Migrants and Other Persons in the Context of Human Mobility in Mexico* (2014), and *Report on Immigration in the United States: Detention and Due Process* (2011).[194]

2) Limitations of International Remedies

In assessing whether to seek a remedy in international forums, one should keep in mind the limitations of these remedies: (1) special access criteria; and (2) lack of binding force of final views or interim measures requests of the treaty bodies.

Most international forums require both the exhaustion of domestic remedies and the absence of any other international complaint. Consequently, international remedies will generally be available only to an individual who has unsuccessfully applied for judicial review. More im-

192 *Ibid.*

193 Inter-American Commission on Human Rights, above note 21.

194 Inter-American Commission on Human Rights, "Thematic Reports," online: IACHR www.oas.org/en/iachr/reports/thematic.asp.

portant, an individual will likely be able to seek redress only through one of the international forums in question. The particular forum chosen will depend on the basis of the challenge to the decision, the jurisprudence on point of the forum in question, and the practical likelihood that an interim or final decision of the forum in question will be observed. As with accessing relief in Canadian courts, requests for relief must be made in a timely manner.[195]

Neither the final views nor the interim measures of international quasi-judicial bodies are formally binding on Canada as a matter of international law, much less as a matter of domestic law.[196] This point can be vividly demonstrated by the case of Mansour Ahani. Ahani was granted refugee protection in Canada, but was later detained on security grounds and ordered deported to Iran, a country where he alleged he would face execution. Following exhaustion of domestic avenues of review, Ahani filed a complaint with the Human Rights Committee in an effort to challenge certain aspects of the Canadian immigration process and to prevent his deportation to Iran.[197] The committee made an "interim measures" request that Canada refrain from deporting Ahani until a decision on the complaint was made. The Canadian authorities treated the request as non-binding and intended to proceed with the deportation. Ahani then applied to the provincial Superior Court for an injunction restraining his deportation pending the committee's consideration.

The Superior Court dealt with two questions: (1) whether section 7 of the *Charter* guaranteed the applicant the right to remain in Canada until the Human Rights Committee had considered his complaint against Canada; and (2) whether there was a legitimate expectation of not being deported from Canada pending the committee's consideration.[198] The court answered both questions in the negative. It held that although Canada ratified both the *ICCPR* and the *Optional Protocol*, it remained free to accept or reject the committee's recommendations and interim measures requests.

Demonstrating a high level of deference to the executive, the court noted that it lacked expertise in foreign relations and that it was not for the courts "under the guise of procedural fairness, to read in an

---

195 The Committee on the Elimination of Racial Discrimination requires the submission of a complaint within six months of the exhaustion of domestic remedies.

196 *Ahani v Canada (Minister of Citizenship and Immigration); Ahani v Canada (Attorney-General)*, [2002] OJ No 431 at para 32 (CA) [*Ahani* CA].

197 *Ahani*, above note 186.

198 *Ahani* [CA], above note 196.

enforceable constitutional obligation and commit Canada to a process that admittedly could take years, thus frustrating this country's wish to enforce its own laws by deporting a terrorist to a country where he will face at best a minimal risk of harm."[199]

Ahani was deported before the decision of the Human Rights Committee was rendered. The committee subsequently found that Canada's actions violated *ICCPR* articles 9(4) (arbitrary detention), 13 (expulsion of a lawful alien), and 7 (prohibition of torture and other degrading treatment).[200] Nevertheless, several months after the decision in *Ahani v Canada (Attorney General)* was issued, Canada submitted a report on compliance with the *ICCPR* which maintained that requests for interim measures were non-binding and that it reserved a right to make decisions on a case-by-case basis.[201]

The reluctance of Canadian courts to recognize decisions of international forums is frustrating. However, the willingness of international forums to rule against Canada does provide some recognition that the overall strategy of framing cases of mistreatment of refugees in terms of human rights violations is well-founded. It further suggests that if such strategies can be translated into the human rights language of the *Charter*, they may continue to play a more significant role in the protection of the rights of non-citizens, such as rejected refugee claimants. The *Charter* itself cannot give a more expansive interpretation of the rights of non-citizens or a more "human rights–based" approach to refugee law, but it does make available to courts a tool that can be used to expand such rights. Ironically, the seeming irrelevance of international human rights mechanisms in cases such as *Ahani* may yet be trumped by the usefulness of their decisions in *Charter* interpretation.

I. CONCLUSION

An unsuccessful applicant's ability to challenge a decision to refuse her protection is a fundamental component of the Canadian refugee status determination process. At present, an individual denied protection may challenge the decision through domestic mechanisms (motion to reopen, appeal, and/or judicial review) and international complaints mechanisms (although they are not formally binding on Canada).

---

199 *Ibid* at para 49.

200 *Ahani*, above note 186.

201 Consideration of reports submitted by states parties under the *ICCPR*, above note 177, art 40, 27 October 2004, CCPR/C/CAN/2004/5 at 10–12.

Since the adoption of the *IRPA*, domestic avenues to challenge negative RPD determinations have been rather limited. Between 2002 and 2012, judicial review was the only option available to rejected claimants. Given the limited scope of review, its highly technical and legalistic nature, and the requirements for leave and certification of a question of general importance for further appeals, it could not be considered a widely accessible and effective remedy. Further, it must be remembered that, as a result of the narrow grounds upon which any challenge may be based and the doctrine of judicial deference, the court may refuse an appeal even if it accepts that the underlying decision is incorrect. Thus, an individual who is genuinely believed to be in need of protection may still lose his challenge to a determination to the contrary. However, at least, rejected claimants received an automatic stay of removal upon application for judicial review and could effectively enjoy the outcome of a successful judicial review.

The Refugee Appeal Division, as originally written into the *IRPA*, envisioned an appeal on the merits for all rejected claimants. The RAD's potentially greater accessibility, the lower cost of proceedings (as compared to judicial review), and the institutional and personal proximity of the RAD to the RPD all promised that it would provide an improved degree of protection to individuals in genuine need. However, when provisions on the RAD were finally implemented in 2012, they were accompanied by restrictions on the right to appeal and cancellation of automatic stay of removal upon application for judicial review for some claimants. Those groups now have a much higher likelihood of being removed from Canada without access to any remedy (unless they obtain a court-ordered stay of removal). Viewed together with one- and three-year bars on PRRAs, which effectively prevent consideration of risks prior to removal of most unsuccessful claimants, the current system creates heightened concern of *refoulement* to danger. Ultimately, this must be the primary criterion by which any framework of review and appeal in refugee law must be judged: whether it prevents the *refoulement* of individuals to persecution, torture, and other abuses.

CHAPTER 11

ARREST AND DETENTION

A. INTRODUCTION

The sovereign authority to arrest and detain migrants has traditionally been a significant aspect of a nation-state's power, allowing the nation-state to ensure non-citizens' compliance with immigration procedures and to contain those believed to represent a threat to the state or the public. Unlike criminal detention, immigration arrest and detention is targeted solely at non-citizens (foreign nationals or permanent residents). It serves such purposes as the establishment of a person's identity, the protection of the Canadian public, and the ensuring of a person's appearance for immigration proceedings or removal. Although officially considered non-punitive, immigration detention can become such, especially when used as a tool for deterring asylum seeker arrivals. Australia offered one of the most notorious examples of such a policy, but Canada has recently joined the ranks by introducing mandatory detention of designated foreign nationals.

In Canada, three immigration detention regimes can be distinguished:

1) detention under sections 55(1)–(3) of the *Immigration and Refugee Protection Act*[1] (on such grounds as danger to the public, flight risk, and lack of identity documents);
2) detention of designated foreign nationals;
3) detention under security certificates.

1 SC 2001, c 27 [*IRPA*].

Each of these regimes will be discussed in turn.

B. ARREST AND DETENTION: AN OVERVIEW

Depending on the circumstances, the *IRPA* provides for arrest with or without a warrant.[2] A warrant for arrest and detention of foreign nationals and permanent residents may be issued if there are "reasonable grounds to believe" that they are inadmissible[3] and are a danger to the public or are a flight risk.[4] Foreign nationals, other than protected persons, may also be arrested and detained without a warrant if there are "reasonable grounds to believe" that they are inadmissible and are a danger to the public, or are a flight risk, or if their identity is in question.[5] Designated foreign nationals who are sixteen or older are subject to automatic and mandatory detention upon designation.[6] Finally, a non-citizen may be detained if a security certificate has been issued against him and there are "reasonable grounds to believe" that he is a danger to national security or to the safety of any person or is a flight risk.[7]

The standard "reasonable grounds to believe" means more than a mere suspicion but less than the balance of probabilities.[8] It requires more than just a subjective belief of the decision maker; the existence of "reasonable grounds" must be established objectively, that is, that a reasonable person placed in similar circumstances would have believed that reasonable grounds existed to make the arrest.[9]

---

2 *Ibid*, s 55.

3 According to the *IRPA*, *ibid*, ss 34–43, a person can be inadmissible to Canada on the grounds of security, human or international rights violations, criminality, serious criminality, organized criminality, health grounds, financial reasons, misrepresentation, non-compliance with the *IRPA*, or being an inadmissible family member.

4 *Ibid*, s 55(1).

5 *Ibid*, s 55(2).

6 *Ibid*, s 55(3.1).

7 *Ibid*, s 81.

8 *Mugesera v Canada (Minister of Citizenship and Immigration)*, [2005] 2 SCR 100 at paras 114–15; *Chiau v Canada (Minister of Citizenship and Immigration)*, [1998] 2 FC 642 at para 27 (TD), aff'd [2000] FCJ No 2043 at para 60 (CA); *Thanaratnam v Canada (Minister of Citizenship and Immigration)*, 2004 FC 349 at para 12; *Sivakumar v Canada (Minister of Employment and Immigration)*, [1994] 1 FC 433 (CA) (in the context of the UN *Convention Relating to the Status of Refugees*, 28 July 1951, 189 UNTS 150, art 1F exclusion from refugee protection).

9 *Charkaoui (Re)*, [2004] FCJ No 2060 at para 103 (CA).

Arrest and detention may occur upon entry as well as after admission to Canada. For example, a foreign national or a permanent resident may be detained on entry if it is necessary to complete an immigration examination or if there are "reasonable grounds to suspect" that she is inadmissible on grounds of security, violation of human or international rights, serious criminality, criminality, or organized criminality.[10] Caselaw characterizes "reasonable grounds to suspect" as "a lesser but included standard in the threshold of reasonable and probable grounds to believe."[11] "Reasonable grounds to suspect" must be based on more than a mere or subjective suspicion or a hunch. However, unlike reasonable grounds to believe, they need not be supported by compelling evidence; the evidence must be simply credible and objective.[12]

Although there is no legislatively prescribed limit on immigration detention, the *IRPA* does provide for periodic review by the Immigration Division of the Immigration and Refugee Board (IRB) or, in the case of security certificates, by the Federal Court. For detailed detention statistics, see Appendix D, Tables 4–8.

Some groups of persons are considered vulnerable and should not be detained unless absolutely necessary. These include unaccompanied children, elderly persons, pregnant women, and persons with injuries or disabilities.[13] In such cases, alternatives to detention should always be considered.[14] In relation to minors (that is, persons under eighteen), the *IRPA* expressly affirms that they should be detained only as a "measure of last resort, taking into account the other applicable grounds and criteria including the best interests of the child."[15] The *Immigration and Refugee Protection Regulations*, section 249, provide a list of special considerations to be taken into account in relation to the detention of minors. For example, the risk of being under the continued control

---

10 *IRPA*, above note 1, s 55(3).

11 *R v Monney*, [1999] 1 SCR 652 at para 49, cited in *Dupre v Canada (Minister of Public Safety and Emergency Preparedness)*, 2007 FC 1177 at para 27.

12 *Sellathurai v Canada (Minister of Public Safety and Emergency Preparedness)*, 2007 FC 208 at paras 70–71; see also *Canada (Minister of Citizenship and Immigration) v XXXX*, 2010 FC 112 at paras 15–16.

13 Immigration, Refugees and Citizenship Canada, "Procedures for Vulnerable Persons," online: IRCC www.cic.gc.ca/english/resources/tools/refugees/canada/processing/minors.asp [IRCC, "Vulnerable Persons"]; Canada Border Services Agency, "Detentions," online: CBSA www.cbsa-asfc.gc.ca/security-securite/detent-eng.html#s7.

14 IRCC, "Vulnerable Persons," above note 13.

15 *IRPA*, above note 1, s 60; *Immigration and Refugee Protection Regulations*, SOR/2002-227, s 249 [*Regulations*].

of a human trafficker or smuggler is one such special consideration.[16] However, despite the above-mentioned provisions of the *IRPA* and the *Regulations*, designated foreign nationals between the ages of sixteen and eighteen are subject to mandatory detention.

In recent years, the issue of immigration detention of children increasingly attracted attention of international bodies. In 2012, the UN Committee on the Rights of the Child emphasized that immigration detention of children solely on the basis of their immigration status or the status of their parents is a violation of children's rights and is never in their best interests.[17] It called upon states to "expeditiously and completely cease the detention of children on the basis of their immigration status."[18] It also urged states to adopt alternatives to detention that take into consideration the best interests of children. Where detention is nevertheless applied, it should be for the shortest time possible and must comply with established human rights standards.[19] In August 2014, the Inter-American Court of Human Rights issued an advisory opinion where it concluded that states may not resort to immigration detention of children as a precautionary measure in immigration proceedings; may not detain children on the basis of their non-compliance with immigration law, or because a child is unaccompanied, or in order to ensure family unity.[20] In October 2014, the Parliamentary Assembly of the Council of Europe adopted a resolution that called upon states to acknowledge that it is never in the best interests of a child to be detained on the basis of their or their parents' immigration status; to prohibit immigration detention of children in domestic law; and to adopt alternatives to detention that fulfill the best interests of the child.[21]

---

16 *Regulations*, *ibid*, s 249(c). In the United Kingdom, non-governmental organizations have documented the predation of traffickers on unaccompanied minors who are not detained. See ECPAT UK, "Crossing Borders: The Trafficking of Children into the UK" (London: ECPAT UK, 2005) at 3–5.

17 Committee on the Rights of the Child, *Report of the 2012 Day of General Discussion: The Rights of All Children in the Context of International Migration* (2012) at para 32, online: OHCHR www.ohchr.org/Documents/HRBodies/CRC/Discussions/2012/DGD2012ReportAndRecommendations.pdf.

18 *Ibid* at para 78.

19 *Ibid* at paras 79–80.

20 Inter-American Court of Human Rights, Advisory Opinion OC-21/14 of 19 August 2014 on Rights and Guarantees of Children in the Context of Migration and/or in Need of International Protection, at para 160, online: www.corteidh.or.cr/docs/opiniones/seriea_21_eng.pdf.

21 Parliamentary Assembly of the Council of Europe, "The Alternatives to Immigration Detention of Children" (draft resolution and recommendation) (2014), online: COE http://assembly.coe.int/nw/xml/XRef/Xref-XML2HTML-en.asp?fileid=21130&lang=en.

In 2015, the UN Special Rapporteur on Torture similarly called upon states to "expeditiously and completely" cease detention of children on the basis of their immigration status.[22] He wrote:

> The deprivation of liberty of children based exclusively on immigration-related reasons exceeds the requirement of necessity because the measure is not absolutely essential to ensure the appearance of children at immigration proceedings or to implement a deportation order. Deprivation of liberty in this context can never be construed as a measure that complies with the child's best interests.[23]

In 2016, the European Court of Human Rights found, reiterating its earlier jurisprudence, that administrative detention of foreign national children was a violation of article 3 of the *European Convention on Human Rights* (prohibition of torture and cruel or degrading treatment or punishment).[24] It concluded, taking into consideration the applicants' young age and the duration and conditions of their detention, that the French authorities had subjected them to treatment in breach of article 3. The Court noted that children's extreme vulnerability (further heightened in the case of asylum seekers) is the decisive factor, which takes precedence over considerations relating to the status of an irregular immigrant.

C. *CHARTER* ISSUES ARISING UPON ARREST AND DETENTION

The right to counsel under the *Canadian Charter of Rights and Freedoms* arises upon arrest or detention. It is discussed in detail in Chapter 2, Section C(2).

---

22 Juan E Méndez, *Report of the Special Rapporteur on Torture and Other Cruel, Inhuman or Degrading Treatment or Punishment*, A/HRC/28/68 (5 March 2015), online: OHCHR www.ohchr.org/EN/Issues/Torture/SRTorture/Pages/SRTorture Index.aspx.

23 *Ibid* at 17.

24 *AB and Others v France* (no 11593/12), 12 July 2016 (ECHR); *AM and Others v France* (no 24587/12), 12 July 2016 (ECHR); *RC and VC v France* (no 76491/14), 12 July 2016 (ECHR); *RK and Others v France* (no 68264/14), 12 July 2016 (ECHR); *RM and Others v France* (no 33201/11), 12 July 2016 (ECHR).

D. DETENTION

In this section, two detention regimes will be examined: (1) detention under sections 55(1)–(3) of the *IRPA* and (2) detention of designated foreign nationals. In the past, refugee claimants could be detained on one of the grounds stipulated in sections 55(1)–(3) (namely, flight risk, danger to the public, and identity). In 2012, subsection 3.1 was added to section 55, establishing a special regime for detention of designated foreign nationals. As will be shown below, there are several key differences between the two regimes in terms of grounds for detention, frequency of detention reviews, and powers of immigration officers regarding detention and release decisions. Currently, refugee claimants can be detained under either of the two detention regimes, depending on their circumstances.

1) Detention under the *Immigration and Refugee Protection Act*, Sections 55(1)–(3)

Under sections 55(1) and (3) of the *IRPA*, a permanent resident or a foreign national may be detained on the following grounds:

- where there are reasonable grounds to believe he is inadmissible and is a flight risk;
- where there are reasonable grounds to believe he is inadmissible and is a danger to the public;
- where it is necessary for completion of an examination (this ground applies only to detention on entry);
- where there are reasonable grounds to suspect that a non-citizen is inadmissible on grounds of security, violating human or international rights, serious criminality, criminality, or organized criminality (this ground applies only to detention on entry).

In addition to the above, a foreign national (other than a protected person) may be detained where immigration authorities are not satisfied with her identity "in the course of any procedure under this Act [*IRPA*]."[25]

The initial decision on detention is made by an immigration officer. While the power to release generally rests with the Immigration Division, an officer may release a detainee before the first detention review if he considers that grounds for detention ceased to exist.[26] He may impose

25 *IRPA*, above note 1, s 55(2).

26 *Ibid*, s 56.

any conditions on release that are considered necessary, including reporting requirements, posting of a monetary deposit, or finding of a guarantor.

Once a person has been detained, the officer must notify the Immigration Division.[27] The division conducts periodic detention reviews and determines whether detention should continue. The *IRPA*, section 58, creates a presumption that an individual is to be released, except in specified circumstances.[28] The Immigration Division is to order release, unless

- it is satisfied that the detainee is a danger to the public;
- it is satisfied that he is a flight risk;
- the Minister is taking necessary steps to inquire into a reasonable suspicion that the detainee is inadmissible on grounds of security, violating human or international rights, serious criminality, criminality, or organized criminality;
- the Minister is of the opinion that the identity of the foreign national has not been, but may be, established and the person has not reasonably co-operated with the Minister by providing relevant information for the purpose of establishing identity.[29]

In addition, the Immigration Division is to take into consideration factors prescribed in the *Regulations*, sections 245–48 (see discussion below).

In this chapter we will examine only three grounds — flight risk, danger to the public, and identity — as they are most relevant to the situations of refugee claimants.

a) Unlikely to Appear (Flight Risk)

Detention on the basis of flight risk may be ordered if there are reasonable grounds to believe that a person is unlikely to appear for an examination, an immigration proceedings, or for removal. The *Regulations* prescribe factors that should be considered in determining whether a person is unlikely to appear. They are as follows:

- whether a person is a fugitive from justice in a foreign jurisdiction for an offence that, if committed in Canada, would also constitute an offence;
- whether a person voluntarily complied with previous departure orders, orders to appear at immigration or criminal proceedings or

27 *Ibid*, s 55(4).

28 *Canada (Minister of Citizenship and Immigration) v B046*, 2011 FC 877 at para 36.

29 *IRPA*, above note 1, s 58(1).

meet conditions imposed in regard to entry, release, or stay of removal;

- whether a person previously avoided examination, attempted to escape, or escaped from custody;
- whether a person is/was involved in people smuggling or trafficking and might, as a result, be unwilling to appear for an examination or be influenced or coerced not to appear;
- whether a person has strong ties to a community in Canada.[30]

The above factors are not exhaustive. Other relevant factors may include the general credibility of the person concerned, the availability of alternatives to detention sufficient to reduce the flight risk, the presence of relatives or friends willing to provide a guarantee or surety, imminence of removal, presence/absence of fixed place of residence or attachment in Canada, frequent changes of address, and use of aliases to avoid detection.[31] The Immigration Division should also consider whether a person has access to significant financial resources, previously used false documents, or tried to hide his presence in Canada.[32]

While detention on the basis of flight risk may be warranted in many circumstances, there are concerns about its application to refugee claimants at the beginning of a refugee determination process. The reasoning behind such decisions to detain implies that claimants are unlikely to appear simply due to their stated fear of persecution and fear of deportation to the country of persecution. This approach is tantamount to detaining a person on the very basis of having made a refugee claim.[33]

b) Danger to the Public

A permanent resident or a foreign national may be ordered detained where there are "reasonable grounds to believe" that the person is in-

---

30 *Regulations*, above note 15, s 245.

31 Immigration, Refugees and Citizenship Canada, "ENF 20: Detention" (December 2015) at 13, online: IRCC www.cic.gc.ca/english/resources/manuals/enf/enf20-eng.pdf [IRCC, "ENF 20"]; Immigration, Refugees and Citizenship Canada, "ENF 3: Admissibility, Hearings and Detention Review Proceedings" (April 2015) at 36, online: www.cic.gc.ca/english/resources/manuals/enf/enf03-eng.pdf [IRCC, "ENF 3"].

32 Immigration and Refugee Board, "Chairperson's Guideline 2: Detention" at para 2.2.3, online: IRB www.irb-cisr.gc.ca/Eng/BoaCom/references/pol/GuiDir/Pages/GuideDir02.aspx [IRB, "Guideline 2"].

33 Working Group on Arbitrary Detention, "Report of the Working Group on Arbitrary Detention on Visit to Canada," E/CN.4/2006/7/Add.2 (2006) at 19, online: OHCHR www.ohchr.org/EN/Issues/Detention/Pages/Annual.aspx [Working Group on Arbitrary Detention].

admissible and is a danger to the public. For assessing the need for detention on this ground, the *Regulations* prescribe the following factors:

- the opinion of the Minister that the person constitutes a danger to the Canadian public or a danger to the security of Canada on specified grounds;[34]
- association with a criminal organization;[35]
- engagement in smuggling or trafficking in persons;
- conviction in Canada of a sexual offence or an offence involving violence or weapons;
- conviction for an offence in Canada under the *Controlled Drugs and Substances Act* related to trafficking, importing and exporting, or production of controlled substances;
- conviction or pending charges outside Canada for an offence that, if committed in Canada, would constitute a sexual offence or an offence involving violence or weapons; and
- conviction or pending charges outside Canada that, if committed in Canada, would constitute an offence under the *Controlled Drugs and Substances Act* related to trafficking, importing and exporting, or production of controlled substances.[36]

The above factors are not exhaustive, and other relevant circumstances, including history of violent or threatening behaviour, or such behaviour at the time of examination, may be considered.[37] It is up to the Board to determine the weight to be given to each factor in a given case.[38] The existence of one of the above listed factors does not automatically lead to a conclusion that a person is a danger.[39] The probability

---

34 These grounds relate to inadmissibility on the grounds of serious criminality, security, violating human or international rights, or organized criminality, namely, *IRPA*, ss 101(2)(*b*), 113(*d*)(i) or (ii), and 115(2)(*a*) or (*b*).

35 *IRPA*, *ibid*, s 121(2):

> "Criminal organization" means an organization that is believed on reasonable grounds to be or to have been engaged in activity that is part of a pattern of criminal activity planned and organized by a number of persons acting in concert in furtherance of the commission of an offence punishable under an Act of Parliament by way of indictment or in furtherance of the commission of an offence outside Canada that, if committed in Canada, would constitute such an offence.

36 *Regulations*, above note 15, s 246.

37 IRCC, "ENF 20," above note 31 at 12.

38 *Canada (Minister of Citizenship and Immigration) v Thanabalasingham*, 2003 FC 1225 at para 115, aff'd 2004 FCA 4 [*Thanabalasingham*].

39 *Ibid*; *Salilar v Canada (Minister of Citizenship and Immigration)*, [1995] 3 FC 150 at para 18 [*Salilar*].

of danger must be determined in each case individually,[40] taking into account such circumstances as the age of the convictions, the character of the accused, and her behaviour in the community since the convictions.[41] For example, with the passage of time, the danger that the person represents to the public may lessen.[42] Cases that involve foreign convictions will require special consideration to determine whether they are equivalent to the offences described in respective sections of the *Regulations*.

The circumstances of the commission of offences may also be useful in determining the weight or the gravity of one factor as opposed to the other. For instance, an offence committed against a minor may be considered more serious than the same offence against an adult.[43] At the same time, a person found to be in association with a criminal organization may be considered a danger to the public without the need to consider any other surrounding circumstances.[44] The legislation does not require that detainees be personally engaged in violence in order to be considered danger to the public; "[d]irecting others to commit crimes is no less dangerous than the perpetration of these crimes."[45]

c) Identity

Foreign nationals, including refugee claimants, who arrive in Canada without identification, on false documents, or whose identity documents are deemed unsatisfactory may be detained until their identity is established. The responsibility to provide proof of identity rests on the foreign national.[46] After evidence attesting to a foreign national's identity is submitted, the Minister will usually seek to verify it and will determine whether he is satisfied as to that person's identity.[47]

Section 247 of the *Regulations* codifies a list of factors to be considered in cases of detention on identity grounds:

---

40 *Salilar, ibid.*

41 *Thanabalasingham*, above note 38 at para 120 (FC); IRB, "Guideline 2," above note 32 at para 2.1.5.

42 *Canada (Minister of Citizenship and Immigration) v Sittampalam*, [2004] FCJ No 2152 at para 17 (FC) [*Sittampalam*].

43 IRCC, "ENF 3," above note 31 at 37.

44 *Bruzzese v Canada (Public Safety and Emergency Preparedness)*, 2014 FC 230 at para 47.

45 *Ibid.*

46 IRB, "Guideline 2," above note 32 at para 2.4.3.

47 *Canada (Minister of Citizenship and Immigration) v Singh*, [2004] FCJ No 1974 at para 38 (FC).

- the foreign national's co-operation in providing evidence of identity, or assisting the Department in obtaining evidence of identity (e.g., providing the date and place of birth, names of parents, detailed information on route to Canada);
- the destruction of identity or travel documents, or the use of fraudulent documents and the circumstances under which the foreign national acted;
- the provision of contradictory information with respect to identity; and
- the existence of documents that contradict information provided by the foreign national with respect to her identity.[48]

As with the other two grounds for detention, the list of these factors is not exhaustive. For example, a person's general credibility can have a bearing on the decision to release.[49] Consideration of some of the above factors is specifically limited so as not to disadvantage vulnerable groups. In particular, lack of co-operation in establishing identity is determined to not have an adverse impact on the assessment of the cases of persons under eighteen years of age.[50]

In addition to the above factors, the *IRPA*, section 58(1)(d), requires the Immigration Division to continue detention when the Minister is of the opinion that the foreign national's identity has not been established, but may be established, and either the person is not co-operating in establishing his identity, or the Minister is making reasonable efforts to establish the person's identity.[51] The operative phrase in the first condition is that "the Minister is of the opinion" — the objective truth of whether a foreign national's identity has been established is irrelevant. Concerns have been expressed about this ground for detention and particularly the potential for the abuse of this power.[52] For example, in the case of passengers from MV *Sun Sea* who arrived in Canada in 2010 (see Chapter 1), the authorities kept maintaining that the Minister was not satisfied with their identity even after identity documents had been obtained and verified.[53]

---

48 *Regulations*, above note 15, s 247.

49 IRCC, "ENF 20," above note 31 at 14–15.

50 *Regulations*, above note 15, s 247(2).

51 *IRPA*, above note 1, s 58(1)(d).

52 Canadian Council for Refugees, "Submission to the UN Working Group on Arbitrary Detention for Consideration in Guiding Principles on the Right of Anyone Deprived of His or Her Liberty to Challenge the Legality of the Detention in Court" (January 2014), online: CCR ccrweb.ca/files/wgad-submission-jan-2014.pdf.

53 *Ibid.*

As seen from the above, the extent to which a person has co-operated with the authorities in establishing his identity plays a significant role in determining whether he may be released. In cases of migrants, the factors listed in the *Regulations*, section 247, seem reasonable; however, the situation is different with respect to refugee claimants. There are obvious reasons for many claimants to perform exactly the actions that are held against them, that is, travelling on fraudulent documents, destroying their documents, and giving contradictory responses to immigration officers. Due to the difficulty of entering Canada legally, many refugee claimants resort to smugglers who bring them to Canada on fraudulent documents. Having experienced persecution at the hands of the state, asylum seekers often distrust government officials generally and seem not to be co-operative. Further, having just arrived in Canada and being unfamiliar with applicable rules and procedures or lacking competent interpretation, they may feel confused and give incomplete or inconsistent statements to the authorities.

In refugee claimant cases, immigration officials need to be sensitive as to how persons can obtain identity documents without divulging personal information to government officials of their country of nationality or former habitual residence. If a completed application for a passport or a travel document must be provided as a condition of release from detention, the existence of a person's asylum application shall not be divulged to government officials of her country of nationality or habitual residence, as long as the removal order against her is not enforceable.[54]

It is possible to continue detention on a different ground after establishing an individual's identity. In some cases, the established identity may raise new issues concerning the individual's risk of flight or danger to the public. For example, persons who arrived on the MV *Sun Sea* in August 2010 were first detained primarily on the ground of identity.[55] Once their identity was established, the Minister sought detention on security grounds (due to the existence of reasonable grounds to believe that they had been engaged in people smuggling) and subsequently on the basis of flight risk.[56]

---

54 *Regulations*, above note 15, s 250.

55 Maureen Brosnahan, "Ocean Lady Migrants from Sri Lanka Still Struggling 5 Years Later: Of the 76 Men Found on the Ocean Lady, 30 Have Been Accepted as Refugees" *CBC News* (18 October 2014), online: www.cbc.ca/1.2804118.

56 See, for example, *Canada (Minister of Citizenship and Immigration) v B072*, 2012 FC 563 at para 2; *Canada (Minister of Citizenship and Immigration) v B001*, 2012 FC 523 at paras 1–2.

2) Detention of Designated Foreign Nationals

As a result of the 2012 changes to the *IRPA*, the Minister of Public Safety and Emergency Preparedness acquired a new power to designate groups of irregular arrivals as designated foreign nationals (for an overview, see Chapter 3). The designation can be made in one of two circumstances:

- the examinations of the persons in the group (e.g., for the purpose of establishing identity) cannot be conducted in a timely manner; or
- there are reasonable grounds to suspect that the group has been or will be smuggled "for profit, or for the benefit of, at the direction of or in association with a criminal organization or terrorist group."[57]

One of the major consequences of designation is mandatory detention of designated foreign nationals who are sixteen years of age or older. This detention regime is more restrictive than immigration detention under sections 55(1)–(3) of the *IRPA*.

First, the very ground for detention is not based on individual assessment of a person's danger or flight risk or lack of identity. Rather, group designation alone (which does not consider the individual circumstances of each person in the group) is a sufficient basis for detention.

Second, a designated foreign national cannot be released at the discretion of an immigration officer before the first detention review. She is to be detained until one of the following: (1) grant of refugee protection; (2) release by the Immigration Division; or (3) release by the Minister's order.[58] The Minister may release a detainee on his own initiative if the reasons for detention no longer exist or, in exceptional circumstances, on the individual's request.[59]

Third, the timelines for detention review are longer than for detention under sections 55(1)–(3). The first detention review occurs within fourteen days after the designated foreign national was first detained and subsequent reviews take place six months after each preceding review.[60] In contrast, the first review of detention under sections 55(1)–(3) takes place within forty-eight hours, the second, within seven days of the first review, and subsequently, once every thirty days.[61]

Fourth, at the first detention review, the Immigration Division may consider only whether a designated foreign national is a danger to the

---

57 *IRPA*, above note 1, s 20.1(1).

58 *Ibid*, s 56(2).

59 *Ibid*, s 58.1.

60 *Ibid*, s 57.1.

61 *Ibid*, s 57.

public, is a flight risk, is investigated for inadmissibility, or has not established his identity. It cannot consider other factors, such as the availability of alternatives to detention,[62] which can normally be considered in cases of detention under sections 55(1)–(3) at any time.[63] Finally, where release is ordered, the Immigration Division must impose prescribed conditions.[64] Moreover, there is a penalty for failure, without a reasonable excuse, to comply with those conditions: an immigration officer may impose a further one-year postponement (in addition to the five-year bar) on a designated foreign national's application for a permanent or a temporary resident status.[65] In the case of other non-citizens (who are not designated foreign nationals), the imposition of prescribed conditions is not mandatory and the Division maintains discretion on whether and what conditions to impose.[66]

Although the provisions on designated foreign nationals do not specifically refer to refugee claimants and officially seek to deter human smuggling, they are a disguised tool for deterrence of asylum seekers. As discussed above, asylum seekers often have to resort to smugglers and often arrive without proper authorization or identity documents. Thus, as long as they arrive in a group of two or more, they run a risk of being designated under these provisions. As already noted in Chapter 3, such detention may have multiple consequences for asylum seekers, ranging from psychological trauma[67] to difficulty accessing counsel in order to prepare for their refugee hearings. Further, the limited grounds that can be considered at the first detention review preclude consideration of any peculiar circumstances of claimants and reduce the possibility of release. Hence, it is highly likely that a designated foreign national would not be released after the first detention review and would have to spend at least six more months in detention before getting a second chance at release. Such detention can be said to acquire a punitive dimension for the person's choice to seek asylum in Canada.

---

62 For the list of factors, see the *Regulations*, above note 15, s 248.

63 *IRPA*, above note 1, s 58 (1.1).

64 *Ibid*, s 58(4).

65 *Ibid*, ss 11(1.3)(a), 24(7), and 25(1.03).

66 *Ibid*, s 58(3).

67 See, for example, Janet Cleveland, Cécile Rousseau, & Rachel Kronick, "Bill C-4: The Impact of Detention and Temporary Status on Asylum Seekers' Mental Health: Brief for Submission to the House of Commons Committee on Bill C-4, the *Preventing Human Smugglers from Abusing Canada's Immigration System Act*" (2012), online: http://oppenheimer.mcgill.ca/IMG/pdf/Impact_of_Bill_C4_on_asylum_seeker_mental_health_full-2.pdf.

The above-described regime bears resemblance to the Australian policy of mandatory and automatic detention of asylum seekers who arrive without proper documentation or authorization. In fact, in 2010, IRCC Minister Jason Kenney visited Australia's immigration detention centres and discussed strategies to combat human smuggling with Australian counterparts, looking to learn from their practices.[68]

Notably, in September 2014, the Australian High Court concluded that indefinite detention of non-citizens without carefully considering whether it is justified in individual cases is unlawful under Australian law.[69] It remains to be seen whether a similar challenge will be brought in Canada.

3) Conditions of Detention and Detention Practices

Immigration detainees, including refugee claimants, are held in CBSA Immigration Holding Centres (IHCs) or provincial correctional or remand facilities.[70] The Canada Border Services Agency currently operates three IHCs: Ontario (Toronto), Quebec (Laval), and British Columbia (Vancouver). The Toronto centre can accommodate up to 195 persons for short- and long-term stays; Laval — 150; and Vancouver — 24 (only for stays up to seventy-two hours).[71] The IHCs operate as minimum to medium-security prisons with razor wire fences, central locking door systems, and surveillance cameras;[72] they house low-risk detainees.[73] IHCs are managed by the CBSA, but some day-to-day operations, including security, may be contracted out to private security firms (for example, this is the case in Toronto IHC).[74]

---

68 Immigration, Refugees and Citizenship Canada, News Release, "Governments of Canada and Australia Working to Combat Human Smuggling" (19 September 2010), online: IRCC http://news.gc.ca/web/article-en.do?mthd=advSrch&crtr.mnthndVl=10&crtr.dpt1D=6664&nid=560859&crtr.tp1D=&crtr.kw=detention%2C+australia&crtr.yrStrtVl=2004&crtr.dyStrtVl=1&crtr.mnthStrtVl=1&crtr.page=1&crtr.yrndVl=2014&crtr.dyndVl=22.

69 *Plaintiff S4/2014 v Minister for Immigration and Border Protection*, [2014] HCA 34.

70 A remand facility is used to hold persons charged with criminal offences prior to their trial and/or sentencing.

71 The most recent data on their capacity is from 2013–14 [authors' access-to-information request; on file with authors].

72 Cleveland, Rousseau, & Kronick, above note 67.

73 Delphine Nakache, *The Human and Financial Cost of Detention of Asylum-Seekers in Canada* (December 2011) at 31, online: www.unhcr.ca/wp-content/uploads/2014/10/RPT-2011-12-detention_assylum_seekers-e.pdf.

74 CBSA, "Immigration Holding Centres," online: www.cbsa-asfc.gc.ca/security-securite/ihc-csi-eng.html#_s3.

High-risk immigration detainees are housed in provincial correctional or remand facilities. In addition, such facilities are used in areas not served by IHCs as well as when a person is exhibiting mental health or behavioural issues.[75] Further, given the relatively small capacity of IHCs, provincial facilities are used when a large group of new arrivals needs to be detained. This was the case, for example, with MV *Sun Sea* which carried 492 individuals, all of which (including forty-nine children) were detained.[76] The detainees were dispersed among various provincial facilities: male passengers and crew, to a makeshift area set up in the yard of the Fraser Regional Correctional Centre; women, to the Alouette Correctional Centre; and women with children, to Burnaby Youth Custody Services Centre.[77] In general, the use of non-CBSA facilities for immigration detention has increased in the past decade from, on average, 27 percent of detainees during 2004–08 to 34 percent during 2009–14 (in 2013–14, it was at the highest, constituting 42 percent of all immigration detainees).[78] The use of non-CBSA facilities varies by region: in Prairie and Atlantic regions, which have no CBSA facilities, all immigration detainees are held in correctional facilities; in British Columbia, about 50 to 60 percent of immigration detainees are held in non-CBSA facilities; in Ontario, on average, 25 to 38 percent; and in Quebec, 11 to 15 percent (for a detailed yearly breakdown, see Appendix D, Tables 5 and 6).[79]

Over the past years, several evaluations and reports raised concerns about CBSA detention practices. In 2008, the Auditor General found that the CBSA did not have precise data on the number of detainees and the length of their detention; decisions on detention were inconsistent (regions with limited holding space were more likely to release individuals on terms and conditions); and conditions of detention were not always in compliance with minimum standards (e.g., cells were overcrowded). The chances of a non-citizen being detained were found to heavily depend on the availability of detention space and budget in a given region.[80] In 2010, another evaluation again highlighted

---

75 Nakache, above note 73 at 31.

76 Canadian Council for Refugees, "Sun Sea: Five Years Later" (August 2015), online: CCR ccrweb.ca/sites/ccrweb.ca/files/sun-sea-five-years-later.pdf.

77 Stephanie Silverman, "In the Wake of Irregular Arrivals: Changes to the Canadian Immigration Detention System" (2014) 30 *Refuge* 27 at 31.

78 Authors' access-to-information request to the CBSA [on file with authors]. For detailed breakdown, see Appendix D.

79 *Ibid.*

80 Auditor General of Canada, "Chapter 7 — Detention and Removal of Individuals — Canada Border Services Agency" (2008) at para 5.88, online: www.

disparities in detention practices across regions.[81] In the Atlantic, Prairie, and Pacific regions, the majority of individuals were released on conditions prior to the first detention review, while this was not the case in Toronto. CBSA staff also indicated the lack of training in dealing with vulnerable populations, which contributed to the inconsistency in detention practices across regions. A 2011 study for the United Nations High Commissioner for Refugees (UNHCR) similarly found regional disparities in reasons for detention and conditions of release,[82] which, as in the past, were linked, at least in part, to the availability of detention space.

Since 2000, fifteen people died in immigration detention.[83] In several cases, concerns have been raised about lack of proper procedures, lack of timely access to medical care or mental health services, and the cloak of secrecy surrounding circumstances of the deaths. For example, in 2007, Joseph Fernandes died after a transfer from Toronto IHC to Maplehurst Detention Centre. The coroner's inquest recommended establishing a process for communication between federal and provincial facilities with respect to medical conditions. In 2009, Jan Szamko died after being transferred from Toronto IHC to Toronto West Detention Centre. The coroner's inquest made a similar recommendation regarding the need for a clear procedure for information sharing between institutions. In 2013, Lucia Vega Jimenez hanged herself in Vancouver IHC. The jury recommended that the CBSA create a dedicated holding centre for immigration detainees staffed by CBSA employees that allowed for adequate access to legal counsel, medical services, spiritual support, and family visits.[84] In 2016, Melkioro Gahungu hanged himself at Toronto East Detention Centre, and Francisco Javier Romero Astorga died in immigration custody. In both cases, the CBSA refused

---

oag-bvg.gc.ca/internet/English/parl_oag_200805_07_e_30703.html; Working Group on Arbitrary Detention, above note 33.

81 Canada Border Services Agency, "CBSA Detentions and Removals Programs — Evaluation Study" (2010).

82 For example, identity was considerably more prevalent as a ground for detention in Quebec (38.6 percent) than in the Greater Toronto Area (GTA) (3.8 percent); flight risk is a more common reason in the GTA (94 percent) than in Quebec (55 percent): Nakache, above note 73.

83 Muriel Draaisma, "Federal Government Reviewing Immigration Detention Process after String of Deaths" *CBC News* (16 March 2016), online: www.cbc.ca/1.3584700.

84 For more details on these and other cases, see Leslie Young, "Deaths in Detention: CBSA's Fatal Failure to Learn from Its Mistakes" *Global News* (5 November 2014), online: http://globalnews.ca/news/1649523/deaths-in-detention-cbsas-fatal-failure-to-learn-from-its-mistakes/.

to publicly identify the detainees or release any information on the circumstances of their deaths.[85]

There is no independent institutional mechanism to monitor conditions in immigration detention. Currently, the only independent monitoring is exercised by the Canadian Red Cross on the basis of the Memoranda of Understanding with IRCC (signed in 2002) and the CBSA (signed in 2006).[86] It includes visits to federal immigration holding facilities and some provincial correctional facilities in Quebec, Ontario, Alberta, British Columbia, and Manitoba. However, the reports by the Red Cross are not made public. According to the 2012–13 report released under an access-to-information request, facilities failed to comply with several standards, being, for example, overcrowded and lacking in support services for detained children and mental healthcare.[87] In general, however, IHCs were found to provide detainees with a safer environment and better access to support services, legal advice, phone cards, and visitors compared to non-CBSA facilities.[88] Given that during the 2004–14 period, about 45 to 47 percent of all immigration detainees were refugee claimants,[89] this finding raises heightened concern. Detention, in general, imposes not only psychological toll but also multiple barriers to effective access to services, legal advice, and other supports.[90] When held in correctional and remand facilities, refugee claimants endure additional hardship due to restricted privileges, social stigma, and the psychological consequences of being housed together with serious offenders.[91] Further, the success of their refugee claims may be jeopardized due to inadequate access to interpreters and legal counsel.[92]

---

85 Debra Black, "Secrecy Cloaks Death of Immigration Detainee in Toronto Jail" *Toronto Star* (10 March 2016), online: http://on.thestar.com/2246v3S; Nicholas Keung, "Family 'Utterly in the Dark' about Chilean Man's Death in Detention" *Toronto Star* (23 March 2016), online: http://on.thestar.com/1Zuciy5.

86 Red Cross, "Promoting the Rights of Immigration Detainees," online: www.redcross.ca/what-we-do/migrant-and-refugee-services/promoting-the-rights-of-immigration-detainees.

87 Jim Bronskill, "Red Cross Uncovers Problems Facing Canadian Immigration Detainees" *Toronto Star* (25 September 2014), online: http://on.thestar.com/1rokUrf.

88 Authors' access-to-information request to the CBSA [on file with authors].

89 *Ibid.*

90 See, generally, for examples, Nakache, above note 73.

91 See also for discussion of these issues, Silverman, above note 77.

92 Working Group on Arbitrary Detention, above note 33.

Overall, as UNHCR noted, detention of asylum seekers should be avoided in favour of less restrictive alternatives.[93] Such alternatives can include reporting and registration requirements, posting of bond/bail, and deposit of documents. As some studies have shown, multiple factors are likely to facilitate asylum seekers' compliance with release conditions, which, indeed, makes these alternatives a viable option.[94]

4) Detention Reviews before the Immigration Division

Neither the *IRPA* nor the *Regulations* provide a temporal limit on detention. The *IRPA*, however, provides for regular detention reviews[95] and the *Regulations* prescribe safeguards against indefinite detention.[96] Review of detention for both designated foreign nationals and other detainees is conducted by the IRB's Immigration Division.[97]

In the case of detention under the *IRPA*, sections 55(1)–(3), detention reviews are conducted with the following regularity:

1) first detention review — within forty-eight hours after the person is taken into detention or "without delay afterwards";[98]
2) second detention review — at least once during the seven days following the first review;[99]
3) each subsequent review — at least once during each thirty-day period after each review.[100]

A party may request a detention review before the expiry of a seven-day or a thirty-day period.[101] An application for an earlier review may be allowed if there exist new facts that justify the review.[102] As already discussed, detention review timelines for designated foreign nationals are different: first within fourteen days and subsequently six months

---

93 United Nations High Commissioner for Refugees, "Canada/USA Bi-National Roundtable on Alternatives to Detention of Asylum Seekers, Refugees, Migrants and Stateless" (September 2012), online: UNHCR http://unhcr.ca/beta/wp-content/uploads/2014/10/RPT-2012-09-24-detention_alternatives-e.pdf.

94 Cathryn Costello & Esra Kaytaz, *Building Empirical Research into Alternatives to Detention: Perceptions of Asylum-Seekers and Refugees in Toronto and Geneva*, Legal and Protection Policy Research Series (Geneva: UNHCR, 2013).

95 *IRPA*, above note 1, s 57.

96 *Regulations*, above note 15, s 248.

97 *IRPA*, above note 1, s 54.

98 *Ibid*, s 57(1).

99 *Ibid*, s 57(2).

100 *Ibid*, s 57(2).

101 *Immigration Division Rules*, SOR/2002-229, r 9(1).

102 *Ibid*, r 9(2).

after each preceding review; an early review prior to the expiry of a prescribed timeline is not possible.

a) Substantive Aspects of Detention Review

Decision making during detention reviews involves two stages. First, there must be a determination as to whether there exists a valid ground for continued detention. If the Immigration Division establishes that one or more grounds for detention exist, it must proceed to the second stage and examine whether the individual may nonetheless be released, particularly through the imposition of terms and conditions. Section 248 of the *Regulations* provides a list of factors to be considered by decision makers in determining whether to continue detention. They include the following:

- the reasons for detention;
- the length of time in detention and likely length of continued detention;
- any unexplained delays or unexplained lack of diligence caused by the Minister or the person concerned; and
- the existence of alternatives to detention.[103]

These factors are derived from court jurisprudence[104] and seek to ensure that continued detention does not violate detainees' rights under section 7 of the *Canadian Charter of Rights and Freedoms*.[105] Caselaw has provided important interpretive guidelines on the four factors listed in section 248 of the *Regulations*:

1) *Reasons for detention*. For example, the case for continuing detention is stronger where a person is considered a danger to the public.[106]
2) *Length of time in detention and likely length of its continuation*. The fact that a person has been detained for a long time and is likely to continue being detained for a lengthy period tends to favour release.[107] The lengthier the detention, the heavier the onus is on the

---

103 *Regulations*, above note 15, s 248; IRB, "Guideline 2," above note 32 at para 3.1.2; *Charkaoui v Canada (Minister of Citizenship and Immigration)*, 2007 SCC 9 at paras 108–17 [*Charkaoui*].

104 Notably, the Federal Court decision in *Sahin v Canada (Minister of Citizenship and Immigration)*, [1995] 1 FC 214 (TD) [*Sahin*].

105 Part 1 of the *Constitution Act, 1982*, being Schedule B to the *Canada Act 1982* (UK), 1982, c 11 [*Charter*].

106 *Sahin*, above note 104 at para 30; *Kidane v Canada (Minister of Citizenship and Immigration)*, [1997] FCJ No 990; IRB, "Guideline 2," above note 32 at para 3.2.1.

107 *Sahin*, above note 104 at para 30.

government to show that continued detention is required.[108] The continued detention should be examined particularly rigorously where there is no end in sight to the determination in the main proceeding.[109] The wording of section 248 of the *Regulations* obliges the Immigration Division to speculate on how long detention is likely to continue based on information about other pending proceedings. However, such speculation must be grounded in "reliable information and an informed opinion."[110] The Division may review the state of these proceedings and their progress over time, but the estimation of future length of detention must be based on existing facts rather than assumptions.[111] The Immigration Division may make the estimate taking into account only the proceedings that are under way or pending at the time of the detention review; it cannot consider potential but so far non-existent proceedings that a detainee may choose to pursue in the future.[112] The length of detention can also be relevant to the assessment of the danger to the public. The danger may dissipate due to the time in detention. Likewise, evidence that supported detention may turn stale with the passage of time.[113]

3) *Reasons for delay.* Unexplained delay or lack of diligence should count against the offending party.[114] Continuing detention is unacceptable when delay in removal was caused by circumstances beyond the detainee's control.[115] In contrast, where a detainee is responsible for delay in proceedings, she cannot complain of the length of detention as unfair.[116]
4) *Availability of alternatives to detention.* Among alternatives to detention are posting of a bond, periodic reporting, confinement to a geographic location, periodic reporting, and the requirement to report changes of address or telephone number.[117] Before ordering release, the Immigration Division must consider whether the proposed conditions would sufficiently neutralize the danger to the

108 *Charkaoui*, above note 103 at para 113.
109 *Sahin*, above note 104.
110 *Sittampalam*, above note 42 at para 14.
111 *Canada (Minister of Citizenship and Immigration) v Li*, 2009 FCA 85 at para 67.
112 *Ibid.*
113 *Ibid.*
114 *Sahin*, above note 104 at para 30.
115 *Ibid.*
116 *Sittampalam*, above note 42 at paras 15–16. In *Canada (Minister of Citizenship and Immigration) v Kamail*, 2002 FCT 381, the applicant refused to sign the application for travel documents necessary for his deportation to Iran.
117 IRB, "Guideline 2," above note 32 at para 3.6.3.

public or ensure that the person will appear for examination, an inadmissibility hearing, or removal from Canada.[118] For example, a risk may be neutralized by such strict conditions as a curfew, refraining from use of a cellphone or a computer, house arrest, wearing of an electronic bracelet, allowing entry of immigration officials into the person's residence at all times, and the restriction of contact with certain individuals.[119] The conditions must not, however, be a disproportionate response to the threat.[120]

The four above-listed factors are not exhaustive and the weight given to each depends on the circumstances of each case.[121] Although a detention review is not strictly speaking a hearing *de novo*,[122] the Board must decide afresh at each detention review whether continued detention is warranted.[123] It must take into consideration all existing factors that relate to custody, including the reasons for previous decisions.[124] While the Immigration Division should take into consideration reasons for previous detention orders,[125] it would be insufficient to merely accept previous decisions.[126] Each detention review determines whether there are reasons at the time of the review to satisfy the adjudicator that detention needs to be continued.[127] Prior detention review decisions are not binding, but if an adjudicator chooses to depart from them, he should provide "clear and compelling reasons" for doing so;[128] failure to provide such reasons constitutes a reviewable error.[129] This rule is designed to safeguard the findings of the previous member who was in a better position to hear original evidence and assess credibility.[130]

Upon completion of a detention review, the Immigration Division may make one of three orders:

---

118 *Ibid* at para 3.6.1.

119 *Ibid* at para 3.6.6.

120 *Charkaoui*, above note 103 at para 116.

121 IRB, "Guideline 2," above note 32 at para 3.1.3.

122 *Thanabalasingham*, above note 38 at para 6 (FCA).

123 *Ibid* at para 8.

124 *Canada (Minister of Citizenship and Immigration) v Lai*, [2001] 3 FC 326 at 334 (TD) [*Lai*], quoted with approval in *Thanabalasingham* (FCA), above note 38 at para 6.

125 *Lai*, above note 124.

126 *Salilar*, above note 39. Both *Lai* and *Salilar* were cited in *Thanabalasingham* (FCA), above note 38 at paras 5–8.

127 *Salilar*, above note 39 at para 17.

128 *Thanabalasingham* (FCA), above note 38 at para 10.

129 See, for example, *Canada (Minister of Citizenship and Immigration) v B046*, 2011 FC 877.

130 *Sittampalam*, above note 42.

- continue the person's detention;
- release the person;
- release the person, but impose certain conditions, such as, for example, payment of a deposit, posting of a guarantee of compliance,[131] or participation in third-party risk management (e.g., the Toronto Bail Program[132]).

Canada (Minister of Citizenship and Immigration) v Romans[133] provides a good illustration of the above-discussed issues. Romans accumulated an extensive criminal record and, as a result, a removal order was issued against him. Pending removal, he was taken to immigration detention (primarily due to being considered a danger to the public). Romans pursued several avenues to remain in Canada and, in the meantime, remained in detention for some five years. Eventually, the Immigration Division ordered the release as it was unknown when Romans would be removed from Canada (due to outstanding proceedings) and his detention was becoming indefinite. Although the Board concluded that Romans constituted a danger to the public, it declined to impose conditions as it considered that in light of Romans's mental state (he was a chronic paranoid schizophrenic), he was unlikely to comply with any of them. The Federal Court found that the Immigration Division's decision to release Romans was reasonable, but it was unreasonable not to impose any conditions on release in light of the Board's express finding that Romans continued to be a danger to the public.

b) Procedural Aspects of Detention Review

The *Immigration Division Rules* set out the general requirements applicable to proceedings before the Division, including time limits, information disclosure, language of the proceedings, procedure for making applications, and calling of witnesses, but they are not as strict as court rules. In the absence of a rule pertaining to a particular matter raised during the proceedings, the Division is accorded discretion to "do whatever is necessary to deal with the matter."[134]

---

131 *IRPA*, above note 1, s 58(3).

132 The Toronto Bail Program is a non-profit agency that allows for release from detention on conditions of community supervision in cases where other forms of release (e.g., bonds) are not available. The Toronto Bail Program has an arrangement with the CBSA under which it selects clients suitable to participate in the program. The selection criteria usually take into account a person's willingness to surrender travel documents or to complete an application for travel documents prior to release. IRCC, "ENF 20," above note 31 at 18.

133 2005 FC 435.

134 *Immigration Division Rules*, above note 101, r 49.

As is the case in other proceedings before the IRB, a person appearing before the Immigration Division has the right to be represented by counsel.[135] A party who is under eighteen years of age or who is unable to appreciate the nature of the proceedings will be appointed a designated representative.[136] Interpreters are also provided if necessary. The party must notify the Immigration Division of the need for an interpreter as soon as possible, in the case of a forty-eight-hour or seven-day detention review, and in all other cases, at least five days before the hearing.[137]

i) Notification of Detention

The CBSA must provide the Immigration Division with information about a person subject to detention review, including personal data, contact information of person's counsel, the date when the person was first placed in detention, reasons for detention, the need (if any) for non-disclosure of information, and whether the person has made a refugee claim.[138] In the case of a forty-eight-hour review, the above information must be provided as soon as possible; in the case of a seven-day or thirty-day review, it must be provided at least three days before the date of the review.[139]

The Immigration Division schedules a date for a hearing and must notify the parties orally or in writing of the hearing's date, time, and location.[140] The Division may also require the parties to meet to work out the schedule of the proceedings or provide certain information.

Under rule 9 of the *Immigration Division Rules*, either the person concerned or the Minister may make an application for an earlier detention review. The rule applies only to seven-day and thirty-day detention reviews, and the application may be allowed where it sets out new facts that justify an earlier hearing.

ii) Disclosure

The parties are required to disclose to each other and to the Division documents that they wish to use at a hearing. The copies of the documents must be received at least five days before a hearing (except in cases of a forty-eight-hour or a seven-day review, where copies simply must be provided as soon as possible).[141] A document may be provided

135 *IRPA*, above note 1, s 167(1).

136 *Ibid*, s 167(2).

137 *Immigration Division Rules*, above note 101, r 17(1).

138 *Ibid*, r 8.

139 *Ibid*, r 8(2).

140 *Ibid*, rr 21 & 22.

141 *Ibid*, r 26.

in person, by regular or registered mail, courier or priority post, fax (if the document is less than twenty pages long), or electronic mail if the Division allows.[142] Where a document is sent by regular mail, it is considered received seven days after being mailed.[143] If a party, after making reasonable efforts to provide a document in a specified way, is nevertheless unable to do so, it may apply to the Division to be allowed another method of delivery or to be excused from providing the document.[144]

Parties can also call witnesses to provide evidence on the matter at hand. A party wishing to call a witness must provide the other party and the Division with information regarding the number of witnesses that it intends to call, the purpose and substance of their testimony, the time needed for testimony, and the party's relation to the witness(es).[145]

In situations involving national security, the Minister's counsel may make an application for non-disclosure of certain information to a person concerned and her counsel.[146] If the application is granted, the Division schedules an *ex parte* private hearing where the Minister's counsel and the agency providing the confidential information present the information to an adjudicator for examination. The person concerned would be provided with a summary (but not all protected information) that would enable him "to be reasonably informed of the case made by the Minister in the proceeding."[147]

iii) *Procedure at the Hearing*

The hearing is adversarial. The two parties are a foreign national or a permanent resident and the Minister. During detention review, the parties may present arguments and facts, cross-examine witnesses, and make submissions. Proceedings are to be held in public, although they may be held in private in some circumstances.[148] If a party wants to have the hearing conducted in private, it must make an application to the Immigration Division to that effect.[149] Hearings are usually conducted in person, but they may also be conducted by video conference.[150]

---

142 *Ibid*, r 29.

143 *Ibid*, r 31(2).

144 *Ibid*, r 30.

145 *Ibid*, r 32.

146 *IRPA*, above note 1, s 86.

147 *Ibid*, ss 83(e), 86.

148 *Ibid*, ss 166(a) & (b).

149 *Immigration Division Rules*, above note 101, r 15.

150 *IRPA*, above note 1, s 164.

The IRB is not bound by strict rules of evidence. Any evidence considered by an adjudicator as "credible or trustworthy in the circumstances" is admissible.[151] However, parties are to follow the best evidence rule; that is, secondary evidence should not be introduced unless primary evidence is unavailable.

The onus is always on the Minister to show the case for detention and its continuation.[152] However, once the Minister establishes a *prima facie* case, the evidentiary burden shifts to the detainee.[153] The fact that the Minister once established a *prima facie* case for detention does not mean that it stands indefinitely. With the passage of time, the evidence that supported detention may become outdated and no longer meet the *prima facie* case for detention.[154] If the Minister wishes to continue detention, fresh evidence of current danger or flight risk must be presented.[155]

E. SECURITY CERTIFICATES

The security certificate procedure allows for detention and removal of permanent residents and foreign nationals who are inadmissible on grounds of security, violating human or international rights, serious criminality, or organized criminality. Since 2000, security certificates were most commonly applied in national security cases, particularly in relation to suspected members of terrorist organizations. Detention on security certificates can be seen as a special type of preventive detention that seeks to protect Canadian society from criminal and security threats.[156] It follows a different procedure and is governed by different legislative provisions than the detention regimes described earlier in this chapter.

Although the security certificate procedure has been in existence since 1978, it was not used particularly often and has no direct link to the refugee determination process. However, recent application of security certificates to several Convention refugees and the possibility of removal to torture make this procedure relevant to the discussion in this book.

---

151 *Ibid*, s 173(1)(d).

152 *Thanabalasingham* (FCA), above note 38 at para 16.

153 *Ibid* at para 24; *Salilar*, above note 39 at para 17.

154 *Sittampalam*, above note 42 at para 27.

155 *Ibid*.

156 *Charkaoui (Re)*, above note 9 at para 130; *Almrei v. Canada (Minister of Citizenship and Immigration)*, [2004] FCJ No 509 (FC) [*Almrei*].

Mainly since 9/11 the security certificate procedure has begun to attract significant attention on the part of activists and the public. This has been due both to heightened awareness of security as a social issue and to the government's willingness to use the security certificate procedure to effect detention. The restrictive rules of disclosure and review that govern security certificates, along with the dire consequences that their use can entail for individuals, has brought them to the forefront of popular, academic, and judicial debate. The constitutionality of the procedure was challenged in *Charkaoui v Canada*, subsequently leading to a number of changes in the *IRPA*. The revised security certificate procedure has also been subject to a constitutional challenge, but it was upheld by the Supreme Court. This section will first discuss the procedure as tailored under the 2002 wording of the *IRPA*, then the *Charkaoui* litigation, and finally the 2008 amendments.

1) Pre-*Charkaoui* Security Certificate Procedure

The security certificate procedure under the 2002 *IRPA* worked as follows. A security certificate was signed by the Minister of Citizenship and Immigration and the Minister of Public Safety and Emergency Preparedness.[157] Upon being signed, the certificate was referred to the Federal Court, which was tasked to determine whether the certificate was reasonable.[158] If a person named in the certificate was a foreign national, he was subject to mandatory detention; detention could also be applied to permanent residents.[159] The detention of permanent residents had to be reviewed within forty-eight hours and after that, every six months.[160] In contrast, foreign nationals could apply for release only if 120 days had passed since the certificate against them was determined reasonable and they had not been removed from Canada.[161] In practice, this meant that foreign nationals would be subject to detention without review for months and, in some cases, years.

In the course of determining the reasonableness of a certificate, the named person had only limited access to the information presented by the government: evidence, disclosure of which was deemed to be injurious to the national security or the safety of any person, was to be kept confidential.[162] The named person was provided only with a

157 *IRPA*, above note 1, s 77(1).
158 *Ibid*, ss 77 & 78.
159 *Ibid*, s 82 (2002 version; no longer in force).
160 *Ibid*, ss 83(1) & (2).
161 *Ibid*, s 84(2) (2002 version; no longer in force).
162 *Ibid*, s 83(1)(d).

summary of non-disclosed information which would allow her "to be reasonably informed of the case."[163] In addition, the person concerned and his lawyer would be excluded from any hearing where the sensitive information was presented. Further, the usual rules of evidence do not apply to the security certificate proceedings: "the judge may receive into evidence anything that, in the judge's opinion, is reliable and appropriate, even if it is inadmissible in a court of law, and may base a decision on that evidence."[164]

If the Federal Court confirmed the certificate, the certificate became conclusive proof that the named person was inadmissible and constituted an enforceable removal order.[165] It also precluded a person from the benefits of a pre-removal risk assessment.[166] The decision on reasonableness was final and could not be judicially reviewed or appealed.[167]

Some of the major problems with the security certificate procedure become apparent from the review of the brief facts of the following five cases:

1) *Hassan Almrei*: foreign national, citizen of Syria, and a recognized Convention refugee; detained since October 2001 and released on conditions in January 2009; certificate found unreasonable in December 2009;
2) *Adil Charkaoui*: citizen of Morocco and a permanent resident of Canada; detained in May 2003 and released on conditions in February 2005; certificate found unreasonable in October 2009 (key evidence withdrawn by the Minister);
3) *Mohammad Harkat*: foreign national, citizen of Algeria, and a recognized Convention refugee; detained in December 2002 and released on conditions in June 2006; certificate upheld in December 2010;
4) *Mahmoud Jaballah*: foreign national and citizen of Egypt; first detained in 1999, but the certificate was found unreasonable; re-detained in August 2001 and released on conditions in March 2007; certificate found unreasonable in May 2016;
5) *Mohammad Mahjoub*: foreign national, citizen of Egypt, and a recognized Convention refugee; detained in June 2000 and released on conditions in February 2007; determination of reasonableness pending.

---

163 *Ibid*, s 83(1)(e).
164 *Ibid*, s 83(1)(h).
165 *Ibid*, s 80.
166 *Ibid*, s 81(c) (2002 version; no longer in force).
167 *Ibid*, s 80(3) (2002 version; no longer in force).

The security certificate procedure was intended as a summary procedure for quick removal of dangerous individuals from Canada; however, practice has showed otherwise. Given the complicated process of collecting intelligence in national security cases and lengthiness of its examination, non-citizens were often detained for years before resolution of their cases. In addition, other proceedings such as appeals, challenges to removal orders, and applications for PRRA tended to further prolong the process.[168] As the above summary shows, the named persons have spent between two and seven years, three months in detention before being released on conditions. The initial conditions of release were very stringent (although progressively relaxed over time) and included curfew (of various duration ranging from 9 to 11.5 hours); supervision by specified individuals; an order to keep within the specified geographic limits during outings; prior approval of any visitors to the house; screening of all communications by the CBSA; bail of various amounts; residence at a specified address; wearing of an electronic bracelet; prohibition on use of communication devices; prohibition on communication with certain individuals; agreement to allow any CBSA or peace officer to enter the residence at any time; keeping peace and good behaviour; prohibition on possessing any weapons; reporting to the CBSA; and surrender of a passport and all travel documents.

In four above-mentioned cases, the decision on reasonableness was finally made some eight to nine years after the issuance of the initial certificate (it should be noted, however, that following the 2008 amendments to the *IRPA*, new security certificates were issued against the above-mentioned five persons[169] and their reasonableness had to be determined anew, which led to a further lag of time). One case is still pending.

Moreover, even those who were recognized to have links with terrorist organizations often cannot be deported because of risk of torture in a destination country. Although only three of the five cases mentioned above are recognized Convention refugees, in some sense, security certificates raise refugee-like issues for all five individuals. The very designation of an individual in a security certificate may cause a

---

168 It is interesting to note that in earlier cases, the Federal Court determined that detention was not indefinite or unreasonably long because the delays in removal were caused by applicants themselves who chose to challenge their removal orders. *Almrei*, above note 156 at para 91; *Jaballah v Canada (Minister of Citizenship and Immigration)*, 2004 FC 299 at paras 36–37.

169 New certificates were signed on 22 February 2008 and had to go to the Federal Court anew.

risk of mistreatment upon removal to his country of nationality. Given that the Supreme Court decision in *Suresh v Canada (Minister of Citizenship and Immigration)*[170] did not impose an absolute prohibition on removal to torture, it is possible that security certificates may become those "extraordinary circumstances" when removal is possible.

The security certificate procedure under both the old *Immigration Act* and the *IRPA* was criticized by some members of the Canadian judiciary, non-governmental organizations, and international bodies. In 2000, the Inter-American Commission on Human Rights indicated that non-disclosure of information in a security certificate procedure raised serious due process concerns.[171] In 2005, the UN Working Group on Arbitrary Detention expressed concerns about the mandatory nature of detention, its lengthiness, the non-disclosure of information, and a possibility of deportation to the risk of torture.[172] Similarly, the UN Committee against Torture highlighted concerns about security certificates in its concluding observations on Canada's periodic reports and recommended the procedure to be revised.[173]

Canada is not alone in utilizing immigration procedures to contain and remove non-citizens deemed to pose a threat to national security. Comparable procedure exists in New Zealand.[174] In the United Kingdom, detention and deportation of non-citizens under certificates was practised during 2001–04 under the 2001 *Anti-terrorism, Crime and Security Act*. However, the procedure was found contrary to the *European Convention on Human Rights*[175] and, as a result, was replaced by a regime of control orders (applicable to both citizens and non-citizens) in 2005[176] and then a system of terrorism prevention and investigation measures in 2011.[177] Both control orders and terrorism prevention and investigation measures allow for imposition of various constraints and conditions (reviewable by courts) on named persons. Australia employs a system of control orders much like those of the United Kingdom. In

---

170 [2002] 1 SCR 3.

171 Inter-American Commission on Human Rights, "Report on the Situation of Human Rights of Asylum Seekers within the Canadian Refugee Determination System (2000)," online: www.cidh.org/countryrep/Canada2000en/table-of-contents.htm.

172 Working Group on Arbitrary Detention, above note 33 at para 8.

173 Committee against Torture, "Concluding Observations," CAT/C/CAN/CO/6 (2012) at 3–4, online: www2.ohchr.org/english/bodies/cat/docs/CAT.C.CAN.CO.6.doc.

174 *Immigration Act 1987* (NZ), 1987/4, ss 114A–114R.

175 *A v Secretary of State for the Home Department*, [2004] UKHL 56.

176 *Prevention of Terrorism Act 2005* (UK), c 2.

177 *Terrorism Prevention and Investigation Measures Act*, 2011, c 23.

all jurisdictions, the mentioned procedures were subject to litigation, in some cases, prompting changes to respective regimes.

Canada and New Zealand maintain special immigration procedures (security or risk certificates) that can be employed in the case of non-citizens only, while Australia and the United Kingdom have opted for control measures that can be applied to both citizens and non-citizens. It should be noted that in all jurisdictions, there are also criminal law provisions, under which both citizens and non-citizens can be subject to prosecution. Despite this, control orders or immigration procedures are often chosen instead. Such choice is usually due to the fact that evidence is not sufficiently strong to meet the criminal law's "beyond a reasonable doubt" threshold. In fact, in the past the UK authorities expressly acknowledged that control orders were employed where it was not possible or feasible to prosecute individuals for terrorist-related activity.[178]

2) *Charkaoui* Decision (2007)

The security certificate procedure was challenged by three named persons — Adil Charkaoui, Hassan Almrei, and Mohamed Harkat — who argued that it violated the *Charter*, sections 7 (right to life, liberty and security of person), 9 (prohibition on arbitrary detention), 10(c) (prompt review of detention), 12 (prohibition of torture), and 15 (equality).[179] In February 2007, the Supreme Court found that the lack of disclosure violated fundamental principles of justice under section 7 and that the lack of regular detention reviews for foreign nationals violated sections 9 and 10(c) of the *Charter*.[180]

With respect to the limited disclosure, the Supreme Court determined that in the context of security certificates, the principles of fundamental justice required a process that provided for

1) a right to a hearing;
2) a hearing before an independent and impartial magistrate;
3) a decision made on the facts and the law;

178 David Anderson, "Control Orders in 2011: Final Report of the Independent Reviewer on the Prevention of Terrorism Act 2005" (March 2012) at 6 and 18, online: https://terrorismlegislationreviewer.independent.gov.uk/wp-content/uploads/2013/04/control-orders-2011.pdf. A similar admission was mentioned by the UK court in *Abu Rideh v Secretary of State*, [2008] EWHC 2019 at para 23, and *Secretary of State v E*, [2007] EWHC 233 (Admin) at para 124.

179 *Charkaoui*, above note 103.

180 Above note 105.

4) the right to know the case against oneself and the right to answer that case.[181]

The Court found that the first two requirements were met, but the other two were not. Due to the lack of disclosure, the person concerned was not able to know the case to be met and, as a result, to effectively respond to that case. This, in turn, undermined the ability of a judge to make a decision based on all available facts and the law. On the one hand, the judge was not accorded independent investigatory powers to gather evidence. On the other hand, she could not rely on the parties to present missing evidence. This was particularly true with respect to the person concerned as he often would not fully know the case against him and, correspondingly, would not know what information to present to counter the government's evidence.

In relation to detention, the Court acknowledged the concern that detention could become indefinite, particularly in cases where voluntary departure was not possible.[182] It, however, concluded that lengthy detention under security certificates did not violate sections 7 and 12 of the *Charter* as long as it was accompanied by regular detention reviews.[183] The Court confirmed that decision makers on detention reviews should take into consideration the factors that were pronounced in *Sahin v Canada (Minister of Citizenship and Immigration)*[184] and later codified in the IRB Chairperson's Guidelines — Guideline 2: Detention — and the *Regulations*, section 248, namely: reasons for detention, length of detention, reasons for delay, anticipated future length of detention, and alternatives to detention.[185] The Court also provided additional guidance with respect to the assessment of these factors in the context of security certificates. In particular, it stated that the length of detention is an important factor, both from the perspective of the person concerned and from the perspective of national security. On the one hand, the longer the detention, the less likely the person is to remain a threat to national security.[186] On the other hand, the more time the government has to investigate the person concerned, the heavier is its evidentiary onus to establish the case for continued detention.[187] With respect to reasons for delay, the Supreme Court emphasized that recourse to remedies that "are reasonable in the circumstances" or to

181 *Charkaoui*, above note 103 at para 29.
182 *Ibid* at paras 99–105.
183 *Ibid* at para 110.
184 *Sahin*, above note 104.
185 *Charkaoui*, above note 103 at paras 111–17.
186 *Ibid* at para 112.
187 *Ibid* at para 113.

"reasonable *Charter* challenges" by the government or by the person concerned should not count against either party.[188] Finally, the existence and feasibility of alternatives to detention (such as release on conditions) must be considered. Where the danger can be neutralized by conditions, release may be ordered.[189]

3) Post-*Charkaoui* Amendments to the Security Certificate Procedure (2008)

Although the Supreme Court determined that the security certificate procedure was unconstitutional, it suspended the declaration of invalidity for one year to allow Parliament to redesign the procedure to make it consistent with the *Charter*.[190] The amendments to the *IRPA* were passed in February 2008. They have preserved much of the basic framework of the security certificate procedure,[191] but added certain safeguards in response to the *Charkaoui* decision. The major changes to the procedure include these:

1) establishment of the position of special advocate;
2) single detention and detention review regimes for permanent residents and foreign nationals;
3) appeal on the determination of reasonableness of a certificate.

a) Special Advocate

The amended provisions preserve the limitations on disclosure of information related to national security.[192] However, they provide a new

---

188 *Ibid* at para 114.

189 *Ibid* at paras 117–23.

190 *Ibid* at paras 138–42. It should also be noted that the Court did not suspend its declaration of invalidity of s 84(2) of the *IRPA* (possibility of judicial release of foreign nationals if they have not been removed from Canada 120 days after the certificate was determined reasonable). In order to ensure a possibility of detention reviews for foreign nationals after the determination of reasonableness as well as during the process, the Court made the following order: that s 84(2) be stricken; that foreign nationals be read into s 83, and the words "until a determination is made under subsection 80(1)" be stricken from s 83(2).

191 The procedure for issuance of the certificate and its main stages described in Section E(1), above in this chapter, continue to apply. However, detention of foreign nationals is no longer mandatory. Rather, amended s 81 of the *IRPA* gives the ministers power to issue a warrant for the arrest and detention of a person named in a certificate "if they have reasonable grounds to believe that the person is a danger to national security or to the safety of any person or is unlikely to appear at a proceeding or for removal."

192 *IRPA*, above note 1, s 83(1) (as amended).

safeguard in the form of a special advocate who is given access to the non-disclosed information.[193] The Minister must provide a special advocate with a copy of all information and evidence that is provided to the judge and is not disclosed to the person concerned and his counsel.[194]

A special advocate is appointed by the judge who is examining the reasonableness of a certificate;[195] the judge also has the power to terminate the appointment and appoint another person.[196] The Minister of Justice is responsible for establishing a list of persons who may act as special advocates.[197] As of July 2015, twenty-two lawyers were on the list of special advocates.[198] The selection process is ongoing and further additions to the list are possible.

The role of the special advocate is to protect the interests of the named person in proceedings where confidential information is heard in the absence of that person and her counsel.[199] The powers of the special advocate include challenging the Minister's claim that the disclosure of certain information would be injurious to national security;[200] challenging the relevance, reliability, and sufficiency of confidential information provided by the Minister;[201] making oral and written submissions with respect to confidential information;[202] participating in and cross-examining witnesses who testify during proceedings from which the person concerned and his counsel are excluded;[203] and exercising, with the judge's authorization, any other power that is necessary to protect the interests of the person concerned.[204] There are, however, no client–solicitor relations between the special advocate and the person subject to a security certificate.[205]

---

193 *Ibid.*

194 *Ibid*, s 85.4(1).

195 *Ibid*, s 83(1).

196 *Ibid*, s 83(2).

197 *Ibid*, s 85(1). The applications for special advocates are reviewed by the selection committee which then makes recommendations to the minister. Department of Justice, "Special Advocates Program," online: www.justice.gc.ca/eng/fund-fina/jsp-sjp/sa-es.html.

198 Department of Justice, "List of Persons Who May Act as Special Advocates," online: www.justice.gc.ca/eng/fund-fina/jsp-sjp/list-liste.html.

199 *IRPA*, above note 1, s 85.1(1).

200 *Ibid*, s 85.1(2)(a).

201 *Ibid*, s 85.1(2)(b).

202 *Ibid*, s 85.2(a).

203 *Ibid*, s 85.2(b).

204 *Ibid*, s 85.2(c).

205 *Ibid*, s 85.1(3). Despite this, solicitor–client privilege is deemed to apply to exchanges between the special advocates and the named person as long as those

Although the special advocate model allows to partially compensate for the non-disclosure, it has its weaknesses.[206] Most notably, once the special advocate receives confidential information from the Minister, she is prohibited from communicating with anyone, including the person concerned, for the remainder of the proceeding, unless such communication is authorized by a judge.[207]

b) Detention and Detention Reviews

The 2008 amendments to the *IRPA* established a single regime for detention and detention reviews for permanent residents and foreign nationals. The Minister of Immigration, Refugees and Citizenship Canada and the Minister of Public Safety and Emergency Preparedness may issue a warrant for arrest and detention of a person concerned if they have "reasonable grounds to believe" that that person is a danger to national security or the public or a flight risk.[208]

Detention reviews are carried out on a regular basis: first, within forty-eight hours after detention begins; and subsequently, at least once every six months after each preceding review.[209] A person who is released from detention on conditions may apply to the Federal Court for review of the conditions of release six months after the preceding review.[210] The judge may vary conditions of release if satisfied that such variation is desirable because of a material change in the circumstances.[211]

---

exchanges would attract solicitor–client privilege at common law: *IRPA*, s 85.1(4). See also *Canada (Citizenship and Immigration) v Harkat*, 2014 SCC 37 at para 36 [*Harkat*].

206 For example, a report by Craig Forcese and Lorne Waldman, which studied the approaches adopted in New Zealand and the United Kingdom as well as related practices in Canada, highlighted that the special advocate model generally suffers from several shortcomings. The study recommended reinstating the model employed by the Canadian Security and Intelligence Review Committee (the process that was in place under the old *Immigration Act*) instead of following the UK/New Zealand special advocate model. Craig Forcese & Lorne Waldman, *Seeking Justice in an Unfair Process: Lessons from Canada, the United Kingdom, and New Zealand on the Use of "Special Advocates" in National Security Proceedings* (Ottawa: Faculty of Law, University of Ottawa, 2007), online: http://aix1.uottawa.ca/~cforcese/other/sastudy.pdf.

207 *IRPA*, above note 1, s 85.4(2).

208 *Ibid*, s 81.

209 *Ibid*, s 82.

210 *Ibid*, s 82(4).

211 *Ibid*, s 81.1(1).

c) Appeal on the Determination of Reasonableness of a Certificate

A decision on the reasonableness of a certificate may be appealed to the Federal Court of Appeal.[212] However, as in the case of other immigration issues, such an appeal is contingent on the Federal Court judge certifying a serious question of general importance.[213]

In 2013, the Supreme Court heard a second constitutional challenge — now to the revised security certificate procedure.[214] Mohammed Harkat, whose certificate was confirmed by the Federal Court, argued, among other things, that the existence of the special advocate was not enough to provide the named person with a fair process. He argued that the regime is unconstitutional because it provided insufficient disclosure to the named person, did not allow the special advocate to communicate freely with the named person, and allowed for the admission of hearsay evidence.

The Supreme Court acknowledged that the amended security certificate provisions remain "an imperfect substitute for full disclosure in an open court,"[215] but concluded that they did not violate the named person's rights under section 7 of the *Charter.* The Court noted that the judge's broad discretion is a crucial guarantee of the fairness of the process:

> Designated judges must ensure that the named person receives sufficient disclosure of the information and evidence to be able to give meaningful instructions to his public counsel and meaningful guidance to his special advocates, must refuse to admit evidence that is unreliable or whose probative value is outweighed by its prejudicial effects, and must take a liberal approach towards authorizing communications by the special advocates. And in cases where the inherent limitations of the *IRPA* scheme create procedural unfairness, designated judges must exercise their discretion under s. 24(1) of the *Charter* to grant an appropriate remedy.[216]

---

212 *Ibid*, s 79.

213 *Ibid.*

214 *Harkat*, above note 205.

215 *Ibid* at para 77.

216 *Ibid* at para 110.

Table 11.1: Comparison of Immigration Detention Regimes

	Detention under Sections 55(1)–(3)	Detention of Designated Foreign Nationals	Detention under Security Certificates
Grounds	• "reasonable grounds to believe" that a person is inadmissible and is a danger to the public, or a flight risk, or if their identity is in question • Need to complete an examination (on entry) • "reasonable grounds to suspect" that a person is inadmissible on grounds of security, violation of human or international rights, serious criminality, criminality, or organized criminality (on entry)	Designation of a person as a designated foreign national	Issuance of a security certificate and reasonable grounds to believe that named person is a danger to national security or to the safety of any person or is a flight risk
First Detention Review	Within forty-eight hours	Within fourteen days	Within forty-eight hours
Second Review	At least once during seven days	Six months after preceding review	At least once every six months

	Detention under Sections 55(1)–(3)	Detention of Designated Foreign Nationals	Detention under Security Certificates
Subsequent Reviews	At least once during every thirty-day period	Six months after preceding review	At least once every six months
Reviewing Authority	Immigration Division of the IRB	Immigration Division of the IRB	Federal Court

F. CONCLUSION

The detention of individuals is one of the most severe powers of the government. Particularly troubling is the government's broad statutory ability to detain based on issues of identity and its even broader ability, albeit less exercised, to detain based on concerns about national security. While motivated by legitimate concerns, both these powers can easily lead to lengthy detentions based on opinions that are difficult to challenge. Further, a new detention regime for designated foreign nationals provides for detention upon designation, without consideration of individual circumstances, ostensibly even when a person does not pose any threat or constitute a flight risk. The jurisprudence continues to struggle to balance the impact of detention on individuals against the need to protect the host society.

CHAPTER 12

REMOVAL FROM CANADA

A. INTRODUCTION

Similar to immigration arrest and detention, removal can be applied only to foreign nationals and permanent residents. It is used as a tool to protect Canada's security and the Canadian public from dangerous persons and to expel those who are no longer entitled to stay in Canada. Foreign nationals can be removed once their authorization to be in Canada expires or is cancelled due to inadmissibility. Permanent residents may also be subject to removal on specified grounds of inadmissibility (e.g., non-compliance with the residency obligation or serious criminality). These grounds are used as a basis to first strip the permanent resident of his status and then subject him to removal. Convention refugees and persons in need of protection are shielded from removal by the principle of non-*refoulement*, whether or not they became permanent residents.[1] Unsuccessful refugee claimants do not enjoy such protection, so can be removed once refugee determination and any available recourse against a negative decision are completed.[2]

For removal to occur, the following basic conditions must be satisfied. First, the government must have the legal authority to remove

1 *Immigration and Refugee Protection Act*, SC 2001, c 27, s 115 [*IRPA*].

2 Not all applicants enjoy automatic stay of removal upon application for judicial review. Thus, they can be removed prior to completion of judicial review, unless they obtain a court-ordered stay. Please see Section D, below in this chapter, and Chapter 10 for further discussion.

the individual, something that is normally accomplished through the issuance of a removal order. Second, removal must comply with the general obligations of non-*refoulement* of refugees and the prohibition of *refoulement* to torture as well as various other statutory, regulatory, or court-ordered stays of removal that may be in place. However, due to the exception to non-*refoulement* under the *Convention Relating to the Status of Refugees* as well as the Supreme Court decision in *Suresh v Canada (Minister of Citizenship and Immigration)*[3] (see Chapter 2, Sections C(1) and F(3)), it is possible to initiate removal of protected persons. Further, if application for cessation of refugee protection is granted (see Chapter 4), a protected person loses both protected person status and permanent residence (if acquired), becomes inadmissible to Canada, and can be subject to removal. Third, the person facing removal must have a right to enter a destination country, or a country that agrees to accept him. Fourth, a person who is subject to removal must be in possession of the documents required for travel (specifically, those required for admission to the destination country). Given that states are usually willing to admit only their own nationals or permanent residents, arranging for the removal of stateless persons can be particularly difficult.

This chapter will discuss each of the core aspects of the removal process in the sequence outlined above: the various categories of removal orders; stays of removal; pre-removal risk assessment (PRRA); and the making of removal arrangements. This discussion is mainly relevant to cases of rejected claimants, although it also outlines principles that are generally applicable to removal of other non-citizens.

B. REMOVAL ORDERS

When a person makes a refugee claim in Canada, she is issued a "conditional" removal order. The mere fact of making a refugee claim does not result in the removal order. Rather, collateral facts related to or arising from the making of a refugee claim are most commonly the basis of the inadmissibility allegations. These grounds include the inability of the claimant to financially support himself while in Canada[4] and non-compliance with the requirement of the *Immigration and Refugee Protection Act* that, as an individual seeking to remain indefinitely in Canada,

---

3 [2002] 1 SCR 3 [*Suresh*].

4 *IRPA*, above note 1, s 39.

he should be in possession of a passport and an immigrant visa.[5] In a few cases, removal orders based on other grounds, such as criminality, will also be sought against refugee claimants (see Appendix D, Table 10, for a breakdown of all removals by ground).

The removal order is "conditional" on the outcome of the refugee claim: where a claim is successful the removal order is deemed void upon the individual acquiring permanent residence.[6] On the other hand, where a refugee claimant is unsuccessful, the removal order will come into force on the latest of the following days:

1) the day the claim is determined to be ineligible for a refugee hearing under section 101(1)(e) of the *IRPA* (claimant came from a safe third country);
2) in a case other than that set out in paragraph (a), seven days after the claim is determined to be ineligible for a refugee hearing before the Refugee Protection Division (RPD);
3) if a claim is rejected by the RPD, upon expiry of the prescribed time limit for an appeal to the Refugee Appeal Division (RAD) or, if the appeal is made, fifteen days after the RAD rejects the claim;
4) fifteen days after the notification that the claim is declared withdrawn or abandoned; or
5) fifteen days after proceedings are terminated as a result of notice under section 104(1)(c) of the *IRPA* (notice that a claim is ineligible for reasons of misrepresentation or withholding material facts or if it is a repeat claim).[7]

Most rejected refugee claimants fall under the fifteen-day time limit outlined in the *IRPA*, section 49(2)(c). For claimants who have the right to appeal to the RAD, the delay in the conditional removal order coming into effect allows for the filing of an appeal and subsequently, if the appeal is rejected, for filing a judicial review application of that rejection. The *Immigration and Refugee Protection Regulations* establish a fifteen-day time limit for filing of a RAD appeal and give another fifteen days to perfect that appeal.[8] The wording of the legislation does not make it clear whether the removal order under section 49(2)(c) is stayed for the fifteen days for filing the appeal or for the cumulative thirty-day period to file and perfect the appeal. As some authorities note, the section is

5 *Ibid*, ss 20 and 41(a); *Immigration and Refugee Protection Regulations*, SOR/2002-227, ss 6 and 50 [*Regulations*].

6 *IRPA*, above note 1, s 51.

7 *Ibid*, s 49(2).

8 *Regulations*, above note 5, s 159.91(1).

likely to be interpreted as referring to the fifteen-day time limit.[9] Once an appeal application is made, removal is stayed until the application is determined.[10] Claimants' removal is further stayed if they file for judicial review of a RAD decision.

Several groups of claimants[11] do not have a right to appeal to the RAD and do not enjoy automatic stay of removal upon filing an application for judicial review.[12] There is, however, some lack of clarity as to whether removal orders of such claimants are nevertheless stayed for fifteen days under section 49(2)(c). The wording of the section does not make the fifteen-day time limit dependent on a person's eligibility for an appeal and, thus, may be interpreted as applying to all claimants.[13] The issue, however, has not been definitively clarified by courts.

There are three types of removal orders: (1) departure orders, (2) exclusion orders, and (3) deportation orders.[14] They are distinguished by the reasons that led to their imposition and by the consequences that they entail for the person's return to Canada. Depending on the specific grounds of inadmissibility upon which the order is based, the removal order is issued either by an immigration officer or by the Immigration Division of the Immigration and Refugee Board (IRB).[15] Although individuals may also be removed through extradition procedures, this method of removal is outside the scope of this book.

---

9 Lorne Waldman & Jacqueline Swaisland, *Canada's Refugee Determination Procedure: A Guide for the Post-Bill C-31 Era* (Toronto: LexisNexis, 2013) at 242–43.

10 *Regulations*, above note 5, s 231(1).

11 These include designated foreign nationals; individuals whose claims have been determined withdrawn or abandoned; individuals whose claims have been determined to have no credible basis or to be manifestly unfounded; claimants subject to an exception to the *Safe Third Country Agreement*; individuals whose refugee protection was vacated or determined to cease to exist; individuals whose claims were deemed to be rejected because an order of surrender was issued under the *Extradition Act*. *IRPA*, above note 1, ss 105(4), 110. For more on appeals to the RAD, see Chapter 10. Legislation also barred claimants from designated countries of origin (DCOs) from appealing to the RAD. However, in 2015, that provision was found to be unconstitutional. For more, see Chapter 3, Section B(1)(a).

12 *Regulations*, above note 5, ss 231(2)–(3). Designated foreign nationals and claimants from DCOs do not enjoy an automatic stay of removal upon application for judicial review. Persons inadmissible on grounds of serious criminality and residents of the United States or St Pierre and Miquelon also do not enjoy automatic stay.

13 Waldman & Swaisland, above note 9 at 243.

14 *Regulations*, above note 5, s 223.

15 For details, see the *Regulations*, *ibid*, ss 228–29.

1) Departure Orders

The departure order regime seeks to encourage speedy voluntary compliance of persons with removal orders issued against them. Unlike an exclusion or a deportation order, a departure order allows the person to return to Canada without needing to obtain an authorization to re-enter. To take advantage of this "benefit," the person must depart Canada in a prescribed manner (that is, appear before an officer to verify departure, obtain a certificate of departure, and depart[16]) within thirty days of the order becoming enforceable. Failure to physically depart within thirty days in a prescribed manner means that a departure order automatically becomes a deportation order.[17] The calculation of the thirty-day period is suspended when a person concerned is detained under the *IRPA* or when the removal order is stayed.[18]

Despite the receipt of a departure order, rejected refugee claimants are rarely able to take advantage of its "benefit." Most often, they lack the funds to depart within the required thirty-day period. In addition, although departure within the prescribed period allows a rejected claimant to return without special authorization, the usual obstacles preventing travel to Canada still exist: the need for a visa,[19] and the distance and cost of travel. Further, some claimants who have left Canada within the thirty-day period may not be aware of the conditions that constitute the "prescribed manner" of departure, particularly, the need to verify the departure with an immigration officer. The failure to follow the procedure even though the person has departed Canada leaves the removal order unenforced and prevents him from returning to Canada in the future. (For more discussion, see Section F(1).)

2) Exclusion Orders

As a general rule, an exclusion order "obliges the foreign national to obtain a written authorization in order to return to Canada during the one-year period after the exclusion order was enforced."[20] A harsher regime applies to foreign nationals who are issued exclusion orders due

16 *Ibid*, ss 240(1)(a)–(c).

17 *Ibid*, s 224(2).

18 *Ibid*, s 224(3).

19 It is highly unlikely that a visa would be issued to a foreign national who had previously sought refugee protection in Canada. Such a request would almost automatically be refused, either on the ground that the previous refugee claim indicates a desire to remain in Canada other than temporarily or because of the misrepresentation implicit in the failure of the refugee claim.

20 *Regulations*, *ibid*, s 225(1).

to misrepresentation: they are subject to the requirement of obtaining a written authorization to return to Canada for a period of five years after the exclusion order was enforced.[21] Upon the expiration of a one-year or a five-year period, a foreign national is no longer required to obtain an authorization to return to Canada.[22]

3) Deportation Orders

A deportation order has more severe consequences for an individual concerned than an exclusion order. It requires a person to obtain a written authorization in order to return to Canada at any time after the enforcement of the order.[23]

4) Other Consequences for Future Travel to Canada

Apart from the conditions of removal orders, a person may be precluded from returning to Canada if her removal was enforced at public expense and the costs have not been reimbursed. According to the *Regulations*, section 243, ". . . a foreign national who is removed from Canada at Her Majesty's expense shall not return to Canada if the foreign national has not paid to Her Majesty the removal costs of (a) $750 for removal to the United States or St. Pierre and Miquelon; and (b) $1,500 for removal to any other country."[24] Thus, even if it is determined that an authorization to return to Canada can be granted, an officer should next decide if repayment under section 243 is applicable. The reimbursement must be collected before the authorization is granted.

C. ISSUANCE OF A REMOVAL ORDER

The *Regulations* outline circumstances in which a given type of removal order is to be issued. Depending on the ground of inadmissibility and

---

21 *Ibid*, s 225(3). There is one exception to this rule: a foreign national who is subject to such an order for reasons of being an accompanying family member of an inadmissible person does not have to obtain an authorization to return to Canada: *ibid*, s 225(4).

22 *Ibid*, s 225(2).

23 *Ibid*, s 226(1). The only exception from this rule is a foreign national who is subject to a deportation order for reasons of being an accompanying family member of an inadmissible person. Such a person does not have to obtain an authorization to return to Canada: *ibid*, s 226(2).

24 *Ibid*, s 243.

the status of the person concerned (namely, whether the person is a foreign national or a permanent resident), a removal order can be issued either by an officer of the Canada Border Services Agency (CBSA) or by the IRB. In all cases, the process starts by preparation of a report by a CBSA officer setting out the facts suggesting that a person is inadmissible.[25] The report is then submitted to a second officer who, depending on the circumstances, would either issue a removal order[26] or refer the case to the Immigration Division for an inadmissibility hearing. In the latter case, the Immigration Division determines whether a removal order is to be issued.[27]

An inadmissibility hearing is usually held in public and is of adversarial nature (unlike a refugee hearing, which is inquisitorial). The parties may call witnesses, examine them, and cross-examine them. Just like the Refugee Protection Division, the Immigration Division is not bound by legal or technical rules of evidence. Upon completion of a hearing, the Immigration Division is to make one of the following decisions:

- to make a removal order against the person concerned;
- to allow a person concerned to enter Canada for further examination;
- to recognize a right of the person concerned to enter Canada (e.g., if an individual is a Canadian citizen);
- to grant permanent resident status or temporary resident status to the foreign national concerned if satisfied that he meets the requirements of the *IRPA*.[28]

Decisions to issue a removal order can be appealed to the Immigration Appeal Division (IAD) of the IRB, except by individuals found inadmissible on the grounds of security, violating human or international rights, serious criminality, or organized criminality.[29] The IAD may allow an appeal, dismiss it, or stay a removal order and impose certain conditions on the person concerned.[30] The latter option is available as a special relief where humanitarian and compassionate grounds warrant it.[31]

---

25 *IRPA*, above note 1, s 44(1).

26 Section 228 of the *Regulations* prescribes circumstances when a CBSA officer may issue a removal order.

27 Section 229 of the *Regulations* prescribes circumstances when the Immigration Division may issue a removal order.

28 *IRPA*, above note 1, s 45.

29 *Ibid*, s 64.

30 *Ibid*, s 67(2).

31 *Regulations*, above note 5, s 251.

D. STATUTORY AND REGULATORY STAYS OF REMOVAL

The *IRPA* defines an enforceable removal order as an order that came into force and that is not stayed.[32] An enforceable removal order has the following effect: the person concerned must leave Canada immediately and the order must be enforced "as soon as possible."[33] However, if an order is stayed, its operation is suspended for a time and a person cannot be removed from Canada. The purposes of stays are multiple: to allow completion of particular proceedings that affect a person's status in Canada; to ensure the applicant's availability to participate in other proceedings as a witness or a party; or to observe Canada's humanitarian obligations. Most stays expire when a designated event occurs (e.g., when particular proceedings are completed). Stays are different from deferrals, which do not render a removal order formally unenforceable but only delay its enforcement.

There are three types of stays of removal: statutory, regulatory, and court-ordered.[34] Only statutory and regulatory stays will be discussed here; judicial stays are discussed in Chapter 10.

1) Statutory Stays of Removal

Section 50 of the *IRPA* lists the following circumstances that may lead to the statutory stay of a removal order:

> (a) if a decision that was made in a judicial proceeding — at which the Minister shall be given the opportunity to make submissions — would be directly contravened by the enforcement of the removal order;
>
> (b) in the case of a foreign national sentenced to a term of imprisonment in Canada, until the sentence is completed;
>
> (c) for the duration of a stay imposed by the Immigration Appeal Division or any other court of competent jurisdiction;
>
> (d) for the duration of a stay under . . . [the *IRPA*, section] 114(1)(b); and
>
> (e) for the duration of a stay imposed by the Minister.

---

32 *IRPA*, above note 1, s 48(1).

33 *Ibid*, s 48(2).

34 The *Federal Courts Act*, RSC 1985, c F-7, s 18.2, provides that "[o]n an application for judicial review, the Federal Court may make any interim orders that it considers appropriate pending the final disposition of the application."

Sections 50(a) and (c) are subsets of judicial stays and therefore are dealt with in Chapter 10. Section 50(b) is self-explanatory and simply prevents an individual from being removed while he is serving a penal sentence. Section 50(d) deals with individuals who succeed in their pre-removal risk assessment (PRRA) but fall within section 112(3) of the *IRPA*. As discussed in greater detail in Section E(1), below in this chapter, such individuals only receive an indefinite stay of removal to the country in which they are at risk. Section 50(e) of the *IRPA* provides authority for the Minister to impose discretionary stays. These may overlap with some regulatory stays and embrace situations of temporary suspension of removal to particular countries or stays in individual cases for reasons of public policy, or humanitarian and compassionate considerations.

2) Regulatory Stays of Removal

Under the authority of section 53(d) of the *IRPA*, the *Regulations* can prescribe circumstances in which removal orders may be stayed. Regulatory stays encompass stays imposed by the Minister and stays not expressly provided for in the Act. The *Regulations* set out the following types of stays:

1) temporary suspension of removal (moratoria) to countries of generalized risk (section 230);
2) stays upon application for judicial review (section 231);
3) stays upon PRRA application (section 232); and
4) stays for humanitarian and compassionate or public policy reasons (section 233).

Some of these stays are automatic (e.g., those under section 231) while others are discretionary and are based on the specific circumstances of the case (e.g., those under section 233).

Under section 230 of the *Regulations*, the Minister may impose moratoria on removal to certain countries marred by generalized violence against the civilian population as a result of an armed conflict, environmental disaster, or "any situation that is temporary and generalized."[35] Currently, moratoria are in force on removals to Afghanistan, Democratic Republic of Congo, and Iraq.[36] However, a moratorium on removals

---

35 *Regulations*, above note 5, s 230.

36 For discussion of related issues, see Canadian Council for Refugees, Pamphlet, "Lives on Hold: Nationals of Moratoria Countries Living in Limbo" (July 2005), online: CCR http://ccrweb.ca/sites/ccrweb.ca/files/static-files/livespamph.pdf; Canadian Council for Refugees, "Submission to the Senate Standing Committee

does not apply to persons who are inadmissible on grounds of security, violating human or international rights, criminality, serious criminality, or organized criminality, or are referred to in article 1F of the *Refugee Convention*.[37]

In addition to moratoria, the Minister may stay removal in individual cases in the context of section 25(1) or 25.1(1) of the *IRPA* on humanitarian and compassionate grounds or public policy reasons. Such stay is effective until a decision is made to grant, or not grant, permanent resident status.[38]

Finally, a removal order is stayed when a rejected claimant applies for judicial review of a negative decision of the RAD.[39] The stay is effective until the earliest of the following:

1) Leave to appeal is denied by the Federal Court.
2) The application for leave is granted, but the application for judicial review is refused and no question is certified for the Federal Court of Appeal.
3) A question is certified but no appeal to the Federal Court of Appeal is filed within the prescribed time limit, or the Federal Court of Appeal dismisses the appeal and the claimant does not file a further appeal to the Supreme Court of Canada within the prescribed time limit.
4) An application for leave to appeal is made to the Supreme Court of Canada, but it is denied.
5) The application for leave is granted but the appeal is not filed within the time limit, or the Supreme Court of Canada dismisses the appeal.[40]

There is no stay of removal on judicial review for designated foreign nationals, claimants from designated countries of origin (DCO), persons subject to removal due to inadmissibility for serious criminality,

---

on National Security and Defence for Its Study on the Policies, Practices, and Collaborative Efforts of Canada Border Services Agency in Determining Admissibility to Canada and Removal of Inadmissible Individuals" (April 2014) at 5, online: CCR http://ccrweb.ca/files/senate-inadmissibility-study-april-2014.pdf.

37 *Regulations*, above note 5, s 230(3). Article 1F of the *Refugee Convention*, 28 July 1951, 189 UNTS 150, excludes from protection individuals with respect to whom "there are serious reasons for considering" that they committed a crime against peace, a war crime, a crime against humanity, a serious non-political crime, or have been guilty of acts contrary to the purposes and principles of the United Nations.

38 *Regulations*, above note 5, s 233.

39 *Ibid*, s 231(1).

40 *Ibid*.

and persons resident in the United States or St Pierre and Miquelon.[41] Stays upon application for a PRRA will be discussed in Section E, below.

E. PRE-REMOVAL RISK ASSESSMENT

As firmly established in the jurisprudence, foreign nationals do not have a right to be in Canada.[42] Once their authorized stay in Canada expires, they must depart or they will be removed. As a rule, foreign nationals are presumed to be able to return safely to their countries of nationality or habitual residence. However, there may be situations where a person concerned alleges that he would face risk to life, risk of torture, or risk of persecution in the country of intended destination. Pre-removal risk assessment (PRRA) is designed to address specifically these types of situations and ensure that Canada does not not violate its international and domestic obligations.[43] This objective was clearly articulated in *Figurado v Canada (Solicitor General)*:

> The PRRA process was implemented to allow individuals to apply for a review of the conditions surrounding the risk of return prior to their removal from Canada and not after their removal. Indeed, the PRRA emerged as a result of the jurisprudence of the Federal Court of Appeal and the Supreme Court of Canada, which required a timely risk assessment to comply with section 7 of the *Charter* . . . . It is clear that Parliament's primary intention in enacting the PRRA process was to comply with Canada's domestic and international commitments to the principle of non-*refoulement* . . . . The PRRA's fundamental purpose is to determine whether or not a person can safely be removed from Canada without being subject to persecution, torture or inhumane treatment.[44]

There are, however, two important limitations on access to PRRA. First, some individuals are not eligible to apply for a PRRA, namely, claimants ineligible for an RPD hearing because they came from a safe third country; persons who have Convention refugee status in another country and may safely return there; persons who already enjoy refugee protection in Canada; and persons subject to extradition.[45]

41 *Ibid*, ss 231(2), (3).

42 *Canada (Minister of Employment and Immigration) v Chiarelli*, [1992] 1 SCR 711 at 733.

43 *Regulatory Impact Analysis Statement to the IRPA Regulations*, (2001) C Gaz I, 4477.

44 [2005] FCJ No 458 at paras 40–41 (FC).

45 *IRPA*, above note 1, ss 112(1)–(2) and 115(1).

Second, most unsuccessful claimants may not apply for a PRRA for a certain time after their claim was rejected or determined withdrawn or abandoned (and they may be removed from Canada in the meantime). When PRRA was introduced in 2002, it, as a general rule, was open to most persons as soon as they became "removal ready."[46] Thus, for example, rejected refugee claimants could apply for a PRRA once they were "removal ready." However, in 2012, the PRRA eligibility rules were changed, adding the following bar on applications: in most cases, an individual cannot apply for a PRRA once she is "removal ready," but only upon expiration of a certain time. Claimants whose claims were withdrawn, abandoned, or rejected (unless the rejection was based on article 1E or 1F of the *Refugee Convention*) are now barred from applying for a PRRA for one year.[47] Rejected claimants from DCOs are barred for three years.[48] The constitutionality of the above-described "PRRA bar" was upheld by the courts.[49]

It is expected that, in most cases, rejected claimants will be removed from Canada well before they are eligible to apply for a PRRA. In 2014, the then IRCC Minister stated that rejected claimants were removed about twenty-three days from the time the case was referred for removal and, overall, it took about four months from the moment a claim was made until a rejected claimant was removed.[50]

The only persons who are not subject to the one- or three-year bar on application for a PRRA are those who were found ineligible to have a hearing before the RPD due to inadmissibility and those named in security certificates. In addition, the Minister may exempt nationals of certain countries or a class of persons from a given country from the application of the one- or three-year bar.[51] As of March 2017, the following countries were subject to exemption (as long as an applicant received a final IRB or PRRA decision on or between prescribed dates):

---

46 *Ibid*, s 112(1).

47 *Ibid*, ss 112(2)(b.1) and (c).

48 *Ibid*.

49 *Peter v Canada (Minister of Public Safety and Emergency Preparedness)*, 2014 FC 1073, (affirmed in *Savunthararasa v Canada (Minister of Public Safety and Emergency Preparedness)*, 2016 FCA 51); *Atawnah v Canada (Minister of Public Safety and Emergency Preparedness)*, 2015 FC 774.

50 Speaking notes for Chris Alexander, Canada's Citizenship and Immigration Minister, at the news conference regarding Canada's asylum system (22 January 2014), online: http://news.gc.ca/web/article-en.do?nid=831769.

51 *IRPA*, above note 1, s 112(2.1).

Burundi, Central African Republic, Egypt, Ethiopia, Guinea-Bissau, Libya, Mali, Somalia, South Sudan, Sudan, Syria, Turkey, and Yemen.[52]

A positive decision on a PRRA usually results in conferral of refugee protection on an applicant[53] (although there are some exceptions, discussed below); it will allow the person to apply for permanent residence. PRRA decisions, like all other immigration decisions, may be judicially reviewed in the Federal Court.

1) Scope and Effect of Pre-removal Risk Assessment

Although the PRRA usually considers the same grounds as the refugee hearing — risk of persecution, risk to life, and risk of torture — there are several differences between the two procedures. First, PRRAs are decided by IRCC officers[54] rather than the IRB. Second, a PRRA is usually a paper-based process, although a hearing may be held in certain circumstances. Third, the scope of a PRRA is limited to reviewing new evidence that "arose after the rejection or was not reasonably available, or that the applicant could not reasonably have been expected in the circumstances to have presented, at the time of the rejection."[55] Fourth, the purpose of a PRRA is to determine whether an applicant can be safely removed from Canada.

There are two important limitations on a PRRA for the following groups of individuals:

1) persons found inadmissible on grounds of security, violating human or international rights, organized or serious criminality;
2) persons whose refugee claims were rejected because of article 1F of the *Refugee Convention* (exclusion from refugee protection

---

52 Immigration, Refugees and Citizenship Canada, "Pre-removal Risk Assessment — Exemptions to the Bar," online: IRCC www.cic.gc.ca/english/refugees/inside/prra/exemptions.asp.

53 *IRPA*, above note 1, s 114(1)(a).

54 After the establishment of the Canada Border Services Agency (CBSA) in December 2003, certain functions of IRCC, including removals, detention, PRRA, and interdiction, were transferred to the CBSA (order in council PC 2003-2063). In October 2004, the responsibility for PRRAs was transferred back to IRCC (order in council PC 2004-1154). Thus, between 12 December 2003 and 8 October 2004, the CBSA administered the PRRA program. *Say v Canada (Solicitor General)*, [2005] FCJ No 931 (FC), unsuccessfully challenged a PRRA made during this period on the ground of the CBSA's lack of independence and impartiality and the presence of institutional bias in favour of enforcement or removal. The Federal Court of Appeal subsequently upheld the Federal Court's dismissal of the challenge: see *Say v Canada (Solicitor General)*, 2005 FCA 422.

55 *IRPA*, above note 1, s 113(a).

for individuals with respect to whom "there are serious reasons for considering" that they committed a crime against peace, a war crime, a crime against humanity, a serious non-political crime, or have been guilty of acts contrary to the purposes and principles of the United Nations);

3) persons subject to security certificates.[56]

First, a PRRA with respect to the above persons can consider only protection grounds identified in section 97 of the *IRPA*, namely, risk of torture, risk to life, and risk of cruel or unusual treatment or punishment.[57] This range of grounds is in contrast to that of other applicants whose PRRAs can also consider the risk of persecution under the *Refugee Convention*.[58]

Second, in assessing PRRAs of the above-mentioned persons, officers are to consider not only the risks to the applicants, but also the risks that they may pose to the Canadian public or Canada's security.[59] In the case of persons inadmissible for serious criminality, officers are to consider whether applicants are a danger to the public;[60] in the case of other above-mentioned applicants, they are to weigh "whether the application should be refused because of the nature and severity of acts committed . . . or because of the danger that the applicant constitutes to the security of Canada."[61] As a result of this balancing, a person may be removed despite the existence of risk of torture in a destination country. It is also possible for the government to argue that such cases fall within the *Suresh* exception.[62] However, court jurisprudence has not yet authoritatively clarified which circumstances would amount to extraordinary to make removal to torture justifiable.

Third, although, as a rule, a positive PRRA decision results in refugee protection, the above persons will not be able to obtain it. They will receive only a stay of removal in respect of the country where they are considered to face a risk of torture, risk to life, or risk of cruel and unusual treatment or punishment.[63] Further, this stay may be cancelled

---

56 *Ibid*, s 112(3).

57 *Ibid*, s 113(d).

58 *Ibid*, s 113(c).

59 Where these extraordinary grounds of refusal are to be considered, the person concerned must be provided with a written assessment related to the grounds in question and allowed fifteen days to submit a response: *Regulations*, above note 5, ss 172(1) & (2).

60 *IRPA*, above note 1, s 113(d)(i).

61 *Ibid*, s 113(d)(ii).

62 See above note 3 and surrounding text.

63 *IRPA*, above note 1, s 114(1)(b).

by the Minister.[64] If a re-examination of the stay is initiated, the person concerned must be provided with a notice of re-examination; a written assessment on the basis of the factors set out in the *IRPA*, section 97; and a written assessment of whether an application should be refused due to the nature and severity of acts committed or the danger that an applicant poses to the public or security of Canada.[65] A person concerned is given an opportunity to submit a written response within fifteen days from the receipt of the assessments.[66]

2) Notification of Pre-removal Risk Assessment

A PRRA application may generally be made only after one is "notified" by the Minister of the right to apply for a PRRA.[67] A notification can be given in person or sent by post.[68] As part of the notification process, a person is provided with a PRRA application and guide. An application for a PRRA must be made within fifteen days from the date of the notification. Within thirty days of notification, an individual must file any further evidence and submissions that she wishes considered.

If a PRRA is filed within the fifteen-day deadline, the removal is automatically stayed until the application is decided.[69] After the lapse of the fifteen-day period, a person can still apply for a PRRA, but his removal will not be stayed.[70] The legislation does not preclude repeat PRRA applications, but they do not result in stays of removal.[71]

3) Waiver of Pre-removal Risk Assessment

If a person does not wish to apply for a PRRA, she is required to sign a "Statement of No Intention," which allows the authorities to proceed with the removal.[72] In the alternative, she may simply allow the fifteen-day application deadline to lapse.

64 *Ibid*, s 114(2).
65 *Regulations*, above note 5, s 173(1).
66 *Ibid*, s 173(2).
67 *Ibid*, s 160(1). However, persons making repeat PRRA applications and persons issued removal orders at a port of entry may apply without being given notification: *ibid*, s 160(2).
68 *Ibid*, s 160(4).
69 *Ibid*, ss 162 and 232.
70 *Ibid*, s 163.
71 *Ibid*, s 165.
72 *Ibid*, s 232(a).

Where the consideration of a PRRA stays removal, an application period of fifteen days is granted.[73] Thus, even if an individual does not allege any risk upon return, his removal may be delayed for up to fifteen days. This is particularly troubling for individuals in detention. In the case where an individual provides "confirmation in writing" that she does not intend to make a PRRA, this stay will be lifted.[74] While this provision benefits individuals who make a clear statement of a lack of desire (or need) for protection, it can nonetheless lead to situations where a waiver is made either under duress or without a complete awareness of a PRRA's nature. Once a PRRA has been formally waived, a changed intention will not result in a renewed stay.

4) Procedure for Pre-removal Risk Assessment

PRRA applications are usually decided without a hearing based on the written submissions of the applicant as well as new evidence submitted by him.[75] Such a process complies with the principles of natural justice as long as the applicant has an opportunity to present all of his arguments.[76] The onus is on an applicant to file a clear application, collect documentary evidence, and address any concerns in submissions accompanying the application.[77]

a) New Evidence

As mentioned earlier, a PRRA can consider only new evidence that (1) arose after the RPD rejection, (2) was not reasonably available, or (3) the applicant could not reasonably have been expected to have presented at the time of the rejection.[78] This rule reflects the idea that "a negative refugee determination by the RPD must be respected by the PRRA officer, unless there is new evidence of facts that might have affected the outcome of the RPD hearing if the evidence had been presented to the RPD."[79] Section 161(2) of the *Regulations* requires the applicant to

---

73 *Ibid*, s 232.

74 *Ibid*, s 232(a).

75 *Ibid*, s 161(1); *IRPA*, above note 1, s 113(a); *Chen v Canada (Minister of Citizenship and Immigration)*, 2005 FC 1523 at para 13 [*Chen*].

76 *Younis v Canada (Solicitor General)*, 2004 FC 266; *Iboude v Canada (Minister of Citizenship and Immigration)*, 2005 FC 1316.

77 *Mancia v Canada (Minister of Citizenship and Immigration)*, [1998] 3 FC 461 (CA) [*Mancia*].

78 *IRPA*, above note 1, s 113(a).

79 *Raza v Canada (Minister of Citizenship and Immigration)*, 2007 FCA 385 at para 13 [*Raza*].

explain why submitted evidence constitutes new evidence within the meaning of the *IRPA*, section 113(a).

Court jurisprudence provided useful clarification of the contours of the notion of "new evidence." In *Raza v Canada (Minister of Citizenship and Immigration)*,[80] the Federal Court of Appeal provided a list of questions that need to be considered in order to determine whether evidence is new. The questions include the following:

1. Credibility: Is the evidence credible, considering its source and the circumstances in which it came into existence? If not, the evidence need not be considered.
2. Relevance: Is the evidence relevant to the PRRA application, in the sense that it is capable of proving or disproving a fact that is relevant to the claim for protection? If not, the evidence need not be considered.
3. Newness: Is the evidence new in the sense that it is capable of:
   (a) proving the current state of affairs in the country of removal or an event that occurred or a circumstance that arose after the hearing in the RPD, or
   (b) proving a fact that was unknown to the refugee claimant at the time of the RPD hearing, or
   (c) contradicting a finding of fact by the RPD (including a credibility finding)?

If not, the evidence need not be considered.

4. Materiality: Is the evidence material, in the sense that the refugee claim probably would have succeeded if the evidence had been made available to the RPD? If not, the evidence need not be considered.
5. Express statutory conditions:
   (a) If the evidence is capable of proving only an event that occurred or circumstances that arose prior to the RPD hearing, then has the applicant established either that the evidence was not reasonably available to him or her for presentation at the RPD hearing, or that he or she could not reasonably have been expected in the circumstances to have presented the evidence at the RPD hearing? If not, the evidence need not be considered.
   (b) If the evidence is capable of proving an event that occurred or circumstances that arose after the RPD hearing, then the

80 *Ibid.*

evidence must be considered (unless it is rejected because it is not credible, not relevant, not new or not material).[81]

In light of the above factors, the date of a given document alone (namely, that it was produced after the RPD hearing) does not automatically make it new evidence; it is important to consider what event or circumstance is sought to be proven by that document.[82] At the same time, evidence that refers to previously examined risks should not be automatically considered not new if it speaks of a new development of those risks and provides materially different information.[83] If evidence refers to an event that occurred prior to the RPD hearing, the applicant must establish that the evidence was not reasonably available or she could not reasonably have been expected to have presented it at the hearing.[84] If an applicant asserts that the evidence was not reasonably available or could not have been expected to be presented, he must explain why it was not available or could not have been presented.[85]

For example, in *Sanchez v Canada (Minister of Citizenship and Immigration)*,[86] a PRRA officer rejected a report that was published prior to the RPD hearing on the basis that the applicant could have found and presented it at the hearing. The court, however, found that the report should have been considered. It noted that the mere fact that the report was published does not mean that it was easily accessible to the applicant. Even the RPD research unit, which is responsible for producing up-to-date country information, did not find this report, so it was unreasonable to expect that the applicant would be able to do so.

b) Oral Hearing

Although PRRAs are usually paper-based, the Minister may decide, on the basis of "prescribed factors," that a hearing should be held.[87] The "prescribed factors," set out in section 167 of the *Regulations*, include these:

(a) whether the applicant's credibility is in question and is related to the factors set out in sections 96 and 97 of the Act;

---

81 *Ibid*.

82 *Ibid* at para 16.

83 *Jessamy v Canada (Minister of Citizenship and Immigration)*, 2010 FC 489.

84 *Sanchez v Canada (Minister of Citizenship and Immigration)*, 2009 FC 101 at para 25 [*Sanchez*]; *Chong v Canada (Minister of Citizenship and Immigration)*, 2007 FC 584 at para 13.

85 *Elezi v Canada (Minister of Citizenship and Immigration)*, 2007 FC 240 at para 26; *Kaybaki v Canada (Solicitor General of Canada)*, 2004 FC 32.

86 *Sanchez*, above note 84.

87 *IRPA*, above note 1, s 113(b).

(b) whether the evidence is central to the decision with respect to the application for protection; and
(c) whether the evidence, if accepted, would justify allowing the application for protection.[88]

For example, in *PJW v Canada (Minister of Citizenship and Immigration)*,[89] a PRRA officer rejected the applicant's sworn written narrative about her sexual orientation and the mistreatment she experienced in Jamaica because of it. The court concluded that in doing so, the officer made an adverse credibility finding, which was central to the applicant's claim, and therefore the officer was obliged to hold an oral hearing. Similarly, in *Cho v Canada (Minister of Citizenship and Immigration)*,[90] the PRRA officer found that the applicant's allegations about the assaults were not sufficiently proven. The court found that this rejection amounted to a credibility finding, and since credibility was at stake, the officer was under an obligation to hold an oral hearing.

If a hearing is held, notice will be given to the applicant of the time and place and the issues that will be raised. The requirement to state issues for the hearing stems from the principle of procedural fairness that the person concerned must know the case to be met.[91] Failure to identify those issues or to provide clarification where requested by the applicant amounts to breach of procedural fairness.[92] At the hearing, the applicant must respond to the questions posed by the officer and may be assisted by counsel.[93]

c) PRRA Decision Making

Given that PRRA exists in order to ensure compliance with Canada's international obligations, PRRA officers "cannot confine or exhaust its analysis to the exact arguments raised by an applicant or even to the exact evidence presented."[94] Officers have a duty to consult recent and publicly available reports on country conditions even when they have not been submitted by the applicants.[95] In light of this, an important

---

88 *Regulations*, above note 5, s 167.
89 2011 FC 1044.
90 2010 FC 1299.
91 *Chen*, above note 75 at para 21.
92 *Ibid*.
93 *Regulations*, above note 5, s 168.
94 *Jama v Canada (Minister of Citizenship and Immigration)*, 2014 FC 668 at para 17 [*Jama*].
95 *Hassaballa v Canada (Minister of Citizenship and Immigration)*, 2007 FC 489 at para 33; *Lima v Canada (Minister of Citizenship and Immigration)*, 2008 FC 222 at para 13; *Kulasekaram v Canada (Minister of Citizenship and Immigration)*, 2013

question arises: does an officer have a duty to disclose to the applicant the reports and other sources that have been consulted? Without a hearing at which the evidence and issues can be fully discussed and reviewed, the PRRA determination runs the risk of being based on a series of issues or body of evidence not anticipated or addressed in the submissions.

The scope of the duty of a PRRA officer to disclose the issues, analysis, and evidence that is to form the basis of his decision has been subject to considerable litigation. The main rules on the disclosure of extrinsic evidence are set out in the Federal Court of Appeal decision in *Mancia v Canada (Minister of Citizenship and Immigration)*.[96] PRRA officers are not required to disclose documents from public sources in relation to general country conditions which were available and accessible at the IRB Documentation Centres at the time the submission was made by the applicant. However, if an officer intends to rely on evidence that is not normally found or was not available in documentation centres when the applicant filed her submissions, the applicant must be informed of any novel and significant information which demonstrates a change in the general country conditions that may affect the outcome of the case. The general principle of disclosure in a PRRA can be formulated as follows: "fairness requires that documents, reports, or opinions of which the applicant is not aware, nor deemed to be aware, must be disclosed."[97] However, the duty of fairness does not require disclosure of a draft risk opinion to an applicant prior to a final decision.[98]

In *Zamora v Canada (Minister of Citizenship and Immigration)*,[99] for example, a PRRA officer conducted her own Internet research on conditions in the applicant's country of origin. These documents were not from the bank of country conditions maintained by the IRB and were not standard documents such as the Human Rights Watch, Amnesty International, or country reports issued under governmental authority. The court found that the officer was under an obligation to disclose these documents prior to making her decision and to give Zamora an opportunity to comment.

FC 388 at para 42; *John v Canada (Minister of Public Security and Emergency Preparedness)*, 2010 FC 1088 at para 37; *Jessamy v Canada (Minister of Citizenship and Immigration)*, 2009 FC 20 at para 81; *Jama*, above note 94 at para 18.

96 Above note 77.

97 *Chen v Canada (Minister of Citizenship and Immigration)*, [2002] 4 FC 193 at para 34 (FC).

98 *Mia v Canada (Minister of Citizenship and Immigration)*, [2001] FCJ No 1584 (TD); *Chen v Canada (Minister of Citizenship and Immigration)*, above note 97; *Akpataku v Canada (Minister of Citizenship and Immigration)*, [2004] FCJ No 862 (FC).

99 2004 FC 1414.

In addition to consulting recent and publicly available reports even when they have not been submitted by the applicant, PRRA officers are expected to consider risk grounds that are apparent on the record, even if these are not specifically raised by the applicant.[100] Finally, even where an applicant is found not credible by the IRB, PRRA officers must still consider whether the applicant's profile would put him at risk upon return.[101] In some circumstances, there may be a heightened duty on the officer to assess risks apparent on the record even if they were not raised by the applicant. For example, in *Jama v Canada (Minister of Citizenship and Immigration)*,[102] these circumstances included the following: the application was prepared without the assistance of counsel; Jama was from Somalia, which is considered a dangerous country; the applicant would be precluded from seeking another PRRA for twelve months; the PRRA application was decided eighteen months after it was submitted and enclosed country documentation may have become outdated.

d) Interplay of PRRA and H&C Factors

In addition to PRRA, one of the most common applications made by rejected refugee claimants is an application for permanent residence on "humanitarian and compassionate," or H&C, grounds. Under the *IRPA*, section 25, the IRCC Minister has a broad power to "grant the foreign national permanent resident status or an exemption from any applicable criteria or obligations of this Act."[103] Although various factors can be raised on an H&C application, most commonly, they include hardship upon removal from Canada, attachment to Canada, and best interests of children directly affected.

The determination of H&C applications usually involves assessing whether an applicant will suffer either "unusual and undeserved" or "disproportionate" hardship. "Unusual and undeserved" hardship is hardship that is "not anticipated or addressed" by the *IRPA* or the *Regulations* and is beyond the applicant's control.[104] "Disproportionate

---

100 *Viafara v Canada (Minister of Citizenship and Immigration)*, 2006 FC 1526 at paras 6–7.

101 *Bastien v Canada (Minister of Citizenship and Immigration)*, 2008 FC 982.

102 Above note 94.

103 *IRPA*, above note 1, s 25(1). However, a refugee claimant cannot file an H&C application while her application for protection is pending: *IRPA*, ss 25(1.2)(b)–(c). Further, a claimant is not eligible to make an H&C application for twelve months after his claim was determined by the IRB or has been declared withdrawn or abandoned: *IRPA*, s 25(1.2)(c).

104 Immigration, Refugees and Citizenship Canada, "IP 5: Immigrant Applications in Canada Made on Humanitarian or Compassionate Grounds," s 5.10, cited

hardship" is defined as "an unreasonable impact on the applicant due to their personal circumstances."[105] However, the words "unusual and undeserved or disproportionate hardship" should not be interpreted as creating three discrete thresholds; rather, all relevant humanitarian and compassionate issues in a particular case should be considered.[106]

As of the 2010 amendments to the *IRPA*, section 25 explicitly excludes consideration of factors that are taken into account in determining applicants' need for refugee protection under *IRPA* sections 96 and 97(1).[107] At the same time, humanitarian and compassionate factors are not relevant to a PRRA and are more properly considered in an H&C application.[108] For example, the interests of Canadian-born children generally fall outside the scope of a PRRA.[109]

Despite the above, the PRRA and H&C factors are closely connected and, at times, both applications may be decided by the same officer.[110] The latter does not in itself raise concerns about bias and does not violate procedural fairness as long as the decision maker has regard to different considerations relevant to each process.[111] While the courts have not discouraged the practice of having PRRA and H&C decisions made by the same officer,[112] they noted that, in such cases, an officer runs a greater risk of confusing the two analyses; extra care should be applied to ensure that both processes are separate.[113]

---

in *Kanthasamy v Canada (Citizenship and Immigration)*, 2015 SCC 61 at para 26 [*Kanthasamy*].

105 *Kanthasamy*, *ibid*.

106 *Ibid* at para 33.

107 See also *Caliskan v Canada (Minister of Citizenship and Immigration)*, 2012 FC 1190.

108 *Dubrezil v Canada (Minister of Citizenship and Immigration)*, 2006 FC 441.

109 *Sherzady v Canada (Minister of Citizenship and Immigration)*, [2005] FCJ No 638 (FC); *El Ouardi v Canada (Solicitor General)*, 2005 FCA 42; *Varga v Canada (Minister of Citizenship and Immigration)*, 2006 FCA 394; *Chandidas v Canada (Citizenship and Immigration)*, 2013 FC 257 at para 38.

110 For example: the case in *Latifi v Canada (Minister of Citizenship and Immigration)*, 2006 FC 1389; *Ramirez v Canada (Minister of Citizenship and Immigration)*, 2006 FC 1404 [*Ramirez*]; *Liyanage v Canada (Minister of Citizenship and Immigration)*, 2005 FC 1045; and *Santos v Canada (Minister of Citizenship and Immigration)*, 2010 FC 614.

111 *Ramirez*, above note 110 at para 47; *Haque v Canada (Minister of Citizenship and Immigration)*, 2012 FC 469 at para 14; *Hamam v Canada (Minister of Citizenship and Immigration)*, 2011 FC 1296.

112 *Haddad v Canada (Minister of Citizenship and Immigration)*, [2003] FCJ No 579 (TD); *Monemi v Canada (Minister of Citizenship and Immigration)*, [2004] FC 1648 (FC).

113 *Ramirez*, above note 110 at para 47.

In a PRRA, risk (of persecution, of torture, of cruel and unusual treatment or punishment, or risk to life) is the only factor considered.[114] In an H&C assessment, risk is merely one of the factors of hardship (together with other considerations such as, for example, best interests of children).[115] The threshold of risk under PRRA is higher than that of hardship under an H&C assessment.[116] Thus, in some circumstances, risk may be relevant for H&C applications, but not sufficient for a positive PRRA determination.[117] Violence, harassment, and poor sanitary conditions may not amount to personalized risk for the purposes of a PRRA, but may be sufficient to establish hardship under an H&C application.[118] Even if a PRRA decision on risk is negative, the officer should not discount those risks in an H&C assessment as they may constitute hardship.[119]

When the same officer decides both the PRRA and the H&C applications "the totality of the evidence offered by an applicant on both issues is relevant to both determinations."[120] Applicants do not need to "present the same material on each discrete application when they are inextricably linked. Indeed, since the Visa Officer was charged with rendering both decisions, this is absolutely unnecessary."[121] The applicant can reasonably expect that the relevant evidence supplied in support of his PRRA will be taken into account on his H&C application.[122]

5) Pre-removal Risk Assessment Decisions

Assuming no extension of the deadline is requested and granted, a decision may be made as soon as the expiry of thirty days after notification.[123] However, a PRRA officer must consider evidence submitted up to and until a PRRA decision is communicated to the applicant. In *Chudal v*

---

114 *Ibid* at para 42.

115 *Ibid* at para 48; *Dharamraj v Canada (Minister of Citizenship and Immigration)*, 2006 FC 674 at para 22 [*Dharamraj*].

116 *Melchor v Canada (Minister of Citizenship and Immigration)*, 2004 FC 1327 at para 16 [*Melchor*].

117 *Dharamraj*, above note 115 at para 24.

118 *Ramirez*, above note 110 at para 45; *Dharamraj*, above note 115 at para 24; *Beluli v Canada (Minister of Citizenship and Immigration)*, 2005 FC 898 at para 10.

119 *Pinter v Canada (Minister of Citizenship and Immigration)*, 2005 FC 296 at para 5; *Melchor*, above note 116.

120 *Sosi v Canada (Minister of Citizenship and Immigration)*, 2008 FC 1300 at para 12.

121 *Ibid* at para 15.

122 *Giron v Canada (Minister of Citizenship and Immigration)*, 2013 FC 114.

123 *Regulations*, above note 5, s 162.

Canada (Minister of Citizenship and Immigration),[124] the applicant submitted a PRRA application, but subsequently sent in more documents on several occasions, including on 8 October 2004. On 15 October, the applicant was notified that his PRRA was refused on 23 September 2004 and that the documents sent on 8 October could not be considered. The court concluded that a decision cannot be considered to have been made until it was written and signed, and notice of the decision was delivered to the applicant. Therefore, the date of the decision was 15 October — the day when it was communicated to the applicant — and documents sent on 8 October should have been considered. The case was sent back for re-determination.

In *Zokai v Canada (Minister of Citizenship and Immigration)*, the applicant filed a PRRA within the prescribed timeline, but advised the officer that more evidence would be forthcoming. A negative decision was made after the thirty-day timeline elapsed, but before the evidence was received. The Federal Court decided that the sole fact that the officer waited for the minimum statutorily prescribed period of thirty days was not sufficient to comply with the duty of fairness, especially given that the applicant had advised that the evidence was forthcoming and given that the decision had such profound implications for the applicant.[125]

The rate of success for PRRAs is traditionally very low — only 2–3 percent.[126] This low rate has been judicially noted, but the courts have held that

> . . . [t]hese statistics in no way undermine the important function Parliament has assigned to the PRRA procedure . . . namely "to comply with Canada's domestic and international commitments to the principle of non-*refoulement*." It is an important safeguard, which should remain irrespective of the probable result, statistically speaking. However, from the standpoint of the system, this information underscores the fact that there are few instances in which a person who has taken advantage of the remedies provided by the Act remains at risk of persecution, and they highlight the fact that the PRRA exists as a final safety-valve.[127]

---

124 2005 FC 1073.

125 2005 FC 1103 at paras 13–14.

126 Immigration, Refugees and Citizenship Canada, "Evaluation of the Pre-removal Risk Assessment Program" (2008 and 2016), online: IRCC www.cic.gc.ca/english/resources/evaluation/index.asp.

127 *Revich v Canada (Minister of Citizenship and Immigration)*, [2005] FCJ No 1057 at para 24 (FC).

All PRRA decisions (positive or negative) are sent to the Canada Border Services Agency (CBSA) Removals Unit. It is common practice to inform a PRRA applicant of the decision in person.[128] A removals officer contacts the applicant and invites her to attend at the CBSA office; the decision is provided at the office during an interview with the officer. If the decision is positive, the applicant is entitled to stay in Canada. In the case of a negative decision, the applicant becomes removal ready pending finalization of travel arrangements. Depending on the circumstances of the case, the applicant may be subject to arrest in order to ensure his removal.

F. REMOVAL ARRANGEMENTS

Once a removal order comes into force, it must be carried out "as soon as possible."[129] A removals officer is under an obligation to enforce an order and has limited discretion to grant deferral of removal.[130]

A person can either depart voluntarily or be removed by the CBSA. The CBSA Removals Unit is responsible for making the arrangements for persons ordered removed and for providing an escort to deportees when required. The removal arrangements encompass several mandatory steps: obtaining travel documents for a person subject to removal (if these are lacking) and securing visas for transit or re-entry if necessary; determining whether an escort is required; and liaising with transportation companies and CBSA liaison officers abroad. In addition, removal arrangements may be affected by the possible need for diplomatic assurances of good treatment in a destination country. The logistical intricacies of travel from Canada to the country of destination will vary from case to case. Each of these aspects of removal arrangements will be discussed in sequence.

---

128 Immigration, Refugees and Citizenship Canada, "ENF 10: Removals" (2010) at 39, online: IRCC www.cic.gc.ca/english/resources/manuals/enf/enf10-eng.pdf [IRCC, "ENF 10: Removals"].

129 *IRPA*, above note 1, s 48(2).

130 *Canada (Minister of Public Safety and Emergency Preparedness) v Shpati*, 2011 FCA 286; *Peter v Canada (Minister of Public Safety and Emergency Preparedness)*, 2014 FC 1073.

1) Voluntary Departure

When a person decides to depart voluntarily, it is not sufficient to merely leave Canada. To be considered to have departed voluntarily, a person must follow a specified three-step procedure.

First, the person must appear before an officer who will determine whether the individual concerned has sufficient means to leave Canada and verify that the person intends and is able to voluntarily comply with the requirements for departure.[131]

Second, an officer must be advised of the person's intended destination, which shall be approved unless the person concerned is

- a danger to the public;
- a fugitive from justice in Canada or another country; or
- someone seeking to evade or frustrate the cause of justice in Canada or another country.[132]

In any of the above cases, the immigration officer is not required to accept the person's intended destination and may instead elect to remove him to another destination. In such a case, the determination of the country of removal may be based on, among other factors, policy considerations and administrative convenience.

Third, a person's removal is considered enforced (either voluntarily or by the Minister) when the following conditions are met:

1) A person subject to removal appears before an officer at a port of entry to verify departure from Canada.
2) A person obtains a certificate of departure from the Department.
3) A person departs from Canada.
4) A person is authorized to enter, other than for purposes of transit, the country of destination.[133]

Where the above requirements are not met, a removal order remains unenforced, even though the person concerned might have left Canada. The existence of an unenforced removal order will prevent the foreign national's admission to Canada in the future.[134] The *Regulations*, however, allow to remedy situations where a person has departed Canada, but whose removal order remained unenforced (most typically because of the failure to verify departure). Section 240(2) of the *Regulations* gives officers the power to enforce unenforced removal orders outside Canada.

---

131 *Regulations*, above note 5, s 238(1).

132 *Ibid*.

133 *Ibid*, s 240(1).

134 Such a person cannot be issued a visa: *ibid*, s 25.

2) Assisted Voluntary Return and Reintegration Program

In 2012, the government introduced a pilot program, Assisted Voluntary Return and Reintegration, for rejected refugee claimants. It sought to create incentives for the rejected claimants to voluntarily return to their countries of origin by providing plane tickets home and up to $2,000 in reintegration assistance delivered in-kind (e.g., to help set up a business or go back to school). The amount of reintegration assistance depended on whether a person filed an appeal and judicial review. If a person applied before filing an appeal with the RAD or if an appeal was discontinued, he could qualify for up to $2,000 in assistance. If a person filed an appeal and it was rejected, but no judicial review application was filed or it was discontinued, the amount was $1,500. Finally, if a person made both an appeal and a judicial review, the amount declined to $1,000.[135] Rejected claimants from DCOs could receive only cash support for essential needs during their return trip and/or upon arrival in the following amounts: $500 for a primary participant and $200 for each additional non-Canadian family member to a maximum of $1,500.

To be eligible for this program, a person must have been a rejected refugee claimant in the Greater Toronto Area (GTA), must have complied with prescribed terms and conditions during the refugee determination process, and must have completed an application for a travel document. The following groups were not eligible: persons who withdrew or abandoned their claims; persons from countries subject to moratoria on removals; persons with a criminal record or who were inadmissible on the grounds of security, human or international rights violations, or organized criminality; persons with an outstanding application for permanent residence and/or a spousal sponsorship application; persons whose refugee claims were determined by the IRB to have no credible basis; persons who were excluded from refugee protection under articles 1E and 1F of the *Refugee Convention*; persons who failed to comply with imposed terms and conditions; and any person who failed to apply for a travel document when requested by the CBSA.[136]

---

135 Canada Border Services Agency, "Assisted Voluntary Return and Reintegration Pilot Program," online: CBSA www.cbsa-asfc.gc.ca/agency-agence/reports-rapports/pia-efvp/atip-aiprp/avrr-arvr-eng.html.

136 Immigration, Refugees and Citizenship Canada, "ENF 34: Assisted Voluntary Return and Reintegration Pilot Program" (2012) at 5–6, online: IRCC www.cic.gc.ca/english/resources/manuals/enf/enf34-eng.pdf.

During the six months of operation, some 2,700 individuals participated in the program.[137]

A government study of the program found that the pilot met its objectives and operated well. However, it also made broader findings that questioned the feasibility of maintaining the program. For example, the study determined that there was a questionable need for voluntary return arrangements, that the program was not cost-effective, and that it "was designed based on a set of assumptions that could not be validated prior to launch, some of which proved not to be accurate."[138] In 2015, the program was discontinued.[139]

3) Enforced Removal

When an individual does not voluntarily depart Canada, the CBSA will enforce his removal. An enforced removal is not restricted to those situations where an individual resists removal. It may also include situations where an individual is unable to remove herself from Canada due to financial or logistical constraints.

Where a removal is carried out by the CBSA, a person is usually removed to one of the following destinations:

- the country from which he came to Canada;
- the country in which she last permanently resided before coming to Canada;
- a country of which he is a citizen; or
- the country of their birth.[140]

There may be situations when none of the above countries is willing to admit the person concerned. In that case, the Minister can select any other country that authorizes the person's entry and remove her there.[141]

---

137 Speaking notes for Chris Alexander, Canada's Citizenship and Immigration Minister, at the news conference regarding Canada's asylum system (22 January 2014), online: http://news.gc.ca/web/article-en.do?nid=831769.

138 Canada Border Services Agency, *Evaluation of the Assisted Voluntary Return and Reintegration Pilot Program* (December 2014), online: CBSA www.cbsa-asfc.gc.ca/agency-agence/reports-rapports/ae-ve/2014/avrrpp-pparvr-eng.html.

139 Stephanie Levitz, "Ottawa to End Contentious Refugee Return Program" *Toronto Star* (22 January 2015), online: www.thestar.com/news/canada/2015/01/22/ottawa-to-end-contentious-refugee-return-program.html.

140 *Regulations*, above 5, s 241(1).

141 *Ibid*, s 241(2).

4) Travel Documents

As described in the previous chapters, refugee claimants often arrive in Canada on false documents or with no identity documents. To effect removal, CBSA officers work with rejected claimants to facilitate issuance of new documents. In addition, where a person is transiting through another country or countries, a CBSA officer must ensure that a transit visa (if required) is obtained.

Travel documents are usually obtained through the foreign diplomatic mission of a given nation in Canada. Officers are prohibited from advising a foreign mission of whether an individual has sought asylum in Canada. Such information can frequently be inferred, however, from the circumstances of the request for a travel document.

In some cases, removal may be possible even without a valid passport if a person does not require a valid passport to enter the country of his nationality. In some countries, admission may be granted upon presentation of an expired passport, birth certificate, or identification card. However, if a person is being removed without a valid passport, CBSA officers must generally obtain the consent of a transportation company and any countries of transit. In such a case, CBSA officers will verify that the destination country is willing to accept the person without documents and issue a Canada Single Journey Document.[142]

5) Diplomatic Assurances

Diplomatic assurances are formal representations on the part of one government to another concerning a particular matter. In the context of removal, diplomatic assurances normally would be sought in cases where one state attempts to remove a person to another state known to engage in torture or persecution. They would include an assurance of a receiving state that a deportee will not be subject to torture or ill-treatment. The practice of diplomatic assurances is found in various countries, including the United States, Canada, the United Kingdom, the Netherlands, and Sweden.[143]

In practice, diplomatic assurances are usually obtained before any IRB hearing or PRRA determination. As such, in Canada at least, they have been considered as part of the risk assessment. In *Suresh*, the Supreme Court stated that the assessment of the risk of the person's return

---

142 IRCC, "ENF 10: Removals," above note 128 at 52.

143 Human Rights Watch, "Still at Risk: Diplomatic Assurance No Safeguards against Torture" (2005), online: HRW www.hrw.org/sites/default/files/reports/eca0405.pdf.

should consider the "human rights record of the home state, the personal risk faced by the claimant, any assurances that the claimant will not be tortured and their worth and, in that respect, the ability of the home state to control its own security forces, and more."[144] Further, it elaborated on the reliability of diplomatic assurances:

> A distinction may be drawn between assurances given by a state that it will not apply the death penalty (through a legal process) and assurances by a state that it will not resort to torture (an illegal process). We would signal the difficulty in relying too heavily on assurances by a state that it will refrain from torture in the future when it has engaged in illegal torture or allowed others to do so on its territory in the past. This difficulty becomes acute in cases where torture is inflicted not only with the collusion but through the impotence of the state in controlling the behaviour of its officials. Hence the need to distinguish between assurances regarding the death penalty and assurances regarding torture. The former are easier to monitor and generally more reliable.[145]

Canada is a party to the *Convention Against Torture and Other Cruel, Inhuman or Degrading Treatment or Punishment*,[146] but the *IRPA* does not contain an absolute prohibition of deportation to torture. Further, *Suresh* has infamously left a possibility of deporting a non-citizen to the risk of torture in extraordinary circumstances. Although this disturbing exception has not been invoked yet, it is feared that diplomatic assurances may be used as an alternative to it.[147]

In *Mahjoub v Canada (Minister of Citizenship and Immigration)*,[148] the Federal Court provided useful elaboration on the *Suresh* framework for the analysis of trustworthiness of assurances. The court wrote:

> . . . a government with a poor human rights record would normally require closer scrutiny of its record of compliance with assurances. A poor record of compliance may in turn require the imposition of additional conditions, such as monitoring mechanisms or other safeguards which may be strongly recommended by international human rights bodies. Conversely, a country with a good human rights record would often likely have a correspondingly good record

144 Above note 3 at para 39.

145 *Ibid* at para 124.

146 10 December 1984 Can TS 1987 No 36, 23 ILM 1027 [*Convention Against Torture*].

147 Human Rights Watch, above note 143.

148 2006 FC 1503.

of compliance, and therefore additional conditions may be unnecessary to enhance the reliability of assurances.[149]

The court found that it was patently unreasonable for the executive to have relied on Egypt's assurances as it did not take into consideration the human rights record of the Egyptian government as well as its record of compliance with assurances. *Lai Cheong Sing v Canada (Minister of Citizenship and Immigration)*[150] provided further elaboration on the parameters for the evaluation of diplomatic assurances. The applicants were accused of smuggling and bribery and were requested to be returned for prosecution to China. The government of China provided a "diplomatic note" with assurances that they would not be subject to the death penalty or torture. The applicants' refugee claim and PRRA had been denied. The PRRA officer was not convinced, among other things, that China would not comply with the assurances given and considered that the Lais' notoriety would protect them against the risk of mistreatment. On judicial review of the PRRA decision, the Federal Court found that the officer's decision regarding assurances was unreasonable for two main reasons.[151] First, the officer failed to examine whether it was appropriate to rely on diplomatic assurances in light of reports about the widespread use of torture in China. Second, she did not analyze whether the assurances met the essential requirements to make them meaningful and reliable.

A number of international bodies and non-governmental organizations have expressed concern about the growing practice of using diplomatic assurances.[152] Such assurances are usually unreliable and ineffective and are often sought from countries with systematic practices of torture; they are not legally binding and have no effective post-return monitoring or accountability mechanisms.[153] The Special Rapporteur

149 *Ibid* at para 87.

150 The case involved a family where the husband and wife were suspected of running a massive smuggling operation in China, and if convicted could face the death penalty. The family made an unsuccessful refugee claim in Canada.

151 *Lai v Canada (Minister of Citizenship and Immigration)*, 2007 FC 361.

152 See, for example, Amnesty International, *Dangerous Deals: Europe's Reliance on "Diplomatic Assurances" against Torture* (London: Amnesty International Secretariat, 2010), online: www.europarl.europa.eu/document/activities/cont/201101/20110118ATT11882/20110118ATT11882EN.pdf.

153 *Ibid* at paras 30–31; Office of the United Nations Commissioner for Human Rights, "Interim Report of Mr. Manfred Nowak, Special Rapporteur of the Commission on Human Rights on Torture and Other Cruel, Inhuman or Degrading Treatment or Punishment," UNGA A/60/316 (2005) at paras 40–52, online: OHCHR https://documents-dds-ny.un.org/doc/UNDOC/GEN/N05/476/51/PDF/N0547651.pdf?OpenElement [OHCHR, "Interim Report"].

on Torture noted that assurances are often "nothing but attempts to circumvent the absolute prohibition of torture and *refoulement*"[154] and opined that they cannot be used as a proper safeguard against *refoulement* to torture.[155] The Council of Europe's Commissioner for Human Rights similarly wrote that diplomatic assurances "are not credible and also turned out to be ineffective in well-documented cases."[156] In its 2006 concluding observations on the report submitted by the United States, the UN Committee against Torture recommended that diplomatic assurances should be relied upon only in regard to states that do not systematically violate provisions of the *Convention Against Torture*, and after a thorough examination of the merits of each case.[157]

In *Mohammed Alzery v Sweden*,[158] the UN Human Rights Committee noted that the content and implementation of enforcement mechanisms in regard to assurances are relevant to determining whether the risk of ill-treatment exists. In this case, the assurances provided no details on the monitoring of their implementation, and the monitoring visits by Swedish officials that took place did not conform to international good practices. As a result, the assurances procured were insufficient to eliminate the risk of ill-treatment and removal of the applicant amounted to a violation of article 7 of the *International Covenant on Civil and Political Rights*.[159] A similar finding was made by the Committee against Torture in a complaint against Canada.[160] The committee found that the system of diplomatic assurances was not designed carefully enough to effectively safeguard against torture and that the complainant's extradition to Mexico was a violation of article 3 of the *Convention against Torture*.

---

154 Office of the United Nations High Commissioner for Human Rights, "Report of the Special Rapporteur on Torture and Other Cruel, Inhuman or Degrading Treatment or Punishment (Mr Manfred Nowak)," E/CN.4/2006/6 (2006) at para 32, online: https://documents-dds-ny.un.org/doc/UNDOC/GEN/G05/168/09/PDF/G0516809.pdf?OpenElement .

155 OHCHR, "Interim Report," above note 153 at paras 51–52.

156 Thomas Hammarberg, "Viewpoints: Torture Can Never, Ever Be Accepted" (27 June 2006), online: Council of Europe, Office of the Commissioner for Human Rights http://archive.is/c7GS.

157 Committee against Torture, "Conclusions and Recommendations of the Committee against Torture: United States of America," CAT/C/USA/CO/2 (2006) at 5, online: www.refworld.org/publisher,CAT,,USA,453776c60,0.html.

158 CCPR/C/88/D/1416/2005, 10 November 2006.

159 19 December 1966, 999 UNTS 171 [*ICCPR*].

160 *Boily v Canada*, Communication No 327/2007, UN Doc CAT/C/47/D/327/2007 (2007).

The jurisprudence from the European Court of Human Rights (developed in the context of the *European Convention on Human Rights*)[161] also expressed a note of caution on the use of assurances. As set out in *Saadi v Italy*, "[t]he weight to be given to assurances . . . depends, in each case, on the circumstances prevailing at the material time."[162] The Court opined that assurances are not sufficient to protect against the risk of mistreatment where reliable sources had reported practices resorted to or tolerated by the authorities which were manifestly contrary to the principles of the *European Convention on Human Rights.*[163] The sending state must examine whether assurances practically provide such protection.[164] For example, in *Baysakov and Others v Ukraine,*[165] the Court found that assurances given by the Kazakh authorities were unreliable and extradition of applicants to Kazakhstan would be in violation of article 3 of the *European Convention on Human Rights*. A similar finding was made in *Ismoilov v Russia* regarding assurances given by Uzbekistan.[166]

In *Othman (Abu Qatada) v the United Kingdom*, the European Court of Human Rights provided further guidance on the assessment of assurances.[167] It is necessary to consider first, the quality of assurances given, and, second, whether, in light of the receiving state's practices, they can be relied upon. The assessment is to take into account several factors, including whether the assurances are specific or are general and vague; who has given the assurances and whether that person can bind the receiving state; whether the assurances concern treatment that is legal or illegal in the receiving state; the length and strength of bilateral relations between the sending and receiving states, including the receiving state's record in abiding by similar assurances; whether compliance with the assurances can be objectively verified through diplomatic or other monitoring mechanisms; whether the applicant has previously been ill-treated in the receiving state; and whether the reliability of the assurances has been examined by the domestic courts of the sending state.[168]

---

161 *Convention for the Protection of Human Rights and Fundamental Freedoms* as amended by Protocols No 11 and No 14 (1950) ETS No 005 [*European Convention on Human Rights*].

162 Application No 37201/06 (28 February 2008) at para 148.

163 *Ibid* at paras 147–48.

164 *Ibid.*

165 Application No 54131/08 (18 February 2010).

166 Application No 2947/06 (24 April 2008) at para 127.

167 Application No 8139/09 (17 January 2012).

168 *Ibid* at para 189.

6) Making of Travel Arrangements

In finalizing travel arrangements, the CBSA will determine whether an escort is necessary and will make arrangements with transportation companies and liaison officers abroad.

An escort can be assigned to persons being removed by the CBSA to minimize the risk to the safety and security of the persons, the travelling public, and transportation company personnel.[169] For example, an escort may be necessary in the following cases: a person is unwilling to be removed or has made threats against persons intending to remove him; a person has been charged with, or convicted of, a serious offence involving violence; a person has been determined by the Minister to be a danger to the public; a person has a medical condition that requires close supervision; and a person poses a safety or security risk.[170] Unaccompanied minors under thirteen years of age are also normally escorted. Persons between thirteen and eighteen may be removed without an escort on direct flights if the airline accepts responsibility for a young person during the trip and no safety or security risks exist.[171] As a rule, two officers are assigned to escort a person considered to pose a safety or security risk; in all other cases, one officer may be assigned.

G. CONCLUSION

The power of removal remains one of the key methods by which the state can enforce immigration law and protect the host society from persons representing a real or perceived danger. While the power is vast, it is subject to two major limitations.

First, the scope of its application is limited to foreign nationals and permanent residents; citizens cannot be expelled from their country of nationality. This distinction further highlights the divide between citizens and non-citizens in an area with serious implications for one's life and security.

Second, removal cannot violate the fundamental human rights to life, security of the person, and freedom from torture. The non-*refoulement* provision of the *Refugee Convention* and the prohibition of expulsion to risk of torture under the *Convention Against Torture* serve to safeguard those rights. The PRRA is specifically tailored to assess potential risks that may be faced by persons subject to removal and to ensure that their

169 IRCC, "ENF 10: Removals," above note 128 at 56.
170 *Ibid* at 57–58.
171 *Ibid* at 59.

removal does not violate Canada's international obligations. However, as noted above, not every person subject to removal is entitled to a PRRA. Further, the *Refugee Convention* and the interpretation of non-expulsion to torture under *Suresh* create room for balancing individual rights against state interests in ensuring the safety and security of the host society. Finally, due to the 2012 changes to the PRRA eligibility, most rejected claimants will not have an opportunity to even make submissions regarding the risks that they may face on return. Thus, Canada's approach to its non-*refoulement* obligations has become even more problematic in recent years.

In addition to the considerations of fundamental rights, there may exist practical impediments to removal. As discussed above, removal arrangements require interstate co-operation and coordination among government and private agencies. Further, the resources committed to effect removal are often inadequate.[172] In any given year, the number of individuals who receive removal orders is greater than the number of individuals subject to enforced removal (for statistics, see Appendix D, Tables 10 and 11). The operation of removals, in many ways more than any other aspect of refugee law, is constrained by the mundane reality of paperwork and resources. In sum, removal represents a complex and multi-dimensional process that, in many respects, reflects the values of a host society and the realities of interstate migration management.

---

172 See, for example, Adrian Humphreys, "Canada's Immigration Enforcement System Suffers from 'Orchestrated Mismanagement,' Whistleblower Claims" *National Post* (10 July 2014).

CHAPTER 13

CONCLUSIONS

A. OVERVIEW OF THE FEATURES OF CANADIAN REFUGEE LAW

This book has examined many aspects of refugee protection in Canada: inland and overseas refugee determination, formal law and government policy, the historic and contemporary context of refugee law, and the domestic and international principles of refugee protection. It has sought to present Canadian refugee law as an independent system, yet one that is open to and influenced by other branches of domestic law, international law, the practices of other jurisdictions, and the general global trends in forced migration.

Refugee law generally — and Canadian refugee law, in particular — is no longer only about refugees understood in the traditional sense of the *Convention Relating to the Status of Refugees*.[1] Both in the inland refugee determination system and the overseas selection of refugees, Canada offers protection to many individuals who fall outside the classical definition of "Convention refugee." Canadian refugee law now embodies categories defined by Canada's obligations under the *Refugee Convention*, the *International Covenant on Civil and Political Rights*, and the *Convention Against Torture and Other Cruel, Inhuman or Degrading Treatment or Punishment*. It does so through the concepts of "Convention refugee" and "person in need of protection" as well as categories

1 28 July 1951, 189 UNTS 150 [*Refugee Convention*].

based on the humanitarian goals of our immigration policies reflected in the definition of the "humanitarian-protected persons abroad" class.

As noted at the outset, the organization of this book mirrors the arc of a refugee claim. Although refugee law is about protection, it is also about the refusal of protection, or, stated in a different way, the (perceived) protection of the prospective host society rather than the protection of the prospective refugee. Thus, Canadian refugee law also includes provisions for the arrest, detention, and forced removal of rejected refugee claimants and others deemed undeserving of protection. While perhaps not practised with the vigour found in other countries, these harsh measures result every year in the incarceration and deportation of individuals who have unsuccessfully sought protection here. Refugee protection is therefore as much about exclusion as it is about inclusion; both reveal different characteristics of a given refugee protection system.

After a relatively rapid development, refugee law is now quite a complex body not only of substantive criteria for protection but also procedural protections. The inland refugee status determination system is the embodiment of this complexity. As the largest quasi-judicial tribunal in Canada, the Immigration and Refugee Board has responsibility for determining whether to offer protection to thousands of refugee claimants each year. In striving to arrive at these determinations both fairly and efficiently, it has developed and applied rules and common law principles that have significantly advanced the state of administrative law. In contrast, the overseas selection of refugees is less characterized by a well-developed set of procedural protections than by an equally well-developed set of procedures encouraging co-operation between refugee-sponsoring groups of the Canadian public and the government.

B. FUTURE DEVELOPMENTS IN REFUGEE LAW

The field of refugee law, in Canada and elsewhere, is fairly young. While the *Refugee Convention* may have celebrated its half century, formal refugee law in Canada is a more recent development. Comprehensive inland and resettlement schemes in Canada date back only as far as the 1970s. However, even during this relatively short history, refugee policies have been amended a number of times. The most recent comprehensive revision of immigration and refugee legislation, in 2002, introduced several new terms and procedures to Canadian refugee law. A further set of significant changes in 2012 redefined both the operational side of refugee determination and the nature of asylum seekers' rights within the system. This last wave of changes has been characterized largely by a more restrictive approach to provision of refugee protection and increased emphasis on safeguarding the host community from perceived abuse and dangers posed by foreigners.

Post-2012, it appeared that the then Conservative government perceived no urgent political need to adjust the refugee system further; however, the election which brought the Liberal Party to power in October 2015 created an opportunity for the re-evaluation of Canada's refugee determination system. The Liberal Party's electoral platform promised a number of improvements to the system, including expanding the intake of Syrian refugees; a $100 million new contribution to the United Nations High Commission for Refugees to support the critical relief for persons affected by the Syrian crisis; fully restoring the Interim Federal Health Program coverage for refugees and refugee claimants; establishing an Expert Human Rights Panel for determination of designated countries of origin (DCOs); providing a right to appeal to the Refugee Appeal Division (RAD) for citizens from DCO countries; and ending the practice of appointing individuals without subject-matter expertise to the Immigration and Refugee Board.[2] The Liberal government has already acted upon the first three promises.[3] Further, in July 2016, it conducted stakeholder consultations, asking how the refugee determination system could be improved, among other things, in relation to the DCO policy and limitations on access to the RAD.

---

2 Liberal Party, "A New Plan for Canadian Immigration and Economic Opportunity," online: www.liberal.ca/realchange/a-new-plan-for-canadian-immigration-and-economic-opportunity/?shownew=1.

3 Immigration, Refugees and Citizenship Canada, "#WelcomeRefugees: Canada Resettled Syrian Refugees," online: www.cic.gc.ca/english/refugees/welcome/; Immigration, Refugees and Citizenship Canada, "Canada Announces $100 Million in Funding to United Nations High Commissioner for Refugees" (26 November 2015), online: http://news.gc.ca/web/article-en.do?nid=1022219; Immigration, Refugees and Citizenship Canada, "Notice – Changes to the Interim Federal Health Program" (11 April 2016), online: www.cic.gc.ca/english/department/media/notices/2016-04-11.asp. In July 2015, in *YZ v Canada (Minister of Citizenship and Immigration)*, 2015 FC 892 [*YZ*], the Federal Court ruled that the bar on RAD appeals for citizens of DCOs was unconstitutional. The Conservative government, which was in power at the time, launched an appeal to the Federal Court of Appeal. However, the subsequently elected Liberal government discontinued the appeal in January 2016. Immigration, Refugees and Citizenship Canada, "The Government Discontinues Its Appeal in the Y.Z Litigation" (7 January 2016), online: http://news.gc.ca/web/article-en.do?nid=1027049.

Although it remains to be seen whether these consultations will lead to any further changes in the refugee system, the opening up of such dialogue is a welcome development. The Conservative government's reign was characterized mostly by the lack of community-based consultations and an often contentious relationship between the government and immigration/refugee advocates and stakeholders, including instances where non-governmental organizations were accused of making false statements on government policies.[4] In the past few years, some of the Conservative government's changes were subject to court challenges (e.g., in relation to restrictions on the Interim Federal Health Program,[5] limitations on the right to appeal for claimants from designated countries of origin,[6] temporal bars on access to pre-removal risk assessment,[7] and revised security certificate procedure[8]). While not all challenges have been successful, several cases led to judicial recognition of the arbitrary and discriminatory nature of certain aspects of the 2012 refugee "reform" and once again highlighted the strong need to re-evaluate the approach taken.

A further push for a change may come due to the developments in the US. The imposition of a travel ban on seven Muslim-majority countries[9] and the suspension of the refugee program[10] created fears of further restrictions and deportations, prompting some to leave the US for Canada. In fact, the number of asylum-seekers crossing the border

---

4 Jason Kenney, "Opinion Letters" *Welland Tribune* (23 May 2012), online: www.wellandtribune.ca/2012/05/23/immigration-minister-jason-kenny-responds.

5 *Canadian Doctors for Refugee Care v Canada (Attorney General)*, 2014 FC 651.

6 *YZ*, above note 3.

7 *Peter v Canada (Minister of Public Safety and Emergency Preparedness)*, 2014 FC 1073 (affirmed in *Savuntharararasa v Canada (Minister of Public Safety and Emergency Preparedness)*, 2016 FCA 51); *Atawnah v Canada (Minister of Public Safety and Emergency Preparedness)*, 2015 FC 774.

8 *Canada (Citizenship and Immigration) v Harkat*, 2014 SCC 37.

9 On 27 January 2017, President Trump issued Executive Order 13769 "Protecting the Nation From Foreign Terrorist Entry Into the United States," 82 Fed Reg 8977 (2017), which banned for ninety days the entry into the United States of individuals from the following countries: Iraq, Iran, Libya, Somalia, Sudan, Syria, and Yemen. On 3 February, a district court suspended the operation of the order. *Washington v Trump*, 2017 US Dist LEXIS 16012, 2017 WL 462040 (WD Wash Feb 3, 2017). On 6 March, a new order was issued, which removed Iraq from the list. Legal challenges to this order are underway. "Hawaii Formally Files Lawsuit to Stop Trump's Revised Travel Ban" *Chicago Tribune* (8 March 2017), online: www.chicagotribune.com/ news/nationworld/politics/ct-travel-ban-hawaii-lawsuit-20170308-story.html.

10 Executive Order 13769 also suspended for 120 days the United States Refugee Admissions Program and suspended indefinitely the entry of all Syrian refugees.

from the US into Canada has increased in the past months.[11] Many trekked for miles in freezing temperatures in order to avoid detection at border crossings.[12] In light of these developments, Canadian advocacy groups renewed their calls to suspend the operation of the *Safe Third Country Agreement*[13] and a new legal challenge to the Agreement may soon be in the works.[14]

C. REFUGEE LAW, GLOBALIZATION, AND HUMAN RIGHTS

The purpose of this book is to provide a practical guide to refugee law. As such, it has largely avoided some of the more abstract debates that accompany the analysis of refugee law. In concluding the book, however, it is useful to situate the practice of refugee law within these broader debates. These debates, particularly the relation of refugee law to the twin phenomena of globalization and human rights, have been alluded to and mentioned *en passant* previously. The following remarks are designed simply to serve as a reminder (rather than a survey) of certain key issues arising from the human rights and globalization discourse.

At the outset, it was stated that this book is based upon understanding refugee law as embodying two principles: (1) states owe obligations to certain individuals who are at risk of persecution in their country of origin, and (2) these obligations are governed, at a certain

11 "Fleeing North: Why Asylum Seekers Are Crossing the U.S.-Canada Border" *CTV News* (17 February 2017), online: http://ctv.news/W3stHGM; Allan Woods, "Is Trump's Refugee Crackdown Threat Pushing Asylum Seekers into Canada?" *The Toronto Star* (10 February 2017), online: www.thestar.com/news/canada/2017/02/10/is-trumps-refugee-crackdown-threat-pushing-asylum-seekers-into-canada.html; "22 Refugees Entered Manitoba near Emerson Border over the Weekend: Number of Asylum Seekers Walking from U.S. to the Province Continues to Grow" *CBC News* (6 February 2017), online: www.cbc.ca/1.3969874.

12 Alan Freeman, "Refugees Are Risking a Freezing Winter Trek to Escape the U.S." *The Washington Post* (7 February 2017), online: https://wpo.st/D82d2; "Refugees Lose Fingers to Frostbite as They Walk to Canada from the U.S." *Reuters* (6 February 2017), online: www.dailymail.co.uk/news/article-4197078/Worried-Trump-asylum-seekers-walk-cold-road-Canada.html.

13 Canadian Council for Refugees, "Calling for a suspension of the Safe Third Country Agreement," online: http://ccrweb.ca/en/safe-third-country.

14 Alexander Quon, "Canadian Law Students Research Ways to Challenge the Safe Third Country Agreement" *Metro News* (4 February 2017), online: www.metronews.ca/news/halifax/2017/02/04/canadian-law-students-research-safe-third-country-agreement.html.

level, by the operation of international law and policy. While this book has discussed the latter principle frequently, it has largely focused on the formal legal interaction between international law and various national regimes. There is, however, another dimension of this principle that bears explicit mentioning. The internationalization of refugee law is not only about the interaction between abstract systems of law and legal principles; it is also about the complex and mutually determinative relationship between migration and globalization. The task of migration regulation, which is what from a certain perspective refugee law is fundamentally about, becomes ever more formidable in this context.

Globalization brings with it both challenges and opportunities for refugee protection and migration regulation generally. On the one hand, international migration has grown in scope and intensity, thereby giving rise to fears of mass influxes of migrants and calling for more restrictive immigration rules. On the other hand, expansion of information flow and media coverage has exposed the interconnectedness of national migration systems and subjected them to greater scrutiny. The effects of state policies on migrant populations have become much more visible and immediate; media coverage shows the faces of real people stranded in refugee camps, fleeing bombings, and embarking on perilous boat journeys. Domestic practices are increasingly being judged not only against national values and standards, but also in a comparative, international context. Canadian refugee law and policy can no longer simply address refugee protection in and by Canada — the boundaries of such a discrete territory have been dissolved by globalization.

Globalization, therefore, requires greater interjurisdictional co-operation and coordination as well as interjurisdictional learning. Unfortunately, this opportunity is utilized not only to improve and refine, but also to dismantle and upset. Although in the area of competition for skilled immigrants interjurisdictional learning has led to the wider implementation of more favourable and open admission requirements, refugee law has followed a different trajectory.

States have been very inventive in developing tools for limiting access to their territories for asylum seekers. Refugee law has been at the forefront of "innovation" in efforts to deter unwanted migration. Not only has it firmly incorporated more traditional methods of interdiction such as visas and interception at sea, but it has reinterpreted the meaning of "state territory" for the purposes of claiming asylum. The current emphasis on control over access to territory and preference to keep asylum seekers out of potential countries of refuge makes a stark contrast to the pre-1950s approach to forced migration which sought to facilitate the international movement of persons from the country of first asylum.[15]

Globalization and the ambiguities that it embodies notwithstanding, territorial and population control by states remains a reality, and the study of national refugee laws does not become obsolete. States are the only entities possessing the power to grant refugee protection and to carry out large-scale resettlement efforts on a continuous basis.

The development of human rights seems to have an ambivalent relationship with refugee law. Notwithstanding the fact that refugee claims have intricate connection to the most fundamental human rights such as the right to life, liberty, and security of person, and the freedoms of expression, religion, and more, the framework of the *Refugee Convention* bars the broad interpretation of refugee protection as a human right. Historically, such an interpretation was affirmed by the failure of the *Convention on Territorial Asylum* in 1977 and has begun to be revisited in the scholarly and policy literature only recently.

Given that states parties have both an obligation to assist generally only those in their territory and the ability to exclude certain persons from protection, the ability to claim asylum cannot be said to meaningfully belong to every human being. Rather, such ability is attached to a person's presence in a particular territory and to the particular circumstances of a case (often including both the specifics of a refugee claim and the asylum seeker's travel route and mode of entry into a state's territory).

D. CONCLUSION

The Canadian refugee determination system is not without its critics. It has been criticized as too lax by both domestic and foreign, particularly American, commentators. For example, in a 2005 "Report on Terrorism," the US Department of State concluded that "[t]errorists and their supporters have capitalized on liberal Canadian immigration policies to raise funds and undertake other activities."[16] More recently, Canada's own Conservative government lamented that the country's refugee

---

15 James C Hathaway, "The Evolution of Refugee Status in International Law: 1920–1935" (1984) 33 *International and Comparative Law Quarterly* 348 at 350–61.

16 US Department of State, Office of the Coordinator for Counterterrorism, "Country Reports on Terrorism 2005" (2006) at 160, online: www.state.gov/documents/organization/65462.pdf.

system is vulnerable to abuse.[17] At the same time, many refugee advocates contend that many aspects of the process are unjust, discriminatory, or plainly irrational. The existence of critics on both sides of the spectrum vividly demonstrates the presence of competing approaches and interests that permeate both political discussion of refugee policy and refugee law itself.

As much of the caselaw discussed in the book establishes, the competing interests must be balanced one against the other. In some senses, the recent approaches to how this balance must be struck increase the importance of refugee advocates and public awareness of refugee issues. As the Supreme Court suggested in *Suresh v Canada (Minister of Citizenship and Immigration)*,[18] the principles of fundamental justice, rather than the *Convention Against Torture*, with its prohibition of torture, are what generally deter Canada from deporting people to torture. The Court has noted that these principles will be violated by *refoulement* because it "shakes the conscience" of Canadians. Although the analysis of this concept is complex, it indicates the continuing presence of the values of the Canadian community at the core of refugee protection. As such, it also provides hope that through engagement with and the education of the wider community, the continued protection of refugees can be assured.

This book is intended to introduce Canadian refugee law. It does not aspire to provide a comprehensive catalogue of the field, but rather, to demarcate the field's general topography. The authors hope that this book will provide an entry point into refugee law — and into the conscience of the community — for students of law, consultants, lawyers, researchers, and interested community members. Refugee law is in a state of continual development so it urgently requires new voices and perspectives. Because of that, our further hope is that this book will prompt, and in a small way encourage, such contributions to the debate.

---

17 Speaking notes for the Honourable Jason Kenney, Minister of Citizenship, Immigration and Multiculturalism, at a news conference following the tabling of Bill C-31, *Protecting Canada's Immigration System Act* (16 February 2012), online: www.cic.gc.ca/english/department/media/speeches/2012/2012-02-16.asp; see also Sponsor's speech at second reading (23 April 2012), online: www.parl.gc.ca/HousePublications/Publication.aspx?Pub=Hansard&Doc=108&Parl=41&Ses=1&Language=E&Mode=1.

18 [2002] 1 SCR 3.

APPENDIX A

SELECTED PROVISIONS OF THE *IMMIGRATION AND REFUGEE PROTECTION ACT*

Immigration and Refugee Protection Act
2001, c. 27

[Assented to 1 November 2001, as subsequently amended, as of 15 February 2017]

An Act respecting immigration to Canada and the granting of refugee protection to persons who are displaced, persecuted or in danger

Her Majesty, by and with the advice and consent of the Senate and House of Commons of Canada, enacts as follows:

Short Title

1. This Act may be cited as the *Immigration and Refugee Protection Act*.

Interpretation

Definitions
2. (1) The definitions in this subsection apply in this Act.

Board means the Immigration and Refugee Board, which consists of the Refugee Protection Division, Refugee Appeal Division, Immigration Division and Immigration Appeal Division.

Convention Against Torture means the Convention Against Torture and Other Cruel, Inhuman or Degrading Treatment or Punishment, signed at New York on December 10, 1984. Article 1 of the Convention Against Torture is set out in the schedule.

designated foreign national has the meaning assigned by subsection 20.1(2)

foreign national means a person who is not a Canadian citizen or a permanent resident, and includes a stateless person.

permanent resident means a person who has acquired permanent resident status and has not subsequently lost that status under section 46.

Refugee Convention means the United Nations Convention Relating to the Status of Refugees, signed at Geneva on July 28, 1951, and the Protocol to that Convention, signed at New York on January 31, 1967. Sections E and F of Article 1 of the Refugee Convention are set out in the schedule.

. . .

Objectives and Application
Objectives — immigration

3. (1) The objectives of this Act with respect to immigration are

- (a) to permit Canada to pursue the maximum social, cultural and economic benefits of immigration;
- (b) to enrich and strengthen the social and cultural fabric of Canadian society, while respecting the federal, bilingual and multicultural character of Canada;
- (b.1) to support and assist the development of minority official languages communities in Canada;
- (c) to support the development of a strong and prosperous Canadian economy, in which the benefits of immigration are shared across all regions of Canada;
- (d) to see that families are reunited in Canada;
- (e) to promote the successful integration of permanent residents into Canada, while recognizing that integration involves mutual obligations for new immigrants and Canadian society;
- (f) to support, by means of consistent standards and prompt processing, the attainment of immigration goals established by the Government of Canada in consultation with the provinces;
- (g) to facilitate the entry of visitors, students and temporary workers for purposes such as trade, commerce, tourism, inter-

national understanding and cultural, educational and scientific activities;

(h) to protect public health and safety and to maintain the security of Canadian society;

(i) to promote international justice and security by fostering respect for human rights and by denying access to Canadian territory to persons who are criminals or security risks; and

(j) to work in cooperation with the provinces to secure better recognition of the foreign credentials of permanent residents and their more rapid integration into society.

Objectives — refugees

(2) The objectives of this Act with respect to refugees are

(a) to recognize that the refugee program is in the first instance about saving lives and offering protection to the displaced and persecuted;

(b) to fulfil Canada's international legal obligations with respect to refugees and affirm Canada's commitment to international efforts to provide assistance to those in need of resettlement;

(c) to grant, as a fundamental expression of Canada's humanitarian ideals, fair consideration to those who come to Canada claiming persecution;

(d) to offer safe haven to persons with a well-founded fear of persecution based on race, religion, nationality, political opinion or membership in a particular social group, as well as those at risk of torture or cruel and unusual treatment or punishment;

(e) to establish fair and efficient procedures that will maintain the integrity of the Canadian refugee protection system, while upholding Canada's respect for the human rights and fundamental freedoms of all human beings;

(f) to support the self-sufficiency and the social and economic well-being of refugees by facilitating reunification with their family members in Canada;

(g) to protect the health and safety of Canadians and to maintain the security of Canadian society; and

(h) to promote international justice and security by denying access to Canadian territory to persons, including refugee claimants, who are security risks or serious criminals.

Application

(3) This Act is to be construed and applied in a manner that

(a) furthers the domestic and international interests of Canada;
(b) promotes accountability and transparency by enhancing public awareness of immigration and refugee programs;
(c) facilitates cooperation between the Government of Canada, provincial governments, foreign states, international organizations and non-governmental organizations;
(d) ensures that decisions taken under this Act are consistent with the *Canadian Charter of Rights and Freedoms*, including its principles of equality and freedom from discrimination and of the equality of English and French as the official languages of Canada;
(e) supports the commitment of the Government of Canada to enhance the vitality of the English and French linguistic minority communities in Canada; and
(f) complies with international human rights instruments to which Canada is signatory.

. . .

Designation — human smuggling or other irregular arrival

20.1 (1) The Minister may, by order, having regard to the public interest, designate as an irregular arrival the arrival in Canada of a group of persons if he or she

(a) is of the opinion that examinations of the persons in the group, particularly for the purpose of establishing identity or determining inadmissibility — and any investigations concerning persons in the group — cannot be conducted in a timely manner; or
(b) has reasonable grounds to suspect that, in relation to the arrival in Canada of the group, there has been, or will be, a contravention of subsection 117(1) for profit, or for the benefit of, at the direction of or in association with a criminal organization or terrorist group.

Effect of designation
(2) When a designation is made under subsection (1), a foreign national — other than a foreign national referred to in section 19 — who is part of the group whose arrival is the subject of the designation becomes a designated foreign national unless, on arrival, they hold the visa or

other document required under the regulations and, on examination, the officer is satisfied that they are not inadmissible.

. . .

Application for permanent residence — restriction

20.2 (1) A designated foreign national may not apply to become a permanent resident

(a) if they have made a claim for refugee protection but have not made an application for protection, until five years after the day on which a final determination in respect of the claim is made;
(b) if they have made an application for protection, until five years after the day on which a final determination in respect of the application is made; or
(c) in any other case, until five years after the day on which they become a designated foreign national.

Suspension of application for permanent residence
(2) The processing of an application for permanent residence of a foreign national who, after the application is made, becomes a designated foreign national is suspended

(a) if the foreign national has made a claim for refugee protection but has not made an application for protection, until five years after the day on which a final determination in respect of the claim is made;
(b) if the foreign national has made an application for protection, until five years after the day on which a final determination in respect of the application is made; or
(c) in any other case, until five years after the day on which the foreign national becomes a designated foreign national.

Refusal to consider application
(3) The officer may refuse to consider an application for permanent residence if

(a) the designated foreign national fails, without reasonable excuse, to comply with any condition imposed on them under subsection 58(4) or section 58.1 or any requirement imposed on them under section 98.1; and
(b) less than 12 months have passed since the end of the applicable period referred to in subsection (1) or (2).

. . .

Humanitarian and compassionate considerations — request of foreign national

25 (1) Subject to subsection (1.2), the Minister must, on request of a foreign national in Canada who applies for permanent resident status and who is inadmissible — other than under section 34, 35 or 37 — or who does not meet the requirements of this Act, and may, on request of a foreign national outside Canada — other than a foreign national who is inadmissible under section 34, 35 or 37 — who applies for a permanent resident visa, examine the circumstances concerning the foreign national and may grant the foreign national permanent resident status or an exemption from any applicable criteria or obligations of this Act if the Minister is of the opinion that it is justified by humanitarian and compassionate considerations relating to the foreign national, taking into account the best interests of a child directly affected.

Restriction — designated foreign national
(1.01) A designated foreign national may not make a request under subsection (1)

(a) if they have made a claim for refugee protection but have not made an application for protection, until five years after the day on which a final determination in respect of the claim is made;
(b) if they have made an application for protection, until five years after the day on which a final determination in respect of the application is made; or
(c) in any other case, until five years after the day on which they become a designated foreign national.

Suspension of request
(1.02) The processing of a request under subsection (1) of a foreign national who, after the request is made, becomes a designated foreign national is suspended

(a) if the foreign national has made a claim for refugee protection but has not made an application for protection, until five years after the day on which a final determination in respect of the claim is made;
(b) if the foreign national has made an application for protection, until five years after the day on which a final determination in respect of the application is made; or
(c) in any other case, until five years after the day on which they become a designated foreign national.

Refusal to consider request
(1.03) The Minister may refuse to consider a request under subsection (1) if

- (a) the designated foreign national fails, without reasonable excuse, to comply with any condition imposed on them under subsection 58(4) or section 58.1 or any requirement imposed on them under section 98.1; and
- (b) less than 12 months have passed since the end of the applicable period referred to in subsection (1.01) or (1.02).

Payment of fees
(1.1) The Minister is seized of a request referred to in subsection (1) only if the applicable fees in respect of that request have been paid.

Exceptions
(1.2) The Minister may not examine the request if

- (a) the foreign national has already made such a request and the request is pending;
- (a.1) the request is for an exemption from any of the criteria or obligations of Division 0.1;
- (b) the foreign national has made a claim for refugee protection that is pending before the Refugee Protection Division or the Refugee Appeal Division; or
- (c) subject to subsection (1.21), less than 12 months have passed since the foreign national's claim for refugee protection was last rejected, determined to be withdrawn after substantive evidence was heard or determined to be abandoned by the Refugee Protection Division or the Refugee Appeal Division.

Exception to paragraph (1.2)(c)
(1.21) Paragraph (1.2)(c) does not apply in respect of a foreign national

- (a) who, in the case of removal, would be subjected to a risk to their life, caused by the inability of each of their countries of nationality or, if they do not have a country of nationality, their country of former habitual residence, to provide adequate health or medical care; or
- (b) whose removal would have an adverse effect on the best interests of a child directly affected.

Non-application of certain factors
(1.3) In examining the request of a foreign national in Canada, the Minister may not consider the factors that are taken into account in

the determination of whether a person is a Convention refugee under section 96 or a person in need of protection under subsection 97(1) but must consider elements related to the hardships that affect the foreign national.

...

Division 4
Inadmissibility

...

Security
34 (1) A permanent resident or a foreign national is inadmissible on security grounds for

- (a) engaging in an act of espionage that is against Canada or that is contrary to Canada's interests;
- (b) engaging in or instigating the subversion by force of any government;
- (b.1) engaging in an act of subversion against a democratic government, institution or process as they are understood in Canada;
- (c) engaging in terrorism;
- (d) being a danger to the security of Canada;
- (e) engaging in acts of violence that would or might endanger the lives or safety of persons in Canada; or
- (f) being a member of an organization that there are reasonable grounds to believe engages, has engaged or will engage in acts referred to in paragraph (a), (b), (b.1) or (c).

Human or international rights violations
35 (1) A permanent resident or a foreign national is inadmissible on grounds of violating human or international rights for

- (a) committing an act outside Canada that constitutes an offence referred to in sections 4 to 7 of the *Crimes Against Humanity and War Crimes Act*;
- (b) being a prescribed senior official in the service of a government that, in the opinion of the Minister, engages or has engaged in terrorism, systematic or gross human rights violations, or genocide, a war crime or a crime against humanity within the meaning of subsections 6(3) to (5) of the *Crimes Against Humanity and War Crimes Act*; or

(c) being a person, other than a permanent resident, whose entry into or stay in Canada is restricted pursuant to a decision, resolution or measure of an international organization of states or association of states, of which Canada is a member, that imposes sanctions on a country against which Canada has imposed or has agreed to impose sanctions in concert with that organization or association.

Serious criminality

36 (1) A permanent resident or a foreign national is inadmissible on grounds of serious criminality for

(a) having been convicted in Canada of an offence under an Act of Parliament punishable by a maximum term of imprisonment of at least 10 years, or of an offence under an Act of Parliament for which a term of imprisonment of more than six months has been imposed;
(b) having been convicted of an offence outside Canada that, if committed in Canada, would constitute an offence under an Act of Parliament punishable by a maximum term of imprisonment of at least 10 years; or
(c) committing an act outside Canada that is an offence in the place where it was committed and that, if committed in Canada, would constitute an offence under an Act of Parliament punishable by a maximum term of imprisonment of at least 10 years.

Criminality

(2) A foreign national is inadmissible on grounds of criminality for

(a) having been convicted in Canada of an offence under an Act of Parliament punishable by way of indictment, or of two offences under any Act of Parliament not arising out of a single occurrence;
(b) having been convicted outside Canada of an offence that, if committed in Canada, would constitute an indictable offence under an Act of Parliament, or of two offences not arising out of a single occurrence that, if committed in Canada, would constitute offences under an Act of Parliament;
(c) committing an act outside Canada that is an offence in the place where it was committed and that, if committed in Canada, would constitute an indictable offence under an Act of Parliament; or
(d) committing, on entering Canada, an offence under an Act of Parliament prescribed by regulations.

Application
(3) The following provisions govern subsections (1) and (2):

(a) an offence that may be prosecuted either summarily or by way of indictment is deemed to be an indictable offence, even if it has been prosecuted summarily;
(b) inadmissibility under subsections (1) and (2) may not be based on a conviction in respect of which a record suspension has been ordered and has not been revoked or ceased to have effect under the *Criminal Records Act*, or in respect of which there has been a final determination of an acquittal;
(c) the matters referred to in paragraphs (1)(b) and (c) and (2)(b) and (c) do not constitute inadmissibility in respect of a permanent resident or foreign national who, after the prescribed period, satisfies the Minister that they have been rehabilitated or who is a member of a prescribed class that is deemed to have been rehabilitated;
(d) a determination of whether a permanent resident has committed an act described in paragraph (1)(c) must be based on a balance of probabilities; and
(e) inadmissibility under subsections (1) and (2) may not be based on an offence
  (i) designated as a contravention under the *Contraventions Act*,
  (ii) for which the permanent resident or foreign national is found guilty under the *Young Offenders Act*, chapter Y-1 of the Revised Statutes of Canada, 1985, or
  (iii) for which the permanent resident or foreign national received a youth sentence under the *Youth Criminal Justice Act*.

Organized criminality
37 (1) A permanent resident or a foreign national is inadmissible on grounds of organized criminality for

(a) being a member of an organization that is believed on reasonable grounds to be or to have been engaged in activity that is part of a pattern of criminal activity planned and organized by a number of persons acting in concert in furtherance of the commission of an offence punishable under an Act of Parliament by way of indictment, or in furtherance of the commission of an offence outside Canada that, if committed in Canada, would constitute such an offence, or engaging in activity that is part of such a pattern; or

(b) engaging, in the context of transnational crime, in activities such as people smuggling, trafficking in persons or laundering of money or other proceeds of crime.

Application
(2) Paragraph (1)(a) does not lead to a determination of inadmissibility by reason only of the fact that the permanent resident or foreign national entered Canada with the assistance of a person who is involved in organized criminal activity.

. . .

Cessation of refugee protection — foreign national
40.1 (1) A foreign national is inadmissible on a final determination under subsection 108(2) that their refugee protection has ceased.

Cessation of refugee protection — permanent resident
(2) A permanent resident is inadmissible on a final determination that their refugee protection has ceased for any of the reasons described in paragraphs 108(1)(a) to (d).

Division 5
Loss of Status and Removal

. . .

Enforceable removal order
48 (1) A removal order is enforceable if it has come into force and is not stayed.

Effect
(2) If a removal order is enforceable, the foreign national against whom it was made must leave Canada immediately and the order must be enforced as soon as possible.

In force
49 (1) A removal order comes into force on the latest of the following dates:

(a) the day the removal order is made, if there is no right to appeal;
(b) the day the appeal period expires, if there is a right to appeal and no appeal is made; and
(c) the day of the final determination of the appeal, if an appeal is made.

In force — claimants

(2) Despite subsection (1), a removal order made with respect to a refugee protection claimant is conditional and comes into force on the latest of the following dates:

(a) the day the claim is determined to be ineligible only under paragraph 101(1)(e);

(b) in a case other than that set out in paragraph (a), seven days after the claim is determined to be ineligible;

(c) if the claim is rejected by the Refugee Protection Division, on the expiry of the time limit referred to in subsection 110(2.1) or, if an appeal is made, 15 days after notification by the Refugee Appeal Division that the claim is rejected;

(d) 15 days after notification that the claim is declared withdrawn or abandoned; and

(e) 15 days after proceedings are terminated as a result of notice under paragraph 104(1)(c) or (d).

Stay

50 A removal order is stayed

(a) if a decision that was made in a judicial proceeding — at which the Minister shall be given the opportunity to make submissions — would be directly contravened by the enforcement of the removal order;

(b) in the case of a foreign national sentenced to a term of imprisonment in Canada, until the sentence is completed;

(c) for the duration of a stay imposed by the Immigration Appeal Division or any other court of competent jurisdiction;

(d) for the duration of a stay under paragraph 114(1)(b); and

(e) for the duration of a stay imposed by the Minister.

Void — permanent residence

51 A removal order that has not been enforced becomes void if the foreign national becomes a permanent resident.

No return without prescribed authorization

52 (1) If a removal order has been enforced, the foreign national shall not return to Canada, unless authorized by an officer or in other prescribed circumstances.

Return to Canada

(2) If a removal order for which there is no right of appeal has been enforced and is subsequently set aside in a judicial review, the foreign national is entitled to return to Canada at the expense of the Minister.

. . .

Division 6
Detention and Release

Immigration Division
54 The Immigration Division is the competent Division of the Board with respect to the review of reasons for detention under this Division.

Arrest and detention with warrant
55 (1) An officer may issue a warrant for the arrest and detention of a permanent resident or a foreign national who the officer has reasonable grounds to believe is inadmissible and is a danger to the public or is unlikely to appear for examination, for an admissibility hearing, for removal from Canada or at a proceeding that could lead to the making of a removal order by the Minister under subsection 44(2).

Arrest and detention without warrant
(2) An officer may, without a warrant, arrest and detain a foreign national, other than a protected person,

- (a) who the officer has reasonable grounds to believe is inadmissible and is a danger to the public or is unlikely to appear for examination, an admissibility hearing, removal from Canada, or at a proceeding that could lead to the making of a removal order by the Minister under subsection 44(2); or
- (b) if the officer is not satisfied of the identity of the foreign national in the course of any procedure under this Act.

Detention on entry
(3) A permanent resident or a foreign national may, on entry into Canada, be detained if an officer

- (a) considers it necessary to do so in order for the examination to be completed; or
- (b) has reasonable grounds to suspect that the permanent resident or the foreign national is inadmissible on grounds of security, violating human or international rights, serious criminality, criminality or organized criminality.

Mandatory arrest and detention — designated foreign national
(3.1) If a designation is made under subsection 20.1(1), an officer must

- (a) detain, on their entry into Canada, a foreign national who, as a result of the designation, is a designated foreign national and who is 16 years of age or older on the day of the arrival that is the subject of the designation; or

(b) arrest and detain without a warrant — or issue a warrant for the arrest and detention of — a foreign national who, after their entry into Canada, becomes a designated foreign national as a result of the designation and who was 16 years of age or older on the day of the arrival that is the subject of the designation.

. . .

Release — officer

56 (1) An officer may order the release from detention of a permanent resident or a foreign national before the first detention review by the Immigration Division if the officer is of the opinion that the reasons for the detention no longer exist. The officer may impose any conditions, including the payment of a deposit or the posting of a guarantee for compliance with the conditions, that the officer considers necessary.

Period of detention — designated foreign national

(2) Despite subsection (1), a designated foreign national who is detained under this Division and who was 16 years of age or older on the day of the arrival that is the subject of the designation in question must be detained until

(a) a final determination is made to allow their claim for refugee protection or application for protection;

(b) they are released as a result of the Immigration Division ordering their release under section 58; or

(c) they are released as a result of the Minister ordering their release under section 58.1.

Review of detention

57 (1) Within 48 hours after a permanent resident or a foreign national is taken into detention, or without delay afterward, the Immigration Division must review the reasons for the continued detention.

Further review

(2) At least once during the seven days following the review under subsection (1), and at least once during each 30-day period following each previous review, the Immigration Division must review the reasons for the continued detention.

. . .

Initial review — designated foreign national

57.1 (1) Despite subsections 57(1) and (2), in the case of a designated foreign national who was 16 years of age or older on the day of the arrival that is the subject of the designation in question, the Immigration Division must review the reasons for their continued detention within 14 days after the day on which that person is taken into detention, or without delay afterward.

Further review — designated foreign national

(2) Despite subsection 57(2), in the case of the designated foreign national referred to in subsection (1), the Immigration Division must review again the reasons for their continued detention on the expiry of six months following the conclusion of the previous review and may not do so before the expiry of that period.

. . .

Release — Immigration Division

58 (1) The Immigration Division shall order the release of a permanent resident or a foreign national unless it is satisfied, taking into account prescribed factors, that

- (a) they are a danger to the public;
- (b) they are unlikely to appear for examination, an admissibility hearing, removal from Canada, or at a proceeding that could lead to the making of a removal order by the Minister under subsection 44(2);
- (c) the Minister is taking necessary steps to inquire into a reasonable suspicion that they are inadmissible on grounds of security, violating human or international rights, serious criminality, criminality or organized criminality;
- (d) the Minister is of the opinion that the identity of the foreign national — other than a designated foreign national who was 16 years of age or older on the day of the arrival that is the subject of the designation in question — has not been, but may be, established and they have not reasonably cooperated with the Minister by providing relevant information for the purpose of establishing their identity or the Minister is making reasonable efforts to establish their identity; or
- (e) the Minister is of the opinion that the identity of the foreign national who is a designated foreign national and who was 16 years of age or older on the day of the arrival that is the subject of the designation in question has not been established.

Continued detention — designated foreign national
(1.1) Despite subsection (1), on the conclusion of a review under subsection 57.1(1), the Immigration Division shall order the continued detention of the designated foreign national if it is satisfied that any of the grounds described in paragraphs (1)(a) to (c) and (e) exist, and it may not consider any other factors.

Detention — Immigration Division
(2) The Immigration Division may order the detention of a permanent resident or a foreign national if it is satisfied that the permanent resident or the foreign national is the subject of an examination or an admissibility hearing or is subject to a removal order and that the permanent resident or the foreign national is a danger to the public or is unlikely to appear for examination, an admissibility hearing or removal from Canada.

Conditions
(3) If the Immigration Division orders the release of a permanent resident or a foreign national, it may impose any conditions that it considers necessary, including the payment of a deposit or the posting of a guarantee for compliance with the conditions.

Conditions — designated foreign national
(4) If the Immigration Division orders the release of a designated foreign national who was 16 years of age or older on the day of the arrival that is the subject of the designation in question, it shall also impose any condition that is prescribed.

Release — on request
58.1 (1) The Minister may, on request of a designated foreign national who was 16 years of age or older on the day of the arrival that is the subject of the designation in question, order their release from detention if, in the Minister's opinion, exceptional circumstances exist that warrant the release.

Release — Minister's own initiative
(2) The Minister may, on the Minister's own initiative, order the release of a designated foreign national who was 16 years of age or older on the day of the arrival that is the subject of the designation in question if, in the Minister's opinion, the reasons for the detention no longer exist.

. . .

Minor children
60 For the purposes of this Division, it is affirmed as a principle that a minor child shall be detained only as a measure of last resort, taking into account the other applicable grounds and criteria including the best interests of the child.

. . .

Division 8
Judicial Review

Application for judicial review
72 (1) Judicial review by the Federal Court with respect to any matter — a decision, determination or order made, a measure taken or a question raised — under this Act is, subject to section 86.1, commenced by making an application for leave to the Court.

Application
(2) The following provisions govern an application under subsection (1):

(a) the application may not be made until any right of appeal that may be provided by this Act is exhausted;
(b) subject to paragraph 169(f), notice of the application shall be served on the other party and the application shall be filed in the Registry of the Federal Court ("the Court") within 15 days, in the case of a matter arising in Canada, or within 60 days, in the case of a matter arising outside Canada, after the day on which the applicant is notified of or otherwise becomes aware of the matter;
(c) a judge of the Court may, for special reasons, allow an extended time for filing and serving the application or notice;
(d) a judge of the Court shall dispose of the application without delay and in a summary way and, unless a judge of the Court directs otherwise, without personal appearance; and
(e) no appeal lies from the decision of the Court with respect to the application or with respect to an interlocutory judgment.

Right of Minister
73 The Minister may make an application for leave to commence an application for judicial review with respect to any decision of the Refugee Appeal Division, whether or not the Minister took part in the proceedings before the Refugee Protection Division or Refugee Appeal Division.

Judicial review
74 Judicial review is subject to the following provisions:

(a) the judge who grants leave shall fix the day and place for the hearing of the application;
(b) the hearing shall be no sooner than 30 days and no later than 90 days after leave was granted, unless the parties agree to an earlier day;
(c) the judge shall dispose of the application without delay and in a summary way; and
(d) subject to section 87.01, an appeal to the Federal Court of Appeal may be made only if, in rendering judgment, the judge certifies that a serious question of general importance is involved and states the question.

Rules
75 (1) Subject to the approval of the Governor in Council, the rules committee established under section 45.1 of the *Federal Courts Act* may make rules governing the practice and procedure in relation to applications for leave to commence an application for judicial review, for judicial review and for appeals. The rules are binding despite any rule or practice that would otherwise apply.

Inconsistencies
(2) In the event of an inconsistency between this Division and any provision of the *Federal Courts Act*, this Division prevails to the extent of the inconsistency.

. . .

Division 9

Certificates and Protection of Information

. . .

Referral of certificate
77 (1) The Minister and the Minister of Citizenship and Immigration shall sign a certificate stating that a permanent resident or foreign national is inadmissible on grounds of security, violating human or international rights, serious criminality or organized criminality, and shall refer the certificate to the Federal Court.

Filing of evidence and summary
(2) When the certificate is referred, the Minister shall file with the Court the information and other evidence that is relevant to the ground of inadmissibility stated in the certificate and on which the certificate is based, as well as a summary of information and other evidence that

enables the person named in the certificate to be reasonably informed of the case made by the Minister but that does not include anything that, in the Minister's opinion, would be injurious to national security or endanger the safety of any person if disclosed.

Effect of referral
(3) Once the certificate is referred, no proceeding under this Act respecting the person who is named in the certificate — other than proceedings relating to sections 79.1, 82 to 82.31, 112 and 115 — may be commenced or continued until the judge determines whether the certificate is reasonable.

Determination
78 The judge shall determine whether the certificate is reasonable and shall quash the certificate if he or she determines that it is not.

Appeal
79 An appeal from the determination may be made to the Federal Court of Appeal only if the judge certifies that a serious question of general importance is involved and states the question. However, no appeal may be made from an interlocutory decision in the proceeding.

. . .

Effect of certificate
80 A certificate that is determined to be reasonable is conclusive proof that the person named in it is inadmissible and is a removal order that is in force without it being necessary to hold or continue an examination or admissibility hearing.

Detention and Release

Ministers' warrant
81 The Minister and the Minister of Citizenship and Immigration may issue a warrant for the arrest and detention of a person who is named in a certificate if they have reasonable grounds to believe that the person is a danger to national security or to the safety of any person or is unlikely to appear at a proceeding or for removal.

Initial review of detention
82 (1) A judge shall commence a review of the reasons for the person's continued detention within 48 hours after the detention begins.

Further reviews of detention — before determining reasonableness
(2) Until it is determined whether a certificate is reasonable, a judge shall commence another review of the reasons for the person's continued

detention at least once in the six-month period following the conclusion of each preceding review.

Further reviews of detention — after determining reasonableness
(3) A person who continues to be detained after a certificate is determined to be reasonable may apply to the Federal Court for another review of the reasons for their continued detention if a period of six months has expired since the conclusion of the preceding review.

. . .

Protection of Information

Protection of information
83 (1) The following provisions apply to proceedings under any of sections 78 and 82 to 82.2:

(a) the judge shall proceed as informally and expeditiously as the circumstances and considerations of fairness and natural justice permit;
(b) the judge shall appoint a person from the list referred to in subsection 85(1) to act as a special advocate in the proceeding after hearing representations from the permanent resident or foreign national and the Minister and after giving particular consideration and weight to the preferences of the permanent resident or foreign national;
(c) at any time during a proceeding, the judge may, on the judge's own motion — and shall, on each request of the Minister — hear information or other evidence in the absence of the public and of the permanent resident or foreign national and their counsel if, in the judge's opinion, its disclosure could be injurious to national security or endanger the safety of any person;
(c.1) on the request of the Minister, the judge may exempt the Minister from the obligation to provide the special advocate with a copy of information under paragraph 85.4(1)(b) if the judge is satisfied that the information does not enable the permanent resident or foreign national to be reasonably informed of the case made by the Minister;
(c.2) for the purpose of deciding whether to grant an exemption under paragraph (c.1), the judge may ask the special advocate to make submissions and may communicate with the special advocate to the extent required to enable the special advocate

to make the submissions, if the judge is of the opinion that considerations of fairness and natural justice require it;

(d) the judge shall ensure the confidentiality of information and other evidence provided by the Minister if, in the judge's opinion, its disclosure would be injurious to national security or endanger the safety of any person;

(e) throughout the proceeding, the judge shall ensure that the permanent resident or foreign national is provided with a summary of information and other evidence that enables them to be reasonably informed of the case made by the Minister in the proceeding but that does not include anything that, in the judge's opinion, would be injurious to national security or endanger the safety of any person if disclosed;

(f) the judge shall ensure the confidentiality of all information or other evidence that is withdrawn by the Minister;

(g) the judge shall provide the permanent resident or foreign national and the Minister with an opportunity to be heard;

(h) the judge may receive into evidence anything that, in the judge's opinion, is reliable and appropriate, even if it is inadmissible in a court of law, and may base a decision on that evidence;

(i) the judge may base a decision on information or other evidence even if a summary of that information or other evidence is not provided to the permanent resident or foreign national;

(j) the judge shall not base a decision on information or other evidence provided by the Minister, and shall return it to the Minister, if the judge determines that it is not relevant or if the Minister withdraws it; and

(k) the judge shall not base a decision on information that the Minister is exempted from providing to the special advocate, shall ensure the confidentiality of that information and shall return it to the Minister.

Clarification

(1.1) For the purposes of paragraph (1)(h), reliable and appropriate evidence does not include information that is believed on reasonable grounds to have been obtained as a result of the use of torture within the meaning of section 269.1 of the *Criminal Code*, or cruel, inhuman or degrading treatment or punishment within the meaning of the Convention Against Torture.

Appointment of special advocate
(1.2) If the permanent resident or foreign national requests that a particular person be appointed under paragraph (1)(b), the judge shall appoint that person unless the judge is satisfied that

(a) the appointment would result in the proceeding being unreasonably delayed;
(b) the appointment would place the person in a conflict of interest; or
(c) the person has knowledge of information or other evidence whose disclosure would be injurious to national security or endanger the safety of any person and, in the circumstances, there is a risk of inadvertent disclosure of that information or other evidence.

. . .

Special advocate's role
85.1 (1) A special advocate's role is to protect the interests of the permanent resident or foreign national in a proceeding under any of sections 78 and 82 to 82.2 when information or other evidence is heard in the absence of the public and of the permanent resident or foreign national and their counsel.

Responsibilities
(2) A special advocate may challenge

(a) the Minister's claim that the disclosure of information or other evidence would be injurious to national security or endanger the safety of any person; and
(b) the relevance, reliability and sufficiency of information or other evidence that is provided by the Minister and is not disclosed to the permanent resident or foreign national and their counsel, and the weight to be given to it.

For greater certainty
(3) For greater certainty, the special advocate is not a party to the proceeding and the relationship between the special advocate and the permanent resident or foreign national is not that of solicitor and client.

Protection of communications with special advocate
(4) However, a communication between the permanent resident or foreign national or their counsel and the special advocate that would be subject to solicitor-client privilege if the relationship were one of solicitor and client is deemed to be subject to solicitor-client privilege. For

greater certainty, in respect of that communication, the special advocate is not a compellable witness in any proceeding.

Powers

85.2 A special advocate may

(a) make oral and written submissions with respect to the information and other evidence that is provided by the Minister and is not disclosed to the permanent resident or foreign national and their counsel;
(b) participate in, and cross-examine witnesses who testify during, any part of the proceeding that is held in the absence of the public and of the permanent resident or foreign national and their counsel; and
(c) exercise, with the judge's authorization, any other powers that are necessary to protect the interests of the permanent resident or foreign national.

. . .

Obligation to provide information

85.4 (1) Subject to paragraph 83(1)(c.1), the Minister shall, within a period set by the judge,

(a) provide the special advocate with a copy of the information and other evidence that is relevant to the case made by the Minister in a proceeding under any of sections 78 and 82 to 82.2, on which the certificate or warrant is based and that has been filed with the Federal Court, but that is not disclosed to the permanent resident or foreign national and their counsel; and
(b) provide the special advocate with a copy of any other information that is in the Minister's possession and that is relevant to the case made by the Minister in a proceeding under any of sections 78 and 82 to 82.2, but on which the certificate or warrant is not based and that has not been filed with the Federal Court.

Restrictions on communications — special advocate

(2) After that information or other evidence is received by the special advocate, the special advocate may, during the remainder of the proceeding, communicate with another person about the proceeding only with the judge's authorization and subject to any conditions that the judge considers appropriate.

Restrictions on communications — other persons
(3) If the special advocate is authorized to communicate with a person, the judge may prohibit that person from communicating with anyone else about the proceeding during the remainder of the proceeding or may impose conditions with respect to such a communication during that period.

. . .

Part 2
Refugee Protection

Division 1
Refugee Protection, Convention Refugees and Persons in Need of Protection

95 (1) Refugee protection is conferred on a person when

- (a) the person has been determined to be a Convention refugee or a person in similar circumstances under a visa application and becomes a permanent resident under the visa or a temporary resident under a temporary resident permit for protection reasons;
- (b) the Board determines the person to be a Convention refugee or a person in need of protection; or
- (c) except in the case of a person described in subsection 112(3), the Minister allows an application for protection.

Protected person
(2) A protected person is a person on whom refugee protection is conferred under subsection (1), and whose claim or application has not subsequently been deemed to be rejected under subsection 108(3), 109(3) or 114(4).

Convention refugee
96 A Convention refugee is a person who, by reason of a well-founded fear of persecution for reasons of race, religion, nationality, membership in a particular social group or political opinion,

- (a) is outside each of their countries of nationality and is unable or, by reason of that fear, unwilling to avail themself of the protection of each of those countries; or
- (b) not having a country of nationality, is outside the country of their former habitual residence and is unable or, by reason of that fear, unwilling to return to that country.

Person in need of protection

97 (1) A person in need of protection is a person in Canada whose removal to their country or countries of nationality or, if they do not have a country of nationality, their country of former habitual residence, would subject them personally

(a) to a danger, believed on substantial grounds to exist, of torture within the meaning of Article 1 of the Convention Against Torture; or

(b) to a risk to their life or to a risk of cruel and unusual treatment or punishment if

(i) the person is unable or, because of that risk, unwilling to avail themself of the protection of that country,

(ii) the risk would be faced by the person in every part of that country and is not faced generally by other individuals in or from that country,

(iii) the risk is not inherent or incidental to lawful sanctions, unless imposed in disregard of accepted international standards, and

(iv) the risk is not caused by the inability of that country to provide adequate health or medical care.

. . .

Exclusion — Refugee Convention

98 A person referred to in section E or F of Article 1 of the Refugee Convention is not a Convention refugee or a person in need of protection.

Requirement to report

98.1 (1) A designated foreign national on whom refugee protection is conferred under paragraph 95(1)(b) or (c) must report to an officer in accordance with the regulations.

Obligation when reporting

(2) A designated foreign national who is required to report to an officer must answer truthfully all questions put to him or her and must provide any information and documents that the officer requests.

Division 2
Convention Refugees and Persons in Need of Protection

Claim for Refugee Protection

Claim

99 (1) A claim for refugee protection may be made in or outside Canada.

Claim outside Canada

(2) A claim for refugee protection made by a person outside Canada must be made by making an application for a visa as a Convention refugee or a person in similar circumstances, and is governed by Part 1.

Claim inside Canada

(3) A claim for refugee protection made by a person inside Canada must be made to an officer, may not be made by a person who is subject to a removal order, and is governed by this Part.

Claim made inside Canada — not at port of entry

(3.1) A person who makes a claim for refugee protection inside Canada other than at a port of entry must provide the officer, within the time limits provided for in the regulations, with the documents and information — including in respect of the basis for the claim — required by the rules of the Board, in accordance with those rules.

. . .

Examination of Eligibility to Refer Claim

Referral to Refugee Protection Division

100 (1) An officer shall, within three working days after receipt of a claim referred to in subsection 99(3), determine whether the claim is eligible to be referred to the Refugee Protection Division and, if it is eligible, shall refer the claim in accordance with the rules of the Board.

Burden of proof

(1.1) The burden of proving that a claim is eligible to be referred to the Refugee Protection Division rests on the claimant, who must answer truthfully all questions put to them.

Decision

(2) The officer shall suspend consideration of the eligibility of the person's claim if

(a) a report has been referred for a determination, at an admissibility hearing, of whether the person is inadmissible on grounds of security, violating human or international rights, serious criminality or organized criminality; or

(b) the officer considers it necessary to wait for a decision of a court with respect to a claimant who is charged with an offence under an Act of Parliament that is punishable by a maximum term of imprisonment of at least 10 years.

Consideration of claim
(3) The Refugee Protection Division may not consider a claim until it is referred by the officer. If the claim is not referred within the three-day period referred to in subsection (1), it is deemed to be referred, unless there is a suspension or it is determined to be ineligible.

Documents and information to be provided
(4) A person who makes a claim for refugee protection inside Canada at a port of entry and whose claim is referred to the Refugee Protection Division must provide the Division, within the time limits provided for in the regulations, with the documents and information — including in respect of the basis for the claim — required by the rules of the Board, in accordance with those rules.

Date of hearing
(4.1) The referring officer must, in accordance with the regulations, the rules of the Board and any directions of the Chairperson of the Board, fix the date on which the claimant is to attend a hearing before the Refugee Protection Division.

. . .

Ineligibility
101 (1) A claim is ineligible to be referred to the Refugee Protection Division if

(a) refugee protection has been conferred on the claimant under this Act;
(b) a claim for refugee protection by the claimant has been rejected by the Board;
(c) a prior claim by the claimant was determined to be ineligible to be referred to the Refugee Protection Division, or to have been withdrawn or abandoned;
(d) the claimant has been recognized as a Convention refugee by a country other than Canada and can be sent or returned to that country;

(e) the claimant came directly or indirectly to Canada from a country designated by the regulations, other than a country of their nationality or their former habitual residence; or
(f) the claimant has been determined to be inadmissible on grounds of security, violating human or international rights, serious criminality or organized criminality, except for persons who are inadmissible solely on the grounds of paragraph 35(1)(c).

Serious criminality
(2) A claim is not ineligible by reason of serious criminality under paragraph (1)(f) unless

(a) in the case of inadmissibility by reason of a conviction in Canada, the conviction is for an offence under an Act of Parliament punishable by a maximum term of imprisonment of at least 10 years; or
(b) in the case of inadmissibility by reason of a conviction outside Canada, the conviction is for an offence that, if committed in Canada, would constitute an offence under an Act of Parliament punishable by a maximum term of imprisonment of at least 10 years.

Regulations
102 (1) The regulations may govern matters relating to the application of sections 100 and 101, may, for the purposes of this Act, define the terms used in those sections and, for the purpose of sharing responsibility with governments of foreign states for the consideration of refugee claims, may include provisions

(a) designating countries that comply with Article 33 of the Refugee Convention and Article 3 of the Convention Against Torture;
(b) making a list of those countries and amending it as necessary; and
(c) respecting the circumstances and criteria for the application of paragraph 101(1)(e).

Factors
(2) The following factors are to be considered in designating a country under paragraph (1)(a):

(a) whether the country is a party to the Refugee Convention and to the Convention Against Torture;

(b) its policies and practices with respect to claims under the Refugee Convention and with respect to obligations under the Convention Against Torture;
(c) its human rights record; and
(d) whether it is party to an agreement with the Government of Canada for the purpose of sharing responsibility with respect to claims for refugee protection.

Review
(3) The Governor in Council must ensure the continuing review of factors set out in subsection (2) with respect to each designated country.

Suspension or Termination of Consideration of Claim

Suspension
103 (1) Proceedings of the Refugee Protection Division in respect of a claim for refugee protection are suspended on notice by an officer that

(a) the matter has been referred to the Immigration Division to determine whether the claimant is inadmissible on grounds of security, violating human or international rights, serious criminality or organized criminality; or
(b) an officer considers it necessary to wait for a decision of a court with respect to a claimant who is charged with an offence under an Act of Parliament that may be punished by a maximum term of imprisonment of at least 10 years.

Continuation
(2) On notice by an officer that the suspended claim was determined to be eligible, proceedings of the Refugee Protection Division must continue.

Notice of ineligible claim
104 (1) An officer may, with respect to a claim that is before the Refugee Protection Division or, in the case of paragraph (d), that is before or has been determined by the Refugee Protection Division or the Refugee Appeal Division, give notice that an officer has determined that

(a) the claim is ineligible under paragraphs 101(1)(a) to (e);
(b) the claim is ineligible under paragraph 101(1)(f);
(c) the claim was referred as a result of directly or indirectly misrepresenting or withholding material facts relating to a relevant matter and that the claim was not otherwise eligible to be referred to that Division; or

(d) the claim is not the first claim that was received by an officer in respect of the claimant.

Termination and nullification
(2) A notice given under the following provisions has the following effects:

(a) if given under any of paragraphs (1)(a) to (c), it terminates pending proceedings in the Refugee Protection Division respecting the claim; and
(b if given under paragraph (1)(d), it terminates proceedings in and nullifies any decision of the Refugee Protection Division or the Refugee Appeal Division respecting a claim other than the first claim.

Extradition Procedure

Suspension if proceeding under *Extradition Act*
105 (1) The Refugee Protection Division and Refugee Appeal Division shall not commence, or shall suspend, consideration of any matter concerning a person against whom an authority to proceed has been issued under section 15 of the *Extradition Act* with respect to an offence under Canadian law that is punishable under an Act of Parliament by a maximum term of imprisonment of at least 10 years, until a final decision under the *Extradition Act* with respect to the discharge or surrender of the person has been made.

Continuation if discharge under Extradition Act
(2) If the person is finally discharged under the *Extradition Act*, the proceedings of the applicable Division may be commenced or continued as though there had not been any proceedings under that Act.

Rejection if surrender under Extradition Act
(3) If the person is ordered surrendered by the Minister of Justice under the *Extradition Act* and the offence for which the person was committed by the judge under section 29 of that Act is punishable under an Act of Parliament by a maximum term of imprisonment of at least 10 years, the order of surrender is deemed to be a rejection of a claim for refugee protection based on paragraph (b) of Section F of Article 1 of the Refugee Convention.

Final decision
(4) The deemed rejection referred to in subsection (3) may not be appealed, and is not subject to judicial review except to the extent that

a judicial review of the order of surrender is provided for under the *Extradition Act*.

Limit if no previous claim
(5) If the person has not made a claim for refugee protection before the order of surrender referred to in subsection (3), the person may not do so before the surrender.

Claimant Without Identification

Credibility
106 The Refugee Protection Division must take into account, with respect to the credibility of a claimant, whether the claimant possesses acceptable documentation establishing identity, and if not, whether they have provided a reasonable explanation for the lack of documentation or have taken reasonable steps to obtain the documentation.

Decision on Claim for Refugee Protection

Decision
107 (1) The Refugee Protection Division shall accept a claim for refugee protection if it determines that the claimant is a Convention refugee or person in need of protection, and shall otherwise reject the claim.

No credible basis
(2) If the Refugee Protection Division is of the opinion, in rejecting a claim, that there was no credible or trustworthy evidence on which it could have made a favourable decision, it shall state in its reasons for the decision that there is no credible basis for the claim.

Manifestly unfounded
107.1 If the Refugee Protection Division rejects a claim for refugee protection, it must state in its reasons for the decision that the claim is manifestly unfounded if it is of the opinion that the claim is clearly fraudulent.

Cessation of Refugee Protection

Rejection
108 (1) A claim for refugee protection shall be rejected, and a person is not a Convention refugee or a person in need of protection, in any of the following circumstances:

- (a) the person has voluntarily reavailed themself of the protection of their country of nationality;
- (b) the person has voluntarily reacquired their nationality;

(c) the person has acquired a new nationality and enjoys the protection of the country of that new nationality;
(d) the person has voluntarily become re-established in the country that the person left or remained outside of and in respect of which the person claimed refugee protection in Canada; or
(e) the reasons for which the person sought refugee protection have ceased to exist.

Cessation of refugee protection
(2) On application by the Minister, the Refugee Protection Division may determine that refugee protection referred to in subsection 95(1) has ceased for any of the reasons described in subsection (1).

Effect of decision
(3) If the application is allowed, the claim of the person is deemed to be rejected.

Exception
(4) Paragraph (1)(e) does not apply to a person who establishes that there are compelling reasons arising out of previous persecution, torture, treatment or punishment for refusing to avail themselves of the protection of the country which they left, or outside of which they remained, due to such previous persecution, torture, treatment or punishment.

Applications to Vacate

Vacation of refugee protection
109 (1) The Refugee Protection Division may, on application by the Minister, vacate a decision to allow a claim for refugee protection, if it finds that the decision was obtained as a result of directly or indirectly misrepresenting or withholding material facts relating to a relevant matter.

Rejection of application
(2) The Refugee Protection Division may reject the application if it is satisfied that other sufficient evidence was considered at the time of the first determination to justify refugee protection.

Allowance of application
(3) If the application is allowed, the claim of the person is deemed to be rejected and the decision that led to the conferral of refugee protection is nullified.

Designated Countries of Origin

Designation of countries of origin

109.1 (1) The Minister may, by order, designate a country, for the purposes of subsection 110(2) and section 111.1.

Limitation

(2) The Minister may only make a designation

- (a) in the case where the number of claims for refugee protection made in Canada by nationals of the country in question in respect of which the Refugee Protection Division has made a final determination is equal to or greater than the number provided for by order of the Minister,
  - (i) if the rate, expressed as a percentage, that is obtained by dividing the total number of claims made by nationals of the country in question that, in a final determination by the Division during the period provided for in the order, are rejected or determined to be withdrawn or abandoned by the total number of claims made by nationals of the country in question in respect of which the Division has, during the same period, made a final determination is equal to or greater than the percentage provided for in the order, or
  - (ii) if the rate, expressed as a percentage, that is obtained by dividing the total number of claims made by nationals of the country in question that, in a final determination by the Division, during the period provided for in the order, are determined to be withdrawn or abandoned by the total number of claims made by nationals of the country in question in respect of which the Division has, during the same period, made a final determination is equal to or greater than the percentage provided for in the order; or
- (b) in the case where the number of claims for refugee protection made in Canada by nationals of the country in question in respect of which the Refugee Protection Division has made a final determination is less than the number provided for by order of the Minister, if the Minister is of the opinion that in the country in question
  - (i) there is an independent judicial system,
  - (ii) basic democratic rights and freedoms are recognized and mechanisms for redress are available if those rights or freedoms are infringed, and
  - (iii) civil society organizations exist.

Order of Minister
(3) The Minister may, by order, provide for the number, period or percentages referred to in subsection (2).

. . .

Appeal to Refugee Appeal Division

Appeal
110 (1) Subject to subsections (1.1) and (2), a person or the Minister may appeal, in accordance with the rules of the Board, on a question of law, of fact or of mixed law and fact, to the Refugee Appeal Division against a decision of the Refugee Protection Division to allow or reject the person's claim for refugee protection.

Notice of appeal
(1.1) The Minister may satisfy any requirement respecting the manner in which an appeal is filed and perfected by submitting a notice of appeal and any supporting documents.

Restriction on appeals
(2) No appeal may be made in respect of any of the following:

- (a) a decision of the Refugee Protection Division allowing or rejecting the claim for refugee protection of a designated foreign national;
- (b) a determination that a refugee protection claim has been withdrawn or abandoned;
- (c) a decision of the Refugee Protection Division rejecting a claim for refugee protection that states that the claim has no credible basis or is manifestly unfounded;
- (d) subject to the regulations, a decision of the Refugee Protection Division in respect of a claim for refugee protection if
  - (i) the foreign national who makes the claim came directly or indirectly to Canada from a country that is, on the day on which their claim is made, designated by regulations made under subsection 102(1) and that is a party to an agreement referred to in paragraph 102(2)(d), and
  - (ii) the claim — by virtue of regulations made under paragraph 102(1)(c) — is not ineligible under paragraph 101(1)(e) to be referred to the Refugee Protection Division;
- (d.1) a decision of the Refugee Protection Division allowing or rejecting a claim for refugee protection made by a foreign national who is a national of a country that was, on the day

on which the decision was made, a country designated under subsection 109.1(1);

(e) a decision of the Refugee Protection Division allowing or rejecting an application by the Minister for a determination that refugee protection has ceased;

(f) a decision of the Refugee Protection Division allowing or rejecting an application by the Minister to vacate a decision to allow a claim for refugee protection.

Making of appeal
(2.1) The appeal must be filed and perfected within the time limits set out in the regulations.

Procedure
(3) Subject to subsections (3.1), (4) and (6), the Refugee Appeal Division must proceed without a hearing, on the basis of the record of the proceedings of the Refugee Protection Division, and may accept documentary evidence and written submissions from the Minister and the person who is the subject of the appeal and, in the case of a matter that is conducted before a panel of three members, written submissions from a representative or agent of the United Nations High Commissioner for Refugees and any other person described in the rules of the Board.

Time limits
(3.1) Unless a hearing is held under subsection (6), the Refugee Appeal Division must make a decision within the time limits set out in the regulations.

Evidence that may be presented
(4) On appeal, the person who is the subject of the appeal may present only evidence that arose after the rejection of their claim or that was not reasonably available, or that the person could not reasonably have been expected in the circumstances to have presented, at the time of the rejection.

Exception
(5) Subsection (4) does not apply in respect of evidence that is presented in response to evidence presented by the Minister.

Hearing
(6) The Refugee Appeal Division may hold a hearing if, in its opinion, there is documentary evidence referred to in subsection (3)

(a) that raises a serious issue with respect to the credibility of the person who is the subject of the appeal;
(b) that is central to the decision with respect to the refugee protection claim; and
(c) that, if accepted, would justify allowing or rejecting the refugee protection claim.

Decision
111 (1) After considering the appeal, the Refugee Appeal Division shall make one of the following decisions:

(a) confirm the determination of the Refugee Protection Division;
(b) set aside the determination and substitute a determination that, in its opinion, should have been made; or
(c) refer the matter to the Refugee Protection Division for re-determination, giving the directions to the Refugee Protection Division that it considers appropriate.

Referrals
(2) The Refugee Appeal Division may make the referral described in paragraph (1)(c) only if it is of the opinion that

(a) the decision of the Refugee Protection Division is wrong in law, in fact or in mixed law and fact; and
(b) it cannot make a decision under paragraph 111(1)(a) or (b) without hearing evidence that was presented to the Refugee Protection Division.

. . .

Decision
111 (1) After considering the appeal, the Refugee Appeal Division shall make one of the following decisions:

(a) confirm the determination of the Refugee Protection Division;
(b) set aside the determination and substitute a determination that, in its opinion, should have been made; or
(c) refer the matter to the Refugee Protection Division for re-determination, giving the directions to the Refugee Protection Division that it considers appropriate.

Referrals
(2) The Refugee Appeal Division may make the referral described in paragraph (1)(c) only if it is of the opinion that

(a) the decision of the Refugee Protection Division is wrong in law, in fact or in mixed law and fact; and
(b) it cannot make a decision under paragraph 111(1)(a) or (b) without hearing evidence that was presented to the Refugee Protection Division.

Principle of Non-*refoulement*

Protection
115 (1) A protected person or a person who is recognized as a Convention refugee by another country to which the person may be returned shall not be removed from Canada to a country where they would be at risk of persecution for reasons of race, religion, nationality, membership in a particular social group or political opinion or at risk of torture or cruel and unusual treatment or punishment.

Exceptions
(2) Subsection (1) does not apply in the case of a person

(a) who is inadmissible on grounds of serious criminality and who constitutes, in the opinion of the Minister, a danger to the public in Canada; or
(b) who is inadmissible on grounds of security, violating human or international rights or organized criminality if, in the opinion of the Minister, the person should not be allowed to remain in Canada on the basis of the nature and severity of acts committed or of danger to the security of Canada.

Removal of refugee
(3) A person, after a determination under paragraph 101(1)(e) that the person's claim is ineligible, is to be sent to the country from which the person came to Canada, but may be sent to another country if that country is designated under subsection 102(1) or if the country from which the person came to Canada has rejected their claim for refugee protection.

. . .

Part 4
Immigration and Refugee Board

Composition of Board

Immigration and Refugee Board

151 The Immigration and Refugee Board consists of the Refugee Protection Division, the Refugee Appeal Division, the Immigration Division and the Immigration Appeal Division.

. . .

Chairperson and other members

153 (1) The Chairperson and members of the Refugee Appeal Division and Immigration Appeal Division

(a) are appointed to the Board by the Governor in Council, to hold office during good behaviour for a term not exceeding seven years, subject to removal by the Governor in Council at any time for cause, to serve in a regional or district office of the Board;
(b) [Repealed, 2010, c. 8, s. 18]
(c) are eligible for reappointment in the same or another capacity;
(d) shall receive the remuneration that may be fixed by the Governor in Council;
(e) are entitled to be paid reasonable travel and living expenses incurred while absent in the course of their duties, in the case of a full-time member, from their ordinary place of work or, in the case of a part-time member, while absent from their ordinary place of residence;
(f) are deemed to be employed in the public service for the purposes of the *Public Service Superannuation Act* and in the federal public administration for the purposes of the *Government Employees Compensation Act* and any regulations made under section 9 of the *Aeronautics Act*;
(g) may not accept or hold any office or employment or carry on any activity inconsistent with their duties and functions under this Act; and
(h) if appointed as full-time members, must devote the whole of their time to the performance of their duties under this Act.

. . .

(4) The Deputy Chairperson of the Immigration Appeal Division and a majority of the Assistant Deputy Chairpersons of that Division and at least 10 per cent of the members of the Divisions referred to in subsection (1) must be members of at least five years standing at the bar of a province or notaries of at least five years standing at the Chambre des notaires du Québec.

. . .

Chairperson

159 (1) The Chairperson is, by virtue of holding that office, a member of each Division of the Board and is the chief executive officer of the Board. In that capacity, the Chairperson

(a) has supervision over and direction of the work and staff of the Board;
(b) may at any time assign a member appointed under paragraph 153(1)(a) to the Refugee Appeal Division or the Immigration Appeal Division;
(c) may at any time, despite paragraph 153(1)(a), assign a member of the Refugee Appeal Division or the Immigration Appeal Division to work in another regional or district office to satisfy operational requirements, but an assignment may not exceed 120 days without the approval of the Governor in Council;
(d) may designate, from among the full-time members appointed under paragraph 153(1)(a), coordinating members for the Refugee Appeal Division or the Immigration Appeal Division;
(e) assigns administrative functions to the members of the Board;
(f) apportions work among the members of the Board and fixes the place, date and time of proceedings;
(g) takes any action that may be necessary to ensure that the members of the Board carry out their duties efficiently and without undue delay;
(h) may issue guidelines in writing to members of the Board and identify decisions of the Board as jurisprudential guides, after consulting with the Deputy Chairpersons, to assist members in carrying out their duties; and
(i) may appoint and, subject to the approval of the Treasury Board, fix the remuneration of experts or persons having special knowledge to assist the Divisions in any matter.

. . .

Functioning of Board

Rules

161 (1) Subject to the approval of the Governor in Council, and in consultation with the Deputy Chairpersons, the Chairperson may make rules respecting

- (a) the referral of a claim for refugee protection to the Refugee Protection Division;
- (a.1) the factors to be taken into account in fixing or changing the date of the hearing referred to in subsection 100(4.1);
- (a.2) the activities, practice and procedure of each of the Divisions of the Board, including the periods for appeal, other than in respect of appeals of decisions of the Refugee Protection Division, the priority to be given to proceedings, the notice that is required and the period in which notice must be given;
- (b) the conduct of persons in proceedings before the Board, as well as the consequences of, and sanctions for, the breach of those rules;
- (c) the information that may be required and the manner in which, and the time within which, it must be provided with respect to a proceeding before the Board; and
- (d) any other matter considered by the Chairperson to require rules.

. . .

Provisions That Apply to All Divisions

Sole and exclusive jurisdiction

162 (1) Each Division of the Board has, in respect of proceedings brought before it under this Act, sole and exclusive jurisdiction to hear and determine all questions of law and fact, including questions of jurisdiction.

Procedure

(2) Each Division shall deal with all proceedings before it as informally and quickly as the circumstances and the considerations of fairness and natural justice permit.

Composition of panels

163 Matters before a Division shall be conducted before a single member unless, except for matters before the Immigration Division, the Chairperson is of the opinion that a panel of three members should be constituted.

Presence of parties

164 Where a hearing is held by a Division, it may, in the Division's discretion, be conducted in the presence of, or by a means of live telecommunication with, the person who is the subject of the proceedings.

. . .

Proceedings — all Divisions

166 Proceedings before a Division are to be conducted as follows:

- (a) subject to the other provisions of this section, proceedings must be held in public;
- (b) on application or on its own initiative, the Division may conduct a proceeding in the absence of the public, or take any other measure that it considers necessary to ensure the confidentiality of the proceedings, if, after having considered all available alternate measures, the Division is satisfied that there is
  - (i) a serious possibility that the life, liberty or security of a person will be endangered if the proceeding is held in public,
  - (ii) a real and substantial risk to the fairness of the proceeding such that the need to prevent disclosure outweighs the societal interest that the proceeding be conducted in public, or
  - (iii) a real and substantial risk that matters involving public security will be disclosed;
- (c) subject to paragraph (d), proceedings before the Refugee Protection Division and the Refugee Appeal Division must be held in the absence of the public;
- (c.1) subject to paragraph (d), proceedings before the Immigration Division must be held in the absence of the public if they concern a person who is the subject of a proceeding before the Refugee Protection Division or the Refugee Appeal Division that is pending or who has made an application for protection to the Minister that is pending;
- (d) on application or on its own initiative, the Division may conduct a proceeding in public, or take any other measure that it considers necessary to ensure the appropriate access to the proceedings if, after having considered all available alternate measures and the factors set out in paragraph (b), the Division is satisfied that it is appropriate to do so;

(e) despite paragraphs (b) to (c.1), a representative or agent of the United Nations High Commissioner for Refugees is entitled to observe proceedings concerning a protected person or a person who has made a claim for refugee protection or an application for protection; and
(f) despite paragraph (e), the representative or agent may not observe any part of the proceedings that deals with information or other evidence in respect of which an application has been made under section 86, and not rejected, or with information or other evidence protected under that section.

Right to counsel
167 (1) A person who is the subject of proceedings before any Division of the Board and the Minister may, at their own expense, be represented by legal or other counsel.

Representation
(2) If a person who is the subject of proceedings is under 18 years of age or unable, in the opinion of the applicable Division, to appreciate the nature of the proceedings, the Division shall designate a person to represent the person.

. . .

Decisions and reasons
169 In the case of a decision of a Division, other than an interlocutory decision:

(a) the decision takes effect in accordance with the rules;
(b) reasons for the decision must be given;
(c) the decision may be rendered orally or in writing, except a decision of the Refugee Appeal Division, which must be rendered in writing;
(d) if the Refugee Protection Division rejects a claim, written reasons must be provided to the claimant and the Minister;
(e) if the person who is the subject of proceedings before the Board or the Minister requests reasons for a decision within 10 days of notification of the decision, or in circumstances set out in the rules of the Board, the Division must provide written reasons; and
(f) the period in which to apply for judicial review with respect to a decision of the Board is calculated from the giving of notice of the decision or from the sending of written reasons, whichever is later.

Refugee Protection Division

Composition

169.1 (1) The Refugee Protection Division consists of the Deputy Chairperson, Assistant Deputy Chairpersons and other members, including coordinating members, necessary to carry out its functions.

Public Service Employment Act

(2) The members of the Refugee Protection Division are appointed in accordance with the *Public Service Employment Act.*

Proceedings

170 The Refugee Protection Division, in any proceeding before it,

- (a) may inquire into any matter that it considers relevant to establishing whether a claim is well-founded;
- (b) must hold a hearing;
- (c) must notify the person who is the subject of the proceeding and the Minister of the hearing;
- (d) must provide the Minister, on request, with the documents and information referred to in subsection 100(4);
- (d.1) may question the witnesses, including the person who is the subject of the proceeding;
- (e) must give the person and the Minister a reasonable opportunity to present evidence, question witnesses and make representations;
- (f) may, despite paragraph (b), allow a claim for refugee protection without a hearing, if the Minister has not notified the Division, within the period set out in the rules of the Board, of the Minister's intention to intervene;
- (g) is not bound by any legal or technical rules of evidence;
- (h) may receive and base a decision on evidence that is adduced in the proceedings and considered credible or trustworthy in the circumstances; and
- (i) may take notice of any facts that may be judicially noticed, any other generally recognized facts and any information or opinion that is within its specialized knowledge.

No reopening of claim or application

170.2 The Refugee Protection Division does not have jurisdiction to reopen on any ground — including a failure to observe a principle of natural justice — a claim for refugee protection, an application for protection or an application for cessation or vacation, in respect of which the Refugee Appeal Division or the Federal Court, as the case may be, has made a final determination.

Refugee Appeal Division

Proceedings
171 In the case of a proceeding of the Refugee Appeal Division,

(a) the Division must give notice of any hearing to the Minister and to the person who is the subject of the appeal;
(a.1) subject to subsection 110(4), if a hearing is held, the Division must give the person who is the subject of the appeal and the Minister the opportunity to present evidence, question witnesses and make submissions;
(a.2) the Division is not bound by any legal or technical rules of evidence;
(a.3) the Division may receive and base a decision on evidence that is adduced in the proceedings and considered credible or trustworthy in the circumstances;
(a.4) the Minister may, at any time before the Division makes a decision, after giving notice to the Division and to the person who is the subject of the appeal, intervene in the appeal;
(a.5) the Minister may, at any time before the Division makes a decision, submit documentary evidence and make written submissions in support of the Minister's appeal or intervention in the appeal;
(b) the Division may take notice of any facts that may be judicially noticed and of any other generally recognized facts and any information or opinion that is within its specialized knowledge; and
(c) a decision of a panel of three members of the Refugee Appeal Division has, for the Refugee Protection Division and for a panel of one member of the Refugee Appeal Division, the same precedential value as a decision of an appeal court has for a trial court.

No reopening of appeal
171.1 The Refugee Appeal Division does not have jurisdiction to reopen on any ground — including a failure to observe a principle of natural justice — an appeal in respect of which the Federal Court has made a final determination.

. . .

Schedule
(Subsection 2(1))

Sections E and F of Article 1 of the United Nations Convention Relating to the Status of Refugees

E This Convention shall not apply to a person who is recognized by the competent authorities of the country in which he has taken residence as having the rights and obligations which are attached to the possession of the nationality of that country.

F The provisions of this Convention shall not apply to any person with respect to whom there are serious reasons for considering that:

(a) he has committed a crime against peace, a war crime, or a crime against humanity, as defined in the international instruments drawn up to make provision in respect of such crimes;
(b) he has committed a serious non-political crime outside the country of refuge prior to his admission to that country as a refugee;
(c) he has been guilty of acts contrary to the purposes and principles of the United Nations.

Article 1 of the Convention Against Torture and Other Cruel, Inhuman and Degrading Treatment or Punishment

1 For the purposes of this Convention, torture means any act by which severe pain or suffering, whether physical or mental, is intentionally inflicted on a person for such purposes as obtaining from him or a third person information or a confession, punishing him for an act he or a third person has committed or is suspected of having committed, or intimidating or coercing him or a third person, or for any reason based on discrimination of any kind, when such pain or suffering is inflicted by or at the instigation of or with the consent or acquiescence of a public official or other person acting in an official capacity. It does not include pain or suffering arising only from, inherent in or incidental to lawful sanctions.

2 This article is without prejudice to any international instrument or national legislation which does or may contain provisions of wider application.

APPENDIX B

SELECTED PROVISIONS OF THE *IMMIGRATION AND REFUGEE PROTECTION REGULATIONS*

Immigration and Refugee Protection Regulations

[*Regulations* pursuant to the *IRPA*, including SOR/2002-227 and subsequent amending statutory instruments as of 15 February 2017]

. . .

Part 8
Refugee Classes

Division 1
Convention Refugees Abroad and Humanitarian-Protected Persons Abroad

Interpretation

Definitions
138 The definitions in this section apply in this Division and in Division 2.

group means

(a) five or more Canadian citizens or permanent residents, each of whom is at least 18 years of age, who are acting together for the purpose of sponsoring a Convention refugee or a person in similar circumstances; or
(b) one or more Canadian citizens or permanent residents, each of whom is at least 18 years of age, and a corporation or unincorporated organization or association referred to in subsection 13(2) of the Act, acting together for the purpose of sponsoring a Convention refugee or a person in similar circumstances.

referral organization means

(a) the United Nations High Commissioner for Refugees; or
(b) any organization with which the Minister has entered into a memorandum of understanding under section 143.

sponsor means

(a) a group, a corporation or an unincorporated organization or association referred to in subsection 13(2) of the Act, or any combination of them, that is acting for the purpose of sponsoring a Convention refugee or a person in similar circumstances; or
(b) for the purposes of section 158, a sponsor within the meaning of the regulations made under *An Act respecting immigration to Québec*, R.S.Q., c.I-0.2, as amended from time to time.

undertaking means an undertaking in writing to the Minister to provide resettlement assistance, lodging and other basic necessities in Canada for a member of a class prescribed by this Division, the member's accompanying family members and any of the member's non-accompanying family members who meet the requirements of section 141, for the period determined in accordance with subsections 154(2) and (3).

urgent need of protection means, in respect of a member of the Convention refugee abroad or the country of asylum class, that their life, liberty or physical safety is under immediate threat and, if not protected, the person is likely to be

(a) killed;
(b) subjected to violence, torture, sexual assault or arbitrary imprisonment; or
(c) returned to their country of nationality or of their former habitual residence.

vulnerable means, in respect of a Convention refugee or a person in similar circumstances, that the person has a greater need of protection than other applicants for protection abroad because of the person's particular circumstances that give rise to a heightened risk to their physical safety.

General

General requirements

139 (1) A permanent resident visa shall be issued to a foreign national in need of refugee protection, and their accompanying family members, if following an examination it is established that

- (a) the foreign national is outside Canada;
- (b) the foreign national has submitted an application for a permanent resident visa under this Division in accordance with paragraphs 10(1)(a) to (c) and (2)(c.1) to (d) and sections 140.1 to 140.3;
- (c) the foreign national is seeking to come to Canada to establish permanent residence;
- (d) the foreign national is a person in respect of whom there is no reasonable prospect, within a reasonable period, of a durable solution in a country other than Canada, namely
  - (i) voluntary repatriation or resettlement in their country of nationality or habitual residence, or
  - (ii) resettlement or an offer of resettlement in another country;
- (e) the foreign national is a member of one of the classes prescribed by this Division;
- (f) one of the following is the case, namely
  - (i) the sponsor's sponsorship application for the foreign national and their family members included in the application for protection has been approved under these Regulations,
  - (ii) in the case of a member of the Convention refugee abroad class, financial assistance in the form of funds from a governmental resettlement assistance program is available in Canada for the foreign national and their family members included in the application for protection, or
  - (iii) the foreign national has sufficient financial resources to provide for the lodging, care and maintenance, and for the resettlement in Canada, of themself and their family members included in the application for protection;
- (g) if the foreign national intends to reside in a province other than the Province of Quebec, the foreign national and their family

members included in the application for protection will be able to become successfully established in Canada, taking into account the following factors:

(i) their resourcefulness and other similar qualities that assist in integration in a new society,

(ii) the presence of their relatives, including the relatives of a spouse or a common-law partner, or their sponsor in the expected community of resettlement,

(iii) their potential for employment in Canada, given their education, work experience and skills, and

(iv) their ability to learn to communicate in one of the official languages of Canada;

(h) if the foreign national intends to reside in the Province of Quebec, the competent authority of that Province is of the opinion that the foreign national and their family members included in the application for protection meet the selection criteria of the Province; and

(i) subject to subsections (3) and (4), the foreign national and their family members included in the application for protection are not inadmissible.

Exception

(2) Paragraph (1)(g) does not apply to a foreign national, or their family members included in the application for protection, who has been determined by an officer to be vulnerable or in urgent need of protection.

Financial inadmissibility — exemption

(3) A foreign national who is a member of a class prescribed by this Division, and meets the applicable requirements of this Division, is exempted from the application of section 39 of the Act.

Health grounds — exception

(4) A foreign national who is a member of a class prescribed by this Division, and meets the applicable requirements of this Division, is exempted from the application of paragraph 38(1)(c) of the Act.

. . .

Sponsorship of foreign national — requirement to attach applications

140.2 (1) If the foreign national making an application for a permanent resident visa under this Division is being sponsored, the application for a permanent resident visa shall

(a) be accompanied by a sponsorship application referred to in paragraph 153(1)(b) by which the foreign national is being sponsored; or
(b) be attached to the sponsorship application sent by the sponsor in accordance with subsection 153(1.2).

. . .

Referral requirement
140.3 (1) If the foreign national making an application for a permanent resident visa under this Division is not being sponsored, a foreign national making an application for a permanent resident visa under this Division shall submit their application with one of the following referrals, if the referral has not yet been submitted to the immigration office by its issuer:

(a) a referral from a referral organization;
(b) a referral resulting from an arrangement between the Minister and the government of a foreign state or any institution of such a government relating to resettlement; or
(c) a referral resulting from an agreement relating to resettlement entered into by the Government of Canada and an international organization or the government of a foreign state.

Exception
(2) A foreign national may submit the application without a referral if they reside in a geographic area as determined by the Minister in accordance with subsection (3).

Minister's determination
(3) The Minister may determine on the basis of the following factors that a geographic area is an area in which circumstances justify the submission of permanent resident visa applications without a referral:

(a) advice from referral organizations with which the Minister has entered into a memorandum of understanding under section 143 that they are unable to make the number of referrals specified in their memorandum of understanding for the area;
(b) the inability of referral organizations to refer persons in the area;
(c) the resettlement needs in the area, after consultation with referral organizations that have substantial knowledge of the area; and
(d) the relative importance of resettlement needs in the area, within the context of resettlement needs globally.

. . .

Non-accompanying family member

141 (1) A permanent resident visa shall be issued to a family member who does not accompany the applicant if, following an examination, it is established that

(a) the family member was included in the applicant's permanent resident visa application at the time that application was made, or was added to that application before the applicant's departure for Canada;
(b) the family member submits their application to an officer outside Canada within one year from the day on which refugee protection is conferred on the applicant;
(c) the family member is not inadmissible;
(d) if the applicant is the subject of a sponsorship application referred to in paragraph 139(1)(f)(i), their sponsor has been notified of the family member's application and an officer is satisfied that there are adequate financial arrangements for resettlement; and
(e) in the case of a family member who intends to reside in the Province of Quebec, the competent authority of that Province is of the opinion that the foreign national meets the selection criteria of the Province.

. . .

Member of country of asylum class

147 A foreign national is a member of the country of asylum class if they have been determined by an officer to be in need of resettlement because

(a) they are outside all of their countries of nationality and habitual residence; and
(b) they have been, and continue to be, seriously and personally affected by civil war, armed conflict or massive violation of human rights in each of those countries.

. . .

Protected Temporary Residents

Protected temporary residents class

151.1 (1) The protected temporary residents class is prescribed as a class of persons who may become permanent residents on the basis of the requirements of this section.

Member of the class
(2) A foreign national is a protected temporary resident and a member of the protected temporary residents class if the foreign national holds a temporary resident permit and

(a) became a temporary resident under a temporary resident permit for protection reasons after making a claim for refugee protection outside Canada under section 99 of the Act; or
(b) was issued a Minister's permit under section 37 of the former Act after seeking admission to Canada under section 7 of the former Regulations or section 4 of the *Humanitarian Designated Classes Regulations*.

. . .

Division 2
Sponsorship

Sponsorship agreements
152 (1) The Minister may enter into a sponsorship agreement with a sponsor for the purpose of facilitating the processing of sponsorship applications.

Contents of agreement
(2) A sponsorship agreement shall include provisions relating to

(a) settlement plans;
(b) financial requirements;
(c) assistance to be provided by the Department;
(d) the standard of conduct expected of the sponsor;
(e) reporting requirements; and
(f) the grounds for suspending or cancelling the agreement.

Sponsorship requirements
153 (1) In order to sponsor a foreign national and their family members who are members of a class prescribed by Division 1, a sponsor

(a) must reside or have representatives in the expected community of settlement;
(b) must make a sponsorship application that includes a settlement plan, an undertaking and, if the sponsor has not entered into a sponsorship agreement with the Minister, a document issued by the United Nations High Commissioner for Refugees or a foreign state certifying the status of the foreign national as a refugee under the rules applicable to the United Nations High

Commissioner for Refugees or the applicable laws of the foreign state, as the case may be; and

(c) must not be — or include — an individual, a corporation or an unincorporated organization or association that was a party to a sponsorship in which they defaulted on an undertaking and remain in default.

. . .

Ineligibility to be a party to a sponsorship

156 (1) The following persons are ineligible to be a party to a sponsorship:

(a) a person who has been convicted in Canada of the offence of murder or an offence set out in Schedule I or II to the *Corrections and Conditional Release Act*, regardless of whether it was prosecuted by indictment, if a period of five years has not elapsed since the completion of the person's sentence;

(b) a person who has been convicted of an offence outside Canada that, if committed in Canada, would constitute an offence referred to in paragraph (a), if a period of five years has not elapsed since the completion of the person's sentence imposed under a foreign law;

(c) a person who is in default of any support payment obligations ordered by a court;

(d) a person who is subject to a removal order;

(e) a person who is subject to a revocation proceeding under the *Citizenship Act*; and

(f) a person who is detained in any penitentiary, jail, reformatory or prison.

. . .

Definition of "special needs"

(2) In this section, "special needs" means that a person has greater need of settlement assistance than other applicants for protection abroad owing to personal circumstances, including

(a) a large number of family members;

(b) trauma resulting from violence or torture;

(c) medical disabilities; and

(d) the effects of systemic discrimination.

Division 3
Determination of Eligibility of Claim

. . .

Definitions
159.1 The following definitions apply in this section and sections 159.2 to 159.7.

Agreement means the Agreement dated December 5, 2002 between the Government of Canada and the Government of the United States of America for Cooperation in the Examination of Refugee Status Claims from Nationals of Third Countries. (Accord)

claimant means a claimant referred to in paragraph 101(1)(e) of the Act. (*demandeur*)

designated country means a country designated by section 159.3. (*pays désigné*)

family member, in respect of a claimant, means their spouse or common-law partner, their legal guardian, and any of the following persons, namely, their child, father, mother, brother, sister, grandfather, grandmother, grandchild, uncle, aunt, nephew or niece. (*membre de la famille*)

. . .

Designation — United States
159.3 The United States is designated under paragraph 102(1)(a) of the Act as a country that complies with Article 33 of the Refugee Convention and Article 3 of the Convention Against Torture, and is a designated country for the purpose of the application of paragraph 101(1)(e) of the Act.

Non-application — ports of entry other than land ports of entry
159.4 (1) Paragraph 101(1)(e) of the Act does not apply to a claimant who seeks to enter Canada at

(a) a location that is not a port of entry;
(b) a port of entry that is a harbour port, including a ferry landing; or
(c) subject to subsection (2), a port of entry that is an airport.

. . .

Non-application — claimants at land ports of entry

159.5 Paragraph 101(1)(e) of the Act does not apply if a claimant who seeks to enter Canada at a location other than one identified in paragraphs 159.4(1)(a) to (c) establishes, in accordance with subsection 100(4) of the Act, that

- (a) a family member of the claimant is in Canada and is a Canadian citizen;
- (b) a family member of the claimant is in Canada and is
  - (i) a protected person within the meaning of subsection 95(2) of the Act,
  - (ii) a permanent resident under the Act, or
  - (iii) a person in favour of whom a removal order has been stayed in accordance with section 233;
- (c) a family member of the claimant who has attained the age of 18 years is in Canada and has made a claim for refugee protection that has been referred to the Board for determination, unless
  - (i) the claim has been withdrawn by the family member,
  - (ii) the claim has been abandoned by the family member,
  - (iii) the claim has been rejected, or
  - (iv) any pending proceedings or proceedings respecting the claim have been terminated under subsection 104(2) of the Act or any decision respecting the claim has been nullified under that subsection;
- (d) a family member of the claimant who has attained the age of 18 years is in Canada and is the holder of a work permit or study permit other than
  - (i) a work permit that was issued under paragraph 206(b) or that has become invalid as a result of the application of section 209, or
  - (ii) a study permit that has become invalid as a result of the application of section 222;
- (e) the claimant is a person who
  - (i) has not attained the age of 18 years and is not accompanied by their mother, father or legal guardian,
  - (ii) has neither a spouse nor a common-law partner, and
  - (iii) has neither a mother or father nor a legal guardian in Canada or the United States;
- (f) the claimant is the holder of any of the following documents, excluding any document issued for the sole purpose of transit through Canada, namely,

(i) a permanent resident visa or a temporary resident visa referred to in section 6 and subsection 7(1), respectively,
(ii) a temporary resident permit issued under subsection 24(1) of the Act,
(iii) a travel document referred to in subsection 31(3) of the Act,
(iv) refugee travel papers issued by the Minister, or
(v) a temporary travel document referred to in section 151;

(g) the claimant is a person
(i) who may, under the Act or these Regulations, enter Canada without being required to hold a visa, and
(ii) who would, if the claimant were entering the United States, be required to hold a visa; or

(h) the claimant is
(i) a foreign national who is seeking to re-enter Canada in circumstances where they have been refused entry to the United States without having a refugee claim adjudicated there, or
(ii) a permanent resident who has been ordered removed from the United States and is being returned to Canada.

. . .

Division 3.1
Claim for Refugee Protection — Time Limits

Documents and Information

Time limit — provision of documents and information to officer
159.8 (1) For the purpose of subsection 99(3.1) of the Act, a person who makes a claim for refugee protection inside Canada other than at a port of entry must provide an officer with the documents and information referred to in that subsection not later than the day on which the officer determines the eligibility of their claim under subsection 100(1) of the Act.

Time limit — provision of documents and information to Refugee Protection Division
(2) Subject to subsection (3), for the purpose of subsection 100(4) of the Act, a person who makes a claim for refugee protection inside Canada at a port of entry must provide the Refugee Protection Division with the documents and information referred to in subsection 100(4) not later than 15 days after the day on which the claim is referred to that Division.

Extension
(3) If the documents and information cannot be provided within the time limit set out in subsection (2), the Refugee Protection Division may, for reasons of fairness and natural justice, extend that time limit by the number of days that is necessary in the circumstances.

Hearing Before Refugee Protection Division

Time limits for hearing
159.9 (1) Subject to subsections (2) and (3), for the purpose of subsection 100(4.1) of the Act, the date fixed for the hearing before the Refugee Protection Division must be not later than

- (a) in the case of a claimant referred to in subsection 111.1(2) of the Act,
  - (i) 30 days after the day on which the claim is referred to the Refugee Protection Division, if the claim is made inside Canada other than at a port of entry, and
  - (ii) 45 days after the day on which the claim is referred to the Refugee Protection Division, if the claim is made inside Canada at a port of entry; and
- (b) in the case of any other claimant, 60 days after the day on which the claim is referred to the Refugee Protection Division, whether the claim is made inside Canada at a port of entry or inside Canada other than at a port of entry.

. . .

Appeal to Refugee Appeal Division

Time limit for appeal
159.91 (1) Subject to subsection (2), for the purpose of subsection 110(2.1) of the Act,

- (a) the time limit for a person or the Minister to file an appeal to the Refugee Appeal Division against a decision of the Refugee Protection Division is 15 days after the day on which the person or the Minister receives written reasons for the decision; and
- (b) the time limit for a person or the Minister to perfect such an appeal is 30 days after the day on which the person or the Minister receives written reasons for the decision.

Extension
(2) If the appeal cannot be filed within the time limit set out in paragraph 1)(a) or perfected within the time limit set out in paragraph (1)

(b), the Refugee Appeal Division may, for reasons of fairness and natural justice, extend each of those time limits by the number of days that is necessary in the circumstances.

Time limit for decision
159.92 (1) Subject to subsection (2), for the purpose of subsection 110(3.1) of the Act, except when a hearing is held under subsection 110(6) of the Act, the time limit for the Refugee Appeal Division to make a decision on an appeal is 90 days after the day on which the appeal is perfected.

Exception
(2) If it is not possible for the Refugee Appeal Division to make a decision on an appeal within the time limit set out in subsection (1), the decision must be made as soon as feasible after that time limit.

Division 4
Pre-Removal Risk Assessment

Application for protection
160 (1) Subject to subsection (2) and for the purposes of subsection 112(1) of the Act, a person may apply for protection after they are given notification to that effect by the Department.

No notification
(2) A person described in section 165 or 166 may apply for protection in accordance with that section without being given notification to that effect by the Department.

Notification
(3) Notification shall be given

(a) in the case of a person who is subject to a removal order that is in force, before removal from Canada; and
(b) in the case of a person named in a certificate described in subsection 77(1) of the Act, when the summary of information and other evidence is filed under subsection 77(2) of the Act.

. . .

Submissions
161 (1) Subject to section 166, a person applying for protection may make written submissions in support of their application and for that purpose may be assisted, at their own expense, by a barrister or solicitor or other counsel.

. . .

Application within 15-day period

162 An application received within 15 days after notification was given under section 160 shall not be decided until at least 30 days after notification was given. The removal order is stayed under section 232 until the earliest of the events referred to in paragraphs 232(c) to (f) occurs.

Applications after the 15-day period

163 A person who has remained in Canada since being given notification under section 160 may make an application after a period of 15 days has elapsed from notification being given under that section, but the application does not result in a stay of the removal order. Written submissions, if any, must accompany the application.

. . .

Subsequent application

165 A person whose application for protection was rejected and who has remained in Canada since being given notification under section 160 may make another application. Written submissions, if any, must accompany the application. For greater certainty, the application does not result in a stay of the removal order.

Application at port of entry

166 An application for protection by a foreign national against whom a removal order is made at a port of entry as a result of a determination of inadmissibility on entry into Canada must, if the order is in force, be received as soon as the removal order is made. Written submissions, if any, must accompany the application. For greater certainty, the application does not result in a stay of the removal order.

Hearing — prescribed factors

167 For the purpose of determining whether a hearing is required under paragraph 113(b) of the Act, the factors are the following:

(a) whether there is evidence that raises a serious issue of the applicant's credibility and is related to the factors set out in sections 96 and 97 of the Act;
(b) whether the evidence is central to the decision with respect to the application for protection; and
(c) whether the evidence, if accepted, would justify allowing the application for protection.

Hearing procedure

168 A hearing is subject to the following provisions:

(a) notice shall be provided to the applicant of the time and place of the hearing and the issues of fact that will be raised at the hearing;
(b) the hearing is restricted to matters relating to the issues of fact stated in the notice, unless the officer conducting the hearing considers that other issues of fact have been raised by statements made by the applicant during the hearing;
(c) the applicant must respond to the questions posed by the officer and may be assisted for that purpose, at their own expense, by a barrister or solicitor or other counsel; and
(d) any evidence of a person other than the applicant must be in writing and the officer may question the person for the purpose of verifying the evidence provided.

. . .

Division 5

Protected Persons — Permanent Residence

. . .

Family members
176 (1) An applicant may include in their application to remain in Canada as a permanent resident any of their family members.

One-year time limit
(2) A family member who is included in an application to remain in Canada as a permanent resident and who is outside Canada at the time the application is made shall be issued a permanent resident visa if

(a) the family member makes an application outside Canada to an officer within one year after the day on which the applicant becomes a permanent resident; and
(b) the family member is not inadmissible on the grounds referred to in subsection (3).

. . .

Prescribed classes
177 For the purposes of subsection 21(2) of the Act, the following are prescribed as classes of persons who cannot become permanent residents:

(a) the class of persons who have been the subject of a decision under section 108 or 109 or subsection 114(3) of the Act resulting in the rejection of a claim for refugee protection or nullification of the decision that led to conferral of refugee protection;

(b) the class of persons who are permanent residents at the time of their application to remain in Canada as a permanent resident;

(c) the class of persons who have been recognized by any country, other than Canada, as Convention refugees and who, if removed from Canada, would be allowed to return to that country;

(d) the class of nationals or citizens of a country, other than the country that the person left, or outside of which the person remains, by reason of fear of persecution; and

(e) the class of persons who have permanently resided in a country, other than the country that the person left, or outside of which the person remains, by reason of fear of persecution, and who, if removed from Canada, would be allowed to return to that country.

Identity documents

178 (1) An applicant who does not hold a document described in any of paragraphs 50(1)(a) to (h) may submit with their application

(a) any identity document issued outside Canada before the person's entry into Canada; or

(b) if there is a reasonable and objectively verifiable explanation related to circumstances in the applicant's country of nationality or former habitual residence for the applicant's inability to obtain any identity documents, a statutory declaration made by the applicant attesting to their identity, accompanied by

(i) a statutory declaration attesting to the applicant's identity made by a person who, before the applicant's entry into Canada, knew the applicant, a family member of the applicant or the applicant's father, mother, brother, sister, grandfather or grandmother, or

(ii) a statutory declaration attesting to the applicant's identity made by an official of an organization representing nationals of the applicant's country of nationality or former habitual residence.

Alternative documents

(2) A document submitted under subsection (1) shall be accepted in lieu of a document described in any of paragraphs 50(1)(a) to (h) if

(a) in the case of an identity document, the identity document

(i) is genuine,

(ii) identifies the applicant, and
(iii) constitutes credible evidence of the applicant's identity; and

(b) in the case of a statutory declaration, the declaration
(i) is consistent with any information previously provided by the applicant to the Department or the Board, and
(ii) constitutes credible evidence of the applicant's identity.

APPENDIX C

TABLES ON PERMANENT RESIDENCE ADMISSIONS

Numbers of Persons Who Have Acquired Permanent Residence (by Category), 1996–2015[1]

Year	Economic immigrants	Family class	Refugees	Total permanent residents
1996	125,370	68,359	28,478	226,071
1997	128,351	59,979	24,308	216,036
1998	97,911	50,898	22,842	174,195
1999	109,255	55,277	24,398	189,950
2000	136,299	60,612	30,092	227,455
2001	155,719	66,795	27,919	250,636
2002	137,861	62,304	25,124	229,049
2003	121,047	65,129	25,984	221,349
2004	133,745	62,260	32,687	235,822
2005	156,310	63,352	35,768	262,242
2006	138,338	75,142	32,510	251,649

1 Immigration, Refugees and Citizenship Canada, "Facts and Figures 2014," online: IRCC www.cic.gc.ca/english/resources/statistics/facts2014/index.asp; Immigration, Refugees and Citizenship Canada, "Facts and Figures 2015," online: IRCC http://open.canada.ca/data/en/dataset/2fbb56bd-eae7-4582-af7d-a197d185fc93?_ga=1.251008578.577896951.1468435762.

Year	Economic immigrants	Family class	Refugees	Total permanent residents
2007	131,271	72,141	27,965	236,762
2008	149,111	71,899	21,861	247,261
2009	153,548	71,990	22,857	252,218
2010	186,968	65,565	24,699	280,730
2011	156,120	61,344	27,876	248,732
2012	160,790	69,870	23,095	257,809
2013	148,254	83,379	24,139	259,039
2014	165,188	67,647	24,070	260,282
2015	170,398	65,490	32,115	271,847

Refugees Admitted for Permanent Residence in Canada (by Category), 1996–2015[2]

Year	Government-assisted refugees	Privately sponsored refugees	Refugees landed in Canada	Refugee dependants	Total refugees
1996	7,869	3,189	13,462	3,958	28,478
1997	7,711	2,742	10,634	3,221	24,308
1998	7,432	2,267	10,181	2,962	22,842
1999	7,444	2,348	11,797	2,809	24,398
2000	10,671	2,933	12,993	3,495	30,092
2001	8,697	3,576	11,897	3,749	27,919
2002	7,505	3,052	10,546	4,021	25,124
2003	7,506	3,252	11,267	3,959	25,984
2004	7,411	3,116	15,901	6,259	32,687
2005	7,416	2,976	19,935	5,441	35,768
2006	7,327	3,338	21,845	n/a	32,510
2007	7,572	3,587	16,806	n/a	27,965
2008	7,296	3,512	11,053	n/a	21,861
2009	7,429	5,037	10,391	n/a	22,857
2010	7,266	4,833	12,600	n/a	24,699
2011	7,363	5,584	14,929	n/a	27,876

2 *Ibid.* The 2015 version of Facts and Figures no longer lists data for refugee dependants, so that information is not available in this table.

Year	Government-assisted refugees	Privately sponsored refugees	Refugees landed in Canada	Refugee dependants	Total refugees
2012	5,426	4,227	13,442	n/a	23,095
2013	5,726	6,330	11,930	n/a	24,139
2014	7,626	5,070	11,197	n/a	24,070
2015	9,488	9,746	12,070	n/a	32,115

Targets for Sponsored Refugee Admission for Permanent Residence in Canada (by Category), 1996–2017[3]

Year	Government-assisted refugees	Privately sponsored refugees
1996	7,300	2,700–4,000
1997	7,300	2,800–4,000
1998	7,300	2,800–4,000
1999	7,300	2,800–4,000
2000	7,300	2,800–4,000
2001	7,300	2,800–4,000
2002	7,300	2,900–4,000
2003	7,700	2,900–4,000
2004	7,500	3,400–4,000
2005	7,300–7,500	3,000–4,000
2006	7,300–7,500	3,000–4,000
2007	7,300–7,500	3,000–4,500
2008	7,300–7,500	3,300–4,500
2009	7,300–7,500	3,300–4,500
2010	7,300–8,000	3,300–6,000
2011	7,400–8,000	3,800–6,000
2012	7,500–8,000	4,000–6,000
2013	6,800–7,100	4,500–6,500

3 Immigration, Refugees and Citizenship Canada, "Reports on Plans and Priorities," online: IRCC www.cic.gc.ca/english/resources/publications/rpp/; Immigration, Refugees and Citizenship Canada, "Key Highlights - 2016 Immigration Levels Plan," online: IRCC http://news.gc.ca/web/article-en.do?nid=1038709; Immigration, Refugees and Citizenship Canada, "Key Highlights - 2017 Immigration Levels Plan," online: IRCC http://news.gc.ca/web/article-en.do?nid=1145319.

Year	Government-assisted refugees	Privately sponsored refugees
2014	6,900–7,200	4,500–6,500
2015	5,800–6,500	4,500–6,500
2016	24,600	17,800
2017	7,500	16,000

APPENDIX D

TABLES

Table 1: Refugee Claim Statistics and Aggregate Acceptance/Rejection Rates, 2004–16

Year	Claims Referred to Refugee Protection Division	Claims Decided by Refugee Protection Division	Acceptance Rate	Rejection Rate
2004	25,725	40,551	40%	47%
2005	20,732	27,307	44%	43%
2006	22,910	19,880	47%	41%
2007	27,876	13,937	43%	39%
2008	34,772	18,276	42%	37%
2009	34,003	26,817	42%	37%
2010	22,565	32,638	38%	42%
2011	25,074	34,258	38%	47%
2012	20,245	29,531	35%	49%
2013	10,381	20,721	38%	48%
2014	13,690	20,024	49%	39%
2015	15,262	16,339	58%	33%
2016	23,619	16,449	62%	30%

(Source: Authors' access-to-information requests to the IRB No A-2014-04527 and A-2016-05520)

Table 2: Top Countries of Origin of Refugee Claimants (by the Number of Finalized Claims), 2004–16

Country	2004	2005	2006	2007	2008	2009	2010	2011	2012	2013	2014	2015	2016
Mexico	3	1	1	1	1	1	1	1	2	4	-	-	-
Colombia	2	2	3	3	2	2	3	5	4	3	4	5	8
Haiti	-	-	10	9	5	3	2	2	5	7	10	-	-
Hungary	-	-	-	-	-	-	5	3	1	1	3	2	2
China	4	4	2	2	4	4	4	4	3	2	1	1	1
Pakistan	1	3	4	5	8	10	-	-	8	5	2	3	6
India	7	5	7	6	6	9	-	-	-	9	7	8	9
Nigeria	8	6	8	7	7	8	8	6	6	-	6	4	3
Sri Lanka	6	7	5	4	3	5	10	-	9	6	-	-	-

(Source: Authors' access-to-information requests to the IRB No A-2014-04527 and A-2016-05520)

Table 3: Acceptance Rates (in Percent) for Top Countries of Origin of Refugee Claimants (by the Number of Finalized Claims), 2004–16

Country	2004	2005	2006	2007	2008	2009	2010	2011	2012	2013	2014	2015	2016
Mexico	25	19	28	11	11	8	11	17	19	18	–	–	–
Colombia	81	79	77	78	79	76	52	37	36	38	51	49	62
Haiti	–	–	54	50	41	42	55	48	47	40	41	–	–
Hungary	–	–	–	–	–	–	2	8	11	20	35	61	61
China	52	48	49	64	61	58	53	53	37	34	42	49	33
Pakistan	35	40	46	49	51	59	–	–	67	71	78	79	74
India	27	25	34	12	25	32	–	–	–	15	18	37	32
Nigeria	50	41	40	43	54	66	63	62	55	–	53	56	44
Sri Lanka	63	67	73	88	94	91	76	–	56	51	–	–	–

(Source: Authors' access-to-information requests to the IRB No A-2014-04527 and A-2016-05520)

Table 4: Appeals to the Refugee Appeal Division (RAD), 2013–16

Year	Appeals Filed with the RAD	Appeals Heard by the RAD	Allowed	Dismissed
2013	1,147	691	19%	78%
2014	2,386	1,930	18%	78%
2015	2,517	2,777	25%	58%
2016	3,446	2,965	27%	55%

(Source: Authors' access-to-information requests to the IRB No A-2014-04527 and A-2016-05520)

Table 5: Breakdown of Immigration Detainees by the Type of Facility (CBSA vs Non-CBSA), 2004–16

Province /Region	2004	2005	2006	2007	2008	2009	2010	2011	2012	2013	2014	2015	2016 (as of July 26)
Quebec													
CBSA facilities	1,378	1,163	1,405	1,870	2,182	1,644	1,065	1,196	1,180	1,087	1,055	1,134	572
Non-CBSA facilities	234	242	223	235	272	244	197	203	164	175	182	176	122
Total	1,525	1,314	1,555	1,995	2,350	1,796	1,194	1,320	1,286	1,213	1,181	1,276	685
Pacific region													
CBSA facilities	1,696	1,682	2,144	2,035	1,892	1,455	1,305	1,327	1,476	1,174	808	814	525
Non-CBSA facilities	1,071	1,101	1,032	898	1,300	1,303	1,661	1,271	1,052	932	1,210	1,346	809
Total	1,998	2,016	2,518	2,352	2,490	2,014	2,143	1,862	1,775	1,473	1,289	1,380	857
Ontario													
CBSA facilities	4,335	4,664	5,317	5,694	6,159	3,505	3,012	3,635	3,768	3,260	2,806	2,383	1,323
Non-CBSA facilities	2,173	2,320	2,442	2,364	2,462	2,154	1,877	1,980	2,092	1,862	1,520	1,429	841
Total	6,294	6,739	7,552	7,916	8,473	5,527	4,748	5,339	5,624	4,887	4,096	3,621	2,049
Atlantic region													
Non-CBSA facilities	32	59	38	65	52	54	46	51	35	31	23	35	11
Total	32	59	38	65	52	54	46	51	35	31	23	35	11
Prairie region													
Non-CBSA facilities	302	238	249	282	320	363	356	371	436	488	496	341	166
Total	302	238	249	282	320	363	356	371	436	488	496	341	166
Canada													
CBSA facilities	7,382	7,492	8,811	9,563	10,203	6,591	5,362	6,133	6,400	5,507	4,669	4,331	2,420

Province /Region	2004	2005	2006	2007	2008	2009	2010	2011	2012	2013	2014	2015	2016 (as of July 26)
Non-CBSA facilities	3,758	3,875	3,936	3,809	4,388	4,092	4,129	3,853	3,762	3,475	3,419	3,326	1,950
All immigration detainees	9,867	10,057	11,568	12,356	13,492	9,528	8,296	8,757	8,972	7,908	6,978	6,516	3,690

(Source: Authors' access-to-information requests to the CBSA No A-2014-10606 and A-2016-09918)

Note: The totals of detainees in each province may not add up because some detainees may have been transferred between CBSA and non-CBSA facilities on one or more occasions and, hence, would be counted towards the numbers for both CBSA and non-CBSA facilities.

Table 6: Detention of Refugee Claimants, 2004–13

Province/Region	2004	2005	2006	2007	2008	2009	2010	2011	2012	2013
Quebec										
CBSA facilities	818	715	777	940	1,051	858	634	703	772	685
Non-CBSA facilities	100	93	88	79	102	101	78	68	52	65
Total	872	759	832	983	1,099	910	677	741	807	730
Pacific region										
CBSA facilities	485	425	380	315	365	386	399	390	474	387
Non-CBSA facilities	615	679	483	384	515	570	951	600	459	375
Total	598	587	538	426	559	629	1,006	558	576	477
Ontario										
CBSA facilities	2,034	2,315	2,772	2,874	3,125	1,653	1,444	1,841	1,967	1,320
Non-CBSA facilities	748	805	909	846	775	739	627	788	931	751
Total	2,712	3,029	3,516	3,656	3,823	2,321	2,021	2,491	2,781	1,951
Atlantic region										
Non-CBSA facilities	14	22	11	17	16	13	14	19	8	6
Total	14	22	11	17	16	13	14	19	8	6
Prairie region										
Non-CBSA facilities	65	64	63	96	92	100	112	133	194	171
Total	65	64	63	96	92	100	112	133	194	171
Canada										
CBSA facilities	3,329	3,448	3,826	4,125	4,538	2,891	2,475	2,923	3,196	2,386
Non-CBSA facilities	1,529	1,649	1,537	1,405	1,487	1,521	1,774	1,588	1,630	1,364
All immigration detainees	4,119	4,319	4,777	5,075	5,546	3,905	3,767	3,969	4,280	3,272

(Source: Authors' access-to-information request to the CBSA No A-2014-10606)

Table 7: Detention of Minors (Seventeen Years and Under), 2004–13

Province/Region	2004	2005	2006	2007	2008	2009	2010	2011	2012	2013
Quebec										
CBSA facilities	76	64	63	106	129	90	46	84	75	44
Non-CBSA facilities	1	4	0	0	1	1	3	0	2	1
Total	77	66	63	106	130	91	49	84	77	45
Pacific region										
CBSA facilities	57	76	86	63	43	36	22	21	7	9
Non-CBSA facilities	4	5	11	4	9	6	11	0	3	4
Total	58	77	88	64	48	38	28	21	8	10
Ontario										
CBSA facilities	332	464	432	590	652	178	128	202	233	161
Non-CBSA facilities	10	22	20	8	4	15	3	4	4	1
Total	341	484	458	600	656	191	130	207	236	162
Atlantic region										
Non-CBSA facilities	1	2	0	1	0	0	0	0	1	0
Total	1	2	0	1	0	0	0	0	1	0
Prairie region										
Non-CBSA facilities	2	1	2	2	0	1	4	2	0	0
Total	2	1	2	2	0	1	4	2	0	0
Canada										
CBSA facilities	464	604	579	757	823	303	195	303	309	214
Non-CBSA facilities	17	35	38	17	14	23	21	7	10	6
All minor immigration detainees	470	613	599	767	833	313	208	310	315	217

(Source: Authors' access-to-information request to the CBSA No A-2014-10606)

Table 8: Grounds for Detention, 2004–16

Legislative Grounds	2004	2005	2006	2007	2008	2009	2010	2011	2012	2013	2014	2015	2016 (as of July 26)
Criminality	0	0	0	0	0	0	0	0	5	161	155	125	53
Serious criminality	0	0	0	0	0	0	0	0	1	48	41	50	14
Organized criminality	0	0	0	0	0	0	0	0	0	7	9	6	4
Security	9	19	25	15	6	9	50	71	10	5	5	7	3
Human or international rights violations	21	15	4	2	3	3	3	3	5	0	2	1	0
Danger to the public	47	60	53	40	44	62	23	44	48	29	40	40	33
Flight risk	7,169	7,553	9,823	9,538	10,615	7,508	6,629	7,433	7,636	6,253	5,765	5,380	3,119
Danger/flight risk	906	956	939	860	853	795	731	691	726	951	546	421	213
Identity	773	629	609	653	670	529	943	573	526	350	331	330	209
Examination	1,097	1,017	286	1,448	1,493	733	93	87	156	302	211	277	107

(Source: Authors' access-to-information requests to the CBSA No A-2014-10606 and A-2016-09918)

Table 9: Detention of Designated Foreign Nationals, 2012–13

Designated Foreign Nationals	December 2012 (when DFN provisions came into force)	2013	2014 (as of 30 October)	Number of Detention Days
Minors (seventeen and under)	3	0	0	7
Adults	12	10	0	469
Total	15	10	0	

(Source: Authors' access-to-information request to the CBSA No A-2014-10606)

Table 10: Removals, 2004–14

Year	Total Number of Persons Removed	Number of Rejected Claimants Removed	Wanted
2004	12,184	8,710	2,044
2005	11,289	8,082	1,450
2006	12,662	9,238	1,402
2007	12,506	8,878	1,503
2008	12,849	8,802	2,047
2009	14,864	10,595	2,526
2010	15,391	10,926	1,695
2011	15,712	10,861	1,740
2012	18,953	13,874	1,447
2013	15,489	10,654	886
2014	12,495	7,654	558

(Source: Authors' access-to-information request to the CBSA No A-2015-03765)

Table 11: Breakdown of Removals by Ground of Removal, 2004–14

Ground for Removal	2004	2005	2006	2007	2008	2009	2010	2011	2012	2013	2014
Criminality	365	368	409	364	386	458	406	459	468	440	429
Serious criminality	623	588	638	580	637	664	659	696	738	714	712
Organized criminality	19	10	18	25	19	67	41	31	48	39	47
Security	4	3	4	1	7	3	4	8	6	12	9
Human rights violations	4	5	9	6	3	7	3	7	6	7	8
Financial reasons	21	23	24	17	13	12	11	17	15	11	16
Health	19	19	11	15	21	36	24	10	16	12	25
Misrepresentation	135	83	108	72	62	59	98	106	138	92	116
Non-compliance with the Act	10,818	10,056	11,300	11,245	11,553	13,185	13,869	14,238	17,418	14,055	11,044
Inadmissible family member	176	134	141	181	148	373	276	140	100	107	79

(Source: Authors' access-to-information request to the CBSA No A-2015-03765)

TABLE OF CASES

INDEX

ABOUT THE AUTHORS

Sasha Baglay (LLB, Kiev National Economic University; LLM in Comparative Constitutional Law, Central European University; LLM, Dalhousie University; PhD, York University) is an Associate Professor of Legal Studies at the Faculty of Social Science and Humanities, University of Ontario Institute of Technology; and an Adjunct Professor at Osgoode Hall Law School. She has written and presented on various issues of Canadian and comparative immigration and refugee law and policy. In 2009–10, she was president of the Canadian Association for Refugee and Forced Migration Studies.

Martin Jones (BA Hons, Queen's University; LLB, University of British Columbia) practised as an immigration and refugee lawyer in Canada for seven years. During that time he represented more than one thousand immigrants and refugee claimants in all stages of the immigration and refugee protection process. Currently, Martin is a senior lecturer in international human rights law at the Centre for Applied Human Rights at the University of York (UK). He has previously taught and served as a visiting researcher at Osgoode Hall Law School (Canada), Queen's University (Canada), the Centre for Refugee Studies (Canada), the University of East London (UK), Georgetown University (US), the University of Michigan (US), the American University in Cairo (Egypt), and the University of Melbourne (Australia). Martin has widely presented and published on various topics in refugee and migration law.